Praise for *The Last Assassin*

'Clear and urgent as the day's news, *The Last Assassin* is a grim study of unintended consequences. It brings into sharp focus events that many of us only half-know, and tells a story sadder and more complex than we can imagine, giving a new life not only to Caesar and his killers but to the common people who filled the mass graves of the Roman wars. It is written with authority, passion and insight – a political thriller, and a human story that astonishes' Hilary Mantel

'Peter Stothard is a master of modern writing about ancient Rome'
Mary Beard

'A compelling true-life thriller, profoundly researched, beautifully written, and a dire lesson in what happens when idealism meets tyranny and political freedom dies'
Christopher Hart, *Daily Mail* 'Book of the Week'

'A riveting, fast-paced thriller that makes one think of the brutal settling of scores at the end of *The Godfather*'
Patrick Kidd, *The Times*

'[A] gripping, gorgeously written new account of the killing and its consequences . . . Stothard explores the familiar ground with fresh, engaging and learned eyes, displaying a novelist's knack for redolent and evocative detail'
Philip Womack, *Spectator*

'Stothard writes with a poet's eye for atmosphere and a novelist's imagination in reconstructing events . . . a striking and evocative treatment of this transformative period'
Edwin Shaw, *BBC History Magazine*

'Told with the genuine elegance we have come to expect from this author'
Roy Gibson, *TLS*

'A writer of rare talent . . . he weaves a tense, fast-paced tale from the many strands of a turbulent era. The vigor of Mr. Stothard's prose, and the acuity of his insight, will propel many readers . . . into an ancient Roman world that is startlingly real'
Wall Street Journal

Also by Peter Stothard

Thirty Days

On the Spartacus Road

Alexandria

The Senecans

The Last Assassin

Crassus

PALATINE

AN ALTERNATIVE HISTORY
OF THE CAESARS

PETER STOTHARD

WEIDENFELD & NICOLSON

First published in Great Britain in 2023 by Weidenfeld & Nicolson,
an imprint of The Orion Publishing Group Ltd
Carmelite House, 50 Victoria Embankment
London EC4Y 0DZ

An Hachette UK Company

1 3 5 7 9 10 8 6 4 2

A CIP catalogue record for this book is
available from the British Library.

ISBN (Hardback) 978 1 4746 2099 4
ISBN (Export Trade Paperback) 978 1 4746 2100 7
ISBN (eBook) 978 1 4746 2102 1
ISBN (Audio) 978 1 4746 2103 8

Map by handmademaps.com
Images: Shutterstock

Typeset by Input Data Services Ltd, Somerset

Printed in Great Britain by Clays Ltd, Elcograf S.p.A.

MIX
Paper from
responsible sources
FSC® C104740

www.weidenfeldandnicolson.co.uk
www.orionbooks.co.uk

To Adam and Eliza

There is a high road called the Milky Way. This way the gods pass to the halls of the mighty Jupiter. To right and left are the houses of the greater gods, doors open and crowded. The lesser gods live elsewhere. This is the place I would not fear to call high heaven's Palatine.

Ovid, Metamorphoses (8 CE)

CONTENTS

MAIN CHARACTERS

THE VITELLII

PUBLIUS VITELLIUS (*c.*40 BCE–*c.*30 CE), palace official from the south of Italy, later a personal procurator for Augustus.

LUCIUS VITELLIUS (*c.*10 BCE–51 CE), son of Publius, consummate courtier for three emperors and their wives and three times consul.

PUBLIUS VITELLIUS (*c.*12 BCE–*c.*31 CE), brother of Lucius, soldier, lawyer.

VITELLIA (*c.*6 BCE–*c.*45 CE), sister of Lucius and Publius, mother of Aulus Plautius, leader of the conquest of Britain.

SEXTILIA (*c.*5 BCE–69 CE), wife of Lucius, mother of Aulus and the younger Lucius.

AULUS VITELLIUS (*c.*12 CE–69), son of Lucius and Sextilia, master of the dining table, eighth emperor of Rome.

LUCIUS VITELLIUS (*c.*16 CE–69), son of Lucius and Sextilia, family enforcer.

PETRONIA, first wife of Aulus Vitellius.

GALERIA FUNDANA, second wife of Aulus Vitellius.

GERMANICUS VITELLIUS, son and heir to Aulus Vitellius.

VITELLIA, daughter to Aulus Vitellius.

AT THE EMPERORS' COURT

PALLAS, Palatine treasurer (*c.*1 CE–62), ally of Lucius Vitellius, former slave.

NARCISSUS (*c.*1 CE–54), palace official in charge of correspondence for Claudius, enemy of Pallas, former slave.

CALLISTUS (*c.*5 CE–*c.*50), correspondence secretary of Caligula and alleged conspirator in his death, former slave.

RUBELLIUS BLANDUS (*c.*25 BCE–*c.*40 CE), provincial courtier who caused a scandal by marrying into the imperial family.

GNAEUS CALPURNIUS PISO (44/3 BCE–20 CE), grandee of the senate prosecuted by Publius Vitellius for murder.

PLANCINA, wife of Piso.

LUCIUS AELIUS SEJANUS (20 BCE–31 CE), captain of the palace guard, chief courtier to Tiberius, patron of Publius Vitellius.

THRASYLLUS (*c.*20 BCE–*c.*35 CE), Greek-Egyptian court astrologer to Tiberius in Rome and Capri.

AKA II OF COMMAGENE, wife of Thrasyllus.

ENNIA THRASYLLA, Thrasyllus's granddaughter, married to Sejanus's deputy and successor, Macro.

MARCUS GAVIUS APICIUS (*c.*10 BCE–*c.*35 CE), court gourmet and attributed author of luxury Roman recipes.

APICATA, wife of Sejanus and said to be daughter of Apicius.

'TIBERIUS CLAUDIUS LIBERTUS', father of Claudius Etruscus, uncertainly named freed slave from Smyrna.

CAECINA ALIENUS, young and colourful commander for Aulus Vitellius.

FABIUS VALENS, older, dissolute commander for Aulus Vitellius.

CAENIS (c.20 CE–74), former slave of Antonia, long-time mistress of Vespasian.

EPAPHRODITUS, former slave and correspondence secretary to Nero, owner of the philosopher slave Epictetus.

WRITERS

QUINTUS HORATIUS FLACCUS (Horace) (65 BCE–8 BCE) son of an ex-slave, lyric poet and favourite of Augustus who avoided too close an association with the Palatine court.

PUBLIUS OVIDIUS NASO (Ovid) (43 BCE–17/18 CE), exiled for unspecified, probably sexual, offences within the court.

PHAEDRUS (first century CE), satirist and adapter of Aesop's fables.

CLUTORIUS PRISCUS (c.20 BCE–21 CE), professional flatterer poet, paid and executed for his panegyrics.

SILIUS ITALICUS (c.26 CE–101), friend and adviser to Aulus Vitellius, author of the longest surviving Latin poem.

CLUVIUS RUFUS (*c.*20 CE–*c.*70), friend and adviser to Aulus Vitellius, author of a lost political account of the early empire and a history of acting.

GRATTIUS FALISCUS (*fl c.*20 BCE–*c.*15 CE) author of *Cynegeticon*, a poem on breeding dogs and hunting.

IMPERIAL FAMILY

JULIA LIVIA (5/7 CE–43), granddaughter of Tiberius, married to Nero, son of Germanicus, and then to Rubellius Plautus.

LIVIA (59/8 BCE–29 CE), mother of Tiberius, creator with Augustus of the *domus Caesaris*.

AGRIPPINA THE ELDER (14 BCE–33 CE), granddaughter of Augustus, wife of Germanicus, starved to death on orders of Tiberius.

GERMANICUS (15 BCE–19 CE), first heir to Tiberius, patron of Publius Vitellius.

AGRIPPINA THE YOUNGER (15 CE–59), daughter of Germanicus and Agrippina the Elder, married to the Emperor Claudius with help from Lucius Vitellius, murdered by her son, the Emperor Nero.

ANTONIA (36 BCE–37 CE), niece of Augustus, patron of Lucius Vitellius and Pallas.

DRUSUS JULIUS CAESAR (14 BCE–23 CE), son and heir of Tiberius, subject of premature obituary panegyric by Clutorius Priscus.

JUNIA CALVINA (*c.*25 CE–*c.*80), great-great-granddaughter of Augustus, first wife of the younger Lucius Vitellius

EMPERORS

AUGUSTUS (63 BCE–14 CE)

TIBERIUS (42 BCE–37 CE)

CALIGULA (12 CE–41)

CLAUDIUS (10 BCE–54 CE)

NERO (37 CE–68)

GALBA (3 BCE–69 CE)

OTHO (32 CE–69)

VITELLIUS (12/15 CE–69)

VESPASIAN (9 CE–79)

THE VITELLII

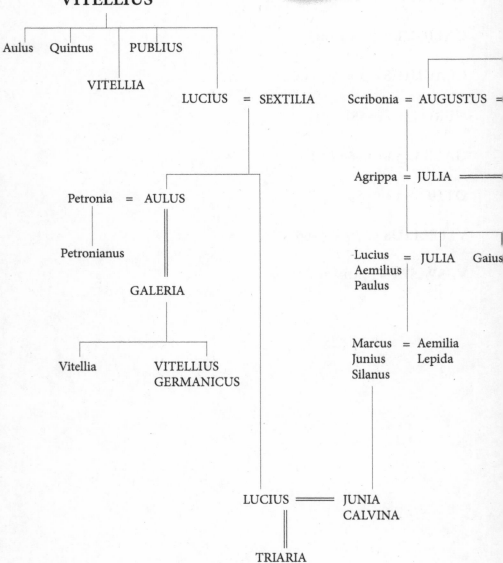

PUBLIUS VITELLIUS

Aulus   Quintus   **PUBLIUS**

VITELLIA

LUCIUS = SEXTILIA

Scribonia = AUGUSTUS =

Petronia = AULUS

Petronianus

Agrippa = JULIA =

GALERIA

Lucius = JULIA   Gaius
Aemilius
Paulus

Vitellia   VITELLIUS
GERMANICUS

Marcus = Aemilia
Junius   Lepida
Silanus

LUCIUS === JUNIA
CALVINA

TRIARIA

THE JULIO-CLAUDIANS

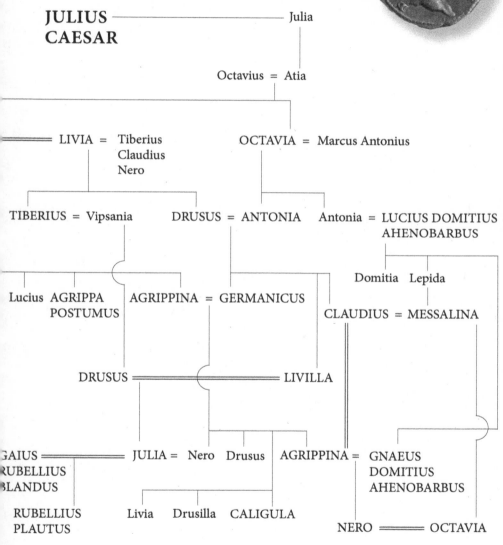

JULIUS ——————————— Julia
CAESAR

Octavius = Atia

==== LIVIA = Tiberius   OCTAVIA = Marcus Antonius
             Claudius
             Nero

TIBERIUS = Vipsania   DRUSUS = ANTONIA   Antonia = LUCIUS DOMITIUS
                                                              AHENOBARBUS

                                                    Domitia Lepida

Lucius AGRIPPA   AGRIPPINA = GERMANICUS
       POSTUMUS   CLAUDIUS = MESSALINA

          DRUSUS ════════════════════ LIVILLA

GAIUS ══════════════ JULIA = Nero Drusus AGRIPPINA = GNAEUS
RUBELLIUS   DOMITIUS
BLANDUS   AHENOBARBUS

RUBELLIUS   Livia Drusilla CALIGULA
PLAUTUS   NERO ════════ OCTAVIA

BRITANNIA
GERMANIA
GERMANIA INFERIOR
RHINE
COLONIA AGRIPPINENSIS
GERMANIA SUPERIOR
GALLIA
DANUBE
PANNONIA
LUGDUNUM
BEDRIACUM
PO
HISPANIA
TIBER
ITALIA
CORSICA
ROME
TIBUR
CAPRI
NOLA
MEDITERRA
CARTHAGE

THE·ROMAN·WORLD IN·69·CE

•TOMIS

BLACK SEA

DANUBE

PONTUS

ACEDONIA

ARMENIA

COMMAGENE

ASIA

•ATHENS

•ANTIOCH

SYRIA

JUDAEA

EAN SEA

JERUSALEM•

•ALEXANDRIA

INTRODUCTION

This is a view of the early Roman Empire that its own historians never wanted us to see. Set inside the houses of the Palatine hill, high on the edge of the ancient Forum, it is a book about two men in particular, a father and son, also a brother and others from the chorus-line in the theatre of imperial Roman life, some with ambitions for bigger parts themselves, almost all of them in one way or another reviled. Many of the characters, thanks to writers over 2,000 years, have been dismissed as poisoners of bodies and minds, informers, selfish gorgers, fabulists, fakes and facile toadies, bureaucrats at best. But Rome, like many later cities and states for which it set the standard, lived by men and women such as these.

Palatine shows the birth of Western bureaucracy. It is a history of the big rooms seen from the small, of the top table told from the lower tables. Its themes are flattery and gluttony, charges that need often to be challenged. Its events include the Roman invasion of Britain and Jewish unrest in the time of Christ but, until its final climactic year of four rivals fighting for the throne, it is a tale of peace more than war. It is a story of a single ruling household and of tactics for domestic times. It is a resonant story for our own times, of dimming memories of a glorious past, downwardly mobile aristocrats, sideways-moving provincials, upwardly advancing immigrants, personal excesses within the wheels of a powerful, often incomprehensible, machine.

It describes a world in flux, a Roman imperial world seen through the eyes of men and women on a hill that gave its name to every palace that followed. Amid a cast of slaves and former slaves, self-appointed lawyers, chancer arrivistes and the fabulously extravagant, it includes the lives of an old-fashioned soldier, snared in the politics of the new age, an exceptionally sycophantic courtier of that age, and a genial sluggard who became a notorious emperor of the banqueting table. Vitellius was their family name.

The most significant at the start of this history was the future emperor's uncle, Publius Vitellius (c.12 BCE–31 CE), an ambitious man of the army, not as clever or lucky as he needed to be. The longest-lasting was the father, Lucius Vitellius (c.10 BCE–51 CE), one of those quiet flatterers recognisable in many eras, a placid toad of the palace corridors, who lived and died in imperial service, ever more powerful as he lived through the successive reigns of Tiberius, Caligula and Claudius. Both were players on a stage newly distorted by one-man rule, its demands needing to be managed, its aims and rules rarely clear.

It was Lucius's son, Aulus Vitellius (12 CE–69) who briefly became an emperor of the Roman world, who was despised by everyone who told his story, and who, against tough competition from both predecessors and successors, set his own standards for the vice of gluttony. Aulus had a brother, brutal and mostly loyal, who was called Lucius like his father. Over half a century, one of the most important periods in the whole history of empire, the Vitellii competed against other ambitious bureaucrats, among the first in Europe to earn the title 'public servants'.

Images of the Vitellii exist only as traces. A fat-faced portrait bust in Venice, the so-called 'Grimani Vitellius', became an artist's model for gluttons. Publius the uncle, for all his efforts in the field and duties in the law courts, did not leave any picture for the history books. Nor is there an image of Lucius the father from his own lifetime: the man who rose silently in the treacherous court of Tiberius, who humoured Caligula's desire to be called a god, who both flattered and prosecuted the notorious empress Messalina was a great effacer of himself.

Lucius was one of those Romans who made the Rome of the early emperors what it was. He worked behind the scenery. He held the highest offices abroad as well as at home, but the man who failed to control Pontius Pilate in Judaea was in every way an unassuming provincial governor and slipped quietly out of every future. Lucius ran Rome while Claudius was pretending to conquer Britain, three times held the consulship, the highest office of old Rome, but, as a knowing survivor of show trials and purges, did not seek credit for himself except in imperial gratitude.

Lucius skilfully used the opportunities of a new era when a few family houses became a single house, a symbol of power as well as a fact of architecture. The imperial Palatine was the house of all power, its dining tables the place of diplomacy, political decisions and death sentences. The Roman Forum, once fought over so fiercely in fiery speech, had become almost a museum. The court was taking its place.

Different kinds of characters were beginning to make history. The Vitellii were just one family among many. A few of the newcomers were writers themselves. Most were not. Most became instead the victims of writers. *Palatine* is a different history of Rome under the descendants of Julius Caesar. It is a book less about the larger-than-life than about almost everyone else.

PART ONE

*Seldom has anyone honourably bought loyalty to the extent
that Vitellius bought loyalty with worthlessness.*

Tacitus (*c.*105 CE)

1

IN THE PALACE DOGHOUSE

In December 69 CE, on one of the last days in a calendar like no other, only a mattress and a wooden door stood between the pale winter light and the panting body of that year's third emperor of Rome. The mattress smelt of dogs, but most of the dogs had gone. This was a small room in a palace of large rooms, but even its smallest rooms looked large to Aulus Vitellius when there was no one left behind.

Not long ago there had been many palace dogs, intimidating, entertaining, scavenging whatever meat had fallen from the loaded tables. Dogs knew how to get what they wanted with the lick of a flattering tongue and the low look of a deep-brown eye. So did the household staff, the lowest and the highest of them. Now they were gone.

Outside in the smoking streets of Rome there were dogs from near and far, some from thousands of miles away, from Britain, Syria, Africa, Greece, the endless steppes, the Danube and the Rhine. Each breed had its virtues and vices, wild bravery for the British, caution for Ukrainians, gluttony for most, fastidiousness for a few. Corinthian dogs were great sniffers of pigs.

In recent years there were rumours of racing dogs. Aulus had once been the governor of Africa and knew all about the dogs of Rome's old enemy, Carthage. Dogs from Cologne, known to all his soldiers from the northern frontier, preferred hares; if anyone were hungry enough to eat dog meat, it tasted like hare. He was not that hungry yet.

Every country had its own unique kind of dog. That was one of the reasons for visiting and invading other countries. Servants too had their special characteristics of places ruled by Rome. But all the living creatures that normally occupied the palace seemed to have gone or, if not gone, were hiding, as he himself was hiding, from the hunters beyond the mattress, bed and door. The guard dogs might already have found new masters among the soldiers from the east whose leader wanted him dead. He did not know.

Aulus's grandfather and uncle had known these dark halls well. His father, Lucius, had been their most faithful servant, celebrated in marble for his service, a diplomat and courtier, flattering when he had to be, ferocious only very rarely, carefully commanding fellow flatterers and rivals, ambassadors, conmen and cooks, even ruling the whole city and far beyond when the fourth emperor of Rome was away on his conquest of Britain.

That perilous regency – only a few months – had been a memorable part of Aulus's education, but none of his family had otherwise ever seen much purpose in educating him. Certainly, neither of his parents ever thought that their son might be Rome's eighth emperor. His mother, Sextilia, was pessimistic at his birth and merely amused when, urged on by senators and soldiers, he added the names Germanicus Augustus to his own. She never knew that he was back now, in power no longer, with only the names she had given him. Sextilia was dead, the news reaching him only a little ahead of his hunters.

Unshaven inside a kennel, even in a palatial kennel with a fortune in gold coins around his waist, he did not look like a son to make a mother proud. He had always been tall, a virtue for a Roman, but his limbs were loose and his stomach huge, his money belt stretched tight. He had a deep scar on his thigh, testimony to the dangers of chariot-racing with Caligula. He limped. He was famed for gluttony. He was prone to belching loudly, a virtue to those, including some very sophisticated thinkers, who thought a man should always follow nature. The grander disagreed with his philosophy of the fart.

He had for half a year been a popular leader of an ungovernable army, men who had marched out of Germany for miles of murder, looting and eating, men who had, merely by mistake, just burnt Rome's most holy place, the temple of I.O.M., Jupiter Optimus Maximus, the Best and Greatest. Aulus had not had many jobs in his life, and in one of them men had accused him of swapping precious temple ornaments for cheap replacements. That seemed unlikely now to be the desecration that anyone would remember him for. He was no Nero, an emperor forever blamed for theft and fire, merely one of Nero's friends. Anyway, maybe the latest burning had been his rival's fault. The Vitellians were not the only ungovernable army out in the streets of Rome in the winter of 69 CE. The acrid smoke from cracked marble still seeped into the palace.

From the Rhine to the Tiber he had ridden the waves of his popularity like a drunken sailor whose destination was chosen by chance. He had wanted to be a worthy successor to Nero. The massive walls of Cologne, birthplace of Nero's much-feared mother, Agrippina, had been his first capital. His final choices had only been where to hide, his family house in Rome or in the country, and whom to bring with him, his baker or his cook or both.

Even his friend, Silius, had gone. Silius Italicus had been consul when Nero died, a writer who had turned words into vast wealth in the law courts. He was a flatterer and a fighter who owned many houses where he too could be hiding. He was a collector of poetry and a poet himself, with ambitions for a long writing life if he could survive this latest wound in the body of Rome. Silius saw wounds everywhere, blood flowing from the swords and spears of ancient Carthage, from the dogs of Crete and Sparta, a nostalgist for the days when Roman soldiers fought Hannibal and not each other.

An emperor without a cook, a baker and without even a poet was no emperor at all. He did not want to be in his family homes. The palace had lured him back to the rooms where he had done the best he could. There were so many rooms, once the places for so many of the once enslaved, Greeks called Claudius and Claudia, Julius and Julia, the bread-makers and poisoners, shoppers and shit-shifters who proudly bore Roman names.

Here was the office of Pallas, the controller of the cash, of Polybius, who wrote poetry for posterity and letters back to kings, of the accountants and clerks whose names he had forgotten or never known. Not far away were the rooms of Beryllus, the little man who took so much money in bribes to deny the Jews, of Posides, the most potent eunuch at the court, of other eunuchs who made beds or offered their bodies in them, of fish-scalers, book-gluers, hair-dressers, of Halotus, the food-taster who sometimes stopped poi-sonings and sometimes did not, of Locusta, mistress of the deadly atropine, and Crispinilla, African costume mistress and mistress of so much more. There was the room of Doryphorus, dead critic of Nero's mistress, of Epaphroditus the detective, of Narcissus, that unforgettable name, the places for so many forgotten names. Now he was alone. It was not yet clear how close the danger had yet come. Every sound in the bitter air was muffled by the blankets that blocked his door.

There were so many clashing noises. This was the season of Sat-urnalia, the time of parties and public gambling, the brief pretence that everyone shared the same ancient liberty. From his dark room of the dogs any scream or cry could be a soldier's or a celebrating slave's. The soldiers of his rival might be celebrating too. Slaves might be killers. This was the time for reversing roles – even in this year, when the rise and fall of three emperors had been just a few of Rome's reverses.

There was a crash and a cry, then screams dulled by walls, silences punctured by the clang of iron, the sharp smell of smoke when wood burns stone. The kennel door opened. Empty rooms loomed before his eyes. The bed and mattress gave way, a rushing sound followed by a crash. An officer grabbed him by what was almost a beard. There was the sharp pain of a dog bite. It was a December of dogs.

2

MR GLUTTON AND MR FOOL

Aulus Vitellius's whole life was of one emperor following another –
Augustus, then Tiberius, then Caligula, then Claudius, then Nero.
He knew no other form of government. The age of rule by the senate
and popular assemblies, the S and P of the SPQR on his soldiers'
standards, ended in vicious violence half a century before his birth.
Recent history was not required reading in the schools of Rome.
Heroic antiquity was preferred.

Aulus could not remember the first succession, the hot southern
Italian morning in the last week of the first emperor's life, August
14 CE. He was only two years old at the time, but he knew the stories. Everyone on the Palatine knew the stories.

A prized personal slave, one of hundreds in the imperial service, had the honour of the last combing of Augustus's hair, the
last holding of a bronze mirror before his Roman nose and thick,
grey eyebrows (so very different from his official portraits), the last
encouragements in his struggle to ensure that neither sickness of
stomach nor foreboding of death would be on show to his friends. It
was important to keep up appearances when one man's appearance
had become the reality of Roman power.

Aulus's brother Lucius was not yet born. His father, Lucius Vitellius, was around twenty-five years old and making his careful way,
alongside Publius and two other brothers, in the imperial systems
of Rome. His grandfather, also called Publius Vitellius, was a procurator, a personal representative of the emperor in the same service.
He was around fifty-five and still remembered the aftermath of the
assassination of Julius Caesar, when the Roman republic had failed
its last test before monarchy began.

The health of Emperor Caesar Augustus mattered most to those
in the household which he had built and ruled since then, helped by

the elder Publius and a growing host of servants who had become public servants too. Within this *domus Caesaris*, Caesar's house and household, the master had attached the rule of Europe's greatest city, where his health also mattered, a country, Italy, where it mattered to a degree, and a wider empire, from Germany to Jerusalem and beyond, where in many places, whatever the public servants might pretend, it mattered hardly at all.

In a small room at Nola, at the western edge of Naples, on the landward side of Mount Vesuvius, it mattered to everyone. This was Augustus's palace, his *palatium*, whether he was on the Palatine hill in Rome or not. This was a modest part of his court in a modest part of his domain, but the name of where he lived and worked was always the same. The season was high summer. In the end there were no consoling sea breezes for the dying emperor, only men and women with fans made from leaves and silk, the slave with the comb and mirror, other slaves, doctors, cooks, other companions on the road who were free men but hardly free, all part of the travelling court which for fifty years had judged, taxed, threatened, used the minimum of force and turned the moving parts of the world.

The day was not yet at its hottest, the nineteenth day of August, the day on which the man who had given the month its name was home at his father's modest house. Born in 63 BCE, the son of a man of respectable success, adopted two decades later to be the son of the new god, Julius Caesar, Augustus had won his domination by diplomacy and force. As death came close in his seventy-eighth year he was back in the room where his natural father had died, where his own life, as the heir of Caesar, was entering its final hours. It was as if he were in a family hospital, a family theatre, staffed by retainers who owed him their every place in a family play.

He checked on the health of his chosen successor's granddaughter, nine years old and one of many called Julia, who was ill. The combing of his hair, the tilting of his mirror, the ointment for his weak left eye, the suggestion that he should thrust forward his jaw for his final speech, perhaps the very shutting of his stricken jaw: all help came from those who were his servants. He no longer had any equals. In the nearby towns, in Naples, Pompeii, Puteoli and Cumae, he was already worshipped almost as a god.

Augustus spoke as firmly as he could. He was never a strong speaker, just as he was never a strong fighter. He preferred to use others to win his battles and debates, to give him the authority that he reflected to the world. His last words, his hair and jaw in place, his eyebrows in a trimmed unbroken line, conveyed the modesty that he most liked to display. He saw himself as a common actor, taking the curtain-call of a comic play among the stock characters beloved by Roman audiences, Mr Glutton, the fat man, Mr Fool, the village idiot, Mr Chew, the ponderous sloth and Mr Toad, the flatterer.

Like the players of a travelling farce, when their night's work was done, the world's most powerful man asked for affirmation. Had he done well? Had he played his part? That was the last question he asked. If he had done his best, let him be given applause in return. Hands clapped like the clattering of tiles. Back in Rome the vaster mass of his palace servants, a class that extended from slaves to senators, each had their own anticipated role for the future. But not till the news came from Nola could the next act begin.

The original home of the Vitellii was only a few miles from Nola, at Nuceria on the south-east side of Vesuvius. In 14 CE they were still a family known by few, their ancestry, noble or otherwise, not yet even imagined. For four centuries Roman history had been a history of great families competing for votes and military glory, competing with gladiatorial spectacles and free food for voters, with cash and land for soldiers. At the beginning of the first century CE the Vitellii were not from one of those families. They did not pretend that when Romulus and Remus sucked wolf's milk on the Palatine, fighting each other before Rome's foundation, some Vitellian ancestor had been a spectator. But this was less of a disadvantage than it once had been.

Aulus's grandfather, Publius, held a mid-level place in the family that was already supreme over all rivals. He was one of Augustus's many procurators, part official, part servant, in the household of which the emperor was head, the only household that mattered, a fact that the Vitellii accepted faster than others who were grander.

This elder Publius had a brother, Quintus, who wrecked his prospects by fighting as a gladiator. Nuceria, like Nola, was rich from gladiator-training and less than 100 years before had been sacked in revenge by Spartacus and his slave army. Gladiators had glamour, but mostly the Vitellii were rising in more conventional ways, quietly, faithfully, sometimes ambiguously, and mostly with very great care.

From his middle-ranking place in the *domus Caesaris*, the modest procurator, Publius Vitellius, saw the advance of all his sons, Aulus, Quintus, Publius and Lucius – and a daughter, Vitellia. The repetition of the same names through the generations was not confusing on the Palatine hill. It was what Romans aiming at lineage routinely did.

Publius, the modest old servant, saw his son Lucius become close to Antonia, daughter of Augustus's sister, one of the women closest to the emperor. Lucius's friendship at court with Augustus's powerful and independent niece was his first step on the household ladder. Antonia was famed for choosing her partisans with care and she was there to help when Lucius went on to have two sons of his own, Aulus, the second Lucius, and another daughter, Vitellia.

After Aulus was born, as was the common custom, Lucius and his wife, Sextilia, ordered auguries to be taken for the boy. The reports were discouraging, particularly if he ever were to command an army. Lucius took careful note. He may not himself have believed in auguries, but prophets, soothsayers and sibyls were everywhere in Rome and Lucius was a very practical man. Sometimes emperors sought their advice and sometimes they banned them. Sometimes it became a crime to see the future and a safer course to keep people pinned in the present tense of their lives. Whatever his belief, Lucius acted as though the prophecies were true. Sextilia, breaking the imperial pattern of mothers fighting fiercely for their sons, was even more sceptical of Aulus's prospects in life.

3

SUCCESSION

From the death room in Nola in 14 CE news came only slowly back to the houses of the Palatine. Colonnades, corridors and tunnels connected what had once been separate homes but increasingly were one. It was a network of offices, dining rooms and halls in which truth was power and rumour spread like fire.

This was one of the three principal places of Rome's foundation, a steep hill where the marshes of the Tiber could most easily be crossed before anyone had ever thought of Rome. It was made from rough volcanic rock, lava and pebbles in a natural concrete that had been easy to carve for defensive walls.

According to myths much encouraged by Augustus, a small hut of reed and straw had been a home to Romulus there. This was a place of survival by suckling a wild beast under a fig tree. In the more certain history of the city it had become the home of the exotic goddess *Magna Mater*, and the eunuch priests who had saved Rome from Hannibal.

In the age of Julius Caesar the Palatine became a site for the rich to build luxurious houses and to look down on the Forum below. Some of those clinging to power in the old world that the Caesars had ended still had houses there. Many more did not, their homes belonging instead to newcomers, provincials, those who had arrived in Rome as slaves, the disrupters of old rules, the builders of empire.

Publius and Lucius Vitellius were born into imperial service and were in their late twenties in that August when Augustus's life was over. They were two ambitious young men who knew that Tiberius, the emperor's adopted son, the elder son of his wife Livia's previous marriage, was ready to take the throne. But, like everyone else at court, there was much that they did not know.

Their likely next master was aged fifty-six, an old man in the eyes
of Rome, a pimply, surly soldier with a prominent chin, his upper
lip hanging over the lower, a learned man but ponderous in speech,
a heavy drinker, short-sighted, needing his own serious attention
from a hair-dressing slave. It was common knowledge that Augustus had taken some time to accept this succession. He had forced
Tiberius away from Rome for years, far from the halls and tunnels
of his court, as a general in Germany and the Balkans or a retiree
in island retreats. Each man was forever suspicious of the other. No
one could rule out a last betrayal.

Around Vesuvius, local loyalists recognised both the emperor
and his heir. Drinking cups were perfect for reinforcing the ambiguity. Along the lip of an Augustus cup might run pictures of the
emperor's kindness to captured barbarians and his easy manner
with Mars and Venus and other Roman gods. On a Tiberius cup
there could be scenes of the next emperor sacrificing before a triumph, celebrating in Augustus's own chariots, listening attentively
to the slave whose job was to remind the victor of his mortality. The
owners of these cups could toast the imperial line with every quaff
of wine and, if by any chance the line took a different direction, they
could order their silversmiths to adapt. Adaptability was the key to
survival everywhere, the more essential a key the closer the loyalist
was to the imperial court itself.

After weeks of uncertainty in Rome there came new word from
Nola to the servants of the emperor's bedchamber and banqueting
halls. Augustus and Tiberius, it seemed, had met and talked before
the comic-play farewell, the stomach-cursed emperor patronising
his stolid stepson for the last time: 'O unfortunate Roman people to
be chewed by such slow jaws.'

Exactly what had he meant by that? That Tiberius was a dullard,
that he deliberated too long and acted too slowly, that he treated
people like produce to be eaten, like objects to be exploited? Or
was his comment a joke, just another line from the comic play on
his mind as he faced his death? It was the job of the courtier to
offer answers to such questions, whispering from the inside to those
waiting outside.

It seemed quite likely a joke. The area around Nola was the home of comedy as well as killing in the arena. Both arts were practised sometimes by rich as well as poor. Thirty years before, the playboy consul Lucius Ahenobarbus, once married to the sister of Lucius Vitellius's patron, Antonia, was encouraging the most respectable rich men and their wives to play parts. Coarse wit entertained the highest tables.

On the nearby island of Capri, which Augustus had purchased for Rome and for his family, Greeks and Italians sang rumbustious comic musicals called the *phlyakes*. The most popular farces were called *Atellane*, after a town barely ten miles away. For fifteen minutes at a time, rarely more, and on temporary stages that travelled with their players, people of all ranks were used to watching men in masks mix the language of food, sex and the latest news, stock characters in stock plots, the slow and stupid, the guileful and the gluttonous – reassurance that everywhere and at all times the powerful pretended, the powerless laughed and life was more or less the same.

The high-summer heat beneath Mount Vesuvius was a haze between what was official news and household gossip. There was 'a sale of smoke', the name for the flow of rumour from the house of the Caesars. Lead drains softened, wood gables sweated, marble paths channelled water and lies. The body of Augustus cooled slowly for some hours, stiffening in the dampness of death, ringed by slaves in a tight noose of security, before the approved account of what had happened left Nola.

4

CARE FOR WHAT WE EAT

Augustus's wife, Livia, even more the matriarch when her husband was dying, controlled the time of death with a fig laced in deadly nightshade, atropine, as it was called in Greek after the Fate who cut the last thread of human life, belladonna as it became known for its use in giving women beautiful big eyes. Or so it was said.

Atropine was a popular drug for poisoners. It had long had its place in the line of the Caesars. The Egyptian queen Cleopatra, lover of Julius Caesar, loved the nightshade as both a cosmetic and a killer. It was Cleopatra's defeat that had brought Augustus to his decades of power before an end maybe hastened by her signature make-up in his fruit.

Poisoning was not easy. Like so much else, from putting on a toga in the morning to preparing for bed, it required trusted staff (some four or five slaves for the toga alone). Few could ever be trusted enough. It was never certain that Livia was a poisoner. She had a luxurious garden of rare herbs and a decorated dining room which reminded her guests of her opportunities to poison them as they ate. She had many enemies who might have made up the story, not least Tiberius himself.

The fig is less a matter of maybe. Augustus enjoyed the produce of his own gardens as the Roman aristocracy long had done, liking to praise the produce of Italy and, by patriotic contrast, diminish that of everywhere else. There were popularly believed reasons why food grown in Italy was finer than any other. The precious metals under its soil were not mined. They were left untouched to add flavour to vegetables and fruit. Augustus knew that there was no gold or silver or even copper and tin in Italy. If there had been it would most certainly have been extracted for sale, not left to make sweeter figs. But many patriots preferred the myth.

Food was part of an individual's character and the character of a whole people. A tongue was for talking and for eating. In street language, poetry and the farces of the stage, it was for sex. The Latin tongue was as special for the Romans as their land. The flatterer and the glutton, the names already beginning their life on the Palatine, were extremes of the same use of the *lingua Latina*.

Augustus liked it to be known that small figs and second-class bread were the staple of his diet at home. This was one of many self-conscious Roman virtues that for a while survived the rise of empire while others faded. The poet Horace, often a promoter of Augustus's ideals, was the son of a former slave and seller of cheap salted meat and fish. He wrote of how the simple vegetables from his farm outdid the feasts of kings. Horace was a pioneer of the satire, a word originally meaning the most mundane mincemeat, and invited grandees in elegant verse to his modest table, gently mocking the fashion for goose liver stuffed with figs. Love of plain country food was the official story from the court for the world outside, whatever the luxuries that its cooks could provide from all ends of the empire.

In 14 CE, whatever the roles of figs and belladonna, Livia delayed the death notice until her son had his preparations in place. For ten years Tiberius had been also Augustus's son. Together, Tiberius and Livia were left with the reins with which to rule and the servants who would help to hold them.

Rome's first emperor left a will prepared in part by his former slaves, Hilarion and Polybius. He bequeathed a household account book of the empire, along with a warning that its responsibilities not be expanded. His private legacy ranged from the tax due from provinces to the list of slaves and other former slaves, those who bore his name and from whom his successor could demand account. There was money in the treasury, not a huge sum since Augustus had not been a hoarder, and a successful economy based on high public expenditure and imperial taxes. There were poets and historians who knew their patriotic duty. It was not yet clear how Tiberius stood towards his political, economic or cultural inheritance.

Although there was nervousness on the Palatine and ignorance in the empire far away, the news of Tiberius's succession was at least the outcome most expected. The Vitellii depended on the succession of a Caesar. Already it was important for the men and women of the palace to be able to think beyond weeks and months towards far-extending years of family rule, consolidating gains and keeping rivals out.

Augustus's adoption of Tiberius in 4 CE, though guaranteeing nothing at first, had signalled his intentions for a hereditary monarchy. The legitimacy that he had won by himself in civil war and subsequent peace would continue through his descendants. What he could not decide was whether that first descendant needed to be a man like himself, inventive, original, an inspirer; or whether his hard-won legacy would best be served by a plodder, a consolidator, a man who slowly chewed his food.

There were other choices from within his own family, but the number was small and had shrunk over his reign. He had a massive mausoleum for himself, but few to follow him inside it. He had no son of his own and the eldest son of his sister was already buried there. A list of his achievements in bronze and marble, his *Res Gestae*, 'What I achieved in my life', stood at the gates as though a courtier permanently flattering his person. But the best chance of real permanence would be successors who owed their place to him alone.

Augustus had only one natural child, Julia, the daughter of a brief second marriage made to cement a political alliance in his rise to power and ending in divorce within days of her birth. There was never a suggestion that a woman could inherit in her own right. Julia had been strategically engaged, married and remarried – eventually to Tiberius – with results as unhappy as her mother's. For the past sixteen years she had stood condemned as a dangerous adulteress, the danger political more than moral. In 14 CE she was still in exile, allegedly starving. Not even the palace servants knew precisely why.

Before her disgrace Julia had produced five children as the wife of Augustus's greatest general, Agrippa, three sons, two of them dead at eighteen and twenty-three – one judged by her father as hardly better than a beast – and two daughters. From her marriage to Tiberius there had been only one child, a son, who had died soon after birth. After that her links to ambitious men at the court aroused Augustus's constant suspicions.

The emperor who wanted a dynasty had been peculiarly implacable against the one woman who could directly give it to him. Even Ovid, Rome's most popular poet, was in exile, and for mysterious reasons connected to Julia and her daughters. Ovid was a supreme artist in many forms. His works included not just *Metamorphoses*, an erotic literary guide to the borders between gods, men and beasts, but *Ars Amatoria* (*The Art of Love*), practical poetic advice for male and female seducers. The Augustus who promoted virtuous eating habits did not mind the higher literature but did not, it was said, want the sex guide.

Ovid was in a world of art way above the bawdy street farces of the Glutton and the Chewer, but he used the same sexual ambiguities when it suited him, more subtly but more woundingly too. In an archery competition Ovid's word for bow was not just a bow. No part was just a part, no service just a job, and a goal was an ejaculation as much as any other end in mind. Ovid had many enemies: those he had hurt, those he had let down and those who had read his poems with guilts about themselves.

The author of *The Art of Love* was an early victim of the courtly truth that what was amusing when the emperor was relaxed, might be treason when courtiers whispered that he needed to assert himself. Some connected Ovid specifically to the immoralities of the imperial family. In as much as anyone could be sure, that was enough for him to be exiled to the Black Sea and still be there at Augustus's death.

The elder Julia was her father's first and last hope of his own descendants, but no part of his future plans. She had not even known that her father was dying at Nola. She knew only that two of her surviving children were also exiled. Her son, Agrippa Postumus, named after her husband, Agrippa, and born after his death, stood condemned by Augustus as a waste of Palatine space. His strength of body was not matched by strength of mind: he liked not just to fish but to style himself Neptune. There was also her namesake daughter, condemned on similar sexual political charges to her own.

Instead, Julia's estranged husband, Tiberius, was at the head of the succession race and for further reassurance for the future he had a nephew, Germanicus, son of Antonia and his brother, Drusus, who carried the bloodline of Augustus and stood next in line. Germanicus was famously unlike Tiberius. In the summer of 14 CE he was in Gaul keeping the peace for tax collection. He was charismatic, popular and also neatly married to Julia's other daughter Agrippina, the only grandchild of Augustus neither dead nor banished from Rome.

This was a complex structure of exclusions, inclusions, expectations and hopes. Adopting Tiberius, after the early deaths of Julia's elder sons, his direct male heirs, was part of a programme of merging the emperor's Julian family, grown smaller by ill luck and ill feeling, with Livia's own much larger, and historically more eminent, Claudians. The whole was the Julio-Claudian house, but the Julian side, as Augustus knew, lacked the numbers to stay equal over time. A ruling family headed by Tiberius, with Livia still in place and Germanicus ahead, was a reasonable certainty for those who served the increasingly Claudian house of Julius Caesar's heirs.

It was not clear, however, what sort of ruler Tiberius would be, or how the court would have to adjust to him. Charisma had been the oil in the old machine. Augustus was a populist. The people and the army had backed him against the aristocratic senators who had murdered Julius Caesar. He had returned the favour with public works and the always careful acknowledgement that the people had the power. His family story and personal charms had made the system run. Tiberius was not a populist. He was not a charismatic man. There needed to be new ways to make the running smooth.

Those who worked in libraries could already know about the theory of flattery. In a house of Julius Caesar's family on the Bay of Naples there were at least three different theoretical studies on rivalries for a master's attention, whether the opposite of flattery was frankness or friendship, the kinds of scholastic dispute which enlivened debates after dinner. But there were few readers, and no clear route from theory to practice for anyone who did read. The whim of the master overseeing the discussion was the way that mattered.

Meanwhile, at her father's death, in her exile from the halls of the Palatine, the elder Julia was already part of half-forgotten history. The only daughter of the Emperor Augustus was already fading away, at first both alive and remembered, then alive but dead in the household memory, then hardly more than a ghost, not visited, not even visible with a backward look. She was allowed her last starving breath in the year of her husband's arrival on the throne. Agrippa Postumus, her son who called himself Neptune, died in that year too, leaving few mourners.

5

A WOLF BY ITS EARS

For the servants of the *domus Caesaris*, as for any Roman household, the hereditary succession of a new head was in one way as normal as death itself: a son replaced a father and the house went on, upwards or downwards depending on the skill and fortune of the next generation. So it was with the Vitellii. But it was novel, even strange, for this process to apply to everywhere and everyone. Rome had occasionally been ruled by autocrats before, appointed for emergencies or the pretence of emergency; never in the 500 years since it expelled its kings had it experienced autocrats in a dynastic succession.

The powers of most officials lasted only a year, were awarded by election and were shared. The assassins of Julius Caesar had killed – and died – in order to keep that principle alive. Augustus ruled under the standard of ending civil war and stopping its return. He flattered the citizens of Rome, the high and the low, that they were still the ones in charge and that he was merely a *princeps*, their first citizen, the head of Caesar's house. They, in return, gave him respect that at some points came close to worship. It was a double deceit which the months after his death made all too clear. Augustus's legitimacy came from victory in war and the concealment of a military coup in comfortable disguise; Tiberius's right to rule – or even to be considered for rule – came only by being the son of the emperor's wife.

After the news from Nola there were immediate army revolts, disputes over pay and conditions of service, signs of more than mere disquiet. Even the celebration of a new festival for Augustus produced riots over actors' pay. Troops restored order, but they could not run an empire. The occupants of the Palatine needed new rules, new conventions, new flexibilities to manage an empire in the manner of a house.

Tiberius was reluctant to show the way. This simple indecision, the truth that he was not like Augustus, may have been the very reason why Augustus had chosen him. Germanicus would have been more likely to bring ideas and energy, but energy was arguably not what was most required. Consolidation and caution were more important.

In his military middle age, on the borders of the empire, Tiberius had grown used to the predictable obedience that comes with army rules. He had enjoyed too the simplicities of leisured life in island Greece. Even early in his reign he spoke of wanting to retire and of returning Rome from his one-man rule to rule by the few and the many. But he was 'holding a wolf by its ears', he sighed. Was it safer to keep holding the wolf and endure its struggle or to let the wolf go and risk the jaws of civil war? He could not let it go.

Any Caesar, any ordinary, unexceptional Caesar, however sluggish, however dull, was the way by which the destruction of war would be kept at bay. That seemed to have been Augustus's dying view. Peace might bring its own problems, but the household could deal with those. The staff could adapt. The lesson for anyone with an Augustus cup and a Tiberius cup was that there was new power but still also old power: the emperor among the gods would still be watching from around the rim.

For those on the Palatine adjustment was not simple. There were many different players, the surviving remains of Augustus's way of rule, the falling but not yet fallen and the rising, whose path was hard to see. There was still a cadre of senior men of the senate whose authority Tiberius said he wanted to restore but whose restored authority he feared. New men might aim to supplant them, but no one could be sure of when and how.

Even execution and exile could not destroy threats from those using his own family name. A man in Gaul had claimed to be Julia's fisherman son, Agrippa Postumus. The impostor was a former slave of Postumus who had succeeded in raising a small army, though not in protecting his infant court from a Palatine spy. This pseudo-Agrippa, once captured, saw no purpose in flattering Tiberius. Tortured on the rack and with no prospect of survival, he revealed the names of none of his fellow conspirators, replying to the emperor's own question 'How did you come to be Agrippa?' with the answer 'The same way that you became Caesar.'

This was an irresistible story, also a dangerous one to tell, descending, as it did, into the deepest source of Tiberius's insecurity. The favour of the new master was the currency that courtiers needed most, a fact to be hidden by a range of face-saving deceits. Under Augustus's one-man rule it had become normal to pretend that he was only the *princeps*, the first among equals. The pretence required for Tiberius was already different.

When Augustus concealed his autocracy, he first cowed the senators with memories of the civil bloodshed he had ended, secondly encouraged the second order of society, the *equites* or businessmen knights, with commercial opportunities in a booming economy of public works at home and abroad, some of it overseen by Tiberius. And thirdly he empowered a small household bureaucracy.

That domestic office, promoting little overall policy but answering queries from across the empire, was where Lucius Vitellius aimed to thrive. The new emperor would be known not just for what he did (in a time of peace there were fewer opportunities for doing) but for what he might possibly do, or what people thought he might do. The Palatine currency was in signs and words, not just on the coinage itself but in letters that were answered and, hardly less important, those that were not.

Many of Lucius's colleagues were slaves and former slaves, men and women whose names were the same as their master's: a 'Tiberius Julius', not so long ago enslaved in the Asian port of Smyrna, might be as unique in his skills as he was nominally indistinguishable from many others. These men understood the minds of the emperor's subjects much better than did those of the old Roman military and political class. They knew the local codes.

The enslaved could be free. The Palatine household was no different from those on the city's other hills. Romans for the most part did not see slavery as an unchangeable state of nature. A Greek nurse, bought and sold in Athens, had more chance of freedom in Rome than if she had stayed at home. She could be a Claudia, like her mistress. There were promotions, jobs bought and sold. 'Sales of smoke' might mean the passing-on of news or the offer of appointments that never quite happened. The seeds of later bureaucracies were there at these beginnings.

Lucius Vitellius was skilled at picking winners. He had the example of his father, the first of his family with a career at Rome, a man whose status rose to that of procurator, one of the many overseeing domestic tax receipts, sometimes doing the same job abroad in large provinces governed by senators or even a few small ones which they could govern themselves. The prefects in charge of Egypt, the corn supply and the city guard also reported directly to Augustus, a policy designed to stop unreliable senators having too much independent power. It was uncertain whether Tiberius would work in the same way, whether the system would work properly if he did and how much, beyond the Palatine itself, it really mattered who was emperor.

The exiled Ovid, desperate for return, saw his salvation in the whole *domus Caesaris*, not in the new sole occupant of the throne. In his *Metamorphoses*, his epic of possibility and change, he had compared the Palatine to the home of the Olympian gods. Soon after Augustus's death Ovid sent a poem to Rome praising not the ascent of Tiberius to the throne but the ascent of Augustus to those heavens beyond the Milky Way. He asked for it to be recited in the palace, to be heard by hundreds as well as read by the few.

This stratagem did not help Ovid: his crime, whatever it was, was not so easily forgiven. But although he had been outlawed for six years and could sense the political wind of Rome only by letters and visitors, his general sense was acute. There was an important pretence at Rome that Augustus was still the primary figure in politics – even after his death.

At the same time, however, Tiberius held power's reins and might choose to pull them one way or another. This was the new reality of one man, one house. Proximity to Tiberius brought the chance to learn about the new power – at dinners, at diplomatic meetings, at visits to soldiers. Food and force fuelled the machine. Flattery greased it.

Tiberius was not a confident populist like Augustus. He was not a charismatic leader. He avoided crowds. He wanted to trust those immediately around him, and if people failed the test, he would find others. Flattery quickly became the new oil, applied from those close below rather than flowing down from above. That was the beginning of the household's slippery truth.

Early every morning the Vitellii became part of a packed crowd of permitted admirers, a *salutatio* at which Tiberius showed himself in the portico of the palace, reviving the tradition of Augustus, who had strictly enforced attendance in formal dress except on days when the senate was sitting. This was the political theatre for Augustus the actor, also the place where his body had been brought to lie in state. It was as though he had never left.

Augustus never said goodbye to the Palatine. At the end of his life he had been too ill to take the *salutatio*. At Nola he had made his final bow only in his mind and to a very few, seeking an answer in applause to the question of how well he had performed.

The restoration of the *salutatio* by Tiberius was both the same and not the same. There was no stardust and no star, only a way of seeing who was greeted in person, who was kissed and how, who was a power and who might not be. Senators entered first, then the richer men of business, the *equites*, then sometimes some from the *populus*, the city mass who had luck and the time. The *amici*, the emperor's friends, were there all the time.

Already jostling for position, enduring the daily acceptance of an autocrat's right to rule, were the sons of the elderly Publius Vitellius, Publius and Lucius to the fore, Quintus and Aulus a bit behind. A curious enquirer into who mattered (or might matter) in the first year of Tiberius's reign heard names in a shifting list – the emperor's Claudian cousins, Julian nephews, slaves, ex-slaves, Greek prophets, gentlemen soldiers and lawyers.

Most were present in Rome, but not all. Germanicus was the most potent name, the newly designated heir, deemed suitable but not quite yet, a man with plans, but ones best kept for a future time. Tiberius's brother's son, aged twenty-nine, was away taxing Gaul when Augustus died at Nola. An immediate return seemed unlikely.

There was Germanicus's wife Agrippina, a power in herself, new mother of a daughter, named after herself and born in an army camp beside the Rhine; there was Julia's daughter, Julia, Augustus's granddaughter; and their many younger children in the imperial bloodline. Most of these were daughters too. The very model of government by a household meant maybe bigger roles for women.

As well as the young Agrippina there was a boy, Gaius, called Caligula in his father's camps because of his little *caligae*, the Roman soldier's standard-issue boot. There was the emperor's own son, named Drusus after Tiberius's dead brother, aged twenty-eight, wilful and insecure. In the next generation there was Tiberius's grandson and namesake, Tiberius Gemellus, the single survivor of the younger Drusus's twin sons, also Gemellus's sister, the sunny-tempered Julia, whose health had so concerned Augustus on his deathbed. All these and more had homes, slaves and ex-slaves on the Palatine.

6

PUBLIUS AMONG THE FISHES

A year after Augustus's death, while the courtly Lucius Vitellius was at the slow-shifting centre of the empire, his bluff elder brother, Publius, was at its northernmost edge facing a clearer and more present danger. Lucius was in Rome with his wife and their son, Aulus, who the augurs had said should never be in charge of an army. Publius, whose birth auguries were unrecorded, was in Germany proving that the family prophets might have barred the wrong man from army service. In temporary command of two legions for Germanicus, he was leading an unnecessary march that had become a mass drowning.

Indistinguishable from his men, the military standard-bearer for the Vitellii was stumbling through salt ponds that were with every minute less distinguishable from the great grey surrounding sea and sky. Winds filled with rain were roaring over banks of sand that had been land only an hour before. With every cloud of freezing air or fleeing birds came whips of grass like leather, shards of razor shells, goggle-eyed fish, lurid, orange, purple and alive, blood-red parts of what may once have been fish, prawns as clear as water, spiked fins and gills hardened and heading for the few rocks that anyone could see.

All around him was chaos that had so recently been order. Men were swept away by the waves or sucked under as though by unseen mouths. The air was a roar. Only under water was there silence. Horses, oxen, baggage, lifeless bodies floated about and blocked the soldiers' way. Separate marching groups became confused, their orders confused, struggling sometimes with their heads only above water, losing their footing, their comrades and their lives. Cries of encouragement to one another died against the North Sea sky. Nothing distinguished the brave from the coward, the careful from the careless, forethought from chance. The same grey power swept everything before it.

Publius began his day on a dry shore where the waves were coming in gently, not as warm as in the Mediterranean but as calm as marble, grey-blue lightened by curls of foam. His orders were directly from Germanicus himself, who wanted two of his legions to be marched back to their camp along the shore rather than overloading his ships. It seemed a simple enough command, one that his young courtier-in-arms, Publius Vitellius, could follow with ease.

Germanicus was a soldier-scholar who knew some of the principles of weather. He made his own translations from the Greek meteorological poet, Aratus. But Aratus, writer of the *Phaenomena*, observer of Macedonia and the eastern Mediterranean, had never seen the German sea. Nor had Publius. The Vitellii were not known for literary interests at all.

Publius was part of a raiding party sent by Germanicus eastwards across the Rhine, not an invasion force marching to conquer new territory (that would have been in contravention of Augustus's still-active will) but far enough to slaughter, humiliate and avenge losses of the past. It was a carefully calibrated exercise in propaganda, through the territory of friendly tribes.

Then came the first signs of the north wind in the high tide season, a flowing together of nature which, across the sea in Britain, once destroyed the fleet of even so meticulous a planner as Julius Caesar. Germanicus was no Caesar, not on the beaches or battlefield, even if he could claim the heritage at Rome. His name suggested a knowledge of Germany that he did not have.

Publius's 10,000 soldiers knew no more than their commanders. They did not smell the tides before they came, before the flat marble waters became a surging limestone white. The sea swelled. The sky fell. Daggers of ice flew as though thrown from miles away or hauled from hundreds of feet below. Publius's whole force – the first time that one of the Vitellii had held command – was pushed back on to quicksand indistinguishable from solid ground, shallows that became the sudden deep.

Previously Publius was happy to be strengthening his position in the entourage of the heir to the empire. Presently he was facing mass loss of life, the kind of disaster that in Rome would be political death even if he did not commit suicide first. The last commander to lose whole legions in Germany, just a short distance to the south and only a few years before, killed himself to save the honour of his family. The Vitellii might expect nothing less of Publius. All around him men breathed in the roaring air or found the silence of drowning.

Eventually the horror ended. After uncountable hours, in a world where counting had died with every other sign of order, Publius was among the survivors, struggling from the grey on to the few patches of ground that were still black. Around them was the seasonal harvest of that night-fishing in the day, nothing but dead parts of creatures that none of them had ever seen before, still less eaten, and ghostly, green-boned eels that were somehow still alive, able to live in air as well as water.

The rocks were a parody of a dining table at Rome. The vomit from the deep was like that from the stomachs of gluttons who puked where they ate. It was no more use to the hungry than the floor when the palace banqueters had left, shells without oysters, prawns still raw, serrated razors soaked in salt and sand.

Those who lived had lost their weapons and armour, emerging with bare or bruised limbs, conscious that they would rather have been attacked by Germans, with an opportunity at least of battle honours, than assaulted by such forces of nature. But when dawn came, they pushed their way to the meeting place where Germanicus had arrived with the fleet, silencing the rumour that all were drowned instead of, as was embarrassingly clear, merely so many of them.

7

BETWEEN THE EMPEROR
AND HIS HEIR

Back in Rome, when the elder Publius Vitellius, Augustus's veteran procurator, assessed the most successful of his sons for the new age, they were shaping into ever more contrasted pairs. His elder and namesake, survivor of a near-catastrophe, was a traditional politician of the army, his younger, Lucius, a subtle courtier of the new administration.

Publius had linked himself closely to Germanicus. He was looking to the future. It was common in eastern courts for ambitious courtiers to look far ahead, sometimes too far, to back the next leader while the current leader was still alive. The danger came from seeing inevitability where the incumbent saw a threat, but few in Rome had studied examples from Alexandria or Babylon such as those. Publius may not have had much choice in 15 CE than to join the new heir to the throne in the northernmost part of the empire. Or he may have seen the move as his main chance. It had quickly almost cost him his life before his life in politics could even begin – a near-death not just by drowning but by failure too.

When Germanicus was away from the court and his mother Antonia, during Augustus's last week in Nola, he was organising a census for taxing Gaul. He had then moved through the German forest on an exercise of propaganda and expiation, the kind of military manoeuvre valued most in the new era in which the empire was neither expanding nor contracting but consolidating what Julius Caesar and Augustus had won.

His chief destination was the long, thin battleground where the army of Quinctilius Varus, friend of Tiberius and fellow consul with him, had six years before suffered the most humiliating possible destruction, the loss of five legions, some 30,000 men, ambushed and extinguished on a rain-soaked road. His target, after burying any dead that still remained, was to punish any of the guilty victors he could find or pretend to have found.

Germanicus's father, Drusus, Antonia's husband and Tiberius's younger brother, was remembered as a ruthless hammer of the Germans. His son carried both his added name and the expectation that went with it. Publius Vitellius was not alone in wanting to march alongside Germanicus. Youth, vigour, learning in Greek and Latin, the translator of a prophetic (if unhelpful) weather poem all fitted admirers' idea of what an emperor should be.

Germanicus was thirty years old. Augustus had been nineteen when he began his vengeance against Julius Caesar's assassins, only a little older than Germanicus when he took sole power at Rome. Tiberius was almost twice as old, and his best days under arms were at least a decade before. It seemed reasonable, even prudent, for an ambitious man like Publius to look forward.

The new emperor seemed at first content with a burnished image of Germanicus, a prince of both the Julians and the Claudians and a useful link between them. Tiberius and Drusus, who was only twenty-nine when he died, had been friends as well as brothers. But even if there had been no sibling sentiment, predictability for the future promoted stability for the present, a stability on which Tiberius by himself could not rely. A celebrity heir cast stardust on the emperor. Flattery of Germanicus as the 'new Alexander' was welcome to Tiberius as long as there were no new acts of conquest to make the name more than a badge.

Even in faraway Tomis, by the Black Sea, hardly less cold than the German Sea, Ovid cast his pleas to be allowed home to Rome in language laudatory of Germanicus. After Augustus's death he changed the dedication of his poem celebrating Rome's religious calendar, the *Fasti*, to Germanicus. This was a suitable gift for a scholar heir, but one not driven by literary taste alone. Germanicus was an asset to Tiberius and a poet's flattery of the young prince, as long as it stayed within bounds, was useful to Tiberius too.

The right flattery of Germanicus could be a benefit for the ruling family as a whole. Germanicus was the first priest, the *flamen*, of Augustus. He had a new daughter, Agrippina, born in his German headquarters, as well as Caligula, his already swaggering son. When a legionary on the Rhine frontier studied the sheath of his sword, he saw Germanicus offering a statue of the goddess Victory to Tiberius while Augustus protected the good fortune of them both.

When Publius Vitellius left Rome for Germany, the aim to cement the heir's status without rousing the insecurity of Tiberius was not hard to understand. But the balance was already uneasy. The emperor sometimes seemed to be favouring the succession of his own son Drusus, from his first marriage, who was only a year younger than Germanicus.

Petulant and conscious of his status, Drusus held the title of consul and seemed to be being marked as the more legitimate alternative, particularly if Tiberius were to live long enough for Augustus's instructions to fade and his bloodline be forgotten. There were, and never would be, any rules about whether Augustus's natural heirs had primacy over the children of an incumbent emperor. A courtier, even one who preferred military tradition to the domestic arts of the palace, had to judge with care.

Some 1,000 miles from the Palatine, the Rhine was the border between the lands which, thanks to Julius Caesar, were seen as already on their way to Roman civilisation and those which were not. For Tiberius the tribes of Gaul were chiefly a challenge for tax-collectors. Those called Germans were different and still needed pacification. The distinction between the two groups was not as clear in the cold swamps and forests as it sometimes looked in Rome, but Tiberius knew the terrain – of both politics and geography – as well as anyone. He did not need his courtiers for that. Men were what they ate. German food of fresh fruit, forest meat and cheese, as well as their fighting spirit, came from a more primitive age. Dangerous, and dangerously admirable, the German tribes still needed the kind of hammer blows delivered by Tiberius's brother, Drusus, Germanicus's father, also the hammer of Germanicus himself.

Rome could not afford to extend its borders. That was Augustus's last statement of truth. Tiberius could not afford an heir who was too successful in his soldiers' eyes. Augustus would have understood that, even though it was not a problem he himself had had. Trips to seize money and ceremonial visits to rescue standards, bury bodies and expunge the shame of Augustus's greatest military disaster were different from conquest. Publius Vitellius was part of a new kind of imperial mission.

What he found within the Rhine army was a defensive force with little glory ahead and the job of looking backwards to its worst past. The massacre in the Teutoburg forest in 9 CE cost a fifth of Rome's military strength and threatened the invincibility of the empire. It came closer than any setback to shattering Augustus's image of calm. He was reported as tramping the palace floors at night and shouting *Quinctili Vare, redde legiones*, 'Varus, give me back my legions'. But six years later, with tax-collectors and tame reporters in the entourage, Germanicus could begin to right the wrong.

Publius arrived several months into the mission, but Germanicus's legions were still scarred by what they had found in the waterlogged Teutoburg forest. Here were the scattered remains of men whose commander, five years before, had led them into a trap. Human and animal bones lay in the same shallow pits beside rotting goat-skin shields and tents. There were skeletons in armour, bells stuffed with grass, designed vainly to muffle the sound of pack-mules, coins of bronze, the remains of a last imperial pay day that the Germans had not even bothered to recover. This was a disaster that required continuing revenge – and also explanation.

To the troops of Germanicus it was Varus's own responsibility that was clearest, the failure of a bureaucrat, not a fighter, an impoverished aristocrat whose father had killed himself after the defeat of Julius Caesar's assassins, a tax-collector whose travelling treasury had been his top priority in the forest mud. Germany was not ready for lawyers and office men.

The Germans were savages whose rules, in as much as they had rules, were not yet ready to be refined into those from Rome. The German conqueror of Varus was a treacherous Roman ally, educated and trusted, who gave Roman banquets for his enemy and made fake requests for the judgment of Roman law. The barbarians' torture pits, the cages in which they had burnt their prisoners, the trees to which they had nailed Roman skulls, all became a lesson in the difference between Palatine conflicts and the real thing.

Varus was a favourite of Augustus, a valued fellow consul of Tiberius, but the wrong sort of favourite friend. He was too courtly for Germans. Before even the last act of what was quickly called Varus's catastrophe, the *clades Variana*, Varus took his own life. Publius Vitellius, one of Varus's avengers, was lucky not to die as a lesser Varus himself. Two lost legions in a time without war would have been a massive loss.

Publius hardly contributed much to Rome's limited aims – or to any other advance for his family. Instead he led a march which only narrowly avoided being a *clades Vitelliana*, a mass drowning rather than a mass slaughter, but a potential catastrophe nonetheless. On this occasion his political luck was good. It did not suit Tiberius to damage Germanicus any more so early in his reign. Germanicus stood by his friend while focusing Publius's future efforts on tax collection, a family skill of his namesake father and of Lucius Vitellius, his already very useful younger brother.

8

FLATTERY AND FEAR

The courtiers of Tiberius's house had a strong interest in the ruling house being that of the Julio-Claudian family rather than any other. After fifty years few Romans wanted the instability of the old republic. But that did not mean to everyone in every other house that the emperor should forever be a descendant of Julius Caesar.

In his final years, Augustus had been clearly frustrated – clearly at least to those who were close – that neither his own family nor that of his wife could provide a suitable candidate to succeed. There was much reasonable ambition in grand men's minds. The aristocrats Marcus Lepidus, Gnaeus Piso and other family heads with heirs to come might all see their own claims to command Rome's armies, control provinces and be the final judge of the law for Romans and the world. Those closest to Tiberius found quickly that they could both flatter him with his natural right to rule and play upon his fears of rival claimants.

When Tiberius took the throne, he did not pretend to be a new Augustus. His continuing argument – in words and signs – was that the old Augustus was still present in all their lives. His aim was that rule by a single Caesar was instead to be as ordinary as all the previous conventions of the past, no more requiring a man of god-like status than the consulship had. Just as it was a matter of routine for there to be a Roman Empire, a fact of geography long preceding any act of Augustus, so too the rule of the Caesars would be made routine.

But what was routine behaviour around an autocrat? Tiberius's accession raised ever more starkly the question of what an emperor really did once there was no more expansion of the empire. The answer was that he responded to thousands of requests from all across the Roman world. His responses rarely required the enactment of a principle: mostly they required knowledge of individual people and places, taxes and exemptions, subjects on which any single man would need specific advice.

Tiberius affected to believe that the senate should provide this wisdom of experience, as it had in the best years of the past. He tried to present himself to the elite as one of their own, merely the grandest Claudian of his father's family, no radical, no populist. He vigorously encouraged senators to seize their responsibilities last shown before the era of Julius Caesar.

This was quickly a failure. Tiberius flattered the senate as a whole, but individual senators were reluctant to believe him and frightened to take what he seemed to offer. Like Augustus he rebuked any member of the senate who called him *dominus*, a word too flagrantly signalling a relationship of master over slaves. But even at the beginning, softer language only partially concealed hard facts. An imperial smile from Tiberius hid many realities, some imagined, others all too real, thoughts and visions of an uncertain future. For those slow to adapt it was easy to fail and fall.

Ambassadors, supplicants and allied kings alike needed guidance they could trust. They found that personal aides, *liberti* (freedmen who had once been slaves), army friends and old imperial servants had the best claim to know the emperor's true mind. And if Tiberius had no view on an issue (which inevitably was very often), they needed advice on how to flatter him into believing that, from his own wise mind, he had come to favour the cause that was their own.

There was almost no systematic government or policy formation. Making the arbitrary slightly more predictable was worth fortunes to petitioners from Rome and across the empire. It also made the whole system work. It was useful to know when the emperor was drunk and when he might be sober. The emperor's routine exercise of power was by legal business. But there were no timetables or state lawyers to organise the courts. There were virtually no state functionaries of any kind.

In the remaining Greek monarchies of the east, those from the age of Alexander the Great that had not been brought under Roman control, there was a simpler model of rule. The kings there had no surviving sources of power that they had supplanted or wanted to supplant. They were the sole power. Augustus had kept the traditional republican institutions of Rome on a form of political life-support, flattering the senators and magistrates that they still mattered, accepting their flattery in return. This was an act – and a hard act to follow.

The 'dictator's dilemma', already a dimly expressed problem of government, became more acute. How could the emperor spread responsibility without losing control? How could he know that the courtier was being frank in his opinion? How could the courtier know that the emperor would do what he promised? Neither side could know. Only the most intimate could even pretend to know. Power shifted to friends, family members and personal servants who began to be public servants. The dining table became the desk. Flattery and gluttony began to be arts of survival as well as government.

Some of the ingratiating and greedy became famous – and then infamous. Many more survived quietly for decades, unknown or almost unknown. There were courts within courts, one of them headed by Germanicus's mother, Antonia, a daughter of Augustus's sister. Unusually, Antonia had the independence to remain unmarried after the death of her husband, Tiberius's brother Drusus, in 9 BCE. Lucius Vitellius owed much to this *grande dame* of Rome. Influential slaves in Antonia's house included Pallas, a teenage Greek accountant, and Caenis, a slave who claimed to carry in her mind 'everything that you have written and anything else you tell me'. In a court of wax tablets, a memory that no one could erase was both a useful and a dangerous asset.

There were also men whom Tiberius found good company, respectful and not too ambitious, whom he had taken on his military campaigns. Typical among these was Gaius Rubellius Blandus, whose family had never boasted a senator and whose house was in Tibur, Rome's nearest pleasure resort. Blandus's name stood for smooth-talking flatterer, an example to all.

Pre-eminent on the Palatine was Lucius Aelius Sejanus, the chief of the palace guard and, just as importantly, a man whom Tiberius could trust with almost any task that he had no appetite for himself. Sejanus was the master of what was not quite yet an imperial private office, also of its banqueting tables. In a very visible Palatine house, decorated as though for a party, was Piso, a grandee close to the Claudians who thought he was already their equal. In their different ways, both of these men – and others too – thought that the house of the Caesars needed new management, maybe without any Caesars. Lucius Vitellius moved between all sides.

9

WORDS FOR A PALACE

As the courtiers of Tiberius adjusted to his power, outside the gates of the *domus Caesaris*, guarding the path down to the Forum, were ever more parades of gifts to him from abroad. A wise diplomat kept his flattery short and his offerings effusive. The mass of the Roman people appreciated the respect shown to their emperor by exotic slaves and animals, a man who was nine feet tall, a hunchback, a dwarf, a giraffe or a giant fish.

Monsters massaged the egos of those citizens who, if not wealthy or well fed, could at least feel comfortingly normal. In the absence of regular gladiatorial games, generous feasts and other necessities of electoral politics, this was flattery to the whole city population. Dead monsters were popular too, massive bones and tusks which, in an age long before the knowledge of dinosaurs, might be relics of beasts dispatched by Hercules. Gifts of more tradable value, gold crowns and silver tableware, were kept in the emperor's personal treasury or in the official treasury, the distinction between the two being fuzzy under Augustus and set to be fuzzier as time went on.

Along with the leadership of its greatest household, the Palatine was changing. It was becoming ever more like an imperial palace. It had ever fewer neighbours. More great houses of the old elite were mere palace annexes, linked by covered lanes, the corridors of the new power. Tiberius himself took a massive site, facing away from the Forum towards the stadium known as the *Circus Maximus*. There he ordered the house that would hold the courtiers and cooks, the enslaved and the free, who were closest to him.

The scale of this was new. Augustus had taken over a few houses of his father's assassins to provide public space and the great temple to Apollo, its pediment floating on only four columns, one of the wonders of his Rome. When he moved to the Palatine it was not even into one of the grandest houses. Augustus did not like to be associated with personal extravagance. He was happy to live and work on the site of Romulus's hut, to look down from his study and see the rooms where his nephews were learning the history of great men that he and his writers were busy constructing.

The exiled Ovid was the first writer to note how Augustus had created a place from which to rule which would soon define ruling itself. The civic crown of oak leaves, a soldier's decoration for saving Roman life, stood above the main entrance flanked by laurels of victory. Yellow marbled walls supported red-tiled roofs. Colonnades stood against the stare of the sun, nut trees among vines, bronze birds next to beasts spewing water into bowls. Tubs of oil scented the principal hallways. Tubs of urine awaited the wool-fullers who needed the acid for their work. Palatine games, theatre and gladiatorial shows, celebrated Rome's founding emperor inside his own home.

Palatine and palace: it was a metaphor that never died. Ovid, in Rome and with a guarded irony, compared it to the home of the gods. Then, in exile, he imagined more of what had not quite arrived in the age of Augustus but was rapidly on its way. The new architecture – of place and mind – came from the needs of autocracy and from the east, where autocracy was the only way to rule. Apollo's prophets looked out eastwards. When ambassadors from Judaea met advisers of Augustus to partition the kingdom of Herod the Great, the easterners must have felt much more at home in Apollo's temple, architecturally and politically, than were the hosts. The public space in front of the palace had room for some 8,000 Jews opposing Herod's complex plan of succession.

Much of what later became familiar as Roman architecture was then wholly new in Rome. The marble oxen on Apollo's walls were as though alive. It was beautiful but treacherous political terrain. Good government required guides. Even Tiberius's mother said she never understood her son's jokes. There were no guides paid at public expense. In 17 CE one of Lucius's less successful brothers, Quintus, lost his status as a senator in a purge of those too poor for their place. Another, Aulus, survived quietly and gained the status of a minor gourmet. Under the republic the succession to the consuls who ran Rome, however corruptly conducted, was clear and by election. Under the Emperor Tiberius, success and failure came from a cloud of imperial will and routine, a haze that the Vitellii had to see through or die.

PART TWO

High in a high tree, safe at ease,
A happy Crow held stolen cheese,
Till on the ground a flattering Fox
Knew just the way to fill his lunch box.
'Darling, how fine are your feathers of black,
How divine your face and your shining back.
If only just a little you could sing,
You'd have no rival on the wing.'
Then she, too eager to display
Her beauty in the vocal way,
Let go the cheese of luscious taste,
Which Foxy seized with glutton's haste.

Phaedrus (first century CE)

10

THE FOX AND THE CROW

While the Vitellii and their rivals manoeuvred their way around the Palatine, surviving present dangers and thinking how to survive the future, there was one man keeping a written record. It was not a direct history of this time. It was instead a rejection of the reality of that, even its possibility. The fables by a writer who called himself Phaedrus were guides to the problems of court life. They looked as though they were for children, certainly to later readers and probably at the time. They starred animals and servants. They were seemingly simple stories about dogs and underdogs in the voice of an underdog, slave stories maybe written by a slave but maybe someone aping that role. No one was ever quite sure.

Phaedrus adapted Greek stories, the already famous fables of Aesop, and invented his own. He translated Greek, but like all the great poets of Rome he made them Roman as well as mere translations. His characters ranged from dogs to frogs, mice to lions, and from courtiers to the emperor himself. The settings were in both town and country. Food and flattery were their persistent themes, the way that they were intertwined and how they explained the world.

Aesop had been his own man of mystery, a captured slave from a golden age of writing some 500 years before, contemporary with the best-known philosophers and playwrights but given only the barest outlines of a character himself. He was said to have been a very ugly member of a great Greek household, a stutterer and clown who won his freedom by his art.

Perhaps he was. Comedy from the weak, both mocking and flattering the powerful, has a persistent history. The story of Aesop's road to freedom may have been in itself a fable. His origins as a slave, if true, would have allowed his life story to be fabricated by anyone in as much as anyone might care to tell it at all. Aesop was either an imaginative man or an imagined man, an inventive genius or a gatherer of tales by others. It was a long time since anyone had known.

Phaedrus was more imaginative than imagined. His identity was concealed, but he existed somewhere in or around the court of Tiberius. He understood the ways of survival for the weak among the strong, some of the weapons which the weak have and which the strong lack. He may not have known much more about Aesop's life than Aristotle did. What he did know, much more importantly than any facts of biography, was that Aesop's work had been successful. It told neglected truths. Just as Roman poets had adapted the sexual torments of Sappho for the age of Julius Caesar and the heroism of Homer for Augustus, Phaedrus adapted Aesop for the reign of Tiberius.

One of the best-known of all Aesop's fables was *The Fox and the Crow*. A hungry fox is at the bottom of a tree looking at a crow on one of the highest branches with some stolen cheese in its beak. The fox is not a climber. He will never reach the top of the tree. Instead he flatters the crow, calling it glossy and glamorous, worthy to be king of all the birds if its voice were as sweet as its looks. When the thieving bird lets out a caw to prove its perfection, the cheese falls to be eaten by the fox.

Various lessons could be learnt from this – about the credulity, stupidity and insecurity of those at the tops of trees, about the necessary cunning of those at the bottom. A piece of flattery, skilfully delivered, was certainly a useful way for a flatterer to be fed. No real harm was done. The fox was hungry, the crow one of the least musical of birds. The cheese was stolen anyway. It was a gentle story of ordinary life.

Aesop's fables of very human beasts – the *Frogs Who Wanted a King* and *Why Dogs Lick Their Arses* – preached good sense and proportion while pricking the pride of the pompous. *The Goose who Laid the Golden Egg* was a warning to the reader to recognise when he was lucky. A Greek philosopher of Tiberius's time both praised Aesop's power and likened it to the art of simple food: 'Like those who eat well off the plainest dishes, he used humble events to teach great truths, and after serving up a fable he adds to it the advice to do a thing or not to do it.'

'Aesop', the philosopher went on, 'was really more attached to truth than the poets are; for the latter do violence to their own stories in order to make them probable; but he, by announcing a story which everyone knew not to be true, told the truth by the very fact that he did not claim to be relating real events.' In the new age of emperors, these fantasy characters in fables delivered their messages about real life not in the Greek of slaves and the elite but in the Latin of the Romans in the street.

Phaedrus, like Aesop, was said himself to be a former slave, freed by Augustus and probably around thirty years old at Augustus's death. That was all. Whether in Greek or Latin, there was no more need for a writer to record the life of a fabulist than the life of a cook. Whoever he was, his work presented an accomplished variety of different faces: poet, reporter, preacher, accomplished ironist. In five books of fables he warned against listening too much to fabulists, including too much to the tale-teller known as Phaedrus. He prefaced his Latin version of *The Fox and the Crow* with the warning against flattery for both its subject and object, the human fox as much as the human crow. As a writer of his age he was a realist. He focused on what went on.

Horace, the poet whom Augustus had wanted in his court as a personal secretary, also knew the story. He used it to warn against both the smooth-talking and the open-mouthed, the vain and the over-reaching. But Horace, writing from his rural retreat, was read only by the elite; Phaedrus, whoever he really was, was for everyone.

11

WHO KILLED THE PRINCE?

Four years after the near-catastrophe on the northern German shore, Publius was a lucky man with a career still on the rise. He was back in Rome and in the service of Germanicus again. The difference this time was that Germanicus was dead, last seen on duty in distant Antioch, and Publius was prosecuting the man accused as his killer. To have won the brief was already a sign of his status; it was an honour to champion the heir who, even more so after his mysterious end, was a popular hero. It was also an assignment that could be the ruin of himself, and maybe his family too, as surely as if he had lost his legions in the sea.

The accused was Gnaeus Calpurnius Piso, a close friend of Tiberius, one of those whom Augustus was once rumoured to have seen as his best successor. The law court was in the senate house, the *curia*, at the foot of the Capitol hill. Behind it was the *carcer*, the prison, where the condemned might be strangled if the prosecutor won a guilty verdict. Above them both wound the notorious Groaning Steps from the summit, a mythical place of public humiliation for the damned. The people of Rome were already showing their interest in the case. There were crowds on the plateau at the top of the hill from where the body of the convicted man might be pushed and pulled, tumbling down these steps before being hurled by hook into the Tiber.

The *curia* was intimidating to lawyer and defendant alike, in some parts like a bare cell, in others like a temple and a luxurious dining room. Beneath Publius's feet were bright mosaics, roses, sheaves of corn and horns of plenty. At the end of the rectangular room, eighty feet away, was a statue of Victory standing on a globe, offering a wreath of triumph, representing the result of the sea battle that had brought the Caesars to power fifty years before.

Plain plaster covered the walls above his head. Marble shone on the sections below. On three broad steps, some fifty feet wide, sat several hundred senators of Rome, their togas striped in purple, their slippers red. This was a day on which Tiberius was affecting the role of just another one of his peers, one judge among many. Publius was dressed in the same way, as a civilian not a soldier, arguing for his future, not fighting for it, navigating a political terrain that was no less perilous than that distant sea.

The brief was not simple. It comprised both the facts surrounding Germanicus's death in October, 19 CE, few of them clear, and what Tiberius wanted the facts to show, a fact that was even less clear. Tiberius could have taken the case for judgment inside the *domus Caesaris*, but he had not. Publius would have preferred to know the emperor's preferred verdict before he began, but he did not. He was in the kind of trap that was becoming ever more dangerous in court politics. He had to present the illusion of being free, the appearance of being in a traditional trial when only the appearance was left.

Was Tiberius pleased that Germanicus was no longer a rival? Had he perhaps even ordered Germanicus's poisoning in distant Antioch? Or was he displeased that he had lost a popular heir since now he had to organise a succession to himself without the prop of Augustus behind him?

The jury on the marble benches was like a painting designed to trick the eye, like the mosaic floor whose corn and fruit seemed solid, almost real. He could see all the senators, but only one of them stood out. The only mind that mattered was the mind that was hardest to read.

If Tiberius was pleased at Germanicus's death, did he want to appear so? Probably not. If he was displeased, did he want to appear vengeful against the assassin? Possibly. Publius's task was to steer through quicksands that made the seas of Germany seem kind. It would have tested the skills of Rome's greatest advocates and flatterers of juries from the past. And Publius was no such man.

Everything about the trial showed how much had changed in the five years since Augustus's death. When Publius had served in

Germany with Germanicus, he had been there as one of the new heir's supporters and friends. But when Germanicus had moved on to govern the entire east of the empire, Tiberius had provided his own choice of helper, a friend, a rival according to some, a man who was also a minder.

The company of Piso had not been welcome to Germanicus. Piso and his wife, Plancina, were supremely grand and self-confident, a vivid reminder of the years of aristocratic independence that Augustus had steered towards its end. Tiberius had promoted him both to share his heir's administrative responsibilities and to keep a close eye on his plans, anxious to ensure that Germanicus and Agrippina, Augustus's direct descendants, including their eight-year-old-son Caligula, did not find further ambition within themselves while their emperor was alive.

It had been a perilous pairing from the start. Piso, as Tiberius well knew, was ambitious for himself. Plancina was a close friend of Livia, the matriarch of the Julio-Claudians but a Claudian first. Piso's elder son held the rank of Tiberius's personal quaestor, a junior position which bound the holder in loyalty for life. Piso's family was filled with long-standing supporters of the Claudians, of Livia, her son Tiberius, and Tiberius's son Drusus. Even after Germanicus's death, Piso had exuded confidence, sailing slowly back to Rome as though on a holiday cruise, holding a great feast for his friends in 20 CE on his return.

As he climbed the steps to the *curia* Publius could have been forgiven for his fear. He was about to prosecute Piso, one of the highest representatives of the respectability to which his own family aspired, a man whom Tiberius might have deliberately used to solve his own family problem. The Vitellii, like others senior to them in the court, needed to recognise force, counter-force and rapid change. So too did Blandus, who had reached the consulship in the previous year, not as grand as Piso or even the Vitellii, but advancing in his own courtly way. Tiberius's mother, Livia, was still a power in her own right. The Vitellii owed their allegiance to her as much as to him. That was one of the simpler of their divided loyalties.

*

Publius had swum for five years in these shifting political currents. Barely had he returned from Germany before the household was filled with rumours that Germanicus was eyeing an early succession, or that his friends were plotting on his behalf, or that the emperor feared that they were. Germanicus left again for Egypt and was acclaimed in worshipful terms as a saviour of the human race by the people of Alexandria. His rejection of the honour was not firm enough for Tiberius, who soon wanted Germanicus further out of his sight, though not beyond his oversight. Piso had been part of his solution, or so it was believed by many.

Then suddenly, and in faraway Syria amid one of many quarrels with Piso, Germanicus was gone. The distant death, its news delayed, confused and lurid, convulsed the court, the senate and the army. There was silence in the streets, a cessation of business, pleasure and all the buzz and hum of the city. The heir was lost, but it was as though a great battle had been lost, legions sacrificed and poison were passing through every house. Agrippina brought back her husband's ashes in an elaborate ceremony. There was even a rare public appearance by Germanicus's brother, Claudius, a stumbling, shambling figure but still a presence to remind watchers of their mother, Antonia, the bloodline of Augustus.

Tiberius did not react immediately. He did not have Piso arrested, or brought back by palace guardsmen. The guard captain, Sejanus, was himself thought to be involved but no one knew exactly how. Piso's slow cruise was allowed to continue. When the silence of the people turned to rumblings around the Groaning Steps, a trial seemed a necessary minimum response. But that did not make necessary a guilty verdict.

This was going to be neither a trial before the people nor a secret trial within the *domus Caesaris*. Tiberius had given judicial responsibilities to the senate soon after taking the throne and this was to be a senate trial, announced on the day after Piso's return, the morning after his welcome banquet for himself. The floor of his great dining hall was hardly cleared before Piso knew of the threat, also that the trial would not be hurried, that he had time to prepare his defence, and that there was a good possibility of acquittal before a jury of his peers.

For Publius there was time too for assembling evidence. As a friend of Germanicus he had formed a firm view of what had happened in Syria, but for his role as a prosecutor facts were few. Piso had not been with Germanicus in Antioch on the hot summer day when he died. That did not make him innocent. If he and Plancina had already poisoned him, or previously arranged his poisoning, that would have been merely wise.

Piso had certainly celebrated when he heard the news of the death, garlanding his ships and holding days of on-board banquets for his friends. But it was well known that each man would have been happy at the death of the other. Antioch was a diseased and dangerous place.

There was no doubt that Piso was a proud and ambitious man, one of those who both fully recognised the legitimacy of the emperor and did not accept that a successor had forever to be a Julio-Claudian. This would be perilous territory to cover in open court. Even in the quietest corridors of the palace it was best put in code.

Everyone who mattered knew that Piso had quarrelled with Germanicus about power and precedence, about relations with local kingdoms and who was responsible for them. He had mocked when Germanicus and Agrippina flattered the Athenian crowd and accepted heavy gold crowns from the king of Parthia. He had disagreed even about kingdoms whose existence was unknown to most in Rome, exotic names like Commagene, which had become part of Roman Syria, and Armenia, which had not. Any border on a map or banquet in a tent had the potential to enrage.

The charges covered not just the death of Germanicus but the disrespect to Germanicus's authority and division of their army into rival factions. Publius could persuasively charge that Piso had relaxed military discipline to win the loyalty of the local legions, paying imperial bonuses under his own name, encouraging Pisoniani to spar with Caesariani. These were serious accusations. Plancina was personally imperious and vicious, a mistress of magic arts. Whether Piso was a murderer was harder to turn into a charge.

But whether he was a murderer mattered much less than what Tiberius, whose seat in the senate was as visible as his motives were opaque, most wanted him to be.

Popular anger against Piso and Plancina was already intense, enflamed by long and loyal support for Germanicus and new sympathy for Agrippina. Piso's ornate Palatine house, impossible to hide, was an added incitement to the resentful. Many still thought that the accused would escape. Tiberius had allowed Piso every possible legal help, a signal that he was seeking an acquittal.

The emperor seemed more confident with his heir gone. He gave a generous reward to the poet Clutorius Priscus for a panegyric safely praising Germanicus's posthumous virtues. Observers of Tiberius's moods, schooled by six years in which this was the currency of their lives, noted his pleasure at the birth of his twin grandsons to Drusus and his wife, brothers to the teenage Julia whom Augustus had asked of as he died. Their arrival in the world had come on the same day as Germanicus's departure.

12

THE ONLY VERDICT THAT MATTERED

Publius Vitellius was about to speak to a brief for which life had prepared him well. He had spent time with Germanicus in Syria, as he had in Germany. He had shared the easy familiarity of military life. For three months he had been collecting evidence against Piso and Plancina and preparing an indictment. He could say that he himself had seen signs of poison on Germanicus's body and had arranged to send to Rome a local poisoner as a potential witness, Martina, a close friend of Plancina.

All this he was preparing to argue to Piso's fellow senators. Among the people of Rome this was a popular cause in support of the prince whose troops he had led to near-disaster on the German beaches; on the Palatine it was a perilous risk. It was possible that Tiberius wanted not only Germanicus dead but Piso saved. No one could be sure. Publius's risk was a risk too for all the Vitellii. One brother, Quintus, was disgraced by extravagance. Another, Aulus, was beginning to earn the glutton's reputation that would later stick to his nephew – and then to the whole family. Only Lucius was quietly climbing the household ladder.

Piso's defence, due to be made a week after the case for the prosecution, was to be led by serious figures, the kind whom Augustus, when he had been thinking of a successor from outside his family, had considered for the throne itself. Piso's supporters were a powerful alliance of the senatorial old guard, even though many of his most distinguished friends had refused to join. On the question of the poisoning, the case for Piso was strong. Although Agrippina believed that her husband had been murdered and Germanicus, she said, had believed so himself, evidence was slight, the accounts of the killing implausible and divergent.

Publius's speech for the prosecution would be the last of three, the summation of the charges at the end of two days of evidence. Though an eloquent climax, he hoped, it was never going to be impregnable. There was barely a dispute about Piso's contempt for Germanicus, his encouragement of divisions between Pisoniani and Caesariani, the promotion of the worst soldiers, who called him 'father of the legions', and punishment of the best, particularly Germanicus's friends. But while serious for a charge of sedition, it did not prove murder.

Nor did celebratory banquets prove Piso's guilt, still less the stories that he had opened up temples to allow others to celebrate. Much of the evidence from the first two prosecutors had been of extortion in Spain, common enough in a Roman trial to denigrate a man's character but of no relevance to the case. Unless Piso was a master revolutionary, aiming to bring down the whole system of rule by the Caesars, the principal advantage from a crime of murder would come to Tiberius's own son and grandchildren. Piso might have had his dreams of a new imperial house, headed by himself and continuing for his own heirs, but none of these points of succession were ones that could be discussed in the open.

Publius could not prove the poisoning. He had no last-minute evidence. His star witness, Plancina's friend Martina, had not survived the journey, poisoned either by her own hand or that of another whose identity was unknown. He could put before the senators only the discovery of body parts, the name Germanicus on charms pierced by nails and the paraphernalia of witchcraft by his bed.

As he began his speech, as the senators listened with due concentration, Publius did not advance anyone's understanding of the facts. As he stared down at the mosaic floor, turned sideways to the bare walls, gesturing with his hands in the way that orators were taught, he changed nothing. Gradually, however, watching not too obviously for Tiberius to indicate whether he would stand by his friend or let him fall, Publius saw that he was on the right side.

Piso watched Tiberius too. Tiberius sat still. He was as silent as
the streets had been when the news of Germanicus's death reached
Rome. Piso read the same signs as his prosecutor and saw that he
was abandoned. The people outside the senate had already decided
– and for once they would have their way. Lest Tiberius should be
in any doubt of their view, the rumbling band of demonstrators had
dragged a statue of Piso up to the Capitol, ready to be smashed,
dismembered and hurled down the Groaning Steps.

On the morning after Publius's closing statement, Piso was
found with his throat cut and a sword beside his body. The last
person to have seen him alive was his wife, unless someone else had
entered his room to create the appearance of a suicide. A sword, it
could be thought, was an unwieldy weapon with which to slit one's
own throat, but a judgment of suicide brought the justice that was
required. It proved his guilty conscience and helped his family's
inheritance of his property. Tiberius's mother successfully pleaded
the innocence of her friend Plancina.

After the trial came the phantoms of promotion, property and
pretence. A priesthood came to Publius as a mark of the emperor's
and the public's approval. He had done a good job. He had been
as eloquent as was desirable in the Rome of the emperors, where
minds did not need to be moved. The Vitellii had a new honour for
their rising family, one of the old honours that still had a purpose
under the rule of the Palatine.

The dead Piso was condemned for treason. The public popularity
of Germanicus, the enthusiasm of the crowd at the Groaning Steps,
made that a popular move. Tiberius did not want to encourage the
exercise of the popular will but would enjoy it when it suited him.
Piso's family was spared the forfeiture of assets and guilt by association that might have come to them. The men called Piso did not
fall far.

The principal problem for the *domus Caesaris* was how to present for the future a legal case which, unlike most of the dramas
within the household, had been a play on the stage of the whole
Roman Empire. The legions and the provincial leaders were still

restless about the fate of Germanicus and what it might mean for themselves.

The result was the most sacred and permanent trial record that Roman craftsmen could produce. Words that had once been sounds in the Palatine air became engravings on tablets of bronze. Every big city in the empire and every camp where the legions spent their winters was to have a detailed account of Piso's trial, the case brought by Publius Vitellius, the virtue shown by Tiberius, the gratitude due to him and his own heirs now that Germanicus and the iniquitous Piso were dead. The rule of Caesar's house for the future, and the principle of heredity within it, was set out not in nods and nudges but in letters of tin fused with copper, the traditional formula for the permanence of law.

On bright-polished tablets more than a metre wide, placed where parts would survive for 2,000 years, was a new version of both a past and an eternity. First, the name of Tiberius was joined with that of Augustus in public gratitude for ending civil war, a role in which Tiberius himself had played no part bar the suppression of some legionary revolts over pay. Secondly, Tiberius was hailed as the paragon of old Roman virtue, of justice, clemency and greatness of spirit, *magnitudo animi*. Germanicus became a hero of all time. An arch would stand in his honour in Germany, the land whose River Rhine he had defended for Rome and whose Roman victims he had avenged. Thirdly, Tiberius's descendants were to stand in line to succeed. Tiberius was not merely emperor, but the father and grandfather of emperors. His son Drusus, an infamous drunk, stood newly and clearly next in line. After him would come his grandsons, twins, Tiberius and Tiberius Gemellus, born on the day of Germanicus's death.

This *Senatus consultum de Pisone*, the decision of the senate in the case of Piso, was Tiberius's answer, brazen in every sense, to the lists of 'What I achieved in my life' outside Augustus's mausoleum. It said who would continue the work which the son of Julius Caesar had begun. Bronze stood for what was genuine, true and needing to be obeyed. As Ovid had observed (he had died in exile three years before), bronze was a medium of threat as well as information.

Not everyone would read the tablet's words, tightly inscribed as in a dedication to a deity. Many soldiers and citizens could read nothing. But they could hear and they could know. They could know what had happened in the recent past and how they should think and speak about their emperor in the eternal future.

The last words of the announcement noted that one of its authors was the son of Lucius's sister Vitellia, Aulus Plautius, who was a personal quaestor for Tiberius alongside the forgiven son of the reviled Piso. Lucius needed a careful response to his brother's role in Piso's trial.

He had to adjust his balance. He had long watched over Germanicus's interests at Rome while assuring Tiberius that any succession by Augustus's choice of heir would be both far off and part of the natural order of the house. Tiberius's personal soothsayer had helpfully agreed. Germanicus's death had brought an end to this order.

But for Lucius the adjustment of balance did not mean precipitately changing sides. The message of the tablets was clear, but a story was still just a story. He did not abandon the family of Germanicus, the prospects of Agrippina and the battered – but still surviving – hopes of her children to inherit in the future.

Publius was more impatient. The loss of Germanicus left a personal gap in his life. He sought a new standard-bearer to replace the one he had lost. Sejanus was the prime candidate, and not for Publius Vitellius alone.

13

TIBERIUS, TIBER AND TIBUR

On the Palatine no courtier would likely be hungry. The fox's cheese or the meat of a dog stood for what might be gained by flattery, a metaphor more than a meal. Not far away, however, it was a different story. Empty stomachs were a mass misery. Rome's food supply was frail. Whatever the boosters of Italy might write, or even think, its land was not able to feed and water its cities.

Essential food came from abroad. There was no alternative at a time of rising populations and unproductive farms. Water needed aqueducts if the fresh streams high above Rome were not to become useless mud before they reached the city. The provision of both required economic and political instincts that Tiberius lacked.

Transport by sea was much cheaper than by land. But when corn came by ship from Sicily and Africa, supply was vulnerable to weather in distant fields and stormy seas. Augustus knew how grain shortages threatened hunger and unrest. He twice faced famine in his reign, worst in 6 CE, when he had publicly had to send his slaves into the countryside, order the senate into indefinite recess and double the grain rations for the starving who stayed in the city.

Augustus encouraged the freeing of slaves for loyal service and exceptional talent, promoting small businesses and farms. He stimulated the circulation of cash throughout the country by building roads and aqueducts as well as temples. On succeeding to be the head of a household that was also a government, Tiberius's first policy was massively to cut expenditure, winning praise from conservatives in the senate who took a similar approach on their own estates. A follower of Augustus's will abroad, he did the opposite at home. The result for Rome was a reduction in paid employment and opportunities for commerce with no gain in the security of food and water.

The death of Germanicus opened a window on to what was happening both near and far beyond the court. In Rome the people began protesting, not just about the fate of their hero but against sharp rises in the price of corn. Tiberius was content, when it suited him, to flatter the men and women of the Forum that he cared about their views on the guilt of Piso. He was compelled, whether he liked it or not, to keep the citizens fed.

The Romans around the Groaning Steps, pushing Piso's marble head and hands, were hungry as well as angry. This was a dangerous combination, the hunger a ready fuse for rage. The Vitellii and their rivals needed to understand that, to balance flattery of Tiberius for their own survival against telling truth to power. The closer the courtiers stood to the object of their obsession, the less close they were to what was happening outside. No one had to travel far to see the problem, but it was safer for most to keep their eyes on Tiberius than on the people he ruled.

Gaius Rubellius Blandus was a slightly different kind of courtier, a man from just outside Rome whose final name meant smooth and obsequious, a good start for his journey through life. Even more useful was the place where he lived, Tibur, the future Tivoli, fifteen miles to the north-east of the Palatine, a place for luxury but also for reflection, with a spa, a marketplace and a university.

The success of the Vitellii was already part of a pattern. Other provincial families were following the same route by which wealthy fathers secured seats in the senate for their sons, and the sons picked their way through the dangers of Rome. Blandus's family had never been able to boast a consulship but, as a smooth-talking companion, a rare friend whom Tiberius liked and trusted, he had become a consul of the previous year. He had a base sufficiently close to Rome to do his job, but sufficiently far away to see something of the countryside.

Tibur was the city's resort for the rich, closer than Nola and the towns around Vesuvius where Augustus had ended his life. Just as the Palatine gave its name to future palaces, so did Tivoli become a label for future gardens of entertainment. Romans with homes in Tibur boasted of a paradise, a place for extracting Italy's finest water, as well as its fashionable limestone, Tiburtine, which, under the name Travertine, became sought after across the empire.

Before marble floors and walls were common in Rome they were the glory of Tibur. There was local food and wine as well as water, welcoming relief from city sounds, smells and responsibilities. Mosaic floors in the Greek style looked like the remains of a banquet, bones scattered among scales and claws. Men dined to the illusion of walking among prawn shells, broken fins and backbones.

Tibur's greatest glory was the river on which it stood. The Anio's bright streams fed apple trees on the heights, falling spectacularly for some eighty feet before crashing through pools to the figs and plums below. Its drinking water was famed and smelt of orchards. At the bridge below Tibur the Anio waters were fresh and bitter, astringent to the skin of those who bathed in it, settling to the stomachs of those who drank.

Tibur's water was as much needed at Rome as the food from its markets and fields. As Blandus, or any traveller, could see, that same water became useless as slowly it turned towards the sewers that led to the sea. Rome's demands were growing fast. Even in good times there was never enough and, even on the Palatine itself, Rome lacked all the water that it needed as it grew. The bitter, clear clouds that cascaded in Tibur were wasted into the sweet, brown Tiber before they could reach the baths, still less the luxurious dining rooms and cramped kitchens, of the capital of the empire.

Aqueducts were not yet a symbol of Rome, were too few and, for the taste of Tiberius, too high in cost. In the interests of the city, a mountain spring needed to flow into a basin with other springs, then flow on not as a torrent but gently, metre by metre, down slow inclines, raised on high arches or buried in tunnels. Rome's first aqueduct, the *Appia*, built by the man who constructed its first road, had carried water from springs south-east of Tibur for 300 years. Six others followed, financed by conquest, but failing to match the demand.

Tibur, Tiber and Tiberius were joined by more than their names in the murky history of Latin. They were linked in a chain of poor information and difficult decisions. The assessors of the Palatine had to balance the water-needs of city people and country farmers, taxing the producers' profits, securing grain at reasonable cost for the Roman poor and the army when imports were impeded. It was a very modern challenge with no modern tools. Grants, licences and regulations struggled against water-theft and all the tricks of grain producers who hoarded in times of scarcity.

In the year of Germanicus's death, and Publius Vitellius's survival in the courts, a journey to Tibur was a better chance to learn about politics than a walk across the Forum. In fields to the east stood hot blue bathing pools where sulphur belched from the sand. To its west the rocks were dry except in winter. On either side of the road to Rome stood a story of struggle very different from that seen in the senate or on Capitol hill. The harvest had failed. Where there was food, there was not enough and the price was too high. Gaius Rubellius Blandus had a view less easily seen by Publius and Lucius Vitellius, men inside the household and looking ever further in.

In good times Tibur's markets amid its temples and villas were packed, its long hillside loved by leisure-seekers for its air and waterfalls, but also by farmers for its access to Rome. It was the crowded gateway from the Apennine mountains to the capital's countryside. Its presiding god was Hercules, not in his role as clubber of monsters but as guardian of the herdsmen who moved their flocks, as regular as the seasons, between the low ground and the high.

Lambs and goats moved through Tibur in rich flocks. In Tibur the sellers sold grain from everywhere. Fruit and vegetables were the local crop, from salad gardens whose produce needed buyers while it was fresh, small fields whose owners made big profits and whose customers were well fed. When food and money flowed freely over Tibur's trading floor, coins with the heads of Augustus and his family preached the necessity of the *domus Caesaris* for the safety to eat, drink and spend. A shopper's bag of denarii commemorated the worship of *Divus Augustus*, emphasising the importance not just of a palace but of a holy house, the *domus divina* of the Palatine. The security of the *res publica* was inextricably enmeshed with the security of the *domus divina*. But when food and money did not flow, nothing was secure.

14
HERCULES THE HERDSMAN

In his youth in his home town, before any journey down on to the Palatine, Blandus knew where to find out what the court needed to know. The market in Tibur stretched down, stall by stall, over winding paths past the country houses of some of the greatest men of Rome. A patient traveller, one like Blandus who was known to all, would know ever more as he descended.

At the highest point was the broadest terrace with the best views, not the finest house in the town but probably the largest, fifteen flat acres from which to look down on the capital. It belonged to the family of Quinctilius Varus, pioneer courtier of Augustus and successful looter of Syria who would be forever known for losing his legions in the Teutoburg forest. Publius Vitellius had almost lost his life and reputation thanks to Quinctilius Varus. The Quinctilii Vari still had their clients and their farms, sources of vegetables and fruit regardless of any standing, or lack of it, at court. Varus's son was a rival of Blandus and the Vitellii, part of the club of young men making their way but not one who caused much disquiet.

Further down there were shrines to Faunus and to the fire goddess, Vesta, both divinities traditionally entwined with Rome. On the next levels sat a temple to the water nymphs, friezes of bulls' heads and flowers, hibiscus and fruit, the market office itself, tables of measures and weights, marble bowls for corn and oil. Traders bought and sold under the still, stern gaze of Augustus, seated as if in a chapel of his personal divinity. The richest of them had built a market temple to mark their emperor's return from a trip on which they feared he might die. One of them ensured that his name be carved where the corn was weighed.

Gaius Rubellius Blandus knew the great and the lesser of Tibur, the titans of the Capitol as well as the traders in carrots and corn and the priests who predicted the future. He was a modest man with a family interest in the local temples and antiquities. His grandfather had taught rhetoric to politicians, but had not used his arts on his own behalf. His father had briefly governed Crete, one of the lowest posts in the imperial service.

The proudest concern of the Rubellii sprawled over the next level on the downward path, the restored local temple which Hercules, protector of herdsmen, killer of animal giants, half man and half god, had dedicated during his labours on earth. This Hercules ensured the provision of milk, cheese and yoghurt, as well as the commemoration of his famous labours. Through every known age, stretched across the landscape, it had stared down on visitors from Rome, the first to greet them and accept their favours, the last to bid them goodbye.

Augustus once pillaged its treasury to pay his troops. But that, like so much strife, was safely buried in the recent past. Augustus had become a Hercules, demi-god of trade and prosperity brought by peace. For the Rubellii the temple was the pride of Tibur, his family's restoration its own greatest pride.

Gaius Rubellius Blandus was not an exceptional man. He began his courtly career as a reliable friend at Tibur, additionally rich from family land beside a very different river in the province of Africa, a good companion, lightly flattering as befitted his family name, *blandus* being a favourite word of the love poets, and used by Ovid for flattery to the goddess of love herself. As a consul he held an office more of honour than power. As an orator he was more smooth than forceful. As an historian he was no more than an antiquary.

The local came first. The Rubellii were leaders among the old Tibur families, provincial in the eyes of the Roman aristocracy but proud that Tibur had been a town with its own ancient sibyl, prophesying to kings when Rome was mere mud, an enemy of Rome when Rome was struggling to survive. The Rubellii were grander than the Vitellii in their provincial origins but milder in their ambitions. All of the senior members had the additional name, Blandus, not a description of which to be ashamed in the new age.

Blandus was a regular traveller on the routes to the capital. Beyond the temple the road ran straight towards the single bridge across the Anio, then south and west to Rome, the start of a journey which, while suburban, was notoriously wild even at a time without famine. The poet Propertius, dead for thirty years, once a careful critic of Augustus but, like so many a convert to flattery, famously weighed its delights and dangers. On the one hand there was the anticipation of sex with his mistress; on the other a landscape of lost paths, muggers and wild dogs. Propertius in his poem travelled to Tibur from Rome for sex; when Blandus travelled the other way, from Tibur to Rome, he was answering the calls of power, service for a year in a minor office in the imperial mint and as one of the public magistrates allocated to the *domus Caesaris*. That was how he came to know Tiberius, who found him agreeable and invited him as a companion on military manoeuvres.

Walkers descended either past the lakes and quarries already abandoned as a lost antiquity, or more steeply and directly through the stinking sulphur ponds either side of the main road. Those who were more relaxed might take the more gradual decline through fields and small farms which, when the city was smaller, had produced its food. Like most of the rest of Italy, ruled from the resorts around Naples and Rome, the farmers along the way had little in common with the luxury of Nola, Nuceria or Tibur.

For 400 years, food and politics had been indissoluble at Rome, in bribes and on stage, in farce and as brutal force. The Forum was a food market before it was a centre for politics. There were many early *fora*, for meat and fish and vegetables as well as rhetoric. *Fora* for wine and luxuries followed quickly on.

Starvation was a weapon and feasting a still-remembered political reward. The earliest feasts, at Tibur as elsewhere, were visible to the many, created and consumed in the open. They were political. They displayed power – over peoples near and far. Ambitious politicians, their coffers filled from eastern conquest, saw the benefit of banquets for votes at home.

The collapse of the states created by Alexander the Great brought into Rome for the first time bronze couches, tapestries in purple and gold and tables on pedestals of marble. Greek slaves revolutionised Roman banquets. Guests came to expect more elaborate meals prepared by skilled chefs, served by elegant waiters, and accompanied by girls who played the harp. Cooking used to be done in Rome by the lowest orders of a great house, but now it came to be looked upon as art, divided among specialists who saw themselves as proudly distinctive, one from another, as members of an orchestra: the man who made the white bread would no more make the brown than a flautist would play the drums.

These changes happened very quickly. Within a generation, the flow of money and slaves generated by Rome's wars changed Roman political competition. Established politicians who were too old to take command in one of these lucrative campaigns had no hope of matching the glory, wealth and popularity of successful younger men. The losers could only contrast their supposed fidelity to traditional Roman virtues with the love of luxury that these young warlords displayed.

For the winners liberality became a signature virtue, a proof of power. Julius Caesar, characteristically, made his own personal impact. His public banquet to mark one of his earliest offices, in 65 BCE, ensured that no one remembered again the efforts of his predecessors. At the feast to mark his third consulship in 46 BCE, two years before his assassination, he for the first time presented four different wines at every table. More than 100,000 dined on lampreys, eel-like delicacies gathered by supporters for whom catering became a critical political art. Whether the food was fish or fowl, it was important that the sudden demands for banqueting did not create shortages and higher prices in other parts of the market.

Caesar himself, who presided wearing bright costume and garlands of flowers, left a legacy of feasting which his successors had to match and adapt and sometimes curb if the custom risked public disorder. Tiberius, to celebrate a military victory in almost his final act as heir to the throne, gave a public banquet on 1,000 tables.

Curbs on public largesse were never popular. By the time that Tiberius was emperor, 'The Inspector of Morals' was the title of a play for holidays. Its central character was one to be mocked. No one liked the feast-inspector. Any banquet was a modest economic redistribution, and the people did not appreciate official curtailment of the menu in the cause of improving their characters.

Food had to be the first demand of politics. Flattery was a way to being fed. Cooks consolidated their status as artists. Companies of cooks made their owners as rich as any men in Rome. A man called Cestius, a member of the priesthood that oversaw public banquets, built himself a pyramid fit for a minor pharaoh. Eurysaces the baker had a tomb that elaborated every part of his trade as though he were a conqueror.

The poor took whatever they could get. It was a responsibility of the emperor to ensure that the voters of Rome should at least have bread. At any time, dangerous hunger might be only a few days of failure away. The wisest of the court kept that truth close to the top of their minds. Some knew when choice between cheeses was possible, when it was too costly and when shortages of everything, even starvation, loomed. Others were more concerned with how banqueting advanced their own interests, others still with how their behaviour might look to those who were hungry. The loaded plates, like every other part of politics, began to disappear indoors, joining the pleasures of those very many, not to be forgotten, who always preferred to live out of the public gaze. Notorious among the conquerors content without politics was Lucius Licinius Lucullus, pillager of Pontus in 70 BCE, who became an early Roman to gain a bad Vitellian reputation for fine dining, finally falling into a fatal insanity and leaving as his legacy his gardens of eastern cherries.

15

CARE FOR CUCUMBERS

The gastronomic rules of the court were unpredictable. It was pious to praise the people of Italy for living modestly on corn and vegetables even when these were soon to become merely a banquet's 'first course'. It was prudent to eat the second and third courses if the emperor was doing the same.

As the heir to the throne, Tiberius had feasted the people but also curbed what he saw as excess in his dining rooms. His cooks served leftovers to those who had previously plotted over camel heels and roasted ostrich. He served only one side of a wild boar, saying that it contained every variety of meat that the other side did. As emperor he would have legislated to ban excess at banquets if he had not feared derision and a general ignoring of the law. He did, however, forbid the selling of pastries in the street.

One man's excess was another's proof of power. To be known as a gourmand at court might be a good thing. It showed discernment. A gourmand was one who asked the gods to give him a crane's neck so that he could savour delicacies the longest. Or so Aristotle had said, and Aristotle was much to be trusted. A glutton simply wanted to stay the longest at table. That was a crime even if its boundaries were hardly clear.

A man might have a good reputation for judging wine. Tiberius supported the principle of good vintages and bad, the discrimination that Caesar had introduced to the public with his four different flasks per table. He was not pleased when his soldiers on the Rhine had called him Biberius the imbiber. A reputation as a drunk meant more about a man than mere drink.

Tiberius's official favourite vegetable, as passed down by later writers, was the humble cucumber. His imperial luxury was to have it on his table at all seasons. His slaves used frames on wheels to catch the sun's heat at every time of day, moving the vegetable beds like patients in a care home, with sheets of sparkling mica, *lapis specularis*, as reflectors, thick mirror stones as blankets for the winter.

Augustus had had his little figs. Tiberius had his little cucumbers. Larger gourds were less attractive. Stuffed marrows signalled luxury, pumpkins an empty head and obsession with sex. Tiberius sensed the truth that the charge of gluttony was about more than food, that like sexual slurs it was an accusation of weakness and bad character. The glutton fish licked the leftovers tipped into the Tiber. A *tripatinium* of bass, lampreys and mixed fish was the height of sophistication. Lines of distinction were fine.

The language of eating was closely linked to sex in the Latin of the streets – and in grander literature too. A slow chewer was a slow sucker; a pot or ladle used by women in the kitchen was a ready metaphor for a vagina; butchery shared the verbs of buggery. Gluttony was a slur from the same vocabulary. It was always different from being a gourmand, an art only for the rich, or greediness, which everyone might like to enjoy. Gourmands could be addicts, obsessed with a rare fish or thrush to the exclusion of all else. But gluttony was a definition that extended beyond the table. It was a character flaw, a permanent part of a man.

The hungry were not always hungry. The fox in Phaedrus's fable saw a single chance. The crow deceived by flattery made a single mistake. But the glutton was always a glutton. Gluttony was persistent, shameful and a private vice shared only with other gluttons. To typify someone as a glutton was to accuse him of lacking a cool head and the sense of proportion and priority necessary for leadership. It meant laziness and thoughtlessness for the future.

Excess at the table was a charge that stood easily for other crimes but, most importantly, it would come to stand for the crime of political failure. Losing power was a far bigger fall than overeating, but lurid details of guzzling and vomiting would stay longer in later memories. Over the next fifty years the charge of gluttony was ever louder heard against those on the Palatine.

Phaedrus told a fable about a hard-working Hand and Foot who grew tired of being attached to a greedy Stomach. They decided to be slaves no longer. They deprived Stomach of food. Stomach rumbled, grumbled and then starved. Hand and Foot starved. By the time the limbs changed their mind, it was too late and all three were dead.

In Aesop's original version of the story Stomach succeeds in taunting Foot back to work. For Phaedrus, writing in imperial Rome, there was a harsher message about what happened when the greedy and the hungry grew too far apart.

16

VITELLIA'S NIGHT OUT

Vitellia, Aulus Vitellius's aunt, watched the success and failure of her four brothers from the house of her husband, Aulus Plautius, a former consul from a quarter of a century before, the suppressor of a minor slave revolt for Augustus. She was the mother of the son, also called Aulus Plautius, whose name was at the foot of the bronze tablets setting out the future of the empire.

Vitellia had only one name because that was still the style for women at Rome. Rule by the *domus Caesaris* helped some women to extend their household power over the empire, but it no more extended their names than it protected them from being abused in histories for lusting after sex and power. All Roman women, with very rare exceptions, had only one name, and Vitellia was very respectable but no grandee.

The little-recorded sister of Lucius and Publius Vitellius became briefly known only for attending a party in 21 CE. It was a poetry reading, the kind of event that Augustus had encouraged on the Palatine. But the poet on this occasion was not of the calibre of the great survivors of Latin poetry, not an Ovid, a Horace or a Virgil, but a writer of flattery-on-demand.

The man reading aloud his work at the party was the same Clutorius Priscus, lover of luxury food, beautiful eunuchs and profitable praise, who had benefited so well from his poem flattering the dead Germanicus. Vitellia's brother, Publius, had provided the prosecutorial prose against Piso, but Priscus had produced the poem.

Priscus was a star. After his first triumph he paid one of the highest-known prices for a eunuch, a much-desired sexual partner known as Paezon who had been the property of Sejanus. The poet next dreamt of being even closer to the centre of power, the laureate of the new age. With his new poem for Vitellia and her fellow guests Priscus was hoping to repeat his previous success and go further.

His chosen subject was not, however, dead. Nero Claudius Drusus was the son of Tiberius whose succession had been promised to the empire in bronze after the trial and death of Piso. He had been seriously sick but was still alive, and particularly alive to any real or imagined slight. This did not discourage Priscus. Despite his all-too-visible excesses at the dining table, Drusus was much doted upon by his father, and the prince's latest illness had been enough to remind Priscus that some well-prepared praise might be a good investment of his writing time. He needed words for every eventuality. A poem could not be produced at the speed of a poison or an emperor's whim.

Vitellia's party was an opportunity for testing lines and themes. Priscus's portrait of Drusus in words would, of course, be flattering. The young man's well-known drunkenness and ill temper would not have been part of the poem, much more his Homeric bravery in battle and his assured path to the immortals on gilded wings. That was the kind of verse that had won Priscus his first big pay day and might reasonably do so again if the right words were ready for the moment of grief.

If Priscus had restricted himself to preparation, all might have been well. His poem continuing the tradition of the great Greek praise-makers might even itself have survived, likening Drusus to stars and planets and the heroes of epic times. If Drusus had been newly dead, Priscus might have earned an even bigger reward than he had for Germanicus. Instead he read aloud a work in progress, a premature obituary which, however flattering, could never be flattering enough.

Vitellia and her friends were his audience. Everyone knew that Drusus was still among the living, that the poem was only a draft, but its imperfections were perhaps less obvious than its simple existence. Someone in the audience described the entertainment to someone who was outside. Someone outside passed the story on. Palace guards descended to interrogate the guests. Was the poem a proof that someone wanted Drusus dead? Or did such praise of the heir prove that someone wanted the emperor himself dead? The guests gave their answers. The Praetorian guard's prison cells, with their racks, whips and other encouragements, stood ready if they did not. Only Vitellia said she had heard nothing.

Tiberius was away from Rome near Naples at the time. The news reached the Palatine first. It might be another day before a considered version of the night's events was in the hands of the emperor. In the meantime, senior senators did not wish to seem complacent.

To some, a vain and greedy flatterer wanting to impress a party did not seem the worst of offenders. Rubellius Blandus was one of those who thought that exile and a loss of ill-gotten gains would be punishment for Priscus enough. To others, even the possibility of a plot against Tiberius was enough for seeking safety in trial and execution.

Drusus chaired the court. No one knew what Tiberius thought, but without even the slightest delay Priscus was tried, found guilty and strangled in the cells at the foot of the Groaning Steps. The eunuch Paezon needed a new owner.

When Tiberius eventually responded from Naples, he commended the senate for its loyalty but criticised the haste of the execution. Maybe he would have shown clemency, maybe not. He was content that few would ever know. For poets the lasting lesson was the same as that of the fable of the fox and the crow: beware the vanity of testing out your voice.

The servants of the *domus Caesaris* knew of its insecurities, alcoholic excesses, manufactured antiquities and dust-covered lies, even while those outside the house increasingly did not. There were different rules of reality for different places. In faraway northern Gaul, almost as far as Britain, there could be a temple pro *perpetua salute divinae domus*, to the everlasting health of Caesar's holy house. Nearer to Rome this was a flattery too far. The insiders grew used to games that could not be won, games played in ways that could not be known. Personal judgement, arbitrary judgement being better than none at all, was the essence of understanding an emperor's will.

Loyalty to the house of the Caesars was not easy. Despite the clear sight of the future on the bronze plaques distributed to the empire after Piso's trial, the household knew that no succession was assured. There was Drusus, proud of the praise that had cost Priscus his life, and other younger Claudian heirs of Tiberius, their swaggering entitlement paraded to all. But there were also still the children of Agrippina and their different claim to be the Caesars of the next generation. And there was Sejanus, the man who might now get back his expensive eunuch, the man whom Tiberius seemed increasingly to treat as his deputy. Some even thought that Sejanus might be the first emperor who was not a Caesar.

Vitellia's brother, Publius, survivor of the German beaches and the law courts of Rome, seems to have liked clarity in his strategies for survival. He eased himself into the circle of Sejanus, a group of gourmets, poets and actors as well as guardsmen. Vitellia may thus have known more about the motives of Priscus than her fellow guests, even more than the senators who put him on trial. Her other brother, Lucius, stood back a little from the guard captain. He prized flexibility and would soon become quietly renowned for it. Like Tiberius he preferred ambiguity about what and whom he needed most.

Publius and Lucius both survived and prospered in a house of servants who would be masters, masters forced to be servants, wealthy soldiers, wily children and would-be successors. Publius was the bolder, Lucius the longer-lasting, the master courtier who saw the emperor's need in myriad matters of day-to-day government, satisfied it but did not parade the need that Tiberius had of him. A successful courtier had to walk a slippery stage. Lucius was flexible and forward-thinking. He understood tax and cash reserves. He was a master of both the political and the practical. He was happy to abase himself. With abasement came some, but not all, lessening of responsibility. At the birth of Western bureaucracy, he was useful, the ultimate accolade.

Tiberius was surviving in power as a master of courtly management, an emperor of ambiguity, of seeming neutrality, of concealing a closed mind, obscuring where he stood, of accepting the flattery that he claimed to detest. Tiberius resisted moves to make him 'Father of his Country'. He was menacing towards those who called his concerns for food distribution 'divine'. But none could ever be sure. Proximity was the key to understanding, flattery the currency. Politics was less the manipulation of the many by the few but the one by the few. A successful flatterer required the skill of a man on a razor's edge.

Success might come in many forms. There might be a difference between a flatterer of Tiberius who was ambitious on his own account, on Rome's account, or in fear of the imminent death of his family or himself. It was not easy at the time to see what that difference always was. Motives were hard to discern. The stages were both the law courts where Lucius and Blandus, with the new status of being an ex-consul, worked in different ways, and the couches around low dining tables which no one seeking advancement or survival could avoid.

Tiberius had both to adjudicate like an emperor over free men and to entertain like an emperor. Meanness ruled alongside excess. Unpredictability always ruled. Tiberius once appointed an obscure candidate over one more distinguished because he had watched the first drink a huge flask of wine at a dinner. There was light as well as dark. Without the uncertainties of light and dark, the household would not manage itself, still less a vast world beyond. Lucius was a master of the shades.

17

PEN AND KNIVES

Sejanus's unique source of power was the Praetorian guard, an elite force that he had taken over from his father and hugely enhanced. When Augustus had used the Praetorians for his personal security, they had been mostly out of sight and in billets divided around the city. Sejanus, seeing new dangers in a less secure regime (and maybe new opportunities too), concentrated them in a single, much more visible camp.

His was a role that gave him his own sword and control over the only armed men allowed in the city. It was not an inheritance as grand as that of a Piso, but in the imperial halls of smoke and mirrored marble it was a permanent reminder of reality. Publius took the important role of army paymaster, but the sharpest weapon that he carried was the writing stylus of a bureaucrat. Day by day the sometime soldier scratched notes and orders in a wax-filled wooden box.

Sejanus's power was military but his skills were courtly, not confrontational in the conventional warrior way. He was a soldier trained in household service, more adept than those who burnished their independent pasts, a soldier whose command was not over imperial expansion but over Rome and the *domus Caesaris*. When the emperor said that he hated flatterers, Sejanus was there to be the military man, the type of straight-dealing officer that Tiberius had admired on manoeuvres. When it was time for a banquet of congratulation, Sejanus ruled the tables.

Sejanus's father had been an only moderately distinguished soldier and landowner, remembered best as a pioneer of force-feeding geese for the livers later known as foie gras, adding the flavours when the bird was still alive rather than after its death as satirised by Horace. Food mattered, alongside the force of the knife. Sejanus's enemies said that in his youth he had been the lover of Marcus Gavius Apicius, the most notorious gourmet of the age, master of minced seafood, stuffed dormouse and sow's belly, an influential figure prepared to scour the Mediterranean for the largest prawns. Sejanus's wife was Apicius's daughter, Apicata.

Apicius was an important name in the story of flattery and gluttony at the courts of the Caesars. He was probably linked sexually to Sejanus in order to smear him, but the story may have been true. Food was, as ever, an easy weapon. Many recipes attributed to Apicius survived like the fables of Phaedrus, even if most other details of his life did not. If Apicius deemed cabbage sprouts too common even when the court was dining modestly, they stayed off the menu – and off other menus that lived on long after his death.

Apicius became synonymous with a certain very Roman way of eating and dying. He stood for luxury, complexity and the consequent ease by which goose liver or fine wine could aid the poisoner. Sejanus became notorious for adding death to fine dishes or watching while the condiments, ideally slowly, did their work. The two men's names were in many ways entwined.

The truth of these charges hardly mattered. Paranoia was part of reason. A poisoner might be in the pay of a fellow diner, a potential heir or the emperor himself. Cooks were allowed to be secretive about their more complex recipes. The Sybarites of southern Italy had given their chefs a year's exclusive copyright on a new dish, the first of any known sort of copyright. Knowledge of fish and meats was an ideal education for a kitchen killer.

It was useful to know what one was eating, but not always possible. Conformity was prized. Vegetarians had to beware: hostility to meat might be misunderstood at court as devotion to the cults of Judaea or some other kind of disloyalty or doubt. To eat seated on a chair, rather than reclining on a couch, might recall the vow of Julius Caesar's last civil war enemy, Marcus Porcius Cato, who said he would never lie back comfortably to eat while the tyranny of Caesar survived.

The tyranny of Julius Caesar, if that is what it was, did not survive. It died at the hands of his assassins. The one-man rule of his heirs did more than survive. It prospered. If Cato in defeat were still alive, and had not cut out his intestines with his own knife, he would still have been sitting down to eat.

On any day the dining tables of the Palatine made a stage. If the emperor was there, he was the star. If the emperor was not there, there had to be an understudy, a dangerous role. There were couches for all the players in sets of three, like a crescent moon around its own low table. Each place on the couch had its own name and status, the *summus*, the *imus*, the *medius*, the *consularis*, the top, the bottom, the middle, the consular. The diners ate reclining on their left elbows. There were some conventions on which the emperor might insist and others on which he might not. Anyone might eat and drink enough to blur fears into hopes.

The dishes themselves began with staples of the poor, the bread and wine, the eggs, always something with eggs at the start of a meal, the little vegetables, cucumber, asparagus, sweet carrots, a mullet, something stuffed, a marrow or a sow's udder or both, apples, pears, usually apples. On some days they moved on to more elaborate luxuries, presented as in a theatrical show then taken away to be served in tiny bowls, like Apicius's honey-smeared nightingales, stuffed with prunes, garnished with rose petals and served in a sauce of herbs and grape juice. Sometimes they would discuss the latest dish, sometimes how luxuries were sapping the Roman spirit. Tiberius, stooped, bald, face pale and spotted by dressings, was as unpredictable about food as he was about his favourites.

The most palpable tension was between Drusus and Sejanus, rivals for meeting Tiberius's needs. The prince thought that the courtier had ambitions above his status. The courtier thought that princely status, while probably necessary for succession, was not a necessary condition for giving advice. If Priscus's poem had been better timed to praise Drusus in death, Sejanus would have happily applauded the best lines.

The effort to create a single family of Julio-Claudians continued. Drusus had his already worldly daughter, Julia, aged sixteen, who was married to Nero Caesar, seventeen, the eldest of Agrippina's sons. If Tiberius's Drusus was first in line to succeed to the throne, as the empire had been assured in solid bronze, Agrippina's Nero Caesar might be second. The two young men themselves were quite friendly, a rarity worth noting by those who lived on such indications of truth.

Agrippina would sometimes be at a table herself, with the Vitellii, Lucius ever watchful, Publius more bold, sometimes too the comfortable Rubellius Blandus. Four years after the death of Germanicus and the trial of Piso, Tiberius was still in a barely concealed conflict with Agrippina and her children who, as well as Nero Caesar and Agrippina, her dominant daughter, included Gaius, known still as Caligula.

These young men and women could not simply or safely be murdered. Agrippina could be accused of lusting for power, gagging and gasping for it as though power were food: Latin had a precise word for such abuse, *inhiare*, to gape with open mouth. But the family of Germanicus remained popular with the people of Rome and maybe necessary, in a last resort, if the Julio-Claudians were to keep power. Caligula, tall and awkward as a youth, no longer with his childlike charm, needed constant surveillance. Tiberius required both informers on their plans and an enforcer who could make plausible threats when these clashed with his own.

Agrippina and her allies had to be kept down but not immediately out. They found themselves pursued through the courts, mostly on the evidence of informers associated with Sejanus. Her friend, Claudia Pulchra, a great-niece of Augustus, was condemned for witchcraft and plotting to poison the emperor. She was the widow of Quinctilius Varus, whose suicide in the Teutoburg forest was designed to save her fortune and her life – and had done so from 9 CE until this time of peace that was turbulent in a very different way.

Tiberius was discovered privately worshipping the spirit of Augustus. In 26 CE Agrippina accused him of simultaneously offering sacrifices to Augustus while prosecuting his descendants. She fought back fiercely on behalf of her friends and sons. Like Antonia, she had her own court within the court. There were the warring Caesars and there was Sejanus. The cautious would try not to be too visibly part of parties, whose membership was ever fluid. Drunken words might be useful evidence in the courts – or more likely in Palatine rooms where a quieter verdict could be given.

In the stories of Aesop was a warning to those trying to back both sides. There was once a bat, anxious in an age when the kingdom of the birds was at permanent war with the kingdom of the animals. The battles swung one way and then the other, but the result was never clear. When the birds were on top, the bat joined the birds; when the beasts were winning, the bat was animal. As long as there was open conflict the bat was safe, but when a peace was made its treachery was laid bare, and it was condemned to life in a dark cave for a cell.

18

THE WAY OF THE
GUARD CAPTAIN

After a decade of the new reign, the captain of the guard was ahead of all his rivals at court. Tiberius, giving flattery as well as receiving it, referred to him as 'my partner in my toils', raising him through the senatorial ranks as well as those of the Palatine. He would eventually become consul, without having held any previous office, but this was barely more than a bauble beside his swords and psychological sway.

Sejanus held physical power as the Vitellii, the freedmen accountants and other courtiers did not. In the middle years of Tiberius's reign he outdid every competitor for the emperor's trust and attention, combining the arts of the Palatine table with the threat of military force. Beyond the emperor himself Sejanus's base of power was a wide network, threatening, bribing, charming as he chose. He gained the reputation as a poisoner of rivals, both their minds and their bodies, someone with whom it was in every sense dangerous to dine. Whether he ever mixed the atropine with the apples will never be known. His most enduring contribution to the history of the imperial court, and all their many successors, is that he may not have needed to.

The guard captain kept close everyone to whom Tiberius listened. From happier days in retreat in the Greek islands the emperor kept an astronomer, astrologer and prophet called Thrasyllus whose wife, Aka, was a princess from her father's tiny realm of Commagene, south of the Black Sea. Commagene was an absolute monarchy, home to Armenians, Iranians and the subjects of Alexander's generals. Thrasyllus understood the licence and limits of autocracy better than those less experienced. Sejanus stood beside him. All swam in a swirling vortex. For no one was the water calm.

There were flatterers at court who called a man what he was not and the jealous who did not call a man what he was. There were men and women, like Thrasyllus and Aka, whose time Tiberius owned, and those he could merely command. There were scholars and aesthetes, learned buyers of the new art and architecture. There were washers and cleaners, keepers of the many more ancient masks and statues, tasked to brush away the dust and flies between the marble fingers of history, the wrinkles in bronze of powers gone by. Others still yearned for those lost powers.

Prophecy and flattery were closely entwined. Tiberius believed that Thrasyllus had predicted his ascent to the throne – and that his predictions of a long life for the emperor would come true too. There was no more critical fact about the future than the age at which the emperor would die. Phaedrus wrote that if he ruled the world himself, men would be as long-lived as crows, the most venerable as well as most flatterable of birds. This was the issue regularly highest in Tiberius's mind.

Thrasyllus had huge courtly power. Melting down a statue of the emperor to make silver plates should have been a capital crime. Thrasyllus used his authority to save a member of his family accused of that ultimate transformation of flattery to gluttony. Sejanus stood close to Thrasyllus and Publius close to Sejanus. But Sejanus looked outwards into Rome, not just inwards into the palace. He was popular and generous to those who brought him news from the street.

The guard captain earned public praise, and his own gleaming statue in Pompey's Theatre, for controlling a massive fire. A senator who criticised this statue for ruining the legacy of Pompey more than the fire ever could have done found it soon politic to starve himself to death. Sejanus was decisive when he needed to be, skilled at using others to execute his decisions, a rising master of the court, able to hold Tiberius's limited affection as, for a while, none other could.

The rivalry between Drusus and Sejanus took a more dangerous turn. Whether for Tiberius's sake or his own, Sejanus fanned further the emperor's fears of his own family's popularity. Drusus, drunk after dinner, struck Sejanus with his fist and accused him of failing to show appropriate respect. Sejanus did not forget. The vortex tightened its grip. He was adept at poisoning Tiberius's mind even if he was innocent of poisoning the bodies of his fellow diners: his message was that the young son always wants the father gone, that the younger generation was a permanent threat to the old. That was the way of some of the great myths of Rome, the history adopted by the Caesars and their poets.

In intrigues that must have tested the tactics of any courtier – and have tested historians since – Sejanus risked trying to join his own family to the Caesars. He planned an imperial marriage for his four-year-old daughter. The unknowing girl was briefly set for a life with the son of Germanicus's brother, Claudius, when her future husband died by choking on a pear in a game of catch. Only then did Sejanus, it was said, turn his attention towards eliminating Drusus, seducing his wife and, with her help, and that of his favourite eunuch Lygdus, slowly poisoning the bibulous heir until he died. Drusus's wife, advised by Thrasyllus, may herself have been active in promoting the same plan.

Or there may have been no plan. Drusus's notable gluttony might have been enough. At the time there was no suspicion. Lygdus was not tortured for a confession of whether he was a rival in bed or accessory to murder. Drusus was loaded with honours at his funeral, the same processions and statues that had been given to Germanicus, flattery being by this time a currency, subject to inflation and needing to be shared equally in public sight. Only Priscus's poem was missing from the wake.

Sejanus then made a second attempt to join the family by marrying Drusus's widow himself. Tiberius forestalled this in a restatement of the claims of Julio-Claudian blood. Sejanus was still a provincial seducer in the eyes of the grandees, useful but not to be allowed beyond due bounds.

Phaedrus skirted around the drama. He mocked another crow, not a prey to trickery by a fox but one who dressed in peacock feathers, a more deliberate form of vanity. He wrote of the frogs who, fearful of drying ponds, wanted Jupiter to stop the marriage of the Sun and any chance of new suns. The frogs were the Roman people, Jupiter was Tiberius and Sejanus the sun.

The jilted bridegroom responded by fuelling further Tiberius's paranoia against potential successors both in and out of the family. In 23 CE Tiberius's sixteen-year-old granddaughter Julia, whose childhood health had worried Augustus on his deathbed, married seventeen-year-old Nero Caesar, son of Agrippina. This was another bid for stability which failed in its purpose. Julia told all Nero's secrets and more to her mother, who passed them to Thrasyllus and Sejanus. The Roman guard captain, quietly backed by the Greek prophet, responded by persuading Tiberius to leave Rome for his own calm and safety and to settle finally, aged sixty-eight and even more jaded than he had been at his succession, on the island of Capri.

The official reason for the departure had been to consecrate a shrine to Augustus at Nola over the house where he had died. The room in which he had asked for an actor's applause and warned of his successor's slow-chewing jaws was to be erased by a temple. Along the route Tiberius received none of the direct petitions from local worthies that Augustus had accepted as he moved through Italy. There was no public feasting. Few people saw Tiberius at all.

On the way south he enjoyed a private dinner in a lavishly reconstructed grotto, a place where the real blended into the fantastical and life was art. Statues there depicted one of Greek literature's great cave stories, the blinding of the Cyclops, Polyphemus, by Odysseus. Homer's account was one of the most disturbing dinner party stories, with the host as gaoler, the guest as assassin and wine drunk to deadly excess. Between the grotto and the sea were artificial ponds for fish and eels. There was a marble Scylla, looming out as though to snatch unwary passers-by. The *Odyssey* was alive – and with Tiberius as its star.

On this occasion the cooks and artists had too big a role in the show, the engineers too little. A rock-fall over the couches gave Sejanus a lucky opportunity to hurl his body over his master's and save Tiberius's life. He also had the means to make his service known. Sejanus's ability to control the household was at its height. Through his guards, he managed almost all the news that passed between Tiberius and the Palatine.

Sejanus let Tiberius hear what would keep him calm. The emperor's successor on the Rhine, Lucius Domitius Ahenobarbus, died at this time at a great age, the grandfather of Agrippina's little son, Nero. Ahenobarbus's long-ago marriage to Antonia's elder sister had been a grand event. His memories stretched back far before the *domus Caesaris* began its rule. Ahenobarbus had succeeded Tiberius in his German commands. He had put married women on stage in his farces. His feasts for supporters were some of the most excessive before the definition of excess had changed. This was the kind of news, helping to tell the story of Tiberius's life, that an emperor could safely hear.

Other news – the petitions, letters, tax exemptions, the routine reality of imperial rule – became more sporadic. The organisation of the Roman Empire meant that this did not matter much. Governors, once appointed in the Palatine intrigues, governed until they were recalled. Tax-collectors collected. Soldiers patrolled distant villages, married those whom they were patrolling, and rarely thought of the city of Rome at all. They themselves were Rome – and in an age of rare peace for those outside the court.

19

WATER ON DUST

On the road to Capri stood the imperial villa on Cape Misenum, headquarters of the Roman fleet, just a few miles from where Augustus died at Nola. This was the setting for twenty-five lines by Phaedrus starring Tiberius in person, relaxed, conversational, verses which the emperor himself might have enjoyed.

This fifth poem in Phaedrus's second book begins with a protest against a scene familiar in every court – and in every business office that came later – the sight of people busy doing nothing.

> *There is a breed of rush-abouts at Rome,*
> *Hurrying to meetings, occupied in idleness,*
> *Pointlessly puffing, lots to do and little done,*
> *Harming themselves, hated by everyone else.*
> *These are the ones I want to put right,*
> *With a true story, if I'm up to the task.*

The hero of the task comes in the very first line, Caesar Tiberius, on his way down from Rome to Naples. It is a hot day. He stops at his villa on Cape Misenum. One of the house slaves, a top man in this country court, fashionably and somewhat effeminately dressed, makes a huge fuss of dampening down the dust for his master's walk. It is as though he were flicking dead flies from ancestral furniture inside the house not outside, flaunting his wooden ladles of water. This is a peculiarly pointless effort. Tiberius laughs at it. The garden is not a state room and the dust is hardly an intruder.

The slave is not deterred. Suddenly he is out of sight. He has slipped ahead through a gap in the maze of garden paths to make another opportunity to impress, to show off his bared shoulders and the dangling tassels below his tunic, continuing to sprinkle in the hope of winning favour, reward or even a slap around the head, the traditional gesture for giving freedom.

Tiberius stops and calls, '*Heus*', 'Hey you!'. Surely there will be a tip at least. But no. The slave is told sternly that all his scurrying about is for nothing. He is taking liberties, not winning them. A man who wants his life back from this emperor will have to pay a much higher price than wiggling a water bucket.

> *You've done nothing, your effort is withering.*
> *You'll need to pay much more*
> *For a box around the ears from me*

The end of this miniature story is not much of a punchline in any sense. But then Tiberius was never known for the sharpness of his wit. He was better known for his reluctance to give slaves the freedom which they might earn from many other Roman owners. The prophetic Thrasyllus, whose new freedman name was Tiberius Claudius Thrasyllus, was a noted exception. Phaedrus was maybe telling a true story, embroidering a piece of gossip, or writing a fiction which fitted his readers' known facts.

Whatever the case, this was a fable, with characters and a miniature plot more Roman than Greek. This was not a translation from Aesop, or even an adaptation, but a Latin poem in Aesop's style. Phaedrus's target was not the emperor but the courtier watering the dust. Perhaps the emperor even smiled when he heard it. Any nearby flatterers might have laughed with him, as they normally would, forgetting that they were the butt of Phaedrus's wit and that Tiberius was the poem's hero for seeing through their designs.

Aulus Vitellius, at the beginning of his teenage years, was an early arrival at the court on Capri, entering a world which produced enough gossip for a whole school of fabulists and writers of satire. To those who weren't there he was one of the emperor's playmates for princes, an unpaid companion, an object for sexual pursuit. He was one of many, it was said, no one special, just a part of the party.

The name of Capri was linked (probably falsely) to *caper*, that most dissolute of creatures, the goat. Latin etymology was a favourite Roman hobby among those with private libraries. The local drama of Capri, the *phlyax* play, took its name from a Greek word for gossip. Goats and gossip came to define the court on Capri.

The best known *phlyax* writer, Blaesus, wrote plays which mixed characters from the Olympian gods with human gluttons and fools, recognisable figures with those from the stock. Another described the improvisations on Capri as tragic farce. By the time of Tiberius the art of the local players was merging with the Atellane sketches of the mainland. But the tradition of gossip, the mixing of news, religion and comedy, remained strong. No period of imperial history ever produced the flow of salacious rumour and innuendo that Tiberius's long retirement to the island would bring.

The Palatine was suddenly far away. With Sejanus and Thrasyllus by his side, the emperor set up an island court, inviting the useful, the learned, the amusing and those who might be butts for his amusement and aids to his relaxation. Although Aulus was not from one of the grand senatorial families whose heirs Tiberius liked most to humiliate, he was invited nonetheless, a genial, gangly boy whose family was politically useful if he himself was not.

Lucius Vitellius, a father not to be excluded from his son's preferment and maybe helped by Antonia, bought a house on Capri of his own. As a rising man of palace administration he needed to stay in touch. His brother, Publius, undamaged by neither his near-disaster in the sea marshes of Germany nor his defence work for Agrippina, was close to Sejanus and in charge of finance for the army. Young Aulus, son of a third generation of servants, discouraged from an army career by the auguries at his birth, was deemed ideal to be a *spintria*, a brothel boy for sexual entertainments with large casts.

There were twelve imperial villas on this, the most southerly island in the Bay of Naples, which Augustus had bought towards the end of his life in a part-exchange deal for Ischia, its bigger northern neighbour. The largest villa was the Villa Jovis on the eastern cliffs, which Tiberius intended to be soon on the same scale as the

Palatine. He would retain full imperial power, judging, making appointments, setting and exempting taxes, delivering some, at least, of the daily mass of decisions demanded of him. There was ample room for his guests and travelling staff. Not every request got an answer, but that was not unusual. An emperor anywhere received many more letters than he sent.

This retreat was not, at first, an exceptional decision. Rich and educated Romans had long taken their work to the towns around Vesuvius. Capri was not the most fashionable destination. Young men like Aulus Vitellius might have preferred many others. Aulus was less subtle, stronger in language, clumsier in action than his father, but by proximity to power in his own right he might sometimes be more powerful. Thus the next chapter in the history of the Vitellii began, the rising of the son.

For Tiberius, Capri was secure and close to two strategic centres which protected Rome, Misenum, where the emperor's ships were moored, and Puteoli, where the city's corn supplies arrived from Sicily and Africa. In the Villa Jovis he had peace away from unwanted petitioners, ambassadors, their promises and praise. He could enjoy the museum of heroic giants, boars' tusks and bones which Augustus had created to house gifts from foreign ambassadors. He could watch the stars with Thrasyllus and bathe in sulphur pools, which his doctors believed were good for his scarred and flaking skin. He had libraries where he could indulge his pedantries and oversee the education of his young visitors.

The night sky, for Thrasyllus and his emperor pupil, was an education in itself. The poet Aratus, writing 300 years before, described how Zeus had drawn the constellations as messages to mankind. His *Phaenomena*, both in Greek and in its Latin form translated by Germanicus himself, was an essential text for any library. It showed how the Great Bear and the Seven Sisters, the stars on the shield of Achilles in Homer's *Iliad*, moved through the heavens as a celestial code for learned watchers to read. The verse was the universe. Thrasyllus was its reader. Aulus Vitellius and other fortunate young men might be its beneficiaries.

Capri had few harbours where the hopeful or hostile might land, each of them guarded by Sejanus's men. Unwelcome messengers or unwilling guests were hurled down from high cliffs. A fisherman who evaded security to present the gourmand emperor with a mullet had his face rubbed in it. When he joked that he was pleased not to have given Tiberius the crab from his catch, he had the crab ground into his face too. This was a story, whatever its specific truth, that warded off intruders with each retelling.

The navy provided any food and water for banquets which the locals could not supply. The villa had some dozen ovens, a bakery and a staff schooled in specialised culinary tasks. No imperial villa could ever lack a *pistor candidarius*, a skilled maker of white bread. The corridors were floored in white mosaic, trimmed with black. Smooth marble columns, swirling colours of grey and green like a lizard's skin, supported the roof of the main banqueting room.

The rooms of the most distinguished guests, or those requiring most surveillance, were above a tower of massive cisterns that collected winter rain, with pumps to recycle waste to the kitchens, the dusty gardens and the baths. The latest curator of Rome's own water supply, Cocceius Nerva, was one of Tiberius's first and long-staying companions, an assignment that did little to advance the building of aqueducts for the capital.

The baths of Capri became notorious. The hot mineral pools were not just good for an old man's skin but enjoyed, so the gossips said, by boys and girls who catered to an old man's entitlements. Oral sex was always a good joke for gossips. A mouth used to speak the truth was surely best not polluted. A tongue used for flattery was best not polluted further. This was the wit of the rural stage. Tiberius became the butt of the Atellane farce actors as 'the old goat lapping up the doe'.

In Capri, the sex of tongues went beyond Tiberius taking a reluctant woman to his bedroom. He had boys called little fishes who licked between his legs as he swam. He demanded that breast-feeding babies be brought to suck him. He hung a painting in which the mythical hunters, Meleager and Atalanta, barred by prophecy from risking her virginity, simultaneously suck between each other's legs. He commissioned elaborate scenes of troilism. Aulus was not the only *spintria* required so that life could imitate art.

The painting of the virgin and the hero was by Parrhasius, the classical Greek master of realism. If further technical advice were required, the library of Tiberius extended far beyond Thrasyllus's copies of Aratus's *Phaenomena*. On Capri there were erotic romances and genealogies of the gods, pornography and Plato, mathematics and tragedy, Italian farce and the legacy that Blaesus and the *phlyakes* had left, the local tragic farce.

An easy way to lower a man was to imagine him with sexual submissives and sycophants. Often these tales were more about the unpredictability for those around an emperor than the capricious excesses themselves. But it was the excess which survived the longest. Phaedrus's poem about the pompous slave of Cape Misenum was never as popular as those starring crows, frogs and dogs. Capri was a place where an autocrat could both indulge his full freedom – and be abused for living beyond imagination.

The island purchased by Augustus was more like a court of the Greek east than anything yet in Rome. It had no counterweight institutions, not even weakened ones, which could impede an imperial whim. Thrasyllus's wife, Aka, perhaps understood it best. She had been born a princess of Commagene. Her home was north of Syria on the road to Persia, the last remnant of the empire of Seleucus founded by one of Alexander the Great's successors. She knew the licence and limits of autocracy as her husband knew the stars.

Commagene had a royal shrine, high on a mountain, in which the statue of the founder of her own family dynasty, Antiochus I, stood at five times his size in life, flanked by eagles, lions, local gods and the gods of Greece. Hercules, Hermes and Apollo served in local dress. The death of his no less absolutist successor, Aka's brother, leaving no heir old enough to succeed, left a vacuum. To the delight of the Commagene aristocracy, Tiberius, in his third year on the throne, filled it with direct rule from Rome.

Aka was proud to become Claudia Aka. Thrasyllus's granddaughter, Ennia Thrasylla, married Q. Naevius Sutorious Macro, prefect of the watch and Sejanus's deputy. The common people of the kingdom would have preferred a new young king to none, but their views had easily been ignored. Commagene, like all of the Mediterranean from Spain to Judaea, had to take its orders, if any orders happened to come, from the east coast of Capri.

There was occasional bad news from the mainland that the island court could not ignore. In 27 CE a wooden stadium at Fidenae, a town about five miles north of Rome, collapsed during a public entertainment and tens of thousands of spectators were killed, probably the biggest civil disaster of the age. Tiberius briefly visited the site, ordering help for the wounded and punishment for the builder. He did not return via the Palatine.

The main news for Tiberius from Rome came in the autumn of 29 CE. Fifteen years after overseeing her son's succession, Livia died, leaving much of her personal fortune to an ambitious favourite, Servius Sulpicius Galba. Again Tiberius did not return for the funeral. Neither did he pay Livia's legacy.

Only a few miles further out to sea from Capri was the windy island of Pandateria, where Augustus had once exiled his daughter Julia. Tiberius, his fears fuelled by Sejanus, sent her daughter Agrippina, Germanicus's power-hungry widow, to Ponza, a different island between Naples and Rome, but to the same death as Julia by neglect and starvation.

20

PROFITS FROM PROPINQUITY

What was worrying to the senate, the people and the members of the *domus Caesaris* left behind was not Tiberius's retreat to Capri but the length of his stay there. On the Palatine when the emperor was away, there was an empty space. Tiberius's power was barely visible until it was absent. Without regular sightings of the man from whom authority fell, fewer knew where it was falling or where safety might be. Courtiers needed to show to themselves and to others that they were in the inner circle, or even an outer circle.

The military and legal power of the past had been facts that a man might touch; the new power, proved through an almost theatrical ritual, was not. New men could bend long-standing social structures. Information from even the unknowing staff could win huge rewards from buyers who thought they were paying for knowledge.

If a man was for any reason deemed down and out of favour, there might be only a short step to his prosecution for treason, the simple charge of no longer being the emperor's friend. Prosecutors could gain a quarter of the wealth of those they successfully drove to suicide or execution. The names of the accusers were secret. There was sharing of fear and, alongside it, a massive redistribution of wealth from old power to new, from country landowners to courtiers of the city, the *bona damnatorum*, the goods of the condemned. In his miserable exile, Ovid had been pleased, and lucky, that his property at least survived in his own possession and was not given to flatterers or gluttons or the emperor himself.

The emperor had first claim – and could either add to his wealth or distribute the gains to the public, directly or indirectly, as acts of liberality or freedom from tax. Tiberius was either reluctant – or insufficiently understanding – to spend his public money. Business opportunities for constructors were fewer. The corn supply slowed.

Water shortages increased. New aqueducts were still needed. Anyone close to the emperor could hope to claim and gain a bigger share of such chances for wealth that were available. Flattery and denunciation were arts seen as a curse by those under threat. To newcomers they were the arts of opportunity.

Despite rumblings that he should return, murmurs from within his household and wider family, Tiberius remained away from Rome, making occasional trips with Sejanus only to the coast around Naples to show that he was still alive. Thrasyllus, supported by Sejanus, had the vital role of keeping Tiberius calm, reinforcing his predictions of a long life to ensure the succession of his seven-year-old grandson, Gemellus.

The news from Rome of trials and executions, some but not all of them orchestrated by Sejanus, matched the news from Capri of cruelty and decadence. Both avenues of information were distorted in the interests of the tellers. There were more treason trials when the emperor was away, and those who profited from disorder and redistribution were less constrained. But the total number of successful prosecutions in the whole of Tiberius's long reign was only about twenty-five, and about the same number failed.

Tiberius enjoyed the results but affected at least to disapprove of them. To a degree he did disapprove. He was not anxious for prosecutors to create too much social disorder simply to curry favour with himself and make themselves richer. Lawyers were regular butts of the emperor's mockery. He liked to see them at each other's throats.

Flattery of the emperor at Rome had to lessen when its recipient was away. But it did not cease. Flatterers might even have been less embarrassed when Tiberius was not there to hear them. Court life was frozen. It was like a masque, different to the rumbustious improvisations from Naples and Capri and the sketches of Mr Glutton and Mr Fool. The new plays had an almost formal script. The star stood forever in the wings. The cast wrote subplots in which the same routines happened again and again.

Succession was still the main story. In 31 CE the order came from Capri that Agrippina's youngest son, nineteen-year-old Caligula, should be sent to join the boys in Tiberius's entourage. Thrasyllus joked that the awkward newcomer had as much chance of becoming emperor as of riding on water over the Bay of Naples. But the last male heir to Germanicus stayed alive and in the race. Tiberius indulged the boy's love of theatre in the hope that it would soften any violent side to his nature. Aulus Vitellius became his friend.

Meanwhile Sejanus, the archetype apparatchik, was promoted alongside Tiberius to the consulship. He pulled strings that the Vitellii could not. He controlled swords as well as pens. His supporters saw a rising tide. Sejanus's sister, Aelia Paetina, was already married to Tiberius's uncle, Claudius, the slobbering cripple who was nonetheless a Caesar. The age of the Sejano-Julio-Claudians still seemed a possibility, and maybe not far ahead.

Tiberius ordered the banishment from Rome of the farce actors whom Augustus had aped on his deathbed. They were at the same time 'so indecent and so popular'.

21

DEATH OF THE DAMNED

Two hundred miles to the north in Tibur there was anticipation, excitement and fear. Gaius Rubellius Blandus, long one of the town's leading men in Rome, seemed set to marry Tiberius's granddaughter, Julia, whose sickness as a girl had troubled the dying Augustus. Although many, both rich and poor, were facing economic disaster, this was at least a boost to local pride in troubled times. Any grand wedding meant a feast, meat and wine in the street for all comers, nuts for children to chase as the bride passed by.

Julia, by this time in her mid-twenties, was already the widow of one potential heir to the throne, Nero, son of Germanicus and Agrippina. She was already a veteran of the court in which Sejanus, her own mother's former lover, remained supreme. Maybe Julia herself had been once set to marry Sejanus. That was merely rumour. By marrying Blandus she might be merely the leading lady of Tibur, perhaps a safer place. Even in the hardest days, the Anio still fell there from the mountains to the plain and the ancient temple of Hercules, older than Rome, still stood proud.

The financial shocks of the decade came from old banking rules newly enforced in the courts. A law once designed to favour investment in Italian land simultaneously caused reluctance of lenders to lend and buyers to buy. Food was short. Farmers without land were falling into bankruptcy. Thousands of slaves, without work and with no right to free food from the treasury, were abandoned and ever more visible beside the roads.

It was not many years since freedom for the enslaved was a punishment more than a gift, an expulsion from the only place that would feed and house them. That had begun to change. Freedom for an individual was becoming more clearly a right worth having in itself. But a reduction in the supply of money, happening for reasons that no one well understood, showed how quickly the past might return and the starving free might again envy the enslaved and fed.

While money was plentiful in the personal bank of Tiberius, it had almost ceased to flow through what was not yet known as the economy. Gold and silver continued to leave the country to pay for imported luxuries. Less returned in tribute and tax. There were no new conquests. The richest lost fortunes in the treason courts and, while some of the new owners, informers, freedmen and provincial prosecutors, spent extravagantly, there were not enough of them and not enough money went on roads, aqueducts and ships, on payments to the free who needed work.

Most of the property of the prosecuted, the *bona damnatorum*, went directly to Tiberius. His appetite for public spending was never high. No major building was commissioned from Capri. Cocceius Nerva, the *curator aquarum*, was a successful servant of the emperor in his retreat but no aqueduct had been completed for forty years. The waters of the Anio were still decorative in Tibur, but still ended splashing uselessly into the muddy Tiber before it entered Rome.

The courtiers of Capri reacted more intelligently than their critics later complained, making large loans available and allowing more time for borrowers to adjust their affairs. The shock was still harsh. Among the senatorial elite, those not exclusively beset by their bankers, there was the additional social shock when Rubellius Blandus, a mere provincial knight, was set to marry Julia. It was not necessary to love the Julio-Claudians to think that this was yet another disruption to the established order.

Then suddenly, at the end of 31 CE, there came the kind of news which, more than the marital, the minor judicial or military, the electoral, the social, even more than the monetary, provided a household court, and its historians, with their drama. In a single day Sejanus lost his prime place at Tiberius's side. He fell spectacularly from his great height. He had risen slowly, inexorably as his supporters thought, until his authority collapsed, threatening all who had associated themselves with his cause, Publius Vitellius among them.

The art of the courtiers was always to protect themselves from the buffetings that might come from above. Knowledge was one buffer, caution another. Even when the Palatine play seemed every day the same, openness to the possibility of a changed plot was the greatest protection of all, requiring the subtlety and patience that Lucius showed in almost everything he did and Publius much less so.

Tiberius, it seemed, had gradually made himself less dependent on Sejanus during his seven years on Capri. He had communication lines to Rome of his own. He had used handwritten letters to communicate with the city prefect. His prophet, Thrasyllus, who had grown closer to Caligula since his arrival, had useful links to a likely successor as commander of the Praetorian guard, his own grandson-in-law, Naevius Sutorius Macro. Lucius and Aulus were also beginning to favour Macro. Caligula had his own informant in Rome, a favourite charioteer and former slave, Eutychus, who claimed to have news of a threat to Tiberius's life. Macro took the details to his growing camp of supporters.

Eutychus was hardly a perfect witness. His story first emerged under routine interrogation about a theft of clothes in a changing room at the baths. Even when he was sent in chains to Capri Tiberius was still unconcerned until Pallas, Lucius's ally, succeeded in seeing Tiberius secretly with a letter from Antonia, the mistress of his house.

In Antonia's letter, whose contents Lucius was very likely to have known, were details of Sejanus's alleged role in the murders of Tiberius's son, Drusus, as well as Agrippina's children. Her court still included Caenis, now Antonia Caenis, a freedwoman and her secretary, whose beauty was renowned but whose mind, more importantly, forgot nothing. At what point, Antonia asked, might Sejanus move against the only other obstacle to his ambitions, Tiberius himself?

Tiberius then interrogated Eutychus, who confirmed the story, either because he knew it or because he now knew what would best suit his survival. The emperor suddenly had what he wanted to hear. As long as Sejanus had been threatening would-be successors, he was useful. When the threats had worked he was less so, even maybe a danger. The maybe did not last for long. He was suddenly a clear and present danger.

Sejanus might have seen the signs, but he did not. If there was the same 'smoke for sale' around Naples as in the rumours around the death of Augustus, neither he nor his allies smelt or bought it. As at the banqueting tables, words which at one moment were as clear as glass goblets at another were as cloudy as the wine swilling within. Tiberius tricked Sejanus by the promise of yet higher promotion. At dizzying speed he was recalled to Rome, stripped of his captaincy of the guard, arrested and replaced by Macro.

Tiberius and his court stayed in Capri. The man who had so long flattered Tiberius's judgement, ruled his banquets and manoeuvred as best he could through miasmas of uncertainty died far from his former master's sight. For the last time he passed below the broad eaves of the Capitoline temple to Jupiter, Best and Greatest, beyond its massive colonnades and towards the Groaning Steps to the Forum below. It was an easy execution for the executioner, a slow fall to death. Sejanus's financial fortune, swelled by flattery, useful-ness and threat, quickly swelled the emperor's funds. The months after his fall were golden times for treasury receipts. Tiberius took emergency measures to ease the supply of money in circulation for everyone.

This was a much greater jolt for the players on the Palatine than the passing of power to Tiberius from Augustus. Those who had cheered Sejanus for twenty years abused his body for three days. Sejanus's wife, Apicata, incriminated her husband before killing herself. Whether she was a good witness, or even a possible witness, to his alleged seductions and poisonings counted for nothing. The case for the posthumous prosecution was clear.

Sejanus's children followed their father down the Groaning Steps. The female members of his family, once the means for his dynastic dreams, played the most prominent part. According to a law that barred the execution of virgins, his daughter had first to be raped by the executioner. His sister, Aelia Paetina, was divorced before her murder. The name of Sejanus became a byword for a monster, used by Phaedrus, the master of the moral fable, almost as mothers might frighten their children.

In his portrayals on page and stage Sejanus soon paid the price of failure. Hardly a man of virtue, he was merely one of many who were concerned whether the empire would survive, who should be its emperor and how. He played the game, succeeded for more than a decade and lost. By losing he became a seducer of princesses, a pimp and traitor, with a love of fine food too, that common code for monstrous behaviour.

These public executions brought more panic than poison ever had. In Rome it was not only the weakest at court and in the streets who became obedient because they were afraid. The strong obeyed too, and some found added strength for future battles by obeying. The senate was convulsed. Vengeance followed vengeance. Excess pursued excess. With so much in life dependent on the sheerest chance, gluttony was as likely to succeed as watchfulness. Obliteration by drink was as plausible a tactic as verbal obfuscation.

Bodies fell in piles at the foot of the Capitol hill. One prominent victim was Decimus Haterius, an ex-consul known as a somnolent glutton, depraved when awake but too inactive most of the time to be a threat. If this was a tactic, it was successful for Haterius, but only for a while.

Haterius the glutton joined the flattering dead. When a flatterer fell, any who had flattered the flatterer were at high risk of falling too. In a swill of accusations, random more than systematic, none produced new evidence of a plot to seize the throne. Thrasyllus helped to stabilise the court by assuring Tiberius he would survive another ten years. Certain that he would live longer than any plotting against him, he settled back into the routines of Capri. The business of empire had still to go on. The court continued to be run by those who stayed safe and unknown.

At the end of 33 CE, at the height of the financial crisis, Blandus married Julia and joined the imperial household on the Palatine. Just as Tiberius had not returned to Rome for the funeral of his mother, he did not return to celebrate the wedding – or to face those who disapproved. A provincial marrying a princess was still an affront to social standards for some. In the goat island of Capri the reports of sexual licence were like those from the sack of a captured city.

With Sejanus gone, Lucius Vitellius rose again among the ranks of the useful and reliable. Bankers and landowners found common cause. With support from young Aulus, his well-placed son on Capri, he achieved the consulship in 34 CE and the governorship of Syria, a job which did not require his permanent residence in the province. Deciding when to and when not to be in Rome required as much of the flatterer's skill as ambiguity in words. Lucius Vitellius knew how to watch, wait and adjust his loyalties.

Publius Vitellius, successful survivor of his closeness to Germanicus, faced treason charges for having been too close to Sejanus. This time he did not escape. His father, old Publius, was too near death to help behind the scenes. He had support from his quieter gourmet brother, Aulus, famed for his generous feasts, who was respectable enough in the new era to have become consul for half of the year 32 CE. But this was not enough.

Facing the horrors of prison at the foot of the Capitol, Publius attempted suicide with a stylus he requested for his bureaucrat's wax tablet. Blood flowed from his body in a thin stream. Encouraged by friends, he allowed himself to be bandaged and brought back to consciousness but died soon afterwards. His wife, Acutia, would be convicted too. Her failed defender was a young balding libertine, Marcus Salvius Otho, with ambitions of his own.

Lucius and Publius had for a short time been on opposite sides in a struggle for Palatine power. Lucius may or may not have been in a position to warn Publius of the case against Sejanus. What seems certain is that he did not. With neither Publius any longer alive, the future of the Vitellii from this point depended upon Lucius, the forty-year-old consummate flatterer, and his playboy son Aulus, twenty-one and already beginning to match his uncle's reputation at the dining table.

22

LUCIUS VITELLIUS AND THE SON OF GOD

'If you release him, you are no friend of Caesar,' the Jewish crowd taunted Pontius Pilate as he pondered the fate of the man known as 'King of the Jews' and 'Son of God'. Jerusalem was not in Syria, but its peace was the responsibility of the neighbouring governor of Syria. The hecklers were picking at the most vulnerable part of Pilate's armour, his status as the emperor's friend, his source of power. To a man of ambition, away from the latest ebbs and flows within the imperial household, that friendship was evanescent, ever vulnerable to intrigue, also everything that he had. Pilate could confidently tell protesters that there was no legal case against the accused; he could not face the charge that he was 'no friend of Caesar'.

There were always problems facing a Roman ruler of Judaea, year by year many of them the same ones. A claimant to be 'King of the Jews' was nothing new. The prospective crucifixion of a 'Son of God' would be hardly a novelty either, neither the punishment itself, still routine for non-citizens, nor the idea of a god's son on earth (Tiberius was a son of a god just as Augustus had been), nor the accompanying noise. What mattered to Pilate was his status within the court.

For Roman administrators Judaea had for more than 100 years been an incomprehensible nuisance, a place of male sexual mutilation as well as peculiar absolutism about god and seafood. King Herod the Great held Judaea with a firm hand till he died in the middle of Augustus's reign. His divided successors, carefully kept divided by Rome, were allowed to squabble and murder to their mutual content as long as Rome received its tribute and faced no costs.

Pilate, like all servants abroad, needed to follow events in the capital much more closely than his masters ever followed the trials of Jerusalem. The Jews recognised that truth as well as their governor did, not just when the issue was the fate of a self-proclaimed king and 'Son of God'. The various Jewish leaders had cultivated many allies on the Palatine. So had their rivals. A battle beneath Capitol hill produced results; one by the Mount of Olives usually not so much.

The governorship of Roman Judaea came with no legions. Pilate had acquired some military experience with Tiberius and Germanicus on the Rhine, but his job in Jerusalem, like that of Quinctilius Varus in Germany, was as an administrator. He needed calm and taxes, no news of disturbances to reach Capri, no tales told against him by religious leaders or local royalty. If he failed, the army that would have to intervene was controlled by Lucius Vitellius, the governor of Syria from 35 CE, for whom friendship with the emperor was the aim always most paramount.

Syria's previous governor had been a friend of Ovid. He was said to have won the job by joining the emperor in a banquet and drinking session that lasted a night and two days. At the end of the party Tiberius judged his companion 'the most agreeable of friends and at all hours' before appointing him to rule Syria and keep whatever eye was needed on the Jews. This champion eater and drinker had since died and Lucius, weighing the risks and rewards of absence from Rome, was on his way east to replace him.

Syria, as the Romans then defined it, was a narrow coastal zone along the eastern Mediterranean, its capital at Antioch, the base from which Rome managed relationships with various neighbouring kings. Freedoms were forever up for negotiation, liberty for loyalty. For the past sixteen years Syria had included Commagene, the former home of Thrasyllus's wife, Aka. There remained a question mark over whether Commagene might be made independent again if its young heir, Aka's nephew, proved suitable. Thrasyllus's granddaughter, Ennia, was being prostituted by her ambitious husband to Caligula.

Each kingdom had a dynasty of the intermarried. No one troubled by the trials of the Julio-Claudians could fail to note the solution favoured by the heirs of Alexander the Great's generals. Aka's brother, Antiochus III, was married to another of his sisters, Iotapa. Their son, possibly set to become Antiochus IV, was also set to marry his own sister, also called Iotapa. As a check on outsiders' ambitions the custom of intermarriage was ideal.

As an added check on the young children's loyalties several were currently held as Roman hostages. Possible rulers of Commagene were currently living in the house of Lucius's patron, Antonia, permanently spied upon, free to observe the pet eels in the ponds of her house on Cape Misenum but not much more. At many a Palatine banquet the lower couches would be taken by princes and princesses living in luxurious confinement. As long as their parents behaved well back home their sons and daughters could eat the finest prison food that anyone could imagine. The price of any slackening of loyalty to Rome was paid in the permanent threat of poison.

Lucius already knew something of Syria from prisoners and slaves, both highborn and low, also from its place in the death of Germanicus and the trial of Piso. Judaea was always a special fascination to those who cared for strange rules about politics and food. The principle of arcane attention to pigs and prawns, animals' hooves and sea creatures' scales had attractions for gourmands even if the obduracy of the eaters did not.

Although Lucius knew more about the dead Piso than Piso's former province, the promotion was a good opportunity that might not quickly recur. Despite the death toll from informers and prosecutors, in and after the time of Sejanus, profitable public offices did not come up as often as in the past. Tiberius liked to leave men for long periods in post if he could, arguing that Romans abroad were like flies on open wounds and, once gorged and sated by extortion, would do less harm. Pontius Pilate had already served eight years in Judaea.

Lucius Vitellius, longer-sighted than many friends of Caesar, was well prepared for the risk in leaving Rome. Antonia was still his

strong supporter. He was one of the consuls for the year 34 CE. He
was the principal organiser of the anniversary celebrations for two
decades of Tiberius's rule. His son, Lucius, was about to marry Junia
Calvina, a descendant of Augustus's daughter Julia, a connection no
longer one of disgrace. His close friend Valerius Asiaticus, a wealthy
grandee from Gaul, was set to be consul in 35 CE. In Capri Aulus
had the responsibility of representing the family interest. The Vitellii were faring fine.

In Capri itself the main news from the east was not the aftermath of a routine crucifixion but a rare sighting of the Phoenix, a
bird whose rebirth every few centuries was held to celebrate a royal
son's piety towards his father. This was the kind of news that Tiberius liked to hear. If Lucius could maintain the flow of favourable
bulletins, alongside stable taxes and the empire's finest dried fruits,
he would be a success. News of the decision by a tent-maker from
Tarsus that Jesus had not been merely 'King of the Jews', the new
king that the Jews quite reasonably had not wanted, but the 'Son
of God' awaited by all Jews, had not needed to trouble the imperial
household. Saul's re-emergence as Paul on the road to Damascus
mattered much less than the new Phoenix, sitting in its nest of fra-
grant herbs and cinnamon as though scripted by Apicius.

While Lucius and Sextilia were in Syria, Blandus, with Julia, his
imperial wife, was governor of Africa. He too was trusted to have a
legion under his command. His prime responsibility in 35 CE was
to maintain Rome's corn supply. Both men had experience of the
court; they were courtiers first and senators second. Both knew how
to avoid the emperor's anger, to divide the issues on which it was
necessary to consult from those when it would be stupid and dangerous. They had seen closely the mistakes of others. Any scratch
in wax on Capri could become a blade of blood in Carthage or
Jerusalem, but the wax was only rarely scratched. Tiberius, in what
was already the pattern for imperial rule, reacted much more than
he initiated.

The prime task for Lucius and Blandus was to avoid trouble. Lucius gained favour with Jewish leaders by restoring some

confiscated robes to their high priests, a costless act. He saw Pilate as a continuing risk to good order. With courtly skill, Lucius gave him more than enough freedom to ruin himself, sending him back to Rome to answer charges over the clumsy crucifixion of some Samaritan protesters. In being the breaker of Pilate's career he had linked himself inadvertently, quietly, and somehow very characteristically, to what was not yet the most far-reaching event of his time.

Lucius knew what, by contrast, would be appreciated on Capri. This had nothing to do with anyone called Jesus Christ. He had on his staff the refined Spanish food and wine connoisseur Lucius Junius Columella, an enthusiast for poetry and prose, dogs and natural rarities. Columella was, publicly at least, a critic of the excesses of his day, praising hard work in the garden over instant gratification. He criticised gluttony. His work on wine began with a flattering dedication to Eprius Marcellus, a feared prosecuting lawyer and professional flatterer of others. He was a useful companion on the razors' edges of life under Tiberius.

Thanks to Columella, readers throughout the empire also learnt of the export to Rome of a nine-foot Jewish prodigy for public exhibition on the Palatine. Lucius and Columella knew that Tiberius had a special interest in the Judaean town of Jamnia and its famed date palms, which Herod the Great had left to Livia in his will. New varieties of dates and figs, almost any novelty for a banquet, would be better received than the latest news of Jewish opinion.

In Antioch Lucius was not only far from his emperor but also further from his already difficult son. Aulus Vitellius had married and become quickly estranged from a wealthy woman in his own extended family. Petronia was the granddaughter of the same Vitellia who had stayed silent before execution of the rash poet Priscus. They had a son, Petronianus, who was blind in one eye. Showing a fierce view of her family, Petronia insisted that her estate could pass to her son only if Aulus was excluded from any part of it.

The future emperor, lacking money to match his lifestyle for almost all his life, was said to have had his son poisoned to thwart his wife's wish. The official verdict, not widely believed, was that the dead boy had intended to poison his father and had killed himself out of guilt and shame. Aulus's second wife was Galeria Fundana, from a more modest family, who bore him a son and a daughter, the first suffering from such a stammer that he could hardly speak at all. This was perhaps not hard to understand.

Lucius showed that his diplomatic skills could work away from the Palatine. He settled a border dispute between neighbouring Armenia and Parthia. He made a brief military intervention in support of one Parthian king over another. He came close to an invasion into the territory of the Nabataeans around Petra which, in an age of money-saving peace, would have been a rare example of legions marching into the territory of friendly kings. But, to his likely great relief, he was able to halt his offensive plans when all-changing news arrived, not from Capri but from the setting for Phaedrus's fable of the flatterer with the watering can, the mainland villa on Misenum.

Tiberius was dead. Thrasyllus's promises of ever-longer life to postpone the problem of succession had finally failed. A few days earlier his tower on Capri for astronomy, prophecy and for matching Greek verse to the universe had been destroyed in an earthquake. Although Rome's second emperor might not have lived as long as his prophet had promised, he had reached the age of seventy-seven, a long, ancient life. He had ruled for twenty-three years, matching the hopes as well as the fears expressed at the death of Augustus just a few miles away in Nola. It was spring, 37 CE. Gardens were coming to life, a time of heavy-scented flowers for anyone ready to celebrate.

Lucius Vitellius, it was said by his critics, had an uncanny sense of who would be a future despot and how a despot needed to be served. Antioch was as much his place of study as the Palatine. He was not the first Roman to enhance his own kitchens and gardens from hotter, drier lands, nor the first to note the art of bowing down to kiss the ruler's feet. But the timing for his education was good: obeisance might look bad, but it might also be a means of surviving: flattery was as essential an oil of government as any from a palm tree.

Though late to receive the news from Misenum, Lucius ordered immediate celebrations for the succession of his son's friend,

Agrippina and Germanicus's son, the survivor of Capri, Gaius Caligula. Blandus did the same in Carthage. Everywhere, from the servants of the *domus Caesaris*, who had their third master, to the soldiers in Syria, who had another ruler whom they had never seen, there was enthusiastic welcome.

Pontius Pilate had a particular cause to rejoice. His was a lucky escape, the avoidance of any appearance in Tiberius's courts and a disappearance into obscurity. Supporters of the crucified Son of God began retelling the fables that their master had taught them, parables as they became known, short lessons on sheep and goats, wine and banquets, fig trees and fish in a form that Phaedrus would have readily recognised from his own.

23

GOAT WORSHIP

For the massed courtiers of the Palatine, each individual calculating for the future, every day was a gamble and Caligula's very survival was a triumph over poor odds. The new emperor was not only the son of Germanicus, whose poisoning in Antioch was possibly ordered by Tiberius, and of the elder Agrippina, whom Tiberius had certainly sent to her death. He had also been the only heir in the way of Gemellus, Tiberius's own grandson. Caligula, while on Capri, had had to disguise any ambitions of avenging his parents and anything but his most devoted support for Gemellus. He had done both very well.

In the senate there was brief talk of abandoning the Julio-Claudians. One consul promoted a return to a republic. Others sought the throne for themselves. The Praetorian guard preferred the problems that they knew to those of the long unknown. Caligula had been a favourite of the military since his mother and father had let loose his charm in the marching camps of the Rhine. He had learnt the arts of a court by observing and practising them at the very highest level. An accomplished actor, he continued Tiberius's persecution of actors. He had survived by acting, by shifting roles and rarely playing himself. He would rule in the same way.

Gaius Caligula was not as glamorous as he wanted to seem. He was tall, heavy-bellied, thin-legged, hairier on his body than on his head, a somewhat goatish figure, although to use the word *caper* in his presence was perilous accuracy, one of many new dangers in the third court of the Caesars. Caligula was an emperor whose brief reign, marked by innovative diplomatic and construction projects, acute sensitivity to slights, whimsical mass executions and fantasies of his own divinity, was notoriously hard for those nearby to understand. Tiberius, who had once described Rome as a wolf held by its ears, had likened his successor to a 'viper for the Roman people'.

To understand him and survive, as the Vitellii needed to do, it helped to know how during six years on Capri he had been so extremely adept at surviving. Never, it was said, was there a better servant or a worse master. The maker of that judgement, a wealthy senator, Passienus Crispus, was an autocrat in his own house but adept at always walking humbly in the emperor's train, eating massively or serving at table as required, flattering beyond the rules of normal reason and answering questions with tact.

'Have you had sex with your sister?', Caligula asked Crispus. 'Not yet,' came the careful reply. Crispus saw that Caligula was both keen to boast of incest but maybe not so keen that an ordinary mortal might have committed the same offence. Caligula would dress up in new, god-like clothes for seductions banned by law. A great flatterer learnt to note just how different from the common herd his master needed to be. The Vitellii were well placed to prosper under a head of the *domus Caesaris* whose sense of exceptionalism, sensuality and display was of a different order from that of either of his predecessors.

The young Aulus Vitellius knew how Thrasyllus and Aka had enthralled Tiberius on Capri, reading the stars for communication from the heavens, predicting a long life for their master and the justified postponement of hard choices about who would follow him. Even if the emperor were not a god, he could be made to feel close to the gods. That was a challenge which well repaid those with the wit to understand it. Lucius Vitellius had the experience of his son as well as his own. He became a leading figure on the new Palatine.

Capri had been a laboratory for autocrats, a place to learn how in Commagene a single family had successfully extended what little power the Romans had not taken for themselves. Aulus had ample opportunity to listen and observe – and to watch Caligula doing the same. Although Lucius had been away from Rome at the time of the succession, he brought back from Syria his own practical appreciation of what eastern monarchs expected for themselves and from their people. These, he decided, were not necessarily unreasonable expectations.

Julius Caesar had accepted praise for his 'divine virtue' and personal embodiment of the state. Eighteen months later he was murdered by friends who thought such hubris a threat. The Ides of March turned out to be just a pause in the process of blurring the difference between men and gods. Caligula made up for lost time.

Augustus had been careful. He encouraged historians and poets to flatter his claim of historic right to rule, to say that his house was on the site of Romulus's hut and that his lineage began from the goddess Venus. He began to allow worship of his *genius*, his divine spirit, even in the suburbs of Rome, by those who wanted to be his worshippers. This was particularly popular among the Greek-speakers of Naples.

The concept of divinity at Rome was never as confined as later religions would insist. In the towns around Vesuvius Augustus had allowed shrines to his *genius*, which, while not quite making him a god in Italy, came very close. The Alexandrian sailors who burnt incense for him as he lay dying, and gained new clothes as a reward, were doing only what they might have done at home. Augustus's priest in Pompeii was quickly keen to clarify his status from *sacerdos Augusti* to *sacerdos divi Augusti*, priest of Augustus the god, as soon as the news from nearby Nola allowed.

Writers played their roles. There was a thriving business in stories of descent from ancient demi-gods and glorious victories in Rome's early wars. A Roman general in his triumph had been dressed as a god for a day. Legendary genealogies helped newly ascendant families to elevate their prestige. The Vitellii became one of many beneficiaries of reconstructed history, the elevation to historical status of events that, even if they had ever occurred, were not ones that had ever mattered before.

Tiberius had not needed to manufacture any more ancestry. Being a Claudian and an adopted Julian was enough. He did, however, need to draw his own line between earth and the heavens. Those who wanted to show support for Rome in the east had long worshipped some symbol of the city, sometimes a statue of Augustus and Tiberius, sometimes a more ancient focus of loyalty. Julius Caesar was a somewhat fading divinity. Tiberius needed the benefit of both being divine, which he knew was absurd, and not being divine, which might disappoint would-be worshippers. He could refuse to be venerated as a junior descendant of Venus and yet still stand for Rome, a divine entity of a different kind. The distinction between the two, while important on the Palatine or Capri, was easily blurred by distance.

After the second transfer of power within the first family of the Palatine, the world without emperors was over. Any emperor might readily be a god in places where that was the sort of ruler required. Caligula declared Tiberius unworthy of divine honours, a verdict that Tiberius would have approved, and of unsound mind, which he would not. Only the mint at Lugdunum in Gaul, the future city of Lyons, made the mistake of issuing gold coins showing the newly dead emperor as a god. The judgement that he was mad was, however, one which Tiberius would on many days have made of Caligula.

Later in the same year, 37 CE, a boy called Lucius Domitius Ahenobarbus was born. His mother was Caligula's sister, the Agrippina born in the camp in Germany who would forever be known as the Younger. Waiting to care for the new entrant in the race for power were the nurses who would give him their milk. Both women were former slaves who carried the Claudian name, Claudia Ecloge and Claudia Alexandria, just two specialist members of what was now a ruling household of thousands.

The *domus Caesaris* was the absolute centre of the Roman world. Reasoning about what made good government was still in flux, but the core truth, still uncomfortable to some, was not. The arguments of those who had killed Julius Caesar were studied by the nostalgic. They were no longer of relevance to the Vitellii. The balance of Senatus and Populus in SPQR, the senate and the people, was becoming antiquarian fiction. The balance that mattered much more was between those in the senate and the court who appeased and flattered – and those in the city streets who were appeased, flattered and fed in return.

24

ILL WILL FOR THE TWIN

In serving Caligula, Lucius and Aulus Vitellius had different but complementary points of vantage. Lucius was among the first men of empire. He had never held those older republican certainties that goodness came from Rome and badness from everywhere else, a confidence that had so long applied to wine and fruits as well as constitutions. He was comfortable with words of worship and deeds of abasement, with scenes of absolute power changing the absolutely powerful. Aulus, in the second imperial generation, had already watched Caligula as closely as any man, sharing parties on Capri and chariot racetracks at Rome. Between them they had a fine sense of the new dangers and opportunities.

In the court of the Palatine the terms of Tiberius's will were an early casualty. Like Augustus at Nola, the dying emperor had been suspicious of his successor till close to the end, convinced by Thrasyllus that he would live long enough to pass over Caligula. His preferred choice was his own teenage grandson, Tiberius Gemellus, only surviving twin son of the heavy-drinking Drusus whom Sejanus had manoeuvred to his death.

Gemellus was brother to the young Julia whom Augustus had asked of as he died. His birth had been commemorated on coins. He had his own distinction: no twins had previously been born to the Caesars. The quiet and capable Blandus was Gemellus's brother-in-law and might be his protector. But, when Tiberius's death eventually came, Gemellus was still too young and unsupported within the household.

Tiberius felt able to stipulate instead only that the two young men, Caligula aged twenty-five and Gemellus aged eighteen, should share power. This was a ploy comprehensible within the republican tradition of joint consuls, but not in a government based on

the *domus Caesaris*. A Roman household had only one head. For
challenging that necessity Tiberius's will was deemed invalid on
grounds of his insanity, a regular device at Rome but made ironic
by its exercise in favour of a man whose own mind so wavered into
imaginary worlds.

Caligula promised to adopt Gemellus instead of sharing power
with him, a perilous offer to any recipient. Gemellus, a dark and
brooding teenager, became ever more reasonably anxious. He had
been born on the day that Germanicus had died, a cause for nervousness among the superstitious. Even when he had only a cough,
he suspected worse. He began adding to his diet some daily anti-
dotes to common poisons.

This might have been common sense if the protection were easily
available. Cretan carrots and Gallic nard, wild poppy and parsley,
myrrh and frankincense, rhubarb and ginger, iris from Illyria were
all recommended. For added efficacy there was the blood of a duck
that lived on poisonous plants by the Black Sea, served with aniseed,
acacia juice, turpentine and malabathrum leaves. But none of these
more exotic items would be accessible without risking attention.

Like all cough medicines, they left an odour on the breath. Gemellus took the risk nonetheless. The closeness of the dining couches
betrayed him. Caligula sniffed the air. A reasonable precaution
was an act of ungrateful distrust, an 'antidote against Caesar'. On
the charge of thinking that he would be poisoned at the emperor's
dinner table, Gemellus was ordered to kill himself.

The third head of the household of Augustus had long watched and
learnt the theatrical arts necessary to survive as an heir and to prosper as an emperor. He had also absorbed lessons that brought benefit to Rome beyond the Palatine. Water had been always precious on
Capri, a dry island with few underground springs. It did not need
to be so scarce in the capital, a city on a major river surrounded by
streams from volcanic hills.

Caligula did not accept that the fountains and waterfalls of the
Anio should serve only the neighbours of Rubellius Blandus at
Tibur. He ordered the construction of the *Aqua Claudia*, forty-five

miles of tunnels and arches from new mountain lakes, changing the river's course, spending huge sums from the treasury, easing economic recession long before the aqueduct itself improved the water supply. The *Aqua Claudia* soared over the lavish tombs of successful tradesmen like Eurysaces the baker.

Tibur was Caligula's birthplace, or rather it was one of the places that claimed the credit. Those who lived near the famous temple of Hercules appreciated the claim that it was the emperor's home. Any connection to Hercules, the most famous half-man-half-god in the pantheon, would appeal to the emperor and might be good for business. Business was important if the flight of cash and credit four years before was not to be repeated. Business throughout the empire improved.

Other changes that Caligula ordered to the natural order were less useful. On Capri he endured the joke from Thrasyllus that he had as much chance of becoming emperor as of riding on water over the Bay of Naples. One of his acts after inheriting the throne and proving the prophecy wrong was to order construction of a three-and-a-half-mile floating bridge over which he rode in the armour of Alexander the Great. His most favoured advisers followed from Baiae to Puteoli in chariots, recalling the processions of eastern kings. Wise courtiers applauded the feat. The watching people, fuelled by feasts from thousands of sacrificial beasts, enthusiastically concurred.

Caligula was a popular replacement at Rome for a recluse who rarely left Capri. His visibility was an advantage. To be tall and pale made a Roman stand out from the crowd. If his hair was thick on his body and thin on his head, if he corrected these defects by threats as well as artifice, this was not a problem for a veteran of Palatine manners. He allowed the exiled actors back to Rome.

Whether the subject was himself or something more challenging, Caligula's mantra was change. For the first six months that change seemed good for the household and beyond. The Palatine had an emperor in residence again, a man whom his courtiers could not only see but sell to the world outside, to ambassadors, to supplicants, to all those seeking an emperor's decision. By explaining

Caligula to those who needed to understand him, they could both earn and exert their own influence.

This optimism at court did not last long. Quite quickly, the now almost traditional role of an interpreter, recognisable even to the few who remembered Augustus, became impossible to play. Some said that Caligula had a sickness of the mind, even that he as well as Gemellus had been poisoned. Whatever was the cause, the subversion of the expected soon became the only result that a courtier could expect. The frail slave from Smyrna, 'Tiberius Julius', already skilled with Caligula's account books, became a master of what was virtually a circus art, the ability to place his head in a lion's mouth and live to tell the tale.

Caligula increasingly needed men to magnify and multiply his pretences. All obstacles became affronts. Like a conjuror gripped by his own magic he began to present himself as one who could challenge any rule of nature. Not only, he said, were his sisters his sexual partners, his sisters had to have sex with his eunuchs. The impossible was possible, the invisible visible. One day came the order for a vast economic construction; on another day for a ruler's artifice, designed to cow and impress, a construction of his own mania for the crowds.

The new normal created new stories. The older men and women of the house remembered having to adapt to Augustus's daughter's and granddaughter's exile for adultery, to Ovid's exile for encouraging it. They now saw an entire section of the Palatine as a brothel for the daughters of the aristocracy, a whim that had of necessity to be wise.

The unfortunate had to join Caligula on a fake invasion of Britain. 'Tiberius Julius' joined a jaunt to a destination as far from Smyrna as any man could imagine. The emperor saw himself in the steps of Julius Caesar, conquering the northern ocean as he had conquered the Bay of Naples. His troops did no more than collect shells on the Channel beaches. The result was proclaimed a triumph.

To survive in Caligula's Rome required a new sense of what was real and what might be made real. Patience was the essential virtue. The careless or backward-looking were quickly caught. Like any returning provincial governor, Lucius Vitellius was regularly under threat, for having been either too successful or not successful enough. He looked after himself. He promoted himself. He flattered himself. He flattered Caligula.

Flattery, like taxation, became ever more necessary for civilised life. It might be deplored, even denounced. There were different kinds of flattery, different levels and purposes, but the exchange of sincerity for advantage spread and flowed from bedrooms to banquet room to business rooms, pervasive like a scent, as natural and necessary as breathing.

25

MAN TALKS TO A MOON

Before the Palatine was a palace it was the home of an old Roman hero, Quintus Lutatius Catulus, a saviour of his city against invading German tribes a century before, one of many models for his fellow citizens to match for vigour and virtue. Catulus was not only a soldier. He was a poet. He read and borrowed from the Greeks before it was fashionable, setting a trail that Horace and Ovid would follow. He was a connoisseur of the theatre, so enamoured of one stage star that he had likened his entrances to the sunrise: 'though he is human, he seems more beautiful than a god'.

In art the human and divine could walk together, heroes with gods, even men and women who were less than heroic. That was what happened in poetry and that was what poets could make happen. Caligula took past precedent – from poets, orators and the merely passionate – and twisted it as no one ever had. He was happy in his own house to be addressed as a god. Sometimes he was insistent. Catulus's sunrise was a metaphor. Caligula presented himself as the Sun itself.

Distinctions blurred. Stories of blurred distinctions blurred into each other. Tiberius had once compared Caligula to the sun as an insult: the young prince was a Phaethon, the Sun god's son, who by reckless chariot-driving came close to setting the mythological world on fire. Caligula, however, spoke of himself as Sun the father, not Phaethon the son, bringing universal light and not destruction. Whether Caligula believed in his own divinity or merely wished to press the limits of flattery was as unimportant as it was unclear.

This presented peculiar problems for those around him. In courtly culture a man who presented himself as the Sun might reasonably imagine himself alongside the Moon. This was a kind of logic. The Sun and Moon were like each other. They were both gods that could be seen, visible by their very nature, not hidden like Hercules or Minerva. Both watched over the seasons for growing food and keeping Rome alive, a constant male and female symbol in the sky.

The Moon was also the goddess of every scheme that came to men at night in their dreams. To Horace, writing as the poet laureate of Augustus's Rome, she was the *siderum regina bicornis*, the twin-horned queen of the stars, a charioteer who drove a two-horse racing chariot, nimbler than the four-horsed kind that had dragged the son of the Sun god too close to the earth. She even had a temple on the Palatine, close to where Caligula spent his nights. In the new realism of the court it might seem natural that the chariot-riding emperor and his neighbour should be friends.

Lucius was quick to absorb these new rules of what was real. He promised prayers and sacrifices, setting a new standard of study for those who thought that humouring alone would be enough to keep them in their jobs. 'I am talking to the Moon,' Caligula told him. 'Can you see her with me too?' Lucius, his head veiled in the eastern style, showed no surprise. He replied that he could not see the emperor with the Moon because 'gods were visible only to other gods'.

This was the wit of an experienced man. It was pitched so as to protect himself, whether Caligula was sane and cleverly testing his courtier or deluded and genuinely believing in his own divinity, or merely experimenting with his own dreams. If he had answered, as the cruder flatterer might have done, that he could clearly see Caligula conversing with the Moon, he risked being drawn deeper into a trap. He might then have been asked what else he could see, which other gods were there, until the laughing emperor could snap out of his pretence and mock him as a charlatan. If he had admitted that he could see nothing, he risked the accusation of doubting the emperor.

Lucius did not know what Caligula genuinely believed about himself. He might have been referring to dining-room furniture, the Moon that was the name for the highest crescent tier of the dining couches. He might have meant almost anything. He might have been simply mad. Men still remembered Tiberius's rival, Agrippa Postumus, fishing and holding the trident of Neptune before he was consigned to his island asylum. In the court of Caligula it was safest to assume that the highest demand for flattery was what the emperor was intending. And, like the crow with the cheese at the top of the tree, he wanted the flattery of those on the ground to be true.

Lucius Vitellius needed to be as insincere as was necessary. Flattering Tiberius had required political calculation, a balancing of factors that the courtier could know. Flattering Caligula required something more. The line that 'gods were visible only to other gods' entered history like one from a famous play. Lucius had to think deeply, drawing from all that he had seen in Rome and in the east, but, most of all, he had to think fast, like an improviser on a stage. When Caligula was the star, everyone had to be in the same play.

As a supporting actor to an autocrat actor-manager, Lucius had an audience of one, the star himself. He had to anticipate, to catch his cues. He had to see the walls and fences within the emperor's mind, between common governance and aggrandisement close to mania, between management of nature and challenge to its laws. Sometimes Caligula saw himself in an oriental paradise of applause; at other times there were the usual garden lines to be drawn, dead flowers to be cleared and damp beds of work to be dug. Lucius learnt fast to serve his master both in his labours as emperor and his delusions about what an emperor was.

A popular professional actor and singer at the court was less nimble than Lucius. Apelles was a confidant of Caligula more in the mould of Aulus Vitellius than Lucius, a companion of play more than administration. When the emperor stood by a statue of Jupiter on the Palatine and asked the unfortunate entertainer which of the two was the greater, Apelles hesitated.

It was not hard for watchers to see why. To say that Caligula was lesser than any god might offend an emperor whose weapons of revenge were closer at hand than any thunderbolt on Mount Olympus. To say that the king of the gods was a lesser god than Caligula might just as surely offend an emperor who affected to be an intimate of the Olympian deities.

The greater flattery would have been the lesser risk. Caligula had begun to experiment with putting his own marble head on the heads of statues of Jupiter and Apollo. An extravagant response praising the new presentation of a sculpture might have both preserved Apelles's self-respect and avoided his punishment. It was the hesitation that brought him down. Caligula had Apelles bound and flogged, his skin falling from his body while his cries and screams brought praise from Caligula for their sweet sound. The singer played his most miserable role – and also survived to tell the tale, to pass on his horror story and to play other roles.

The story spread, just as the quick wit of Lucius had done. Brutal violence was everywhere in Rome. There was nothing unusual in a man with power flogging one who lacked it. But a good story of violence and cruelty was still worth telling.

Caligula was a master of the quick, impromptu reply – in both Greek and Latin. Like Tiberius he enjoyed the company of philosophers, although he sometimes tested their metaphysics by execution. Once he had a man killed and for days continued to invite him to dinner. The empty space had its own meaning. The household adapted or died, sometimes both adapting and dying. Lucius was a great adapter, a skill all the more tested when what was real was increasingly only in the emperor's mind.

Phaedrus told a story of a stork who served dinner party food to a fox in a deep, narrow dish where his guest could not reach; when the fox returned the invitation the food appeared on a wide, shallow plate impossible for the stork. Awkwardness for the guest was comedy for the host. Diners at Caligula's court could see themselves in the fable, as in so many others.

There were traditional dinners for senators, their wives and children where Caligula gave presents, togas for the men, purple scarves for their families. There was the illusion of equality, one of the purposes of men and women taking food together as guests or hosts. There were also novel dinners at which some of the food was made of gold, temptations to one human appetite while destructive of another. His own new clothes included flowing eastern robes and floral tunics. Like Tiberius he gave a huge promotion to a man who had impressed him with greed.

While Caligula played god, Lucius Vitellius became a priest of Rome, a member of the *Fratres Arvales*, the Brothers of the Fields, a body that proudly traced its roots to the prehistory of the city. The Arvals, like the Sun and the Moon, were responsible for the harvest. Few institutions were more determined than the Arvals to boast their importance, producing annual stone lists and minutes of their activities, records of feasts and sacrifices, the rolling of jars down hills and the award of rose petals.

Others seemed not to rate the Arvals as significantly as they rated themselves. At a time when there were many writers of history, handing on their stories to each other, the true and the merely good, the name of the brothers barely appeared in history at all. The Arvals did not matter. Lucius was a pioneer of flattering the man who did matter, and whose place in history was built on some of the strangest stories of flattery ever told.

26

GOOD WATER, GOLDEN MEAT

The Palatine palace was growing fast, piece by piece, house by house. An ancient temple of the Forum became a new entrance. The twin divinities, Castor and Pollux, one with a Greek king for a father, the other sired by Jupiter, were Caligula's doormen. This was a world of blurred lines. A gold statue of Caligula had to be daily dressed in whatever the emperor was wearing, served by priests who were themselves flattered by sacrifices for their table, peacocks, pheasants and black grouse.

Those who had shared the parties of Caligula's youth, like Aulus Vitellius and Eutychus the charioteer, shared the riotous street-rampages permitted by his impunity. Aulus became a charioteer himself, the sport of the Moon and Sun in the heavens, where victory depended on manoeuvring the sharpest turns of the circuit, listening to a man ahead on horseback shouting advice, spinning a pair of wheels made in different sizes to make the turning easier. Aulus's single gashed thigh was a lucky escape.

Caligula also played the benevolent patriarch, restoring elections for minor offices, allowing the candidates to feast and entertain their voters. He held the consulship and allowed Germanicus's brother Claudius to hold it with him in 37 CE. He bought support in cash. Then he squandered what he had paid for. He distributed food. Then he would close the grain stores and condemn the city people to a few days' hunger, just to show that he could.

He had a showman's contempt for the dull. He hoped for a great disaster, like Augustus's *clades Variana* or Tiberius's stadium collapse, anything to mark his reign and ensure it was never forgotten. 'A man ought either to be frugal or a Caesar,' he would say. Guests at his banquets might be hungry if their bread and meat had been made of gold, but they would have something to talk about when they went home.

In the east he appointed Antiochus, Thrasyllus's wife's nephew and another of his party favourites, to be the new king of Commagene, sending him home with the entire revenue exacted during its time as a Roman province. Then he pulled away the throne, hardly before Antiochus had settled on it, as though in a party game. In the west his trophy shells from a beach facing the coast of Britain were just another illusion. He made pearls disappear in glasses of wine, dissolved or cunningly saved for the next show.

He paraded his Julian descent from Augustus's only daughter over the merely Claudian claim of the clearly insane Tiberius. But whatever his family line and whatever the name of the show, the administration of empire had to go on – and the staff of the Palatine had to make it happen. He tried to reduce the power of courtier ex-slaves within the palace. He deemed his own decisions both sanctified and the best. But those decisions could never be enough to achieve results, even the most bizarre ones. Eutychus became suddenly extraordinarily rich – and powerful enough to build a new home for his chariot horses by the labour of Roman legionaries. A Greek freedman, Callistus, corrupt, competent and a close reader of Caligula's mind, became as grand as any courtier of Tiberius.

Long pipes were laid for the *Aqua Claudia*, each section fractionally lower than the last to ensure the smooth passage of water when the testing and then the full flow would begin. Great arches maintained the height of the pipes where the natural terrain would have brought a crashing fall. The treasury paid the slave-masters and the brick-makers, the engineers and their assistants while one of the walks used by Rubellius Blandus on his way from Tibur to Rome became an industrial highway.

'Tiberius Julius' from Smyrna became a quiet accountant of aqueduct projects. Blandus, who had done good service rebuilding parts of Rome destroyed by fire, never saw the result. He had survived the dangers of a marriage above his station. He died before seeing the *Aqua Claudia* deliver any useful water to the hydrants, baths and pleasure domes of Rome.

Caligula approved another imperial marriage. Valerius Messalla Barbatus was a senator, a distinguished grandson of Augustus's sister Octavia, and a loyal servant of Caesar's house. His daughter, Messalina, was allowed to marry the brother of Germanicus and the emperor's uncle, hardly a gracious permission since Claudius was a disabled antiquarian not expected to climb further the career ladder of the Palatine. Caligula, in what may have seemed a disarmingly modest act, married Lollia Paulina, the wife (quickly ex-wife) of a senator from Gaul. Lollia was quickly Caligula's ex-wife too, supplanted by a mother of three daughters, Milonia Caesonia, whom he was said to like parading naked at court. Caesonia won the reputation as her new husband's poisoner – although any dose seemed to make his behaviour even more like a madman's.

The prudent view on the Palatine was that no act of ingratiating flattery could be too much, no applause too loud. A wise man might make a speech in the senate thanking Caligula for an invitation to dinner. Since Gaius could on one occasion spend the annual tribute of three provinces on a single dinner, on gold and liquid pearls to match sums not expendable even on seafood, flamingos and giraffe, this was maybe justified. The practice of senators kissing the emperor's cheek did not return. Caligula preferred to proffer a foot.

A writer of Atellan farces who made a *double entendre* of doubtful taste found himself on a theatrical funeral pyre, deemed to have had the opportunity of flattery and missed his chance. His screams came as interval entertainment. If anyone made a noise during a show by his favourite actor, Mnester, Caligula would have him dragged from his seat and flogged. Sometimes he himself would flog the offender. Antonia, mother to Germanicus, protector of Lucius and Pallas and veteran of the Palatine since its beginnings, committed suicide in a lonely protest. Lucius survived within a shrinking group of those upon whom he could rely.

In the third of his fables of contemporary court life Phaedrus offered a cautionary tale of a man called Princeps, that very useful title invented by Augustus but also the name of a fashionable flute-player. Princeps was a very superior slave who had broken his leg in an accident on stage, an acrobatic soaring that was too high for his own good. After three months in straps he was about to make a comeback, keen to earn a good pay-day, preening himself for the applause he had missed so much in his forced recuperation.

Musicians, unlike actors, did not wear masks. This Princeps was therefore a familiar face. Phaedrus described how a rumour surged around the theatre that the long-absent celebrity was about to appear. Even a rumour brought excited applause. The flautist finally appeared and blew out kisses to his fans.

Unfortunately, at the same time, the real Princeps arrived to take his seat in the stands. The flautist Princeps was unaware. The crowd roared its devotion to their emperor. The flautist thought that the roar was for himself. The crowd delighted in the confusion.

The Princeps in the audience was the master of the *domus divinae*, the holy house. The Princeps on the stage, his leg strapped in snow-white bands, looked more like a server at the Palatine tables. The deluded artist was lucky to escape with nothing worse than a dying on stage, a few catcalls, a kicking back out into the street, a gentler end than Phaedrus himself, so recently so fearful of Sejanus, might have predicted in any other form than a fable.

The new world was a stage. Stealing an emperor's thunder might once have meant winning a military victory that Augustus or Tiberius would have preferred to win themselves – a dangerous enough success. Phaedrus described a different theft of thunder, the mere mistaking of an emperor's applause for one's own. This might be no less dangerous.

The fable was an extended metaphor for a shifting landscape of politics. Just as gluttony had become different from greed, flattery had become different from exaggeration or lying. There was a new pattern which stretched beyond any act or instance. It was a web.

27

TORTURE OF AN ACTRESS

Diplomacy required its own kind of flattery. Flattery was built from lies, and going to lie abroad for one's country was what diplomats did before there was a Roman Empire and for long after it had fallen. Any official from Syria or Egypt might be used to addressing a self-styled king of kings. When representing his country in Rome, the deal was whatever the diplomat had to do.

Caligula's expectation to receive worship as a god was none the less perilous for diplomats at his court. The differences between Jews and Greeks, never-ending squabbles in many tiny pimples of the Mediterranean empire, unusually violent in 38 CE, became much more dangerous when Caligula had to be appeased. An embassy of Alexandrian Jews expressed contempt at any suggestion of a man's divinity. Caligula was even more contemptuous of their disbelief. The rival Greeks responded by giving the emperor even more divine titles.

Caligula asked the Jews why they avoided pork. They replied cautiously that there were also some who avoided lamb. Caligula agreed. He himself, he said, did not like lamb. This small measure of agreement about dinner was as much as the meeting achieved. Caligula showed more interest in the gardens where the talks were taking place, ordering windows and art for his pavilion walls. Adjudication, if it ever came at all, was not immediate. For courtiers there were months of money to be made from taking bribes from both sides.

Caligula saw worship as his right. And, if he were to receive any lesser form of flattery, the decision to do so, he thought, should be his own, not a choice of some barbarian dietary obsessives. When he dictated letters to the new governor of Syria, Publius Petronius, Lucius's successor and one of the Romans who best understood the delicate politics of Judaea, he added threats in his own handwriting. The clash of incompatible beliefs was not long in coming.

Barely eighteen months into his reign the Greek population of Jamnia, the date town of Judaea, erected an altar for the imperial cult. The resident Jews tore it down. Caligula saw a personal insult and ordered Petronius that the great temple at Jerusalem itself should be converted into an imperial shrine. It should house a giant statue of the emperor as Jupiter. The governor was to use two legions to enforce this decree.

Petronius was horrified that what might be harmless, even useful, flattery elsewhere was being imposed where it could cause riot, rebellion and religious war. He used first the bureaucratic tool of delay, easier when in a remote border province than in Rome. He ordered the building of the statue, but told the sculptors not to hurry. When he marched his Syrian legions to the border of Galilee he met a massive demonstration from those who saw the statue as their prime anxiety. The harvest was being neglected. Famine loomed.

Petronius withdrew and wrote to Caligula with a direct appeal to change his mind. This was a dangerous tactic from a distance. Even for Lucius, watching closely at Caligula's shoulder, the emperor's mood was hard to predict. Caligula told Petronius first to obey orders and secondly to commit suicide. But Petronius, in the same way as Pontius Pilate, survived.

Suddenly, courtly expertise had become of no account. Before the suicide instruction to Petronius reached Syria came the reports of Caligula's own death. This was a matter of vital importance on the Palatine, and only a little less in Syria, even if elsewhere the news mattered much less. His fantastical aspirations were a burden to those who had to see and skirt around them, but to most citizens of the empire they meant no more than they did to the Moon. Details of his departure were anyway scarce at first.

Every day, at Caligula's last week of Palatine games, 41 CE, there was some sort of free lunch: apples, pears and pomegranates, dates and figs, beef steaks and chicken wings, live ducks and hens, deep-filled baskets hurled into a tight-packed crowd as bounty from the emperor. It was just like the very best of old times, when men who wanted votes fed those who wanted feasts, or perhaps a parody of those days. On the familiar wooden benches in the courtyard of the marble palace, in the pale January sun, most were not bothered about memory or mockery. Quail and partridge scuttled around their feet to be caught for later.

Before the assassination, anxiety gripped only the very few. Cassius Chaerea was an undistinguished officer of the palace guard, a soldier softened by court life whom Caligula enjoyed mocking as effeminate, giving him erotic daily passwords to hand on to his men, turning his own security into a sexual comedy of cocks and eunuchs. Quintilia was an actress, suspected of knowledge of an assassination plot. Caligula hoped that Chaerea would be so determined to prove his masculinity that he would be her especially brutal torturer.

Chaerea did what he was told to do. Quintilia revealed nothing of whatever she knew about the would-be killers. Maybe she had not known much. Chaerea so wrecked her body and face that even Caligula felt guilty. When the emperor ordered compensation for the no longer beautiful actress, Chaerea was as confused as he was ridden by guilt.

The plotters were disorganised in every way. Each had his own very different reason for thinking that this last day of the games in honour of Augustus, in the place where his body had lain in state, was the day when his great-grandson should die. The chance of success must have seemed low. Among the hopeful who had failed to act before were Cornelius Lentulus Gaetulicus, one of the boosters of Caligula's connection to Tibur, and Valerius Asiaticus, the wealthy Gaul who had endured Caligula's critique of his wife's performance in bed. Many had spoken. Some had spoken to each other. None had acted and time was running out.

Yet when, towards the end of the performance, Caligula left his seat to judge a visiting choir from Greece and take a bath, Chaerea, consumed by his own behaviour as much as by constitutional nicety, followed him into one of the twisting Palatine passages and hacked him with his cavalryman's sword. Others added their blows. Loyal bodyguards briefly fought the assassins, but there could be little loyalty to Caligula once he was dead. Soon there was none.

Chaerea then escaped through the corridors and covered paths to the sometime house of Germanicus. On the side of the Palatine where Caligula's father and mother had once lived there was the usual panic of assassins, echoes of the Ides of March eighty-five years before, the uncertainty whether the killers would be hailed as heroes or killed in turn. At the heart of the court, those who had run the real business of empire under the dead emperor prepared for life under a successor whom they hoped better to control.

Their choice was Germanicus's brother, Antonia's son, Messalina's husband. The new Emperor Claudius was the senior member of the Julio-Claudian house, an unexpected successor except in the sense that the expected successors were becoming rather few, a survivor on account of his all too visible disabilities for office – slurred speech, a limp and a genuine preference for ancient Etruscan texts over the politics of his own time. Palace guardsmen were said to have found him cowering behind a curtain. Maybe he was close enough to one of the plots to have been less than wholly surprised. Certainly he was backed by Callistus, the most powerful freedman of the old court.

Claudius's disabilities and eccentricities would throughout his reign remain a useful cloak, discouraging to those who did not see him operating day by day but of less concern to those who knew him. His ways might not be wholly predictable but, by the standards of the past four years, he was a man who shared some of the reality that others saw. Chaerea was executed on the very normal grounds that any assassin should die to discourage others.

With Caligula's death Aulus Vitellius had lost his friend and fellow charioteer. But Lucius, long-time protégé of Antonia, would work with Claudius and his wife Messalina very well. The status 'friend of Caesar', as the crowd had taunted Pontius Pilate, was the greatest, and most fragile, status of all. The new Caesar found many old friends.

28

GARDEN ORNAMENTS

Lucius did not attract the charges of corruption that clung to many in the court. None of the Vitellii was known for susceptibility to bribes, not even Aulus, whose laxity with money was much more famed than any greed for it. Lucius was wealthy nonetheless. Being a powerful man on the Palatine was still a path to profit. The honest avoiders of risk made money as well as the gamblers. Lucius Vitellius invested in land, as Roman senators always had, and some of it was around his house in Aricia, just a few miles south of Rome on the Appian Way.

Aricia stood for freedom from Rome. '*Egressum!*', 'Phew, I'm out of there!' wrote Horace as he began his part in a diplomatic mission for Augustus during the civil wars. *Egressum magna me accepit Aricia Roma*: Aricia welcomed me when mighty Rome was left behind. But Aricia was also near enough to the capital for messages to flow quickly back and forth and for a cautious courtier to be able to return if the new emperor needed him. The first months of Claudius's reign were calm compared to Caligula's last. It was unwise to be complacent, but the family could still enjoy a few meals under their fig trees.

Lucius in his late forties was still a fit man, known no more for sickness than for greed. He was a more venerable figure in his own garden, less wired within the latest dramas, with his wife Sextilia, veiled and grander in bearing, albeit from a family less close to the *domus Caesaris*, their taller sons, Aulus and Lucius, the first somewhat stouter too, both in their twenties, survivors of Tiberius in Capri and Claudius's Rome. Food was simpler where the country met the city: vegetables in little dishes, salted meat, honey cakes, quince, pistachios, flasks of spring water and spiced wine, and at the table centre statues taller than the flasks, though miniature nonetheless, the household gods of the Vitellii, the wooden Peace and Plenty that his old father, Publius, had worshipped in Nuceria.

Although these guardian witnesses to the family's progress were looked after by more household slaves than Publius would have had, they were still recognisably the same, some painted, some in stone, still garlanded and looking after the food as they did in every family, claiming, like garden birds, the first call on anything that fell from a plate. Old Publius would have been surprised only by a few interlopers among the statuary.

Amid the featureless figures in stone and wood were others in gold, robed in the Greek style and recognisable as individuals: Pallas, *a rationibus*, the accountant, Narcissus, *ab epistulis*, master of the post, and Callistus, *a libellis*, the sifter of petitions. To those familiar with the court there was also Polybius, the speechwriter and secretary, Posides, literary and refined, recognisably the eunuch, all of them former slaves themselves, once victims of vicious assaults, newly loyal outsiders as the Vitellii once had been, the men with the greatest power over every family table. Every public servant had his job. Their statues were a reminder that men could grant favours just as could gods. Rome was not so very far away.

The new emperor was content with the idea of a household being a government. Physical frailty had kept Claudius from following Tiberius into the army or Caligula on to the racetrack. He had few links to the clubs of Roman life. His nervousness in speech separated him from the senate. A crippled survivor of childhood disease and an even more aggressive childhood tutor, at key moments he had been deemed too weak to be even worth killing. The weapons of the weak, insincerity and flattery, were the ones he knew best.

He stared at his courtiers from small, deep-set eyes, short, fleshy and lopsided whether he stood, sat or reclined to eat from a couch. Freed slaves, scribes, cooks and accountants, eunuchs for food-tasting, sex or book-keeping were the people with whom he had passed most of his life. The posts held by the men in Lucius's garden were not new, but it became quickly clear that they were more powerful than before.

Claudius gave out gold rings with his own portrait to designate those who had free access to his presence. As Ovid had pointed out sharply in his exile from Augustus's court, anyone who knew an emperor at all would pretend to be his friend. In a single house, without distinctions of rank or constitutional office, some sort of ordering of intimacy was essential. All were more confident once knowing where they stood, or should be standing.

Gaius Julius Callistus had gained his first two names as a freed slave of Caligula and his third from the Greek for beautiful. He soon became as intimate with the new emperor as he had been with the old. Some said he had himself engineered the change of regime, happy for the doubtful credit of assassination to go elsewhere. Callistus had been as important in Claudius's ascent to power as the guardsmen searching behind the curtain. In an age of only rudimentary maths, he studied risk and accounts and, like Claudius, the art of gambling.

There was the beginning of a career structure for courtiers. 'Tiberius Julius' from Smyrna was freed at this time, promoted, allowed to marry into the aristocracy and prepared for a career as a procurator, the rank of old Publius Vitellius under Augustus. There he showed further the courtier's art of not only serving the emperor but identifying his successors. A machine of new opportunity was being born, as perpetuating of itself as the senate and the army.

In the countryside beyond Aricia, where courtly promotions mattered hardly at all, money moved more quickly from purse to purse, buying support as it was spent and spent again. Claudius held games. He put on shows. He expanded Caligula's projects of public work. He took control of the corn supply from the senate and began a new harbour to protect the transport ships and prevent local floods. East of Rome he ordered the draining of the Fucine Lake through three miles of mountain tunnel, levelling high ground, employing 30,000 men, promising new fields for food.

The *Aqua Claudia* was meanwhile slowly reaching Rome from the nearer hills above Tibur, bending along the contour lines by minutely measured gradients. Rome's imperial *aquarii* worked in a *familia aquarum* of 700 people, both slave and free, funded through

Claudius's own treasury and by water taxes. They were supervised by another Imperial freedman, a *procurator aquarum*, conducting an endless routine of calibrated inspection interrupted by emergency.

Seen from the palace tables, there was a power in applying numbers to politics too. According to the revered Greek thinker Solon, those who had influence with tyrants were like pebbles used in maths, the same stone sometimes representing a very large number and at other times a very small one. So too were the men of a court. To Lucius Vitellius, no great soldier himself and much more comfortable behind a desk, calculators like the men represented in his dining-room shrine were the future.

Lucius flattered Pallas in particular, the chief of the imperial treasury and sometime slave and freedman of Claudius's mother, Antonia. It was Pallas whom she had trusted to deliver her allegations about Sejanus's crimes to Capri. Almost as important was the man who filed most letters as pending, Polybius, the emperor's writer of speeches, a translator of Homer into Latin and Virgil into Greek, or so those claimed who wanted a word said on their behalf. Then, and not least, came Narcissus, who controlled the flow of all letters to and from the Palatine. These men were essential for the working of the empire.

On most days Claudius ate simply with his own children and the children of his friends. The newly prominent freedmen did not need to be invited to the extravagant banquets. Their influence came from more exclusive proximity, becoming notorious for protecting their clients from harm, cancelling any excess generosity by their master, rewarding flattery of the kind that Caligula had demanded, sometimes rejecting it, reversing judgments, altering documents. The year 41 CE was a good year for Antiochus IV of Commagene, reinstated to the throne by order of Caligula, then deprived of it by the same caprice, then restored to his inheritance by the brother of Germanicus.

When Claudius declared war on other people's gluttony, venturing where Tiberius had feared to go, a ban on stuffed dormice was piloted into law, if probably not into common practice. Little more noticed was his ban on stewed meats in the streets. Both were expressions, not exertions, of his power. When Claudius wanted his own seaside dining cave, matching those of Tiberius and the garden-lover, Lucullus, the builders of Baiae received their due instructions.

Emerging bureaucracy brought practical reform. There was a crackdown on theatrical carpenters whose seating failed the spectators, as it did in the catastrophe at Fidenae, or whose stage machinery failed the actors, as in Phaedrus's fable of Princeps, the flautist with the broken leg. There was more than a moral to be learnt about stealing an emperor's applause. There was a problem and a solution. Sloppy circus builders would be food for the circus lions.

Freedmen and friends took their own homes around the Palatine. The renowned house of the republican orator Lucius Licinius Crassus, with its shady garden of lotus trees, became just another house of a confidant of Claudius. The homes of the freedmen, particularly those of Callistus and Posides, were sites of wonder in themselves. The dining room of Callistus had thirty pillars made from precious onyx and was notoriously barred to the man who had been his master when he had been a slave. Rotundus Drusillianus, from the household of Caligula's sister, Drusilla, was a collector of massive silver plates from Spain.

Posides lived in splendour alongside the eunuch priests of the *Magna Mater*, perhaps gaining his own quiet satisfaction for the crushing of his testicles as a slave child or the cutting of his scrotum as an adolescent, operations that had extended his sexual appeal at the cost of a high-pitched voice, hormonally elongated limbs and a powerful sense of difference. Phaedrus wrote sympathetically of a eunuch's plight in public life, the disgusting jokes and abuse about lost body parts that he had to endure in court, his struggle to argue that he should not be judged for bad treatment inflicted upon him but only for bad things he himself had done.

Phaedrus's fable was formed from a legal quip, the double meaning of a *testis*, the similarity of the words in Latin for witness and testicle. Although eunuch was a Greek word, a keeper of the bed, the fable was not a translation of anything by Aesop. The court setting was Roman, not the only one in the fables, almost as though Phaedrus himself, if he was an ex-slave, was a lawyer too.

Some grandees of Rome found their dependence on former slaves hard to endure; some thought that the damage done to a man by slavery would forever be a bar to virtue; but few thought they could turn back time. Any senators accused of plotting against Claudius found that an obsequious pleasantry to Polybius, Posides or Narcissus, perhaps a payment too, might save their lives.

Within this new system with new rules there was no shame in flattery, and for gluttony no blame. Household management of the Roman world – based on friendship not elections, responsive rather than initiating, more often random than systematic – was set to stay. The machinery of government and its oil were both essential. Both would remain the essence of court life for centuries, the oil lasting longer than almost any act, for good or ill, of the machine itself.

Forged around a court of characters ripe for satire, most of Phaedrus's fables, like Aesop's originals, were not about named human individuals. They were peopled by birds and beasts, safer subjects but sometimes bolder too, subversive, even directly attacking identifiable figures. A powerful animal, a lion or a great ape, would be shown abusing its power over the weak and gullible. When frogs in a pond asked Jupiter for a king and sneered at the god's first offer of a floating log, their next anointed monarch was a frog-eating snake. Men asked who was the old log and who was the new snake.

Canine characters showed the greedy and the flattering in ways that dogs peculiarly can, sniffing each other's arses, chasing their own reflections or being so gluttonous as to give up their own lives and freedom for a snack. A dog swimming with a piece of meat in his mouth would drop his meal to get the meat in the mouth of another dog appearing to swim beside him. A pack of dogs, desperate to lick some meat at the bottom of a river, would nearly drown themselves trying to drink the torrent dry. Dogs accepted the slavery of the collar in order to have fine food from the banqueting tables in their bellies; a wolf, however hungry, would not. Dogs were a means by which Roman readers in the age of Augustus's successors could look obliquely at themselves. Phaedrus was their guide.

Augustus himself had known a very different poet of the kennels, named, though not very certainly named, as Grattius Faliscus. Grattius's work on hunting explained what a Roman master of dogs might more practically expect: not a mirroring of his own morals but help on the hunt. Comparison of the two dog men, Phaedrus and Grattius, however dimly seen through their art, can begin to define what had changed at Rome since the death of Augustus at Nola.

Grattius was more a teacher than an artist. His dogs were only for the chase, not at all for chastising flatterers or gluttons. It was Grattius who set out in huntsman's verse how every country had its own kind of dog and how useful this was for visitors and invaders. Take a Persian dog. It was hard to tame but wild in battle. A Ukrainian dog disliked fighting but had wise instincts. A dog from China was fierce beyond all imagination. Corinthian dogs pursued pigs. Rhine dogs, known to all returning soldiers from the northern frontier, helped men hunt hares.

Dogs could be improved by foreign mates. African dogs had a bestiary of mates. Around the Caspian Sea the bitches bred with tigers, toughening the stock with every generation. Mountain Greek dogs, fit only for barking, would shut up when mated with mastiffs. The British dog, as long as an owner was not too fussy about looks and manners, was usefully careless of its own life in battle, even comparable to a hunting partner of the heroic Greeks.

Grattius was not a court poet like Virgil or Horace. He was not a troublemaker like Ovid. He represented a blunt, expansive, martial Rome. Unlike Phaedrus, Grattius was never a popular poet, his work surviving only in a single long fragment and datable only from a reference in Ovid's failed pleas to be released from exile by the cold Black Sea. In one line among thousands on love and myth, Ovid's essential guide to the Rome of his time, his companions and rivals, stood Grattius the dog-poet, listed in the architecture of place and mind that the universal poet was missing.

Compared to Grattius, Phaedrus's fables were more tricky. Their popularity came, like the Atellan farces which the emperor had banned, from their licensed dissection of old authority. Gluttons and flatterers were both seen as dogs. Phaedrus satirised the strong and also undermined the weak. He was both a flatterer and a critic of flattery, much more than a moral jester, an artist as hard to read with certainty as any of the courtiers among whom he moved.

Grattius had not used dogs to say what a poet might not dare to say about men. His hounds were hunters for food, helpers in war. German dogs were like German people, either to be subdued or to help Romans subdue. All dogs did vital tasks. If they did not, they would not be there. Breeding was a domination of nature. A poisoner could test his arts on the tongue of a dog.

29

LUCIUS RULES THE WORLD

Two years into his reign Claudius divided the senior men of Rome into three groups: those whom he needed for the conquest of Britain, the task in which Julius Caesar had failed and which Caligula had failed to begin; those whom he needed with him to stop them exploiting his absence by a coup; and those whom he trusted to run the city and empire while the emperor was away. The leader of the third group, consul in 43 CE for the second time, was Lucius Vitellius. This was the highest position that the Vitellii had reached so far.

It was almost 100 years since Caesar had twice crossed the Channel, or, as he called it, the Ocean, the name which made his efforts sound fabulously difficult in case he failed, which, unusually for him, he did. Tides had broken his ships. Gauls, not yet knowing the cost in their own deaths, revolted behind his back. Not even Caesar, the great self-praiser and author of his own history, could write that away.

Britain had been a conquest too far. Twice he gave up and went home, satisfied only that the southern British tribes seemed bribed enough to be loyal. What he most immediately wanted was to be richer and more powerful than his son-in-law back home, the irritatingly acclaimed Pompey the Great. Britain had not helped. Caesar's carefully edited version put his failure in the best possible light.

Augustus later considered another try. His flatterers even promised for a while that he would finish his father's task. But he had always bigger problems than a mere tempting irritant. Conquest had to justify its cost and the conquest of Britain, he thought, would not. Tiberius continued this policy of long oblivion and as his favourite island preferred Capri. Caligula thought about Britain briefly before finding easier fantasy schemes.

For Claudius in 43 CE this unfinished business was a chance to fashion himself in the best tradition of a Caesar, a great-great-grandnephew of Julius Caesar, as long as Rome could be kept secure while he was away. Neither Tiberius nor Caligula had dared to leave Italy as emperor. Claudius was the proudest writer, observer and thinker to rule Rome since Caesar. He knew how he might flatter himself – and be flattered – when he came back in triumph.

Claudius chose as the leader of the invasion force his commander in distant Pannonia, Aulus Plautius, one of his key supporters after Caligula's death, a man of no great family himself but a former consul, allegedly trusted by Tiberius, and related to the Vitellii. Plautius seemed a sound choice and proved to be so, neither too close to the grandees of Rome nor too far away.

Narcissus had to leave the comfortable Palatine tables where he sifted the empire's letters to its emperor. He too took the road to the mysterious island where the priests were Druids and people were their sacrifices. Plautius brought his nervous army to the pebbled beach of northernmost Gaul, showed them the shifting sea, and they refused to cross. Britain was more unknown than any place they had ever been, more bizarre than anywhere of which they knew. They needed reassurance.

Plautius stood on a podium, not a famous face except to the men who had followed him from the Danube, and visible only to a few. His speech failed to change their minds. Impatiently, and it did not at first seem wisely, Narcissus tried his own plea on behalf of the emperor. Nothing changed until the horror of taking orders from such a man became clear to the troops. An ex-slave affecting to lead an army was a crossing too far from Palatine to camp. Such reversal of roles had once been kept to the one day in the year when the low lorded it over the high, the festival of Saturn. 'Io Saturnalia', they shouted, 'Happy holidays', mocking both one of the most powerful figures in the empire and themselves. The ships sailed for Britain.

Posides the eunuch sailed too, further outraging traditionalists in the army when he was given one of their highest bravery awards, the *hasta pura*, an ornamental spear, probably not, it was thought, for bravery: there were to be no last-ditch struggles on this British campaign, nothing to require a writer to become a fighter. Also on the trip was one of the many Palatine doctors, Scribonius Largus, famed for whitening Messalina's teeth and easing Antonia's tonsillitis. Claudius's personal doctor, Stertinius Xenophon, was one of the highest-paid members of staff. Even greater than his loyalty to the emperor was his devotion to his home island of Cos in the southern Aegean. The mud of Kent and Essex must have been an even greater ordeal for him than for the rest of the travelling court.

Claudius in Britain was an emperor in a hurry, not in the way that Julius Caesar was always in a hurry, circling and extending the edges of the Roman world, but in a hurry to get home. All his problems were at home, apart from those he had brought with him and would have to stay with him, the rivals whom he needed closely to watch. Those who reluctantly made the trip included Valerius Asiaticus, the rich Gaul who had tentatively plotted the killing of Caligula, Lucius Livius Galba, the heavy-faced favourite of Livia whom Tiberius had deprived of her legacy, and Titus Flavius Vespasianus, both protégé and protector of Narcissus. Vespasian was a politician and general whose mistress was Antonia's secretary, Caenis. Behind his military demeanour he was a fierce flatterer. With or without Caenis's advice, he had once made a senate speech thanking Caligula for a dinner invitation.

Lucius Vitellius was left in the *domus Caesaris* to run the normal business of government as best he could. His son, Aulus, had learnt early about power, swimming with Tiberius in Capri as a child, gambling and racing with Caligula. But his first close sight of administration came while Claudius was away invading the island that every predecessor had failed to win. Aulus, from his great height, was free to watch.

For all those left at Rome there were the permanent problems of corn supply, the new harbour at Ostia, the slow, snaking progress of the *Aqua Claudia* from Tibur, the drain for the Fucine Lake which for 1,900 years would be the longest tunnel in the world. Abroad there was the plan to end discontent in Judaea, the funding of a small war in Mauretania to the south of the straits of Hercules, and some consolidation of the tax base in Gaul. Senators had to be flattered that they had at least some of the power of their ancestors. The people always needed to be fed – and a new system of dated tickets for collecting the free corn was designed to prevent the queues at the end of each month.

In Britain itself there was little to interest the Vitellii except the glory that Claudius might find there and, if he didn't find, Lucius would have to promote and invent. Druids, their secret language and human sacrifices, were of much more interest to Claudius than they were to his hard-working man in Rome. Flattering the old antiquarian that he was also a great general was the central aim of the project. How much Claudius, an emperor with new military clothes, believed the flattery or merely pretended to believe it, was never clear.

Britain had oysters, mysterious creatures which grew fatter and thinner with the phases of the moon. That was indeed clear. There was tin in the western British mines, gold allegedly in the hills, several friendly native kings and even those that were unfriendly had sons who might betray them. There were traders who knew Rome well and were well known at Rome. There were slaves everywhere. According to Caesar the British population was immense. So too was the number of its animals for human consumption, a class that did not include chickens, geese or hares, which the people kept as pets.

The less civilised Britons lived inland and clothed themselves in skins. Even Rome's friends on the coast wore blue tattoos. The hair on their heads and upper lips was long. Otherwise they were close-shaved. Groups of up to a dozen men, including fathers and sons, took to bed the same women, the children deemed always to belong to whichever man had done so first.

The British dogs, according to Grattius, Augustus's poet of the kennels, were usefully courageous, although they had well-known limitations: ugliness, ill-discipline, just like most of the people. It was necessary to penetrate the Britons to bring home their dogs, as he had ambiguously put it. Rape and enslavement were what Romans abroad did so routinely as to be rarely worth mentioning.

Claudius, whose own favourite was a small white dog, would have read his Grattius, omnivorous student that he was. Aulus Plautius might have pretended to know this author's list of national dogs which, behind its canine growls, was a window into how its writer and his readers saw their expanding world. The doctor, Scribonius Largus, made a speciality of treating dog bites. But otherwise the expectation of the courtiers was of nothing much bar mistletoe and superstition, surrounded by the same vicious waves, clinging mud and cloud that Publius Vitellius and his men had found on the German shore.

Good things, especially good food, came from the east. Those campaigning in Britain never felt further from Rome than when they ate. But, through good planning, Claudius and his travelling court had to eat in Kent and Essex for only sixteen days of a six-month absence from Rome. They landed on what was still then the island of Thanet, crossed the oyster-filled channel to the mainland, marched with elephants to what was not yet London and on to Colchester, where the local tribes, knowledgeable about Rome and well understanding Claudius's temporary need to be flattered, made a tactical surrender.

It had been a gamble, the kind of calculated risk that Claudius and Callistus understood well. Their men knew about gambling too. In the ground behind the invasion beach they left behind squares made from Italian marble, a rarity for Kent, their surface scratched with crosses within smaller squares. There were also pieces of a box made of bone, a simpler game, holes at top and bottom and slats inside to ensure the random falling of dice. For the many soldiers who preferred a still greater simplicity of decision there were wave-worn pebbles for the palm of a hand: make a fist, take a guess, two stones or one, one or none, in or out, easy money.

As soon as the Danube legions had subdued Britain's flat lands, with a respectable count of bodies on what could be deemed battlefields, Claudius could leave with a victory and forget the rest. The lands that were newly Roman were the only parts of Britain that anyone would know or care about. His elephants had shown the showman's touch that few would forget.

On his return, via the dedication of a fountain for himself at Lugdunum, the Gallic town of his birth, Claudius awarded himself what his courtiers agreed was a well-deserved triumph. This was his chance to be driven in a chariot through the streets of Rome, accepting applause like the heroes of old for an achievement which, while not wholly real, had more substance than the imagination of Caligula. He issued commemorative coins to praise himself for conquering the Ocean. He did not give himself the name Britannicus, bestowing it instead on the young son whom Messalina was obsessively protecting from rivals.

Claudius was grateful to his commander. Aulus Plautius would nonetheless have to live off the damp northern fields for a little longer, the diets of himself and his men supplemented from the holds of a chain of transport ships, a virtual wooden bridge across the Channel. He would be allowed an appropriate lesser honour at a later stage.

All Claudius's companions, the eager and the pressed, won honours in Britain to secure their loyalty. These honours were of far greater importance on the Palatine than anything happening in Colchester. After Julius Caesar's failures in Britain, Augustus's caution and Caligula's fantasies, success was a fact. An emperor had made a difference in the empire that everyone had to recognise.

30

ASHES OF A SWALLOW

When Claudius was back in Rome, Lucius again had to balance the roles of the flatterer and administrator, the dark arts of the courtier's day squeezing practical governance into whenever it could be done. Flattery is always an inefficient use of time, requiring watchfulness and patience amid bouts of high activity. Gluttony is for some an easy accompaniment, a way of spending wasted time and obliterating the sense of its consequences.

This was, however, the way that Lucius's world was run. His sons were still in good positions to learn for themselves. The wife of Lucius, his younger son, was the ambitious Junia Calvina, a great-great-granddaughter of Augustus whose family saw itself as no less entitled to rule than the throne's recent occupants. Alongside the court of freedmen were also the rival grandees. Again there arose the older jealousies within the *domus Caesaris*.

Claudius's wife, Messalina, was the figure whom Lucius watched most closely. While somewhat easier to understand and predict than Caligula had been, she was behind much of the palace turbulence and accused of being behind it all. Lucius made her his special object of flattery, different in form from humouring Caligula about his place in the heavens but in outcome, he hoped, the same.

Messalina had turned Claudius against Julia Livilla, one of Caligula's notoriously beloved sisters, who was briefly recalled from exile after her brother's assassination. Livilla was executed while her alleged lover, the Spanish orator at court, Lucius Annaeus Seneca, was exiled to Corsica. This was a generous fate, though rapidly unappreciated by Seneca himself, whose flamboyant letters from exile, widely read later but not at the time, were a masterclass in flattery. Their recipient was the freedman Polybius, a man of literary taste who may have appreciated their style but did nothing to ease their writer's return home.

The new empress also moved early against Tiberius's grand-daughter, Julia, whose husband, Rubellius Blandus of Tibur, had died before enjoying his imperial status for very long. Julia had a son, Rubellius Plautus, who was about ten years old. Tiberius had ordered Julia's marriage to Blandus to keep her heirs out of the succession race. But a provincial background was an insufficient guarantee to the anxious empress, who had hopes for a two-year-old son of her own.

Julia was charged with incest, immorality and use of poisons, persuasively enough for the newly triumphant Claudius to order her execution. The woman who for thirty years since Augustus's death at Nola had been married to a regal son of Germanicus and a respectable man from Tibur faced an executioner's sword. The object of Augustus's last anxiety made no defence. Her friend and relative, Pomponia Graecina, wife of Aulus Plautius, never forgave Claudius.

Pomponia might have herself suffered for that but instead sur-vived for a further four decades. Her path of survival was twisted and dark. She may even have worshipped the man whose cruci-fixion Pontius Pilate had been incompetent to prevent. Christians were becoming a small problem. Jews and Greeks were still a much larger one. Quickly there would be the not-very-conquered Britons too.

Much banqueting marked Claudius's return from his conquest. Scribonius Largus had new experiences from his trip to Britain to improve his textbook, soon to be dedicated with due flattery to Callistus, some useful thoughts on damp and cold, snake bites and yew tree juice. Back home his more valuable expertise was once again in cosmetic toothpaste, breath fresheners, earache, vomiting and the cure of those whose excrement signalled their excess.

Like Apicius and the Palatine cooks, Largus used dozens of rare ingredients because his patients could afford them – and maybe because his rivals could not. His recipe book of drugs showed a man keen to assault the reputations of others while promoting his own.

'*Bone deus!*', 'Good god!', he interjected at the failings of those he deemed to fall outside the profession. Like Phaedrus, but with sage and saffron rather than satire, he gave his readers an insight into the daily jealousies of the court.

Time with the emperor brought a doctor profit just as it did for a diplomat. If a drug was popular with the imperial family, it was saleable beyond the Palatine. Largus mixed celery seeds, cinnamon, myrrh and the ashes of an overcooked swallow to calm the throat of the emperor's mother Antonia. The protector of Lucius Vitellius, Pallas and Caenis, destroyer of Sejanus, had a throat much used in the interests of the *domus Caesaris*. Her satisfaction was a profitable sign for others.

In remote Britain there arose a temple to the Divine Claudius. Colchester was distant enough from Rome to fit the convention that emperor worship be permitted to those far away. Augustus had set that rule, not explicitly but clearly enough. Britain was in the west, not the east, but there could hardly be any place where the natives were stranger. Even Tiberius, who did not become a god after his death, had permitted some of the wilder northern Gauls to flatter him with worship. The Britons would have the same privilege to prove themselves loyal.

There may have been also a tactical purpose – as in Alexandria, where an altar to a Roman gave Greeks a weapon with which to irritate the Jews and balance local power. Perhaps it was hoped that the new temple would replace the Druidism that Aulus Plautius and his legions saw as their enemy in the mist. Before he took the throne the emperor would have had a greater interest in studying Druids than in substituting himself for them. But his brief trip to the mud of eastern Britain, and the grovelling welcome from its chieftains after their defeat, may have encouraged him to advance the process of civilisation.

There were benefits from dividing the loyalties of foreign wor-shippers. At Rome those who benefited most from a changing face of flattery were the flatterers themselves, protected by their arcane knowledge of what was right or wrong and prepared to sell that knowledge to outsiders. Scribonius Largus, who used Augustus's name to promote an ointment that the first emperor had used on his weak left eye, called Claudius *deus noster Caesar*, Caesar our god, a phrase that Augustus would not have allowed in Nola except from an Alexandrian sailor.

31

FLATTERY'S TEXTBOOK

Just as flattery was a means for survival at court, so was anonymity. When Phaedrus published his fables he dedicated them to a man called Eutychus, a figure hardly less mysterious than himself. Maybe this Eutychus existed or maybe he did not. Quite likely he was a type of man, not an individual. Many of the missing occupants of the halls where Aulus was to hide in the December of 69 CE were types of men, book-keepers, bakers of white bread, breeders of dogs; or types of women, wet-nurses, voluptuaries or magicians. Their names were their work; their work was their identification and all the mark on memory they would make.

Eutychus was a common name for a slave. It meant good luck, appropriately for the Eutychus who had been one of Caligula's charioteers, even more so for the Eutychus who betrayed Sejanus. It was possible, though never likely and maybe never known, if Phaedrus's Eutychus was one of these lucky men or just a type. When Phaedrus dedicated his book of fables, with a sideswipe at the monstrosity of the safely dead captain of the imperial guard, some readers would have seen a connection between two real men. More readers, perhaps those enjoying from further away Phaedrus's flattering foxes and arse-licking dogs, would have just seen Eutychus as any slave on the make, anyone that they might know.

A lucky slave was a particularly popular type for Roman readers. It was natural for a master to think that a man was lucky to be his slave or, at least, lucky not to be someone else's. Sometimes that thought was justified. A loyal slave might be truly lucky, well paid, promised freedom and then officially freed, slapped around the face in a ritual act of sending him or her on his way. Freed slaves would often then stay on in the master's house, still telling the master what he liked to hear about himself, maybe more likely to be believed, fortunate in a different way, particularly so if the household was the sprawling Palatine and they could profit from knowing its rules. An unlucky slave could be kept enslaved or cast out into an unwelcoming world, not just profitless but starving.

Phaedrus might have been a slave or former slave himself, or a witty Roman citizen pretending to be an ex-slave, a lawyer perhaps of some kind (there is a lawyerliness about some of his jokes) with an interest in Aesop and a desire to entertain. Whatever the truth, Phaedrus was sufficiently cautious about his own anonymity that the learned Seneca could claim never to have heard of him. Writing one of his pleas to the powerful freedman Polybius from his exile in Corsica, he could claim that the task of translating Aesop into Latin had still to be undertaken. Polybius, despite all his burdensome duties, was, Seneca argued, the perfect writer to make the attempt.

This letter later became much more important for students of flattery than any fable by a man known as Phaedrus about an animal or even an emperor. Seneca was a courtier of rare breadth of intellect, an orator, teacher, pioneer playwright, hypocrite courtier and elegant justifier of hypocrisy, a revolutionary guide to the interior of characters' minds, soon to be perhaps the most powerful and richest great writer of all time. Seneca's letters taught philosophy and politics and the etiquette of how to survive. But, at the time when Claudius was newly back from Britain, the author was still in Corsica and as low as a hungry fox at the bottom of a tree.

Messalina was implacable against Seneca. Courtiers might rule upon most of what mattered at court, the tax queries, the building contracts, the diplomatic give and take, but on personal matters they were wise to stand a little further back. Managing the personal (much of it with origins that were obscure) was as important as managing the political. The two might sometimes be the same. Lucius knew the arts of anonymity. Seneca was not in the least anonymous. He was a courtier in very public disgrace.

Corsica was a larger place of imprisonment than the Mediterranean islands on which so many junior members of the *domus Caesaris* had starved. It was a trading post between Italy and Gaul. It had fertile fields as well as malarial swamp. There was familiar food for a man who had been a vegetarian until, in the reign of Tiberius, vegetarianism, like so much else, became a potential sign of dissent. Messalina may have thought she was being generous. She might have incited Claudius to be much harsher. He would probably have done what she said.

Seneca's nights were much warmer than Ovid's on the Black Sea had been. Ovid had died in exile. Seneca feared the same fate. He was not a fit man. His chest heaved every day of his life. His throat was a cave of coughs. Much worse, he claimed (almost certainly falsely) that there was no audience on Corsica for his words and no readership for his work. Any passing ship might bring an executioner as well as letters from friends. He was hardly less determined to be back in Rome than if he had been on Pandateria or Ponza, the harsher prisons used by Augustus, and he thought he knew the levers of release. Even in his faraway place he heard that Polybius, Claudius's secretary, speechwriter and minister of many portfolios, had lost his brother. In around 44 CE he sent back a letter of extraordinary flattery, a *consolatio*, a knowing manipulation of the only world that he thought worth knowing.

To anyone ever studying the flattery required for court life this letter would be an essential document. Lucius Vitellius might easily have left such an embarrassment behind, but he was lucky; he was never in exile and he left the arts of writing to others.

Seneca's opening thoughts were about the need for humility. After some conventional words about the nature of life and the inescapable reality of death, he moved swiftly on to his gratitude that Polybius might be reading his letter from distant Corsica at all. There were so many in the empire who needed the genius of so great a man as he, the power he had earned both by his love of his master and his translations of the poetry of Homer into Latin prose and of Virgil into prose in Greek. Literature, he wrote, elevated Polybius even higher than did the letters of business and politics, from all over the world, that he sifted each day for the emperor's eyes.

Seneca knew, as only politicians who were writers knew, that a speechwriter prefers to be praised for his art than his power. The pressures of the Palatine, he went on, were preventing Polybius from using his more important literary talent. Like Claudius, who had lost his freedom for the sake of the world, so too was Polybius kept from his books. Both men were like planets, pursuing their course without rest.

Seneca advised that Polybius be wary of letting his grief for his family loss keep him from the *domus Caesaris*. Only outside the Palatine did he risk despondency. A dead brother did not much need to be mourned. In Seneca's kind of *consolatio* the dead man was irrelevant and did not need even to be named. The mention of him was merely to provide the appearance of honest criticism that gives flattery its greatest power.

Since Polybius always said that Claudius was dearer to him than even his own life, still more his brother's, it was wrong, wrote Seneca, for the courtier to complain about the triviality of death while the emperor's divinity was by his side. Polybius should instead, with dry and happy eyes, continue to write his works that equalled the greatest poets, even exceeding their stature by bringing them readers in the Roman world. And then, with his best powers and with his emperor as model and guide, Polybius should compile an account of the deeds of Claudius himself, so that, being heralded by one of his own household, they will be repeated throughout all ages.

But, he added, Polybius also needed a rest, or at least a change of pace. After such weighty matters as Homer, Virgil and Claudius, Seneca had what might seem some lesser suggestions, the highest of these in Seneca's mind being his own liberation, but that ought not to be raised too early. He had a little idea. He hardly dared venture to suggest (but he did anyway) that Polybius might agree to turn into Latin, with his characteristic elegance, the Greek tales of Aesop, a task that 'Roman intellect has not yet tried'.

That was not quite true, but in a piece so full of falsity it was hardly the worst offence. Perhaps Seneca didn't see Phaedrus as Roman intellect. Perhaps Phaedrus was still writing in the shadows, not a member of the Roman writers' club. Perhaps Seneca hoped that thinking about Aesop would be good for Polybius, bringing him down to earth from his pretence to be a planet. That would have been a subtle point, certainly by contrast with what was to come next once Polybius was caught by his own vanity.

Lift yourself up, Seneca continued with his *consolatio*, 'and every time that tears for your brother well in your eyes, fix these upon the emperor. At the sight of the splendour of his divinity they will be dried. His brilliance will dazzle them so that they will see nothing else.' This was a grotesque advance on Lucius's advice to Caligula that he could not see him talking to the Moon because gods were only visible to each other.

Seneca went beyond Thrasyllus's reassurance of Tiberius's longevity on the throne. He predicted Claudius the lengthiest imaginable reign. 'May gods and goddesses lend Claudius long to earth. May he rival the success, may he surpass the years, of the god Augustus. So long as he remains among mortals, may he not learn that any one of his family is mortal. May he offer his son as ruler to the Roman Empire and see him ruling by his side before he is his successor. Known only to our grandchildren may rise the day on which he rises to the skies.'

He went on in words taken from the same books used by those following the crucified 'King of the Jews'. 'Suffer him to heal the human race, that has long been sick and evil, suffer him to restore and return all things to their place from the madness of the reign now past. May this sun, which has shed its light upon a world that had plunged into the abyss and was sunk in darkness, ever shine.'

Only at this point did Seneca slide his praise towards less weighty matters, though not less weighty to him, his own predicament as an exile in Corsica. He did not, he said, wish such messianic events to occur in his absence. He too wanted to be a witness to the emperor's glory. That was his reason for adding to the millions of words on Polybius's many desks.

He was confident. 'The Emperor's mercy raises the hope that I will not fail to see his glories. For he has not thrown me out with no thought of ever lifting me back. Even when I was first hit by Fortune and was falling, he checked my fall, and with his divine hand let me down gently.' That was why he was alive in Corsica rather than the decaying corpse that Messalina, with Lucius Vitellius at her side, would have preferred.

'Meanwhile,' he moans, 'my great consolation in wretchedness is to see his compassion spreading across the world. Since his mercy has unearthed many who were buried long years ago, I do not fear that I shall be the only one it will pass by. He himself knows best the time for each man's rescue. I shall strive that he should not feel ashamed to rescue me.'

Seneca did not show any sign of shame himself. He was not too proud to beg attention from the emperor who was 'the consolation of all mankind'. He was anxious only that the form be right. He appealed to Polybius writer to writer. He had composed his letter 'as best I could, with a mind now dulled by long rusting. If it shall seem to be ill suited to your intelligence, or to fail to heal your sorrow, think how he who is gripped by his own misfortunes is not at peace to comfort others, and how Latin words do not suggest themselves easily to one in whose ears there is nothing but the noise of barbarians.' The language of Corsica, he complained, was distressing even to the more civilised barbarians, still more so to himself.

And there he stopped, with himself, where he had hoped to direct attention from the start. Much of Seneca's language about 'the universal consolation of all mankind' would soon become more familiar. Some Christians became sufficiently impressed with it to pretend that Seneca was somehow a Christian himself, an exchanger of letters with Saint Paul, struggling nobly to escape the shackles of his place and time.

For Seneca, however, in the pressing present of Corsica in 44 CE, even this rhetorical command of flattery was not enough to free him. Perhaps he had misread Claudius's appetite for praise. Being a courtier at a distance was always hard. Lucius Vitellius preferred to stay close. Being close was all. Perhaps Polybius, piled around with papyri for his attention, never even read the *consolatio*.

32

A BEDROOM SLIPPER

Gaius Julius Polybius controlled the letters, but Antonius Pallas controlled the money. Both men were former slaves, both bearing proudly the Roman names of the families who had freed them. Pallas was the most powerful freedman at Claudius's court, the prime minister of the empty rooms, known to the emperor since he was a child in his mother's house, vastly wealthy, proud of his reputation for virtue, prickly about any contradiction suggested between these two.

Pallas was increasingly a person of suspicion to Messalina, too close, she thought, to Agrippina, the granddaughter of Augustus's only child, the most direct descendant of Augustus still alive. Agrippina and the former slave were lovers, it was also said, a smear against each of them, the same smear by which the empress had put Seneca on a beach in Corsica.

Lucius took the contrary side, the side of the established power. That was his way and his skill. He was the most powerful man at Claudius's court who was not a freed slave. Like Polybius, his sympathies were with Messalina, who was also in the imperial bloodline as a direct descendant of Augustus's sister. More importantly for the present, she was Claudius's wife and the mother of his son.

Polybius and Messalina, the secretary and the empress, were also allegedly lovers, an allegation about freedmen and their mistresses so common as to be worth repeating only as gossip. As gossip, of course, it was very frequently repeated. There was never a suggestion that Messalina and Lucius were lovers, although her slipper was often in his hand, on occasions ostentatiously kissed, to show whose side he was on.

Lucius preferred to be a fixer than a player. Court life was more complex under Claudius than in the reign of Caligula. There was not just one man with the Moon who had to be humoured, there were two women, Messalina and Agrippina, and their open champions. There was less space for the role of diplomat in the shadows.

The senate too tried to adjust itself to the changing times. It was not helpful to grandees for them to look down upon Pallas, the freed slave who was establishing his own household of freed slaves, the Pallantiani. Anxious senators passed a decree welcoming him to the status almost of a former consul. Lucius seemed to his colleagues to be a man moving in the opposite social direction, a senator who behaved like a flunky at a court of Commagene or Persia, simpering over the toe of an imperial shoe. Old social distinctions were blurring, a marker of bureaucracy's birth and the new courtly life.

Neither Lucius nor Aulus Vitellius ever had a reputation for sexual excess. Both were known as uxorious in a place and time when fidelity was more a political aspiration than an individual one. But at this perilous part of his life at court Lucius could not avoid being drawn into the charge and counter-charges of who was sleeping with whom. He did have one passion, it was said, for the saliva of one of his own ex-slaves which he mixed with honey for his throat after a hard day at work. This was at a time when his champion, Messalina, was accused of competing with prostitutes for the prize of greatest sexual staying power. Lucius's sin seemed more like a medicine by Scribonius Largus, honey, herbs and bodily fluids – without the ashes of a swallow.

Sexual charges, like charges of gluttony, were verbal weapons whose relationship to reality was often the least important fact about them. Any kind of oral sex – with man, woman or footwear – was especially good to use against a man whose words needed to be brought into disrepute. In the rhetoric of the street a befouled tongue could not be trusted as a conveyor of truth. Medicinal saliva was, however, hardly much of an entry in the annals of food and flattery. Lucius was still a problem-solver more than a problem in himself.

Messalina herself was the rising problem. She was fast succumbing to imperial fantasies of her own, flattery from a younger husband (there were various candidates), a firmer position at the head of the

Palatine tables, and maybe a more official form of power behind the same throne. It was never fully clear whether the empress or Claudius himself was the prime executioner when prominent senators began to disappear. But the death of one distinguished senator who had rejected her initiated a terror in which she denounced other senators too. It became a lasting mark of courtly law that an accused might never know who was whispering to the judge. Julia, object of Augustus's dying concern and widow of Rubellius Blandus, was just a preliminary victim.

Lucius found a new role when Messalina wanted ownership of what were seen as Rome's finest gardens. In the eyes of her enemies, using the same hostile language once used against Germanicus's widow, Agrippina, she was gasping for them, gagging for a possession that she desired as though it were the latest delicacy or a new lover. Getting the gardens of Lucullus, the site of cherry trees and other pioneering luxuries a century before, required a man who could work both the law courts and the imperial courts, comfortable when both were sometimes the same. Lucius was a friend of the gardens' owner, an unwilling seller, as well as of the woman who coveted them. He could no more avoid Messalina's commission than could his brother, Publius, have avoided the prosecution of Piso for the murder of Germanicus three decades before. He had to betray his friend to stay alive.

The name of the latest owner of Lucullus's pleasure park was Valerius Asiaticus, the senator from Gaul whose wife had once been insufficiently imaginative in bed to please Caligula between courses at a banquet. Caligula had then expressed his dissatisfaction to the rest of the guests. Asiaticus, a calm and popular man, became subsequently sympathetic to the conspiracy to murder Caligula but had held back from acting himself. Like Lucius he preferred realism to revenge.

Claudius was neither hostile to Asiaticus nor keen to extend his wife's collection of vines and shady trees. He was also strongly in favour of more senators from Gaul as a dilution of the power of old Roman families. None of that, nor his record of generous hospitality, was any help to Asiaticus. The charge chosen by Messalina was

that of attempting to supplant the House of Caesar. Lucius's task was
to portray the owner of the gardens not as a sympathetic observer of
Caligula's death but its prime instigator.

Lucius's co-prosecutor was a professional lawyer, Publius Suillius
Rufus, despised by traditionalists in the senate for earning high fees
but supported by Claudius on the grounds that legal practice should
not be preserved for the already rich. Suillius, like so many in the
empty rooms of this story, was either a sleazy man-on-the-make
or a breaker of tired moulds, depending on who was writing the
history. For most writers he was a man of sleaze.

The trial took place in late 47 CE, not in the senate house where
Publius Vitellius had once done his duty in denouncing Piso, but in
Claudius's private rooms in the *domus Caesaris*. Messalina was one
of the few spectators. Lucius led the main charge. Suillius tried to
humiliate Asiaticus by accusing him of passive homosexuality (the
only kind that was deemed humiliating). Asiaticus was as calm as
when Caligula had humiliated his wife. He said that Suillius's sons
had their own direct knowledge of his active sexual performance.
Before slitting his wrists, he added that he would rather have died
under Caligula or Tiberius than by words from the mouth of a Vitellius who had licked and sucked between so many women's thighs.

In treason trials the language of sexual abuse came in from the
street. It became a legal commonplace to compare the foul mouths
of informers to those who fouled their mouths in sex. Phaedrus had
a fable about it which the censors of his only surviving manuscript
found too strong for survival. Asiaticus's last act was as cold and
calm as his last words, ordering a new site for his funeral pyre so
that the flames did not damage the trees for which he had died.

For Lucius the price of survival was higher than it had ever been
before. He was angry at what Messalina had made him do and the
abuse he had received in return. He was no longer above the fray.
He was a highly visible actor on a stage in which food, flattery and
sex were combined within the vocabulary of farce.

Meanwhile, away from the emperor's chambers, the court had
more matters to consider than merely itself. There were food riots
in Rome, a political threat at all times. The first water flowed into

Rome from the *Aqua Claudia* and, although the work was not completed, it was continuing well. The gardens and bath houses of Rome gained water at a minimal expense to Tibur but, in a court increasingly divided at the very top, good administration did not win much advantage. The man who made an art of walking the tightropes was risking everything on one side. Pallas and Agrippina saw clearly how close Claudius was to rejecting his wife. Lucius stayed almost too long with Messalina's slipper.

The empress's hopes for continued power lay, securely it once had seemed, with her and Claudius's son, the newly named Britannicus, the boy whose succession Seneca had insincerely urged should be smooth, unopposed and far into the future. Agrippina's ambitions lay in her son, Lucius Domitius Ahenobarbus, known as Nero, her supporter, Pallas, and her own growing popularity with her uncle Claudius.

Messalina had her personal hopes too, and not only in her desire for finer vines and shadier trees. She was said, sometimes with sympathy, to prefer the beds of actors and aristocrats to that of her older and disabled husband. She was not very discreet. She pursued the same stage star, Mnester, who had captivated Caligula, arranging his obedience to her by means of an imperial decree and a statue of him cast in bronze.

In 47 CE, Lucius was consul for the third time, a rare distinction, but the focus of political attention was not on Syria and Judaea, where the Christians had a new promoter in Paul of Tarsus, nor even much on Britain, where Aulus Plautius was finally allowed to leave his post, but on the bedrooms of the Palatine. Messalina's reach was beginning to exceed her grasp. Mnester was an unwilling seducer. He had to be ordered into her bed. After his much-rumoured role in the end of Caligula he maybe thought that another political performance would be one too many.

When the empress's attention turned instead to the consul designated for the following year, Gaius Silius, Mnester's name, usually familiar only from programmes for the stage, appeared on the lists of those charged with conspiracy. The famous actor, beloved by palace and public alike, was condemned to death in

Claudius's private Palatine rooms, his silent plea for mercy a final success in dramatic effect but a failure in saving his life. Life was exceeding art. Phaedrus's fabled stage star had merely stolen an emperor's applause: Mnester had stolen rather more and met his end like the tragic heroes he liked to play.

Pallas, Narcissus, Callistus and Polybius, still the senior four among the Palatine freedmen, were in growing disagreement about the damage that Messalina was bringing to the *domus Caesaris*. The containment of dissent within his household court was, for Claudius, one of the system's chief advantages. But when Messalina secured the execution of Polybius too, the courtiers closed ranks. Lucius, staging a diplomatic retreat, discarded the slipper and moved against his patron.

Narcissus seized the opportunity to move decisively further, convincing Claudius that Messalina and Silius had held a public wedding ceremony and were plotting to seize the throne. On his own authority, ensuring that neither Pallas nor Callistus knew what was about to happen, he had Messalina murdered by a freedman called Evodus, a victim in her own new gardens, dying in such a way that Claudius, calming himself at a drunken dinner, did not have to be implicated himself.

Lucius too was kept away from the final act. He did not see Messalina being wheeled around in a cart like so much garden rubbish. Narcissus suspected that long service as the empress's slipper-holder might bring him to her aid at the critical time. Claudius called for more wine. Public response was quiet. Messalina had not been an empress with popular appeal. The work of building alliances and aqueducts continued. As well as developments in Syria and Britain there were revolts along the Rhine and struggles within the courts of Commagene and Parthia, all of which, like the water supply of Rome, needed attention from behind a Palatine door.

33

OF UNSHAKABLE LOYALTY TO HIS EMPEROR

Rivalry between the freedmen did not cease. They each had their prime responsibility but, like senior officials in future courts, they did not fear to stray beyond their allotted roles. Some were famous, others virtually unknown beyond the Palatine, others still anxious to climb the greasy poles of early bureaucratic power. Some stayed in the background: Dionysius, a rich Greek eunuch, was so anxious for a role that he abandoned his free status in order to insinuate himself into the court. Others were flagrant: a freedman called Arpocras was proud to gain permission for a luxurious private carriage, for slaves to carry him through the streets and for personal sponsorship of games and feasts.

There was broad agreement that Claudius would at some point need a new wife. The issue was who it should be, the kind of question where senior freed slaves, intimates of the family, had a stronger responsibility than those, like Lucius, who had their own families and stood at a greater distance. The whole *domus* needed clarity on who would succeed to the throne. The prospects of Britannicus were dimming with the demise of his mother. Three men, Narcissus, Callistus and Pallas, played the main parts in a marital selection story that became both theatrical and mythical in its retellings.

The power of Narcissus, the writer and reader of Claudius's letters at home and abroad, had also dimmed from its peak after Messalina's murder. The role of assassin was insufficient to counter his previous loyalty to the empress he had killed. His benign suggestion to Claudius was that he remarry a woman to whom he had been married before, Aelia Paetina, a sister of Sejanus and already the mother of Claudius's daughter, Claudia Antonia.

Callistus, the chief official in charge of the law courts, had been both close to Caligula and part of the plot to assassinate him. But after a successful career on the line between the two kinds of courts he was increasingly an invalid. The dedicatee of Largus's book of cures was in constant pain with kidney stones. Showing a conservatism hardly less than that of Narcissus, he proposed a previous wife of Caligula, the usefully wealthy Lollia Paulina.

Pallas, the financial secretary and at most times the senior of the three, proposed Agrippina, whose big advantage was her son Nero, grandson of Germanicus, at the centre of the line of the Caesars, and, unlike Britannicus, almost ready to succeed. She was, however, arguably too close to the family. A special law would be required to make a legal marriage between the emperor and his niece.

Thus, as it seemed, there were three plausible candidates: Paetina, maybe too familiar, Paulina, surely very tolerant if somewhat scarred by her six months as Caligula's empress, and the third certainly the most trouble. Paetina had the weakest backer and was still maybe tarnished by her connection to Sejanus. Paulina's disadvantages included her not unreasonable suspicions of life at court and her fondness for astrology. Agrippina would need a change in the law on incest for her to have the right to Claudius's bed. This was where Pallas needed Lucius Vitellius.

Lucius sensed that Agrippina was the one most likely to succeed. There was no greater courtly art than seeing the immediate future. But the mere kissing of a slipper was not the kind of loyalty Agrippina required. She needed a false prosecution and a change in ancient law. Thus, late in his career, Lucius Vitellius had to risk himself out in the open in the courts where household and senatorial politics met, where his brother had first fought the family cause in the trial of Piso almost thirty years before.

The first task was to make possible a teenage marriage between Nero, whom he knew as a friend of Aulus, and Octavia, the daughter of Claudius and Messalina. This would strengthen Agrippina's cause. The only obstacle was that Claudius had already promised Octavia to someone else, Junius Silanus, another descendant of Augustus, popular, respected and not readily shifted from his place.

Lucius had no subtle way forward. Silanus suddenly found himself accused of incest with his sister, Junia Calvina. Incest was about to become Lucius's speciality. He had some credibility in proposing this slur since Junia had only just been divorced from his own younger son, Lucius. On this occasion neither the legal niceties nor the bedroom evidence needed to be tested. Before the case was heard, Silanus chose to resign his public offices rather than face public humiliation.

Lucius and Pallas were now firmly in league to promote the interests of Agrippina and Nero. This was good for the Vitellii and conveniently, Lucius could argue, in the best interests of the *domus Caesaris* and the empire that it controlled. Claudius remained indecisive. It became necessary for Narcissus, Callistus and Pallas to make their cases directly before an emperor whose role was both presiding judge and subject of the case. The process must have looked like a fraud, though, by the standards of the recent past, not perhaps an egregious one.

Some real testing of arguments certainly took place. Paetina was maybe too arrogant: she had earned a fearsome dowager reputation since Claudius had divorced her two decades before. Paulina's experiences with Caligula had left her too crazy. Agrippina would be hardest to control even if the legal obstacles could be removed. The rhetoric moved back and forth. How much the outcome was genuinely in doubt was hard to say.

The choice seemed more like a work of art than a personal or dynastic plan. The judgment of Pallas was a parody of the Judgement of Paris, the mythical beauty competition between three goddesses for the Golden Apple, the argument which began the Trojan War. The mythical question was would the winner of the apple be Juno, the queen of the gods, offering Paris the bribe of power, or Minerva, the goddess of fine design, offering the gift of victory in exquisite armour, or Venus pimping out Helen, the peerless beauty married to a Greek king and causing the maximum chaos. There was only one answer, but the plot required at least the possibility of others. This was one of the founding stories of Rome. Without Paris taking Helen as his prize to Troy, there would have been no war, no

Trojan defeat, no Trojan Aeneas to flee to Italy as the hero of Virgil's epic poem.

Claudius deliberated and followed Pallas. His empress would be Agrippina, the Venus of the debate. One popular version of the Judgement of Paris, written early in the reign of Augustus, was by Ovid before he became himself a victim in the sexual politics of the Caesars. His poem showed Helen happily taking part in the pimping process, though with proper reluctance at first. Agrippina was not reported as having the slightest doubts.

This was a major household victory for Pallas, the former slave who had so faithfully served the emperor's mother. While the theatrical show was going on perhaps he already knew best what Claudius's real wishes were. Agrippina was an acknowledged beauty, favourite of the court sculptors and possibly already sharing the bed of her uncle. Lucius had the final job of making the planned incest fit with the law – and quickly, before the question could loom too large.

Inside the senate Lucius had certain formal privileges as censor, an antique office which Claudius the antiquarian had revived and given to his trusted counsellor. In addition to vague responsibilities for public morality, he could initiate and control business. He again exercised this power, which he had already used to drive Silanus from office, requesting that he be allowed to speak first on a matter of highest importance to the state. While Claudius waited at the palace, Lucius made his argument for the new marriage, beginning with how much a hard-working emperor deserved a wife, gaining easy agreement for this uncontroversial proposition, then moving on to how only a woman of the noblest birth, the most proven fertility and the best of character would suffice.

Agrippina's right by birth was as high as it could be in the imperial family. The name of her father Germanicus was the most popular in memory bar that of Augustus himself. She already had a son and might have more. Her good character might readily be debated but was superior, everyone would now agree, to the promiscuous dead traitor she was attempting to replace.

Lucius's switch from Messalina's slipper-bearer to Agrippina's advocate was smooth. He argued that marriages within families were a protection against emperors becoming sexual predators on outsiders. The senate, he said, should always be consulted on such vital decisions. Marriages with the daughters of brothers might be unfamiliar in Rome, but in the great imperial families of the east such unions were common. Why should the *princeps* of Rome have any less freedom than the princes of Commagene?

The speech was a triumph. The senate voted its agreement. Individual senators rushed out towards the Palatine gates to demonstrate. Enough people joined to allow the claim that the full SPQR was behind the marriage. Lucius won his case – and with it a new lease on power under the new regime.

Aulus Vitellius became consul in succession to his father, whose final term in office was his third. The family was entering the aristocracy, new men no more. The father helped the son, as the son in Capri had once helped the father. As censor, Lucius could keep a close watch over his consular son. There was need for some delicate argument over whether Claudius's personal representative in Syria or the Jewish authorities owned the robes of their high priests that Lucius had returned to them while he was governor. Aulus never became known for tact, but he survived without dishonour.

On the first day of 49 CE, Agrippina and Claudius were married. Junius Silanus, who had unwittingly stood in the way of Nero's marriage to Claudius's daughter, killed himself in protest on the same day. His sister, Junia Calvina, was exiled. No longer the wife of the young Lucius Vitellius, she was barred from Rome by the determination of her ex-husband's father. She would not see either Lucius of the Vitellii family again.

Agrippina, aged thirty-three, was empress. She was already a veteran of imperial high society. Her mother had been a formidable, if finally failing, fighter. Her previous husband, the father of Nero, dead for eight years, was the son of Lucius Domitius Ahenobarbus, the wealthy promoter of married women on stage whose extravagant shows had so alarmed Augustus. The Ahenobarbi were prominent, sometimes controversial, but she had surpassed them all. Her new husband was ruler of the *domus Caesaris* and of the Roman world. Her son was married to her new stepdaughter. Together Nero and Octavia were well poised for the future. Admirers noted Agrippina's double canine teeth, a further sign of her sudden great good fortune.

The face of the new empress became famous. She was portrayed in pale-green translucent stone, her tiny nose and mouth suggesting modesty and a high moral tone. She spread her good fortune to her supporters and even to the small town in Germany where she was born. It became Colonia Claudia Ara Agrippinensis – Cologne as it later came to be known, with the letters 'g' and 'n' in her honour. Those who had feared Messalina's anger could sleep more easily. More than thirty senators had been executed or murdered since the death of the more famously murderous Caligula but, with Messalina dead too, the killings almost ceased.

There was particular good fortune for Seneca. The self-interested comforter of a freedman's grief was brought back from Corsica to give political tutorials to Nero. The need for an educator in rhetoric produced success where Seneca's rhetoric itself had miserably failed. A year later Nero was adopted as Claudius's son as well as his son-in-law. Messalina's son, Britannicus, whose easy glide to the throne Seneca had called for in his *consolatio* to Polybius, was now yesterday's prince.

Lucius joined Claudius in a census of office-holders and citizens. They barred a distinguished Greek judge because he knew no Latin. They purged the senate of some of its more dubious members by an unprecedented 'volunteer' programme of retirement. As a flatterer Lucius had lost none of the agility that had kept him alive under Caligula. 'May you often do it,' he said when Claudius opened Secular Games that would not be expected again for around 100 years.

Phoenix birds were supposed to appear even more rarely than Secular Games. A new sighting like the one a mere fifteen years before in its flaming nest of cinnamon was best ignored in order to maintain due order. The people were given other entertainments.

Nero's coming of age was celebrated by stage performances. In the spirit of Agrippina's impresario father-in-law there were strict decrees against barracking young aristocrats who appeared as actors. One of these was a rising star, more ambitious in the military and sexual arenas than on stage. His name, not yet famous, was Fabius Valens. The *Aqua Claudia* had its formal opening. Claudius could take the credit for the permanent supply of more clean water past Tibur into Rome.

Pallas's brother, Marcus Antonius Felix, became the latest governor for the Syrians and another sign of outsiders taking over the traditional centres of power beyond the *domus Caesaris*. Those in the senate who would have liked – and profited from – the job themselves accused him of unreasonable corruption, a charge that would be amplified in Judaea. Lucius remained close to Pallas, continuing to buy information for their shared ends and ensure that the sellers were paid.

A successful prosecutor from a undistinguished family, Eprius Marcellus, dedicatee of Columella's wine guide, was promoted to the rank just below the consulship to replace the unfortunate Junius Silanus. He served only for a single day in an office normally held for a year. Even those who despised his origins and his work had to agree that he could not do much harm. But his appointment, to critics of the household in the senate, was just one more case of changing times and people of whom they disapproved.

Callistus gave up his struggle for life as well as power. He had backed the wrong contestant in Claudius's Judgement of Paris. The long-time stone in his bladder was a condition only curable by the knife, a process as dangerous as that which had once taken the testicles of his Palatine rival, Posides. Scribonius Largus advised a diet of insects from stone quarries for bladder stones, a sympathetic cure by the rules of Roman medicine, maybe especially sympathetic for a man notorious for his taste in rare marble, but in Callistus's case not an effective one.

No mere doctor could stop the statuette of Callistus being the first of the Palatine courtiers to leave the dining-room shrine of Lucius Vitellius. There was no point in having an image of a dead freedman among his household gods. Callistus's head, if it were deemed too recognisable, could be lightly recast for a successor. The master of the courts had been a huge cog in a government machine; he had a daughter and a grandson ready for imperial service in the court he had helped to create; his name was on lead pipes bringing water to Rome. But Callistus, the bureaucrat behind the scenes, was not going to last in flattering memories, nothing like a god of Peace or Plenty, one of the statues of plaster, wood and pastels that would be passed down as an heirloom for the Vitellian dining rooms of the future.

Lucius himself had not long to live. Still influential, he was also approaching his sixtieth year and vulnerable to new versions of himself. Accused of treason and designs upon throne, he could not avoid the day in court he had so often watched destroy others. Agrippina protected him from execution and outlawed his unfortunate accuser, but two days after his arrest he died, peacefully of a paralytic stroke. A credit to his trade, he was awarded a marble memorial statue by Claudius inscribed 'of unshakable loyalty to his emperor'.

34

GOD-GIVEN MUSHROOMS

When Lucius Vitellius died in 51 CE, his elder son had already achieved as much as his family had expected of him and more. Aulus was thirty-nine, a courtier of the *domus Caesaris* who was also a former consul and senator. Being a former consul was not what it had been when his grandfather first came to Rome, but it did not mean nothing. His father had been three times consul. This was a record which Aulus showed no wish to match. He did not live in the past, even the very recent past. He did not ape his older senate colleagues in distant nostalgia. He cared nothing for ancient times when there were no Vitellii except those imagined by the gullible. Aulus lived in the present, with a survivor's half-closed eye on the near future. He was a large and genial man with a limp, a low-slung belly and long experience of watching his superiors. He understood power. He knew what the powerful wanted. In that respect, if not in intellectual range and subtlety, he was his father's son.

In his single consulship, three years before, he had successfully promoted Claudius's plan to appoint 'long-haired Gauls' to the senate. Opponents then argued that, because Gauls had sacked Rome almost five centuries before and then resisted the divine Julius Caesar, their experience, power and, most of all, their money should be denied to the highest offices in Rome. Aulus spoke for the emperor. He introduced to the senate the very proposal that so many of its members, in fear and in their own interests, opposed. His was not the speech that counted. Only Claudius's words told their hearers how they ought to vote. But when Claudius lacked support – in the senate and even among his own freedmen – a Vitellius had been with him.

Aulus took over his father's place in the social and religious clubs of Rome. A Vitellius would still be one of the twelve *Fratres Arvales*, the Brothers of the Fields, who had their ancient duty, traced to earlier than Rome itself, for making sure that the gods smiled on Italy's food. Their own feasts, celebrated in the country four miles west of Rome, were notorious for ensuring their own food supply: each brother dined wearing an ear of corn on his head secured by a white band.

The revival of the club had been part of Augustus's reinvention of Roman history, the connection of his own favoured institutions with ones which may or may not have existed in the past. Claudius was a Brother of the Field, as, soon, was the teenage Nero. Aulus also joined the Club of Fifteen, the *Quindecimviri Sacris Faciundis*, another priestly college famed for its banquets as much as for its responsibility to read secret books of prophecy in the present interest.

At around the same time as his father died Aulus remarried. These two events were probably connected. His relations with his first wife, approved by Lucius in the Roman way, had been fractious, not only financially. His second wife, Galeria Fundana, was more tolerant.

His brother, the younger Lucius, was also divorced – from Junia Calvina, the imperial wife whose faked incest had helped their father destroy Messalina. He was soon to be married to a second wife, Triaria, whose vision was also more forward than back – sometimes, it seemed, the most militant Vitellian of them all.

With their father safe among the respected dead, the two brothers were more free to enjoy the dining rooms of the Palatine and the surrounding streets of bars which Aulus in particular preferred. This was a time of imperial peace, except in Britain and Parthia, which were far enough away not to worry much the people of Rome. Shortages of food, not always prevented by the fine-dining Brothers of the Fields, were of greater concern than conquest.

Aulus made it his business to know Nero well. He did not share the new heir's passions for poetry and theatre, but for more than two decades Aulus had watched and learnt how to live among the powerful. Gluttony was a family trait for which he was already known, but flattery helped him to the positions from which he was worth knowing at all.

*

The Vitellii had survived the deaths of Augustus at Nola, Tiberius at Misenum and Caligula in the palace corridors. Aulus and Lucius, the new leaders of the family, had next to survive the aftermath of Claudius's death, hastened, it was said, by poison. The administer was possibly Xenophon, his ungrateful household doctor, or Locusta from Gaul, on whom many poisonings were blamed, or Halotus the eunuch food-tester, maybe bribed by Claudius's wife who was, now more importantly, Nero's mother. The poison was probably atropine, the cosmetic of Cleopatra and the spice allegedly sprinkled by Livia on Augustus's figs. The deadly food for Claudius was a mushroom.

Halotus was one of the most successful survivors behind the office doors of the Palatine. Food-tasting, like many specialised responsibilities at court, was conducted by a hierarchy of slaves and former slaves. Just as there were different bakers of bread and cakes, headed by the most high-skilled baker of white bread with expensively refined flour, so too there were junior and senior food-tasters. Together they operated a reverse version of the normal pecking order at table, the grander being last to taste and the lesser first. Halotus was the senior taster, just as Locusta, surviving in and out of prison according to her rates of success, was the highest-regarded of the poisoners. Neither's task was as simple as it was sometimes made to seem.

Claudius died while being less well than usually watched. Narcissus, his most loyal courtier and constant enemy of Agrippina, was conveniently convalescing away from Rome. He was taking the warm volcanic waters around Vesuvius for relief of his gout, the glutton's disease, as his many enemies might have been tempted to say. The emperor himself was watching the performance of a farce at the time he took his mushrooms, not going as far as Augustus in making an actor's last request for applause, but continuing the theatrical theme of the Caesars. His last reported words were a joke that he had 'shat himself', a standard from the comic play-book of the street.

Claudius was deified in death. Nero, aged sixteen and still out to impress his mother with his wit, joked that mushrooms must be the food of the gods because Claudius had become a god by eating one. Most mushrooms were simple food, not much favoured in the recipes of Apicius. Some were greater delicacies. Green-capped, white-gilled *Amanita phalloides* were the most useful for promoting an elevation to Mount Olympus, their venom impervious to the heat of cooking.

35

AULUS THE EDUCATOR

In October, 54 CE, the *domus Caesaris* was not united in its acceptance of Nero as the fifth emperor of Rome. Although Pallas remained strongly in support of Agrippina and her sixteen-year-old son, Narcissus led a faction which preferred Britannicus, aged only thirteen but with the potent claim that he was the grandson of Germanicus. Narcissus's influence was not what it once had been, but gout and ill temper had not completely cut the web that he had spun around the Palatine in so long a term of service.

Either boy, the senior courtiers agreed, would need experienced guidance. Nero had his mother while Britannicus did not. Agrippina, even to her greatest critics, was a woman determined to educate her son and there was hope – as there was always hope at a transfer of power – that youth would be an opportunity for improvement. Aulus was characteristically in the party of hope and established power, a rejecter of nostalgia, fear and subversion. In that he was truly his father's son.

Aulus was an educator in princely play. Nero needed his mother's praise, his tutors' praise and his playmates' praise; if he could not have all three, the third came to be the praise that mattered most. He was not drawn to gladiatorial shows: this form of Roman theatre provided no opportunities for himself. He wanted stages on which to tread, not an imperial box to sit in. He wanted flatterers to clap him, not just friends who would join him in applause.

Nero's studies were directed first by two freedmen from the pool of court teachers. Seriousness quickly became the responsibility of Seneca, who repaid for his rescue from Corsica with both lessons in the rhetoric of politics and speeches which made it appear that his efforts had already borne fruit. Seneca gave his pupil lessons

on clemency and constitutionalism that aimed to revive the best
memories of Julius Caesar and Augustus.

Their shared effort was at first much admired. Nero enjoyed
the flattery he received as a generous constitutionalist and Seneca
played on that need for applause. As long as the flattery that Nero
received was for doing good, Seneca saw himself as a success. But in
order to stay successful a tutor had to be more than a virtuous bore.
That was the more difficult task.

Seneca made little use of direct flattery of Nero, preferring instead
to contrast him with his predecessor. He composed a vicious assault
on the dead Claudius, a contemptuous reversal of the flattery he
had sent to the Palatine from exile. The tutor who soon became
Nero's closest adviser mocked the 'pumpkinification' among the
gods of Olympus of the man who had condemned him to Corsica.
In a short satirical essay, the *Apocolocyntosis*, Claudius was depicted
in a heavenly court where no one took any notice of what he said:
'You would think they were his freedmen, so little attention did
they pay him.' The man accused of killing 'as easily as a dog shits'
became deified as a vegetable, not one of Tiberius's little cucumbers but a pumpkin, a desiccated gourd never seen on a decent
table, a hollow joke whom the gods of Olympus were horrified
to receive.

In life Claudius never believed in the ultimate flattery that he
was divine. Unlike Caligula, he discouraged convoluted deceits
and allowed temples to himself only in places, like Britain, where
the natives themselves might be flattered by a Roman deity in their
midst. Only in death, in Seneca's theatrical imagination, did he
become a god, a slobbering, slurring, incomprehensible monster,
greeted by Hercules as a hairy sea-beast, convicted of mass murder
and condemned by his new colleagues to their worst imaginable
fate, living in the Hades household where Caligula was rightly eking
out his own afterlife. Claudius's new servants were the same as the
old, the freedmen whom he had 'sent ahead' to look after his needs,
individually named and known to Seneca's audience. Polybius stood
ready to the fore, but there was also Myron, Amphaeus, Pheronac-
tus and Arpocras, the former slave who had been allowed his own

carriage through the streets and to put on entertainments like an ambitious vote-seeker of a century before.

The occasion for the 'pumpkinification' was Nero's first Saturnalia on the throne, the traditional time in the centuries before the *domus Caesaris* for household roles to be reversed, for masters to serve their slaves, for abuse and flattery to flow against the normal tide. Claudius's reversal was exceptional even for a Saturnalia.

At the same festival Britannicus sang what he hoped was a witty song about his failure to succeed his father. Maybe Agrippina encouraged him, fearing that she had served her purpose in the life of her ungrateful son and making Saturnalian threats that Rome had the wrong young emperor, that the grandson of Germanicus was the better man. These were mistakes in a court where to use traditional subversion was a naivety. Ovid was not the last to learn the courtier's truth that what was funny one day might be fatal the next.

By the evening of his fourteenth birthday, Britannicus had already survived attempts on his life in the new era. He was cautious. He had watched the ways of the table as carefully as had Aulus Vitellius. Finally, a way was found, but Locusta the poisoner failed to provide a strong enough dose. For that failing she was racked and whipped by Nero himself. Shortly afterwards, four months after Nero's joke about the god-given mushrooms, Britannicus was in the part of the imperial dining rooms reserved for children and succumbed to sudden sickness. The son of Messalina and Claudius, both his parents vilified and dead, asked for a hot drink tested by his food taster. He found it too hot and asked for it to be cooled. The poison, a higher dose this time, came with the cold water.

Nero said that Britannicus was suffering from an epileptic fit. The dead boy was not only an emperor's natural son, as his song had made clear, but he had also sung his offence in a fine singing voice. This was a double affront to Nero, the second a deeper cut than the first. The death was in full view. The pyre was already built. The funeral was held quietly on a rainy night.

*

The methods of the Vitellii were changing with the times. Aulus's father flattered Caligula like a doctor humouring a patient. When Claudius came to power, Lucius sat alongside the secretaries for correspondence and finance. He helped the emperor to be a statesman and to feel like one when he was not. Aulus's method was more to be a companion in eating, drinking and incognito wanderings around town. He saw what made Nero feel good about himself and ensured that he had it. Nero wanted praise for his poetry, inspired by and maybe borrowed from the best in the empire. Most of all, what Nero wanted was applause for his frail and husky singing, practised with great determination, with diets of leeks in oil, laxatives and lead weights on his chest.

On certain days each month Nero ate nothing but leeks. Chopped with their vegetable cousin, chives, they were for Nero what figs were for the first Roman emperor and cucumbers for the second. In Greek Nero was the *porrophagus*, the leek-eater. Apicius recommended leek with laurel berries wrapped in cabbage leaves, a vegetarian voice-tutor's version of the ducks stuffed with dormice enjoyed at more traditional banquets at court. Augustus and Tiberius were trying to signal their simple Roman virtues. Nero was trying to be a Greek singing star.

The successful at court were, as ever, those who sensed the latest truth. When others cavilled to pretend that they were in the presence of a musical genius, Aulus flattered Nero's voice and lyric skill. He joined Nero's teenage parties, in and out of the Palatine, helping the new head of the *domus Caesaris* to find an audience that his predecessors had never sought.

Aulus was a tall, strong, heavy man. Nero was slight and frail, with distinctive deep-set eyes. Even as a thirteen-year-old he had been a subject for sculptors, dressed in the toga of a man beyond his years, stretching his hand downwards in acceptance of respect. His young face was easily recognised on the coins that Aulus exchanged for food and drink. Out in the streets Nero would sometimes protect himself by dressing as a slave. This was not necessarily so demeaning a role to play. In the court where he had spent his childhood some of the most powerful men and women were slaves or former slaves. If a Caesar so required it, everyone might be a slave.

When greater security for the emperor seemed necessary, their revelling band was backed by guardsmen and gladiators disguised in the everyday dress of Rome. With them too were the sons of senatorial families, ideally the poet sons or those prepared to pretend themselves poets or, if without even the slightest literary aspiration, to applaud Nero's lines.

Prominent among these was Marcus Salvius Otho, the defence advocate who had failed to save Publius's wife, Acutia, after the fall of Sejanus. Otho was from an ancient Etruscan family and had a wife, Poppaea, whom Nero came to covet as a mistress. The period of coveting did not last long. Otho retreated into a distant but respectable banishment as a twenty-six-year-old governor of Lusitania. Without his wife he survived and waited for applause of his own.

Being applauded was becoming almost synonymous with being an emperor. Nero jealously guarded his flattery. He did not only want it, he wanted it for himself alone, just as emperors had long demanded every bit of military glory. Nobody but an emperor could celebrate a triumph; nobody but Nero could please an audience.

What made actors dangerous was not so much what they said and did, the satirical crimes of the Atellane farce men, but the sound of their being clapped. Their masks, as Phaedrus had pointed out, might have no brains behind them but their celebrity was a threat in itself. The dying Augustus had used actors' language to ask for the traditional reward from an audience to a stage. The last in his line preferred not to have to ask.

Seneca tried hard to keep both control and good relations with his pupil. The theorist of flattery was no purist. He urged what he saw as philosophical restraint. Preserving the body, like preserving Rome itself, was a matter of balance, with pleasure to be had in the low parts of the city and virtue to be won on the high ground. The whorehouses and the cookhouses, the temples and the Forum were all part of the body politic as long as proportion was maintained. Nero's way of life was a useful education in the lives lived around him.

A good emperor, Seneca said, should show restraint in accepting cheap praise from the senate. Nero did not need the title *Pater patriae*, father of his country, that Augustus had held. Nor did he need the calendar to be restarted in December to mark his birthday. What he needed was a reputation as a reasonable man. Some small degree of unpredictability was acceptable in a ruler. When Nero held his morning salutations, he might dress down while others dressed up, dress Greek when he was expected to dress Roman. That kept his people alert. But excess was the enemy, excess in gluttony and vanity the worst.

Hypocrisy was essential to politics. Strictly speaking (that was whenever Seneca was writing essays of general instruction), a proper Roman man was supposed to be devoted to the gods, his family, and to the state – not to his lust or belly. From his Corsican exile he had directed some of his harshest critical theory at those who spent their fortunes on exotic dishes: 'They vomit so that they can eat, and they eat so that they can vomit. They don't even consider the dishes which they have assembled from across the earth worthy of digestion.' Excess in food or sex was a sign of inner moral laxity. If Romans desired anything more than basic food and drink for sustenance, they were fulfilling not their needs but their vices.

In less strict practice (when Seneca was giving personal advice), the lessons were more forgiving. A useful philosophy also included elegant arguments about why beliefs need not be put into practice in every case at every time. That was the means by which Seneca hoped both to survive and be useful. His influence, both in theory and practice, grew and then gradually faded. The likes of Aulus Vitellius were more amenable counsellors.

36

OEDIPUS AND ACTORS

As a former consul, Aulus remained a senator. That rule had not changed while so much else was being transformed. Early in Nero's reign it became even easier to combine the roles of senator and courtier. A senate meeting was held at the palace so that Agrippina could listen from behind a curtain. When the senators used coins to borrow, lend and gamble, they might see Agrippina as the obverse figure and Nero relegated to the back, or sometimes the two heirs of Augustus together like a kissing couple.

But Agrippina, like Seneca, began running out of ways to control what she had created. After losing Britannicus as a lever against her ungrateful son, she looked for others who might keep him in line, perhaps Aulus Plautius, the real hero of making Britain Roman, or, more threatening, Rubellius Plautus, son of Blandus of Tibur and Julia, memorably one of the last names on the lips of Augustus.

As her influence further waned, the mother was reduced to seeking any affection from her son that she could. She played the seductress – whether by sex or heavy flirtation, few could certainly say. At least one writer at court, Cluvius Rufus, whose books included a history of acting, was a close observer of Agrippina's roles as an incestuous mother, her boasting about her success after a heavy lunch, and the confusion that this caused.

Even in the Palatine court incest was something of an affront, a practice that, though fine in Commagene and further east, was alien to Rome. Sex between mother and son was a plot line of myth and tragedy, safest kept to the stage, ideally to the very private stages where Seneca's own plays, including his *Oedipus*, were performed. Seneca had to send a warning to Agrippina that an Oedipal *princeps* of Rome, paraded in lurid accounts to all, would be intolerable to the distant legionaries whether or not they were true.

Seneca waxed and waned as master of both flattery and its opposite. His intellect gave him power. He wrote much of what Nero said,
criticising Claudius not just in pumpkinifying farce but in early para-
graphs pronouncing on good government. He understood money.
He was a rare force within the *domus Caesaris* at this and any time
– with his own personal staff, his Spanish background, respectable
but not part of the Roman aristocracy, and his memories of exile.
He also had two useful brothers: an elder, Gallio, who would claim
a place in later histories by rejecting a lawsuit in Greece brought
by the Jews against the Christian leader, Paul of Tarsus ('but Gallio
cared for none of these things') and a younger, Mela, who acted as
one of the emperor's personal representatives, a procurator as old
Publius Vitellius had been.

Aulus, with his own brother actively alongside him, watched and
weighed the family loyalties. Their father had been too loyal to Messalina for almost too long. Their uncle, Publius Vitellius, had stayed
too long in the shadow of Agrippina's mother. The next generation
needed to avoid the same fate with Agrippina, the formidable but
weakening daughter.

Less than a year after Nero's succession, Pallas left the Palatine,
a further sign that Agrippina's power was falling. Pallas had been
her man as much as Claudius's. Marcus Antonius Pallas departed
with his head held high, with the name of a Roman of the imperial
house, the status of a Roman praetor, almost that of a consul, and
a deal that no questions be asked about the sources of his wealth.
He would owe the state nothing and nothing would be owed by the
state to him.

This was a relief for Nero. Power for freedmen was part of the
legacy from Claudius that he wanted to reduce and, rhetorically at
least, to end. Pallas had been envied, even hated, by senators who
resented the influence of a former slave and hoped that their own
influence might rise to fill the gap. Some of those hopes were met,
since Nero preferred to keep business out of his bedrooms. He had
little interest in bringing policy battles into his palace. Opportunities for bribery fell.

Seneca supported Pallas's departure. It was increasingly his sole task to manage both the machinery of the Palatine rooms and a maddened mother of the emperor. He had to warn Agrippina against her too-public affections, a dangerous task for Seneca in itself. Agrippina claimed to be protecting Nero's wife, Octavia, from threats to her position from outside the imperial family, an argument which must have tested the most flexible master of philosophical argument.

Agrippina's chief target was Claudia Acte, a former Greek slave with whom Nero liked most to share his nights. The daughter of Germanicus railed against even the slightest chance of a servant in the *domus Caesaris* joining the masters. Seneca agreed, but thought that Acte would be less trouble than many alternatives. He fabricated a story to protect her claiming that she was instead the lover of his relative, Annaeus Serenus, the chief of Rome's fire brigade. Nero supported the deceit by wooing his mother with even more expensive gifts than those for his mistress. Agrippina had the same appetite for gardens that had signalled the end of Messalina, a bad omen it seemed to some. Serenus, an emotional man whose moods belied his name, was rewarded by Seneca with the dedication of a treatise on how to acquire a quiet mind.

The humiliation of Octavia, Nero's wife and Claudius's daughter, sent danger signals to the court. Aulus Vitellius, educated in Capri, had learnt to watch the doors to the bedroom as well as the banqueting hall. A female former slave might be less threatening than a male, but the emperor's mother was not alone in seeing the risk to Nero's legitimacy from abandoning Octavia. Without her he would have no children in the direct line of succession from Augustus. Agrippina, appeased by grand fabrics from the emperor's wardrobe, returned to uneasy favour, but not for long. Her open-mouthed ambition, as her critics complained, began to recall that of her mother as well as her predecessor.

Two years after coming to power, Nero ordered the exile of all actors. Maybe he felt that he was being mocked on stage. Maybe he saw unwelcome competition or sensed, farcically even in the realm of farces, that the actors saw competition from him. Popular actors, like popular fables, were inevitably subversive and an easy affront to those who affected the higher arts. Those who won applause in the streets risked the double wrath of a jealous politician and an even more jealous artist.

Nero's grandfather, Lucius Ahenobarbus, had famously produced farces. Nero wanted to go well beyond that, to take the stage himself, not at first in Rome under the eyes of his hostile mother and a suspicious senate but in one of the theatres around Nola or in Greece. This would be a parody of the Roman virtue of living up to one's ancestors, certain to meet censure from Agrippina wherever his show took place, but an ambition even early in his reign.

Aulus was an encourager of that ambition. His great-uncle, Quintus, had lost social standing by his performances in public. Fashions had moved both back and on since then. A courtier had better to be nimble than frank. Survival required seeing how Nero saw himself. The most necessary skill was not only flattery itself but a careful observation of the flattery of others.

With his hopes of acting operatic parts held back by his mother, Nero settled first on literature to show himself in what he considered his true light. When the poet Calpurnius Siculus praised both Nero's literary skill and his commitment to lower taxes, his likeness to Apollo and his love of world peace, that was – and still is – a fair indication of how his subject wanted to be seen.

Siculus was a bucolic poet whose other subjects were safely in the realm of nymphs and shepherds. His predecessor, Virgil, in the time of Augustus had succeeded in introducing subversive commentary among the shady trees and flocks, but under Nero the bucolic was back where it began. Siculus's most striking innovation was replacing the standard peasant farmer with a more metropolitan gardener.

Nero planned to match Virgil's greater work, his twelve books of the *Aeneid*, the authorised foundation myth of Rome, honoured by readings aloud as work in progress at Augustus's court. Flatterers of this new project to write an epic on the deeds of the Romans urged that it should comprise at least 400 books. Another relative of Seneca, Annaeus Cornutus, prolific in Latin and Greek poetry himself, retorted that no one would read so many. This rare impatience in the imperial presence became merely an opportunity for further flattery. Did Cornutus not know that Chrysippus, one of the most distinguished of all Greek philosophers, had written on a Neronian scale? Why should the emperor do less?

Many at court knew the work of Chrysippus. He was a writer highly regarded in Rome. He wrote on the philosophy of almost everything and was also famous for drunkenness at banquets and dying of laughter at his own joke about feeding figs to a donkey. Cornutus snapped back that Chrysippus's 700 books on morality and logic were at least useful to people's lives, an act of candour about the contrasting likely usefulness of Nero's epic which won him both further fame and exile.

Nero liked to share his dining rooms with poets. He encouraged spontaneous composition and appropriated others' best lines. He was keen on poets who satirised other people, the fat, the thin, the incompetent, particularly the medically incompetent. He financed a Greek epigrammatist who dedicated to Nero his second book, telling the gods that he would have been nothing if the emperor had not been his paymaster. Nero himself wrote a poem attacking a young courtier as 'a one-eyed man', a penis, a prick, a Cyclops blinded by Odysseus in his cave. To weep with one eye was to ejaculate. There were many allusive possibilities for students of Greek to pass carefully around a table.

Aulus Vitellius was at the centre of this literary salon. He promoted a book of Nero's poems, the *Liber Dominicus*, the Master's Book. Gallio, the eldest Seneca brother, introduced Nero's public readings. Mela, the youngest, more than made up for his aversion to public life through his son Lucan, Marcus Annaeus Lucanus, a highly political poet who hailed Nero as divine, though not, of course, the son of the newly reviled 'pumpkin god', Claudius – without whose adoption of him Nero would not have been emperor at all.

Lucan declared that every horror of civil war had been worthwhile because it led to the new reign. At the first literary festival in Nero's honour Lucan won a crown for verse flattery. Nero's own themes included a mistress's fair hair and a rewriting of the Trojan

War with a new hero, Paris, the judge who gave Venus her apple for beauty. He took the Latin poetry prize himself.

Some of the tactics of these poet flatterers were not as new or necessarily shocking as their critics claimed. Poetry and praise had for centuries been the same. If a politician could find no one to be his flatterer, it was not unknown for him to write the poem of eulogy himself. Some of the best-loved Greek poets were professional flatterers, praising for pay, sometimes asking for money in the poems themselves.

A mercenary approach did not make a poet bad, either in the judgement of his peers or of later critics. Pindar, who 500 years before had profited from praising princes and charioteers in central Greece, was still much admired despite the difficulty and density of his language, sometimes because that difficulty restricted its appeal to the few. Poetry was perfect for both the flatterer and the flattered. It was ritual even before the addition of rituals from the court. It was reciprocal. At Nero's table a poet gave praise and accepted praise. He flattered and hoped to be flattered in return.

The dinner table itself encouraged a sense of idealistic Greek equality, though it was a brave man who used it. Flattery was like a deterrent weapon. No one could opt out since, if they did, their rivals might not. It seemed safer to increase the power of praise rather than reduce it. This was the new Roman way. Phaedrus's hungry fox was more pleading in Latin verse than Aesop's had been in Greek prose. Cornutus used Latin for his day-to-day works while reserving Greek for anything subtle or important. Greek eulogy had its ancient rules which great Roman poets could adapt into high art and which the mere hungry versifier could copy for a living, for a free meal and to stay alive.

World peace was, meanwhile, an ambition not merely boasted by Calpurnius Siculus and his fellow artists but almost achieved. This was a result of reduced Roman ambition on the advice of Augustus, a secure succession by the skill of Agrippina, the lack of need for Nero to show military prowess and his personal preference for other skills. Seneca's Gallic ally, Sextus Afranius Burrus, commanded the palace guard. There seemed no risk of a return to the age of Sejanus.

Around the Mediterranean there were still a few skirmishes between Jews and Greeks, the former rejecting any kind of worship of the emperor, the latter flattering Nero all the more in order to do their rivals down. This brought not public expense but profit to certain parts of the court even when opportunities for lesser corruption were lower. Beryllus, one of Nero's freedman and, like Seneca, a former Palatine tutor, took massive bribes from the Greek side for an imperial judgment denying Jewish rights in Caesarea.

Between Roman Syria and Parthia lay the disputed state of Armenia, whose king had to be kept independent. But the Parthian king, whenever there was potential disturbance, preferred diplomacy to battle. Nero's court offered numerous diplomatic avenues. Commagene, restored to independence by Claudius after its troubles under Tiberius and Caligula, remained quietly loyal to its liberator, its dissidents driven out and stateless further east.

In Britain there was desultory progress in creating a firm border, a merely rhetorical ambition to conquer Wales and some minor trouble among the then little-known Iceni tribe on the eastern side of the country. Claudius had gained all the easy kudos likely from penetrating the land of dogs and oysters. The best hopes of expansion were financial, the building of towns in the civilised south of the country, a concern for Seneca more in his personal role as banker than as senior adviser to Nero.

As long as the *domus Caesaris* was providing a source of unambiguous authority, it was serving its function. In Syria and Britain, even in Tibur and Nola, it mattered much less who was Caesar, less still whether they ate peacocks or had sex with their mothers, than that there was an emperor whose decisions could (or just as frequently could not) be received.

37

DISH OF MINERVA

The Great Food Market on the Caelian Hill south-east of the Forum, the *Macellum Magnum*, was one of Nero's prized projects, a square of shops arranged two storeys high around a courtyard, with a ring of domed columns, a marble-countered area for butchers with drains to sluice away blood, a separate place for selling fish, and fountains for discarding small change to the gods.

Nero was a great banqueter but not a notorious glutton. He had other vices by which he would be defined. He did care about feeding the people. He promoted himself on his coins alongside Ceres, the goddess of corn, and Annona, the spirit of the free food by which the emperor kept the poorer citizens from starvation. Closer to the mood of the streets than any of the Caesars since Julius, he knew what would keep him popular and what would not.

He knew too that the court and its Palatine guard was even more important than public opinion. The new *Macellum* was more for the delicacies of the rich than the needs of the poor. Like the riverside market of Tibur, it was a temple to fine food. Families who wished to boast of their best businessmen built shrines to them among the shops. Lucius Calpurnius Daphnus would have been as unknown as so many thousands in the Palatine rooms had not his heirs portrayed him in stone, prosperous and chubby, with a fish in one hand and a banker's book in the other.

A fresh mullet was a major asset, but a fading one. A live fish, transported in water barrels from the coast, might rate the same price as gold, weight for weight, *uncia* for *uncia*, pound for pound. A dead fish was worth less every hour. Salted fish, the kind sold by Horace's canny father as he began to make his fortune, had a much lower price but held it over time. The *Macellum Magnum* was for lenders and speculators. From the marble slabs anyone might become an Apicius for a night, buying spiny lobster with lovage and pepper, diced crab, pumpkin in the style of Alexandria, melon in raisin wine. Aulus Vitellius became a notorious abuser of credit.

Nero needed his new buildings to be big successes. In March 59 CE he had made the biggest mistake of his reign. His courtiers knew nothing in advance of the plan to murder his mother. They needed every possible means to distract attention from what they had not stopped. Nero was harder than usual to distract. Applause did not work when night after night there was dinner at which the shade of Agrippina, dead for days, weeks and even after months, still loomed in her long-allotted place.

The scenes were all familiar, Halotus the food-taster, still hovering, two of Nero's childhood tutors present, Anicetus and Seneca, Nero's mistress, Poppaea, on the couch where Agrippina would have been if Anicetus had not run his sword through her womb and Seneca were not left with the task of explaining the murder to the senate and the people of Rome. Nero, more panicked than liberated, was still seeing his mother as a very angry ghost.

Not even the dining room's keenest flatterers could persuade Nero that his plan to rid himself of Agrippina after a party on the Bay of Naples had gone well. The emperor had been too nervous to ask for help. He considered various ways of removing the main obstacle to his singing stardom and a new marriage, not to Acte but to Poppaea, the ex-wife of the comfortably exiled Otho. He ended with absolutely the worst way.

A poisoning in public seemed impossible. Agrippina had too many clients who owed her loyalty. She had seen too many deaths by deadly nightshade to fall for an atropine cocktail. Seneca was still a determined protector of the empress who had rescued him from Corsica when his flattery of Polybius failed. Burrus backed Seneca. They saw Agrippina as the only brake on Nero's worst ambitions.

The *Quinquatria* banquet for Minerva, Italy's goddess of wisdom and memory, was held at Baiae, the notorious resort where Caligula had once begun his equally notorious water walk. It was part of a women's festival for the goddess, a chance to highlight feminine values, to praise Minerva's protective shield over Rome, to eclipse for a night the rival swords of Mars, the war god. It was a party for enjoying the fruits of the sea, for silver shields to be used as dishes for lobster, crayfish and sturgeon – and for prophets to tell the peace-loving guests their most intimate futures.

To Seneca, who for once knew nothing, Baiae was where girls went to play at being girls and where men and old women played as girls too, an unpredictable and almost public place, unpropitious for a killing even if the killing were a good idea. The plan of the more biddable Anicetus, Seneca's predecessor in Agrippina's school for her son, recently promoted to command the imperial fleet, was to murder Nero's mother on her quiet sea journey home.

Anicetus took the job. His method was more ingenious than practical, more like a rhetorical exercise than the plan of a ruthless killer. He used his position as admiral to build a sinking ship. On board was a lead-weighted, collapsing bed in which Agrippina would sleep off the fine wines of the *Quinquatria* before quietly drowning in the wreck of a broken cabin.

For all its ingenuity on a classroom blackboard, the accident failed to happen, the bed merely tipping its occupant overboard for a short and easy swim to the shore. Anicetus had to stab Agrippina himself as she stumbled to what she thought was safety. Seeing death instead, she opened her legs to his sword. She screamed about the ingratitude of a son to the mother who had given him birth. There were many witnesses to the murder.

Even within a few days a mass of myths and stories had attached to the daughter of Germanicus and mistress of the *domus Caesaris* whose lucky double dog teeth had let her down after a night under Minerva's tragically inadequate shield. Not even Seneca, drafted from Rome to write an explanation for the senate, could claim an accidental death. Not even Nero, a man trained at blurring art and life, could deny to himself what he had done.

Seneca did his best. The killing, he said, prevented Agrippina's own plans to kill Nero. The messenger she had sent with the news of her lucky survival at sea was carrying his own assassin's sword. In and out of the Palatine, most saw no choice but to accept the story and move on. Only the emperor himself was struggling. Star of the stage in his own mind, free without his mother's disapproval to become a bigger star, he was in that same mind a mother-killer, a matricide, an unforgivable criminal who in the great Greek plays was forever pursued by avenging spirits.

Seneca's own plays, composed in some of the quieter times throughout his life, were masterpieces of deep emersion in minds distorted by excess and guilt. He wrote Greek tragedies in his own dense Latin, an *Oedipus*, a horror story of sex between mother and son, a *Medea* about a child-killing mother and a *Thyestes* in which a king banqueted on his own children. But neither his literary genius nor his political skill could help Nero once Agrippina was dead. No new marketplace for food, no banking or business, could drive a mother's murder from the minds of the men and women of Rome. Art and flattery were not enough to undo what the desire for art and flattery had done.

Nero ordered a new villa at Sublaqueum in the hills where the *Aqua Claudia* began its route to Rome. This was deeper in the countryside than Tibur, too far to be reached from the Palatine in a single day. When the court moved it had to stop for the night. The farmhouse that had once belonged to Horace, his symbol of the simple life, was newly aggrandised, with more bedrooms and a bathhouse fit for a small town. In front of the court's latest country home a vast artificial lake improved the emperor's view without improving the supply of water to the city.

At Sublaqueum Nero gathered his courtiers to dining tables where his mother had never reigned. There was still Halotus, the food-taster, Poppaea and Aulus Vitellius but also poets, singers and masters of oratory. Orators were increasingly popular for prosecuting Agrippina's alleged accomplices, particularly those who were rich and whose wealth was deemed due for redistribution. Food was an accompaniment to singing and dancing, an obliterator of unpleasant necessities, blasting away the news of the latest trials for fabricated treason.

Chicken breasts were softened with oil and shaped into cakes, lampreys stewed with coriander. Others might praise the choice of beans from Baiae, a paste of peas with ginger, hard-boiled eggs and honey, duck scalded in its feathers with turnip. For readers of Greek comic melodramas (and Nero was an avid reader), eating a favourite eel or fowl was as close as anything could come to making a man feel like a god. Food could bring back the dead to life. In Nero's mind his murdered mother was always on the brink of new life.

Sublaqueum was a hotel hard to leave. Seneca wanted to spend more time at his own country houses. He blamed the constant banqueting for damage to his health. Nero wanted his former tutor at his side, citing the long loyalty of Lucius Vitellius to the Divine Claudius. Praise of Lucius was a commendation of Aulus too. Any mention of Claudius was worth a smirk at Sublaqueum. His daughter Octavia, still Nero's wife, was rarely at the house where recipes were a rejection of reality, a reinforcement of status, a reminder of what it meant to be on the inside rather than the outside.

This was the world which Seneca had helped to create and never wanted to see again. He had had enough. He had done enough. The offices of the Palatine still worked well. Burrus was keeping the guard under control. But Nero's closest companions had become a bodyguard of mirrors, men and women who reflected both his view of himself, his hopes of a yet more celebrated future and the threats that they saw all around.

There was no longer a chance of the clear succession that the court needed above all else. With the death of Nero's mother, and the consequent collapse of his marriage to Octavia, the *domus Caesaris* lost its hope of a new Caesar. Some new family had to be standing ready, just as Augustus had considered at Nola. Seneca wanted no part of that future.

When the companions came together in the hills above Tibur, the ghost of Agrippina was best not mentioned. The spirit of the local landowner of Tibur, young Rubellius Plautus, was all too present too. When Nero looked for threats to himself Plautus was arguably, and ever more visibly, the greatest threat.

38

BLACKENED TABLES

It was almost thirty years since Tiberius had scandalised the grandees of Rome by marrying his disgraced granddaughter, Julia, to the respectable, but hardly grand or ambitious, Rubellius Blandus from Tibur. Even in a time of food and water failures, sudden debt and economic collapse, the wedding had been a social offence. And if the aim had been to weaken Augustus's most direct descendants, to dilute the line with an outsider merely of good repute, it had been an even bigger failure.

The son of Julia and Blandus, Rubellius Plautus, was still seen – fearfully in Sublaqueum and hopefully elsewhere – as a man who might rule Rome as it had not been ruled since the death at Nola. For four months a comet fell across the sky, the sign that Augustus had used to show his own right to take the place on earth of Julius Caesar. Gossips had time to speculate who Nero's heir might be. It was a dangerous time for a contender, however retiring Plautus might be, however content to continue the local antiquarianism of his father.

Nero was well aware of Plautus's potential to rule. Agrippina had taunted her son with his name. Plautus himself may have played no part, but Nero's flatterers fanned his insecurity. Seneca advised caution in dealing with Plautus but Seneca, increasingly, was in retirement. Nero was becoming happier to accept his excuses.

Nero's rights to rule included his being both the adopted son of Claudius and the husband of Claudius's daughter. This had once looked incestuous, but was now accepted. Had he and Octavia had a son together, there would be no need to gossip about Plautus. But there had been no child at all, and no sign of one. If Nero were to divorce Octavia, who was popular at Rome, he would lose part of his legitimacy; if he were to stay married, he was risking his chance of a legitimate heir by a new wife.

Maybe marriage to one's sister had been wrong all along, acceptable only as long as it was useful. It was the sort of practice that Romans still associated with the eastern kingdoms of Commagene and beyond. The legal arguments of Lucius Vitellius had been more expedients than precedents. Poppaea, who had proved her ability to give birth with a previous husband, had her own supporters at the dining tables, demanding divorce and remarriage for herself.

Seneca wanted to protect Octavia and saw his advice as far superior to anything in the past from Lucius Vitellius. The man celebrated in the Forum for loyalty to Claudius had indulged his patrons too much. He had encouraged Caligula to see himself talking to the Moon. A desperate exile might be excused for placing his patrons among the planets but Lucius, unlike Seneca, had never been an exile.

Even more importantly, Lucius was dead. His son might as well have been dead too for all the good he did. Seneca's advice was subtle and fragile, vulnerable to being overturned in his own ever-longer absences. He stood for maintaining the awkwardness of the match between sister and brother. It was hard to be heard.

While the comet was still low overhead, a new contribution to the argument came from the sky. A night of autumn lightning lit the road from Sublaqueum to Rome, illuminating the temples of Tibur, the new lakes behind new dams and the new course of the *Aqua Claudia*. The waters were in black shadows split with jagged flashes. In the morning the tables by the lake where Nero and Poppaea had entertained themselves and their friends were black-scarred and smouldering.

Professional prophets for an emperor, like Thrasyllus for Tiberius, were skilled at improving the most unpropitious signs. But no one at Sublaqueum could see the shattered wood above Tibur as anything but doom for the emperor and a mark of heavenly approval for Rubellius Plautus. Nero ordered a letter sent to Rome advising that his reluctant rival would be safer in the fields of Asia that he had inherited through his imperial wife.

Plautus might have expected worse. He swiftly followed the travel advice that might easily have been for suicide instead. He would never see Tibur again. For two more years Nero refused to decide between his younger and older courtiers, the crudest flattery and the subtler kind he had been educated to expect, between divorce and staying married, eliminating Plautus and letting him live.

Shortly after the lightning storm, the emperor fell ill at Sublaqueum after bathing in the upper pools of the River Anio. His coterie expressed the classic fears of the flatterer's repertoire, asking how will the empire survive if its great leader is gone? Nero rebuffed rather than rewarded the idea of such dependence. The system would cope, he told those anxiously observing his sweats, before naming as his heir a man called Memmius Regulus, Rome's oldest ex-consul, a man of otherwise no great distinction whose closest link to the *domus Caesaris* was a brief and unprotesting loan of his wife to Caligula.

Like Rubellius Blandus, Memmius was known as modest in wealth and talent. He had not even married into the edges of the imperial family. His naming must have aroused comment about others similarly lightly connected, men such as Aulus Plautius, commander of Claudius's British campaign, cousin of Claudius's first wife, a war hero linked closely to the Vitellii. There was also Galba, almost a son to Augustus's wife, Livia, and Otho too, if his ex-wife Poppaea were to become Nero's empress as she intended.

There was a Cassius, descended from Julius Caesar's leading assassin but married to a granddaughter of Augustus. With the options spread so wide, anyone might dream at Sublaqueum of someday taking the head of the table. Success would produce any number of flattering genealogists and prophets to improve their claims.

Aulus Vitellius was part of no one's calculations. He had no tested talents. There was rumbling local warfare around Nuceria, his family's home town, but Nero did not choose him to bring peace when attempts by the senate failed. Instead, the son of Lucius Vitellius was about to take a gentle job abroad, one requiring little but loyalty, his first job of any kind since serving as consul under the watchful eye of his father twelve years before.

In 60 CE Aulus became Nero's governor of Africa, the quiet province based on the lands of Rome's greatest old enemy, Carthage. The fields of Africa were important. They provided most of the corn that Nero needed to give away in Rome. But the province was not usually challenging to administer; Blandus and Julia seemed to have had no trouble there. When Augustus had allowed it to be rebuilt after the defeat of Hannibal 200 years before it was as a grandiose version of what he hoped Rome might become, filled with marble and men loyal to himself.

Carthage was still a place of dreams, the mythical home of Dido, the queen whose passion for Aeneas had failed to prevent the founding of Rome. There was always the hope that Dido's magnificent mythical treasure, rescued from the murderer of her husband in the exotic east, made famous in Virgil's *Aeneid*, might be found and be more than a myth. Aulus took his brother, Lucius, to Carthage too. Together they managed their domain of bread-flour, pomegranates and hopes of ancient treasure. Aulus's wife gave birth to their first son.

In Sublaqueum and Rome succession anxiety eased. Nero recovered from his cold. He ordered the death of Pallas who, in prosperous retirement, with a grand tomb prepared on the road to Tibur, was still too much a reminder of Agrippina's grip on his life. When Pallas left the Palatine it was a major political event; when he left his life it was not. That was one of the differences between those who inherited power and those selected to serve it.

Nero had already tested the appetite of himself and the people for a modest Neronia festival of sport and poetry, hosted by the consuls of the year and attended, with their due blessing, by the Vestal Virgins. Both the popular appetite and his own were high, although the crowd would have preferred more Atellane farce and less poetry in Greek. Nero was next planning grander stages, celebratory banquets, charioteering around the *Circus Maximus* and mass spectacles starring, if he dared, himself. There were great Greek parts for matricides like Orestes, murderer of his mother Clytemnestra after the Trojan War. Nero was going to play them.

Seneca was still available when needed, taking care of his own great fortune and the fortunes of the state, balancing them and sometimes allowing one to influence the other. Britain was the biggest test in his preparations to retire. In 61 CE, in distant Colchester the temple of the Divine Claudius was suddenly as blackened a ruin as Nero's picnic tables at Sublaqueum.

As many had predicted when Aulus Plautius led Claudius's invasion, Britain had proved as dangerous and useless as Africa was profitable and peaceful. Nero gave the job of subduing Wales to one of Claudius's favourites, who died after only a year, leaving a long and flattering will in favour of the imperial treasury but little else of strategic use.

The most threatening rebellion against Rome, by Queen Boudica and her Iceni tribe, began in the east of the country, reduced London as well as Colchester to damp embers, and spread terror everywhere before finally failing in the west. Boudica killed herself. The legions restored order but there needed to be new determination, and new military leadership, to finish the job that Julius Caesar had so long ago begun – or, at least, to decide what finishing the job might mean.

One reason for the revolt was the sudden withdrawal of credit from Rome, sharply rising rates of interest and brutal retribution upon those who could not pay. Seneca, in the midst of reorganising his affairs, was prominent among those demanding rapid repayment, a leader of financial opinion not just because of his wealth but because he was held to know whether Nero might be considering a withdrawal from Britain altogether. Even Nero's dispatch of a personal ambassador to Britain, his freedman, Polyclitus, with a massive retinue of lesser courtiers, succeeded chiefly in showing how much bureaucracy had been born, how little progress made in emptying the Palatine rooms. The Romans stayed. So too did the trade in slaves and dogs.

Dog-racing came to Rome – or at least the threat of it during a dispute between chariot-owners and the emperor about prize money. Grattius had set out the ways in which dogs and foxes of different national characters might be bred to produce a greyhound. A British and an African might be a winner. On this occasion the row ended in negotiated compromise with the owners of the horse-drawn chariots before any new sport could come to the stadia.

The Palatine had new connecting tunnels between bedrooms and banqueting halls and a new and influential *arbiter elegantiae*, a style counsellor, Petronius Arbiter, who made decisions about what was appropriate for the emperor's table and what was not. Petronius also wrote a secret satire on his own role, the *Satyricon*, a surviving story of food raised to art and of slave boys' hair used for washing after defecation. He did not live long but left a lasting fantasy. The court remained enough of an attraction for Nero to impose financial penalties on those who pretended to be imperial freedmen when they were not. This was a new and unusual problem.

Two years of light duties later, Seneca asked Nero if he could move in the opposite direction and withdraw from court altogether. He wanted to write more about the theory of flattery than to exercise his old-fashioned flatterer's skills, to portray guilt-haunted characters in tragedy rather than live a life with the ghost of Agrippina. He wanted to live more like his nephew, his brother Mela's son, who was rising in reputation as a poet. He cited the example of how Augustus had let go his own long-serving counsellors. Nero responded with a detailed rebuttal, referring again to the example of Aulus's father, Lucius Vitellius, who had stood by Claudius till he died.

Seneca remained at court, a further diminished force. There was a successful response to the mass sinking of corn ships in the Tiber, subsidies and other moves to stop panic. Images of the *Macellum Magnum* food market began to appear on coins. But Seneca could not stop the murder of Rubellius Plautus in Asia in 62 CE after he was rumoured to be plotting a bid for the throne. Nero sent his eunuch freedman, Pelago, to ensure that the suicide happened as required. When Nero held Plautus's head in his hand he mocked how frightening its long nose was. This was not the *clementia* he had once claimed to prize.

Nor could Seneca stop the divorce of Octavia, her execution on the grounds of an alleged relationship with Agrippina's killer, Anicetus, and the extravagant marriage of Nero and Poppaea. His relative, Annaeus Serenus, who had pretended an affair with Acte so that Nero could progress his own, died after eating mushrooms at a palace banquet. Nero's freedman, Doryphorus, successor to Callistus as *a libellis*, sifter of requests for imperial help, was poisoned on suspicion of organising public opposition to the marriage.

The Brothers of the Fields sacrificed a cow with gilded horns to Minerva, adding the offspring of Nero and Poppaea to their list of those who would ensure health and happiness for all. 'Their end is destruction, their god is their belly,' Paul of Tarsus, promulgator and propagandist for the new Christianity, wrote to his followers from Rome, warning of gluttons, evil-doers and dogs.

39

FOOD AND FIRE

When fire raged through Rome in the summer of 64 CE, it was not an unusual disaster for a city built of more wood than stone. It lasted ten days, but the firefighters had better access to water than those who had done the same job in the past. Nero's managers of the corn supply organised food to be brought in from the fields at public expense. Subsidies were paid and prices controlled. The emperor's lasting failure was what he himself saw as his instant success, his personal performance of *The Capture of Ilium*, the song of the fire at Troy from which Rome had arisen through the heroic virtue of Aeneas, the theme of Virgil's *Aeneid*, the poem which had brought lasting glory to his ancestor, Augustus.

Nero expanded his repertoire of epic heroes from Troy, strengthening his lungs with bricks piled on his chest and calming his throat with honey and spiced wine as well as leeks. He played Nauplius, the mythical Greek who avenged his dead son by luring sailors on to rocks with false fires and slaughtering any who swam to the shore. Niobe was one of his female roles, a mother whose pride brought divine destruction on her children and whose husband was the son of Zeus and played a golden lyre.

After the fire an audience was invited to watch Nero play the part of Hercules, not as a protector of Italy in the temple of Rubellius Plautus's family but as a madman in chains who had murdered his wife and children. A vast palace of theatres and banqueting halls, revolving ceilings and stages was added to the imperial domains in Rome in place of what the fire had destroyed. Nero's builders ordered coloured marbles from across the empire. Glass sparkled in the mosaic ceiling like night sky. Frescoes and floors filled with sea monsters. More houses of the old senatorial elite disappeared.

The *Domus Aurea*, the Golden House, was a wonder of the age. It was not a disaster until Nero's other failures made it so. It provided employment before it attracted opprobrium. Its workers were proud of their roles. Some of its increasingly specialist staff, Eumolpus and his daughter, Claudia Pallas, planned memorials to boast their responsibilities for its furniture. Others tended the rare fluorspar glasses that reputedly improved the taste of wine. There were new jobs for *triclinarii* around the dining-room couches, *fornacarii* to stoke the furnaces, *ministratores* for the many demands of administration. The successors to the slave who combed the hair of the dying Augustus were *tonsores* and *ornatores* or holders of other grander titles.

When critical citizens began to suspect that Nero himself had deliberately set Rome ablaze so as to rebuild it in grander style, there were feasts to placate them. Imperial expansion brought more public benefits than did the houses of the senatorial elite. There were garden parties like stadium games. Walkways were lit with Christians clothed in burning pitch. Two decades after the disgrace of Pontius Pilate, Rome finally had a hideous use for those who worshipped the 'King of the Jews'.

The fire caused more damage than at first sight to the *Aqua Claudia*. Nero ordered repairs and then diverted its water to make a great lake. He wanted power for a revolving domed banquet chamber to represent the earth and the sky, the paths of the Moon and Sun gods, new water to spray scented fountains and to sluice a block of forty lavatories, more than in most large towns. The stories of the *Domus Aurea*, good and bad, spread wider and faster from Rome than did the imperial edicts and replies to tax questions which occupied most of the men of the Palatine.

The impact on normal administrative life, even on the management of disaster, was small. The cogs in the Palatine machine continued to turn; most of the empire did not need the Palatine machine or rarely asked for its verdicts. The *Aqua Claudia* still brought the fresh springs of the Anio into Rome. A new extension of the underground pipes ran west into the Palatine and beyond.

*

If Nero had to be an entertainer, Seneca would have preferred him to be a charioteer, the sport of the Moon in which Aulus Vitellius had both proven skill and a thigh wound to prove it, than a singer following Apollo, the Sun. Racing, like singing, required its own unusual diet. Draughts of dried pig shit, mixed with water to strengthen muscles, were just part of the regime. The track was a much lesser disgrace than the stage. The *Circus Maximus* was central to old Rome, the view of every emperor from the windows of the Palatine.

The chariot was a sport of ancient kings and epic heroes. The poet Pindar produced some of his most florid praise for charioteers. Seneca loathed everything that happened in a stadium, but he still saw the wearing of a high Homeric helmet to drive horses as less offensive than wearing olive leaves to recite poetry and play the lyre. Nero did not agree. In his final years at Nero's side, Seneca had no choice but to praise his former pupil's skill as a musician, comparing his voice to that of Apollo, watching while his initial high hopes fell further.

Nero wanted to compete on merit and was confident that he could. In quinquennial games in 65 CE he played the harp, obeying every rule followed by other competitors, using only his cloak to mop his brow, and waiting with a persuasive display of nerves for the inevitable announcement of his victory. In suburban streets supporters founded clubs called the Neropoppaenses to show their approval of the emperor and his new wife.

Although Nero lapped up these layers upon layers of flattery, as for any addict it was not enough. He began to resent Seneca's own literary skill and that of his nephew Lucan even more. The object of flattery envied the very skills used to flatter him. Petronius Arbiter was forced to suicide. The emperor wanted the applause of both the court and the public too, a lust for artistic celebrity which drew him gradually further away from the *domus Caesaris* at home and to entertainment abroad.

Aulus Vitellius was a loyal booster of Nero's showmanship. The first of the emperor's personal performances on stage were in a regional experiment around Naples, close to his family home, and to where Augustus had died among the adulatory Alexandrian sailors. Popular demand soon brought a transfer to Rome. Aulus's own personal service was to rouse the crowd to demand what the emperor affected shyness to supply. When Nero left a theatre without performing, he could rely on Aulus to ensure that the retreat was merely a tactic. Aulus was never a competitor. He played no instrument except, like his father, the emperor himself, whom he wanted to sound good, look good and be good too – as long as the third was consistent with the first and second.

The audiences of Rome were flattered by Nero's attention and happy to reciprocate. Whether or not Nero was a good tragic heroine (opinions varied even at the time), he must have made an extraordinary spectacle, well worthy of Phaedrus's pen. This *princeps* was not being merely confused with a preening musician of the same name, winning the applause that a comeback flautist thought was his own due: this *princeps* was himself the musician. The son of a great courtier, Aulus son of Lucius Vitellius, was the master of the ceremonies. No one needed Augustus's fat men of Atellane farce – or cared whether Mr Glutton and his friends were exiled or not – when there was entertainment like that.

Aulus stayed away from even the best-supported opposition to Nero in the senate. There was a plot to replace the emperor with a member of the same Piso family that had been disgraced and driven to death by the efforts of his uncle, Publius. Piso was himself a noted singer but avoided the charge that singing was his only love. One of Nero's Greek secretaries for replying to citizens' petitions, Epaphroditus, was the first to see the danger. Seneca was accused of involvement, probably unjustly, and had to take his own life. His subversive nephew, Lucan, a flatterer whose poetry protested too much, was more likely to have been a plotter and died in the same way.

Out in the provinces and in the army, attitudes began to be harsher and louder. A centurion on the Rhine did not need to believe every bizarre story from the Palatine, but there was no doubting that the emperor was a singer and lyre-player who had murdered his imperial mother and humiliated his imperial wife.

Piso's conspiracy caught the innocent as well as the guilty in Nero's revenge.

Epaphroditus bought grand gardens by the Golden House with the financial reward for his detective work. One of his personal court of philosophers, Musonius Rufus, a friend of Rubellius Plautus and a critic of gluttony, took the punishment of exile. A promoter of a simple diet, Rufus suffered from association with Seneca and, like Seneca under Claudius, had to do his thinking on a distant island. His gains, he said, were to his Stoic understanding of deprivation.

More distant observers included the elderly Galba in Spain, supported by a flamboyant and much younger financial secretary, Caecina Alienus. Further west in Lusitania was Poppaea's banished husband Otho, more famed as an effeminate fop than a warlord, a gourmet whose use for common bread was as a paste to keep his body free from hair. Neither was a feared man of resistance and Otho, like Aulus Vitellius, had been one of Nero's intimates on their nightly riots through the Roman streets. Aulus Plautius, the hero of Britain, was a candidate for some. No one would have thought of Vitellius himself, especially not his closest family and friends.

Nero took hope from the arrival of a conman from Carthage who claimed to have seen the location of Dido's treasure in a dream. Like the emperor with no clothes, Nero was easy prey. His courtiers shared the enthusiasm and the hope. When Nero believed, his flatterers pretended to believe. Aulus, the courtier most recently in Africa, must have had his doubts – but also the best command of the story. Quite quickly the fact was exposed as fantasy, but not before Nero had spent the new money anyway on new stages on which to perform and receive applause.

40

TUTOR IN VICE

The last time that an emperor had left Italy was when Claudius went to Britain in 43 CE, leaving Lucius Vitellius to manage business in his absence. Almost a quarter of a century later, when Nero left for a singing tour of Greece, Aulus did not get the chance to match his father. Left behind in Rome was Helius, one of his freedmen, a less successful pair of eyes and ears. Every member of Nero's entourage was in the wrong place to sense the events on the Palatine and in the empire that would bring the year when four men were emperors, none of them an heir of Julius Caesar.

The focus for the planners of the trip was that all the main Greek festivals should be rearranged into a single season. Nero had to be able to win every possible prize in the shortest time that it was safe for him to be away. The stages had to be perfect, the audiences appreciative but not too obsequious. The competition had to seem to be real.

Nero's sexual and emotional needs also needed court attention. Poppaea had survived only three years as empress, leaving a daughter and dying, it was said, during a violent row about the time Nero was spending at the races. He was taking to Greece his less controversial third wife, Statilia Messalina, also Sporus, a boy castrato who had to be dressed like Poppaea. Among his closest courtiers on the journey was his African 'mistress of the Imperial wardrobe', Calvia Crispinilla, known to her enemies as Nero's 'tutor in vice'.

By the final years of his reign Nero's bodyguard of mirrors was a musical troupe the size of a legion, a parody, to his critics, of Augustus's young soldier bands, but to Nero a sign of progress and civilisation. Its purpose was art, not war. Its numbers rose quickly to some 5,000, rehearsed to provide synchronised applause of the kind that Augustus had once heard from Alexandrian visitors to his beloved Naples. Those with memories as long as the Vitellii's could recall those last days of Augustus, the clapping of the sailors and their reward in new clothes from their emperor. Nero enjoyed a triumphant tour. His hosts were expert at creating the greatest dramatic tension before hailing Nero Victor. Crispinilla organised his marriage to Sporus.

Back in Rome, there was a rather different reality. Helius had to deal with a more than usually serious revolt in Judaea and the defeat of four legions. There was a massive earthquake. A tidal wave destroyed corn ships and warehouses and damaged the *Aqua Claudia*. New gold coins displayed Nero's elegant new marketplace. In gold the emperor's face was just as symbolic and imperious as in his youth, if somewhat fatter around the neck. His eyes were deeper in his head, with just a slight tilt upwards to the sky as though the master were solving every problem.

Aulus Vitellius began another of his rare public roles, the supervision of contracts in Rome for the repair and rebuilding of temples. There were complaints that gold and silver ornaments, candleholders, lamps and plates were being mysteriously swapped for tin and brass copies. Whether this was the result of incompetence or corruption was never clear. Throughout his life Aulus was never accused of greed for money. In Africa he was deemed unusual in his probity, even if frequently short of cash. Unlike his father and uncle, he was no orator and could not earn legal fees.

The treason courts were still profitable places to work. Vibius Crispus, a dangerous wit, and Eprius Marcellus, the gourmet friend of Columella the wine writer, were newly rich men in Rome. Aulus's friend, Silius Italicus, designated to be consul in 68 CE, prosecuted many men whose private wealth the emperor thought would be better public. Nero personally took over 'half of Africa'. The estates that had made Rubellius Blandus rich and paid for the ornamentation of Tibur gained a different function for Rome. Italicus was also planning their appearance in his inspirational epic of the war against Carthage.

These trials were not for the incompetent. The arguments had to be persuasive, some of the substance real. Italicus was an artist.

Marcus Aquilius Regulus, an orator whose art was comparable to the best of the old Republic, won a death sentence for three members of the senate and massive transfers of wealth out of the old order. But, without Seneca, Nero had no one in the cowed ranks of the senate who could do what Lucius Vitellius had done for Claudius, getting his master's bidding done while making the senators feel that they still mattered.

Aulus was certainly not that man. Mildly mired in scandal, he retired as best he could with his wife and brother. His son was five years old, tall and gangling and had a nervous stammer, probably not the only member of the court so afflicted.

Revolts within the Gallic legions – the kind of protest beyond the palace walls that Tiberius and Claudius had crushed without too much trouble – led more quickly than anyone expected to a collapse in Nero's support and the end of the dynasty. Some in the court began to sense the winds from the world outside. Others looked only inwards. Calvia Crispinilla, a true mistress of costume changes, helped to turn a legion against him in her native Africa. Rome again faced famine from the blocking of African corn.

Nero heard the news of the revolts at a dinner in Naples on the ninth anniversary of his mother's murder. He overturned the table, smashed two crystal cups engraved with scenes from Homer and for a week abandoned the normal business of replying to letters. He ordered corn ships to carry stage sand needed by his court wrestlers.

On his return to Rome he sent a letter to Spain ordering the death of Galba. He spent the rest of the day discussing how organ pipes could be powered by aqueducts. His inner court was quickly reduced to four former slaves, Epaphroditus, the loyalist who had saved him from danger before, Sporus, the castrato who looked like his second wife, Neophytus, hardly known outside the Palatine, and Phaon, his financial controller and the last of Pallas's successors. Phaon owned a villa outside Rome where they thought they might hide if the news from the armies required retreat.

It took three weeks for Nero to learn that Galba had somehow intercepted his death sentence and was still alive. The movement of other commanders was unclear, but their lack of loyalty to himself was not. The last band from the Palatine court set off for Phaon's villa and waited. It did not take long for Galba's soldiers to reach Rome, for the senate to recognise the right of might, and for Nero's whereabouts to be known. On 9 June 68 CE, Nero heard the horses approach. His box of poison was missing: one of his household had taken a final payment before fleeing into the future. He attempted to stab himself in a more suitably theatrical suicide. His last recorded words were *Qualis artifex pereo*, 'When I die, what an artist dies.' Epaphroditus assisted him to ensure success.

PART THREE

Take a cooked sow's belly, with the teats still on it, fish, chicken, breasts of thrushes, strictly fresh eggs and raisins. Boil and spread on pancakes. An expensive silver platter would materially enhance the appearance of this dish.

Apicius (attr.) (first century CE)

41

MR STINGY

The news of Nero's death was at first uncertain. It blew from room to room through the Palatine, from house to house and town to town less like the 'smoke for sale' at the death of Augustus than the smoke that had seeped through the roof tiles in the great city fire, twisting, turning, changing colour and substance. The first reports were sharp, those following ever more blurred, more bloody and also more bloodless. Not everyone believed that Nero was gone.

Household members, few of whom were ever popular, took much of the blame for the perilous uncertainty. The dead emperor still retained respect on the streets he knew so well. There was hunger for food but not necessarily for a new Caesar, even if one could be found. The fear of the unknown was still strong. His nurse, Claudia Ecloge, and his long-time lover, Claudia Acte, arranged a suitable funeral pyre, dressing him in white robes embroidered with gold, laying him in a white crystal coffin in the family tomb of his fathers.

If Galba were to succeed, he seemed certain to repudiate Nero, his friends and his works. Aulus Vitellius slipped into obscurity as best he could. He had lost his last sponsor among the heirs of Augustus.

Aulus's wife, Galeria, was possibly of some assistance. She was no Neronian. She was famed for virtue just as his father, according to the inscription in the Forum, had been. She had her own connections to Silius Italicus, the would-be new Virgil of whatever era came next. But she was linked to the age of Nero, if a successor chose to purge the court too far. Men would later accuse Aulus Vitellius of many crimes against convention and good taste, but neglect of his second wife was never one of them. His first had paid money to keep him from their children. He was determined to care for his second.

In the early days of enforced retirement Aulus could also assess how the last successor to Augustus had ended the family line. Nero and his court had been looking out for the wrong kind of opponents in the wrong direction. On his triumphant tour of Greece the emperor had won hundreds of competitions in poetry and singing, scattering the competition from coast to coast. Meanwhile, an unknown Roman Gaul called Julius Vindex was leading a revolt.

Vindex himself had not defeated Nero, but he had encouraged Roman generals to think that they might do better, or to fear that someone else might do better if they did not. Servius Sulpicius Galba, with a nearby army in Spain and already one of the consuls designated for the following year, had been just one of these. Another was Marcus Salvius Otho, former husband of Nero's murdered wife, Poppaea, who was still in comfortable exile in the furthest part of Spain as governor of Lusitania.

Aulus was twenty years younger than Galba and did not know him well. Otho had been his companion at Nero's court, sharer of banquets, concerts and flattery of their master's voice. Those who sought certainty of succession wondered if Galba, who was abstemious, strict, vain and, most importantly without living children, might adopt Otho. Aulus might hope for future advancement if such certainty could be achieved. So might his stammering son, the highest of Aulus's concerns.

But this was primarily a time for survival, seclusion and forgetfulness in the hope that others would forget. It was a time for family matters. A stammer had to be cured. The boy needed calm. Romans distrusted those with impediments to speech. In whatever way a man spoke – as a public orator or as a court flatterer – a stammer was a handicap. Aesop's stutter had not contributed to his reputation for wisdom, only for being a clown. Claudius had not made disability fashionable and even Claudius, along with Lucius Vitellius, his faithful minister, was slipping into the distrusted past. Ahead was the new and unknown.

What was already certain was a fact more significant than the choice of any particular emperor. The new truth was that the choice for the first time since the death of Augustus need not, and would

not, be made at court. The *domus Caesaris* no longer had a Caesar
in Julius Caesar's line and would have to wait for whichever successor might choose the name (or another name) as his title.

The future was clouded by distance and ignorance. Soldiers in
different places, from west to east, stood ready to take the decisions
that for more than fifty years had been made within the palace.
Senior officers whom he knew, such as Fabius Valens and Caecina
Alienus, previously judged on the Palatine by what they might do
for Nero, became suspected of conspiring in their own interests and
against one another.

Aulus did not have many friends in the army. In his time in
Africa he had no direct responsibility for the legion in the province.
Valens had made his first public appearance at Rome as a volunteer
performer at the Neronia festival. His home was a holiday resort in
the hills south-east of Rome and his reputation was as a libertine, as
notorious for taking the sexual opportunities of power as was Aulus
for exploiting the kitchens. He had thrown his weight into turning
troops from Nero to Galba and was expecting a rapid reward. He
was one of many.

Caecina was also prominent in Galba's service, a younger war
hero, tall and eccentrically dressed in multicoloured coat and Gallic
trousers, fast-talking in the officers' mess, conspicuous on the battlefield, dangerously so if his superiors were looking too long in his
direction. He was the kind of adventurer who, in earlier days, would
have appealed to Julius Caesar. A mutual loathing made Valens and
Caecina very useful allies to anyone else. But this was of no immediate concern to Aulus.

Galba, the new man of the moment, had the advantage of looking as an emperor ought to look, even if few ever did. He was tall
and blue-eyed, with a downward-curving nose. He was bald and
sensitive about it, and as soon as he had the chance he added hair to
the image on his coins. Even before he was emperor, he had a family
tree claiming descent from Jupiter and the Sun, a distinction which
others had to wait for until they reached the throne.

Galba had prospered in his youth as a protégé of Livia, Augustus's wife. He was sufficiently dangerous to Claudius – or possibly

valuable too – for the invasion of Britain to be postponed until he was fit enough to travel. (Aulus could remember that well, the high point of his father's career in service.) He survived the enmity of Agrippina, who allegedly wanted to marry him. Many absences abroad came to his aid. He was rich, not least from Livia's legacies, but notorious for frugality, an antique virtue all the more appreciated in the senate, which gratefully acclaimed him as Nero's successor. His army then waited for the money that a new emperor traditionally paid his troops. This menacing military presence close to Rome made the senate's gratitude useful, but not absolutely necessary.

Galba had used secret informants at the court of Nero. Prime among them was Calvia Crispinilla, the woman from exotic Africa seen as Nero's 'mistress of vice' but with influence well beyond the bedrooms and banqueting halls. It had always been the most important courtly skill to sense the direction of the political wind. Crispinilla was the mistress of that art, as well as those for which she was better known – and had no need to worry if grander people thought her merely a pimp.

The new emperor was neither a courtier nor the master of an influential court. He was a man who presented himself as the past. In an antique custom, he made all his slaves and freedmen parade before him twice a day. He had an inner circle of only three, an undistinguished soldier, his lawyer and his male lover. Supporters could only hope that this group might be widened by the pressures of power.

Otho, hoping to exploit his knowledge of how a court ought to work, offered the newly acclaimed Emperor Galba an early gift of some of his own most cultured slaves. He met with a sharp rebuff. Vitellius kept himself out of the way with his wife and children.

News at Rome was scarce. In Galba's army it seemed that Caecina had suffered a setback, an investigation on suspicions of theft and fraud. Otho and Valens were more visible on the march south from the Alps, joining in the massacre of a force hastily produced by Nero on the last bridge into the city; the emperor's mind had still been on the stages of Greece. His battalions of ballerinas dressed as Amazons put up appropriate resistance. A key last concern for Nero had been the escape of himself and his Greek theatrical equipment. That was what Aulus and his friends knew. That was what Galba soon learnt, and some of it was true.

Galba did not care for the machinery of the stage. In as much as he had a taste for theatre it was closer to that of the dying Augustus at Nola. At his first celebratory games, designed to show himself to the people, a team of Atellane satirists played the stock roles of Mr Glutton, Mr Fool, Mr Toad and Mr Chew. These were characters who had entertained in Italy before the arrival of competitors from the highbrow east. There was an especially enthusiastic response for a figure called Onesimus, Mr Stingy, the parent who is mean to his children. The audience joined in and the line was sung that *Venit Onesimus a villa*, 'Onesimus is back from his farm', a sign that might have sounded good to the new emperor but quite quickly was not. His soldiers wanted their money.

42

A GOOD JOB FOR A GLUTTON

Galba's only autumn in power was mild before what would be an unusually warm winter. The mosquitoes of Rome rolled in clouds around the damp alleys. The house of the Vitellii was poor by the standards of Aulus's childhood. He was no longer part of the *domus Caesaris* which Nero had so confidently expanded beyond the Palatine. He had lost his creditworthiness at the fall of his guarantor and his creditors were pressing him hard. It was a good time to be leaving and Galba, solely for his own interests, gave him his chance.

One of Aulus's distant and wealthier relatives, notorious for little more than his indecisiveness, had already received the governorship of Pannonia and its possibilities for plunder along the banks of the Danube. Tiberius in his youth had made his military reputation beside the border river which ran west to east across Europe as the Rhine ran south to north. That was no part of Galba's plan. A general who had just led an army to Rome did not want other generals with the initiative to do the same.

Lower Germany was an even more strategic province than Pannonia. It stretched down the Rhine from the North Sea to its capital at Colonia Agrippinensis, a camp that had won its walls and towers from being Agrippina's place of birth during Germanicus's campaigns. To general surprise, even of Romans for whom the new world was nothing but surprise, Galba gave Lower Germany to Aulus Vitellius – with a brief to do as little as possible.

It was hard to see what advantage Galba thought he might gain from this. Perhaps the most immediate was that Aulus did not belong to that large class of the imperial household whose ill-gotten gains Galba was hoping to recoup for the treasury. If, as was occasionally alleged, he had swapped gold ornaments for bronze during a minor administrative role, there were no gains remaining. Or, as his wittier critics remarked, he had eaten them all. Galba was apparently content that his governor should gorge himself on the food of the northern seas as long as that was the extent of his ambition.

Aulus's departure was less than elegant. He had to move Galeria and their children, Aulus and Vitellia, into a small apartment, borrow a pearl from his mother and dodge those who thought he was merely fleeing his debts. He was lucky that the moneylenders in Rome, like the food traders and the builders, faced a range of much bigger problems than himself in the new age without the Caesars.

There was no longer even the very limited certainty for the future that was necessary for banking and building. There was again no clear succession. A necessary decision, pressing before Galba had found the slightest comfort on the throne, was whom he might identify as his son and heir. Otho looked the man most likely. Almost as impoverished as Aulus, he was highly enthusiastic for the role, borrowing money and distributing it at a banquet to the palace guard, hastily organising a marriage for his daughter with a senior adviser to Galba.

But there were other hopefuls too to test the moneylenders' confidence. In the last weeks of November the issue was still unresolved. Aulus left Rome, feasting, glad-handing, showing an early common touch and leaving his debts behind. When locals along the route north asked if he had enjoyed his breakfast, he belched loudly to prove it.

Aulus was a man for all men. He saw nothing wrong with a belch or a fart. These bodily functions were forces of nature, and many of the grandest philosophers he had heard at the tables of emperors had argued for following nature's calls. A dish of beans in sweet and sour sauce, attributed to Apicius himself, became known as the Vitellian. Stoicism was about more than a stiff upper lip; it was about the undigested decay of food.

Within a month he was at the birthplace of Agrippina, Colonia Agrippinensis. The welcome for Aulus was at first no warmer than the weather. About half his troops claimed loyalty to Galba, but the other half, much noisier, felt that there was more plunder to be had from the tribes whose opposition to Nero had brought Galba to power. They wanted to fight Germans, not call a halt on the orders of someone whose authority was hardly that of a Caesar.

The legionaries did not trust the locals, whose married women wore their hair in turbans and worshipped goddesses that did the same. Their most profitable German partners were the local traders in slaves, the *mangones*, who bought captured prisoners and dressed them up to get a higher price in Rome. This was a business that a man could proudly boast on his tombstone.

Few wanted the inactivity which Galba's representative was demanding. To a visitor from Rome – and Aulus's military inexperience made him little more than a visitor – the Roman soldiers in Germany looked disconcertingly like Gauls and Germans themselves. The legions seemed like just another tribe wanting war. The flamboyant Caecina, resentful at his accusation for fraud further south, was not alone in wearing multicoloured patched Gallic trousers any more than he was alone in disaffection with Galba.

Aulus set about making himself popular as best he could. He had always liked to be liked; it was the skill that had kept him alive. The officers of Aulus's new legions ate from field tables without the couches and entertainments of Capri and the Palatine. Dogs chased hares across the white clay mugs from which they drank the local beer. He ensured that they ate well. Their best wine glasses may have been stamped with the head of Augustus, in glowing bottle-green, but their devotion to the line of the Caesars did not extend as strongly to anyone who merely lived in Caesar's house, particularly if his policies did not seem profitable to themselves.

It was not yet clear how much loyalty and discipline was at risk with the loss of the last man to boast the imperial bloodline. Julius Caesar himself had cleared the land of Cologne in retaliation for a native uprising and massacre of his soldiers. One of his many daggers was a talisman in the temple of Mars. This temple itself was a gift to Cologne because of the birth there of Agrippina. Cologne was a town of the Caesars from its creation.

No living soldier had served anyone but a descendant of the victim of the Ides of March, 44 BCE. The grid of streets was built around the east–west line of the sunrise on the birthday of Augustus.

Capricorn, Augustus's constellation among the gods, adorned the temple to the dead. It was more than 100 years since a teenage heir had discovered the power of his father's name and defeated larger armies that lacked that unifying force. Caligula and Nero had many failings as commanders, but the Caesar in their name was not one of them.

After the suicide of the last of Caesar's line, a laudatory red-lettered inscription to Nero was used as a sewer cover. There was panic and uncertainty. But all loyalty in Lower Germany was still fluid. Galba was little more than an ungenerous disciplinarian to those who had served him. He looked like an emperor, but he lacked the capricious generosity which troops had come to expect. He was grim and antiquarian in his brutality. He was not a Caesar, and he was a long way away in Rome. From the capital came rumours of demotions, decimations and a dogged refusal to pay bounties and bonuses which the legionaries believed they were owed.

Aulus looked as much like an emperor as Galba did. He was just as tall. His nose bent towards his chin. He was inexperienced in warfare but highly experienced in survival. He had never been a flatterer with words as his father had been. But he was a master of making himself popular by deeds, by cavorting with Tiberius, riding chariots with Caligula, applauding Nero's poetry and organising others to applaud. He had known hard times. He understood people whose times were much harder. If one set of soldiers could make Galba emperor, another might do the same for someone else.

43

FILL ME UP!

Rumours of how Galba was consolidating his power reached as far as Cologne. It seemed that in the *domus Caesaris*, which no longer had a Caesar, the new emperor was keen to clean house. Locusta the poisoner, mistress of the atropine, was condemned to a more public death than she had dispensed to others. Galba ordered her to be led in chains through the city before her execution. Along the same route clanked a long line of courtiers whom he deemed 'the scum that had come to the surface in Nero's day'.

Acte survived, escaping to Sardinia where she freed her own slaves as Actiani. Crispinilla too survived; she had helped to give Galba the confidence to challenge Nero. The people knew her name from stories of the Neronian court but she was close to Otho too, both of them sharing information that those seeking success under Galba would prefer to stay hidden. She knew what was in the food, and who was flattering whom in the bedrooms. She was as quick-witted as the consummate courtier needed to be, a quality no less valuable because Romans attributed it to the blood drawn to her brain by the African sun.

Once his purges were over, Galba began the task of staying in power, but little of his thinking leaked out into the army, not even to the part of it that had raised him to the throne. He still had no court himself, only three advisers of whom one, his former slave Icelus, was also his lover. No one in either of the German provinces knew anything of his plans. It was known that Galba would at some point name a successor, but not when or whom. Only one fact seemed to be agreed. Six months into his time in office, Galba was ever more certain that his task was a break with the recent past, not a continuation of it.

The armies of Germany were anxious most of all for the tradition of buying their loyalty. If there was not to be expansion of the empire, with the opportunities for plunder they had tasted against Vindex's rebels, there had to be gifts in cash paid from some part of the world that was already under Roman rule. Nero had heavily depleted the treasury and Galba had what looked like a principled objection to new public expenditure.

Otho had been popular with his legionaries in Lusitania. He was said to see himself as the man next in line. Many doubted this. Galba, it was feared, had not brought discipline back to Rome, financial and otherwise, in order for the throne to pass after his death to a playboy friend of Nero whose only military experience stemmed from Nero's desire to get him away from a woman married at different times to them both.

The result was a vacuum of the kind that the soldiers of the age without a Caesar, like the courtiers of the *domus Caesaris* before them, most abhorred. The idea that Galba might consider Aulus Vitellius, another playmate of the Caesars, seemed even less likely to the men of the German camps, even to those of them who had considered that option at all. When a wholly new name appeared in the rumours it was an equal shock.

Unknown to the legions of Germany, like almost every other fact in Rome, Galba was beginning to turn against Otho. He was settling instead on Lucius Calpurnius Piso, from one of those many old families who, from the beginning of Tiberius's rule, had considered themselves just as worthy of the throne as any adopted son of Augustus. Several members of the Piso family, for half a century from the death of Germanicus, had paid the price of their presumption.

Piso's family stretched back to Julius Caesar's colleagues and rivals, to Pompey the Great, to Crassus, crucifier of Spartacus's army, and to far beyond. In Galba's mind a young Piso would add lustre to his own line just as the youth's grim seriousness, hardened by the execution of his brothers and his own exile, would continue the style of rule that Rome would continue to need.

The watchwords of his new heir, Galba hoped, would be 'honour, liberty and friendship, the chief blessings of the human mind', and not what he had found on the Palatine, 'flattery, adulation and that worst poison of an honest heart, self-interest'. Otho in Rome, borrowing more and more money on the basis of his imminent adoption, had no more knowledge of the coming rebuff than did the armies far away.

Aulus commanded his own soldiers from his base in Cologne, but most of them lived in scattered camps throughout Lower Germany with little action required and little entertainment beyond grumbling about their prospects. This was a frontier army whose closest contact with the local peoples was with those trading them as slaves. Its great wall, three miles long and six feet thick, with nine gates and nineteen towers protected hardly more than the staff of the governor himself. Triple arches separated military traffic from pedestrians. There was little variety in the local stone – sandstone studded with quartz, dark varieties and pale – and less variety still in the amenities added in the twenty years of Agrippina's colony.

And whatever bars or bath houses there were in Cologne, most of the men were not even near them. They spent the days patrolling the mud of a river bank. They had no Caesar, no action and no certainty of new money. Easily disgruntled with Galba, they also lacked an obviously willing replacement. Aulus Vitellius was accused by his critics of many crimes, but arrogant ambition was never one of them. His men waited for a lead from somewhere else.

In Upper Germany, the part closer to Rome, there was the same disgruntlement but also an ambitious, charismatic commanding officer, Caecina Alienus, who needed a survival strategy of his own. Caecina was only in his mid-twenties. He had neither the name, age nor position to seek the throne for himself. He faced a death penalty from Galba for corruption and little opportunity to defend himself in the purge of those deemed corrupt at Nero's court. He began agitating on Vitellius's behalf. So too did Fabius Valens, once an enthusiastic participant in Nero's military parades for youth, now free for new enthusiasms.

Results came fast. At the new year of 69 CE Aulus learnt that two of the Upper German legions, standing between himself and Rome, had refused the traditional annual oath of allegiance to their emperor. He treated this news with care. Although his formal duty was to enforce that allegiance, that was not necessarily the best way to survive. He had no control over Caecina or Valens. He was not agitating for himself, but excessive modesty might be as dangerous for him as excess ambition.

Anyone who knew of the auguries at his birth could, by the rules of the age, have been reasonably cautious. Anyone who knew the balance of power after the death of Nero had to recognise that an army might want to be the power, not merely follow a leader. Aulus at first showed some of the caution he had learnt on the Palatine and in Capri. From Cologne he sent a message that legions of Rome should either prepare to enforce allegiance to Galba on dissenting colleagues or prepare to support a new emperor.

Aulus maybe hoped for a lengthy period before a reply. If so, he was disappointed. On the second day of January, barely twenty-four hours after the first refusal of the oath, Fabius Valens brought back an answer, not one Aulus had been actively seeking but one he could not for long ignore.

The troops in Upper Germany would not coerce their colleagues who had rejected Galba. Instead, encouraged by Caecina, they had broken such few statues of Galba that they had and declared themselves loyal only to the letters SPQR on their standards, to the Senate and People of Rome. This was a meaningless cover for rebellion. There had to be an emperor for them to accept or deny. The Augustan state could not keep the peace merely by existing, by pretending that the SPQR was still in place. That kind of peace was gone.

In Rome many members of the senatorial aristocracy, former governors and generals or their descendants, would have seen chances for themselves in these events. But none had soldiers at the time when soldiers were needed. On Aulus Vitellius's behalf, the troops in Germany became their own leaders. Valens's route to the centre of Cologne was up the vertical axis of a cross, directly through the south gate of the massive walls, along the muddy north–south road towards the east–west road lit perfectly by the sun on Augustus's birthday. Escorting him was a band of Roman and local cavalry, a ragged retinue of tiny horses and sword-swinging riders. Almost as though Galba were no more alive than was Augustus, they hailed Aulus as emperor.

Valens entered the governor's mansion in search of the beneficiary of his efforts. It was hardly an imperial palace. It was closer in appearance to the cold stone of Julius Caesar's Rome than the marbled splendour that five subsequent Caesars had bequeathed to the Capitol, Forum and the Palatine. Its bricks were stamped with *Ex Germ Inf*, the sign of the brickworks where too many of his soldiers had to labour. The view east to the Rhine reminded no one of that to the Tiber.

The dining room was heated by a wood-burning stove, the bedroom damp and cold. The new Emperor Vitellius had only the authority that he was about to be given. He was following orders, not giving them. He had to emerge from his quarters in trousers and tunic, without time to change into a general's uniform, still less a toga. An enthusiastic soldier handed him the dagger of Julius Caesar that he had taken from the shrine to Mars, the war god.

On his first morning of elevation Aulus was carried high by his troops on a tour of the sodden town, the grim, grey towers, the temple to I.O.M. that was neither Optimus or Maximus to anyone used to the Capitol of Rome. He waved Caesar's dagger as the only visible sign of the difference between that day and the day before until he returned to his headquarters to find it in flames.

It seemed as though Galba or the gods had taken instant revenge. The dining-room stove was quickly decreed the culprit, not the last time that Aulus Vitellius would be pursued by legends of the table. The superstitious troops still saw the blaze as an ill omen until Aulus found sufficient wit for a tricky moment, hardly the sophistication for which his father had been famed but good enough. 'Do not lose heart,' he declared. 'To us a light is given.' He then led his followers to a dining room that had been spared the flames and to a large lunch, with wines from the south, reported and recorded for posterity.

Aulus did not send any announcement to Rome. He neither claimed the throne for himself from the senate and people, nor claimed that he was taking over to end the tyranny of his predecessor. He acted as though wholly satisfied to be emperor of Cologne, enjoying food and drink fit for his new status and delaying the date when he might be required to do anything else.

He saw no need for haste. There was wine from the south as well as local freshwater. There were forests of game, fish delivered from the north, a military harbour, quartz quarries for glass, long pipes from the hills and vast sewers into the Rhine. There were kitchens and echoing halls. The money that Agrippina had released for her birthplace colony had been spent in more useful ways than if she had been born in Tibur. Cologne was ready for a man ready to use what others had built. Drinking cups carried the mottoes *VIVAS*, 'To Life and Health', and *REPLE*, 'Fill Me Up'.

44

A HARD MAN TO FLATTER

Even if Aulus was not communicating with Rome, it was clear to Valens and Caecina that Galba would soon learn of events in Germany, the refusal of the new year oath and the elevation of Vitellius, the first an unwelcome but manageable surprise, the second doubtless a cause for incredulity. It would not have been hard to imagine the mockery at the news that the master of the fowl and seafood courses was claiming the mastery of all lands and seas ruled by Rome.

The legions of the Rhine needed fast to live up to their fearsome reputation in order that Galba's tiny court of advisers, his fellow soldier, his lawyer and his lover, should fall as fast as it had risen. Fortunately the winter stayed warm, the conditions for marching south much easier than in a normal season. Caecina and Valens, sticking to their preference for keeping as far away from each other as possible, divided between them what could now be described as the Vitellian forces.

Caecina was the keenest to leave, Valens as determined that his rival should not race ahead. Caecina took the shorter, more arduous route through the Alps. Valens, with a convenient eagle flying for his soothsayers, took his soldiers, with his personal train of camp-followers, on the longer march through Gaul to the Mediterranean coast.

Aulus needed little persuasion to stay in Cologne with a largely fictional main force ready to follow when required. At his personal communications centre, rebuilt and restored from the fire that was his own 'light' from the gods, he would receive bulletins both on the progress of his army and how Galba was planning to respond.

Soon enough there was news. Soon it was a time of bloodshed like no one had known since Caesar's conquests. Valens, he learnt, had been unable to stop his men from slaughtering thousands of German tribesmen. For most years during the empire, the madness – or even the sanity – of succession politics at Rome made little difference to life in the provinces. But in January 69 CE the men of what would later become Metz succumbed to mass murder driven not by greed for plunder but by a political transformation. The horror was hardly a credit to Valens's authority. Aulus might hope, and see it as a warning against future resistance. Hoping was all that he could do. From Caecina there were few reports of any kind.

Then, after only a few weeks as emperor of the sodden Rhinelands, there was news for Aulus from Rome that was more dramatic than anything from his armies. His enemy on the Palatine, he learnt, was no longer Galba but his old friend from the days of Nero, the newly proclaimed Emperor Otho. Galba had made a massive mistake in preferring the aristocrat over the playboy as his successor. In announcing his choice of Piso, he had not even flattered the palace guard for their exemplary loyalty while the Rhine army was in revolt. Nor did he promise the cash that they still believed was theirs.

Otho had not accepted the demotion of his hopes. He was deep in debt, his creditors were everywhere, even his house was collapsing, and he had secured just enough of a final loan to pay for a team of assassins. He appointed one of his freedmen to organise the murder. He appointed another to be his head of the navy and chief agent for ensuring the loyalty of any unreliable senators.

He and his agents bribed a group of guards to proclaim a new regime and agree to accept their due financial reward as soon as the stingy Galba was dead. Their code word, which would have aroused no suspicion, was that it was 'time to meet with the master builder'. Otho needed many meetings with his master builders for his notoriously crumbling house. He had no money to pay them, but intended that he would soon be housed at the public expense.

By the time that Aulus was reading his dispatches in Cologne, Otho was already master of the halls where both of them had served in the very recent past. Even in faraway Carthage, a freed slave called Crescens was holding a huge feast in support of Otho's claims, a new reminder of how politics and banqueting had been linked in the previous century.

The first plan had been to kill Galba while he was at dinner, not usually a long opportunity. Galba got away and had been confident enough to climb to the temple of I.O.M to give thanks for his preservation. This preservation was not long. An emperor without a court, he had been dragged from his litter while passing through the Forum, finally and desperately telling his attackers that, if they spared his life, they would be paid.

The urban civil war had been short. If Vitellius had any doubts about the launch of a longer war on his own account, it was already too late. Otho, it seemed, had handled the heads of both Galba and Piso and was particularly delighted with that of his aristocratic rival for the succession. Galba's head had reached the palace with a soldier's thumb in its mouth for easier portability.

Aulus knew his new enemy. He knew the courtly facts about him, that he was a small man, with spreading toes, thinning hair and face whitened by make-up. Aulus had been with Nero when the emperor wanted Otho's wife Poppaea as his empress. Otho was not unlike Nero; he was not ashamed of that and at first used the name Nero Otho in his letters.

Otho would not risk being the enemy to the palace guard that Galba had become; the early news was clear about that. At an extravagant banquet, designed to win senatorial support, the eating was interrupted by a revolt of Praetorian soldiers who feared that Otho was planning a surrender. He had to climb on to a couch to calm a revolt that had been launched on his own behalf.

The senate was successfully flattered. Otho was happy to appear as an old servant when he was the new master. That was an easy deception for a veteran of the Palatine. Early news suggested that there would be no purge of Galba's supporters, more a realistic acceptance that men and women had to make their peace with power.

Crispinilla was still surviving the calls from the mob that she be executed for her stewardship of Nero's orgies. Galba's lover, Icelus, had ensured Nero's last wish not to be decapitated before burial.

This had not helped him. He had been crucified as a slave even though he was a freedman. There was no great concern at Rome for a freed slave, however rich he had become by Galba's side – richer, it was said, and certainly more rapidly richer, than any freedman of Claudius or Nero.

Letters directly from Otho began to arrive at Cologne. Aulus's brother, Lucius, was now a hostage. Otho offered safety for Lucius and a luxury retirement for Aulus if the march on Rome by Caecina and Valens were to cease. Assassins began to arrive too, easily identifiable among the tiny population of the army town but a clear statement of intent.

Aulus sent back letters and assassins of his own, threatening dire consequences to Otho's family if any harm befell his mother. The safety of his wife, Galeria, was assured, he believed, because a senior member of Otho's court was a member of her family. His letters offered Otho the same retirement terms that he had been offered himself. His assassins were slightly more likely to survive in crowded Rome than Otho's in Cologne, but there was little expectation that the outcome would be decided by a single dagger.

Otho would not be an easy rival to dislodge. The new emperor, hailed like Galba by a senate without soldiers, was knowing and cunning. When it seemed that Nero's name was not as popular as he had supposed, he stopped using it. Otho knew much more than had Galba about the mechanisms of making a house a place from which to rule. He was hard to deceive by flattery. He knew its rules too well.

Aulus had no option but to stay behind his generals and, since he could not retreat, aim to defeat him by older ways. Little happened in Lower Germany. His few imperial duties were to try prisoners sent back by Caecina. In preparation for what he hoped would be a respected reign ahead, he acquitted several troublemakers who made good speeches before the soldiers' juries.

45

BROTHER BEHIND THE LINES

Lucius Vitellius was the younger brother of Rome's new emperor in Cologne, but that did not necessarily make him an enemy to Otho in Rome. The two brothers had worked together in Africa, Lucius following Aulus as governor in what to the Africans must have been one unbroken regime. But, when the stakes were the rule of the whole empire, it cannot have been obvious to Lucius that his brother was the right man to back, that Aulus would win if he fought Otho or even that he would fight at all.

Lucius knew enough about Aulus to think that he might prefer doing nothing to doing anything. To have two emperors, neither of whom had known about the other's ascent, was clearly ludicrous. It was disorienting for the palace guard, who depended on a single emperor and did not have one. It was a misunderstanding that caused chaos whenever a suspicious guardsman saw something untoward. But it need not lead to civil war.

No one should want civil war, certainly not anyone trained in the *domus Caesaris* that had emerged from so many civil war years. Otho was no Julius Caesar. Aulus was most certainly no Augustus. One of the two might back down and Aulus, feeding his face far from Rome, was perhaps the man more likely to choose luxury retirement.

Aulus's soldiers might want to fight. But civil war was both harder and less profitable than terrorising northern tribesmen. Civil war brought with it not just the prospect of killing former friends but the convention which prevented the defeated being ransomed or enslaved. Neither Otho nor Aulus were from a world where Romans fighting Romans made sense. Otho held the throne in Rome. It made no sense for Lucius to assume that he would lose it. Accepting flattery for himself as a Vitellian, a man of new and greater interest might, temporarily at least, be enough.

Throughout the warm January there was ample time to consider these assumptions and enough ignorance of the facts for encouragement of theory. There were more immediate distractions too. The Tiber was in constant flood, a city bridge collapsed to become a dam and river waters destroyed gardens and shops. The possibility, or not, of hostile armies emerging from the north was a problem for Lucius much further away.

Food may have been plentiful in Cologne, but in Rome prices were soaring, apartments were tumbling into flooded basements and the people were nostalgic for Nero who, while debasing the currency, at least gave them Caesar's bread. Otho, like Nero, ordered the minting of silver coins linking himself to Ceres, the goddess of the corn. It was soon requiring silver even to buy a loaf. Otho's own silver was reserved for paying his troops and avoiding the fate of stingy Galba.

Lucius was probably free to leave Rome for the north and join his brother's forces, but it was a probability that he did not test. There were rumours, no more yet than that, of legions of the Rhine, loyal to Aulus, popping from the Alpine passes like stoppers from a jar. It was all almost fantastical. In Cologne, even if he reached that far, he, Lucius Vitellius, would be merely the younger Vitellius yet again. By staying in Rome he could best be useful to Otho, if required, useful to Aulus, if that seemed appropriate, useful to their mother, which Aulus would surely approve, and useful to himself whoever was the winner.

Otho, however, had no need of Lucius except as a hostage. He already had the service of many Romans who considered themselves useful, even invaluable, and were not the brother of the friend who had become his enemy. The servility of senators and junior officials to a new emperor was astonishing even to those who had attended the court of Nero. Statues of Poppaea, who had been wife to them both, sprung up again as though at a party she had never left. Aulus was no longer part of the party.

In the middle of February the first reliable news came to Rome of the twin attack by Valens and Caecina. Rome itself had no military defence apart from palace guardsmen more effective at court politics than against defenders of the Rhine frontier. Otho summoned the best imperial legions from the Danube, assembled his best generals and prepared for what seemed, unless a deal could be done, to be the most likely battlefield – on the long, broad plain north of the River Po.

For the legionaries from the Rhine Rome would be their destination, not the source of their power. Otho knew enough not to rely on the young men of the Palatine who dressed themselves as Greek heroes and packed their travelling kits for feasting and fornicating along the way. One of his courtly soldiers was Gaius Julius Antiochus Epiphanes, prince of Commagene, nephew of Aka, the wife of Tiberius's Thrasyllus. Antiochus was just one of the many fish struggling without the political water that was all they knew and needed.

Otho needed brute force to meet the brute forces against him. He prepared his own uniform as a regular foot-soldier. He had learnt more in Lusitania than those who remembered his Palatine days expected or would know themselves. He hoped to join his Danube legions and deal separately with Caecina and Valens, either by diplomacy or by battle, before they could unite. Their mutual enmity was his own best friend, he hoped.

His last speech in Rome was a triumph, possibly too good to have been written by its speaker. The likely writer was the orator Publius Galerius Trachalus, whom Aulus was relying upon to protect Galeria, his wife, who was still in Rome with their children. Otho did not even name Aulus and accused the Rhine legions merely of restless credulity. It was met with lengthy applause of the kind given to Nero's singing and Caligula's virtuosity on the chariot. Lucius Vitellius prepared to join Otho on the journey north.

By the middle of March, Lucius was one of some 5,000 men who had marched out with Otho, stopping fifteen miles behind the main forces ahead. His final destination, not of his own choice but very satisfactory for him, was Brixellum, a small town in the fertile flat fields south of the Po, home to farmers of pigs, vines and wool. The land was slowly drying in the spring winds, every day becoming easier terrain for fighting.

A war was beginning but neither Aulus, still in Cologne, nor Otho, nearer but no better an example to his men, would witness the first battle for their futures. Lucius and Otho had to wait in Brixellum for news brought back by messenger to the drainage ditches and grape trellises. Aulus would learn nothing till all was over.

In the first week of April Otho made one brief visit to what had become the front line outside the small town of Bedriacum on the north side of the Po. He did not stay long. Only when he returned to Brixellum with a large escorting force were Lucius and Otho's other camp-followers able to know what had happened since the Vitellians arrived in Italy.

It was a picture without clear prediction for the future. Caecina had been active for almost two weeks. It was no longer a magical success to bring an army through the Alps (Hannibal's pioneering journey was almost 300 years before), but it was still a surprise to the detachments of Otho's force whom he had quickly overwhelmed. Just as reportable, and maybe more disturbing to Lucius, was the arrival of Caecina's wife, with a full cavalry escort, on a horse decorated in purple as though she, not Aulus's wife Galeria, were the next empress.

Caecina had then, it seemed, been beaten badly in a rushed assault on the town of Placentia. He had been keener to defeat Otho's armies before Valens arrived than on any victory itself. Otho's men, by contrast, felt that their own generals were too patient and had not pressed their advantage. Caecina had won a cavalry battle. His men had wounded the prince of Commagene, the kind of detail that looks good in dispatches while making no difference to any outcome. Otho's men were close to revolt again over the caution of their commanders, whom they accused of being at heart on the side of the Rhine army, if not of Aulus Vitellius himself.

Little was clear. The arrival of Valens had not immediately helped the Vitellians' cause. His troops, like those of Otho, accused their commander of insufficient loyalty to their emperor and, even worse, of hiding plunder beneath his tent that should have been shared with his men. They forced him to escape dressed as slave and dug up his quarters, from bed-tents to banqueting tents, before allowing him back. Caecina referred to Valens as 'a disgusting old git' and Valens called Caecina 'a pompous prat'. This was not an alliance that, to Lucius, seemed a secure investment for himself. Until the facts were less like smoke, the peace of Brixellum suited him well.

Otho's own response was to stay in Brixellum too. His brief council of war had decided on a rapid attack while the Vitellians were in disarray, and a role for himself that was wholly behind the scenes. He feared that if Aulus were to be following Caecina through the melted Alpine ice, the soldiers of the Vitellii would be yet further emboldened. Aulus was still in Cologne and in no hurry to leave, but neither Otho nor Lucius could be sure of that.

Bravery would have been foolhardy for Otho's cause. He had announced no heir and thus a victory for his forces in which their commander died would be a total defeat. Lucius too saw no advantage in declaring his loyalty. Brixellum, its vineyards, pig fields and wool-carders, was to remain Otho's base – and Lucius's too until such time as he saw both an opportunity to leave, and a benefit in leaving.

The next news to reach Brixellum, only a few days later in the middle of April, was of the total defeat of the forces fighting for Otho. When Otho's supporters at his base camp showed themselves ready to fight on, Lucius quickly saw the dangers of the rear becoming the front line. He and other senators retreated, bickering and backing further down the road to Rome. Fortunately for everyone, Otho killed himself at dawn after the news came. His last words for Vitellius were that he should enjoy his family. His last part in the drama of court politics was soon deemed his finest.

In their early days on the Palatine and at Capri, both Otho and Aulus had learnt to present themselves for theatrical effect. Otho's death prevented many further deaths, and the reports of it to the retreating party from Bologna ensured that this part of the story was at an end. Reports of it to Rome ensured that Aulus Vitellius, first hailed merely by soldiers at Cologne, was pronounced emperor by the senate and people, where emperors were supposed to be pronounced. The new emperor continued his march south.

46

WINE FOR THE BATTLEFIELD

In Lugdunum, to the west between Cologne and Bedriacum, stood a memorial to one of the most respected side-changers from the entire century of the Caesars. Lucius Munatius Plancus founded the colony in the year after Caesar's assassination while he was still trying to decide whether the assassins or one of Caesar's would-be heirs deserved his support. He was organising banquets for Cleopatra till only a few weeks before her defeat which brought the emperor Augustus to power. While he was flattering his way back to favour with the new regime, Horace wrote for him a wry ode reminding him of his mistaken past, the benefits of bureaucratic peace (not least his home by the waterfalls of Tibur) and of bygones being bygones. Plancus quickly became a pillar of the new order.

His past foundation of Lugdunum, beside a river so slow-flowing that no one could tell its direction, became just one of his achievements, a town of baths fed by foaming aqueducts, with a massive amphitheatre used by emperors on their frequent visits as well as a luxurious place of exile for unwanted eastern kings. Both Claudius and Germanicus were born there. It was a very Roman city where rich men's freedmen boasted freed slaves of their own.

Lugdunum's position on the gold road from Spain made it ideal for the minting of money for troops. This was the place where an incautious master coiner once declared the newly dead Tiberius a god before learning that the official designation by Caligula was maniac instead. It was the empire's only mint until Nero ordered his own coinage struck in Rome. A little more than a century after Plancus's statue first rose from the mud, this was the well-chosen site, still 500 miles from Bedracium, where Aulus Vitellius, moving slowly south, ordered the senior survivors of his victory to meet.

The newly unchallenged emperor did not yet look the part. While the tradesman of Cologne provided food fit for his station, no one offered suitable clothes. Only the governor of Lugdunum gave him the gold and purple that prevented him having to re-enter Italy in the shabby garb in which he had left. Once appropriately dressed, he was keen to congratulate his supporters, accommodate those who had fought against him and plan a long trip to Rome to claim what he already owned.

Vitellius was not alone in getting new clothes. He raised his stammering son to the imperial purple too and renamed him Germanicus, the heir to his father as the original Germanicus had once been to Tiberius. This must have seemed a doubtful double augury for the boy. Many remembered the murder of the first Germanicus and the trial which did so much for the new emperor's uncle. A few too might have recalled the role Plancina, wife of Piso, Plancus's granddaughter.

Once a man was emperor every event of his past became history, a piece of something that mattered as well as merely having happened. Publius Vitellius had not proved that Plancina's husband was a murderer, but now he was important again. That was the relevant truth. The daughter of Lugdunum's founder had been protected by her friendship with Augustus's long-surviving widow, Livia. That too was now part of the story of the Vitellii.

At Lugdunum power began with the personal. Showing a matrimonial jealousy unusual at the highest levels of Rome, Aulus ordered the pursuit and execution of the man who had married his first wife, Petronia. He promised a seemingly modest marriage for his young daughter, Vitellia. Her husband was set to be the governor of north-eastern Gaul, Decimus Valerius Atticus, wealthy and himself from a Gallic family. There was not yet a new web of imperial connections but, even without the Caesars, there were still many traditional roles for the family of an emperor, enemy, heir apparent, mother behind the scenes, brother as protector and maybe heir too if anything were to happen to the son.

Aulus commissioned coins that showed his father, Lucius, as he had never been portrayed in his lifetime, leaner-faced than his son, smug and smiling. Aulus's mother remained a reluctant convert to respect for the new emperor, especially dismissive of her grandson's new name. She had known the original Germanicus, not well but enough to know that the boy presented to the crowd at Lugdunum did not deserve the name. Nor did her son, who had added Germanicus to his own names. She had given birth, she said, only to a Vitellius.

As Aulus left Lugdunum there was already the clash of advisers for which the Palatine was well prepared. Cluvius Rufus, an historian and former supporter of Otho, joined the travelling court from Spain and immediately clashed with one of Aulus's freedmen, Hilarius. Cluvius, an eloquent orator too, found himself accused of trying to establish a breakaway province. Cluvius won his case. He was a supporter of Vitellius now. He understood the senate as he understood the theatre, and he knew the mood in still-faraway Rome.

Lines of responsibility were more fluid than in Rome, where courtiers had clearer roles – for answering letters, writing speeches, vetting appointments and negotiating with supplicants. In Rome only the very senior courtiers crossed boundaries into each other's areas of responsibility. On the road men might be masters of all trades. Cluvius became more than a supporter – a new senior courtier to the Emperor Aulus Germanicus Vitellius.

In Rome the palace guards were the only soldiers close to the men and women running the household. In a military camp there were soldiers in daily attendance. Neither group knew easily how to deal with the other. Aulus flattered his soldiers, and the soldiers flattered him in return by praising his freedmen. They called for one of the grandest of them to be promoted to the status of a knight with the right to wear gold rings on his fingers, the degree immediately below that of a senator. Aulus was reluctant and confused. He agreed the promotion but continued in private to address him as a former slave, soon crucifying him as a slave too for a crime of alleged corruption.

In place of some senior freedmen, Vitellius also promoted Roman businessmen of the class just below the senate, favouring especially those who had witnessed his initial elevation before the northern legions. To have been at Cologne was an honour, to be at Lugdunum too. Household roles were accepted by members of Rubellius Blandus's class as a promotion, an award of jobs which once they would have despised, an expansion of a policy that Claudius had cautiously begun. This began slowly to transform the way in which imperial courts were staffed, if less so the nature of the courts themselves.

The new emperor was keen to attend the gladiatorial games which Caecina and Valens were planning in his honour in local towns near Bedriacum. He also wanted to see the battlefield itself and the tomb of Otho at Brixellum, which he had been assured was suitably small. Word spread that he intended to continue the party of Cologne. Carriages of finest seafood queued to meet the imperial demand. Boxing bouts became drunken riots. The great survivor, Lucius Munatius Plancus, a general once prepared to crawl across Cleopatra's floors in the costume of a mermaid, was the perfect presiding spirit.

It was a long and slow journey into Italy. Not till he was at Bedriacum did Aulus see how he had won his victory – or at least how he might plausibly claim to have won it. He did not lack help. Caecina and Valens explained their exploits. Unusually for court life, despite the chaos, there was enough glory to go round.

Otho's men, he learnt, fought better than expected. Their guardsmen from Rome may have been reinforced with actors and dancers; they may have been more used to watching slaughter in the arena than fighting for a cause; but they had driven back Caecina's troops in the first battle for Placentia, dropping millstones and other heavy agricultural equipment on the heads of attackers who were drunk, hungover or both.

The final victory was clear enough: the enemy commander was dead. But there was great doubt, until a common story could be agreed, over who had fought for whom, how genuinely, how loyally and sometimes whether they had fought at all. Otho's troops had suspected that their own commitment was greater than that of their commanders. It suited those same former commanders for Otho, newly pardoned at Lugdunum, to suggest that this fear had indeed been justified: they had been sympathetic to Aulus Vitellius all along.

Caecina, it seemed, had been both at his boldest and weakest before Valens arrived. He had given no order to attack Otho's men in a single massive strike. He had had to move on to softer targets in order to claim a victory. It was hard to be sure if this had been right or wrong, but there were enough ambushes and raids to enliven the war stories on both sides.

Mutinies were just as numerous. Caecina had to show Aulus his firmness in dealing with a mutiny among his men without taking responsibility for the mutiny having happened in the first place. Valens had to explain his own mutinies. His escape from his men while disguised as a slave had to be turned into a triumph of adventure. The commanders vied with each other to show a valiant progress from risk to reward.

The coordination and final victory of Vitellius's forces had come most from the anxiety of Valens's soldiers that they might be deprived of victory's revenge, the profits of loot. They had raced and joined their comrades from the Rhine while Valens himself was still considering his options. The central truth was that the Rhine army was superior to that from the Danube, even if many of Otho's troops had the fiercer loyalty to their emperor.

Otho, however, had failed to match that loyalty – and doomed himself by his impatience. He was not an easy man to advise or control. His years as a courtier had inured him to most forms of flattery. While some men on the Palatine were forever addicted to false words, Otho in Lusitania remembered enough to make him sick.

Patience might have triumphed for Otho if he had allowed it. The Vitellians had pillaged the ground behind them and were short of supplies. Otho had access to provisions from the whole of Italy and Rome itself. He could have waited. Instead he ordered a mass assault before all his reinforcements were in place.

From the safety of Brixellum, with Lucius Vitellius uneasy at his side, Otho had waited for news of a battle that he need not have fought until his enemy was weaker. Caecina and Valens had subdued their rivalries for a final act of joint intimidation above their enemy's camp. It was this solidarity which persuaded Otho's commanders to surrender. These were all claims and controversies of the kind that battlefield tourists appreciated – and always have. Failings were forgotten, bravery remembered, blame distributed as far as possible to the dead.

Although the battle stories had been cleaned up for the victor from Cologne, the battlefield had not. Ears were more easily deceived than eyes. In civil wars the fallen were often quickly removed, their relatives near, the first scavengers knowing what the dead would have wanted as well as what the living might want from their corpses. But the fighters at Bedriacum were all far from home, not permitted to enslave or take prisoners for ransom, only intermittently obedient to their commanders.

Forty days after the final fighting there was still much around Bedriacum to show what had happened there, corpses of all ranks wearing what had once been the labels of life, faces with papery eyes, cavernous stomachs, severed hands, ditches of blood and spears, cheap dented helmets, arms and men smashed beyond use by any but farmers who would soon again be trimming their vines. Aulus Vitellius was later credited with the line, delivered after much use of medicinal alcohol, that dead enemies smelt sweet but dead Roman enemies even sweeter.

More than half a century before, Aulus's uncle, Publius, had seen the grim impact on Germanicus's men of visiting the Teutoburg forest, where Varus had lost five of Augustus's legions. That journey of expiation had been taken ten years after the *clades* that would forever bear Varus's name. At Bedriacum the evidence of war was fresher, the flat land black with gorging birds, black kites and vultures, black shrikes and crows, mountain birds in a long landscape stretching towards invisible peaks. The bloody fields would soon be vineyards again, but meanwhile the army of Vitellius began its slow progress south, a growing court of wine-sellers and cooks in close attendance.

The men deserved a mighty party to clear their minds. It was several weeks before Aulus finished his journey from Cologne to what became the greatest Roman banquet that anyone could imagine. Lucius Vitellius, conscious perhaps that he had not committed himself to the Vitellian cause as courageously and completely as he might have done, was ready to be the most enthusiastic master of ceremonies.

47

THE SHIELD OF MINERVA

Sea fish travelled alive in wooden barrels of saltwater, heavy cargoes requiring round-bottomed transport ships or carriages capable of dragging artillery to war or silver for soldiers, or whatever was needed at the time. It was a trade whose profits depended on assessing faraway demand. A red mullet from Marseilles might be worth a small fortune one day and nothing the next. A scorpion fish, washed up on the rock beaches of Germany where Publius had almost lost his men, could find a high price as long as it was where men were competing to feed an emperor with a reputation. So could prawns from the most prized Greek islands, anchovies from the Black Sea, the sea urchins of Egypt and the oysters of Britain, sometimes rushed to market by teams of runners if the boats and trucks were too slow. However exaggerated some of the stories of Aulus's gluttony became, there seems little doubt that the victory of Valens and Caecina at Bedriacum was good for the exotic fish trade.

Between Bedriacum and Brixellum there was at first little cause for a party. The roads showed fresher signs of savagery than the battlefield itself. While Caecina and Valens had been warily celebrating in Lugdunum, their men had begun a neighbourhood riot of plunder and destruction. The defeated too had joined in to take their share. For the families farming beside the Po, or fishing coarse carp or catfish in its streams, the aftermath of the battle was more brutal than the fighting. The wiser tradesmen kept their distance. The victorious armies were like an inland sea, controlled by no one but the distant tides. Only the returning commanders, with Aulus Vitellius newly at their head, restored the order of before.

At Brixellum there was the site of Otho's headquarters, closer to the battle than Aulus had ever been but arguably more a sign of cowardice. Here the emperor's brother could add to the family story.

Lucius could explain his frustration at being held behind the lines, even if not all believed him. He could report the stubborn loyalty of the enemy officers, not a group easy for a brother of Vitellius to live among. He could show Otho's personal tents and the remains of documents and letters. Otho had maybe destroyed his records in order that his supporters, or those undecided, should not suffer when Aulus was in power. Or maybe Otho had been burnishing his reputation in other ways; but the murder of Galba would not be so easily expunged.

Aulus and Lucius could discuss tombs, two brothers in a family which now had claims on grandeur. Otho's was small, his body burnt to ash to save it from desecration. Nero, the last of the Caesars, lay in the tomb only of his father's family. The mausoleum of Augustus was filled with many who had hoped to succeed and died too early. There was no such vault for the Vitellii yet.

Lucius was determined to allay any doubts about his own place in the new imperial family. His first marriage had been to Augustus's great-great-granddaughter, Junia Calvina; his second wife, Triaria, was ferocious for her new family's regime. The Vitellii of the third generation, like Lucius and Publius in the second, were a contrasting pair. But Lucius was already Aulus's fiercest defender as their armies swarmed, unopposed, upon the capital, a gastronomic march on Rome.

The most efficient way of cooking for successful troops on the march was to roast meat. As far back as the epics of Homer, this was the way. Roasting needed the fewest dishes and plates. It was not a lesson that the Vitellii brothers intended to apply. Chefs accompanied the soldiers as though they were the cavalry protecting their flanks, a parody, both in the act and in the telling, of the great imperial cavalcades through the countryside, the *comites*, by which Augustus and his successors had dispensed law and power.

The troops ate well off the summer lands, their officers from the wagons from distant seas, and all displayed the easy debauchery that Romans preferred to associate with foreigners. The standard fare may have been little more than *Pisa Vitelliana*, the eponymous paste of peas or beans, pepper, ginger, lovage, hard-boiled yolks and honey. The only memory for later writers was of vastly expensive food, regularly demanded, imported and consumed by Vitellius, sometimes four times a day, in his borrowed imperial regalia.

The finest food for the march was garlanded like the most successful general, wreathed in laurel like a conquering hero. The serving dishes were called *fercula*, the word once used for the carts that hauled the gold and silver in a triumphal parade. The feasting was a form of reward for Vitellius's flatterers, a substitute for the real power he had not yet achieved, and perhaps an obliterating therapy for himself.

Valens and Caecina were becoming even more like courtiers and less like commanders. Valens ordered from Rome a huge cast of actors to add to the entertainment, aiming to impress both Vitellius and, more importantly, all the other would-be members of the emperor's court who were presenting their credentials. The civilians created too much of a party atmosphere for some of the soldiers' tastes. Admiring applause was fine; stealing swords and belts was not. Swords were drawn and spectators killed, a spree that ended only when one of the dead was found to be the father of a man welcoming his son back from the wars.

Lucius began preparation for his brother's *Cena Adventica*, the banquet that would mark Aulus's arrival in his capital. The finest fish needed the finest plate. No pottery dish could be found that was large enough. When Apicius was making his pancakes of fish and thrushes' breasts, he recommended the added satisfaction that would come from a silver dish, not just because of its value but the possibility of its greater size. It was a horrible vice, said Horace, to pay a huge price at market only to squeeze the purchase on to a plate that was too small.

Silver was the favoured metal from which the rich should eat, mined in Spain, hammered and riveted into giant dishes decorated with what they were made to contain. There was no lack of such silver at Rome. Connoisseurs collected examples from the empire, exhibiting the treasures in their homes, buying antiques from the masters of the Greek workshops. In the reign of Claudius the freedman Rotundus Drusillianus, once the property of Caligula's favourite and most notorious sister, had been just one who collected tableware on this grand scale. Fruits of land and sea, dogs and dolphins danced around the rim of many a plate which a new emperor might acquire, or which might be offered for his use.

The Vitellii had not extended the empire, nor even visited very much of it, but on their 'Shield of Minerva', a gleaming dish of epic name and proportions, would lie the produce of everywhere from Parthia, still unconquered, to the Pillars of Hercules between the Mediterranean and the Atlantic, still passed only by the few. Aulus and his new court would dine off Spanish silver on pikes' livers streaked in red and yellow, sperm of lampreys, brains of pheasant and peacock, tongues of flamingos.

Much lesser food would be served to thousands of soldiers and citizens, roasts and fish stew, the lesser parts of the lampreys as once offered by Julius Caesar. Not everyone could celebrate with silver on the delicacies that showed Rome's reach beyond the Euphrates and the Ocean. But every rich variety, more like vomit to later minds, would become a metaphor for wider ills. When Agrippa Postumus was exiled by Augustus for excessive fishing in the guise of the god Neptune, it was a single charge against a soon-to-be forgotten man. The charge against Vitellius of excessive fish-eating would never die.

The final progress to the dining tables was as slow as Aulus's exit from Cologne. Some of the German troops, who had never seen Rome before, rushed ahead to see for themselves the Palatine, the temple of Jupiter Optimus and Maximus and between them in the Forum the place where Galba had died. The narrow streets were awkward for the new arrivals. They found Romans as bemused by their long swords and leather jackets as they themselves were surprised at the massed white togas of officials, and would-be officials, for the new reign. The abundance of ovens for the coming feasts was less of a surprise. Violence of a mostly good-natured kind was no surprise at all.

Behind these men of the Rhine army, as he had been ever since their departure, Aulus Vitellius had to make his own choice of dress. He had options. He was no longer dependent on the hasty packing at his house in Rome when Galba was still alive, nor on the generosity of the Roman governor at Lugdunum who had fitted him for the role he was about to take. His first thought was to wear the red cloak of a conquering general, to ride on a great horse with a conqueror's sword at his side. The theatre of war was beginning to suit him.

But Aulus had advisers too. Those who had fought at Bedriacum did not want their chances of wealth and power to be destroyed by a mad pretence that their leader was a Caesar. The Emperor Augustus had also been the victor in a civil war, but he had dressed his triumph against fellow Romans as a victory over Cleopatra, a dangerous alien. The people of Rome, perplexed and contemptuous as many of them were, might still revolt if Aulus pretended too far to be what he was not. Not yet crippled by the certainty of a Caligula or Nero, he wore the clothes that those who were waiting for him wanted to see.

Aulus Vitellius passed through the city walls on foot. He wore the toga that he had been entitled to wear while Nero was alive. His height made him easy to see, but his modesty was on view too. Behind him were the legions who had made him, their eagles gleaming against the summer sky. Around him were Caecina and Valens and their commanders. But togas took prime place among the armour. His leading centurions wore the white robes of priests. He had Germanicus, his son and heir. He had most of what a Caesar had ever wanted. It was a magnificent display.

Other members of his family were waiting. His elderly mother, no less sceptical of Aulus than on the day of his birth, no less clear that the Vitellii were not the Caesars, had to take the title Augusta. Continuity was what the Senate and People of Rome demanded, the SPQR that was all the more potent in letters than in fact. The Emperor Vitellius walked the broad path up to the Capitol, led the sacrifice to Jupiter and greeted his mother by her new name. He made a speech that flattered himself. Leaders of the popular assembly returned the flattery by urging that he become Augustus.

Meanwhile, Lucius was preparing his banquet. Sea creatures, so far from their home seas and so freshly dead, sprawled over the largest silver plate that Lucius could find. Light was able to pass through the piles of raw flesh, tiny shrimps and slices of mullet and turbot, showing the shadows of animals, vegetables, gods and heroes carved below. Crab and oyster were more solid elements of the gastronomic theatre, blocking the diners' view of any shining corn sheaves or acanthus. Silver was the metal that Apicius had commended for the best display of his cuisine. It enhanced the translucent and reflected what would not let through the light. It was precious but not so precious as to take all attention from the trophies of the Black Sea and Atlantic.

The plate was called the Shield of Minerva, after the protective armour for Rome's goddess of art and memory. This was not a shield for war. Minerva was a rival of the war god, Mars, mistress of flautists, not fighters. Those who were served from this shield would be unlikely to see even a scene of war, nothing more violent than the sword of a swordfish or the backward-pointing teeth of a pike. This *Cena Adventica* was a banquet for when battles were in the past. Neither Lucius nor Aulus had fought themselves to advance the name of Vitellius to barely below that of the Caesars. But when Lucius gathered the roes of rare fish alongside the tongues of rare birds and spread it all over a giant piece of theatrical armour, he ensured how his brother's arrival in Rome would always be remembered.

48

EMPEROR VITELLIUS

Aulus Vitellius found the same easy popularity with the people of Rome as he had with the troops of Cologne. He discovered that the memory of Nero, his long-time companion of the streets, was still warm in the places where they had played together. He ordered that an altar be built to the last Caesar in the Campus Martius behind the Capitol. Crowds outside the great temple to Jupiter were soon able to look out beyond the site of Julius Caesar's assassination and smell the smoke of the latest sacrifices. Nero's priests were to come from the order that Tiberius had established in memory of Augustus. Nero's poems were to be read aloud and admired as though their author were still seeking the flattery of his hearers. A flute-player was urged 'to render something from the Master's Book', and there was no doubt who was the master.

Aulus advertised his support for his favourite team of chariot-racers just as Nero and Caligula had done and as many Romans in the street liked to do. When the Blues triumphed on the racetrack he was as clearly content as when wine was in his cup or prime prawns on his plate. Julius Caesar had dictated routine letters while the horses were wheeling around the track. Everyone could see that Vitellius preferred the stadium to the office.

The offices of the emperor were vastly larger than when Augustus had ruled the Roman world from his tower. Offices, baths and banqueting halls extended out into Nero's Golden House. Aulus's wife disapproved of these additions to the imperial domain, her critics claiming that she deemed it not extravagant enough. The Palatine was still primarily the workplace of the slaves and ex-slaves of the emperor, responding to requests or queries from thousands of miles away as they had for 100 years.

There were no immediate shifts in tone towards the city or the empire between the summer and autumn of 69 CE. At the court of the new emperor were some who had accompanied him from Cologne, for his battlefield tour and on the gastronomic march south. He promoted more *equites* to posts which previously men of their class had been reluctant to take. But there were many more who occupied the same rooms in which they had served for Nero, Galba and Otho, answering letters, selling favours, feeding dogs, some of them even surviving since the reign of Claudius, remembering when Lucius Vitellius the elder ruled the staff and his sons were unruly children.

Aulus alienated some support that was dangerously close to home. There was a new class of impoverished senators whom Nero had exiled and whom Galba had allowed to return. Aulus was persuaded that these senators' freedmen, who had become as rich as his own, should pay a tax to help their masters, a policy which, with insufficient foresight, he imposed on the freedmen of the Palatine too. The people in the streets applauded yet another move which brought their emperor closer to themselves. For the courtiers there came the need for ever more elaborate tax evasion and a first sense that their master was not on their side.

The new emperor returned some of the goods of the damned that had been taken after the treason trials under Tiberius and Caligula. He left untouched the fortunes of those whom he had executed for supporting Otho. But there was no time for these sorts of administrative adjustment to succeed – or fail. Just as the Caesars had sometimes exiled all actors, Vitellius barred from Rome all impudent prophets of the kind that his mother had heeded at his birth. That did not stop them successfully prophesying his imminent death or, like the actors after every exile, slipping quietly back into the city.

The prosecutors still prospered. Nero's master lawyer of the treason trials, Vibius Crispus, joined the Vitellian cause and proved himself as flexible as his predecessors. Like Seneca he pleaded for a leave of absence through illness. If he had not fallen ill, he said, the banquets would have killed him. Though a reluctant glutton, Crispus showed all the survival skills that had been necessary for a public servant during the era of the *domus Caesaris* that had come to its end.

The soldiers who had put Aulus in power profited from higher pay. The new emperor was not about to repeat the mistakes of Galba. But the legions from Germany found their status undermined by the favouring of local recruits for prestigious posts in the palace guard. Some of them were living in swampy areas close to the Tiber, sharing their homes with malarial mosquitoes unfamiliar to them from the Rhine. The heat was the biggest killer since the battle of Bedriacum. The armies who had acclaimed Aulus at Cologne were still loyal, but less enthusiastic in their applause.

Caecina and Valens were also as loyal to Aulus as they had been before, but this did not make them loyal in the way that Augustus or even Nero would have expected. Both were consuls, but neither was the most reliable of aides to an emperor still finding his way. Each hated the other much more than they loved anyone else. Each competed with the other in promoting games across the city, paying the bills with the houses and lands of those who had died supporting Galba and Otho. Valens, though as focused as ever on his varied personal pleasures, was more skilful than Caecina in rewarding his own troops.

Aulus had little time to watch and wait and eat and enjoy as he had done for so much of his life. At the beginning of September there were reports that a single legion in Moesia, modern Bulgaria and Serbia, was in revolt. At first this did not raise serious alarm but, quite quickly, it became clear that another Roman army was marching on Rome, aiming, it seemed, to do from the east what Aulus had done from the west.

This army contained the legions of Judaea and Syria that Lucius Vitellius had once held for Tiberius. It had a commander currently in Alexandria, Vespasian, who was a decorated veteran of Claudius's British campaign. If one army could impose its will on the Palatine court, so maybe could another. The rival force would have to be faced.

It was Caecina alone who led the Rhine legions back north to the battlefields beside the River Po; Valens was either too ill or too cunning to start the trip. Each of Aulus's commanders had to decide how serious was the threat, how likely it was to succeed and how best they should protect and advance themselves. The emperor, who was staying behind in Rome, had never been a totem for his commanders, never a cause in himself worth fighting for. He was liked by his men but not an object of devotion. He was that much more common kind of leader, the man in charge at the time. The question for Caecina, newly back on the road, and Valens, still in Rome, was how long that time would last.

The totem for the armies heading towards them was a man who had been in and out of the lives of the Vitellii for fifty years. Vespasian was more a soldier than a courtier, but he had skilfully trodden the fine line between those roles. He never had to pretend that Caligula was talking to the Moon, but he did once deliver a senate speech of exceptionally flattering thanks for an invitation from Caligula to dinner. Like Aulus's father he was part of the court of Augustus's niece, Antonia, also the long-time lover of her famously unforgetting secretary, Caenis. He was a protégé of Narcissus, and in Britain sixteen years before he had won a fearsome military reputation under Aulus Plautius.

Under Nero the career of Vespasian had seemed to be coming to an end. He had been an unlikely companion on the poetry tour of Greece. Though knowledgeable in courtly manners, he was notoriously hard-faced for musical evenings which required the appearance of relaxation. His expression seemed often held by wire, as though he were permanently adjusting his mask or, as the unkinder noted, just about to have a shit. Already almost sixty years old, he had a reputation for falling asleep during Nero's performances, on one occasion having to be abused for his yawning by Phoebus, one of Nero's freedmen. His elder brother, Titus Flavius Sabinus, the city prefect at Rome, was the head of the family.

Only an unusually serious revolt in Judaea brought Vespasian to the right place at the right time. He had been a hammer of the tribes of west Britain while Aulus's father was the top man at Rome.

In 66 CE Nero needed to choose a man to be a hammer of the Jews when most of the group around him were more fitted for dancing. Vespasian was the best prospect in the emperor's sight, and suddenly he was at the level in the Roman world from which, in 69 CE, he could make a challenge for the throne.

Vespasian's family was only a little grander than the Vitellii had been before the rise of Aulus's father. He was the grandson of a centurion who became a debt-collector, a profitable but hardly respectable trade whose members Aulus knew all too personally. Like Aulus and his brother he had been a governor of Africa. He was notoriously poor, less through excessive spending than by failing to acquire, and often dependent on Sabinus for support.

Aulus's first reaction to the news of an army loyal to Vespasian was that it was fake. He made a speech blaming dissident supporters of Otho for spreading alarm. He ordered troops to break up crowds of potential gossips, an act which merely made the rumours more believed. At the same time he ordered legions from Germany, Spain and Britain to leave for northern Italy in case they were needed.

On the road north from Rome Caecina had many reasons for confidence. Vespasian was not even with his men: his priority was controlling the Egyptian corn supply. The soldiers of the east would be fixed more on their own advantage than that of their absent leader, just as those of the west had been. The Rhine armies who had created Emperor Vitellius were well capable of defeating their rivals.

But Caecina also knew that his troops were not any longer the angry men of Cologne, nor even the banqueters of the march from Brixellum. He could see, more clearly on the march than before he left, that their armour was neglected, their horses tired and their spirits low. They were fine fighters. They could face the jealous armies of Vespasian or any other army. But they lacked the fire they had had before.

A message came to Caecina from Valens in Rome calling for his own soldiers in the army to halt and await his arrival as, he said, had previously been planned. Caecina ignored it. The position, he claimed, had changed. It was important that the Vitellians faced the armies of Vespasian at full strength before any reinforcements made him stronger. Caecina had little faith in the arrival of the new troops that Aulus had ordered from the western provinces; their commanders would be wisely waiting to see which was the winning side. They would claim every sort of local unrest for staying at their posts. It was winter. The roads were hard to travel.

Only with the biggest possible force would Caecina have the chance to prevaricate too. He could then hold Aulus's future in his hand. If he were to defeat the legions of Syria and Judaea, he would have the glory which not even Valens could challenge. A second *Cena Adventica* would be even more splendid than the first. If he were to change sides and persuade the whole Vitellian army to follow, he would cleanly destroy Aulus's cause. Aulus would have nothing left with which to fight, Rome would have its fourth emperor in a year and Caecina would be owed the biggest debt by the new incumbent. Messages soon began to arrive from Vespasian.

49

NO TIME FOR A PARTY

Aulus Vitellius never much wanted to be emperor. Everyone who knew him knew it. His opinion of himself was not so far from that of his father and mother. He did not, however, want to be an ex-emperor. There had never been a living ex-emperor and Aulus was not an innovator, except perhaps in the kitchen, and maybe not even there. He had taken a role into which others had thrust him. He had discovered at Cologne his ability to motivate men by bonhomie and belching and understanding their needs. If the high-minded criticised him for enjoying an execution or a banquet, they were criticising most men of Rome. He was an everyman of Rome. He was happily doing the little that an emperor had to do.

For the second time in his life he had entrusted the same two men to manage his interests. His forces were gathering to repel the invaders. Caecina was ahead and Valens was on the road too, just as they had been on the march from Germany that brought him to the Palatine. Valens had eventually set off from Rome, without fresh troops but, or so it was said, with a generous accompaniment of women and eunuchs to lighten his nights. His pace had been slow, but the two were now manoeuvring in northern Italy as they had before. Beyond that Aulus knew little.

The emperor did not take up arms himself. There was no shame or bad strategy in that. He was closer than Vespasian to the battles about to be fought in their names. His heir was a child. His death would end his family's cause completely. Aulus retired to eat and drink amid the statues and pistachio trees of the villa that had once been his father's. While his protectors went north, he himself went south.

He retreated fifteen miles from Rome to his family estate at Aricia. This was where he had taken meals with his father and mother when he was young, eating simple food under the watchful eyes of their household gods, wooden statues of Peace and Plenty beside those of Pallas the accountant, Narcissus the master of the post, Callistus the sifter of petitions and Polybius the self-styled artist who had ignored Seneca's pleas for help.

In the autumn of 69 CE the shade of the trees was the same, though much else was not. The food owed more to Apicius than in the past and the threats to his peace of mind were more military than the papyri that had pursued his father from the small rooms of the Palatine. The need for the familiar deities was more acute. His boy, Germanicus, not only bore the name of a failure in the Julio-Claudian line; it was a reminder of his family's long service to that line. The Caesars were over, and the Vitellii were under threat.

He rested in his garden and waited. The unkind could compare him to an animal on a hot day before the circus, forever content as long as he was fed. But his loyalist soldiers on their way north would be more understanding. They had never served under his direct command. They would have been content that he was alive – and that they had someone to fight for and gain from. It did not matter whether Aulus was with Silius Italicus, discussing the restoration of Virgil's tomb, or with his cook considering the virtues of the spiny lobster, or by himself with Peace and Plenty. No soldier cared if his emperor was a glutton or an aesthete or neither. If they ever had cared, they did not care that summer.

Silius was important for Aulus Vitellius even though he did not yet have any readers. Augustus Caesar had had a name, a long reign and the poets Virgil and Horace to commemorate his ideals. Aulus Vitellius had a name that was still little known beyond the Palatine, only a short reign at the time he was relaxing in Aricia, and a poet companion who had not yet written what, like all poets, he was always threatening to write.

Yet Silius had plans for what would become the longest Latin poem to survive, the story of Rome's struggle against Hannibal 250 years before. The repetitive brutality of Silius's battle scenes would soon recall perfectly the year when there were four emperors. Aulus's poet was the master of horses toppling and writhing,

swimming fields of gore, the dredging of bodies from ditches of
blood as though they were the sea.

While Aeneas's shield, given to him by the goddess Venus, carried the weight of Augustus's hopes for Rome's future, Silius's shield
for Hannibal was a common gift from man to man. Aulus himself
had borrowed his own armour. His most famous shield carried flesh
from the fishmonger's scales. But none of that meant much to the
soldiers back around the flooded fields beside the Po.

After weeks of silence, news eventually came back to the dining
tables of Aricia. There were more successes to toast, failures to
ignore, loyalties and defections to note for the future. Near Bedriacum, where Aulus had toured the battlefield only weeks before,
drinking to disguise the smell of death, there had been much more
death, brutal clashes of sword and shield, each bout interspersed
with hours for discussion among the commanders about whom the
men were fighting for and why.

Aulus knew the chequerboard pattern of the battlefields, the
squares of land which Augustus had awarded to his victorious vet-
erans, a legacy as lasting as that of his poets. He knew what the
ground was like, brown and gold and red, dogs licking the blood of
the living and dead. He didn't need to see it. Caecina, it was said,
had changed sides, or tried to, a man worse than a dog. He had
made a speech praising Vespasian and tried to persuade his officers
to join him. His men had not agreed. They had objected to being
sold like slaves in a market. Caecina was the one now in chains,
waiting for either Aulus or Vespasian to give him his reward.

The messages were confused. Aulus reluctantly felt the need to
provide clarity where none existed. He returned from Aricia to
Rome, addressed the city guard, praised the loyalty of their colleagues in the field, and removed their commander who was close
to Caecina. He gave a longer speech to the senate on the healthy
state of the empire and heard his brother, Lucius, commend a vote
of censure on Caecina and his removal from the consulship.

There was one day left to run of Caecina's term of office. So, in a
stately adherence to the motions of government, he promoted one of

his friends for the shortest term since Julius Caesar did the same in the year before his assassination. That previous move had promoted the joke that Gaius Rebilus was so vigilant in his consulship that he never slept. The genuine consul for 45 BCE, Gaius Trebonius, had been so offended at the diminution of his office as to move closer to joining the assassins of the Ides of March. Aulus's friend became merely an object of ridicule.

Lucius tightened his grip on his brother's court. With no more knowledge than Aulus of their enemies around the banks of the River Po, he concentrated on those who might be enemies beside the Tiber. Lucius was still insecure about the part he had played at Brixellum. He had not left to fight beside Caecina and Valens. Those with betrayal on their own minds were particularly liable to pursue others on the same charge.

Top of Lucius's list was the man who had given Aulus his first set of emperor's clothes, Junius Blaesus, the governor who had hosted the victors and vanquished of Bedriacum at Lugdunum. Aulus had arrived at Blaesus's palace in the same state of dress that had taken him from bankruptcy in Rome to victory in a battle that he hadn't fought. He had left it in the scarlet cloak and military bronze of a successor to the Caesars.

Back in Rome after his tour of duty, Blaesus might have expected due gratitude. Instead Lucius saw an opportunity to bring him down. Blaesus was unlucky that a party to welcome him home was held on one of the rare nights when Aulus was not in the party mood, when the provider of his new clothes was perhaps not what he wanted to see.

By the standards of 69 CE there was nothing unusual about the homecoming. The host was the freedman son of one of Nero's nurses, a man famously once fired for using a lavatory erected for the sole use of the emperor. The event was the same kind of *Cena Adventica* that Lucius had given for Aulus. There may not have been a Shield of Minerva, but there were blazing torches and other normal signs of revelry, all of which Aulus could see and hear from an imperial villa in one of Nero's former gardens.

Aulus was feeling sick that night and all the less happy that anyone else should be celebrating. Lucius seized this moment when his usually genial brother was open to jealousy – and fanned that feeling into anger. Blaesus, he claimed, was one of those wealthy aristocrats always sneering at Aulus when they thought it safe: he had been close to Caecina from the start and might be so still: he was a threat not only to Aulus but to his son Germanicus. To stress the last point he brought the six-year-old to Aulus's sickroom.

Aulus was grateful for his brother's confidence in the future of the Vitellii. He was lying in a house he had once shared with Nero, and may have thought of what Nero would have done with much less reason than Lucius was presenting. Blaesus, he agreed, must be executed. The means should be poison. He would visit him when he was dying.

Lucius took on the task. He also took an empty space in the membership of the Brothers of the Fields, receiving his personal rose petal to mark his promotion, rolling a jar down a sacred hill, feasting on pork, beef and lamb in the menu order set out in stone.

50

A DRINK TO DEFEAT

While Caecina was in chains, the first news from Valens was a suspicious request for reinforcement. Aulus's remaining general wanted not legions but cavalry and light-armed troops. Aulus paused. What Valens wanted, and very rapidly wanted according to his dispatch, seemed more useful for an escape than for fighting Vespasian.

Further news followed of Valens's determined sexual exploits while he waited for the new troops to arrive, more defections and losses and reports of Caecina with their enemies. Vespasian was accepting allies and deserters. There had been a final battle on a field too blood-soaked and waterlogged for any forces to make camp. Valens had escaped – and his whereabouts were unknown.

Aulus did not give up. He had watched emperors and learnt from them even if he had never wanted to be an emperor. He assembled a band of cavalry and guards and sent it north to block the mountain passes which Vespasian's armies would need to cross to reach Rome. He called up a legion of marines from the fleet in the Bay of Naples. He put Lucius in charge of the defence of Rome itself. He began a programme of buying support with money that he did not have. He sold lucrative appointments, cutting taxes and granting greater freedoms, stretching the credulity of all recipients but flattering them nonetheless.

Behind every door in the court was a man who would normally say no – to a request for a consulship, a proposal for a new aqueduct, a plea that a city be given the same tax advantages as its neighbour. Suddenly the treasury was like a bath with every plug set to open. Some of the doors had no one behind them at all. The cautious and lesser-known had fled, newly prepared to risk their posts in the hope of claiming them back when the view was clearer.

Aulus sent spies north to assess the new balance of power, hoping for answers that would justify his generosity. Vespasian's officers identified the interlopers, organised meetings with their most determined fighters, tours of their disciplined camps, then sent them back to Rome. One was a centurion whom Vespasian's men took on a tour of the bloodiest battlefields beside the Po. From this vivid reversal of Vitellius's tour of Bedriacum it was undeniable that the armies of Caecina and Valens had been destroyed – by defection, but massively by death.

Bodies lay in piles once more in the ditches. Every farm on the chequerboard around the Po had its pieces of a defeated army. Reports from civilian survivors brought more horror than the sights of the dead, torture and burning, rapes of boys and girls, the tormenting of the old to reveal wealth they had long since lost.

When the centurion returned for his interview with his emperor, he found Aulus's confidence still high. To prove his worthlessness when so obvious a truth was not believed, he killed himself. Aulus heard all his spies' stories and ordered all their executions. Morale was his surest remaining strength and he did not want it sapped by truth.

Finally Aulus began his own march north with his cavalry and guards. A crowd of senators followed behind. Gradually their numbers fell. His senior courtiers encouraged him for longer, knowing that their own survival in power might not survive another change of control on the Palatine. The soldiers stayed loyal, but Aulus's military inexperience was insufficient for what became a complex test.

News arrived that the fleet at Naples had defected. Dividing his forces, he sent one half back to quell the revolt and the other forward to the passes of the Apennine mountains. His officers knew that this way both moves would fail. His courtiers panicked that their master was out of their control, and kept from him the advice that might have saved him.

Aulus was a man faraway out of his depth. Reportedly he was drunk much of the time. Drunkenness was a regular charge against failures, but that did not make the charge a falsehood. He was buoyed by the support of the local people who cheered his progress. He accepted their offer to take up arms themselves and registered the first volunteers himself.

These were the fantasies of a drowning man. It was a century and a half since Rome last had a citizen army. He ordered his personal band of gladiators to join the suppression of the naval rebels. He raised cash from freedmen and rich supporters who still saw their best future with Aulus if he could take a grip on events.

There was little sign of that. Ahead of him his soldiers were already defecting. His aides could not protect him from the news that Valens was dead. Hopes that his most loyal commander was raising new armies in Germany were as false as all his present hope. Valens's head on a spear, paraded among his former troops and camp-followers, was seen by too many for the fact to be doubted. There were no reprisals from Vespasian's commanders against the men and women who had supported Valens since Cologne. The testimony of their defeat was enough.

When Aulus had marched on Rome in April he was like a lottery-winner floating on a cloud of popularity and success. Making the return journey he was still popular, but on a darker cloud. Messages arrived in Vespasian's name offering generous terms for surrender, comfortable retirement homes near the town where his family had begun, safety for his family, for the next generation, his son and his future children, a life with money and slaves. He responded with queries about exactly where his houses would be, the quality of sea views and kitchen service.

51

IN AUGUSTUS'S TEMPLE

Tarracina was a high town by the sea, half way between Nuceria, where the Vitellii began, and Rome, where Lucius was charged with defending his brother's reign as emperor, between where Augustus had died after forty-five years in power and where Galba had died after seven months. Some fifty miles both from Naples and from the Palatine, Tarracina stood on a bright white rock, a marker for travellers, an inspiration for poets and, in the early winter of 69 CE, a place where Lucius, after surprising his soldiers by leaving Rome, was planning the next move in his family's fortunes.

Virgil and Horace had passed through Tarracina as part of a sensitive diplomatic mission more than a century before, Horace describing it as *inpositum saxis late candentibus*, 'perched upon the far-shining rock'. Lucius had to seize and fortify that high white rock and from there cow the naval revolt, protect the grain supply for the capital and maybe, if more defeats followed, leave Italy for Africa and renew the fight from where he and his brother had each once been the governor. With him was his wife Triaria, as keen as Lucius himself to defend the family honour with her sword.

Back in Rome Aulus learnt that their mother was dead. Sextilia had supported him as a son if not as an emperor. She was the last link to the second generation of his family's public life. Some soon claimed that he had starved her, in the tradition of Augustus and his daughter, in order to fulfil a prophecy that he would rule longer if his mother died first. Others said that his mother had asked for poison to commit suicide. A reputation as a devoted mourner or a murderous manoeuvrer for advantage: that was the difference between winning and losing.

While Lucius was besieging Tarracina, Aulus began to be besieged, rather more gently, by Flavius Sabinus, the brother of

Vespasian. Sabinus was a very different kind of brother from Lucius: he was older and quieter, the highest hope of a modest family, relied upon for loans in trouble, and, although himself a distinguished veteran of Claudius's British campaign, a conciliator in recent years more than a fighter. Nero had appointed him as city prefect and he had retained the job throughout the reigns of Galba and Otho.

Aulus too had kept him in charge of the city. Sabinus had supporters in Rome who thought him a better prospect for their quiet lives than Vespasian himself. Vespasian was far away. Sabinus was a man with whom Aulus might reasonably hope to do business, to save his life and family in some form of retirement. Offers continued of country homes by the sea and all the seafood that even he might want to eat.

The main negotiation between the two men was set for the Palatine temple of Apollo, Augustus's great addition to the house which would become his family's palace. This was still Aulus's domain. He could still invite Sabinus to look out from its broad colonnades and round-domed chamber to the *Circus Maximus*, where he had ridden chariots with Caligula, and to the banqueting halls which had been the love of his later life. Sabinus too knew the temple well. It was a public space in a private house, as Augustus had always intended it to be.

Aulus brought to the temple two of his most trusted friends, Cluvius Rufus, the historian and governor of Spain whom he had saved from a treason charge at Lugdunum, and Silius Italicus, who had been consul in the previous year. He needed a deal. This was not an occasion for freedmen trained to say no. His court was anyway much reduced, a shadow of that which had run the empire from the time of Tiberius to Nero.

Cluvius was already writing a history of the Caesars, and at the temple of Apollo he would be in the room when the next phase began, whatever that next phase was. He was an authority on the theatre as well as politics, the Latin farces cited by Augustus on his deathbed and the Greek songs preferred by Nero. Cluvius was a man with answers both on the origins of the histrionic arts and on their place in the history of all Rome.

Silius was younger, richer, a former governor of Asia for whom the past was just as important as the present, maybe more so. His passion was for the poetry of Virgil and, if he himself would only rarely match the skill of his hero, that did not stop his ambition or his hopes.

Together they stood with Aulus as he discussed terms with Sabinus. Observers watched as best they could, reading signs from the faces and gestures as though from a theatre's highest seats. Aulus, tall, tired and limping, seemed dejected, maybe humbled. Sabinus looked out more compassionate than triumphant. The outcome was surely an abdication, although when and how could not be known.

The next show for the onlookers in the Forum was a procession from the doors of the Palatine, headed by the emperor in the black toga of a mourner. Behind him was a closed litter, carried by slaves, and behind that a line of his remaining courtiers, listless, their faces lowered like that of their leader. Some citizens shouted encouragement to the man whom they still saw as their emperor. The soldiers of the Vitellian cause, the drivers of that cause since Cologne and Bedracium, kept a sinister, contrasting silence.

Aulus spoke to the simmering crowd. For the sake of peace, the state and his children he announced that he was giving up the throne. He held out a dagger to the most senior man in the crowd. The symbol was refused. At Cologne Aulus had taken a dagger from Caesar's altar to show his acceptance of the throne. In Rome he could not give a dagger back. His son, Germanicus, was in the litter lest anyone be in any doubt. An abdication, accompanied by wife, court and stuttering heir, was a first in imperial history and, unlike the monsters, freaks and other novelties greeted at the gates of the Palatine, was ungratefully received.

The abdicator tried to depart by way of the temple of Concord and leave the dagger there. Next he turned towards his family home on the other side of the *Circus Maximus*. Soldiers blocked every route bar that back to the palace. Aulus was back in the *domus Caesaris*.

It was not clear what this meant. Perhaps the party was changing its clothes: black togas for a funeral were traditionally exchanged for white before a banquet in honour of the dead. There were no reports of banqueting, but to the troops of Vespasian the retreat of Aulus to the Palatine did not look like the abdication promised to Sabinus. Perhaps Aulus was instead hanging on.

The news of uncertainty spread. There were soon two sets of forces in the Forum and surrounding streets, not always easy to distinguish even by each other. The biggest difference was that Vespasian's soldiers were subordinate to Sabinus, and Aulus's were taking orders from no one. The unled won the early skirmishes with ease.

Sabinus did not want to have to fight for Rome. That was neither in his character nor in his commission from his brother in distant Alexandria. He ordered a withdrawal to the heights of the Capitol, where he could consider his next move. The Vitellians followed in pursuit.

Rain poured through the night. Aulus and Sabinus succeeded in exchanging messages as though they were still preparing for the conference that had already happened. Aulus admitted that he had lost control. Sabinus accused him of negotiating in bad faith and never intending to abdicate. Aulus had even fewer powers of an emperor than when he was first hailed by his troops in Germany. Sabinus was in fear for his life and begging by letter for what Aulus was unable to give.

Aulus learnt of the aftermath only when Sabinus was brought before him in chains. The men who had fought for the Vitellian cause (hardly, in truth, his own cause any more) had been frustrated by piles of toppled statues which Sabinus had ordered as barricades. They had no machinery with which to clear their way. The stones were slippery after the storm. Both sides had thrown torches. The battle had spread across the Capitol to the temple that more than any other defined Rome itself. The ancient roof over the marble columns dedicated to I.O.M. Jupiter Optimus Maximus, Best and Greatest, was made of ancient wood. Each blamed the other for the fire that had dried, then cracked and roasted the sacred rocks.

Aulus still hoped to save Sabinus's life. But this was no longer a private meeting at which his advisers were a would-be poet and an historian of the theatre. He was hemmed in by the soldiers who had brought their captive and by citizens who had followed them for the sport of seeing a powerful man die.

Aulus's soldiers feared betrayal by their own leader. They had their emperor and the debts that he owed them – and they wanted to keep them both. Sensing further equivocation, they found their enemy's brother, severed his head and dragged his body to the top of the Capitol hill, treading their way through the ruins of what had only days before been the greatest temple in Rome.

A starfish of stiffening limbs tumbled down towards the Forum. A headless corpse fell faster than a faller who was still alive, bumping and streaking the stones with whatever last meal he had taken. Occasionally a dying man might accelerate his death – or delay it till a drowning in the Tiber. Aulus Vitellius had not seen precisely how his fellow negotiator had died.

He was away from the horror, banqueting in the halls where as a boy he had watched Tiberius. After sufficient men and women had seen that the cause of the Vitellians was still alive, the remains of Flavius Sabinus rolled into the river and out to sea.

In even the worst circumstances Aulus liked to see hope. Some said that Vespasian, the would-be fourth emperor, might possibly be pleased at his brother's death, thinking that even the most helpful member of his family might become a rival once the throne was won. But this was hardly a secure basis for future talks on Aulus's own safety. He had his own brother, still alive and working on his behalf. He was not sure exactly where.

52

OUT OF THE DOGHOUSE

News came to Aulus from inside Tarracina, where the forces of Vespasian were as keen to eat, drink, rape and plunder as were Lucius's besiegers. The defenders were in no state to hold the white rock. It took only a single slave to shift allegiance from one master to another for a gate to lie open and an assault to become a massacre. The forces of Vespasian fled to their ships. Lucius's wife, Triaria, put on her sword and stormed the streets as a victorious Vitellian soldier. For Aulus, unable to concede power, there was a new possibility that he might maintain it.

Yet, on the north side of Rome, his enemies, roused by the death of Sabinus and the destruction on the Capitol, were only ten miles away. Aulus sent towards them a band of guards and slaves and barely trained citizens whose local knowledge brought them further victory in the maze of gardens and narrow streets. He called on the senate to send emissaries, accompanied by vestal virgins, for a truce. The answer from Vespasian's officers was only a pause.

The next sight in Rome was of fierce fighting by troops of both sides, neither trusting their leaders to allow the fighting to last. Even in the season of Saturnalia, it was the most extreme of contrasts and reversals. Friends were enemies, and enemies friends. In one street there was a party, in another a welter of blood and maimings. Dogs fed on their usual scraps or on skulls. Prostitutes plied their trade in one corner, while in another they piled the corpses of their colleagues and their clients.

The Roman Forum, no longer a political museum or place for rhetoric, was a battlefield. Beneath the ruins of the great Capitol lay the wreckage of fighting street by street, damp dust that had once been the state records at the base of the hill. It was an accident, a spark in a musty library, a smoulder of pressed reeds, a flame over taxes and treaties, a new fire like the spread of a rumour around the Palatine and then a roar of destruction. The stuff of much history was gone.

There were tiny victories for both sides, cheered on by citizens watching from open windows as though this urban war were a parade. Soon it became clear that a force with leaders but less knowledge of the terrain was beating those with more knowledge but no leadership at all. Aulus knew no more than did these enthusiastic spectators about the last moves in his military career. Vespasian's cavalry included many who a week before had been its enemies. Legionaries still fighting for Aulus disappeared into a small camp by the city's north-east walls, determined that when Vespasian's main force poured into the city, it would not pass unopposed.

It seemed as though Aulus's troops were deliberately giving their leader time to escape. Whether or not that was true, Aulus did attempt the same route out of the Palatine that he had failed to take after his abdication, first to his family home and then out to the south towards Tarracina. At his side he had his baker and his cook, no longer an historian or poet. This time he was not prevented by force but by a collapse of his own powers to go on. Again he turned back towards the palace.

Behind him the Forum was no longer a battlefield. A few women picked over what the soldiers had left. Inside the gates he sought familiarity in the halls where the Vitellii had so long served, the rooms where his grandfather, Publius, had administered for Augustus, where his uncle, Publius, had argued for Germanicus, where his father, Lucius, had flattered Caligula's wish for worship and Claudius's to be the conqueror of Britain. All were empty, unrecognisable, without even their ghosts.

Every emperor had extended these halls. Nero's Golden House exceeded every predecessor and neighbour, spreading across the southern hills. Banqueters had so many more spaces than before to rouse a jaded palate. When filled, the rooms had seemed perfect for their purposes. When empty, they were vast. His cooks had gone. There was no one to reminisce over his Shield of Minerva. His baker had gone.

He found a smaller room where the guards once kept their dogs, African and British, the hunters from Syria and Spain. It was not so very small, but it was dark. He could not see in every corner. There was a bed and a mattress. He moved them against the door. He waited. He heard clanking from down below. There was the sound of soldiers' voices, the opening of gates and the acrid smell of blackened marble. He would be found if anyone cared to look. He would be recognised, though maybe not if the searcher was from the banks of the Danube and had never seen the Palatine before.

He would not be found dead. He had neither the will nor the sword for suicide. Nero and Otho had killed themselves. Otho had gained credit for that. Otho had stopped a war. Otho had saved lives. Aulus Vitellius Germanicus had tried to stop a war while also staying alive. He had failed. He was just waiting for the soldier who would remind him how far he had failed.

Hard footsteps hammered against mosaic. There was a crash against the door. His barrier fell back softly. The soldier's name was Julius Placidus. That was all he learnt. This Placidus knew whom he had found. Maybe the image on his coins was not so different from the face of Rome's third emperor for 69 CE. Aulus felt the tying of his hands, the tearing of his clothes and the bite of an emboldened dog. His dead master, Tiberius, had held the city like a wolf by its ears. Aulus had let the city go.

Outside in the corridor Placidus checked that he had the right prisoner and led Aulus from the palace. Rome's eighth emperor would have gained many more admirers in future if he had died before being dragged, hands tied behind his back, along the Sacred Way towards the Capitol. Instead he still tried to negotiate. He had important information, he said, too sensitive for anyone to hear except the man who wanted to replace him. He had for half a year wanted his successor to be the son whom he had named German-icus. If he could not have that, he wanted Germanicus's safety to be assured and that of the Vitellii who were left.

The statue of his father was still standing in the Forum where the climb to the Capitol began, its inscription declaring the loyalty of Lucius Vitellius to the house of the Caesars. It had been no part of

Aulus Vitellius's own life to want to be a hero. Other statues that had for a century been the memory of Rome were piled as barricades. The ashes of laws and taxes blew along the streets. Marble arms reached towards the sky. There were still many stone dead standing, enough for many future street fights, but most of the living were gone.

Aulus Vitellius had few illusions about himself or why he was in power. The coinage of his brief time in charge of the mints made no claims in gold, silver or bronze for Justitia, Virtus or Pax. He did not present himself as a man of Justice, Virtue or Peace, still less as the son of a god or the father of the fatherland. An occasional gold coin which boasted his support from the SPQR was a mistaken use of old moulds, maybe those of the hopeful Galba. Aulus had been resistant to believing those who flattered him. His money offered mere assertions of the *consensus exercituum*, the agreed choice of the armies. A glance on one side showed his puffed cheeks, fleshy nose and double chins, on the other the slender figure of a youthful war god, naked except for a cloak. As soon as there was no consensus of the armies Aulus lost his power. He was a very ordinary man, with ordinary vices, an ordinary willingness to go with any flow – and a love of obliteration by food and drink which was ordinary, magnified by his opportunities and exaggerated in his failure.

News of his progress spread fast. Wound followed wound. Outside the palace gates was the place in the Forum where foreign supplicants to Tiberius and Caligula used to leave their gifts, their strange animals, dwarfs and giants. Aulus became just such an attraction himself. People prodded his belly and pulled at the hair on his unshaven face. He made a final attempt to attract the attention that an emperor better deserved. He had information, he said, that would save Vespasian's life. He had to be allowed to tell what he knew to the man who most needed to know it. His captor continued their shared procession to the Capitol. Soon there were more captors and a longer climb to the acrid remains of the ancient temple.

The descent was shorter. The soldiers did not sever his head at the top of the Groaning Steps. They placed a cord around his neck.

He was led like the companion of his kennel, stumbling before he fell. His last sight of the Palatine was in the smoky distance. His last words were a reply to a barracker in the crowd. He cried out that, whatever his failings and present fate, he had been that man's emperor: *ego tamen imperator tuus fui*. He died slowly by blows and cuts, torn to fat, fleshy pieces, tumbling towards the memorial to his father, a sword under his chin to make him face his torturers, his belly protruding forever to stand for his failure to control his appetites, his opportunities and himself. Galeria received what was left of his body. His head disappeared into the spreading crowd.

53

NEW COURTS FOR OLD

This book has been the story of a hill and its people, of a palace and a mostly forgotten palace family. To conclude first the family story, Lucius Vitellius did not try to escape to Africa. He marched his troops towards Rome from Tarracina, tried to negotiate for his life with those hunting for him, failed and died at the pleasure of the victors. The stammering Germanicus lasted only a little longer than his uncle.

The family name was as quickly degraded as the body at the bottom of the Groaning Steps. The name of Aulus Vitellius – and that of Lucius too – was expunged from the stone tablets of the Brothers of the Fields. The fabricated lineage from the local gods of Nuceria was replaced by a hardly less likely line of descent from a freed slave, a shoe-maker, an informer who had married the prostitute daughter of a baker. This was a jibe of farce, easily hurled against a glutton. Suetonius, the biographer of emperors in the early second century, born around the time of Aulus's death, left the truth of the divergent tales to be judged by his readers. Others were less generous. Once its refuge had changed from shady villas to a doghouse, so did the family's past and future.

Aulus Vitellius was left as an exemplary man of the Palatine, over-promoted like so many in administrative machines, the courtier son of a great courtier father, a flatterer's disciple. After he became the eighth emperor of Rome his name was glued to gluttony because he blasted away the madness of his world with peacock's brains and flamingo tongues. He didn't fall from power because he was a glutton; he was a glutton because he fell from power. After Aulus, no other Vitellius ever much mattered. It was a bad name to have.

Of all Aulus's many failings gluttony was merely the most memorable, the most vivid, the one word of abuse into which all others could be wrapped. His father Lucius earnt his place in the stories of his time by management, flattery and intrigue. His son ate his way into history. When Renaissance artists wanted characters for Roman orgies, his face was a favourite. The fat, fleshy marble bust, owned by the Grimani family of Venice, became one of the most repeated images from ancient Rome, coming to symbolise all the sins of the city and empire in which its subject had lived, worked, survived and so briefly ruled. Both gluttons and flatterers were characters of the Palatine that later state servants recognised nervously among themselves.

Many historians praised the civil peace brought by Augustus and the successor heirs to Julius Caesar. A few saw it as ruthless autocracy. But in films and other fictions the first phase of the Roman Empire ended only in stories of flattery, lies and excess. The Palatine was where gluttons sat at their top tables, guzzling and vomiting while regimes rose and fell faster than the plates could move from dormice to giraffe. Flatterers corrupted their masters, made the bad even worse and created the conditions in which anyone might eat themselves to death. Aulus and his father were in the rooms of power and represented that era's end.

The Palatine hill itself quickly lost prestige. The year 69 CE was like a long, low theatre show of the kind that Augustus had cited as he died – an unrolling sequence of uncomfortable, identifiable characters, the young madman, the old martinet, the libertine, the glutton, the soldier – all of them caricatures that Romans were happy to forget for a while. The new emperor Vespasian wanted to mark a difference from the past. His historians were happy to help him. Slaves, ex-slaves and other courtiers were easy scapegoats.

Vespasian took the name of Caesar, but preferred to rule from one of Rome's imperial gardens rather than the rooms left empty when Aulus Vitellius departed for the last time. He ordered the destruction of Nero's palatial extensions – and their eventual replacement by public spaces financed by the proceeds of another Roman repression of the Jews. The Colosseum arose where the

Domus Aurea had briefly stood. Banqueting declined. Cooks and clerks found it wise to choose more modest marble memorials. Vespasian showed virtuous clemency to Aulus's daughter, Vitellia, a reminder of the best spirit of Augustus. The aim of the new regime was to revive as much as was prudent of the simplicity affected by the founder of the empire, to promote beans as food for the poor, to expel the most flagrant wastrels from the senate, to preserve the best disciplines and leave the worst behind.

Yet the system of government did not – and could not – change for long. The Palatine's empty rooms rapidly refilled, many previous occupants returning to their old places or to promotions. Vespasian used courtiers, favourites, slaves and former slaves to run the empire as Claudius and Nero had done. He re-employed as his office gatekeeper the freedman Phoebus, who had rebuked him for yawning while Nero sang. He had ten more years of service from Caecina before, in his own dying days, he had him executed for conspiracy. Crispinilla, once the controller of Nero's new clothes, moved to the edges of political life and profited from the wine trade. Her name survived on amphorae as well as in histories written by those horrified by her role at court and the roles of other upstarts like her.

Caenis, once the slave of Antonia, survived for five years in even greater prosperity as Vespasian's long-time mistress, entrusted with selling priesthoods, governorships and other offices of profit under the empire, freeing her own slaves for office with the name Caenidianus. Famed in her youth for her beauty and powers of memory, she outlived Vespasian's wife and daughter, becoming the single heiress to the legacy of both Pallas and Agrippina, a courtier and a princess, less criticised than they within a court now accepted as a system.

The name of the veteran courtier from Smyrna freed from slavery by Tiberius, advanced by Caligula, Claudius and Nero, did not survive in any inscriptions. Or, if it did, no one has recognised it. But he himself lived till the age of around ninety, husband of a consul's sister, imperial procurator, father of two children, holder of the post once held by Pallas, each day deciding what to spend on soldiers, food supply and aqueducts. He had an administrative skill, in Rome and in the east, which Vespasian and his family appreciated as the heirs of Julius Caesar had done. Like Lucius Vitellius he suffered a demotion at the end of his life, but no fate worse than comfortable exile. Throughout his life on the Palatine he ate and drank modestly, or at least gained that valuable reputation.

Unlike Lucius, this quiet man from Smyrna saw neither of his sons ever become emperor. But the son known as Claudius Etruscus became massively rich, added to Rome's bath houses and commissioned a poetic tribute to his quiet father, a 'wearer of so many yokes and endurer of so much rough sea', a man never even quite securely named. The flattering poet was not Aulus's friend Silius, who under the rule of Vespasian found the peace to begin his epic of Hannibal, but Publius Papinius Statius, another figure of what would become a lesser literary age, a master of praising domestic architecture, public works and the madder of Vespasian's sons. The eulogist of Claudius Etruscus's father was a more than worthy successor to Clutorius Priscus, the praise-seller who had failed to survive his party night with Aulus's sister.

The Palatine title, *procurator*, held under Augustus by Publius, the first courtier of the Vitelli, grew in range and power. Those officials who were governors without needing to be from the senate became familiar, if not always welcome, to the emperor's distant subjects. The princes of Commagene exchanged their authority at home for status in the empire as smoothly as though swapping currency. Those Commagene people who hated government from Rome remained in exile, their complaints loudly made but only to the few who might listen, very few of those in the swollen rooms around the emperor.

Rome held its empire, tightened its rule and the bureaucracy of Rome spread just like the aqueducts. Like the *Aqua Claudia*, it was useful and survived. Below the princes and procurators more than 4,000 names and job titles have survived on memorial slabs, *Claudii* and *Julii*, *tabularii* and *dispensatores*, *adiutorii* and *pedisequi*, proud bearers of a sometime emperor's name, account clerks and stewards, administrators and escorts. Graffiti appeared beside more formal engravings. The name of one Palatine wardrobe slave was commemorated with a donkey head and cross, scratched on a wall to mock his worship of a 'King of the Jews'.

Some inscriptions boasted progress through the ranks on what was almost a career path, others the satisfaction in stone of a life as the emperor's *pistor* or *dulciarius*, his *a lagona* or *a cyatho*, his baker, his sweet-maker, the man who held the silver, the wine jar or the cup. When an emperor needed to wear new clothes, he might use his *a veste privata*, his *a veste castrense* or his *a veste gladiatoria*, the choice dependent on whether he intended to be at home, out with soldiers or at the theatre. Vespasian curbed what he saw as excess but did not stop what others, not least his sons and successors, saw as normal. Much survived into later courts. So did the serious administration of empire with which the courts were inextricably linked.

The Palatine remained as an administrative palace even after the capitol of the empire moved to Constantinople in 330 CE. Later still it became much more than a place, more than any single hill or palace, surviving as a symbol long after there was any Roman Empire anywhere. In the sixteenth century the crumbled walls and terraces of the Caesars became one of the first botanical gardens and bird collections in Europe. Where thrushes and cranes had once been served on silver platters, there were new aviaries and exotic plants for peacocks to eat. But the ideas of the Palatine, codified because they were so useful, moved to wherever there was power. When Peter the Great was designing his new Russian capital in the early eighteenth century, he decreed imaginary hills in the swampy ground: his Palatine was what would become the Nevsky Prospect, the grandest street in the city. A Russian Caesar was already a Czar. A Palatine became the title for officials from Bohemia to Burgundy.

Nero's freedman Epaphroditus, the well-rewarded saviour of his master from assassins, had among his own slaves the philosopher Epictetus, who, even while the first dynasty of Caesars was fading, posed the question of what the court had become, how its members should behave to each other, an insider's guide to the lessons of the recent past. He showed the need for getting the work done, for doing the most good within the system, for recognising that those around an emperor were like fish alive in a tank, rising and falling in the water, promoted, demoted, but in the greatest peril only if they fell outside. Power was a circle, not a triangle, a globe, not a pyramid, a place where the provider and consumer were one, where a flatterer may be as much responsible for flattery's ills as the flattered.

Epictetus compared all human life to being a guest at a banquet of the gods. Men could take gratefully what is offered and be worthy of their invitation. Or they could refuse dishes and attempt perilously to share in the power of their hosts. The court was the model of the world. Everyone had different weapons. Flattery was a weapon of the weak. Exchange was everything. The courtier should expect nothing for nothing. Just as a small coin bought a lettuce, so too did flattery. No one should expect to have both the lettuce and the coin. Men exchanged invitations for personal attention, food for fawning over the host.

Courtiers and emperors were not so very different. The view of both was necessary for understanding history. Epictetus knew that all were liable to inflate their own importance, to believe they were worthy of their roles, to think that when a Caesar put a man in charge of his chamber pot he was suddenly a wise counsellor. But the banquet was theatre. Everyone, for Epictetus, was an actor in a play. Augustus at the end of his life was like all men and women at all times of their life. Their part might be as a grand consul or a lowly cripple, a fat fool or a subtle schemer. The play itself might be long or short. The aim was to be part of the whole.

Epictetus, like Phaedrus, parodied the behaviour of the court. He recognised the desire to worship any source of office or benefit. A god might be anyone who could deliver a favour. Divinity was just another status within a bureaucracy. Even gods were slaves to higher powers, as Statius, in his *consolatio* for the death of Claudius Etruscus's father, agreed. The former slave of a former slave understood the nagging doubts behind even the most successful servant. Epictetus knew the works of Phaedrus. He was a theorist grounded in practice. The court was the old normal and the new normal. It might change, but not change very much.

In the Middle Ages Epictetus was the most read of all ancient philosophers. He had been on the Palatine of the Caesars. He had seen how gluttons and flatterers accepted insults and expressed gratitude for them, how they ran around after favours like children chasing nuts at a wedding party, how they sensed what was necessary to live another day.

NOTES

PART ONE

1 In the palace doghouse

Cassius Dio (*c.*160 CE–*c.*235), one of the five main sources for the early empire, was a wealthy politician who wrote a history of Rome in Greek in eighty volumes, some of which survive intact and others in abridgement and quotations. His aim was to expound and explain the greatness of Rome, with a good eye for vivid detail and many sideswipes at those who disrupted his positive narrative. Dio devoted his books 63–5 to the Year of the Four Emperors, describing Aulus Vitellius's last days (64.16–20) and his last hiding place in a palace room where dogs were kept.

Suetonius Tranquillus (*c.*70 CE–*c.*130), who wrote biographies of Julius Caesar and every emperor up to Vespasian, was himself a courtier and imperial official. In his Life of Vitellius (*Vitellius* 16) he has the dog tied up outside the kennel door rather than inside. The exact site of the kennel, like so much about the sprawling imperial palaces, is clear in none of the sources. For the development of the Palatine see Wiseman (2019) and for the newer palace, the *Domus Aurea* built by Nero, see Ball (2003).

For the variety of dogs in Rome, as set out by the poet Grattius in the time of Augustus, see https://penelope.uchicago.edu/Thayer/E/Roman/Texts/Grattius/Cynegeticon*.html#ref38 p. 167

The pessimism of Aulus's mother, Sextilia, at her son's birth is described by Suetonius (*Vitellius* 3), who also reports Aulus's common touch as a belcher (*Vitellius* 7) and his final days (*Vitellius* 15–17).

Publius Cornelius Tacitus (56 CE– *c.*120), the most influential historian of the period, was damning of Aulus Vitellius at every point. He began his *Histories* (*c.*100 CE) with the Year of the Four Emperors and then went back to write his more famous

Annals, from the reigns of Tiberius to Nero, not least to explain how the antique greatness of Rome had decayed to such a state that Vitellius (*Histories* 3.84–6) might end his reign as a glutton on the Groaning Steps. Tacitus, an aristocrat with a strong sense of the virtues of Rome's senatorial government, is the source most responsible for prejudice against a bureaucracy of former slaves.

2 Mr Glutton and Mr Fool

Suetonius describes the death of Augustus (*Augustus* 97.3–100) and his actor's call for applause (*Augustus* 99). Augustus's apology for Tiberius's slow chewing (*Tiberius* 21.2) is echoed by Dio (56.31).

There is much controversy about the nature of Atellane farce, particularly its longevity and relation to other theatre. See Frassinetti (1967) and review by A. S. Gratwick in *Classical Review* (1970), 20. Also E. Fantham (1989), 'The earliest comic theatre at Rome: Atellan farce, comedy and mime as antecedents of the commedia dell'arte', in D. Pietropaolo (ed.), *The Science of Buffoonery: Theory and History of the Commedia dell'arte* (Toronto).

3 Succession

Dio (31.1) reports the claim of Livia delaying the announcement of Augustus's death.

For Augustan mythology of the Palatine see Virgil *Aeneid* 8.337–61.

For the Augustus and Tiberius cups in the Boscoreale Treasure, buried before the eruption of Vesuvius in 79 CE, see Kuttner (1995).

4 Care for what we eat

Suetonius (*Augustus* 101.1) names the trusted freed slaves who wrote out parts of Augustus's will, Polybius and Hilarion, successors to two of his earliest private servants for public duties, Thyrsus and Epaphroditus, who negotiated with Cleopatra and guarded her after the Battle of Actium (Plutarch, *Antony* 73.1–2). Thyrsus took a flogging from Antony for seeming to him to want from Cleopatra what he and Julius Caesar had already had.

The already-dead son of Augustus's sister, Octavia, was Marcus Claudius Marcellus (42–23 BCE).

Gaius Plinius Secundus, Pliny the Elder (23 CE–79), who died in the eruption of Vesuvius, was an encyclopaedist of the natural world. He notes the idea that Italy's farms were fertile from unmined precious metals in his *Natural History* (33.21:4). For Ovid on the sexual vocabulary of archery see his *Amores* (1.8:47) and Adams (1982) on strings and bows.

Gowers (1993), pp. 126–79 gives a subtle account of Horace and the dining table. Obesity embodied moral and literary excess. A fat book was a bad book. For an invitation to a modest meal see *Odes* 1.20 and for a critique of storks' legs, goose liver and roast blackbird *Satires* 2.8. Suetonius (*Horace* 1) describes Horace's father as a *salsamentarius*, a seller of cheap salted meat and fish.

The library with the treatises on flattery was owned by Julius Caesar's father-in-law, Lucius Calpurnius Piso, at Herculaneum on the Bay of Naples. The house philosopher, Philodemus, a friend of Virgil and Horace, had ample opportunities to see how theory matched practice. See *Herculaneum Papyrus* 222 and Obbink (1995).

5 A wolf by its ears

Suetonius was a master of using detail and quotation to paint his complex picture of Tiberius as emperor, avoiding the moralistic attacks by which Tacitus shows his disapproval of the court. The comparison between ruling Rome and holding a wolf by its ears is attributed directly to Tiberius (*Tiberius* 25); also the reply from the fake Agrippa Postumus that he had gained his title in the same way that Tiberius had – by fraud. Tacitus (*Annals* 2.40) has the same story about the slave who pretended to be Augustus's legitimate heir.

Ovid's comparison of the Palatine to the home of the gods is at *Metamorphoses* 1.168–76. For his pleading praise of the divine

Augustus from exile see *Tristia* (2.22, 4.4) and *Epistulae ex Ponto*
1.1:25–9. For a fine short account of the issues in Ovid's dealings
with the *domus Caesaris* see L. Morgan (2020).

6 Publius among the fishes

Sea conditions for the unwary have changed little in the Channel
over 2,000 years. Publius's two legions were the Second and
Fourth. The Second had fought on both sides in the civil wars
which brought Augustus to power, eventually gaining the title
Augusta for its service to the new regime. Tacitus reports the
drama of the march by the sea (*Annals* 1.70) and the earlier catastrophe for Rome in the Teutoburg forest (*Annals* 1.57–90). See
also Dio (56.19:1–22) and Murdoch (2006) for a modern account.
For Aratus's *Phaenomena* see note on Chapter 19.

7 Between the emperor and his heir

Suetonius (*Augustus* 23) gives Augustus's reaction to the losses in
the Teutoburg.

8 Flattery and fear

Dio (66.14) describes Caenis's reputation for memory. For a survey of Antonia's household, within a detailed account of inscriptions referring to imperial freedmen and freedwomen, see L.
R. Penner (2013), 'The epigraphic habits of the slaves and freed
slaves of the Julio-Claudian household' (University of Calgary).
Penner gives a good account of the opportunities and difficulties of using inscriptions in the *Corpus Inscriptionum Latinarum*
(CIL) for understanding the court of the Caesars. Inscriptions
on stone are usually brief, broken and vulnerable to confusion
when, e.g., every female slave freed by Augustus, Tiberius or
Caligula can have the same name, Julia.

9 Words for a palace

For poetic grappling with the new Palatine see Ovid (*Tristia* 3.1, *Metamorphoses* 1.248).

PART TWO

10 The fox and the crow

For issues surrounding the life of Phaedrus see Henderson (2001) and E. Champlin (2005) in *Journal of Roman Studies*, 95, discussed by R. M. Edwards (2015) in *Rheinisches Museum für Philologie, Neue Folge*, 158. Champlin argues that Phaedrus was not a Greek slave but a Roman courtier writing in the persona of a Roman Aesop.

The philosopher who linked Aesop's tales to simple food was the vegetarian and abstainer from alcohol Apollonius of Tyana (*c.*3 BCE–97 CE), cited by Philostratus, *Life of Apollonius of Tyana* (5.14). Apollonius was said by Philostratus to have entered Rome in Nero's time in defiance of a ban on philosophers. The fable of the fox and the crow (1.13) is discussed by Kapust (2018).

11 Who killed the prince?

For Tiberius's nervousness at Germanicus being seen as a god in Alexandria see V. Ehrenberg and A. H. M. Jones (1955), *Documents Illustrating the Reigns of Augustus and Tiberius* (Oxford University Press), p. 320a.

Tacitus (*Annals* 3.9:3) describes the *irritamenta invidiae*, the incitement to resentment, of Piso's house on the crowded Palatine.

12 The only verdict that mattered

Marcus Aemilius Lepidus was set to lead for Piso's defence. Tacitus (Annals 1.13) describes Augustus's considering him, and others of the old aristocracy, as his successor instead of a member of his own extended family.

Tacitus (*Annals* 2.74, 3.13) reports Publius's speech in the Piso trial. See also Tacitus *Annals* 2.55:5, 2.57:3–4, 2.69, 2.75, 3.9, 3.15.

For the bronze tablets, which add substantially to the details in Tacitus's narrative, see W. Eck, A. Caballos and F. Fernandez (1996), *Das Senatus Consultum de Cn. Pisone Patre* (Munich). Also M. Griffin (1997), 'The Senate's story', *Journal of Roman Studies*, 87, and A. Cooley (2009), 'The moralising message of the Senatus Consultum de Cn. Pisone patre', *Greece & Rome*, 45(2).

13 Tiberius, Tiber and Tibur

For Tiberius on food subsidy and flattery see Tacitus *Annals* 2.87:2.

The builder of the *Via Appia* and *Aqua Appia* was Appius Claudius Caecus (*c*.312–279 BCE).

14 Hercules the herdsman

The night journey to Tibur is at Propertius 3.16.

Marcus Terentius Varro (116–27 BCE) was a politician and polymath who in a late work on agriculture (*De Re Rustica* 3.2:16) wrote of the threats to food prices from the demands of those providing banquets. See J. H. D'Arms (1995), 'Between Public and Private in Epulum Publicum', in *Horti Romani* (L'Erma di Bretschneider) (1998), Maddalena Cima and Eugenio La Rocca (eds).

Pliny (*Natural History* 14.97) credits Julius Caesar with serving four different wines for the first time at a public feast.

15 Care for cucumbers

Pliny refers to *triplatinum*, a luxury of lampreys, bass and other fish, at *Natural History* 35. 162. See Gowers (1993), p. 123 n.

Phaedrus's fable of the hand, foot and stomach is at 3.16.

16 Vitellia's night out

The family tree of the Vitellii is tangled and not everywhere clear.
Vitellia was the sister of Lucius and Publius, thus the aunt of Aulus
the emperor. She was also the grandmother of the Petronia who
became briefly Aulus's first wife. She was the mother of Aulus
Plautius, who would later lead Claudius's invasion of Britain.

Tacitus (*Annals* 3.49–51) reports the performance and trial of
Clutorius Priscus. Also Dio 57.20:3–4.

Suetonius (*Tiberius* 42) notes Tiberius's appointments of fellow
heavy drinkers and his commissioning of a dialogue between
various courses of a banquet – a mushroom, an oyster, a thrush
and a fig-eating warbler.

17 Pen and knives

Plutarch (*c*.40 CE–*c*.120), a Greek priest at Delphi, was one of the
earliest sources for the first-century imperial court, author of the
famous *Parallel Lives* of noble Greeks and Romans. He also wrote
separate lives of the eight emperors from Augustus to Vitellius;
only those of Galba and Otho, two of Vitellius's predecessors in
the Year of the Four Emperors, have survived. Plutarch (*Cato*
56) describes Caesar's puritanical enemy, Marcus Porcius Cato,
as vowing not to recline at dinner while Caesar's tyranny is still
a threat. Cato is paired in the *Parallel Lives* with the Athenian
general known, mockingly by his enemies, as Aristides the Just.

There are various versions of the fable of the bat who cannot decide
between the birds and the beasts. Phaedrus's is fable 18.

Dio (57.195) and Tacitus (*Annals* 4.1) describe Sejanus's relationship
with Apicius. The invention of foie gras is credited to Apicius
himself by Pliny (*Natural History* 8.77). The attribution of recipes, then as now, is notoriously inexact.

Tacitus (*Annals* 4.12) has Agrippina as open-mouthed for power as
for food. He is as hostile to women in public life as to slaves and
former slaves. See M. Beard (1995), 'Imaginary Horti: Or Up the
Garden Path', in *Horti Romani* and note on Chapter 32.

Tacitus (*Annals* 4.52) has Agrippina charging Tiberius with hypocrisy for the simultaneous worship of Augustus and prosecution of his descendants.

18 The way of the guard captain

Phaedrus's fable of the fox and the peacock is 1.3 and of the frogs complaining about the sun 1.6.

Suetonius (*Tiberius* 39) tells the story of Tiberius in the cave. See Conticello and Andreae (1974). Reviewed by A. F. Stewart in *JRS*, 67 (1977). For a modern life of Sejanus see McHugh (2020).

19 Water on dust

For Phaedrus (2.5), the emperor and the watering can, see Henderson (2001).

There is much argument about the content, origins and influence of the *phlyax* plays. See Trendall (1967) and Taplin (1992).

For discussion of Suetonius's account of Tiberius's sexual interests, and the role of the *spintria*, see E. Champlin (2011), 'Sex on Capri', *Transactions of the American Philological Association* 141(2), pp. 315–22. Also B. Gladhill (2020), 'Tiberius on Capri and the limits of Roman sex culture' (McGill). Suetonius (*Tiberius* 45.1) reports Tiberius as the goat lapping up the doe.

Parrhasius (*c*.430–350 BCE), from Ephesus and Athens, is sometimes described as the first pornographer in painting.

Suetonius (*Galba* 5) describes Livia's bequest. Plutarch (*Galba* 3) says that he and Livia were related. Plutarch's *Galba* is one of the most positive portraits of the period, highlighting the attempt by the first of the four emperors of 69 CE to reject the court culture of the Palatine.

20 Profits from propinquity

Suetonius (*Caligula* 19) reports Thrasyllus's prophecy about Caligula being as likely to become emperor as to walk across the Bay of Naples.

Dio Cassius (57, 21, 3) suggests that Tiberius banished all actors from Rome in 23 CE because they debauched women and caused 'uproar'. See also Suetonius (*Tiberius* 37).

For the redistribution of wealth through the confiscations from the condemned see E. Champlin (1992), 'Death and taxes', *Studi Italiani di Filologia Classica*, 10.

21 Death of the damned

For the significance of Rubellius Blandus see R. Syme (1982), 'The wedding of Rubellius Blandus', *American Journal of Philology*, 103(1).

Tacitus (*Annals* 5.8) reports the death of Publius Vitellius. The charges and the suicide belong in Book Six, but the incorrect numbering in Book Five goes back to the sixteenth century and still survives. Also Suetonius (*Vitellius* 2).

For Grattius's *Cynegetica* see J. Henderson (2001), 'Going to the Dogs', *Proceedings of the Cambridge Philological Society*, 47.

For the economic crisis of 33 CE see Tacitus *Annals* (6 16–17). For a modern account, see too P. Temin (2001), 'A market economy in the Early Roman Empire', *Journal of Roman Studies*, 91.

22 Lucius Vitellius and the Son of God

St John's gospel (19:12) has the line that 'If you release him you are no friend of Caesar.' For the limited Roman mentions of the crucifixion of Jesus see Tacitus (*Annals* 15.44) and Josephus (*Antiquities of the Jews* 18.3). Joseph ben Matthias (*c*.37 CE–*c*.100) (Titus Flavius Josephus) is the historian who wrote closest to Vitellius's time as emperor. He was born soon after Lucius organised the recall of Pontius Pilate and moved in his thirties from being a supporter of Jewish revolts to a recogniser of the power and authority of the Roman Empire. His account was later extended and enhanced by Christian sources.

Lucius's predecessor in Syria was Pomponius Flaccus. Suetonius (*Vitellius* 6) gives a dismissive account of Aulus Vitellius' wives.

23 Goat worship

See Dio (59.26:5–10) on Caligula's new god-like clothes for seducing his sisters, and Suetonius (*Caligula* 22.2) for the emperor and the statues of his favourite gods wearing the same clothes. Tacitus (*Annals* 6.20) records Passienus Crispus on Caligula as servant and master.

24 Ill will for the twin

Suetonius (*Caligula* 21) records the start of the *Aqua Claudia*.

25 Man talks to a Moon

Dio (59.27:6) and Suetonius (*Caligula* 22.4) describe Caligula's view of the heavens. Phaedrus (1.26) tells the fable of the fox and the stork.

For the idea that the *Fratres Arvales* had origins earlier than Rome itself see Aulus Gellius (*Attic Nights* 7.7:7) and Pliny (*Natural History* 17.2:6).

26 Good water, golden meat

Suetonius (*Caligula* 22) reports the gold statue and its regular change of dress. Juvenal (*Satires* 6.615–20) jokes of Caesonia the poisoner.

Phaedrus (5.7) tells the story of the actor and the emperor. See Henderson (2001).

27 Torture of an actress

Philo (*c.*20 BCE–50 CE) was a pioneer in connecting Greek and Jewish philosophy. His role (*Legatio ad Gaium, Embassy to Caligula* 361) in the delegation to Caligula in 40 CE and its discussion on the benefits of pork and lamb is his only recorded appearance in political history. Josephus (*Antiquities of the Jews* 19) recounts the death of Caligula. See Wiseman (2013).

28 Garden ornaments

Aricia as Horace's first stop on his diplomatic journey for the future
Emperor Augustus is at *Satires* 1.5. Pliny (*Natural History* 33.145)
reports Rotundus Drusillianus's ownership of a silver plate
weighing 500 pounds (350 modern pounds) and eight others
half the size but still substantial on any table.

The best account of Grattius, the dog poet, is by J. Henderson (2001)
in *Proceedings of the Cambridge Philological Society*, 47, a witty
defence of the poet against those who have treated him as barely
better than a dog himself . Ovid's single mention of Grattius is at
Letters from Pontus 4.16:34. The dogs from what is now Ukraine
are the *Geloni*.

29 Lucius rules the world

Horace (*Odes* 3.5:2–4) echoes Augustus's British ambitions.
Suetonius (*Claudius* 17) and Dio (60.19–23) recount Aulus
Plautius's invasion of Britain for Claudius. Strabo (*c.*64 BCE–24
CE) in his *Geography* (4.5) gives an economic assessment for
invading and holding Britain. For the best modern account see
Hingley (2022).

Josephus (*Jewish War* 7.1.3) describes the award to officers of miniature spears and eagles of silver and gold. To some soldiers the
award of a soft-tipped spear to a eunuch might have seemed less
outrage than irony. The second-century lawyer and writer on
strategy Polyaenus (*Stratagems* 8.23.5) describes the role of elephants in Britain.

Seneca (*Apocolocyntosis* 13.12) mocks Claudius's little white pet dog
once its owner is safely dead.

30 Ashes of a swallow

Largus's recipe for Antonia's throat medicine is from the
Oxyrhynchus Papyri (P.Oxy. 2547) and is in the Wellcome Library
for the History & Understanding of Medicine, London. Largus's

Compositiones are at PHI Latin Texts. https://latin.packhum.org/
loc/1011/1/0#0

31 Flattery's textbook

Seneca's letter to Polybius (*De Consolatione ad Polybium*) is analysed
by L. Gloyn (2014), 'Show me the way to go home', *American
Journal of Philology*, 135 (3). Dio (31–2) refers to an embarrass-
ing letter from Corsica that Seneca later tried to suppress. See
Wilson (2015).

32 A bedroom slipper

Suetonius (*Vitellius* 2) describes Lucius's performance with
Messalina's slipper. Tacitus (*Annals* 11.1–3/ 5–8) reports the prosecution and death of Valerius Asiaticus and Claudius's siding
with Suillius in the argument over legal fees and the importance
of a law career not being restricted to the already rich.

For descendants of Pallas see CIL 6. 00143 and others listed by L.
R. Penner (2013), 'The epigraphic habits of the slaves and freed
slaves of the Julio-Claudian household' (University of Calgary),
p. 128. For the literary use of Messalina's open-mouthed lust for
gardens and lovers see M. Beard (1995), 'Imaginary Horti: Or
Up the Garden Path', in *Horti Romani*. Tacitus (*Annals* 11.29 and
37–8) reports Messalina' death.

33 Of unshakable loyalty to his emperor

Pliny (*Natural History* 12.12) tells how Dionysius from Thessaly,
a wealthy importer of plane trees, on one occasion pretended
to be a freedman in order to join the court in search of power.
Suetonius (*Claudius* 28) tells the story of Arpocras. See also note
on Chapter 35.

Tacitus (*Annals* 12.4) describes Lucius Vitellius's role in Claudius's
marriage to Agrippina. Ovid's version of the Judgement of Paris
is at *Heroides* 16.

The senator who wanted the new rights of Claudius and Agrippina for himself was Alledius Severus. Tacitus (*Annales* 12.7) reports this unusual form of flattery while suggesting that Agrippina had put Severus up to it.

For the Arval Brothers see M. Beard (1985), 'Writing and ritual: A study of diversity and expansion in the Arval Acta', Papers of the British School at Rome, 53.

Plutarch (*Galba* 9.1) and Tacitus (*Annals* 15.72) report the legacy of Callistus. His name on lead pipes is at CIL 15. 07500.

Pallas's younger brother suffered harsh criticism in Judaea from Christian and Jewish writers, some elements of which he may have deserved; others probably fell upon him because of his status within the court. He found it as difficult as his predecessors and successors to deal with the addition of Christianity to the tensions between Greeks and Jews (*Acts of the Apostles* 24.24).

Lucius's accuser on treason charges in 51 CE was Junius Lupus, an otherwise unknown senator whom Claudius, after an appeal from Agrippina, sent into exile (Tacitus, *Annals* 12.42). This last piece of courtly manoeuvring is Tacitus's last reference to Lucius. Suetonius (*Vitellius* 3) records Lucius's death and the honour of his commemoration in the Forum.

34 God-given mushrooms

See V. Grimm-Samuel (1991), 'On the mushroom that deified the Emperor Claudius', *Classical Quarterly*, 42(1).

35 Aulus the educator

Seneca (*Apocolocyntosis* 10, 13) gives the list of Claudius's freedmen, sent 'on ahead' to Hades, and mocks Claudius for killing as easily as a dog shits – also as the owner of a white pet dog, being terrified by the shaggy black hound guarding the gates. Tacitus (*Annals* 13.15) describes the poisoning of Britannicus. Pliny (*Natural History* 19.33) reports Nero's diet of leeks. Phaedrus (1.7) tells the fable of the fox and the mask.

Seneca (*A consolation to Helvia, his mother* 10. 3) consoled his
mother during his exile by stressing the benefits of life away from
the banqueting halls, his absence from those who eat to vomit
and vomit to eat. The letter was written at about the same time as
his pleading flattery of Polybius.

36 Oedipus and actors

The work of Cluvius Rufus was influential on later understanding
of the fall of the Caesars. An enthusiast for the theatre as well as
politics, he is arguably the best candidate to be what is known as
the 'common source' for the Year of the Four Emperors, the lost
contemporary account used by Plutarch, Tacitus, Suetonius and
maybe Dio and Josephus too. The career of Aulus Vitellius, as
recorded by those historians, provides some of the best evidence
for this unrecognised eyewitness. For his life and scraps of identifiable work see Wiseman (2013) and Cornell (2013).

The anonymous author of *Acts of the Apostles* (18.17) describes the
refusal of Seneca's brother Gallio to involve himself in disputes
between Jews and Christians. Seneca's advice to Serenus in difficult times is *On Peace of Mind* (*c.*60 CE), a recommendation
to steer a middle way between sobriety and drunkenness – also
between other extremes.

The dating of Calpurnius Siculus is disputed. T. P. Wiseman (1982),
'Calpurnius Siculus and the Caludian Civil War', makes a pow-
erful case for the time of Nero (*Journal of Roman Studies*, 72).
Calpurnius appears in J. W. Duff and A. M. Duff (1934), *Minor
Latin Poets (Vol. 1)*, Loeb Classical Library.

The Greek epigrammatist was Lucilius. The object of Nero's penis
poem was Claudius Pollio. Lucan's exceptional flattery of Nero is
in his *Pharsalia* (1.33). Cicero wrote a poem praising his own consulship. For the mockery of Cicero the self-flatterer see Tacitus
(*Histories* 2.36) and Seneca (*On Anger* 3.37:5). Tacitus (*Annals*
12.59) reports Agrippina's lust for gardens. See M. Beard (1995),
'Imaginary Horti: Or Up the Garden Path', in *Horti Romani*.

37 Dish of Minerva

The image of the Macellum magnum on Nero's coinage is at https://www.britishmuseum.org/collection/object/C_1958-1101-1

Tacitus (*Annals* 14.1–28) gives a dramatic account of Agrippina's murder, its causes and consequences.

For the need for a staging post between Rome and Sublaqueum see B. Frischer (2010), 'The Roman Site Identified as Horace's Villa at Licenza, Italy', in G. Davis (ed.), *A Companion to Horace* (Wiley-Blackwell).

38 Blackened tables

Pliny the Younger (*Letters* 7.29:2) reports Pallas's tomb on the *Via Tiburtina*. Paul of Tarsus on the Romans for whom 'their god is their belly' is at Philippians 3:19. Tacitus (*Annals* 14.29) gives the name of the short-lived governor of Britain as Quintus Veranius. Suetonius (*Nero* 32) reports the inheritance tax of five-sixths instead of one half for freedmen who died with false imperial names. For Nero's fears of Rubellius Plautus see Tacitus (*Annals* 13.9:3.), for the comet (14.22:21) and for Plautus's death (14.58:9).

39 Food and fire

Cluvius Rufus is the likely source for the main historians' shared and detailed account of the relationship between Poppaea, her husband Otho, and Nero. For the popularity of Nero's marriage to Poppaea, as opposed to the view of it by ancient historians, see the graffiti, *Neropoppaenses*, cited in Opper (2021). For the *Domus Aurea* see Farinella (2020).

40 Tutor in vice

Suetonius (*Vitellius* 5) reports Aulus being accused of swapping gold for brass in temples. Suetonius (*Nero* 49) reports Nero's dying words. See too M. F. Gyles (1962), 'Nero: *Qualis artifex*', *Classical Journal of Middle West and South*, 57(5).

PART THREE

41 Mr Stingy

Depending on who was telling his story, Galba was either prudent with public funds or mean towards the pay demands of his army, an enemy of the Palatine court or an emperor whose fewer advisers pillaged much more money. His mostly good reputation was a product of the wholly bad reputation of Vitellius. Plutarch, who prized moral comparisons over other duties of a biographer, began a lasting trend.

Suetonius (*Nero* 50) describes the loyalty of nurses and mistresses at Nero's funeral. Dio (63.22) and Josephus (*Jewish War* 4.440) recount the Vindex revolt. See too P. A. Brunt (1959), *The Revolt of Vindex and the Fall of Nero* (Latomus).

Suetonius (*Vitellius* 6) describes Vitellius's son as a stammerer and (*Galba* 13) reports Galba being mocked with a line attacking meanness from an Atellane farce.

42 A good job for a glutton

Aulus's relative in Pannonia was Lucius Flavianus. Suetonius (*Vitellius* 7) describes Aulus's appointment to Germany and popularity for belching. For the Nero drain cover in Cologne see Wolff (2003). Tacitus (*Histories* 1.46–55) describes Aulus's adoption by the German armies.

For a commemoration of freedmen's freedmen, see the tribute to Scurranus and his business manager, Venustus, his household accountant, Deciminianus, his doctor, Agathopus, his dresser, Primus, and Tiasos, his cook. CIL 6. 01597, cited by L. R. Penner (2013), 'The epigraphic habits of the slaves and freed slaves of the Julio-Claudian household' (University of Calgary).

43 Fill me up!

Dio (64.3) reports Galba's view of the Palatine court. For Acte's own court see L. R. Penner (2013), 'The epigraphic habits of the slaves and freed slaves of the Julio-Claudian household' (University of Calgary), p. 228 and Appendix K.

For street plan of Cologne see Wolff (2003). Suetonius (*Vitellius* 8) reports Aulus's wit following the fire at his headquarters. Tacitus (*Histories* 1.15, 1.48) explains Galba choosing Piso over Otho as a strike against flatterers.

44 A hard man to flatter

Suetonius (*Otho* 6) reports Otho's password. Tacitus (*Histories* 1.76) tells of the feast in Carthage given by Crescens in support of Otho.

45 Brother behind the lines

Tacitus (*Histories* 2.47–8) describes the suicide of Otho and (2.54) reports the first flattery of Lucius Vitellius as the brother of the next emperor.

46 Wine for the battlefield

Horace's ode (1.7) is addressed to Plancus. For a discussion of Horace's attitude to Plancus and to Tibur see J. Moles (2002), 'Reconstructing Plancus', *Journal of Roman Studies*, 92.

For the site of Lugdunum see J. F. Drinkwater (1975), 'Lugdunum: "Natural capital" of Gaul?', *Britannia*, 6. Tacitus (*Histories* 2.54) reports Aulus's execution of Gnaeus Cornelius Dolabella, the husband of his first wife, Petronia.

Plutarch's narrative of Bedriacum and the battles of 69 CE focuses on the unusual independence of Roman legionaries from their chains of command. Tacitus agrees, while putting somewhat more emphasis on the orders of their officers. For a discussion of these shades of difference see G. Morgan (2006), pp. 5–8. See too E. Manolaraki (2005), 'A picture worth a thousand words: Revisiting Bedriacum', *Classical Philology*, 100. Plutarch toured the battlefield himself; see R. Syme (1980), 'Biographers of the Caesars', *Museum Helveticum*, 37(2).

47 The Shield of Minerva

Pliny (*Natural History* 35.163) and Suetonius (*Vitellius* 13.2) report the Shield of Minerva. Tacitus (*Histories* 2.95.3) gives the cost. Dio (65.2) explains that the silver was necessary not to show extravagant luxury but to make a dish of sufficient size. For Rotundus Drusillianus's silver plate see note on Chapter 28.

48 Emperor Vitellius

Dio (65.2) reports Vibius Crispus's gratitude for the illness that took him away from the table and saved his life. The expulsion of astrologers is at 65.4.

Tacitus (*Histories* 2.82, 3.8) shows Vespasian prioritising control of Egyptian corn and the ability to starve Rome over being with his army in the field. To be in Alexandria Vespasian had the support of the imperial prefect, Tiberius Julius Alexander, a proof that Augustus's policy of banning ambitious senators from Egypt and using personal appointees instead had failed.

49 No time for a party

Rosius Regulus was the consul for one day. The party-giver was Caecina Tuscus. Tacitus (*Histories* 3.12–14) reports Caecina in chains.

50 A drink to defeat

Tacitus (*Histories* 3.42–62) reports the death of Valens.

51 In Augustus's temple

For a discussion of Sabinus, Vespasian's elder brother, see K. Gilmartin Wallace (1987), 'The *Flavii Sabini* in Tacitus', Historia, 36. Tacitus (*Histories* 3.68–79) reports the negotiations with Sabinus and his death.

52 Out of the doghouse

Tacitus (*Histories* 3.71) reports the burning of the records.

53 New courts for old

On Aulus's very public humiliation see Pliny (*Natural History* 34. 24). Tacitus and Cassius Dio record Aulus's last words.

On the father of Claudius Etruscus Statius (*Silvae* 3.3) see Weaver (1965). For Caenis's legacy see CIL. 6. 04057.

See A. Sillett (2018), 'The Prince and the Pauper', whatwould cicerodo.wordpress.com for the Roman procurator in the adaptation of Roman government for empire. For the continuing lamentations of anti-Roman exiles from Commagene see Josephus (Jewish War 7.231–6).

Suetonius (*Vitellius* 1) begins his Life with contrasting accounts of the origins of the Vitellii, the flattering and the dismissive, and does not choose between them, a scepticism which improved his reputation among later writers, such as Vopiscus (fourth century). See H. W. Bird (1971), 'Suetonian influences in the later lives of the *Historia Augusta*', Hermes, 99, p. 131.

For representations of Vitellius in art and the donkey-headed Christian graffiti see Beard (2021). The late punishment of Ephaproditus for his role in Nero's suicide is described by Suetonius (*Domitian* 14.4) and Cassius Dio (67 14.4).

Suetonius (*Vespasian* 4) and Dio (66.11–12) recount the story of Vespasian and Phoebus.

Tacitus (*Annals* 3.55) describes approvingly Vespasian's attitude to banqueting. See also Mommsen (1996).

For the sixteenth-century Palatine see N. Nonaka (2015), 'The aviaries of the Farnese Gardens on the Palatine', *Memoirs of the Academy in Rome*, 59/60 (University of Michigan Press). For the Palatine of St Petersburg see Larmour and Spencer (2007).

Epictetus compares life to banqueting with the gods (*Handbook* 15), arguing that any superior is divine (*Discourses* 4.1). He describes life as a play (*Handbook* 17) and the danger of wanting both the lettuce and the money, the ancient equivalent of having one's cake and eating it (*Handbook* 25). Statius (*Silvae* 3.3:50) in his poem on the father of Claudius Etruscus describes the hierarchy in which everyone is a slave to a higher power.

BIBLIOGRAPHY

Adams, J. (1982), *The Latin Sexual Vocabulary* (Duckworth)

Baldwin, B. (1992), *The Career and Work of Scribonius Largus* (Rheinische Museum für Philologie), Neue Folge, 135, pp. 74–82

Ball, L. F. (2003), *The Domus Aurea and the Roman Architectural Revolution* (Cambridge University Press)

Balsdon, J. P. V. D. (1934), *The Emperor Gaius* (Clarendon Press)

—(1979) *Romans and Aliens* (Duckworth)

Beard, M. (2021), *Twelve Caesars: Images of Power from the Ancient World to the Modern* (Princeton University Press)

—(2015) *SPQR: A History of Ancient Rome* (Profile)

Bédoyère, G. de la (2017), *Praetorian: The Rise and Fall of Rome's Imperial Bodyguard* (Yale University Press)

Brothwell, D. and P. (1998), *Food in Antiquity: A Survey of the Diet of Early People* (Johns Hopkins University Press)

Conticello, B. and Andreae, B. (1974), *Die Skulpturen von Sperlonga* (Mann, Berlin)

Conybeare, F. C. (1911), *Philostratus: The Life of Apollonius of Tyana* (Harvard University Press)

Cornell, T. J. (ed.) (2013), *The Fragments of the Roman Historians* (Oxford University Press)

Corpus Inscriptionum Latinorum (CIL) 1863– (Berlin)

Davidson, J. (1997), *Courtesans and Fishcakes: The Consuming Passions of Classical Athens* (HarperCollins)

Eden, P. T. (ed.) (1984), *Seneca, Apocolocyntosis* (Cambridge University Press)

Farinella, V. (2020), *The Domus Aurea* (Electa)

Frassinetti, P. (1967), *Atellanae Fabulae* (In Aedibus Athenaei, Romae)

Garnsey, P. (1988), *Famine and Food Supply in the Graeco-Roman World: Responses to Risk and Crisis* (Cambridge University Press)

Gowers, E. (1993), *The Loaded Table: Representations of Food in Roman Literature* (Clarendon Press Oxford)

Griffin, M. T. (1984), *Nero: The End of a Dynasty* (Routledge)

Hard, R. (ed.) (2014), *Epictetus, Discourses, Fragments, Handbook* (Oxford University Press)

Henderson, J. (2001), *Telling Tales on Caesar: Roman Stories from Phaedrus* (Oxford University Press)

—(2004) *Aesop's Human Zoo: Roman Stories about Our Bodies* (University of Chicago Press)

Hingley, R. (2022), *Conquering the Ocean: The Roman Invasion of Britain* (Oxford University Press)

Kapust, D. J. (2018), *Flattery and the History of Political Thought: That Glib and Oily Art* (Cambridge University Press)

Kuttner, A. L. (1995), *Dynasty and Empire in the Age of Augustus: The Case of the Boscoreale Cups* (University of California Press Berkeley)

Laes, C. (2018), *Disabilities and the Disabled in the Roman World: A Social and Cultural History* (Cambridge University Press)

Larmour, H. J. and Spencer, D. (eds) (2007), *The Sites of Rome: Time, Space, Memory* (Oxford University Press)

Levick, B. (2001), *Claudius* (Routledge)

—(1999) *Tiberius, the Politician* (Routledge)

McHugh, J. S. (2020), *Sejanus: Regent of Rome* (Pen & Sword)

Millar, F. (1997), *The Emperor in the Roman World* (Duckworth)

—(1964) *A study of Cassius Dio* (Clarendon Oxford Press)

Mommsen, T. (1996), *A History of Rome under the Emperors* (Routledge)

Mooney, G. W. (ed.) (1930), *Suetoni Tranquilli De Vita Caesarum Libri VII–VIII* (Longman)

Morgan, G. (2006), *69 A.D.: The Year of Four Emperors* (Oxford University Press)

Morgan, L. (2020), *Ovid: A Very Short Introduction* (Oxford University Press)

Mouritsen, H. (2011), *The Freedman in the Roman World* (Cambridge University Press)

Murdoch, A. (2006), *Rome's Greatest Defeat: Massacre in the Teutoburg Forest* (History Press)

Obbink, D. (1995), *Philodemus in Italy* (University of Michigan Press Ann Arbor)

Opper, T. (2021), *Nero: the man behind the myth* (British Museum)

Romm, J. (2014), *Dying Every Day: Seneca at the Court of Nero* (Knopf)

Rowe, G. (2002), *Princes and Political Cultures* (University of Michigan Press)

Spawforth, A. J. S. (ed.) (2007), *The Court and Court Society in Ancient Monarchies* (Cambridge University Press)

Sullivan, J. P. (trans) (1986), *Petronius, The Satyricon / Seneca, The Apocolocyntosis* (Penguin Classics)

Taplin, O. (1992), *Comic Angels: and Other Approaches to Greek Drama through Vase-Paintings* (Clarendon Press)

Trendall, A. D. (1967), *Phlyax Vases* (University of London Institute of Classical Studies)

Vehling, J. D. (1936), *Apicius: Cookery and Dining in Imperial Rome* (Walter M. Hill, Chicago)

Vickers, M. and Gill, D. (1994), *Artful Crafts: Ancient Greek Silverware and Pottery* (Oxford University Press)

Wallace-Hadrill, A. (1996), 'The Imperial Court', in the *Cambridge Ancient History,* Vol. 10, *The Augustan Empire 43 BC–AD 69* (1996) (Cambridge University Press)

Weaver, P. R. C. (1964), 'The slave and freedman 'cursus' in the imperial administration', Vol. 10 (Cambridge Philosophical Society)

—(1965) 'The Father of Claudius Etruscus: Silvae 3.3', *Classical Quarterly,* Vol. 15(1) (Cambridge University Press)

Wellesley, K. (1989), *The Year of the Four Emperors* (Routledge)

Wilson, E. (2015), *Seneca: A Life* (Allen Lane)

Wiseman, T. P. (2013), *The Death of Caligula* (Liverpool University Press)

—(2019) *The House of Augustus: A Historical Detective Story* (Princeton University Press)

Wolff, G. (2003), *Roman-Germanic Cologne* (Bachem, Cologne)

ACKNOWLEDGEMENTS

To Mary Beard, Joanna Evans, Ed Lake, Caroline Michel, Ruth Scurr, Andrew Sillett, Stefan Vranka, Paul Webb, *Optimi Lectores*, the very best of readers.

INDEX

New Perspectives in Philosophy
of Education

Also available from Bloomsbury

Authority and the Teacher, William H. Kitchen
Education as a Human Right, Tristan McCowan
Deleuze & Guattari, Politics and Education, edited by Matthew Carlin and Jason Wallin
Teaching as the Practice of Wisdom, David Geoffrey Smith
Critical Narrative as Pedagogy, Ivor Goodson and Scherto Gill
Education in a Post-Metaphysical World, Christopher Martin

New Perspectives in Philosophy of Education

Ethics, Politics and Religion

Edited by David Lewin,
Alexandre Guilherme and Morgan White

Bloomsbury Academic
An imprint of Bloomsbury Publishing Plc

B L O O M S B U R Y
LONDON · NEW DELHI · NEW YORK · SYDNEY

Bloomsbury Academic
An imprint of Bloomsbury Publishing Plc

50 Bedford Square	1385 Broadway
London	New York
WC1B 3DP	NY 10018
UK	USA

www.bloomsbury.com

BLOOMSBURY and the Diana logo are trademarks of Bloomsbury Publishing Plc

First published 2014

British Library Cataloguing-in-Publication Data
A catalogue record for this book is available from the British Library.

ISBN: HB: 978-1-4725-1340-3
ePub: 978-1-4725-1336-6
ePDF: 978-1-4725-1396-0

Library of Congress Cataloging-in-Publication Data
A catalog record for this book is available from the Library of Congress.

Typeset by Integra Software Services Pvt. Ltd.

Contents

Acknowledgements

The editors would like to thank all the contributors to this volume for their scholarship, collaboration and commitment. In particular, we would like to express our gratitude to Professor Paul Standish for his support throughout this project, from his initial agreement to speak at the philosophy of education conference ("What's the Use of Philosophy of Education?") at Liverpool Hope University in June 2012, to his continuing commitment to philosophy of education in the UK and beyond. We would also like to thank Liverpool Hope University for supporting this project and for its ongoing support for philosophy of education.

Notes on Contributors

David Aldridge is Principal Lecturer in Philosophy of Education at Oxford Brookes University, UK, where he is also Programme Lead for Secondary and Post-Compulsory ITE, Master's Programmes in Education and the Educational Doctorate. He taught and led Religious Education and Philosophy in secondary schools for ten years and now serves on the executive committee of the Philosophy of Education Society of Great Britian. His primary research interest is the philosophy of education, particularly from the perspectives of hermeneutics, phenomenology and continental philosophy. He is currently preparing a monograph, *A Hermeneutics of Religious Education*, for Bloomsbury, and is also co-editing a volume, *Realism in Religious Education*.

Alexandre Guilherme has taught philosophy and education at the universities of Edinburgh, Durham and Liverpool Hope, UK, and has held visiting positions at the Université de Neuchatel, Switzerland, Universität Bern, Switzerland, Universitetet i Oslo, Norway, Maastricht University, the Netherlands, and Ponticia Universidad Catolica Peru (PUCP). In 2010–2011, he was awarded Postdoctoral Research Fellowship at the Institute for Advanced Studies in Humanities, University of Edinburgh, UK, to work on his research project entitled *Martin Buber's Philosophy of Dialogue: A Tool for Reconciliation*. As a consequence of this, he has published extensively on the topic of dialogical education as a tool for reconciliation between communities in conflict. He has also published material in the fields of philosophy and theology in connection to Spinoza, Fichte and Schelling and has translated a number of works by Leonardo Boff, the Brazilian philosopher and theologian, one of the founders of Liberation Theology.

David Lewin is Senior Lecturer in Education at Liverpool Hope University, UK, where he leads the Philosophy of Education Special Interest Group. He is the author of *Technology and the Philosophy of Religion* (2011) and has co-edited (with Todd Mei) *From Ricoeur to Action: the Socio-Political Significance of Ricoeur's Thinking* (2012). His recent research has addressed philosophical significance of modern technology, and he is currently working on theological pedagogy, drawing on contemplative religious traditions.

David Lundie is Lecturer in Education at Liverpool Hope University, UK. He is a co-author of *Does Religious Education Work? A multi-dimensional investigation* (2013) and was a member of the Privacy Aware Design Strategies research team at Cornell University, USA, from 2011 to 2012. His research draws attention to an intersubjective phenomenology of learning, and his recent research interests have focused on the design of educational technology to preserve and enhance spaces for intersubjective encounter.

Jon Nixon works as an independent writer based in Cumbria, UK. His most recently authored books are *Hannah Arendt and the Politics of Friendship*, *Interpretive Pedagogies for Higher Education: Arendt, Berger, Said, Nussbaum and their Legacies* and *Higher Education and the Public Good: Imagining the University*. His most recent co-edited book is *Academic Identities and Higher Education: The Changing European Landscape*. He is currently working on a book entitled *Rosa Luxemburg and the Unfinished Revolution*. He has held chairs at four UK universities and is currently affiliated to the Hong Kong Institute of Education.

Adrian Skilbeck has been teaching in the secondary education sector for twenty years and is now undertaking doctoral studies at the Institute of Education, University of London, UK, under the supervision of Professor Paul Standish. His research draws on the work of Stanley Cavell and Raimond Gaita and is focused on the concept of seriousness in education, its personal and impersonal character, and its association with ideas of voice and presence. His wider research interests include moral philosophy, philosophy and literature, drama in education and the application of drama pedagogy to philosophical questions.

Richard Smith is Professor of Education at the University of Durham, UK. He was editor of the *Journal of Philosophy of Education* (1991–2001) and founding editor of *Ethics and Education* (2006–2013). His principal research interests are in the philosophy of education and the philosophy of social science. His most recent book is the edited collection *Education Policy: Philosophical Critique* (2013). *Understanding Education and Educational Research*, co-written with Paul Smeyers, will be published in 2014.

Paul Standish is Professor of Philosophy of Education at the Institute of Education, University of London, UK. He has published widely in the philosophy of education. Recent books include *The Therapy of Education* (2006), co-authored with Paul Smeyers and Richard Smith; *The Philosophy of Nurse Education* (2007), co-edited with John Drummond; and *Stanley Cavell and the Education of Grownups* (2011), co-edited with Naoko Saito. From 2001 to 2011 he was Editor of the *Journal of Philosophy of Education*.

Judith Suissa is Reader in Philosophy of Education at the Institute of Education, University of London, UK. Her research interests include anarchist and libertarian educational theory, political philosophy and parent–child relationship. She is the author of *Anarchism and Education* (2006) and co-author, with Stefan Ramaekers, of *The Claims of Parenting; Reasons, Responsibility and Society* (2012).

John Sullivan was, from 2002 to 2013, Professor of Christian Education at Liverpool Hope University, UK, where he is now Professor Emeritus. He is also Visiting Professor in Theology and Education at Newman University, Birmingham, UK. He has taught, from classroom teacher to Headteacher level, in several secondary schools, served in senior leadership roles in a Local Education Authority and has substantial teaching experience (BA, MA, PhD) in universities. Author and editor of seven books and more than seventy chapters on religion and education, he is interested in the mutual bearing on each other of theology and education and also in continuing professional development.

David Torevell is Associate Professor of Theology and Christian Education at Liverpool Hope University, UK. He has published two monographs – *Losing the Sacred: Ritual, Modernity and Liturgical Reform* (2000) and *Liturgy and the Beauty of the Unknown. Another Place* (2007). He has edited books on theology and aesthetics and published numerous articles on his research interests, which are liturgy, Christian education, aesthetics and philosophy of education. He is the principal editor of the *Liverpool Hope University Studies in Ethics Series*.

Morgan White is a lecturer in education studies at Liverpool Hope University, UK. His research interests are in political theory and the failure of much contemporary political philosophy to attend properly to relationships between education and politics. He has published in the *Journal of Philosophy of Education* and is currently working on research around ideas related to democratic theory, especially the work of Hannah Arendt and Jürgen Habermas, and university education. Prior to lecturing, he worked as a school teacher for over a decade.

Ruth Wills is a doctoral student at the University of Winchester, UK. Her thesis involves a critical appraisal of spiritual pedagogy and reflects philosophically on issues regarding learning and the learner. She is Secretary of the International Association of Children's Spirituality and a member of the Philosophy of Education Society of Great Britain. She also teaches music in a UK primary school, has 18 piano students and is a foster carer.

Introduction

David Lewin, Alexandre Guilherme and Morgan White

The pathos of modern philosophy of education is its false humility. Philosophy of education should not see itself as handmaiden to the purer contemplation of philosophy proper. Nor do the applied fields of enquiry on which policy and practice are constructed stand without founding principles. Rather, philosophy of education lies between two poles of contemplation and application.

So, what is philosophy of education? One possible answer is given in a recent review of the relevance of philosophy to education studies. John Haldane noted that, in the early 1950s, H. M. Knox distinguished between *educational philosophy* and *philosophy of education* (Haldane, 2012, p. 4; Knox 1952). While the former tended to concern the ideas of 'great educators', the latter was about reflective, theoretical conceptual enquiry. Knox was keen to focus attention upon the development of *educational* theory. For Knox, philosophy of education was not so much about discussion of the relevance of what might be seen as the philosophical canon (Plato, Aristotle, Hegel and the like) for educational matters but about educational themes related to philosophical topics themselves: humanism, realism, naturalism, idealism and the assessment of aims and values. In a similar vein, Haldane suggests that philosophical work in the field of education ought to give up on the patronage of mainline philosophy (applying popularized versions of philosophical ideas of the last generation) and instead adopt the approach of case-based reasoning found in *casuistry*. Here analysis is combined with hermeneutic interpretation and ethical evaluation in, for example, addressing questions about the permissable boundaries of agents with particular responsibilities in particular circumstances, or about the ends, values and ideals that might govern a particular practice (Haldane, 2012, p. 14). Theoretical reflection upon cases is capable of generating new concepts and arguments because educational theory is contextual and practical. While Haldane is right to worry about the status of the philosophy of education in relation to philosophy departments in British universities, we should not forget that any social, political, epistemic, ethical or philosophical questions that take seriously issues about how society ought to be organized given fundamental features of human nature must involve questions about education: what to teach, to whom and by what methods? Haldane here revisits the ancient dichotomy of the theoretical and the practical and finds his answer in the case-based approach.

Since the heyday of philosophy of education in the 1960s, when R. S. Peters published his seminal *Ethics and Education*, philosophers now find themselves with fewer opportunities to explore the fundamentals of education in academia. Speak to most philosophers of education in the United Kingdom today and you will get the unmistakable impression that philosophy of education is being increasingly marginalized in educational curricula. This is most obvious in the domain of Teacher Education, where the requirement to conform to a narrowly defined conception of education is now dominant. Historically, university departments of education in the United Kingdom were largely concerned with Teacher Education and so the existence of 'education' as a subject of inquiry was generally pursued within that context. But recent developments suggest this is undergoing significant change.

Over the last few years there has been a considerable growth in programmes of study that aim to widen the perspectives of educational discourse. These courses, generally titled 'Education Studies' or just 'Education', are typically separated from programmes in Teacher Education and often introduce students to educational theory through what in the 1960s were identified as the four disciplines of education: psychology, sociology, history and philosophy (Hirst, 1983) – later this led to the development of other disciplines, such as economics of education and anthropology of education. This surge of interest in the wider questions of education cannot be dismissed as only a reaction to the current constraints of teacher education in the United Kingdom, a 'negation of the negation'; rather they represent a substantive opportunity to reimagine the field of 'education' (cf. Furlong, 2013). It is here, then, that we are likely to find new directions for philosophy of education being explored.

The present volume was first conceived in the context of just such efforts to reimagine the study of education, where in 2011 at Liverpool Hope University a new Education Studies programme was established.[1] A conference to address the relevance of philosophy of education took place in June 2012 at Liverpool Hope, where many of the ideas for this book first came together. So while we must acknowledge that these are difficult times for subjects across the arts and humanities, including philosophy of education, given the social and political climate in which we live, we also believe there are exciting opportunities for philosophers of education and educationalists with an interest in the discipline.

Despite a certain optimism, one must wonder whether philosophers of education can be of help in finding solutions to some of the more acute and intractable problems of our current social and political context; or are they allowing themselves, unwittingly perhaps, to become part of the conventional machinery of socio-political compromise by understanding their role primarily as one of offering solutions? On the one hand, the need to engage in policy discussion and policy formation might involve an impulse to challenge existing structures or to propose radical alternatives in a bid to remain 'policy relevant'. On the other hand, there are pressures to engage in reasonable and realistic debate, but one can wonder whether such reasonableness is too often encoded in something altogether too restrictive. As the prominent environmentalist David Brower once said of his own tendency to engage in environmental debate: 'I was not always unreasonable, and I am sorry for that' (Brower, 2000: 26). The desire to seem reasonable can be regarded by some as the inhibition of the political and social imagination.

In engaging with contemporary social and political discourse, then, we might ask whether philosophers of education are gadflies or sophists. This convenient dichotomy is some consolation to those who are content to remain disengaged from the institutions that constitute our socio-political world. Cynics can simply maintain that the gadflies are too marginal while the sophists are too mainstream, and therefore philosophers of education must indeed walk a fine line. In times when 'education' is a topic so politically charged, to the point of becoming a significant aspect of the election battleground (because 'education' is increasingly regarded as a panacea for our social, political and economic ills) and because research and inquiry, under the banner of the Research Excellence Framework, in Britain are expected to involve a narrowly construed 'impact' upon society (cf. Furlong, 2011), philosophers of education face the pressure to provide some political leverage that makes purely philosophical claims appear equivocal or dilute. However, this is surely an opportunity to do philosophy at the coalface, because it is this interdisciplinary space that will challenge efforts to separate the pure from the applied and the theoretical from the practical. Those directly involved with 'education' – the teachers and lecturers, as well as the students they teach – know only too well that the practitioner cannot simply comply uncritically, just as the critic cannot remain objectively disengaged.

This book seeks to be both specific in concern and wide in scope, at the same time that it develops the field of philosophy of education and engages with some headline issues currently faced by those interested in education. All convenient dichtomies must, then, be put to one side: the pure and the applied, the formal and informal, directed and non-directed, constructivist and objectivist. All such dichtomies are the bread and butter of educational theory, but from the wider vistas that this book opens onto, they conceal as much as they reveal. The chapters contained in this book are not unified by one particular philosophical perspective, methodology or tradition, still less by a single vision of what the purposes of education ought to be. Indeed, the effort to specify schools and traditions within philosophy of education can serve to reinforce a parochialism that this volume hopes to undermine. Not that we should be blind to historical divisions such as continental, analytic and pragmatist philosophical schools, nor should we be unable to speak across such distinctions. It is our perception that too much theory is constrained by arbitrary thematizations, and so the contributors to this volume have been encouraged to speak within their own voice and tradition, while oriented towards shared concerns that are defined in the wide terms that structure the book.

The ethical, political and religious in education

The human being inhabits a world constituted by ethical, political and religious concerns. These themes provide the widest scope for consideration of what is most fundamental to human existence. They also provide properly philosophical contexts in which to explore problems in education. For these reasons we have organized our volume around these three categories. To be sure, these realms can never be entirely discrete: the ethical elides with the political which, in turn, can blur with the religious. This has led to discussion among the editors, for instance, about whether a particular chapter is best located in one section of the book rather than another, and our decisions still appear doubtful to us in some cases. But these considerations suggest a more significant unity operating across these three divisions.

1. As R. S. Peters argued, education is an ethical act (1966). The ethical character of education might be obscured by the role that the state plays in it. The notion that we can locate values in a private domain apart from a neutral public one has come and gone (McLaughlin, 2008). The secular *polis* (if such a term is at all meaningful) is not a value-free space, but it embodies commitments expressed not least within the ethos of education. The ethical character of education, how education is understood and taken up, requires urgent philosophical attention in an age in which the 'performative' has

largely displaced the 'deliberative'. Such focus upon the 'performative' nature of education (say, good education must be education that gets students high grades, to give an obvious example) places unhelpful limits upon the philosophical terrain and the perspectives it might offer.

2. As Paulo Freire demonstrated, education is a political act. The polis is formed to the extent that individuals can be brought into the social world through education. Clearly, the state has an important role to play in terms of defining policy and enabling practice. But perhaps what is seldom understood is the role for education in constituting the political realm. The political significance of education demands urgent philosophical attention in a time in which policy and practice lack a substantive ground.

3. For figures such as John Henry Newman, Martin Buber and Emmanuel Levinas, it would not have seemed controversial to regard education as a religious act. Today we might assume that although we cannot avoid the ethical and political dimensions of existence, surely the religious domain does not apply to all. But, rather like ethics, the religious speaks to the universal human need to express an ultimate concern. Such a concern is typically, though not necessarily, articulated in traditional forms of religious life. Here we have sought to articulate the religious as a human orientation to something that goes beyond the finite.

The decision to structure the book around three key themes should indicate that this work is not intended as a comprehensive account of contemporary philosophy of education. This would be a Herculean task, and the danger with such an approach is the false impression of unity and coherence that can result. It is rather too easy, sometimes, for students to get the impression that the knowledge they need can be gleaned from one volume, or even a set of volumes. Our liberal approach in this book asks the reader to seek the unknown, insecure and problematic and not to settle for seemingly ordered interpretations but to look at issues anew. The new perspectives of the title are not the exclusive preserve of the authors gathered here but are formed and reformed by the readers who themselves participate in the formation and interpretation of those perspectives.

The book begins with a Prelude by one of the foremost philosophers of education working in the United Kingdom today, Paul Standish. In his chapter, 'What's the Use of Philosophy of Education?' Standish provides an examination of the relations and tensions between philosophy of education and contemporary educational theory with broader cultural and philosophical concerns, setting the scene for the more specific discussions that follow. Standish explores the increasingly specialized and fractured intellectual milieu in which philosophers and educationalists are working, a milieu in which the imperative to justify one's existence in utilitarian terms is shown to be not neutral but part of a pernicious technicization of the field.

Part One, 'Ethics', begins with David Lewin's examination of the structure and scope of technological thinking. He argues that the separation of technical reason from ethical reason finds its ground in a wider metaphysical shift identified in Heidegger's philosophy of technology. Lewin contends that the ethical character of education is hidden by unrestrained technological thinking. This is followed by Chapter 3, in which David Lundie explores the information-theoretic account of knowing and learning, a model of knowledge that finds itself reinforced by the prevalence of systems of information technology. Lundie argues that human identity requires a conception of education in which learning is more than just an event in a causal chain of information processes. In Chapter 4, Adrian Skilbeck suggests that the process of thematizing ethical issues within education seeks to erase personal commitments, regarding them as antithetical to the moral seriousness appropriate to ethics. But this negation of the first person distorts the nature of ethical thinking while giving the appearance of offering a rigorous and defensible educational programme. Section one ends with David Aldridge's examination of the role of fables as moral exemplars. Aldridge draws attention to the hermeneutical complexity of Aesop's story of the fox and the crow discussed by Rousseau. Whether moral exemplars can ever be deployed as forms of directive pedagogy is complex, though Aldridge argues that this complexity calls for a reassessment of the fruitful tension between heteronomous and autonomous education.

Part Two of the volume, on 'Politics', begins with Morgan White's chapter on the instrumental nature of contemporary higher education. He argues that the present structure of our universities produces graduates and academics ill-equipped to engage as citizens in the *polis*. Jon Nixon, in Chapter 7, examines the university's hermeneutic tradition. He argues that an 'ethic of deliberation' is fundamental to understanding the humanities and the 'hermeneutical imagination'. In the context of all-too-familiar global, collective problems such as environmental degradation, energy crises and deteriorating labour standards, to name a few, it is a hermeneutical imagination combined appropriately with technical knowledge that is required to tackle such issues. Such problems require a radical reconceptualization of our universities, away from a scientized notion of culture, and towards institutions which enable human conversation. In Chapter 8, Richard Smith explores the monoculture of instrumental reason within neoliberal culture. He argues, rather than challenging such instrumental rationality, our universities are swept up in such thinking. In response the university must reassert its central value as an institution committed to the critical examination of thinking and the development of *phronesis*. In Chapter 9 Judith Suissa offers an anarchist understanding of the philosophy of education which seeks to problematize assumptions about the state and state education as the terrain upon which discussion about the philosophy of education takes place. Her argument draws attention to a latent conservatism in philosophy of education which takes for granted the contextual backdrop of the capitalist state. Suissa seeks to take seriously the possibility of a truly free and equal society and the role education might play in this, without descending into naïve blueprints and the problems usually associated with utopian revolutionary thought.

Part Three, Religion, begins with Chapter 10, in which Alexandre Guilherme provides the standard philosophical reading, as well as an alternative theological one based on the Hasidic roots of Martin Buber's thought, of the *basic words* 'I-Thou' and 'I-It'. This is followed by a discussion on the implications of Buber's philosophy for education, leading to the conclusion that 'education is *inclusive per se*'. In Chapter 11, Ruth Wills highlights a tension in spiritual education in the light of renewed government requirements that schools in England and Wales should promote a spiritual dimension to teaching and learning. This serves as the basis for Wills' discussion on the 'experiential paradigm' and her defence of the claim that the 'middle ground' is not necessarily problematic and that it can provide space for critical reflection during the educational process. In the following chapter, John Sullivan suggests ways in which theology might enrich our understanding of key issues in education, such as *who* we are as teachers and learners, *what* might be taught and learned, *how* education might be delivered and *why* do we teach and learn. Finally, in the last chapter of this volume, David Torevell analyses Xavier Beauvois' film *Of Gods and Men* (2010), a film about the lives and deaths of Cistercian monks in Algeria in 1996, and argues that it is a valuable resource for teachers working in Catholic schools, as well as elsewhere, for it bears a strong connection to Catholic theology and its relation to issues of identity and education.

Philosophers of education are caught on the horns of a false dilemma, a choice between the practical and theoretical. To remain aloof from practical considerations does not speak to the ethical, political and religious contexts in which we live. Yet to speak to and for the practical issues in education today can lead to the sublimation of the utopian imagination. There may not be a straightforward answer to the pragmatic question: 'What is the 'cash-value' of all this reflection?' But the failure to answer certain questions may only be the failure to be unreasonably reasonable. The failure calls for new forms of reason that exceed Haldane's affirmation of the situated and contextual.

One of the pressing concerns of the institutionalized activity of philosophy of education is based upon self-doubt about its status in relation to philosophy more generally. In a moment of supreme irony we are beginning to find that unwelcome changes in the political economy of academia mean that mainline philosophy will be increasingly encouraged to reflect more directly on matters of immediate human concern. This is the business of philosophy of education, the business of philosophy.

Notes

1   It is worth noting that the university initially offered disciplinary courses across both Education Studies and Teacher Education divisions of the Faculty of Education. However, the tight regulatory demands on Teacher Education made this shared endeavour unworkable.

References

Brower, D. (2000) *Let the Mountains Talk, Let the Rivers Run*. Gabriola Island: New Society Publishers.

Furlong, J. (2011) "Universities and the Discipline of Education: Understanding the Impact of the United Kingdom's Research Assessment Exercise", *Power and Education* 3(1): 18–30.

——— (2013) *Education: An Anatomy of the Discipline*. London: Routledge.

Haldane, J. (2012) 'Educational Studies and the Map of Philosophy', *British Journal of Educational Studies* 60(1): 3–15.

Hirst, P. (1983) *Educational Theory and its Foundation Disciplines*. London: Routledge & Kegan Paul.

Knox, H. (1952) "Research in Educational Theory", *British Journal of Educational Studies* 1(1): 52–55.

McLaughlin, T. M. (2008) *Liberalism, Education, and Schooling, Essays by T.M. McLaughlin*. Exeter: Imprint Academic.

Peters, R. S. (1966) *Ethics and Education*. London: George Allen and Unwin.

Prelude

1

What's the Use of Philosophy of Education?

Paul Standish

The curt directness of the question that is our starting point, its air of no-nonsense practicality, is in some ways welcome. What *is* the use? One can almost hear the gruff confidence, or perhaps the glum despair, with which the question might be asked. And it is, is it not, a rhetorical question, which might suggest that anyone who raises it is not really looking for an answer? But let us give this voice, just to see what it is that motivates the question and where it might lead.

In the 1990s Kenneth Clarke, an intelligent and in many ways thoughtful spokesperson for the Conservative party and its one-time Minister of Education, famously castigated teacher education courses as being full of 'barmy theory'. Here at last, then, so it seemed to many, was a minister who was not afraid of exposing and denouncing the ideological interests and the self-indulgent fantasies of those employed to train teachers. What was the use of all that technicist psychology, posturing sociology and abstract philosophy? If Clarke had thought in such terms, he would have been partly out of date, for in fact these disciplines had by the 1990s been displaced in some degree by the new 'sciences' of education – of curriculum theory initially but then more powerfully of school effectiveness and school improvement – with sociology rethinking itself as social policy analysis, and other disciplinary migrations towards social justice research. Had Clarke been more *au fait* with these developments, it is unlikely that he would have been reassured.

Clarke's 'barmy theory' was calculated to strike a chord with conservative Middle England, with its *Daily Mail* philistinism and fear of anything that smacked of the intellectual. But it would be wrong to suggest that such a suspicion of educational theory was isolated in this way. In the 1970s, student teachers themselves had reacted against aspects of their curriculum, especially where this introduced them to seemingly irrelevant sociological or psychological theory, or required them to attend to a apparently remote history of schooling, and some articulated a special unease about philosophical abstractions that struck them as disconnected from the challenges of the classroom; and these were, no doubt, real challenges. It was partly that unease that played into the radical reforms that Margaret Thatcher was able to introduce. Meanwhile, on the other side of the Atlantic, and in a very different educational jurisdiction, Ronald Reagan's government was gleefully encouraging the same kinds of de-skilling, anti-intellectualizing changes.

There is no difficulty then in imaging those sceptical voices that would indeed ask what the use of philosophy of education might be. But a different kind of criticism regarding philosophy has been mounted from within educational research itself. Such research has for some time been dominated by an ideology of empiricism in which it is assumed that the only way in which education policy and practice can be understood is through empirical enquiry. The gathering of empirical data is the stuff of science, and in the absence of this no serious research can be undertaken. Hence, its question to philosophy is not so much 'What is the use?' as 'What is the evidential basis for your claims?' It works with the justified concern within academic enquiry to avoid unsupported assertion, but it then inflates this into a methodological principle that casts out all else. It fails entirely to understand the Wittgensteinian insights that justification must end at some point, that not all our background assumptions can simultaneously be called into question and that our enquiries must start from somewhere.

It is important that to criticize this ideological empiricism is in no way to disparage empirical research, which is most certainly needed in various ways. It is, however, to condemn the unsupported and clearly fallacious assumption that it is only through the gathering of data that educational research can take place. This is clearly fallacious, in that all enquiry derives from assessments about what it is worth enquiring into. Such assessments involve the exercise of criticism and judgement over questions of value. Of course it may be interesting to do a survey to find out what others happen to think about such questions, but this is not going to show that the judgements they make are justified. Nor will it suffice to retreat to formulaic expressions of 'effectiveness' or of 'what works', for these leave open the questions of 'effectiveness in what respect' or 'what works in what respect'. To provide the missing justifications or to fill in the missing specifications of what works requires reasoned argument, and this is not an empirical matter.

But none of this quite takes the sting out of the expression 'What's the use?' The idea of use is intertwined with notions of instrumentality and the taking of a means to an end. Things need not be conceived exactly like this, of course, as Karl Marx's differentiation of, on the one hand, use-value, related genuinely to human needs, and, on the other, exchange-value, characterized by a 'congealing of labour-time', clearly shows. And John Dewey's pragmatism is a philosophy far more hospitable to a holistic conception of use. Let us not avoid the sting in the question, however, by shifting the metaphysical parameters in this way. What must be seen is that when we take the question on its own terms, things are less straightforward than they may seem, because the kinds of relationships that can exist between means and ends are diverse. Utilitarianism presents us with a whole philosophy geared towards a certain kind of instrumentalism, a calculus for evaluating consequences and determining efficient means to the maximization of good outcomes. It may be fashionable today to decry the effects of this way of thinking, but it is reasonable to acknowledge the way that this was an appropriate philosophy for its time: utilitarianism developed in England in the early nineteenth century, partly in response to the scale of the social problems brought about by industrial change, specifically the massive migration into the towns. It was a philosophy that sought to rise to the challenges of the large-scale planning that the situation demanded. No doubt it had its excessive forms then – forms that Charles Dickens would satirize in such novels as *Hard Times* – but its greater excesses became apparent in the twentieth century, when more ideological forms of industrial planning and social engineering came to the fore.

To take a means to an end, however, does not make one a utilitarian, and in fact it is impossible to imagine a human life of which this was not a part. The variety of relationships that is possible here, however, is certainly worthy of attention. An example from British secondary schools of the 1950s and 1960s illustrates this nicely. For many students in their teens, practical education was divided along gender lines: the boys would do woodwork or metalwork, and the girls shorthand and typing. All of these were useful activities, and they were assumed to provide skills appropriate to finding work. But there is a difference in kind between these activities, and this surely worked to the benefit of the boys: while woodwork and metalwork might be regarded as involving intrinsic satisfaction, this is far less obviously the case with the subjects the girls pursued. There can be satisfaction in typing well, but it would be odd for someone to do this without some extrinsic end (the typing of a document for a particular purpose). In other words, this is not the kind of practice that can be seen as a craft, with the inherent richness that that implies: it is purely a means to an end, and if another means were available, it might indeed be preferable. One has only to think of what has actually happened in respect of these activities for this to be seen to be true: the advent of word processors has altered the role of keyboard skills, and their eventual obsolescence with the growing refinement of voice recognition seems highly likely. Typing skills will then be useless. While industrial production continues to change ways in which, say, furniture is made, it seems unlikely that the appeal of carpentry will simply die out.

If one turns to other aspects of the curriculum, further differentiations within means–ends relationship come to light. What, we might ask, is the point of football? Candidate answers would include (i) the enhancement of physical fitness and health, (ii) the development of such virtues as team spirit and competitiveness, (iii) the enjoyment of the game itself and (iv) vocational purposes involving careers in sport. While the first two of these aims might be realized by many other means or perhaps by-passed by the taking of health-producing drugs, this specific sport is internally related to the third and possibly to the fourth too. In reality, for the physical education teacher, these four aims are likely to be unproblematically woven together. In the same way, one can question the use of teaching literature, and here answers proffer themselves, ranging from (i) the development of writing skills and (ii) the expansion of the learner's vocabulary to (iii) moral education and (iv) aesthetic appreciation. While the first three of these seem largely to instrumentalize the activity, the last restores a sense of its intrinsic worth. And again, in reality, these aims would very likely not be clearly articulated: they would sit reasonably happily together, although drawing attention to one or the other might have a telling effect on the texts chosen for study and on the manner of teaching and learning. It would surely, however, be a weak justification for the subject that concentrated only on (i) and (ii); by contrast, a robust justification would give pride of place to aesthetic appreciation, though with plenty of room still available for giving substance to the forms this should take.

These examples indicate the complex differentiations in means–ends relationships that can easily be made in terms of questions of curriculum, and they suggest the inappropriateness of a casual employment of these terms in life as a whole. What does need to be added, however, is that it is still worth identifying and guarding against a kind of ideology of instrumentalism that has infected thinking across the social sphere, including, of course, education. A lexicon of 'aims', 'objectives', 'learning outcomes' and 'mission statements' has come to provide the dominant architecture of educational discourse. The quasi-mechanistic assumptions behind this and its reduction of people to 'end-users', 'stake-holders', 'customers' and of course 'human resources' reinstall this continually in our institutional policies and practices. The familiarity of the suave and now thoroughly naturalized institutional 'HR', which has replaced 'personnel', hides the oddness of thinking of people in this way. That sense of oddness is partly retrieved, however, if we reappropriate the 'use' question and ask, rather pointedly, 'What is the use of people?' 'What's the use' and 'what's the point' are questions that can trip off the tongue too easily.

We shall at a later stage return to these matters, but for now let us take up again the question that was our starting point: What is the use of philosophy of education? When this question is posed, it is quite commonly accompanied by a background unsteadiness about what philosophy (and, therefore, philosophy of education) actually is. Let us take that as an entry point to these problems of definition and use.

Genealogy and the state of the art

It is not uncommon for people to react to the idea of philosophy of education as if it were a very strange kind of animal. What on earth can it be like, they seem to say? But I find myself perplexed at their perplexity. Jurisprudence asks philosophical questions about the nature of the law and legal practice. Philosophy of education asks comparable philosophical questions about the nature of education and educational practice. What then is the problem? Yet this is unlikely to settle the minds of those who are unclear about philosophy itself, and certainly the subject can be difficult to define or explain. So what can be said?

Understanding here is not helped, on the whole, by the summary accounts, the classifications of methods, the typologies that are found in textbooks of research methods and that then proliferate in courses inducting students into educational research. Here it is not uncommon to find tabulated lists and matrices, where, say, ontology is separated from feminism, and phenomenology is contrasted with objectivism. In such contexts, students commonly have impressed upon them the need quickly to establish their 'theoretical perspective', as if this were a precondition for the empirical or other study upon which they are to embark. This reinforces the idea of research as technical and of philosophy as dry and abstract, a matter of '-ologies' and '-isms': it profoundly distorts philosophy's nature and what is at stake when such terms are appropriately employed.

For present purposes I propose instead a more genealogical approach, and here I shall, as it were, take a step sideways and embark on the discussion in a different way. I want to pursue these matters with reference to a historic pictorial representation of the state of the art – that is, the art of philosophy: Raphael's fresco *The School of Athens*. The painting, which was completed between 1509 and 1511, is a fresco that Raphael was commissioned to paint by Pope Julius II. Pope Julius, nicknamed 'the fearsome pope' or 'the warrior pope', was one of the most powerful rulers of the age. It was his ambition to restore Rome to its classical greatness, with grand-scale architectural reconstruction, masterminded by Bramante. Raphael's extraordinary contribution to this project reaches its high point in *The School of Athens*. One of four main frescoes in the Stanza della Segnatura in the Vatican, each of which treats of a different theme, the painting answers to the imperative 'Seek knowledge of causes'. Its subject, as we have seen, is philosophy.

Let us picture Raphael's great work and consider what it reveals.[1] The perspective Raphael grants the viewer is from within the grand, palatial room that is depicted. We are, as it were, at the foot of the large marble steps that lead up to the figures depicted. Through the entrance of the room, at the centre of the painting, two men approach from the light outside. Each makes a simple gesture of the hand, elegant but contrasting gestures. The older man, Plato, rises onto his toes as if drawn upwards, flame-like in the ethereal colours of his cloak: his raised hand and finger point towards the sky. Aristotle, younger, more virile and earthly, his feet planted flat on the ground, reaches out towards us: his fingers are splayed horizontally and his palm turned down. These two gestures, vertical and horizontal, articulate the coordinates of the painting, affirming those properties that ally painting with the rational art of the geometer, taking the measure of heaven and earth.

Each man holds a book, a book he has authored himself: Plato, the *Timaeus*, a cosmological discussion of the divine source of things, the higher towards which thought is led, away from the changeability of the world; Aristotle, the *Ethics*, an enquiry into the good in the practical affairs of human beings, which treats of the flux of experience and sensory engagement with things. But the two men are united pictorially by the arch through which they are walking towards us, and this is amplified by the series of arches that structure the painting as a whole – arches readable simultaneously, and in contrary movements, as entry into the matrix of human becoming and ascension out of the Cave, the cave that Plato depicts in *The Republic* as an allegory of education. Either way, the arches lead the eye towards these two men, making them the focal point of the painting;

moreover, they are at the same time highlighted, even beatified, by the fact that, among the host of characters represented, they are the only ones who are seen against the sky. It is from this that the story unfolds.

The two men converse together, but from them there derive two lineages of thought: Raphael displays these graphically and they are more or less divided in the lower quarters of the picture. Where do these lines of thought lead? From Plato to Pythagoras, from Aristotle to Euclid, Zoroaster and Ptolemy, and from the higher level of pure philosophy down to the realm of the senses, where there is awareness of mass and quantity, the fresco depicts some sixty figures, compressing many centuries, and bringing this range of thinkers within the formal structure of a tableau. The formal properties of the work articulate a dialectical structure, with the two lines of thought unfolding towards us: we follow the figures outwards and down the steps to the lowest level, where they are divided; but then when seen within the overall structure, we find that they are spanned by the receding series of arches and, hence, in this contrary movement, formally united. For all these symmetries and formal satisfactions, however – these and many more, beyond the scope of the present discussion – the painting is far from static. The scene is animated with conversation and movement, and the dynamism of this is accentuated – by the diagonals of raised arms, elbows at angles and legs outstretched, as well as of bodies bending forward in rapt attention.

Two factors in the painting disrupt this ordered scene. The first is the more striking, for here in the open space, on the white steps that descend between the two clusters of thinkers, there sprawls the biggest and perhaps the most ungainly figure, identifiable as Heraclitus. Silent and brooding, the figure is out of place in this animated scene; out of place also in that the sprawling body breaks with the formal properties of the picture. In fact, it is not just the man's body but the stone block on which he leans, which is oddly and inexplicably at an angle to the steps, as if the building were somehow still in progress. Perhaps in philosophy it always is. This may symbolize, then, Heraclitus' pre-Socratic insistence on flux and the mutability of things. But the force of the intrusion lies elsewhere. Raphael had been painting this masterpiece at a time when another work was underway in a large adjacent room, a room that was kept under lock and key. That room was the Sistine Chapel. The story is that one night Raphael bribed his way into this room and saw the work of his rival Michelangelo. The figure we are considering has been described as Michelangeloesque, even as representing Michelangelo himself, as well as resembling Saint Jeremiah, depicted on the ceiling of the Sistine Chapel. In contrast to the philosophers and mathematicians that populate the larger part of *The School of Athens*, the figure on the steps has the body and clothes of a workman, even anachronistically a workman's boots, and for these reasons, and in spite of its brooding qualities, it can seem mildly comic, even slightly absurd. Michelangelo was, by all accounts, awkward in his social and business dealings, in contrast to the assured and genial demeanour of Raphael, the younger man. So here, it seems, Raphael is having fun at the expense of the artist of the room next door.

Yet this is a double gesture, for at the same time the placing of this figure at the centre foreground of this, Raphael's greatest work – that is, the toleration of this intrusion into the work's symmetry – must function as a kind of homage. The placing of the figure in a direct vertical line under Plato's upstretched finger amounts to an acknowledgement of Michelangelo's genius – a genius governed less by the rational laws of symmetry and proportion that have so much contributed to Raphael's masterwork than by divine inspiration.

The force of this homage is increased by the relative self-effacement of Raphael himself. We need to notice his signature appearance on the extreme right of the scene, an appearance that can otherwise seem almost insignificant. His expression is equivocal, perhaps readable initially as a mischievous pleasure at this mockery of his rival, here amidst the comprehensive grandeur of this scene, but any such self-satisfaction is quickly counter-balanced by, even ceded to, this humble, perhaps aching, acknowledgement of the greatness of Michelangelo's achievement. Of course, it may seem ironic that the expression of humility achieved through this disruption contributes immeasurably to the scope of *The School of Athens*: it is its self-effacing masterstroke. We might read this as a fitting complication of philosophy too.

This directness of Raphael's gaze out of the painting, which is tantamount to a breaking of convention, akin to that of the television interviewee's 'mistake' of looking directly at the camera (a right reserved for newsreaders and reporters, anchor-persons, and presenters of the weather), constitutes the second disruption of the scene. It is emulated by two further figures, the more significant of which is the white-clad figure on the steps, two places to the left of the sprawling Heraclitus. And this exceptionally is a woman, the fourth-century Egyptian philosopher and mathematician Hypatia. What, then, is to be made of the fact that Raphael licenses this direct communication with the viewer both to himself and to this woman, aligning himself with her, though from these different points in the scene?

But this question is overshadowed by a further astonishing fact about the painting. The cartoons for the work reveal that Raphael had earlier intended to fill the blank space of the steps at the front of the scene with an image of Hypatia herself. As it happened, however, he was advised by a Vatican official against foregrounding a woman in this way, for reasons it is not difficult to imagine, whereupon, at a late stage, this section of the fresco was replastered and the imposing image of Heraclitus inserted. It may be that we are then tempted to say that Hypatia and Raphael himself are 'in the know' in some way about what has happened, even catching us out as voyeurs of this scene. But this, itself a too-knowing reading, obscures the suggestion here of a feminized intuition and understatement.

The upshot of these thoughts is that these disruptions can be read as partial subversions of the grand plan of the painting. As intimated above, they also invite a reappraisal of the architectonic aspects of the account of philosophy it provides. Moreover, this occurs within a work that is commissioned in part as a kind of self-representation or marketing exercise for Pope Julius himself: such are the political stakes of the representation of the field. It is then to the way that philosophy understands itself, especially in relation to its purchase on education, that I wish now to turn.

What is the philosophy of education?

When philosophy emerged in ancient Greece, the painting tells us, it offered a new means of theorizing, not only about the nature of the world, but about the nature of our knowledge of the world. Knowledge, it turned out, was of different kinds, and the emphasis given to this or that would lay the way for developments of thought that shaped the ensuing development of civilization, in the West and, increasingly, in the East too. When philosophy of education emerged – and, on one account, this was in London in 1962 – it offered a new means of theorizing about educational policy and practice. It was in that year that Richard Stanley Peters was appointed to the Chair in Philosophy of Education at the Institute of Education. He had already made something of a mark in his role as Reader in Philosophy at Birkbeck College, University of London, and significantly he had broadcast talks on education on the BBC's Third Programme. It was not that philosophy had not been considered before in relation to education, but his advent heralded a new methodological rigour in enquiry, inspired by the conceptual analysis that was dominant in mainstream departments of philosophy. In some ways this sanctioned a modest conception of the subject, casting it in the role of Locke's under-labourer to other research in education;

but its confidence in its methodology, and its watchwords of rigour and clarity, caused others to perceive it as speaking with a certain hauteur. It is not to be regretted that the substance of the work that then developed went well beyond this methodological prescription, for in fact some of the most interesting work that was produced extended into a vision of education, a restatement of liberal education, in which the influence of various philosophers was acknowledged. The celebrated forms of knowledge thesis of Paul Hirst consciously gestured towards Plato's forms, though with the acknowledgement that these were human products, the heritage of centuries of human endeavour, not somehow carved in stone. The emphasis on rational autonomy as an aim of education drew not only on Kant but also on John Stuart Mill for its inspiration. And from Michael Oakeshott there derived the notion of education as the 'conversation of mankind'.

Yet, for all the value of the endeavour of Peters and his colleagues, such an account of philosophy of education's genesis seems woefully inadequate. Its self-representation seems blind to philosophy's involvement with education throughout its history. And how else could it be? The central disciplines of philosophy concern not only what it is to know but how it is we come to know (epistemology), and not only the nature of the good but how we learn to live good lives (ethics). Plato, writing dialogues that depict an older man leading a younger towards knowledge, surely understood the intimacy of this relation. And to be more specific, one would need to acknowledge other traditions – say, the extraordinary prominence of education within American pragmatism, as the work of John Dewey makes abundantly clear, and the flowering of the idea of *Bildung* in German thought in the nineteenth century. Philosophy of education, on this expanded view, can be seen to be as old as philosophy itself. In fact, from the point of view of practice, none of this should surprise us. When practical problems in education are confronted, when they are pursued to where the questions lead, they take us to the most central matters in philosophy itself – the nature of knowledge and the nature of the good life. None of this is to disparage the contribution of Peters and his colleagues. It is rather to set their achievement within a broader and more diverse history, in which not only the Western authors identified above but also other cultural traditions will figure, including, for example, the extraordinary legacies of Buddhist and Confucian thought.

As the sociology of knowledge helps to show, however, the history of a discipline is never simply the product of its rationale and logical coherence: it also depends upon the vicissitudes of circumstance. The growth of the philosophy of education, when Peters and his colleagues were in their heyday, was enabled in part by changes in policy regarding teacher education. While this is a UK story, it resonates with experience in many countries. The commitment in the United Kingdom to making teaching a graduate profession led to the establishment of a Bachelor of Education degree in which intellectual substance and weight were provided by the foundation disciplines – that is, by those disciplines through which educational policy and practice could most clearly be studied: history, philosophy, psychology and sociology. This led to a demand in the colleges of education for people trained in these subjects, and the universities rose to the challenge of providing them, with the Institute of Education taking a key role. All this reflected a climate conditioned not only by demographic change and economic prosperity but by a greater faith in education.

As we saw at the start, however, the approaches adopted were not without their problems. Dissatisfaction came not only from frustrated and sometimes intellectually challenged students but from more reactionary sources, including the so-called Black Papers in education. At the end of the 1970s Margaret Thatcher came to power partly through a populist exploitation of negative images of teachers and criticism of the way that they were trained: this laid the way for what was in effect a progressive de-skilling in the decades that followed. As a result, the place of the disciplines in teacher education was challenged, and the numbers of posts in universities in the foundation disciplines declined. Philosophy of education was under threat.

All this is very much to be regretted, but happily the story does not end there. Over the last two decades or so the field has seen a revival, with a spectacular growth in publication and with a new vitality in conference and other research activity. The *Journal of Philosophy of Education*, which Peters established in the 1960s, began by publishing some 90 pages a year. By the first decade of the new millennium it had expanded to more than 700 pages, and recent volumes are realizing over 120,000 downloads of articles per year. The journal is now one of several in the field. Hence, it seems that there is much in philosophy of education that is in a healthy state.

Let me return briefly, however, to say a little more about philosophy of education's relation to its 'parent' discipline – a metaphor of dubious legitimacy, as my remarks above have perhaps shown. It is not uncommon for those in philosophy departments to view philosophy of education with a degree of suspicion and as somewhat amateur. But this needs to be seen very much in the context of a research climate in which academics are under pressure to specialize in less and less. In the face of such an imperative the kinds of questions that philosophy of education raises can seem intractably messy. Addressing them requires an approach in which different aspects of the mainstream are brought together. To the narrow specialist, this can indeed seem amateur. Conversely, where mainstream philosophers attempt to address such matters, the result can be erudite but detached from the demands of practice. Yet this latter connection is vital if philosophy of education is to realize its potential in terms of practical usefulness. It is understandable then if philosophers of education sometimes find themselves poised unsteadily between the demands of the philosophical problems as they are pursued in the mainstream literature and the need to connect meaningfully with the experience of educational practitioners. Let us consider this by way of a further turn to the question of use.

Self-representation and the paradox of use

There is no doubt that the contemporary self-representation of educational research constitutes a technicization of the field, in which the articulation of usefulness is of paramount importance. This is accentuated by the manner in which it is funded and by the way it is positioned by the expectations of politicians. One manifestation of this is found in its emulation of physical science. Supposedly following the model of medical research, randomized control trials come to be taken as the exemplar of useful research in education. At the same time, the now obligatory political emphasis on evidence-based policy translates as the provision of quantitative data. But is this really what is needed in the training of teachers? Is this what the emphasis on the teacher as researcher is about? Does this provide meaningful continuing professional development?

Against the tide of policy initiatives and interventions, philosophy can make explicit the role of practical reason in the professional practice of a teacher. It can also do something else. It can address what we might think of as the existential challenge that is typically felt by anyone when they begin teaching and indeed later, recurrently, in their career. As a teacher, you are exposed, in a way you have not anticipated. The experience of teaching can get to you, in that you are emotionally caught up with what you are doing – in relation to the class, to individual learners, to the subject itself. Hollywood cinema has plainly appreciated this, though its images tend to glamorize the experience at the expense of realistic evocation of the challenges of the work. By contrast, DH Lawrence's recounting of Ursula's experience in *The Rainbow*, for example, captures something of the daily drudgery and desperate despondency that can beset the teacher alongside a sense of the calling to something higher, which together might be more suggestive of the vocation: Lawrence's phrase for this is 'the holy ground'. Much of this is surely drawn from his own real and in many respects successful experience in the classroom.

There is no simple recipe for how this enhancement of practice is to be achieved, but students on courses in philosophy of education often speak with moving conviction of the ways that their reading and discussion of philosophy has helped them in their practical lives as teachers. This may be in part because the subject answers to their more general sense of uncertainty about their lives as a whole – an uncertainty that is typically felt by human beings generally, for all the strategies we have of covering this over or keeping it at bay, and an uncertainty that is characteristically exposed by the challenges of being a teacher. It is in part this that shows the very special importance of teaching and learning in a human life. Rising to these challenges does not depend only on the acquisition of a battery of techniques: it requires what I have called above the acknowledgement of a more existential engagement. Philosophy provides this not through some narcissistic self-examination but through the kind of enquiry into why we think what we do and into the grounds for holding the beliefs we have that, unlike purely technical matters, can only be pursued meaningfully if one is authentically involved in what one is doing. It is through this that the realities of one's professional role and one's life as a whole can more appropriately be confronted and addressed.

Let me finish with a kind of parable. Jeremy Bentham's utilitarian conception of the Chrestomathic University, the one conducive to learning and ideally efficient, had a bearing on the establishment of London University in 1825 (see Young, 1992). It is not difficult to trace the fluctuating influence of this idea through the development of higher education since then, and in recent decades it has its obvious resonances in the notion of lifelong learning and in a general marketization of education, both keynotes of educational policy internationally. But should higher education be useful or useless – that is, devoted to pursuits that are justified in their own right rather than to those that have utility? Consideration of sections of Adam Smith's *The Wealth of Nations*[2] concerned with education is surprisingly instructive here. For Smith, educational institutions are to be justified in terms of how far they are of use. He recognizes that a division of labour is necessary for economic progress and the creation of a civilized society. Yet a consequence of this is that the minds of workers will be dulled by the repetitiveness and narrow range of their tasks, dulled in a way that does not occur in more primitive societies: this, he states, is a basis of moral and intellectual decay. So the virtues of a civilized society are undermined by the development of those very measures that have been set up to bring it about. As a palliative to the alienated condition of the majority of the population in such a society, Smith turns again to education, and now the training in geometry and mechanics, thought a proper preparation for future employment, is supplemented by an introduction to those 'sublime' pursuits that are *not* useful. Because of the way degeneration is, as it were, built into the system of utility, we have the paradox that the useful becomes useless for the society it was designed to create; conversely, the pursuit of useless sublime knowledge becomes useful in ameliorating those worst effects of utility, and hence in sustaining the society. The opposition between usefulness and uselessness, which has characterized and continues to characterize so much of the debate about higher education, and which here prompts the question of the usefulness of philosophy of education, begins to fall apart.

Is it fanciful to find in the lives of contemporary teachers a dulling of experience, brought about not so much by the repetitiveness of their tasks but by their subordination to the efficient delivery of the curriculum and their being enlisted in relentless competition over standards, dulled in a way that did not occur so much in less technicized regimes of teaching and learning? Is it fanciful to imagine that such contemporary practice, for all its good intentions, for all its commitment to efficiency and effectiveness, might harbour a basis of moral and intellectual decay? Unlike in Smith's reflection, however, the benefits to the teacher or policymaker of studying philosophy of education would not be merely palliative in kind, for here it is not just a matter of compensating for the mind-numbing repetition of factory production: their philosophical experience would contribute directly to their professional roles and to the substance of that practice. Call this 'sublime' if you like, but it would have a use-value that no one should doubt.

Notes

1   For a variety of images of the fresco, see http://www.bing.com/images/search?q=school+of+athens&qpvt=school+of+athens&FORM=IGRE. There are useful discussions of the painting at http://www.bbc.co.uk/programmes/b00j7txt and http://www.newbanner.com/AboutPic/SOA.html. The Vatican's website gives the following: http://mv.vatican.va/4_ES/pages/z-Patrons/MV_Patrons_04_01.html [accessed 3 March 2014].

2   First published in 1776, *The Wealth of Nations* (Smith, 1982) was, of course, seminal in the thinking of the New Right, especially of Thatcherism.

References

Smith, A. (1982) *The Wealth of Nations*. London: Methuen.

Young, R. (1992) 'The Idea of a Chrestomathic University', in Rand, R. (ed.) *Logomachia: The Conflict of the Faculties*. Lincoln and London: University of Nebraska Press: 97–126.

Part One

Ethics

2

Technological Thinking in Education

David Lewin

Where does *homo technicus* dwell? Through digital networks I am everywhere anywhere; I am being-with everyone. Does that inevitably lead to the opportunism and narcissism of social networks? Does this access to all erode any possible encounter with the *other*? Is this projection of freedom in terms of that which subjectivity can represent to itself really nothing more than the essence of nihilism, as Heidegger saw in Nietzsche's completion of Platonic metaphysics (Heidegger, 1998; Irwin, 2002)? Heidegger's radical account of the destiny of Western metaphysics, expressed today in modern technology, is finding extraordinary fulfilment in educational thinking and practice. I will begin with the observation that our present educational problems are not simply pedagogical, any more than the problems of the technological age are just technological (Heidegger, 1977, p. 4).

Educational theorists often lament the crisis of educational culture in the present age. Recent work by authorities in the field, such as Roger Brown and Ron Barnett, does little more than draw attention to the failings of educational theory to address the deeper issues behind the crisis (Barnett, 2010; Brown, 2013). Both Brown and Barnett worry about the marketization of higher education but seem unwilling to address the metaphysical issues at stake. I argue that those metaphysical foundations are related to technological thinking. Educational theory struggles to keep pace with technological change at a practical level, so it is hardly surprising that the deeper currents behind technological change are often ignored. If educational theorists have struggled to reflect upon the impact of technological change, philosophers have been even slower to respond to the trajectory of technological society. This is partly a result of technology's neutral facade.

Along with philosophers such as Heidegger, Marcuse and a host of others, I will consider the flattened interpretation of the world characteristic of technological society. This one-dimensionality structures and limits the scope of education today. After sketching the influence of technological thinking, I examine the putative separation of neutral technological means from humanly determined ends. The separation of the supposed value-free technical means from more substantial ends is analysed in terms of a concealment of the subtle ethical demands and commitments characteristic of educational practice. Philosophers of education have discussed this separation but generally have not located its roots in the logic of technological thinking, which I will attempt to do. More recently, thinkers such as Iain Thompson (2005), Kevin Flint and Nick Peim (2012) have related Heidegger's critique of technology with a notion of ontological education, offering an important development of Heidegger's understanding of technological *enframing*. I hope to contribute to this interest in the Heideggerian critique of technological thinking.

Digital divides

Those of us old enough to remember a world without mobile phones are often struck by the profound changes the world has witnessed since the birth of the commercial cell phone in 1978. Those of us young enough to have lived always surrounded by mobile technology might be largely inured to what has been called the 'Future Shock' (Toffler, 1970), or the 'innovation overload', often experienced by older generations. Social theorists have grown accustomed to dividing inhabitants of modern industrialized societies into two camps: the digital natives, born into the digital age, and digital immigrants, an older generation who find themselves having to adapt former attitudes and ways of life to a brave new world (Bennett et al., 2008; Prensky, 2001).

Some have shown that there are problems with these categories (Dixon and Sanders, 2011). It is by no means clear that the younger generation experience technology with the familiarity suggested by the term 'native'; nor does the colonialist terminology seem appropriate. Nevertheless, the categories have struck a chord. And for those less at home with modern technology, for the digital immigrants, the present age is often accompanied by an inarticulate ambivalence – an existential anxiety – about many aspects of technological progress.

Ambivalence to technology is generally muted or diverted by the idea that any problems we have are not with technology per se but with particular technologies that need careful control, to avoid specific social or environmental consequences. There is a tendency to translate fairly amorphous and widespread technological anxieties into the language of risk. The technologies of risk management ensure risks are contained within managed cost–benefit analyses. But technological anxiety goes deeper than this, expressing an unease that goes beyond either risks we avoid or account for or specific dangers relating to particular devices. Of course, we need to be concerned about the damaging effects of particular technologies. But what of uncanny technological anxiety? Technological anxiety is existential, being, as Heidegger would say, 'nothing and nowhere' (Heidegger, 1962, p. 231) but still all around.[1] Insofar as technology is ubiquitous in forming the structures of our being-in-the-world, it renders anxiety almost invisible, and therefore nearly powerless to resist technological thinking. In the guise of benign neutrality, many technological devices present no clear and present danger to existence and therefore no meaningful risks to be managed. Mobile communications and the pervasive information networks, for example, extend the means by which human beings may connect, but the ends to which those means are put must be up to people to decide. Despite the fact that a number of prominent philosophers of technology have tried to complicate or even wholly reject this sort of technological neutrality, this view is culturally dominant (see Borgmann, 1984; Heidegger, 1977; Lewin, 2011; Marcuse, 1964).

But surely it is up to us whether, for example, we use computers in classrooms or whether we develop sophisticated online learning environments. The idea that technological devices are neutral certainly appeals to common sense. It would seem peculiar or quaint to imagine that devices could have subjectivity, desires or could determine their own ends. We naturally assume that devices are subject to *our* will.[2] Yet social scientists and philosophers are disposed to question the binary logic of structural versus individual agency in shaping human action (see Bourdieu, 1977; Giddens, 1984). From the perspective of much social theory, the notion that we should ignore the imperative of social and economic forces in structuring individual choices might seem naïve, and so structuration theory places limitations on free subjectivity without fully conceding human agency to technological determinism. Similarly, the category of the digital native suggests a generation of people who no longer wonder at the presence of digital technologies and do not make autonomous decisions to take them up. The digital native no more chooses to use technical devices any more than they choose to get out of bed in the morning (we might choose not to, but for the most part we do not choose to). Technologies have become integrated, embedded and transparent.[3]

The digital immigrant is an endangered species, and with the digital native in the ascendant, the neutrality of technology withdraws into its transparency. Is the native relinquishing her agency to the thoughtless consensus of technological advance? If technological devices have an impact on the way we understand the world, then we might be alarmed by their increasing transparency, a transparency made possible by a shroud of benign neutrality. To explore this idea a little further, I want to consider how the technical interface structures and limits our being-in-the-world.

Separating means from ends: The technical interface

The technological epoch boils down to this: providing users with access to unhindered functionality. What might seem like a fairly innocuous phrase bears some elaboration. In brief, we are turned into users and the world exists insofar as it provides some useful function for us as users. One obvious way in which we can see this taking place is through the ubiquity of the technical interface. In essence the interface places the user and the device in a narrowly defined relation that foregrounds use and conceals all else: a form of what Heidegger calls 'technological enframing'. The evolution of mobile phones demonstrates well this general tendency for devices to present functionality through interfaces. Modern tablets like Apple's IPad take this further by being virtually all (virtual) interface. User functionality is foregrounded by the touchscreen that constitutes an ever-expanding portion of the visible device, and the complex operations that facilitate device functionality are placed out of sight within the technical operation of the device. As far as possible 'dead space' on such a device is eliminated as the screen offers extraordinary functionality via the near-infinite configurations of apps. This device is an example of a general tendency to separate interface design and development from operational or functional design.[4] In fact, design engineers (particularly software engineers) have developed a design pattern for this approach to product design called *model-view controller*.

Model-view controller defines a common approach in larger-scale software and hardware systems development, where one team of engineers is responsible for developing the operation or function of a device (what the device can actually do), another team develops the interface or view (the way the user interacts with the device) and a third team manages the interaction between these two key aspects of the device (what is called the controller). Within this pattern, the interface design is uncoupled from the core operational design so that interface engineers can think purely about the 'user-experience' without their imagination being impeded by operational limitations that might otherwise compromise the user interface. In other words, the interface designers are encouraged to look at the product from the point of view of the user. This design pattern illustrates well the tendency to separate the ends of a device from its means since the user is thought to be concerned only with ends.

Beyond product design, this pattern is evident throughout the social institutions of modern life. Consider one example from educational theory: the efforts that university managers are currently making to ensure that the view or interface of the university is optimal. Teams of staff examine strategies for how to improve scores on student surveys and university league tables in a way that considers institutional appearances entirely separately from 'realities'. Student experience is managed as though it were a distinct category within the operation of the institution, as though the experience of the students could be uncoupled from the deeper structural issues that form the culture of an institution. Standish eloquently indicted the 'aesthetic appeal' of the allure of presentation which 'fosters a kind of simulacrum of learning' (Standish, 1997, p. 453). Indeed, there seems no need to refer to the university that lies behind the *idea* of the university. It is the idea that is constructed, marketed, attended, graduated from and finally stands for the graduate seeking to place themselves within the *standing reserve* of human resource (Heidegger, 1977, p. 18).

This example provides one illustration of the way in which means are separated from ends: that as long as the institution provides quality assurance through rational consensus, what takes place on the ground is irrelevant. Consequently, university brand management has become an industry in itself. The model-view controller reflects and radicalizes the broad tendency to separate ends from means. This separation allows for the maximization of efficiency while offering optimal user experience. In their book *Rethinking the Education Improvement Agenda*, Kevin Flint and Nick Peim focus in particular on the manner in which this separation of means and ends expresses itself in the technology of assessment, in 'the privileging of examination results as the officially recognized, so-called objective measures that mark the ideological telos of the system'. This ideological telos 'tends to reduce the play of difference in the dominant official language of education' (Flint and Peim, 2012, p. 50). Heidegger is one philosopher for whom the play of language in education is itself the play of being.[5]

The significance of Heidegger's later reflections on the 'technological understanding of being' or 'technological thinking' is increasingly recognized with educational theory (Flint and Peim, 2012; Standish, 2002; Thompson, 2005; Waddington, 2005). Even within philosophy of technology, Heidegger's influence begins and ends with ontology (which might explain why Heidegger's influence has diminished within philosophy of technology since the so-called empirical turn; see Achterhuis, 2001). In essence, Heidegger's concern is the manner in which being is disclosed in the present age. For Heidegger, technological disclosure 'puts to nature the unreasonable demand that it supply energy that can be extracted and stored as such' (Heidegger, 1977, p. 14). Insofar as we regard the world in terms of human will, we relate to an interface of sorts, which for Heidegger can only lead to nihilism. The inevitable outcome of Nietzsche's fulfilment of Western metaphysics, argues Heidegger, is that in constructing itself humanity realizes its own essential negation (Heidegger, 1977, pp. 53–113). This wilful extraction of truth is not the only way in which being might be disclosed; it can also be disclosed by a combination of the extraordinary success with the veil of neutrality that has all but eliminated alternatives. In the wake of Heidegger, thinkers such as Paul Tillich (1988), Herbert Marcuse (1964) and Albert Borgmann (1984) have developed similar concerns that technical reason has a pathological tendency to separate ends and means. The influence of Heidegger on these figures is significant, providing a thread for what has come to be called (rather unhelpfully in my view) technological essentialism (Feenberg, 1999; Thompson, 2005). This tradition of philosophy of technology regards technological devices as the outward expression of a way of seeing and being-in-the-world: a way of being that seeks to foreground usefulness and conceals whatever has no particular use. This way of seeing has effects still more worrying than the environmental threats often associated with technological progress. The dangers to our existential being are that much more pernicious because they are harder to detect, being shrouded by a cloak of technological neutrality.

Before turning more explicitly to the implications of technological thinking for education, there is one more strand that I wish to introduce to this thread, namely philosophical hermeneutics. Human existence is essentially temporal and historical and so our being-in-the-world is at least partially contingent upon the historical moment in which we find ourselves. Philosophical hermeneutics does not seek to escape historicality and the inevitability of what Gadamer calls 'historically-effected consciousness' (Gadamer, 2004, pp. 336–341), but it seeks to explore what arises from it and within it. Thus in the technological epoch, the understanding of being is structured by technological thinking which I have expressed in terms of the separation of means and ends.

If we conceive of this technological understanding of being within the purview of phenomenological hermeneutics, we arrive at what I call the *technological hermeneutic*. It is a hermeneutic that sees beings only in terms of what shows up *for us*. Exemplifying this, the interface reduces the complex and infinite nature of disclosure, to the controllable, predictable and user-friendly.[6] The whole point of the interface is to stabilize what discloses itself. The interface fixes and closes and thereby opposes dis-closure. By its attempt to conceal complex (that is, fragile or insecure) interaction and deliberation, the interface denigrates and excludes the depth of things. Unlike the tree, the river or the mountain, the interface is designed to be, as far as possible, purely operational and therefore functional in the context of total control. Of course, it is an illusion that the interface achieves complete control. The interface discloses a world in an interpretive-historical context like any other hermeneutic disclosure. What for Heidegger distinguishes the totalizing technological hermeneutic is its extraordinary capacity to close off all other possible disclosures, effectively universalizing a particular mediation.[7]

This brings us back to Heidegger's concern with the technological epoch. The problem for Heidegger is not that the world is disclosed in terms of what might be of functional use to us; after all, even the ancient Greeks do this, but that the technological disclosure of being exerts such a force that it excludes all other possible disclosures. We earlier saw an example of this reduction where technological anxiety becomes reduced to something else: risk management of particular technologies. Even the idea that other forms of disclosure are possible is negated. That there might be a life for the trees beyond the plans of human beings becomes unthinkable; that there might be an intelligible logos inherent in things themselves becomes absurd; as Paul Ricoeur puts it, in the present age 'the cosmos is mute' (Ricoeur, 1995, p. 61). As a consequence, beings are exclusively *for us*. That is to say, beings show themselves only in terms of their utility to us; what functional use we can make of them. A further expression of this manner of being is that things become reduced to what can be accessed through the interface. Should no interface exist, then the being of the thing (for all practical purposes) withdraws. The being of things is positioned and actualized by way of the interface. Here we find some support for Heidegger's radical claim that the metaphysical foundations of modern technology are to be found in Platonic idealism. Indeed, through the modern technical interface we are directed to interact with the formal identity of beings (as elaborated by technical architects) and regard the actual as an inconvenient impediment to the formal. This provocative thesis has not been discussed here due to the limitation of space. Flint and Peim have related this Heideggerian reduction of being as *enframing* to an equivalent reduction in education where they describe the 'principle of assessment' (Flint and Peim, 2012). Here 'what is' becomes what is assessable: not only do those elements of education that are not assessed fall outside the frame of assessment, but they are also in danger of being entirely buried.

I argue elsewhere that a consequence of this positioning of beings in one-dimensional terms conceals the hermeneutical nature of existence from us (Lewin, 2012). Insofar as we are aware of the hermeneutics of existence, we are required to make judgements about which interpretation seems right to us. An awareness (perhaps pre-philosophic) of hermeneutics is awareness that the technological mode of being-in-the-world, where things exist *for us*, is but one among many possible interpretations (others being, for example, aesthetic, ethical or spiritual). But the concealment of the hermeneutic process takes place alongside the erosion of the human faculty of practical reason, named by Aristotle as 'phronesis'. It is the manifest complexity of the world that calls Aristotle to inscribe human nature with a virtue that is neither simply contemplative (*sophia*) nor purely practical (*techne*) (Aristotle, 2002, Book VI). This partly synthetic partly pragmatic mode of *phronesis* seems to correspond with an appreciation of the hermeneutic structure of being.[8] Simply put, the presentation of pure function (mediated by the interface) is a concealment of the need for *phronesis*.[9] I now want to explore how technological thinking results in the erosion of the human faculty of practical reason in education.

The erosion of phronesis in education

The emergent culture of performance management, of evidence-based practice, and of improvement in standards, exhibits the climate of control in which education currently exists, as reflected in the behavioural objectives model. As a consequence, the fragile process and purpose of human formation (if 'human formation' was ever the real purpose of education, but then it would be naïve to speak of a singular educational purpose) are in danger of becoming a lost art. The act of decision-making in a climate like this is being reduced to a technocratic process, and the judgement of educators seems increasingly unlikely to flourish where vocational integrity is replaced by professional ethics. Such a shift in educational thinking reflects a broader cultural drift towards instrumental rationality and technological thinking.

In *Back to the Rough Ground*, Joseph Dunne develops a philosophical challenge to the behavioural objectives model, a model in which each lesson has specific outcomes intended to contribute to a planned curriculum (Dunne,

1993). For Dunne, the primary task of the behavioural objectives model is to specify learning outcomes from which instructional methods and techniques can be derived. This appears to be the road to efficiency in teaching and is therefore considered good in itself.

In a way that reflects what I have argued about the tendency of technical interfaces, the process of defining clear objectives and outcomes involves the separation of ends and means – 'ends alone were allowed to be intrinsically valuable... this model enjoins teachers to specify their goals as discrete, observable behaviours' (Dunne, 1993, p. 6). This foregrounding of ends, results or outcomes, reinforces what Clarke and Newman have called 'the logic of managerialism' in which 'managers are accountable for what they deliver, but not for how they deliver it. It is results, not methods that count' (Clarke and Newman, 1997, p. 64). In other words, this management of outcomes involves the separation of the ends of education from the means by which those ends are achieved. If we are to manage those ends effectively, then we must define with absolute clarity the nature of the ends sought. This process of delineating clear, established objectives and outcomes for a planned curriculum leads to the erosion of the hermeneutical dimension of teaching. More specifically, it is the technological hermeneutic that has eroded this professional responsibility. Philosophical hermeneutics recognizes that what is 'true' cannot be contained within a clear 'method', and so is always open to reinterpretation. Dunne shows how the tendency within objectives writing has been to gloss over or pragmatically elide complex and conflicting interpretations: 'remember the iron-clad rule of objective writing: if there is a disagreement about the meaning, don't argue about it, fix it' (Mager, 1984, p. 68).

The presentation of clear objectives is an expression of the technological hermeneutic which foregrounds ends and conceals means by regarding them as merely the neutral activity to achieve substantive ends. In this case means are void of any values or commitments and could be replaced by more efficient means. Indeed, efficiency is the supreme, even the singular value that is attached to means in the technological age, a point made forcefully by the French philosopher of technology Jacques Ellul. For Ellul, the technological society is rule by technique, defined as 'the totality of methods rationally arrived at and having absolute efficiency... in every field of human activity' (Ellul, 1964, p. v).

The separation of technical reason from what can be called moral (or ethical) reason is of crucial significance, especially given the widespread assumption that the remit of educators extends only as far as the development of technical reason, but cannot include the development of ethical understanding. As Robert Bellah puts it:

> There is a profound gap in our culture between technical reason, the knowledge with which we design computers and analyse the structure of DNA, and the practical or moral reason, the ways we understand how we should live. We often hear that only technical reason can really be taught, and our educational commitments from primary school to university seem to embody that belief. But technical reason alone is insufficient to manage our social difficulties or make sense of our lives. (Bellah et al., 1992, p. 44)

It is not that only technical reason can be taught but rather that only technical reason is appropriate to a current conception of education structured by linear curricula, focused schemes of work, objectives and lesson outcomes. These aspects of technical reason are the means by which a certain vision of education is instantiated, a vision informed by the technological hermeneutic. However, that vision is very often inherited, or taken for granted: we assume that we need to produce certain skills and attributes in our students and should be able to determine the right objectives and outcomes that will feed into the skills and attributes taken to be appropriate to this kind of education. The failure to give substantial consideration to the vision of education that informs technical reason is concealed by the fastidious elaboration of clear outcomes undertaken by educators. Perhaps on some level there exists a sense that we are not fully in control of education and this makes us all the more concerned to elaborate the expectations of our students, as if that is equivalent to genuine reflection upon the depth of education. As Heidegger puts it, 'the will to mastery becomes all the more urgent the more technology threatens to slip from human control' (Heidegger, 1977, p. 5). And so there is an expectation that outcomes should drive the process of curriculum development as a whole. In short, we project a narrow conception of the goal of education in order that the means to achieve the goal can be developed relatively easily. The more concretely we are able to operationalize our terms, the more effectively we are able to achieve successful outcomes. But does not the price paid for the clarity render such a victory pyrrhic? This reification is the preliminary task of technological thinking, for means can only be effective if they are directed to clearly identified goals, ends that are far more circumscribed than the formation of transformation of students.

Furthermore, this separation of means and ends encourages us to separate the practical from the ethical. It is assumed that theoretical reason is there to consider ethical matters and develop the vision or end towards which education is orientated, while technical reason exists as the neutral process (the means), is shorn of any deeper reflection on ends, does not require practical wisdom (Aristotle *phronesis*) and is a purely technical operation. Aristotle sought to avoid this radical separation of means and ends, of technical and theoretical reason. The Aristotelian conception of *phronesis* seeks not just the right goal but the appropriate application of principles to practices to bring about right action.[10]

In the work of Dunne, Richard Smith and others, we find philosophers of education seeking to resist the erosion of the human faculty of judgement. Smith is concerned to resist the worst excesses of technical reason. He says, 'The ascendancy of technicism, of technical or instrumental rationality, is sufficiently marked in education, in the English-speaking world at least, to need little illustration' (Smith, 1999, p. 327). Instrumental reason may be all but ubiquitous, but I argue that we do not have a clear grasp of its scope and effects. Smith cites the audit culture and the proliferation of performance indicators that beset modern educational institutions about which we all know too much. But drawing attention to the structures of technocratic society has not protected us from their dehumanizing effects. On the contrary, the improvement agenda shows little sign of slowing, within the present 'aegis of quantification' (Flint and Peim, 2012, p. 2). Just as technological society appears to improve living standards on almost every measure, so educational standards, as we are often told, have shown a consistent improvement. Therefore, the critics of performance management and the audit culture have no rational ground from which to speak and so go unheeded (this reflects the broader sense that critics of technological culture are marginal because their critique can gain no traction on the apparently neutral technological means – a point forcefully developed by Herbert Marcuse in *One-Dimensional Man*). Our anxieties about the educational improvement agenda have no more discursive legitimacy than anxieties about the age of technology. It is at this point that we must recognize that philosophy of education has not had traction – it has failed to resist or overcome the managerial culture within the vast majority of state-controlled educational institutions. And like the juggernaut of progress in general, this failed vision seems inexorably to proliferate within our educational culture.

One reason for this failure is that we fail to take seriously the amorphous anxieties that accompany technological or educational progress. Even where technology is not simply identified with devices and so can be seen as a process, it is regarded as a neutral one which governments can take or leave. But the progressive rhetoric conceals a profound unease which has not yet found full expression. (A more generous and probably more empirically accurate interpretation of the relative failures of philosophers of education would say that philosophy is effective only at the margins as gadfly to the state.)

Paradoxically, the more we focus on defining quantifiable ends, the more pathological our relation to ends becomes. The end that can be circumscribed is only ever a provisional reference point – it is hermeneutically incomplete. Paul Tillich captured this very well when he pointed out that in the technological age we find 'an end that is the endless pursuit of means without an end' (Tillich, 1988, p. 80). So in fact the endeavour to circumscribe clear ends or outcomes postpones or conceals the contemplation of true ends, which cannot be made finite or simply circumscribed. Thus Tillich said that technological culture could only offer 'a telos that negates a telos' (Tillich, 1988, p. 80).

Where educators speak of the formation or transformation of students, what do they mean? Is there any answer to this question that does not diminish the play of language? It is no bad thing that the reference point of this ultimate concern of education remains infinite, always there to be contemplated even though it cannot be fully defined or circumscribed. This dialectical relationship between the provisional concerns for the vision of education to be realized must not be collapsed, avoided or obscured.

Conclusion

There is something of a paradox in the foregoing discussion: on the one hand, I suggested that the paradigm of the technical interface presents us with pure ends unencumbered by means. This view was developed in educational terms as the focus on fixing outcomes and objectives and driving curricula by these defined outcomes. On the other hand, there is a view – only briefly developed here – that technologies are great at developing means but seem to conceal from us ultimate goals, or ends, and that we are so enchanted by technical means that we forget about the ends for which those means are developed. The resolution to this apparent paradox has already been suggested.

The foregrounding of pure ends in education *is* the concealment of reflection on real ends. Real ends (what Tillich called our ultimate concern) are infinite and uncircumscribed and cannot be simply presented or captured in outcomes. Indeed, outcomes provide useful, important provisional ends, but only insofar as they are dialectically disclosing the ultimate concern for education: the transformation of humanity. But what does this mean? The anxieties that tell us we do not know might also suggest that 'it is the nothing that we are seeking' (Heidegger, 1994, p. 98).

The inescapably ethical character of education is hidden by technological thinking which conceals means and presents ends. The technological age has successfully separated fact from value, process from ethics, and in this way has been able to professionalize educational institutions and relations. The task of the philosophy of education must be to question the structures of thought and perception that determine education. Is this to question or reject technological nihilism? Perhaps, but at least we might consider the compulsion to conform to the busyness of educational attainment that itself amounts to very little, but not quite nothing: 'That in the malaise of anxiety we often try to shatter the vacant stillness with compulsive talk only proves the presence of the nothing' (Heidegger, 1994, p. 101).

Notes

1   Of course, Kierkegaard too understands anxiety as constituting an essential feature of the human condition: 'If a human being were a beast or an angel, he could not be in anxiety. Because he is a synthesis, he can be in anxiety; and the more profoundly he is in anxiety, the greater is the man' (Kierkegaard, 1980, p. 155). What clearer manifestation of the nature of humanity could there be for the secular age than the rise of homo-technicus!

2   The question of technological determinism has been discussed at some length by philosophers of technology keen to either claim Heidegger a determinist or to defend him against this charge (see Feenberg, 1999; Lewin, 2011; Thompson 2005).

3   Orlikowski (1992) has argued that either side of the duality between technology as structuring, and technology as a neutral tool for autonomous agents, is incomplete and requires the other.

4   The ubiquity of the interface makes the most obvious recovery of craft seem increasingly unlikely. Standish suggests a typical view: 'The first and most obvious possibility is that there may be a limited recovery of a kind of craft. This is to reclaim the role of the practical, that answerability to materials which the craftman's work embodies, and which the college of technical and further education should be well placed to celebrate' (Standish, 1997, p. 455).

5   Heidegger reverses the oft-quoted idea that we play with language: 'it is not we who play with words, but the nature of language plays with us' (Heidegger, 1976, p. 118).

6   I have avoided the temptation for an excursus here into Heidegger's distinction between the primordial conception of truth as dis-closure (or unhiddenness in the Greek notion of *aletheia*) and the truth of 'correctness' or correspondence between

an object and its representation. Clearly, though, these two conceptions of truth relate to the argument that the interface depends upon the representational truth as correspondence between the concept (or icon in the interface) and its reference. Heidegger goes into the problems with the latter view in many places, but notably for educators in 'Plato's Doctrine of Truth' (Heidegger, 1998).

7   This point encapsulates much of Heidegger's concern about technology. Heidegger is no Luddite but is concerned about the totalizing nature of the technological understanding of being.

8   Aristotle presents *phronesis* in two apparently distinct ways: as the capacity to deliberate about human ends, as 'what is good and advantageous for oneself', and also as the faculty that considers the means by which ends are achieved. This indicates that the distinction between means and ends does not fully hold in the Greek cosmos (Wall, 2005). Dunne prioritizes the phronesis as the deliberation about appropriate ends (to distinguish substantive ends from merely utilitarian ends). But Wall argues that what is needed is also a recognition of the moral character or means (Wall, 2005, p. 65). Wall also presents Alasdair MacIntyre's understanding of phronesis as significant in providing the faculty by which the 'truths' we inherit from our moral tradition are reinterpreted and applied in the particular context of the historical present.

9   In a similar sense, Biblical hermeneutics has often required a mode of fragile and insecure deliberation in order for the complex nature of the Biblical text to show itself. Where that hermeneutic complexity is reduced to literal reading, then, I suggest, a kind of interface has been constructed behind which the interpretive complexity is concealed and the reader is made a user. The text becomes one-dimensional. Whether the historical development of Biblical hermeneutics can be convincingly correlated with technological rationality is beyond my primary concern, which is simply to propose Ricoeur's relevance to understanding technology in terms of his broader philosophical hermeneutics.

10   As Aristotle puts it: 'Whereas young people become accomplished in geometry and mathematics, and wise within these limits, prudent young people do not seem to be found. The reason is that prudence is concerned with particulars as well as universals, and particulars become known from experience, but a young person lacks experience, since some length of time is needed to produce it' (*Nicomachean Ethics* 1142 a).

References

Achterhuis, H. (ed.) (2001) *American Philosophy of Technology: The Empirical Turn*. Trans. Robert Crease, *Indiana Series in the Philosophy of Technology*. Bloomington, IN: Indiana University Press.

Aristotle, (2002) *Nicomachean Ethics*. Trans. Joe Sachs. Newburyport, MA: Focus Publishing.

Barnett, R. (2010) 'Marketised University: Defending the Indefensible', in Molesworth, M., Nixon, L., and Scullion, R. (eds), *The Marketisation of Higher Education and the Student as Consumer*. London: Routledge, pp. 39–51.

Bellah, R., Madsen, R., Tipton, S., Sullivan, W. and Swidler, A. (1992) *The Good Society*. New York, NY: Vintage Books.

Bennett, S., Maton, K., and Kervin, L. (2008) "The 'Digital Natives' Debate: A Critical Review of the Evidence", *British Journal of Educational Technology* 39(5): 775–786.

Borgmann, A. (1984) *Technology and the Character of Contemporary Life: A Philosophical Inquiry*. Chicago: Chicago University Press.

Bourdieu, P. (1977) *Outline of a Theory of Practice*. London: Cambridge University Press.

Brown, R. (2013) *Everything for Sale? The Marketisation of Higher Education*. Oxon: Routledge.

Clarke, J. and Newman, J. (1997) *The Managerial State*. London: Sage.

Dixon, S. and Sanders, R. (2011) 'Dangerous Assumptions – What Our Media Students have taught Us', *Media Education Research Journal* 2(2): 12–25.

Dunne, J. (1993) *Back to the Rough Ground: Practical Judgement and the Lure of Technique*. Notre Dame, IN: University of Notre Dame Press.

Ellul, J. (1964) *The Technological Society*. Trans. John Wilkinson. New York, NY: Vintage Books.

Feenberg, A. (1999) *Questioning Technology*. London: Routledge.

Flint, K. J. and Peim, N. (2012) *Rethinking the Education Improvement Agenda: A Critical Philosophical Approach*. London: Continuum.

Gadamer, H-G. (2004) *Truth and Method*. Second edition, Trans. Joel Weinsheimer and Donald G. Marshall. London: Continuum.

Giddens, A. (1984) *The Constitution of Society*. Cambridge: Polity Press.

Heidegger, M. (1962) *Being and Time*. Trans. Macquarrie. Oxford: Blackwell.

—— (1976) *What is Called Thinking?*. Trans. J. Glenn Gray. New York, NY: Harper & Row Publishers.

—— (1977) *The Question Concerning Technology and Other Essays*. Trans. William Lovitt. New York, NY: Harper & Row Publishers.

—— (1994) 'What is Metaphysics?', in Krell, David Farrell (ed.), *Basic Writings*. Trans. David Farrell Krell. London: Routledge, pp. 155–182.

—— (1998), 'Plato's Doctrine of Truth', in McNeill, W. (ed.), *Pathmarks*. Cambridge: Cambridge University Press, pp. 155–182.

Irwin, F. R. (2002) 'Heidegger and Nietzsche: Nihilism and the Question of Value in Education', in Peters, M. (ed.), *Heidegger, Education, and Modernity*. Oxford: Rowman & Littlefield Publishers, pp. 191–210.

Kierkegaard, S. (1980) *The Concept of Anxiety*. Princeton: Princeton University Press.

Lewin, D. (2011) *Technology and the Philosophy of Religion*. Newcastle Upon Tyne: Cambridge Scholars Press.

—— (2012) 'Ricoeur and the Capability of Modern Technology', in Todd Mei and David Lewin (eds), *From Ricoeur to Action*. London: Continuum, pp. 54–72.

Mager, R. (1984) *Preparing Instructional Objectives*. Belmont, CA: David S. Lake.

Marcuse, H. (1964) *One-Dimensional Man*. Boston, MA: Beacon Press.

Orlikowski, W. J. (1992) The Duality of Technology: Rethinking the Concept of Technology in Organizations, *Organization Science* 3(3): 398–427.

Prensky, M. (2001) 'Digital Natives, Digital Immigrants Part 1', *On the Horizon* 9(5): 1–6.

Ricoeur, P. (1995) *Figuring the Sacred: Religion, Narrative and Imagination*. Minneapolis, MN: Augsburg Fortress Press.

Smith, R. (1999) 'Paths of Judgement: the Revival of Practical Wisdom', *Educational Philosophy and Theory* 31(3): 327–340.

Standish, P. (1997) 'Heidegger and the Technology of Education', *Journal of Philosophy of Education* 31(3): 439–459.

—— (2002) 'Essential Heidegger: Poetics of the Unsaid', in Peters, M. (ed.), *Heidegger, Education, and Modernity*. Oxford: Rowman & Littlefield Publishers, pp. 151–170.

Thompson, I. (2005) *Heidegger on Ontotheology: Technology and the Politics of Education*. Cambridge: Cambridge University Press.

Tillich, P. (1988) *The Spiritual Situation in Our Technical Society*. ed. Thomas, J. M. Macon, GA: Mercer University Press.

Toffler, A. (1970) *Future Shock*. London: Bantam Books.

Waddington, D. (2005) 'A Field Guide to Heidegger: Understanding the 'Question Concerning Technology', *Educational Philosophy and Theory* 37(4): 567–583.

Wall, J. (2005) *Moral Creativity: Paul Ricoeur and the Poetics of Possibility*. Oxford: Oxford University Press.

3

Learning Analytics and the Education of the Human

David Lundie

This chapter highlights and critically examines a fundamental shift which has subtly penetrated the pedagogical practices of schooling, aided by global measures of efficacy. These changes can be traced back to epistemic trends in the philosophy of computing and information but have recently come to redefine core notions such as learning and knowledge. This shift, I argue, requires of educational philosophers a new articulation of the teleological foundations of education as a human practice.

The proliferation of technological interfaces to augment, supplement, enhance and above all to monitor pedagogical engagement in recent years has brought both utopian and dystopian predictions from educational theorists. On the one hand, the potential for the global information age to bridge divides between local knowledge systems and traditional repositories of high status knowledge, while still in its infancy, promises hitherto unimagined pluralist pedagogical encounters. On the other, the threat that the exponential efficiencies promised by increasing technical prowess in the management of the learning encounter may further marginalize those moments of spontaneous, thoughtful or unexpected learning, the simple, joyful and human aspects of education. In what ways may the philosophy of education, in particular perspectives from European personalism, make a contribution to the design of systems that enable pluralist pedagogies while minimizing the threats posed by too rigid a model of technocratic education?

From the beginning of computer systems, philosophers of information have engaged with questions of epistemology and ontology (Shannon and Weaver, 1949; Turing, 1950). Initially, these questions underpinned the authentication of truth values in the communication and manipulation of data by machines: how could one information processor be sure of having received the message correctly from another and of the identity of the sender? Such questions kept the philosophy of information clearly within the realm of the philosophy of mathematics. Until recently, information ethics was largely understood as a function of efficiency – when designing a system to transmit air traffic control signals, an error could result in a crash, so an ethical system is an efficient system, with effective fail-safes. Under such a description, an ethical information system is an efficient one, and the social effects of the system in use can be seen as 'inherently value neutral' (Alder, 1998). Recently, however, concerns have increasingly been raised about the ethical issues which reside in the design process itself (Knobel and Bowker, 2011; Wicker and Schrader, 2010), recognizing that a system may pose ethical problems by being too efficient (Cohen, 2000) and by changing social interactions between human agents in ways unforeseen in their conceptualization (Friedman and Nissenbaum, 1996).

From the estimated 68,000 CCTV cameras in English secondary schools (Big Brother Watch, 2012) to the 155,000 students who registered for MIT's first massively open online course (of whom just 4.6% completed) (Hardetsy, 2012), the sheer scale of change offered by educational technology is momentous. It is not only the scale of the numbers, however, but the nature of the human–computer interaction itself which has the potential to redefine education in the information age. There is a dawning recognition that technology has the potential not only to increase the efficiency of the classroom but to change the nature and meaning of education in ways that have rarely been exposed to scrutiny and debate.

In his *Postscript on the Societies of Control*, Gilles Deleuze (1992) suggests that the information society operates by a new locus of control, decentring the enclosures of earlier disciplinary societies: factories, schools, archetypally prisons. Whether or not this prediction presages the end of schooling as we know it in the post-industrial West, it is clear that teachers face a more porous, less 'enclosed' professional environment, both through the availability of networked resources and the less welcome intrusion of networked camera and recording devices (Parry, 2005). While many of the most vocal critics of the digital society have pointed to a 'digital panopticon' (Barbrook, 2013), evoking Bentham's disciplinary prison *par excellence*, Deleuze argues that the information society no longer needs such enclosed structures to control its subjects. Instead, Deleuze posits the effect of *dividuation*, the dividing of the individual among the ceaseless entailments which make a claim on their person. Unlike the factory whistle or the school bell, which summons the subject to the place of enclosure, dividual identities are 'always on': the work e-mail at 6 a.m; the lecture podcast to listen to at the gym. Deleuze observes:

> [J]ust as the corporation replaces the factory, *perpetual training* tends to replace the *school*, and continuous control to replace the examination. Which is the surest way of delivering the school over to the corporation. (1992, p. 5)

Departing from Deleuze's concern with the corporate and neoliberal agenda served by this new locus of control, this chapter draws attention to a more existentially troubling informational ontology. This ontology offers to corporate interests an illusory sociology of total control, but in the process reduces the definitions of knowledge to information and wisdom to processing. The origins of this ontology and its consequences for education, humanity and society have thus far been largely absent from public discourse, in either the political or academic arenas.

Technology is an elusive concept, both seductive and suspicious; it can be defined very broadly to encompass all forms of *techné*, craft or equipment of use to the endeavour of learning and has been the subject of suspicion ever since Socrates' concerns about the written word supplanting the art of dialogue (Plato, *Phaedrus* 276e–277a). In the interests of clarity, such suspicions and speculations are here laid aside in addressing the specific technologies of learning analytics systems. Nonetheless, the connection which exists between knowledge, being and *techné* is of central importance: in *The Origin of the Work of Art*, Heidegger considers *techné* to denote a form of knowledge or experience of being. The artist, craftsman or technician causes beings to come forth, to be revealed and become present to the technician as knower (Heidegger, 1978, p. 184). In this becoming present, something is known – all technology and all means of mediation have informational content. As with Socrates' concern for writing, analytic technologies mediate informational content in new ways; the mediation itself has informational content. Specifically, learning analytics systems are digital, interactive and data-acquisitive. This informational content may be termed *operational data*; these are data relating to the operation, use and performance of the data system itself (Floridi, 2004, p. 43). While a focus on understanding the workings of this operational data may be beneficial for education *about* technology, as well as media education more broadly, it also has important implications for education *through* technology, which are yet to be fully explored.

The technologies addressed in this chapter have the additional properties of being digital, interactive and data-acquisitive. Digital technologies process data by assigning it numerical (specifically binary) variables. Digital data consists of the answers to a series of yes/no binaries – some theorists have regarded this form of information as not only foundational to all knowledge (true/false binaries) but to the ontology of the physical world (is/is not binaries) (Wheeler, 1990). Regardless of whether digital data has such an ontological foundation, an information-theoretic epistemology, an account of knowledge which we will go on to define, raises important philosophical and pedagogical problems. Further, these technologies are interactive; they are intended to facilitate communication between two or more intelligent agents, the success of which presupposes effective interaction between each agent and the mediating technologies (Ess, 2009). Finally, in being data-acquisitive, data acquisition serves as a supporting and in some cases hidden architectural component of the functioning of the system (Wicker and Schrader, 2010). In order to perform the functions for which they were designed effectively, the system must acquire and distribute information about the user. For example, kinaesthetic game controllers for games consoles collect extensive and fine-grained data on individual gamers' gait and range of motion – while these may be used to improve the gameplay experience, they also enable the system to recognize and identify individuals in ways that would not otherwise be possible.

Education is not immune from the growing interest in 'Big Data', the practice of systematically acquiring and mining fine-grained demographic data with a view to improving business performance through such measures as targeted advertising or the development and refinement of predictive models of corporate behaviour. Privacy and information security in this environment evoke a complex tangle of technological, socio-legal, economic and moral questions (Tse et al., forthcoming), which academics from a range of disciplines have attempted to address. Learning analytics has come to refer to the application of these techniques in the pedagogical domain. Drawing upon the techniques and theories of digital data mining, learning analytics systems attempt to harness granular data on measurable learning interactions with a view to enhancing effectiveness. Such a definition of 'effective' learning, however, is not value-neutral and relies on pedagogical and epistemic assumptions which are drawn from the information-theoretic account of knowledge and which are problematic for a philosophy of the education of the human person.

The information-theoretic account of knowledge, as formulated by Dretske (1981), may be defined as:

K knows that s is F = K's belief that s is F is caused (or causally sustained) by the information that s is F. (Adams, 2004)

My neighbour calls to say that he has bought a new car, and this information causes me to believe that he has indeed bought a new car. This approach seeks to solve the problem of justification which undermines positivist epistemology (Gettier, 1963) by positing only causal, and not justificatory, links. Whereas the positivist account of knowledge as justified true belief encounters a problem in the relationship between justification and truth, the information-theoretic account specifies that all justifications are simply further information about information, or 'metadata'. The information that my neighbour is trustworthy and not given to boasting or lying may be part of the causal account of my believing that he has bought a new car, but this is 'metadata', information about information. Such an account is highly satisfactory when designing systems for information authentication and transmission and consequently occupies a prominent place in the philosophy of computing and information. To define human knowledge, and human educational interactions, in these terms however is potentially penurious.

This attempt to reduce all knowledge to a chain of causes is not new. At the dawn of the Industrial Revolution, as today, new technologies led some to hope that traditional uncertainties and unprovables could be dispensed with. In 1749, La Mettrie posited an early behaviourist account of the brain, attributing to secondary causes the entire explanation of human action, without recourse to values or ends. Challenging Descartes' immaterial ego-soul, which La Mettrie considered 'tantamount to being reduced to the intervention of the Holy Ghost' (1996, p. 29), La Mettrie also posits an information transmission account of knowledge: 'sounds or words, which are transmitted from one person's mouth, through another's ear and into his brain' (1996, p. 13). Such an account reduces all education to transmission; my hearing that my neighbour has a new car, on this account, is substantially the same as if I had heard the sound of its engine – all justification, whether experiential, interpersonal, mediated or reflective, is information. So comprehensive is La Mettrie's causal account that he could be credited with having implied a model of artificial intelligence which later came to dominate the field of information technology. Turing's (1949) natural language use test – that a machine can be considered intelligent if it is capable of using human language indistinguishably from a native speaker of the language – is presupposed by La Mettrie when he predicts (quite presciently) that apes could be taught sign-language, and from this surmises no exceptionalism about human minds. Such a statement only holds true if one holds an information-theoretic account of intelligence – the ape, or the computer, is intelligent if and only if it plays the same role in the causal chain of information processing and transmission as a human subject.

Two subtle yet significant problems with the information-theoretic account of knowledge itself have been well addressed in the literature. A third is worth consideration in an education context, as it is problematic for the interaction between information systems and the phenomenology of consciousness. Briefly touching on the first two, an information-theoretic conception of knowledge appears to solve the justification problem, but arguably this is merely shifted to the level of information. Attempts to resolve this by defining information carefully as well-formed meaningful data (Floridi, 2005) only result in a further regress to the level of data, and this regress is not contingent but inherent in the pyrrhonist ontology of causes in purely second-order terms, which underpins the information-theoretic account. Secondly, attempts to elide out this regress by positing a truth-condition-dependent definition of information, such that x is information that p iff p (Dretske, 1982) may appear effective in theory, but are problematic in practice, in that the information flow of any real system will include both true and false information, data and 'noise'. One attempt to address this problem rests on a mathematical theory of communication (Shannon and Weaver, 1949), which posits the justificatory power of information as an inverse function of probability. The less likely a state of affairs, the greater the quantity of information needed to reduce its probability to 1. To answer the question of whether I have left my door unlocked requires only one piece of information, but to answer which of the 40 people on my street have left their door unlocked takes much more.

As with La Mettrie's transmission account of learning, the information-theoretic account posited above only requires a causal channel, not an act of learning. It is this third and more fundamental problem, I will argue, that is problematic with regard to human subjects. Firstly, a causal channel is necessary for the information-theoretic account, but with regard to first-person consciousness, no such channel can exist. Secondly, a causal channel is sufficient for the information-theoretic account, but for information to be known to a first-person subject, it is insufficient for it simply to be caused. The meaningfulness of information as conceptualized above rests on its usefulness in calculating probability, not in its value to the knower.

If, as Wittgenstein observes, there is no private language (1953), then the general definition of information in which all information is well-formed meaningful data will not suffice for knowledge in a human subject. Meaning presupposes some 'criteria of meaningfulness' which must be found within a given language or discourse (Phillips, 1993, p. 8), which suggests a representational theory of mind. While this may suffice for certain forms of propositional knowledge, it cannot account for knowledge of what may be termed '*ipseity*, the normally tacit or unnoticed "myness" of the experience' (Zahavi and Parnas, 1998, p. 700), knowledge of a self as the subject of our reflections. The self does not represent its own 'myness' as an item of metadata about some sensation, however, but rather that myness is fundamental to the experience of any first-person state. This is true not only when I am reflectively identifying that it is *I* who sits in front of the computer screen but also on a much more basic level, pre-reflectively aware of my feeling of boredom or interest (Zahavi and Parnas, 1998, p. 689). It is not that 'mine' is an item of metadata to be added to the experience of interest in the abstract. It is possible to say that this *ipseity*, 'myness', is fundamental to the experience of any first-person state. My perception is an experience which requires no causal channel to make manifest its myness (Zahavi, 2005). Consequently, the value of information as a calculation of probability and the value of experience to the conscious subject are incommensurable.

The implications of adopting a purely transmission-based account of learning, such as is commensurate with the information-theoretic account in the education of human subjects, are of deep concern. The reduction of learning to transmission and transmission to cause is penurious to the education of the conscious subject as a person. While the educational model which accompanied the Industrial Revolution may arguably be criticized as instrumentalist (Bowles, 1976), it would be a misrepresentation to suggest that it was ever solely the education of *homo faber* or of 'machine man'. The industrial human agent, while alienated from production, must remain engaged in order to be an efficient producer (Spencer, 1996, p. 64), whereas in the societies of control, transmission and production are coterminous, quality control and production are one and the same process. For the programmable information agent, nothing is gained by work which was not already inherent in its programmed nature; cause is no longer separable from effect. This is true not only of traditionally automatable manual tasks but increasingly of the symbolic analysis which characterizes many higher-level professional occupations (Reich, 1992). Because information technology 'operates at the traditionally human level of control in enabling the achievement of any and all objectives, *we cannot expect to discover or design new requirements for control that only people can fulfill*' (Spencer, 1996, p. 73). The formerly human domain of controlling productive processes, now alienated, human education as an education for control of means of production, control of second-order causal processes of efficiency, is no longer solely the preserve of the human.

Such a conclusion may either be accepted, as Floridi (2013) does, for example, accepting that human subjects can no longer claim any ontological distinction from any other form of information processor, or resisted. In the remainder of this chapter, I attempt to plot a course for the education of the person as conscious subject, as distinct from the forms of 'knowledge' synonymous with digital information systems.

Given the criticisms made above of a valueless, pragmatist model of knowledge as a chain of information, it is tempting to resort to a Cartesian dualism. Such an attempt is, however, equally problematic. It is not insignificant that La Mettrie draws an analogy with the intervention of the Holy Ghost, for in a world of increasingly fine-grained analysis of second-order causes, the Cartesian ego-soul becomes increasingly a 'man of the gaps'. As positivist science advances in understanding of the mechanics of the universe, causal accounts of the role of God are reduced to a 'god of the gaps', postulated at the end of the causal chain as far as currently known. 'Either God is in the whole of Nature, with no gaps, or He's not there at all' (Coulson, 1958, p. 35). Likewise, the ego-soul finds itself relegated to the end of the chain in a purely transmissionist account of knowledge – that which cannot (yet) be explained by information, a man of the gaps, a ghost-within-a-computer-within-a-machine. The consequence of proposing a retreat to the cultivation of the ego-soul is the education of an irrelevance for inconsequential ends. The ever-decreasing distance between cause and effect, learning and evaluation, information and knowledge, and the increasing ability to determine outcome through information require another form of response. Either the human subject exists on a level of primary cause and value, exercising justifications incommensurable with information, or the human subject does not exist. A man of the gaps will not do.

Some commentators have responded to this threat by positing the need for a right to underdetermined environment, a space free from analytic micro-management, in which human subjects can develop a sense of their own 'autonomy [which does not] ... degenerate into the simple stimulus-response behaviour sought by direct marketers' (Cohen, 2000, p. 1400). Such attempts, while well meaning, remain fated to failure, firstly because they rely on regulation which is systemically incapable of keeping pace with technology (Tse et. al., *Under review*), but more constitutively because they implicitly accept the information-theoretic account of knowledge. Such an approach attempts to preserve by enclosure a space for the man of the gaps to continue to preserve himself from facing the inevitable consequences that follow from his true status as an information processor like any other. Not only is such a solution insufficient; it is even unnecessary to the cultivation of the human subject, which is either present in the whole acting person or dissolves into the information network.

The information age has given rise to a new epistemic problem-set, with implications for educators, managers and the organization of human capital. The problem, which David Weinberger categorizes as 'too big to know' (2012) may be illustrated by the following example: A team of researchers in physics and engineering from two research-intensive universities in the United Kingdom collaborated on the design of the cooling and vacuum system for the Vertex Locator of CERN's Large Hadron Collider. The complexity of such a system, in which the design of one sub-component exceeds the expertise of any one human agent or single research lab, typifies the problem-set. Our intuitive definitions of knowledge are challenged when faced with a technology, clearly brought forth by human agency, yet about which no one individual can claim to comprehensively 'know' how it works, in phenomenological terms, to have an experience of its being. Problems of this kind illustrate the challenges of 'network learning': Who does the learning in a network? Is the network itself both learner and teacher? In such a situation, learning and evaluation, communication and production, collapse into one another and the critical space in which an individual may be said to be an agent or subject of his own learning, wittingly and willingly, begins to be elided.

Is this elision problematic? The danger of such an agentless learning is that it confronts us with an anti-humanist pluralism. Luciano Floridi suggests that he has pointed us towards a further member of this problem-set, a decentring of human intelligent agency, which is yet compatible with a range of great philosophical traditions, and which subsumes these as levels of abstraction within the information-theoretic account (Ess, 2009). Are the values of all humans, like the minds of those many CERN scientists, best realized by their transference into the information network? At first glance, such a project may suggest itself as a form of positive pluralism (Harrison, 2012); however, its claim to make the experiential and the informational commensurable, to have found a common denominator between 'myness' and informationality, volitionality and efficiency, remains ultimately reductive and penurious to the education of the human person.

Returning to the earlier thesis, a personalistic philosophy of mind, borne out by empirical investigations into personal information (Schrader and Lundie,

2012), offers a refutation of such a project. Human agents are distinguished from robots, zombies and Turing machines not by their response to any given problem-set (Floridi, 2005) but because they value their own information incommensurably with the value of information *simpliciter*. My mother's maiden name is not only of informational value as a password to my bank account but also of a personal value as a link to memory, heritage and family. The former of these values is quantifiable and communicable; the second is of interest only to me. It is an intentional value; its 'myness' is not an attribute to be added to the information but is intrinsic to it. If the 'myness' of learning as a fundamental human activity is incommensurable with the 'data' of an information-theoretic kind of knowledge, then the human subjective perspective is not a level of abstraction of data, because it does not rest on causal chains for its meaning, nor is it an interpretation laid upon data, but rather is made manifest without secondary cause. There is an irreducibility to the first-person perspective which preserves the autonomy of the human, but this must be cultivated, and cannot be so in an overdetermined environment.

The challenges posed by information technology in the societies of control require of us a pedagogy of the human reducible neither to control the means of production (as in the disciplinary societies) nor the cultivation of an abstract ego-self. Technologies of learning which amount to technologies of control, 'analytics' as a function of simultaneous transmission–production–assessment, while they may be in both senses an 'efficient cause' – serving as second-order means and as an increasingly effective link in a chain of information transmission – are ultimately insufficient to develop human education. This requires the intentional reality of personal value. By recognizing that learning technologies are not value-neutral, by initiating a conversation between the normative resources a personalist philosophy of education can bring to the design of systems and the nature of the data gathered and analysed by such systems, it may yet be possible to create an authentic technology of learning. In such an environment, the human subject is not diminished by informational ontology (such that they need to be defended against over-determined technological environment), but rather the system is designed from human values upwards (Knobel and Bowker, 2011). In such an environment, a human ontology is augmented by information and communication technologies, not subsumed within it.

Educators, like many other professionals, find themselves working in collaboration with experts across many fields, bringing with them myriad perspectives and competing systems of what constitutes knowledge, and how it ought to be valued. Such approaches bring with them threats, in particular the threat that unmanageable complexity will lend itself to 'Big Data' taking control of the business of curriculum development. Already, educational technology is one of the largest areas of investment for traditional media companies such as NewsCorp, and the symbiotic relationship between corporate examination providers and publishing companies has been explored elsewhere (Conroy et al., 2013). As content and process are increasingly co-terminous in the societies of control, curriculum materials become inseparable from the learning environment. Without action, corporate interests may well wrest control of the development of materials for the network age out of the hands of an under-prepared and under-resourced teaching profession. Nonetheless, the potential for ground-up pluralistic and humanistic approaches to connecting learning communities, such as the visible fictions project (2013) developed for Scotland's Curriculum for Excellence, promises dynamic resource environments which could enable teachers, students and texts to enter into relational learning encounters across the world. Through ConservationBridge (2013), a participatory web-based method of curriculum delivery, students learning about environmental change in rural China can interface directly with students living in the region and with ecologists studying the region. Instead of learning aims being limited by the printing costs of a textbook, or the order cost to a Local Education Authority, opportunities exist to expand a study in one area to encompass learning across a range of fields and disciplines, making connections not according to an informational framework but as the connections present themselves to the phenomenal consciousness of the learning subject. This is a human education, an education of the person in encounter with the world, however mediated. At present, however, such ground-up approaches to creating networked learning encounters are both variable in quality and often not explicit in their underlying informational or pedagogical values, requiring an entirely new skill set of practical wisdom from teachers and curriculum adopters. How educators and their public paymasters respond to the potential of these new opportunities and threats will be the litmus test for the contribution of learning analytics to a more positively engaged, pluralist, connected and authentically human society.

References

Adams, F. (2004) Knowledge, in Floridi, L. (ed.), *The Blackwell Guide to the Philosophy of Computing and Information*. Oxford: Blackwell, pp. 228–236.

Alder, G. S. (1998) 'Ethical Issues in Electronic Performance Monitoring: A Consideration of Deontological and Teleological Perspectives', *Journal of Business Ethics* 17: 729–743.

Barbrook, R. (2013) *The regulation of liberty: Free speech, free trade and free gifts on the net.* http://www.hrc.wmin.ac.uk/hrc/theory/regulationofliberty/t.11[1].html [accessed 14 October 13.

Big Brother Watch (2012) *Class of 1984: The extent of CCTV in secondary schools and academies* s.l:s.n.

Bowles, S. (1976) *Schooling in capitalized America: Educational reform and the contradictions of economic life.*

Cohen, J. (2000) 'Examined Lives: Informational Privacy and the Subject as Object', *Stanford Law Review* 53(3): 1373–1438.

Conroy, J., Lundie, D., Davis, R., Baumfield, V., Barnes, L. P., Gallagher, T., Lowden, K., Bourque, N., and Wenell, K. (2013) *Does Religious Education Work? A Multi-dimensional Investigation.* London: Bloomsbury Academic.

ConservationBridge (2013) http://www.conservationbridge.org/ [accessed 21 August 2013].

Coulson, C. A. (1958) *Science and the idea of God: The eleventh Arthur Stanley Eddington lecture*, 21 April 1958.

Deleuze, G. (1992) 'Postscript on the Societies of Control', *October* 59: 3–7.

Dretske, F. I. (1981) *Knowledge and the Flow of Information.* Cambridge, MA: MIT Press.

—— (1982) 'The Informational Character of Representations', *Behavioral and Brain Sciences* 5(3): 376–377.

Ess, C. (2009) 'Floridi's Philosophy of Information and Information Ethics: Current Perspectives, Future Directions', *Information Society* 25(3): 159–168.

Floridi, L. (2004) 'Information', in Floridi, L. (ed.), *The Blackwell Guide to the Philosophy of Computing and Information.* Oxford: Blackwell, pp. 44–60.

—— (2005) 'Consciousness, Agents and the Knowledge Game', *Minds and Machines* 15(3): 415–444.

—— (2013) *The Fourth Revolution – The Impact of Information and Communication Technologies on Our Lives.* Oxford: Oxford University Press.

Friedman, B. and Nissenbaum, H. (1996) 'Bias in Computer Systems', *ACM Transactions on Information Systems* 14(3): 330–347.

Gettier, E. L. (1963) 'Is Justified True Belief Knowledge?', *Analysis* 23: 121–123.

Hardetsy, L. (2012) *Lessons learned from MITx's prototype course.* Available at http://web.mit.edu/newsoffice/2012/mitx-edx-first-course-recap-0716.html [accessed 2 August 2013].

Harrison, V. (2012) *The relationship between pluralism and diversity.* Available at http://beyonddiversity.dnr.cornell.edu/node/159 [accessed 30 December 2013].

Heidegger, M. (1978) *Basic Writings: Revised and Expanded Edition.* London: Routledge.

Knobel, C. and Bowker, G. C. (2011) 'Computing Ethics Values in Design', *Communications of the ACM* 54(7): 26–28.

La Mettrie J. O. de. (1996) *Machine Man and Other Writings*. Cambridge: Cambridge University Press.

Parry, G. (2005) 'Camera/Video Phones in Schools: Law and Practice', *Education and the Law* 17(3): 73–85.

Phillips, D. Z. (1993) *Wittgenstein and Religion*. London: St Martin's Press.

Plato, (n.d.) 'Phaedrus' in Trans. Jowett, B., *The Works of Plato*. New York, NY: Tudor Publishing Co.

Reich, R. (1992) *The Work of Nations: Preparing Ourselves for 21st Century Capitalism*. New York, NY: Vintage.

Shannon, C. E. and Weaver, W. (1949) *The Mathematical Theory of Communication*. Urbana, IL: University of Illinois Press.

Schrader, D. and Lundie, D. (2012) The value of privacy and private information sharing in online communications, *Association of Moral Education Annual Conference, San Antonio, TX, November 2012*.

Spencer, G. (1996) Microcybernetics as the Meta-Technology of Pure Control, in Sardar, Z. and Ravetz, J. R. (eds.), *Cyberfutures: Culture and Politics on the Information Superhighway*. London: Pluto Press, pp. 61–76.

Tse, J., Schrader, D., Ghosh, D. and Liao, T. (*Under review*) *The academic discussion of privacy and ethics in IEEE Security & Privacy*.

Turing, A. (1949) *Intelligent Machinery*, s.l.:s.n.

—— (1950) Computing Machinery and intelligence, *Mind* 59(236): 433–460.

Visible Fictions (2013) http://visiblefictions.co.uk [accessed 21 August 2013].

Weinberger, D. (2012) *Too Big To Know: Rethinking Knowledge Now that the Facts aren't the Facts, Experts are Everywhere, and the Smartest Person in the Room is the Room*. New York, NY: Basic Books.

Wheeler, J. (1990) 'Information, physics, quantum: The search for links', in Zureck, W. (ed.), *Complexity, Entropy and the Physics of Information*. Redwood City, CA: Addison Wesley, pp. 309–36.

Wicker, S. B. and Schrader, D. E. (2010) 'Privacy Aware Design Principles for Information Networks', *Proceedings of the IEEE* 99(2): 330–350.

Wittgenstein, L. (1953) *Philosophical Investigations*. Oxford: Blackwell.

Zahavi, D. (2005) *Subjectivity and Selfhood: Investigating the First-Person Perspective*. Cambridge, MA: MIT Press.

Zahavi, D. and Parnas, J. (1998) 'Phenomenal Consciousness and Self-Awareness: A Phenomenological Critique of Representational Theory', *Journal of Consciousness Studies* 5(5): 687–705.

4

The Personal and Impersonal in Moral Education

Adrian Skilbeck

In comments subsequent to giving his 1929 Lecture on Ethics, Wittgenstein told Friedrich Waismann that it was essential to 'speak for oneself' on ethical matters. 'Ethics', he had said in the concluding paragraph of the lecture,

> so far as it springs from the desire to say something about the ultimate meaning of life, the absolute good, the absolutely valuable, can be no science. What it says does not add to our knowledge in any sense. (Wittgenstein, 1965, p. 12)

However, Wittgenstein ambiguously finished by saying that ethics

> is a document of a tendency in the human mind which I personally cannot help respecting deeply and I would not for my life ridicule it. (Wittgenstein, L. 1965, p. 12)

Commenting on this to Waismann, he remarked,

> At the end of my lecture on ethics, I spoke in the first person. I believe that is quite essential. Here nothing more can be established. I can only appear as a person speaking for myself. (Waismann, 1965, p. 16)

I want to highlight two features from within and without the lecture. Firstly, the ethical, however it is characterized, is something Wittgenstein respects. Secondly, it is essentially expressed in the first person and not the third person. This is a perspective that is at odds with one prevailing strand of moral education, although at first glance that might not appear to be the case when it would seem students often are encouraged to voice their own opinions.

It is taken as an unremarkable commonplace that moral issues are necessarily serious in addition to being complex and difficult and one's thinking should duly reflect that. In order to come to a clear understanding of particular issues and to assess the views expressed, thinking should be rational, coherent and free from emotional distortion or personal bias. The teaching of ethics in the English school curriculum, usually but not always as part of Religious Studies, encourages just such an attitude. Appropriately serious issues are included in syllabus material – for younger students topics like the environment, global warming and human rights and for older students social issues with a substantial moral character, such as euthanasia and abortion. Students debate the issues, weigh up the arguments and arrive at conclusions. They engage with ethical theory and contemporary analysis and commentary. In this way they learn to think critically, construct arguments, weigh up evidence and provide their teachers with material by which they can be assessed in their capacity to do just those things. Placing this in the wider picture, the development of such skills in rational/critical thinking can be seen as an important contribution to preparing children to lead active autonomous adult lives by equipping them with the kind of transferrable critical thinking skills that will empower them, as citizens in the adult world, to make informed decisions about complex issues and to detect falsehood and bias in the arguments of others. Therefore, if one aims in one's teaching to encourage students to think independently and freely for themselves, on this account one will be teaching them the formal skills of rational argument, how to construct and support arguments, how to provide counter-examples, how to make a case, how to derive one's conclusion from one's premises and how to analyse the work of others. Our taking seriously such requirements for our thought is therefore demonstrated in an approach which is rigorous, disciplined and essentially impersonal even when students are encouraged to express their own views.

What could be wrong? I will argue it gives a distorted picture of the nature of ethical thinking while appearing to be educationally sound. Why might this be so and what is the nature of the misrepresentation? It is distorted because it locates the seriousness of moral thought solely within the subject matter that Rush Rhees referred to as 'issues of life and death' and in an impersonal, anonymizing characterization of reasoning on such issues which is capable of exhibiting appropriate rigour and analytical clarity and assessable as such. In so doing, it reflects an impoverished concept of the way in which the personal nature of such thought is conceived, which leads to the exclusion of the first-person presence of the individual in their own thought, in effect silencing the personal voice as intrinsic to the assessment of the individual's moral thought in both spoken and written form. I will argue for a richer notion of the personal which makes clear why both reason and emotion are internal to the idea of ethical seriousness and the idea of having a voice, notwithstanding some of the difficulties in giving an ethically conditioned account of personal presence. However, I will consider whether the demand for such a presence in ethical 'debate' is necessarily a good thing for reasons to do with the nature of institutional learning and the age and experience of students. Whether or not it is ultimately a good thing, the underlying point is that this conception of ethical thinking is not visible in moral education because the teaching of ethics is modelled on an academic tradition that has rejected this approach to talking about ethics, the place of the personal within moral deliberation and the different forms it can take. If it were present, I believe it would open up possibilities with respect to our conceptions of moral seriousness and how it is represented, which would free moral thought from its obsession with theory, without diminishing consideration of what is most serious in our lives.

My general concern is captured in the following quote from the Australian philosopher Raimond Gaita, who has written extensively on the theme of the personal in ethics. Of the conception of ethical thought I question, Gaita says that it

> treats the difficulty of seeing what (morally) to do as a difficulty for thought which is no different in kind for the person whose problem it is than for a class of moral philosophy students rehearsing an exercise in 'practical ethics.' And this is because of a general conception of what thinking is and of the way in which it is impersonal: thinking has to do with propositions, their truth-value and their logical bearing upon one another, and these can be assessed by anyone with the requisite capacities of mind, none of which make necessary reference to the individual who has them. Hence it is felt that, if we are to understand the way in which morality is personal, then we must locate its personal character somewhere other than in thought. (Gaita, 1989, pp. 130–131)

The idea of a class of moral philosophy students rehearsing an exercise in practical ethics is what I take to be the model employed in the teaching of ethics to sixteen- to eighteen-year-olds in the English education system, as part of either Religious Studies or Philosophy courses. Similar practices typically epitomize what is widely understood as dealing with ethical 'issues', and they are commonly found in the ethics components in vocational courses, most obviously in medical ethics and dealing with hard case dilemmas.

There is little reference to the idea of a first-person concept of ethics in the language of course descriptions and the academic features that students are required to demonstrate in their work. The following quotes are taken from one of the syllabus course descriptions Students will 'recall, select and deploy specified knowledge' 'identify, investigate and analyse questions and issues arising from the course of study', 'interpret and evaluate ... concepts, issues and ideas, the relevance of arguments and the views of scholars', 'communicate, using reasoned arguments substantiated by evidence'. (OCR, 2008, GCE Religious Studies v2)

The aim is to provide a good grounding in the skills of moral reasoning and to prescribe objective standards in such reasoning by which students can be examined. The emphasis is on reasoning and, more generally, the cognitive skills of critical thinking. Students study the canonical theories of utilitarianism, Kantian deontology and Aristotelian virtue ethics and apply their knowledge of the theories to specific moral problems which come with their own associated moral challenges in order to draw out strengths and weaknesses of the general ethical theory being applied. The following are typical of the kind of questions students are required to answer:

> Kant's theory of ethics is not a useful approach to abortion. Discuss.
> A relativist approach to the issues raised by abortion leads to wrong moral choices. Discuss.

If we take the first question, about the usefulness of Kantian ethics, it looks as if it might at least acknowledge some of the more nuanced personal complexities of the issue. In one of the main textbooks for this syllabus, Jill Oliphant discusses how one might begin to reflect on the question. She writes:

> Abortion would be hard to universalise, as there are so many different situations and motivations for obtaining an abortion – all consideration of emotions is to be disregarded and yet abortion is an emotional decision, especially in situations where the mother has been raped, is very young or is carrying a severely disabled foetus. (Oliphant, 2007, p. 100)

This might seem to be a very quick rejoinder to the earlier point, in that students are being encouraged to reflect on a more personal conception of an ethical problem that makes it more than a mere exercise. The criticism of the formal rational nature of Kantian morality and the function of universalization presents an opportunity for the student to consider the place of emotions in moral deliberation and enter into a discussion of the personal perspective through their moral imagination – their capacity to imagine what it would be like to be faced with the complexity of someone else's position and the way in which the moral picks up on the determining factors of particular circumstances.

This is not the case. The examples – rape, teenage sex and disability – are three typical, well-trodden examples from the literature, taken from specific arguments they are intended to exemplify – the sanctity of life, the rights of the mother and the quality of life. They should be serious but removed from their function as examples within argument they appear exposed as lurid, sensational and over-dramatic, designed either to unsettle or support the serious work, that of rational argument and counter-argument, but not serious in themselves or worthy of being taken seriously as indicative of something that substantially enters into the academic nature of the problem, which is one of how to give an appropriately reasoned account of the problems. As Gaita suggests, the way in which such examples are intended to function, and I would add in the classroom as well as in their original context, does little more than 'add a dramatic psychological dimension' to a 'deliberative difficulty' where 'their application in moral deliberation leaves their "cognitive" grammar unaffected' (Gaita, 1989, p. 127). It can do so because of the essentially impersonal way in which such deliberation is philosophically conceived, which is then replicated in the kind of reasoning that students are expected to exhibit in their study of ethics. This is not to underplay the potency of such examples in the rhetoric of public ethics, but it is unclear how such features will enter into a serious account of moral deliberation in personal consideration about what to do.

That sounds as if I am arguing for a notion of the personal in which emotions are taken seriously in a manner that is reflected in the tone of debate as well as its content, that rather than engaging in an ethical shouting match, students should respond as if they are dealing with someone in the grip of a 'real-life' dilemma, handling discussion with an appropriate sensitivity to the tone and expression of their comments in the language they use. In one respect I am. If the personal character of emotions is important in an account of what it is to engage in serious reflection on ethical matters, any serious account of the personal in ethics must assign a role to the place of both the emotions and the language of emotion in moral deliberation in order to redress the balance of the impersonal. However, I do not want to suggest that the personal voice is predominantly emotional or that the inclusion of such language is what marks the ethically serious nature of the personal. One still needs to be clear about what is ethically significant in our understanding of the reality of 'real-life' that claims serious response from those concerned and how moral theory distorts the ethical in failing to adequately reflect the way in which reality is itself ethically conditioned, as opposed to its presenting us with purely pragmatic or scientific problems, for example. I do not want to confuse a call for moral seriousness in the concept of the personal with a requirement that we should engage sympathetically or empathetically with each other in the classroom. They are distinct forms of engagement that may at times be co-existent, and their independent presence in the classroom is something I will address later. Gaita's comments on the place of emotions in ethical thought are instructive. He writes that

> in matters of value we often learn by being moved, and our being moved is not merely the dramatic occasion of or introduction to a proposition which can be assessed according to critical categories, whose grammar excludes our being moved as extraneous to the cognitive content of the proposition. None of which means that we must surrender critical judgement. (Gaita, 1989, pp. 136–137)

These are still matters of value and as such, regardless of whatever emotions are experienced by someone faced with a moral problem, such emotions are still subject to critical reflection as to what a person has reason to do or believe. I do not want to argue that all examples within the discourse are of this nature. What troubles me is that the way students are encouraged to discuss moral issues does not adequately reflect how such problems are serious to the individual. Of course it is desirable for us to be clear in our thinking, but conceptual clarification is usually conceived as a philosophical concern rather than a lived concern: the problem is the way in which the personal is eliminated as an integral aspect of the moral nature of a decision and the assumption that conceptual complexity and the need for conceptual clarity are alone what make such questions difficult.

How then might we offer a substantial notion of speaking in the first person that locates the seriousness of such speech in personal presence and not 'elsewhere'? Recent work by Matthew Pianalto in this area attempts an account of how this might be done (Pianalto, 2011). Pianalto's paper is a response to Wittgenstein's lecture. He begins by distinguishing speaking for oneself from other forms of speech, which include, but are not exhausted by, such things as 'speaking as an expert (or authority), speaking on behalf of another person or group ..., and speaking hypothetically (as in the case of many philosophical arguments and in debate' (Pianalto, 2011, p. 255). These formal and contextual variations, of which speaking personally is one, are also broadly characterized by the possibility of their being sincere forms of speaking and therefore invite contrast with descriptions of insincere speech that differ in intention and tone, if not necessarily content. However, Pianalto's more important contrast for the idea of speaking personally is with 'other sincere ways of speaking', modes of speech which reflect our serious concern, demand our respect and serious attention but which can best be characterized without necessary reference to the speaker. As such they are distinct from speaking where some kind of personal perspective is internal to the authoritative nature of the speech, both in intention and reception.

For example, to speak as an expert or on behalf of others is to speak out of one's cognitive capacities, including one's knowledge and experience and mastery in a profession. Sincerity in such instances is not a relevant consideration. If I go to see my doctor I hope he or she will have a good 'bedside manner', but I also want an accurate diagnosis or appropriate advice. If my car needs repairing I want the problem identified and fixed. I hope I will be dealt with honestly and decently. While there are basic human qualities we expect as part of the interaction, what ultimately matters is that the person has the requisite knowledge and can be trusted accordingly.

However, the way in which we talk of speaking for oneself on ethical matters seems to demand more than just speaking accurately from a body of knowledge or even just speaking from experience. Sincerity might be thought to be a relevant factor here, that is, we mean what we say. But while one might be sincere in holding certain views, they may still be poorly reasoned, sentimental or simply not have the meaning which we thought they possessed. Being sincere does not guarantee that our views will or should be taken seriously or that we will not end up looking foolish. But neither is it clear how knowledge as the expression of facts about the world helps either. The problem in cases like abortion is not scientific facts per se but what those facts mean to us and how moral considerations enter into our understanding of them. While some features of our life seem to unproblematically admit a quite clear factual description and characterization, Pianalto suggests that for other features fact and value appear entangled and our choice of language and the concepts we use to identify facts as relevant considerations communicates the way in which we evaluate these considerations.

> A clear example of this latter kind of difference is the varying ways people will refer to a fetus – whether as a baby, a person, a human being, none of the above, etc – depending upon their views on the permissibility of abortion. (Pianalto, 2011, p. 260)

This alerts us to the way in which speaking for oneself is much more than just sincerity. But what is it? Pianalto suggests we consider how, in offering our views to others, we are bearing witness 'for a particular ethical orientation toward the world' (Pianalto, 2011, p. 259). In speaking ethically 'we do more than simply describe our attitudes, experiences and values, but also recommend them to others' (Pianalto, 2011, p. 259). Thus speaking for oneself is more than just the expression of feelings, insofar as they are just expressions. We are trying to justify our views, 'make them intelligible to others or likewise trying to understand or critique the position of others' (Pianalto, 2011, p. 260). We do so through the language we use as well as how we structure it, not simply to persuade but to best represent our perspective.

What then are the features of an individual's perspective such that speaking out of that perspective is to speak for oneself and demands we take such speech seriously? From where in our language, tone and presence does the morally authoritative nature of our speech emerge? I raise this point because it is difficult to see how tying the notion of speaking for oneself can be ethically conditioned by the idea that it expresses a perspective on the world unless we understand such a perspective as itself ethically conditioned. Otherwise it is no more than opinion and it could be any kind of subjective perspective, just as the notion of bearing witness needs to be ethically conditioned or it is equally empty as an expression of an ethical perspective. What is it that thought and speech must reflect if they are to have an ethical character and is there a metaphysical emptiness in the way the idea of a personal perspective is expressed? This is a charge that has been levelled at the notion of speaking personally that Raimond Gaita has articulated and which has in turn influenced Pianalto's thinking on the personal voice in ethics. Christopher Hamilton for one (Hamilton, 2008) has argued that Gaita's claim that one can only speak from a personal perspective about the ethical character of events in one's life is open to considerable doubt.

Hamilton's criticism is focused on a passage in Gaita's *A Common Humanity: Thinking about Love and Truth and Justice*. During a discussion of goodness and virtue, Gaita describes his experience of seeing a nun talking to patients in a psychiatric unit where he worked as a volunteer. It was not only that her compassion for those afflicted was visible in 'the way she spoke to them, her facial expressions, the inflexions of her body' (Gaita, 2002, p. 18) but that her demeanour revealed a love which made their humanity visible in a way that would not invite the thought, as Gaita suggests might otherwise have been the case, that it would have been better for these patients if they had not been born. Striving years later to make philosophical sense of this, Gaita finds moral theory inadequate to the task of offering him 'proof' he can point to in order to explain why he characterized the nun's behaviour as he did in what it revealed about the patients. There are no metaphysical or empirical properties one can ascribe to the patients to justify the nun's compassion as he experienced it. He could not indicate facts about the patients which revealed them to be our human equals and therefore 'rightly the objects of our non-condescending treatment' (Gaita, 2002, p. 21). What was revealed to him was 'the quality of her love'. Gaita recognizes the difficulty this might present, because he continues:

But if someone were now to ask me what informs my sense that they were rightly the objects of such treatment, I can appeal only to the purity of her love. For me, the purity of her love proved the reality of what it revealed. I have to say 'for me', because one must speak personally about such matters. That after all is the nature of witness. (Gaita, 2002, pp. 21–22)

Hamilton is troubled by the claim that all one can do is 'speak personally'. He characterizes this as 'a vision of the moral world whose tone is one of absolute conviction' (Hamilton, 2008, p. 193), but that very little is being said with such claims. This thought recalls the quotes from Wittgenstein which opened the essay and that in reflecting the 'tendency of the human mind' that Wittgenstein was so much in sympathy with, little can be said about how things are in the world when, as Gaita himself admits, 'from the point of view of the speculative intelligence … I am going around in ever darkening circles, because I allow for no independent justification of her attitude' (Hamilton, 2008, p. 22).

Hamilton's criticism draws attention to several potential problems in Gaita's concept of speaking personally. Gaita, Hamilton argues, is not entitled to any substantial claim about how things are by using such rhetoric as he does. There is a sleight of hand at work; in saying I can do nothing other than speak for myself, I am in fact making absolute claims about what I am describing and the perspective from which I am speaking. Secondly, Hamilton believes there is an implicit claim to the plural 'we' in Gaita's use of the singular 'I' that he is not entitled to make in so far as his invocation of the way in which he speaks personally reflects an absolute claim on behalf of others. Hamilton argues rather that 'one's temperament will colour deeply how one interprets the example and what its lessons are supposed to be' (Hamilton, 2008, p. 193). The implicit 'we' should be replaced by something like 'I, given the kind of person I am, cannot help thinking that I and the rest of you ought to be judged in the light of the absolutely pure' (Hamilton, 2008, p. 193). I cannot therefore be speaking *for* anyone but only *of* someone – me. If one does not take that step, it is unclear who the 'I' is in the first-person perspective and what we are seriously claimed by. Hamilton jokingly speculates that it could be 'the man with laundry bills' or the authorial voice of the book or even just this section of the book, a distinct authorial voice from other books by the same author. What is it that gives the claim to be speaking personally its morally serious presence? 'To say that one speaks personally is not yet, as such, to settle anything about who is speaking' (Hamilton, 2008, p. 193). Hamilton suggests that 'what Gaita means, at least in part, is that he is speaking out of his deepest sense of things, out of his all-things-considered, best judgments, and that others may not share this way of looking at things' (Hamilton, 2008, p. 193). Hamilton's concern is that such ways of talking about moral perception simply invite doubt 'rather than confidence in one's own judgment' (Hamilton, 2008, p. 194) and there is an emptiness and lack of clarity at the heart of such speech – 'a kind of vertiginous free-fall in which nothing is really made clear save the fact that nothing is made clear' (Hamilton, 2008, p. 193). This links to the third problem, which underlies the first two – that invoking the personal in itself says very little about the ethical conditioning of such speech and presence. But if so, what does?

The first way to make clear what is unclear is to assert that the first-person perspective must itself be a morally conditioned perspective and cannot merely be a sufficient condition for calling such speech moral. The difficulty in establishing how one can ever be sure of this is the problem of 'the man with laundry bills' – that one's speech and action might be shaped by reasons that have nothing to do with moral concerns. Furthermore, on the basis that one feature of our taking moral thought seriously is that notions of partiality and impartiality are themselves moral considerations, 'the man with laundry bills' represents an irreducible partiality that skews any claims to views being objective in as much as they are understood as personal, and there is nothing in the first-person concept of authoritative speech by which to assess this or deny it as a valid expression of how someone views the world. I do not think for one moment that Hamilton is asking us to take 'the man with laundry bills' seriously as expressing a moral perspective. His point is that we cannot know how the immediate circumstances of someone's life motivate someone to speak and act as they do if all we have is their word, taken on trust. It is not that metaphysical claims about the moral character of personal presence cannot be taken as trumping compelling psychological reasons for acting as we do; there are no meaningful metaphysical properties to underpin these claims in the first place. The metaphysical emptiness at the heart of such claims invalidates the idea of a moral perspective in such speech as somehow distinct from individual moral psychology. It is merely subjective.

It is a strong attack, but it is mistaken. The personal is never merely personal nor is it reducible to individual psychology. As such it can apply to 'the man with the laundry bills' (who could be a professor of moral philosophy), just as easily as it might to a student in an ethics class who is having boyfriend troubles or problems with her parents. However, it is one thing to assert this, another to demonstrate it. We need to know what the features of this conditioning consist of. It would be a mistake to completely dismiss the idea of 'the man with laundry bills' as an irrelevance in assessing what can and cannot count as justifiable reasons in moral deliberation. If such features of our lives are contingent, they are not de facto irrelevant. However, the extent to which the events and circumstances of our lives do enter into our ethical reflection is conditioned by our understanding of what kind of things can have moral depth and seriousness and the way in which our arriving at an answer reflects this. The way in which reasons for action are understood to be valid moral reasons is itself morally conditioned by their being reasons that have depth and seriousness. This is something we have to discover through our reflection and is open to both questioning by oneself and others and subsequent modification in the light of reflection. The extent to which aspects of our lives are perceived as trivial or significant, relevant or irrelevant in moral deliberation is part of the process of such reflection, and our understanding of them as such is located in the epistemic vocabulary through which we express this understanding.

Hamilton would not, I think, be satisfied. That the authoritative nature of the personal voice can be caricatured in this way presents a problem of absurdity as well as scepticism. There is nothing to say that a person's perspective might not be pragmatic, instrumental, relative or just plain ridiculous and laughable. If I say to someone 'That's wrong!' and they say, with a look of surprise, 'Wrong? What, morally wrong?' that surprise may be personal but can also come from a perspective that sees decisions about action in pragmatic terms. Political decisions are a good example of this. But in moral matters we are expressing something more than a pragmatic sense of right and wrong. We are inviting someone to perceive something differently. We are offering them a picture of what counts as serious in our own lives, what considerations place limits on what we can and cannot conceive of doing. How is this achieved? Pianalto gives us some idea of what this might be when he suggests that it might consist of 'what he or she (the speaker) takes to be the basis for this way of judging' (Pianalto, 2011, p. 263). He rightly suggests 'a single discrete judgment' would not appear to do justice to this, although it might of course depend on the circumstances. But presumably our speaking in our own voice, taken as authoritatively speaking, is something more than the number of judgements that are made. We need to look at how we assess an individual's account of their judgement and the language we use to do so. If we cannot judge in this way and the vocabulary of critical thinking is inadequate/irrelevant, how do we judge, how do we speak authoritatively and how is it ethically conditioned? Pianalto offers some possibilities. We can, for example, identify those perspectives 'that are characterized by sensitivity, coherence, consistency and conscientiousness' and distinguish them from those 'that are superficial and steeped in sentimentality, dogmatism and incoherence'(Pianalto, 2011, p. 263). Pianalto argues that while we might not be able to establish a perspective as 'absolutely true or correct', these characteristics 'licence us in treating it as a perspective that deserves to be taken seriously (and respected) as a worthy way of looking at and responding to the world' (Pianalto, 2011, p. 263). Furthermore, being known as a person for whom truth matters will enter into our taking the moral claims of such a person seriously. This will not, I fear, satisfy Hamilton, for whom the sceptical problem remains.

Discussing comments on moral deliberation made by Rush Rhees, Gaita describes the confusion that Rhees engendered by arguing that moral judgements could be both personal, absolute and still substantially open to disagreement and the possibility of being wrong. Gaita quotes Rhees as follows:

> They thought that I was saying that any condemnation of a man's action ('That was a foul thing to do') is just an explanation of 'how I see it'; and that, of course, others may see it in a different way 'which is just as good'. As though I had said there are no real disagreements on moral questions. Or: as though I do not deny what another man says when (e.g.) he praises the action which I condemn. It is always hard to see how people can mistake your meaning so completely. (Rhees, 1969, pp. 95–96 in Gaita, 1989, p. 124)

Gaita comments that one will be confused by what Rhees said, firstly, if one thinks that objectivity is essentially impersonal; secondly, if one thinks that morality is not serious unless it is objective; and, thirdly, in response to the first two, if one thinks that morality is personal only because each one of us must choose our morality and that morality acquires its seriousness from such a view. What is here being subverted are the considerations that are normally opposed to each other as conflicting accounts. What is being argued for is a concept of moral seriousness in which the impersonal is internal to the concept of the personal and in turn both ethically conditions and is ethically conditioned by an understanding of how we are individually claimed by what is serious in moral reflection. Hamilton's account does not do justice to the disciplined nature of Gaita's understanding of personal speech because in characterizing the first-person ethical perspective as a psychological one, the perspective becomes both partial and open to doubt as an expression of a specifically moral motivation and intention. To be sure, the context in which Gaita used such language invites such scepticism, but we have fuller, more robust accounts of the personal elsewhere in Gaita's writings on which to draw.

If we are working from within an ethical perspective, the terms on which we assess the worth of a perspective cannot acquire their status merely from any propositional status they possess in the propositional realm. This has the implication that the diverse aspects of authoritatively speaking for oneself, for example certain emotional responses and certain fundamental notions that are internal to the idea of truth such as objectivity and impartiality, are themselves ethically conditioned. Thus, it becomes an ethical requirement that in speaking from a personal perspective one is not only sensitive to the emotional content of one's thought but also that one's views are carefully considered and in both spoken and written form a concern for the truth can be detected as internal to what is being said. It matters to oneself that one is lucid and intellectually disciplined in the articulation of one's thought and not deluded about how things are in reality. The intended parody of Hamilton's invocation of 'the man with laundry bills' when applied to the seemingly absolute nature of Gaita's concept of the personal is effective because it depends on an idea of speech as the undisciplined expression of an inner motivation which is not accessible to scrutiny, or if it is, it is only in the context of an absence of a metaphysic of moral presence that renders the personal as no more than an expression of self-centred, highly partial wants and needs, best understood through psychology. But the demand that in order to assess the veracity of what he experienced when witnessing the nun, others should be able to report on a similarly transformative experience, misses the point because it fails to recognize the way in which it is internal to Gaita's concept of the personal that the content of the claim and its truthfulness are available to others because of the kind of speech that is enacted in speaking personally. We are never the sole arbiters of what is morally serious. In what follows I will discuss how Gaita's work responds to such challenges and I will place it within the context of the teaching of ethics. In so doing I hope to offer a portrait of the ethically serious individual rather than a caricature and how such a person is ethically present in the language and tone of their speech.

At the start of this chapter I raised a doubt about whether the problems I see associated with the established way of approaching ethical thinking were necessarily a bad thing in the context of 'the classroom'. This in turn implies a doubt regarding the place of the personal in moral education with which I have opposed the traditional account, even though I suggest this should be taken far more seriously than it has been to date. As a metonym for a whole range of interpersonal encounters, 'the classroom' is itself conditioned by an understanding of the limits of the personal and the impersonal and what is accordingly acceptable or unacceptable. My worry is that the concept of the personal that I have taken from the work of Gaita and others cuts across this traditional understanding and is therefore a potential source of confusion and misunderstanding. As previously indicated, a call for moral seriousness should not be confused with a requirement that we engage with each other in a sympathetic and empathetic manner. The danger is that in doing the latter one thinks one is doing the former and that such engagement is what it means to take another person seriously. Bringing these two aspects of engagement together points to the difficulty of conceptualizing the personal so as not to give undue weight to emotional expression because that leads to detaching such expression from the critical context in which issues are discussed, that is, that when someone is speaking personally the level of exposure taking place renders serious critical engagement inappropriately insensitive and requires a sympathetic/empathetic response instead – one might engage in a form of (philosophical) counselling but that is not the same as serious philosophical discussion, which in turn is not the same as debate, where the possibility of vigorous, impassioned speech is a patina for essentially impersonal engagement.

My question is whether young people at this age have the experience or capacity to both speak for themselves and equally importantly can listen to someone who is speaking personally, understood as more than merely offering an opinion in an exam class within an institution. How will it be 'heard' in the right way? There is a strong possibility of students experiencing exposure in circumstances where there would not be appropriate support or understanding of this conception of the ethical voice. But why should I be so concerned about 'exposure' in what is no more than the normal, everyday nature of classroom discussion, debate, agreement and disagreement? To understand this I will return to Gaita and to the idea that to speak personally is to speak out of what he calls 'an historically *achieved* individuality' (Gaita, 1989, p. 135), in which 'one cannot acquire moral knowledge in any sense that would make one morally knowledgeable. It is more natural to speak of a depth of moral understanding, or of wisdom' (Gaita, 1989, p. 134). It is perfectly possible to become more knowledgeable in the study of ethics as it is currently conceived and examined. One can do so in a fairly short space of time and be academically successful. But in Gaita's account, the deepening of our moral understanding takes time and it does so in the life of an individual. The idea of 'experience', therefore, is ethically conditioned by what it means for our understanding to deepen, which requires the kind of attention and reflection on the events of our lives that Hamilton's example of the 'man with laundry bills' does not touch, even as Hamilton accuses Gaita of failing to offer a sufficiently objective and verifiable account of ethical realities. The problem is not whether students have limited experience in terms of the kind of things that have happened to them, which may be a lot, but whether they have the conceptual understanding and maturity that will enable them to reflect seriously on features of their own lives and those of others in such a way as to both express a depth of understanding in their own moral perspective and 'hear' when someone else is speaking from such a perspective. My argument is that if this happens through the kind of teaching of ethics that is currently in place, it will do so only accidentally, because our lives are only accidentally relevant to the kind of problems that students are presented with for engagement with the theory they are required to analyse and apply.

However, if one is unsure if personally held views can be appropriately respected or adequately expressed at this stage, then perhaps the discussion and debating of such issues through a theoretical framework is more appropriate. On such a view we have the rough and tumble of essentially impersonal debate contrasted with the more therapeutic approach. Taken individually as phenomenon of impersonal and personal engagement, they represent a distortion of what is serious in the personal conception of moral thought that I have articulated and how it might be developed. Taken together and suitably conditioned, both may exist within the concept of the personal I have been arguing for, along the lines Rhees suggested.

While it is important that one needs to be able to trust those one is with, it is also essential that one can question and challenge without feeling one is treading on egg-shells when presented with other members of a class speaking for themselves. However, that is why it is important to understand the way in which speaking for oneself is disciplined. It has to be understood that speaking for oneself is not a form of confession or therapy or merely an expression of emotion. When one is saying 'This is what I think/believe' and taking responsibility for that thought, what matters is that a critical vocabulary is in place that is broad enough to assess both the coherence of the structure of argumentation but also other ways in which the perspective might be expressed, for example the choice of language used, the nature of description and the characterization of the issue. It is in this way that we are present in our thought in the first person. This is not the case when one looks at the criteria by which students are currently assessed. Gaita argues:

> To have something to say is to be present in what one says and to those to whom one is speaking, and that means that what one says has, at the crux, to be taken on trust. It has to be taken on trust not because, contingently, there are no means of checking it, but because what is said is not extractable from the manner of its disclosure. (Gaita, 1989, p. 136)

I am not sure it is even a matter of trust but a matter of paying very close attention to both what is said and how it is said, the form of argument and the expression of the personal concern. However, when one looks at the vocabulary of cognitive engagement that I outlined at the start of the chapter, there are limits to the language of rationality, which we have seen addressed by Pianalto.

Someone might argue that much of what I have said is beside the point, that what matters is to achieve conceptual clarity on issues that are emotionally, morally and intellectually challenging, and if we are to have disciplined discussion on emotive issues that generate heated, potentially frank exchanges, we must avoid the emotional in favour of clear-headed, calm, rational debate that is conducted in a spirit of intellectual rigour and care for logic and coherence. The best way to achieve that cool, critical distance in form, tone and content is through an impersonal, theoretical approach. On this account students are being initiated into a tradition or discourse, a field of knowledge with its own intellectual requirements. This is a stage where students acquire philosophical concepts and analytical skills and it is a period they must go through before they can begin to critique the way in which such knowledge is constructed and expressed. However, theoretical perspectives themselves need to have the capacity to speak to us in a way that is living and resonant just as the issues themselves are taken to be part of a lively contemporary social and cultural debate that crosses over into areas of public policy, the arts, the law, medicine and so on.

Of course I am aware that this approach has to stretch across a range of 'issues', such as euthanasia, bioethics, just war, stem-cell research and so on, and while some of these raise similar questions to those I have raised with abortion – that speaking for oneself is an irreducibly important part of the reality of the issue, others might appear to be less of this kind and the voice of the expert becomes important. However, if we essentially occupy our own perspective on the world then it would be rash to suggest that we can speak as experts or occupy the territory of experts on ethical matters independent of our own ethical perspective on such matters. While clearly someone can speak with considerable knowledge and we would hope they do so, I would argue that it is from the characterization of speaking for oneself I have outlined that one's perspective is ethical. It would therefore seem to be important to enable students to discuss and write in a manner that pays due attention to ways in which personal perspectives can be articulated and which reflects Raimond Gaita's concern that it should be a disciplined enactment in speech and action.

Given the difficulties that could be envisaged by asking students to articulate personal perspectives, there is a fundamental pedagogical issue that would need resolving. It is about creating the right environment. I would suggest this is an ethical requirement and as such it is more than the normal classroom management requirements of maintaining good order, ensuring clear aims and objectives, keeping discussion focused, lively, thoughtful and relevant and so on. It would also involve developing certain attributes in one's students that enable them to work in the kind of environment that reflects a critical understanding and consciousness of the features of speaking for oneself that I have claimed are ethically important, for example being able to distinguish between what is 'characterised by sensitivity, coherence, consistency and conscientiousness' and what is superficial and 'steeped in sentimentality, dogmatism and incoherence'. Establishing the right kind of tone is vital.

I am not suggesting any of this is easy to achieve. It raises many questions, for example, about the nature of sensitivity and attention and about the way in which critical tone is understood in the epistemic vocabulary of moral seriousness. To sum up, what I have tried to sketch is the difference between two approaches to ethical seriousness, the dominant impersonal model of moral philosophy which is to be found in the classroom and the more nuanced idea of the personal in ethics which I have tried to suggest is a question of a certain kind of first-person presence in both written and spoken form. The defining character of the former is that of the expert, the philosophical advisor who speaks from what they know. The character of the latter is that of the wise person, who speaks out of the life they have lived. The wider question to be answered is whether such a model is useful or desirable for students in educational settings.

References

Gaita, R. (1989) 'The Personal in Ethics', in Phillips, D.Z. and Winch, P. (eds), *Wittgenstein: Attention to Particulars*. New York, NY: Palgrave MacMillan, pp. 124–150.

—— (2002) *A Common Humanity: Thinking about Love and Truth and Justice.* London: Routledge.

Hamilton, C. (2008) 'Raimond Gaita on Saints, Love and Human Preciousness', *Ethical Theory and Moral Practice* 11(2): 181–195.

OCR GCE Religious Education v2. Available at http://www.ocr.org.uk/qualifications/as-a-level-gce-religious-studies-h172-h572/

Oliphant, J. (2007) *OCR Religious Ethics for AS and A2*. Mayled, J. (ed.) London: Routledge, p. 89.

Pianalto, M. (2011) 'Speaking for Oneself: Wittgenstein on Ethics', *Inquiry: An Interdisciplinary Journal of Philosophy* 54: 3, 252–276.

Rhees, R. (1969) *Without Answers*. London: Routledge & Kegan Paul, pp. 95–96.

Waismann, F. (1965) 'Notes on Talks with Wittgenstein', *The Philosophical Review* 74(1): 12–16.

Wittgenstein, L. (1965) 'Lecture on Ethics', *The Philosophical Review* 74(1): 3–12.

5

Rousseau's Pedagogical Hermeneutics and Some Implications for Moral Education

David Aldridge

Rousseau's line-by-line analysis of La Fontaine's verse re-telling of the fable of 'the fox and the crow' sits in chapter two of *Emile, or on Education* between two equally surprising and commonly caricatured positions on – firstly – the uselessness of history, geography and foreign languages in the education of the young, and – secondly – delaying any encounters with books or learning to read (the 'plague of childhood') for as long as possible (Rousseau, 1979). It is hardly my aim in re-reading Rousseau's reading to support or advocate his startling claim that – contrary to the views of most thinkers on moral education either before or since – the employment of fable does more harm than good for the moral development of the youngest children. However, it is my contention that there is an important hermeneutic significance to Rousseau's consideration of the child's *readiness* to understand fables that his critics have not really got hold of. This is all the more important since I hope to demonstrate that this issue of readiness extends beyond Rousseau's close reading of the fable and into a consideration of the place in moral education of both narrative and – wider still – *exemplarity* itself.

The most rigorous philosophical advocacy of moral exemplars in the education of the young (and by extension – sometimes explicitly – of the pedagogical use of fable, as a source of such exemplars) can be found in the literature of what has come to be called 'character' or 'emotions' education. These terms can admittedly designate a relatively broad church. However, I follow Kristján Kristjánsson in attributing to a diverse range of thinkers from a number of related disciplines a certain 'family resemblance' that revolves around a return to some key insights of Aristotle (namely, that a 'habituation' into moral virtue must take in conative, affective and behavioural elements, as well as cognitive), along with the incorporation of the most recent findings in moral psychology (cf. Kristjánsson, 2000, 2002, 2007). These thinkers also share, to a greater or lesser extent, a certain 'othering' of Rousseau (cf. Kilpatrick, 1992; Kristjánsson, 2002). One writer even summarizes the history of Western moral education under the pithy slogan 'Aristotle vs Rousseau' (Sommers, 2002, p. 5). By the end of this chapter I hope not only to have called into question this antithesis and the educational principles that have given rise to it but also to have indicated the essential part that Rousseau plays in considering the working of the exemplar in a specifically pedagogical context. This is an area which the character educators have left surprisingly undeveloped, but in which a significant theoretical aporia can already be detected.

An embarrassment of *Maîtres*

Rousseau acknowledges that the poetic form of La Fontaine's re-telling of the fables of Aesop will make them easier to memorize, and the employment of animal protagonists will no doubt delight the youngest listeners. However, these strengths carry concomitant interpretive difficulties that will lead to the child mistaking the moral message that a tutor intends by selecting any given fable. The gist of Rousseau's condemnation is that 'no matter what effort is made to simplify them, the instruction that one wants to draw from them compels the introduction of ideas he cannot grasp' (1979, p. 113). Furthermore, and seemingly paradoxically, 'If they were to understand them, that would be still worse, for the moral in them is so mixed and disproportionate to their age that it would lead them more to vice than to virtue' (Rousseau, 1979).

The fable of the fox and the crow is selected as an exemplar of La Fontaine's work: 'I take for example the very first because it is the one whose moral is most fitting to all ages, the one children grasp best, the one they learn with the most pleasure' (Rousseau, 1979). The interpretive difficulties begin at the very first word, the Maître of 'Maître Corbeau'. Rousseau asks, 'what meaning has it on this occasion?' (Rousseau, 1979). It seems that even the well-known advocate of 'present interest' (who would rather the child Emile never learned to read than be made to do so against his natural inclination) draws the line when that interest is to be piqued by the incorporation of animals in human roles. The child who does not yet understand the complex nuances of the honorific 'Maître' will be further confused by it being applied to a crow. The child who already understands the social complexities implied in the interactions between the two characters seems little to require their being translated into this animal context ('Let us always make images according to nature'), and for the child who does not yet grasp the complexity of the social and economic activities alluded to in the fable, no amount of effort by talking foxes or crow connoisseurs of cheese ('Was it a Swiss cheese, a Brie or a Dutch?') will provide a bridge from the familiar to the unfamiliar: rather, some awareness of the complex human interactions to be exemplified by the animals seems to be presupposed before the animals' uncharacteristically human behaviour can be grasped as such (113).

A further problem is contained within that first word, however. It is significant that Maître is not only an honorific: it does not simply stand for Monsieur. 'Maître' is also the title by which Rousseau frequently refers to Emile's tutor, because it also carries the sense of both the teacher (master, magister) and the exemplary figure who is to be emulated. With regard to his learning from the fable, the child is from the outset treated to an embarrassment of *Maîtres*. His tutor has of course selected the fable and intends some specific instruction by it, but if the child is to learn from examples (even negative ones), these examples set themselves up as Maîtres in collaboration with (or opposition to) the tutor's efforts. Maître Corbeau we have already met, but later on it is the crafty fox ('Another master!') who claims to have sold the crow a moral lesson for the price of a cheese. Yet this does not exhaust the range of pretenders to the title of *Maître*, since the whole fable *itself* promises to instruct: stories, we know, can have 'morals', and the fable is paradigmatic of this relationship.

The crow hardly seems worthy of the title of Maître until we acknowledge that his example can be of a vice to be avoided as much as a virtue to be imitated. The crow thus perhaps embodies the vice of *amour-propre*, the desire to be applauded by one's peers, that is Rousseau's target elsewhere in the *Emile*. Perhaps there are intellectual virtues at stake here too: the crow is also just a little imprudent, or a little too trusting of apparent praise, such that he failed to see through the fox's flattery where a wiser beast would have. In La Fontaine's version of the fable, to give some credit to the hapless beast, there is perhaps also something positive to be emulated in the crow: the crow finally resolves never to be tricked in such a way again. By example, then, he perhaps promises to teach us that we ought to *learn* from our mistakes.

The fox, however, makes as many as three possible claims to the title of teacher. Firstly, there is his explicit claim to have taught the crow a lesson, presenting his devious machinations as an honest transaction – a lesson for a cheese. A pedagogical relationship between fox and crow is therefore established *within* the fable. However, in a curious twist on the typical form of the Aesopian fable,

La Fontaine directs this pedagogical relationship outwards by placing the moral of the story in the mouth of the fox – 'every flatterer…Lives at the expense of the one who listens to him' (115). The fox's command, 'Learn', is thus directed to the student of the fable as much as to the crow. The third possible claim is one that troubles Rousseau greatly: the fox promises to teach the student a great deal that the tutor has good cause not to wish him taught – how to trick others and use flattery for personal gain, as well as how to hide deception through the protestation of truth. This forbidden knowledge exerts a power over the child that is difficult to resist. Every child, Rousseau reminds us, on reading a fable in which the lion represents the powerful animal who can get his own way (regardless of the moral) identifies with the lion; as soon as he is introduced to the fable in which the gnat's special strengths award him victory over the lion, the child switches allegiance. The guiding principle here is not the identification of virtue but immediate personal gain: the lesson that the child learns from nature is not that 'good will out' but that the most powerful or the most cunning will triumph.

The fox thus represents the *deinos* or 'clever' figure of Aristotelian ethics, who – lacking the virtue that would lead him to the good – reasons in service of bad ends. Such a figure cannot serve as an exemplar for moral conduct except in a negative sense; he has every rational capacity *except* phronesis; it is thus that he operates without constraint and is able to exploit situations to his own advantage. Yet recall that the 'moral' of this fable is placed in the mouth of the fox. He is the privileged possessor of moral knowledge in this fable, although he is himself without virtue. He also demonstrates that one can apply this knowledge for immoral advantage while suffering no long-term harm (that the fable tells us of, at least). Furthermore, the fox claims a moral authority in the story; it is he who teaches a moral lesson to the crow. Gadamer points out that 'it is more than accidental that such a person is given a name [deinos] that also means "terrible". Nothing is so terrible, so uncanny, so appalling, as the exercise of such brilliant talents for evil' (Gadamer, 2004, p. 320). Younger children, Rousseau urges, are susceptible to the 'uncanny' power of the fox. As soon as the idea of obedience to authority is introduced to a child, Rousseau has told us earlier in this chapter, the child will apply his emerging reason to subverting it. What tools the fox can provide him with in service of these ends!

The fable as a whole also makes a claim to the title of Maître: this might seem to stretch the term until we remember the peculiar stylistic convention of the fable, which is to include a moral and thus (in appearance at least) to contain an instruction or guideline about its own correct interpretation. Not only can the fable thus represent a teacher, but it can also exemplify two different approaches to moral pedagogy, what might be called a 'directive' and a 'non-directive' approach. Non-directively, the narrative can offer up examples to the child (the older child, in Rousseau's view) and invite him to make judgements about proper moral conduct. The value of this 'active' learning is then – in Rousseau's opinion – undermined when the moral intrudes into the narrative and asserts a meaning (teaching directively). It is for this reason that Rousseau argues that when he *does* introduce fables later in a child's education, it will be with the morals filed off (1979, p. 248).

Rousseau and the character educators

What I have offered above is not the only way of cashing out the difference between a directive and a non-directive education. As well as describing a pedagogical distinction between direct instruction and discovery, perhaps a more well-known definition, specifically where moral outcomes are concerned, is that advocated by Michael Hand (cf. Hand, 2008), where a directive approach seeks to impart moral knowledge or guide students towards a particular intended moral outcome and a non-directive approach does not. It is possible to be pedagogically non-directive in the first sense mentioned (adopting a discovery-based approach to moral learning, for instance) while being 'directive' in terms of intended outcome, and seeking to guide students towards particular moral perspectives, attitudes or behaviours.

Critics of Rousseau have tended to conflate the two possible senses of this distinction. So Sommers, who offered us 'Aristotle vs Rousseau', argues that 'Rousseau's views inspired the progressive movement in education, which turned away from rote teaching and sought methods to free the child's creativity. Rousseau's ideas are also deployed to discredit the traditional directive style of moral education associated with Aristotelian moral theory and Judaeo-Christian religion and practice' (2002, p. 30). While Rousseau indeed eschews rote teaching, as his condemnation of learning the fables by heart demonstrates, it is not clear that he rejects 'directive' moral education in the second sense offered above. His argument for postponing the time of fables, for example, does not rest on any relativistic claim that the teacher should not aim to instil particular moral values into the student, or any application of an 'epistemic criterion' whereby a moral view might be held to be controversial, so much as a practical claim that – if introduced before the child is ready – the fable will be unsuccessful in bringing about those values (for further discussion, see Cell, 1995).

William Kilpatrick, in his own criticism of Rousseau, emphasizes his origination of the continental idea of *authenticity* – that human beings ought to look inward to find their own moral compass and should take ownership of their own individual and unique path through life. Left free to select their own exemplars or role models without direction, Kilpatrick argues, children will do without heroes or seek out their own aspirations reflected back to them in others, such as the 'successful' celebrities of the day (Kilpatrick, 1992, p. 106). Although he does not attribute moral relativism directly to Rousseau, Kilpatrick argues that progressively or romantically informed forms of moral education have given students the impression (whether or not by explicit intent) that there are no relatively uncontroversial moral truths.

There is a hermeneutic element of Kilpatrick's criticism that draws explicitly on E D Hirsch (cf. Hirsch, 1987). There are shared meanings to moral texts which require an appropriate background of knowledge or cultural literacy to access (Kilpatrick, 1992, p. 117). Given free reign to interpret these texts for themselves, children will project their own meanings into the texts or simply misunderstand them. It is largely to teachers' failure to grasp the mettle here that Kilpatrick attributes the cause of the problem that forms the title of his influential book, the question of *Why Johnny Can't Tell Right From Wrong*. Despite E D Hirsch's own opposition to the hermeneutics of the 'romantics', elements of Rousseau's own hermeneutics appear to anticipate his perspective. If we explore the condemnation of teaching history that immediately precedes Rousseau's discussion of fable, we note firstly that Rousseau – largely in tune with a number of prominent character educators – attests to the morally edifying value of historical narrative (Bennett, 1993; Kilpatrick, 1992; Kristjánsson, 2000). What makes it 'ridiculous' to attempt history with the youngest children is their lack of *readiness* to encounter such narratives as that of Alexander and Philip the Doctor. The 'little professor's' reading of the tale, in which Alexander's bravery in drinking what might be poison is interpreted as an example of putting up with unpleasant tasting medicine, is exactly the kind of reduction to the child's limited frame of reference that Kilpatrick would ascribe to the influence of Rousseau, and yet the latter contends that the story is wasted on the child, who has been unable to comprehend its real meaning – 'that Alexander believed in virtue; it is that he staked his head, his own life on that belief; it is that his great soul was made for believing in it' (1979, p. 111).

Rather than being the result of an unrestrained process of self-discovery, Kilpatrick urges that moral understanding is *hard won* and requires significant external intervention. Kristjánsson offers this external aspect as a significant difference between Aristotle and Rousseau. Where the character educators urge that moral development should be (at least in part) 'extrinsically motivated' and 'heteronomously formed', for Rousseau (Kristjánsson argues) it must strictly be 'intrinsically motivated' and 'autonomously formed' (Kristjánsson, 2007, p. 100). It is certainly true that Emile will not be habituated through reward and punishment: how could he, when he is to have no concept of obedience or duty (Rousseau, 1979, p. 89)? However, on the matter of moral motivation, Kristjánsson goes on to embellish Aristotle with a significant 'intrinsic' component. By citing Nietzsche's claim that 'the true role of a moral exemplar is to waken yourself to your "higher self" – the higher ideals to which you can aspire, the possibilities that lie dormant within yourself', Kristjánsson draws directly on the continental tradition of authenticity that Kilpatrick opposes to the character education movement (Kristjánsson, 2007, p. 102); the intrinsic/extrinsic distinction is not thus as easily drawn as Kristjánsson contends.

Kilpatrick makes more of the necessity for heteronomous intervention into moral development, but he offers a mixed message that illuminates the aporia that I alluded to in the introduction to the chapter. He suggests that even 'twenty minutes of excerpts' of the behaviour of passengers and crew during the sinking of the Titanic in *A Night to Remember* is sufficient to consistently reduce the most blasé students to tears. To have such an effect, he argues, is a defining feature of great art. He adds that the 'film doesn't leave the viewer much room for ethical maneuvering' and that '[w]e are not being asked to ponder a complex ethical dilemma; rather, we are being taught what is proper' (Kilpatrick, 1992, p. 139). Sommers correspondingly offers a traditional Jewish story where (as opposed to Kohlberg's moral dilemmas, in which there are 'no obvious heroes or villains') 'the moral message is clear', even 'contagious' (Sommers, 1993, p. 12). Instead of requiring a hard-won background of moral understanding in order to be intelligible, the claim seems now to be that some moral stories at least (perhaps if they are appropriately told or represented so that they can act appropriately on the emotions) act themselves as teachers, directively conveying their own moral message without ambiguity. While Kilpatrick consistently maintains that moral understanding must impose itself from a source external to the student, it is not clear whether moral exemplars require the careful preparation of teachers in order to be intelligible, or whether teachers must in fact 'step back and not interfere with the power of the stories themselves' (Narvaez, 2002, p. 156).

The psychological research (normally argued by character educators to be consistent with Aristotle's thinking) indicates that even the most cherished and time-honoured moral stories do not act on children in this way. So Darcia

Narvaez, in a review of the available literature, observes that that 'when the text does not fit with the reader's background knowledge or schemas, readers will poorly understand... misrecall... and even distort memory to fit with their schematic form' (2002, p. 158). 'Theme extraction' (or discerning the moral or 'point' of a story) even from simple texts (Narvaez discusses the story of the *Three Little Pigs*) proved difficult until age ten, and 'not automatic or fundamental generally unless the topic is familiar' (162). Narvaez makes this case to emphasize that students require continued intervention by a teacher if they are to understand the approved or legitimate meaning of the story (the author's intention, say, or the educator's intention in selecting the story), rather than a morally subversive but internally consistent alternative.

While the character educators urge the need for a heteronomous source of moral development – the exemplar to be imitated – the part that moral narrative plays here is in question. Is it sufficient to tell a story, or do we need to adopt the 'time honoured' practice of 'driving home its moral' (Kristjánsson, 2000, p. 8)? Perhaps the solution is to be found (and the character educators variously seem to suggest this) in identifying different stages of readiness for moral development: where the older child can be trusted to engage in non-directive discussion around moral narratives, younger children require a more didactic exposition of their significance, and those still younger must be developed through a pre-rational process of habituation, in which the teacher – rather than instructing – acts himself as moral exemplar.

The exemplarity of fable

Recall how the fable itself, with its assertion of a moral, can exemplify the teacher. Rousseau's selection of the fable as a specific example of moral narrative can therefore demonstrate a great deal about how the teacher relates to his chosen exemplar. He observes that the intrusion of the moral into a fable raises a further question about its pedagogical value: it calls into question the power of the exemplar to *speak for itself*, or to guide its interpreter towards a single accepted or intended moral meaning. The moral seemingly intervenes to contain a narrative that threatens to disclose more than is intended in its didactic use. La Fontaine's re-telling of the fable not only creatively puts one moral (about how flatterers flourish by exploiting the vain) in the mouth of the fox but then adds a further coda in the mouth of the crow, who articulates a sort of 'trick me once...' resolution for future action. A student of this fable thus has at least two *authorized* morals to respond to, in addition to any of their own that they might begin to interpolate.

The tutor who chooses to employ this fable with some edifying intent has interventions of his own to perform. If the crow shows us that we ought to learn from our mistakes, then here is a *fool* who *is* to be imitated. If the fox can claim to teach the moral message, then here is a *teacher* who is *not* to be imitated. Why would a tutor choose to educate a young child with this fable, Rousseau asks, when he must then persuade that child to perform such a complicated inversion? One further inversion is implied, and although Rousseau does not elaborate it, we must situate his rather banal exposition of the meaning of the fable (that Emile ought not to be foolish, like the crow) within his wider project for Emile. Emile, we are constantly reminded, is not to be like other children; he is to be protected and preserved from the deceitful social situations that arise from being motivated from a young age by the requirement to obey (or at least, not to get caught), or from being encouraged to employ ideas that do not have their basis in experience.

Before he is ready to encounter the fable (it is held off until chapter 4), Rousseau argues that it is important for Emile to have had a very specific experience. He refers back to the experience he has contrived for Emile in chapter 2, where the child is given the opportunity to humiliate a magician by learning his trick, and then is humiliated himself by the magician, who has colluded with his tutor in preparing this event. The experience of shame and embarrassment enables Emile to realize how the magician felt when he was humiliated by Emile, and thus Emile is able to understand the wrongness of his previous action (for further discussion, see Cell, 1995). This sets him up to identify with the crow when he encounters La Fontaine's poem. Rousseau thus wishes to preserve Emile from the fox's influence until he has the tools to subvert the world that the fable holds out to him and affirm another that it conceals: not a world where wit serves only as a means of exploiting others or protecting oneself against such exploitation, but a world in which virtuous agents are motivated by a desire not to cause suffering to others. This is a truly fabulous world in which, if it could only be made real, *neither of the explicit or directive 'morals' of the fable would need to be learned.*

The child who learns the lesson that there are those who flatter for profit is also in a position to discern that he ought not to do the same, although no element of the story points directively towards this moral. In order to learn from the fable, he must already have the means to resist the uncanny power of the fox, although this presupposes that he has grasped the lesson that the fable conveys.

The young Emile thus joins the ranks of the adults, who are able to read La Fontaine 'discriminately' (Rousseau, 1979, p. 116), because they *already know the moral meaning of the stories.*

What is to be learned here about moral pedagogy? Let us firstly acknowledge that the fable can be interpreted not as a special or limited case of moral narrative but as an *exemplar for moral exemplarity itself.* The failure of the intrusion of the 'moral' to control or contain the reception of the fable draws attention to the failure of any narrative to teach directively in the sense of conveying an unambiguous meaning to its reader: any example, we are shown, can always be read otherwise, whatever authoritative intervention a teacher might make to drive home its significance.

This stands not only for moral narrative but for any moral exemplar, even when the teacher offers his own actions and comportment as an example to be imitated in a process of habituation. When Rousseau urges his tutor to be an example to his young charge, this is not initially as a moral agent to be imitated but as an example of the natural necessity to which Emile must become resigned (1979, p. 91). The teacher who wishes to constitute a different kind of example must demand that his actions be interpreted otherwise, but in so doing he hands over to the child the responsibility of deciding what kind of teacher he is to be, since in the very act of demanding that his actions be imitated he offers an action, the demanding itself, that must not be imitated.

This does not mean that the tutor must give up hope of employing exemplars to communicate a particular moral message (the other sense of 'directive' pedagogy), but it does tell us something about the conditions for a convergence of the child's moral understanding with that of his tutor. We cannot hope – not having our own experimental 'Emile' (as even Rousseau did not) – to contrive for whole classes of children the experiences that would constitute a context of readiness (a 'frame') to receive a particular exemplar in the manner that we intend, so we must do the next best thing, which is rather to attend to a child's moral readiness and to select or employ the exemplars that the child *is* ready for. This requires that we reassess the balance of heteronomy and autonomy that is argued by the character educators. While we do not abandon the aim of guiding the child in a particular virtuous direction, we must acknowledge that the exemplified in all cases is presupposed within or runs ahead of the exemplar, or that the child's moral development begins with who they already are. There is an *anamnetical* element to what we learn from exemplars. As Irene Harvey puts it in her interpretation of Rousseau, 'In thus orienting the pedagogical practice around the child's own possibilities, one does not impose anything on him but rather brings out what is already there' (2002, p. 124). This gives us an insight into Kilpatrick's experience of seeing his pupils weep at the noble conduct on the sinking titanic: Kilpatrick's students are not Arendt's 'tiny barbarians' (see Sommers, 2002, p. 23) who need to be civilized by the redemptive power of great art; rather, they are moved because of who they already are. The emphasis of the character educators on the heteronomous grounding of the working of exemplarity thus can be seen to obscure a final insight: that the child himself is always an exemplar from which his teacher must learn if moral development is to take place.

References

Bennett, W. (1993) *The Book of Virtues: A Treasury of Great Moral Stories*. New York, NY: Simon and Schuster.

Cell, H. R. (1995) 'Rousseau and La Fontaine: Postponing the Time of Fables', in Clark, L. and Lafrance, G. (eds), *Rousseau and Criticism*. Ottawa, ON: North American Association for the Study of Jean-Jacques Rousseau, pp. 219–230.

Gadamer, H.-G. (2004) *Truth and Method*. Trans. Weinsheimer, J. and Marshall, D. G, London: Continuum [original German publication 1960].

Hand, M. (2008) 'What should We Teach as Controversial? A Defense of the Epistemic Criterion', *Educational Theory* 58(2): 213–228.

Harvey, I. (2002) *Labyrinths of Exemplarity*. Albany, NY: State University of New York Press.

Hirsch, E. D. (1987) *Cultural Literacy: What Every American Needs to Know*. New York, NY: Vintage Books.

Kilpatrick, W. (1992) *Why Johnny Can't Tell Right From Wrong*. New York, NY: Touchstone.

Kristjánsson, K. (2000) 'The Didactics of Emotion Education', *Analytic Teaching* 21: 7–14.

—— (2002) 'In Defence of "Non-Expansive" Character Education', *Journal of Philosophy of Education* 36(2): 135–156.

—— (2007) *Aristotle, Emotions and Education*. Aldershot, Hampshire: Ashgate.

Narvaez, D. (2002) 'Does Reading Moral Stories Build Character?', *Educational Psychology Review* 14(2): 155–171.

Rousseau, J.-J. (1979) *Emile, or on Education*. Trans. Bloom, A., New York, NY: Perseus Books [original publication 1762].

Sommers, C. H. (1993) 'Teaching the Virtues', *The Public Interest* 111: 3–13.

—— (2002) 'How Moral Education is Finding its Way Back into America's Schools', in Damon, W. (ed.), *Bringing in a New Era in Character Education*. Stanford, CA: Hoover Institution Press, pp. 23–41.

Part Two

Politics

6

Universities, Citizens and the Public

Morgan White

Universities help create participative citizens, with the skills and dispositions required to engage in the public sphere. Academics also sometimes act as expert citizens, contributing their specialized understandings to public debate. Universities are public institutions that support democracy, not mere providers of training conceived as private or investment goods. Higher education policies are blind to the public dimension of democracy and this blinkered approach to policy undermines the democratic aspects of education.

Liberal and republican citizens

In political thought there are two general approaches to the concept of citizenship: the ancient, republican tradition and the modern, liberal understanding of the citizen (Touraine, 1997, pp. 77–89). Michael Ignatieff compares these:

> The one defends a political, the other an economic definition of man, the one an active – participatory – conception of freedom, the other a passive – acquisitive – definition of freedom; the one speaks of society as a polis; the other of society as a market-based association of competitive individuals. (Ignatieff, 1995, p. 54)

Higher education in the early twenty-first century orients itself firmly towards liberal-economic citizenship. The participative, political citizen is subsumed within the economic, instrumentally rationalist individual. Capacity for *action*, conceived in explicitly political terms, is diminished and replaced by steering mechanisms where individuals respond instrumentally and strategically to their environment. The tensions between the private and the public, between economics and politics, between life and world, between state, market and *polis*

An earlier version of this chapter was published as 'Higher Education and Problems of Citizenship Formation', *Journal of Philosophy of Education* 47(1): 112–127.

can be seen throughout the twentieth century. However, these tensions are particularly clear in education, and clearer still in higher education. 'Austere' governmental responses to the 'fiscal crisis' that has been running since 2008 are pulling these tensions to breaking point. Civic relations between persons pursuing a common good have been replaced by talk of market relationships alleged to result in efficient outcomes. However, these seemingly efficient outcomes occlude the public value of civic virtue and this ought to be regarded as a substantial cost.

The liberal language of contract has entwined these values of citizenship and value for money. The citizen is replaced with the taxpayer, who has been reified, turned into someone concrete who demands his or her money's worth from the public sector. The social contract is reduced to a transaction between consumers and producers. The liberal perspective on the university looks to issues of 'fairness' and seeks that institutions widen participation, but this neglects the broader and, perhaps, deeper issue of the degradation of the good of the university (Sandel, 2012, p. 108). To be sure, there are hidden costs incurred by the liberal market model that are difficult, if not impossible, to measure. What values, for instance, are cultivated among students and academics operating as instrumentally rational agents in a market environment? How might such instrumental rationality corrode the ethical norms associated with professional spheres such as teaching, financial accountancy, law, politics, healthcare, and academia itself, for instance? It is likely that higher education institutions saturated by instrumental rationality will produce graduates who grasp the fable of the bees, but not the tragedy of the commons.

Citizenship and education

Modern political thought displays a tendency to draw a distinction between citizens and state (with an intermediary stage of 'civil society'). But, if we recall Aristotle, we know that citizens are those who are fit to obey and to govern. Citizenship, therefore, implies active participation, not through a civil society which sits below the state, but more directly through office holding, as well as more or less tacitly, through obeying the laws made by all citizens in common. Ignatieff reminds us that

> Civic-virtue, the cultural disposition apposite to citizenship was thus two-fold: a willingness to step forward and assume the burdens of public office; and second, a willingness to subordinate private interest to the requirement of

public obedience. What Aristotle called the "right temper" of a citizen was thus a disposition to put public good ahead of private interest. (Ignatieff, 1995, p. 56)

The importance of civic-virtue and its development is under-emphasized, largely because of the overwhelming influence of the universalistic, liberal idea of the citizen. But, in terms of a political aspect to education, it is this idea of developing virtue, of some kind, which has most often connected political and educational theories.

The Aristotelian idea of citizenship, which combines, at once, ruling and being ruled, is not, however, the only model on offer. The Platonic version of citizenship, for instance, draws a sharp distinction between rulers and ruled, or the *aristoi* and the *pseudo-aristoi*. This idea leads to a conception of civic education which lays stress on the need to inculcate, on the one hand, an ability within the citizenry to choose leaders effectively and, on the other, to foster political loyalty. As Eamonn Callan puts it:

> The efficacy of representative institutions in elevating the *aristoi* to political office and keeping out the *pseudo-aristoi* depends on what ordinary citizens do in that sphere of political participation, modest though it might be, that representation entails. The supposed superiority of democratic aristocracy over plain old aristocracy requires that citizens have the ability 'to discern the talent and character of candidates vying for office, and to evaluate the performance of individuals who have attained office'. (Callan, 1997, p. 110)

For Callan, the development of this ability comes through what Michael Walzer calls 'vicarious decision-making' or a form of 'democratic play'. Callan explains:

> This is the making of vicarious anticipative and retrospective judgements, sometimes in deliberative solitude but more often in dialogue with others, about the proper conduct of public officials.... In a representative democracy, vicarious anticipations and retrospections regarding the decisions of office holders are a profoundly serious endeavour. That is largely because the skill and insight we develop in playing the game are what we rely on to evaluate the performance of office-holders and to measure the talent and character of candidates for office. The talent and character of candidates has to do with the quality of the decisions they are likely to make, just as the merit of current office holders depends on the quality of decisions they have made. So citizens who are inept participants in Walzer's democratic play will be in no position to tell the difference between the *aristoi* and the *pseudo-aristoi*. (Callan, 1997, pp. 110–111)

But Callan now wants to deny that such democratic play is, in itself, an educative process. The ability to play this game of citizenship proficiently comes from practice as well as from some antecedent teaching in the rules of the game. If citizens inhabit an open political culture which encourages democratic play, most will, eventually, learn to play the game well. Moreover, inept participants here are not those who fail to distinguish correctly the *aristoi* from their pseudo counterparts. No one can be entirely sure of this. But those who refuse to take part in the game are more likely to be poor democratic citizens.

Callan misconstrues Walzer's idea. The point of anticipative and retrospective deliberation is not to draw the Platonic distinction between those who are and those who are not capable of rule. Rather, deliberative democracy collapses this dualism. As Walzer clearly puts it:

> Vicarious decision-making precedes and follows actual decision-making. In our minds, if not in fact, we imitate the Aristotelian ideal: We rule and are ruled in turn. We decide and we (usually, but not always) abide by the decisions of others. It's not the case, then, as elitist writers have argued, that citizens merely reaffirm or reject their leaders at periodic intervals.... The study of politics should have this purpose: It should help ordinary citizens reflect upon the most important matters of state. It should prepare leaders, would-be leaders, and vicarious leaders – which is to say, it should prepare all of us – for the democratic business of taking stands and shaping policies. (Walzer, 1980, pp. 159–160)

Through a dialogic process of this democratic play citizens learn to be better citizens. They learn to make up their minds on salient political issues of the day and to make decisions. This democratic play, however, does not teach citizens to discriminate between rulers and ruled. Rather, vicarious decision-making is an act of citizenship in itself. It implies what Hannah Arendt called 'isonomy', or formal political equality in terms of a capacity for action. Now, in an increasingly de-politicized culture it is precisely these sorts of 'skills', or rather dispositions, that universities (and schools) should encourage in their teaching, and not simply focus on those 'employability' skills deemed appropriate by career officers and employers or attractive to students, with at least one eye fixed on future job prospects and the income-generating capacity of a university course. If society is to describe certain abilities as 'key skills', surely the most relevant are those which allow us to engage as citizens. This would mean, in practical terms, an understanding of and an ability to use, rhetoric, logic, grammar (the trivium as it was once known in the mediaeval university) and critical capacities. But formal skills alone are not enough, for some sense of the duties of citizens towards others is also required, as is an understanding of the world that individuals live within. Michael G. Gottsegen sums this up succinctly:

> By one account the paramount need is to equip the youth of today with the practical skills that will be necessary in the world of tomorrow. Especially in a world that is changing as fast as ours, it is argued, there is little point in conveying knowledge which quickly becomes obsolete .... [H]owever, a skill-oriented pedagogy which does not undertake at the same time to bind men to their past, and thus to their world, constitutes a danger to that very world of which the proponents of "relevant" skills believe themselves to be so mindful. More important ... than the imparting of skills is the imparting of an ethos of worldliness and world-concern which the teaching of skills alone will not serve to inculcate. (Gottsegen, 1994, p. 112)

The republican, in addition to an understanding of and attachment to the world, requires an artillery of skills (of reason, empathy and of rhetoric) to engage in the agonal realm of politics; the liberal citizen can call upon a set of formal political and civil rights and duties bestowed by the state. The latter citizen appears politically passive; the former appears active.

However, the republican citizen is active in the public sphere only to the extent that he is already free. Ignatieff writes:

> Since Aristotle assumed that political discussion was an exercise in rational choice of the public good, he also assumed that the only persons fit for such an exercise were those capable of rational choice. And the only ones capable of rational choice were those who were free. Dependent creatures could not be citizens: slaves, those who worked for wages, women and children who were both subject to the authority of the domestic *oeconomia* were excluded from citizenship. Adult male property owners were the only persons vested with civic personality. (Ignatieff, 1995, p. 56)

Citizenship has always been an exclusionary category: exercising political choice and decision-making require an independent mind, and this in turn requires material and social independence. Property holding guaranteed independence and rationality free from material concerns. So, while there is a clear contradiction between a republican, property-based mode of citizenship and its liberal, rights-based counterpart, we can also see such property restrictions in the ideas of liberals like Locke, who saw rights based in property relations. However, the republican view is more than a defence of property or gendered privilege. Citizenship required certain intellectual, social and economic prerequisites for good judgement in the realm of politics. Moreover, as Ignatieff points out, the property required for citizenship was landed, rather than held in moveable assets. As such, property-holding citizens also held a patriotic interest in the state. The point, however, is that political freedom did not stand independent of cognitive capacities, status and material wealth. We might question the degree of political freedom in heavily indebted students, focused on the economic value of their degrees and encultured into an instrumental mode of learning.

In the civic republican tradition, juridified bureaucracy was anachronistic. Offices were rotated among citizens; the establishment of a permanent bureaucracy was resisted because this might invite a separation of specialist bureaucratic interests in opposition to the public interest. This explains why the republican tradition is wary of the concept of civil society, informed, but also dominated, by the state. For republicans, citizenship is self-rule, taken in turns by members of a coherent community.

But, of course, this rule of self-rule is indeed a myth. The profits of office mean that office holders want to hold on to their positions. The civic concept of citizenship has to be supplemented by a discourse on corruption (just as the civic university requires a discourse on the degradation of its purposes). Ignatieff writes that republican 'Citizenship implied a tragic and often nostalgic sense of lost human possibility. Civic life was a ceaseless struggle to preserve the human good – the *polis* – from the forces within human nature bent on its deformation into tyranny' (Ignatieff, 1995, pp. 58–59). From the normative perspective of civic republicanism then, it is little wonder that the empirical history of the university appears as a jeremiad.

Civil, political and social rights

Certain material conditions have to be met to help to ensure the virtue of citizens. Just as private civil and political rights balance civic community, these in turn have to be balanced with social rights. The problem is that reconciling these requires that we accept their contradictions. Formal legal equality is rather empty without the social and economic equality necessary for the exercise of legal equality. Indeed, the formal legal rights of citizenship were concretized in the founding of the modern welfare state. This welfare state should be seen as an expression of those social rights which underpin purely abstract, formal civil and political rights. The state once saw its role as the guardian of equal citizenship balancing the undermining forces of the market economy. It is because of such social rights that citizens could count on protection against illness, old age, illiteracy and unemployment. It was a welfare state founded upon universal benefits which strengthened the civic ties between individual citizens and between their private and the public interest: 'Taxation was thus explicitly conceived as the instrument for building civic solidarity among strangers' (Ignatieff, 1995, p. 67).

Presently, however, the welfare state has a rather different image. In place of acting as a kind of civic cement, the welfare state is often presented as an institution which provides disincentives to work, supports the feckless, removes individual responsibility, is an unnecessary drain on national income and is overly bureaucratic. Far from building solidarity among strangers, the taxation paid to fund the welfare state, *once value for money is demanded from welfare services*, actually serves to undermine civic ties. The welfare state, conceived as a comfort blanket that creates a suffocating culture of dependency and entitlement, is not a civic glue that binds in solidarity but a solvent that individuates and atomizes. Either welfare provision brings people closer together in the spirit of solidarity, creating civic bonds, or public services are delivered in a way which aims at efficiency which will break down civic ties between people. This civic retreat should be regarded as an anomic cost, or inefficiency.

Citizenship and university education

The erosion of civic ties is demonstrated in the case of a higher education system which takes the efficient training for future employment of students as its main aim. Students no longer receive a rounded, civilizing education:

[O]nly 2.6 per cent of American students major in English. Almost as many major in catering, domestic science, and hotel management. The British figures are heading in the same direction. It may or may not be a good thing to teach young persons the art of portion control, or to give them diplomas in the wiles of advertising, but such students are not being turned against western civilization. They are being so unblinkingly trained to take their place in the modern consumer society that to encounter a decent scepticism about western civilization would do them good .... [P]rofessional training is not enough for the whole of life. It is not exactly news that the holders of MBAs have been known to commit fraud, to throw their workers on to the street needlessly, to sacrifice production to financial manipulation, and to behave as badly as Thorstein Veblen complained that financiers behaved a hundred years ago. If they behave badly because they have been badly trained, what they lack is not a training in analytical techniques but a sense of the duties of the powerful and the clever to the less powerful and the less clever. (Ryan, 1999, pp. 154–155)

Veblen's complaint about financiers is prescient, but a 'vocational' education is usually nothing of the sort. How many of the students and graduates of these courses really have a calling for hotel management? Vocational courses are merely those which point towards a training for a future career. Ironically, of course, such career-based courses have flourished at precisely the same time as the idea of a career, in the sense of engagement in uninterrupted professional employment, is disappearing (Williams, 1988, pp. 52–53).[1] While it is still possible to conceive of, and look forward to, a legal career or the vocation of the priesthood with reasonable confidence, for instance, we cannot look forward to a career in politics, or in television, or even hotel management with the same degree of confidence. It only really makes sense to speak of a political career in retrospect. A formal university training is a strict requirement for lawyers; it is not for television producers, journalists or politicians. Formal training may help in some ways, but this only means that we can call such training 'vocational' in the very loosest sense. Intuitively, then, it seems to make more sense to think of a career in hindsight. If the notion of a career as uninterrupted progress can no longer be generally relied upon, then it does seem odd that education, and higher education most markedly, has become much more career oriented. It could be argued that education, and university education with it, has gradually become integrated into the wider framework of the bureaucratized welfare state. After all, the welfare state provides for citizens in need of some assistance, but the need for this should vanish if we educate and train citizens to be able to provide for themselves, usually through employment. In this sense, a university education geared towards future employment would allow the state to step back from its responsibilities to provide wider social rights. Putative students are being misled. The instrumental university has become a tool to provide more efficient labour markets, where vocational education generates a supposedly level playing field that will allow the state to withdraw from other forms of welfare provision, such as unemployment benefit, allows employers to withdraw from work-related training and proposes that the individual student shoulders the brunt of the costs. This credentialist promise, however, of a ticket to a career, is a trade borne of desperation. The degree appears attractive because employment is becoming more precarious.

The transition to a more instrumental idea of the university was begun at the end of the nineteenth century when science became a means of capital accumulation through the application of discoveries in the fields of physics and chemistry to commodity production. This was the result not only of advances in science itself but also because of a greater willingness on the part of capitalists to invest in research and development, a spirit which was fostered by increased industrial competition and a sufficient level of surplus capital. This industrial development created a demand for scientific-technical education which was complemented by the rationalization of state administration which compounded the demand for technocrats. Tony Smith explains:

> No longer was the goal of a university education the formation of character. Rather than being oriented towards the ideal of *Bildung* [self-formation], the university now had the goal of producing persons capable of discovering and applying technically employable knowledge. No longer was the ideal the well-rounded humanist of the *Universitas litterarum*. Instead the ideal became the specialist, one who concentrated on a particular area and was able to produce causal knowledge of the regularities of that object realm. (Smith, 1991, p. 196)

But, although the ideal related to the specialist, this was combined with a notion that we can all be specialists because the logic at work here was to *produce* a band of trained researchers capable of making further efficiency savings or finding or creating new markets for goods and services.

Higher education now cannot be claimed to remain the preserve of an elite. Instead, it has become one agency among others charged with increasing the opportunities of individuals. And opportunity, because it is conceived in a strictly materialist fashion, is synonymous with production and consumption: job opportunities, career prospects and earnings potential. This is most evident in the new subject areas: leisure and tourism studies, media studies, fashion design and business administration (but we might also include things like education studies too). Ronald Barnett points out that these

> newer forms of study are not merely operational but are instrumental in character. That is, they are designed to bring about technical effects on a taken-for-granted world (or slice of it). They are built around a technical interest in the world in which the world is objectified and externalized, and it is understood to be a suitable vehicle for instrumental operations to be wrought upon it. The action that they encourage can be said to be critical, but its critical component is arrested at the instrumental level. It is a critical action that accepts the world largely as given and seeks to produce more effective operations within it. Transformations are entirely acceptable *providing* that they produce greater profitability, power and security. (Barnett, 1997, p. 79)

It could, however, be suggested that this is nothing new. Universities, in their mediaeval form, were, after all, about training for the elite professions of law, medicine and public administration. But Barnett argues that the link between the university and work was entirely different in the mediaeval period. He refers to Basil Bernstein on this point:

> The mediaeval curriculum might, in the professional schools, have contained an operational character, but it was not instrumental.... Not only were the studies framed in the larger curriculum of the Trivium (grammar, logic and rhetoric) and the Quadrivium (arithmetic, astronomy, geometry and music), but the Trivium, "as exploration of the word" took precedence over the Quadrivium, "as the exploration of the world". "The construction of the inner was the guarantee for the construction of the outer. In this we can find the origin of the professions". But we have been seeing the abandonment of the inner world, except that the inner world is now finding its way back in the form of an instrumental control of the self by the self (in other words, *self-control*). As a result, 'knowledge, after nearly a thousand years, is divorced from inwardness and literally dehumanised'. (Barnett, 1997, p. 79)

Knowledge, however, is also divorced from a public form of outwardness. Once knowledge acquires a private instrumental value, a value without a public value, it is also dehumanized because it forecloses the possibility of action. The outer, it should be noted, develops the inner; the Quadrivium builds our understanding of the Trivium. Private, instrumental values attached to knowledge curb the *vita activa*; outward, publicly oriented values enable it to flourish.

It is here that citizenship, earning income and education come together. We are regarded as citizens to the extent that we can partake in social life, and social life has come to mean, for many, little more than production and consumption. And so good citizenship loses its ties to traditional ideas of virtue and worldliness. Instead, virtue is demonstrated by secular signifiers: what we can consume and those things we consume are primarily determined by what we earn, and how we earn it, since leisure time is also required to consume. What we earn has, in the past, been largely determined by educational background (or rather what we earned was determined by class background and this correlated with educational background), and so, it follows, some kind of flow between the roles of citizenship, employment and education can be expected.

Of course, this is all entirely contingent. The idea that those with more material goods live fuller lives is precisely the inequality that democracy attempts to iron out. What we have is a democratic state which reinforces this message which celebrates consumption and encourages fairness through encouraging what it calls a 'meritocracy'. However, the merit rewarded in this system is that which corresponds with the status quo ante. This takes away the critical voice of dissent and leaves us as narrower, more limited, citizens. As citizens we can take part in the life of society but we cannot mount a political challenge to the world we inhabit and the corruption of the goods we value. In short, and in Arendtian terms, the idea of citizenship has shifted from a political to a social meaning.

In our rather impoverished understanding of higher education, learning is either productive, in that it is regarded as an investment which will pay dividends in terms of future earnings, or it is consumptive, in that it is like a leisurely activity, a kind of high-minded frivolity. But this is to mistake education for training or entertainment. While education, Arendt maintains, belongs to the realm of the world, training and entertainment relate to life. Education introduces learners to the world; it teaches them to question it in a process of becoming and ensures the continuance of the world. Training and entertainment, on the other hand, are consumer goods destined to be used up:

> *Panis et circenses* truly belong together; both are necessary for life, for its preservation and recuperation, and both vanish in the course of the life process – that is, both must constantly be produced anew and offered anew, lest this process cease entirely. The standards by which both should be judged are freshness and novelty, and the extent to which we use these standards today to judge cultural and artistic objects as well, things which are supposed to remain in the world after we have left it, indicates clearly the extent to which the need for entertainment has begun to threaten the cultural world. (Arendt, 1993, p. 286)

Arendt here compares the worldly realms of culture and art with the business of earning and entertainment. But the point pertains equally to education. In a rush to provide equality of opportunity, to broaden the range of groups participating in higher education and in connecting efficiency indicators to teaching and research, we have forgotten the purposes of education generally, and higher education specifically. As higher education comes under the fiscal pressures of austerity, the need to recall those purposes is urgent.

Higher education should not be necessary for developing basic democratic virtues, such as toleration, truth-telling and a predisposition to respect others. What universities can do, however, is encourage the kind of vicarious decision-making advocated by Walzer. As Gutmann puts it:

> [L]earning how to think carefully and critically about political problems, to articulate one's views and defend them before people with whom one disagrees is a form of moral education to which young adults are more receptive [than young children] and for which universities are well-suited. (Gutmann, 1999, p. 173)

Democratic citizenship and academic autonomy

But what is taught is not the only directly relevant factor, for the idea of democratic citizenship not only offers a platform from which to criticize the vocational nature of much of what is taught in universities. It also offers a defence of institutional, scholarly autonomy. Academics can (sometimes) be regarded as an especially important category of citizen:

> Control of the creation of ideas – whether by a majority or a minority – subverts the ideal of *conscious* social reproduction at the heart of democratic education and democratic politics. As institutional sanctuaries for free scholarly inquiry, universities can help prevent such subversion. They can provide a realm where new and unorthodox ideas are judged on their intellectual merits; where the men and women who defend such ideas, provided they defend them well, are not strangers but valuable members of a community. Universities thereby serve democracy as sanctuaries of nonrepression. In addition to creating and funding universities, democratic governments can further this primary purpose of higher education in two ways: by respecting what is commonly called the 'academic freedom' of scholars, and by respecting what might be called the 'freedom of the academy'. (Gutmann, 1999, pp. 174–175)

The academic freedom of scholars is neither a right of citizenship nor a contractual right of university employees, though it is most obviously expressed through permanent academic tenure (Shils, 1997, pp. 80–82). It is the democratic purpose of the university, and not contracts held between employers and employees, which grounds the freedom of academic scholars.

> The core of academic freedom is the freedom of scholars to assess existing theories, established institutions, and widely held beliefs according to the canons of truth adopted by their academic disciplines, without fear of sanction by anyone if they arrive at unpopular conclusions. Academic freedom allows scholars to follow their autonomous judgment wherever it leads them, provided that they remain within the bounds of scholarly standards of inquiry. (Gutmann, 1999, p. 175)

In return for this freedom scholars have a duty to observe scholarly standards of inquiry. To neglect this would make the freedom of the scholar indistinct from more general freedoms of speech that all citizens hold. To be sure, it is precisely a blurring of these categories which occurs when an academic scholar takes on the role of a consultant. One way, then, that we might assess the decline in academic freedom would be through the increasing *expectation* that academics behave like consultants and, connectedly, the increasing prevalence of short-term temporary employment contracts for academics. Of course, the notion that academics can also act as consultants reinforces the pressure to keep levels of pay down and to offer temporary employment. The myth we are encouraged to believe in is that good teachers and good researchers will also be able to function as successful consultants in the real world of business. Seldom do we come across the point that education, from a normative point of view, takes as its task the preservation of the world, which entails a cultivation of civilization, while the 'real world' of private business and industry, in fact, belongs to a life process and sometimes does considerable harm to the world in concrete terms.

Now, one form which academic freedom takes is the ability for academics to be able to control the educational environment within which teaching and research take place. The institutional administration of universities, however, varies between cultures in important ways.

> Whereas German universities were generally self-governing bodies of scholars who made administrative decisions either collegially or through democratically elected administrators, American universities (with few exceptions) are administered by lay governing boards and administrators chosen by those boards. Therefore, while the scholar's right of academic freedom in the German context could readily be extended to a right collectively to control the academic environment of the university, the academic freedom of faculty in the American context had to be used as a defense *against* the universities' legally constituted (lay) administrative authority. Recurrent threats by universities' trustees and administrators to the academic freedom of faculty members made it easy for faculty to overlook their stake in defending their universities against state regulation of education policies. (Gutmann, 1999, p. 176)

When we look to the administration of British higher education, we see a marked shift from a more or less Germanic model of governance to an American system of management (Salter and Tapper, 2000). The crucial difference, however, is that in British higher education institutions, professional administrators, teaching and research staff with administrative responsibilities and lay members of universities' governing bodies are all guided by the norms laid down by state-determined performance indicators which attempt to reproduce a market, or at least a competitive, environment. The public good of the university is polluted, degraded and colonized by both state and market.

The managerial argument against the kinds of points I sketched out above claims that academic freedom is the slogan which academics appeal to whenever their authority is undermined. Academic freedom, so the argument goes, is a concept which applies to the freedom of students just as much as academic staff. Therefore, academic freedom entails duties towards teaching students well. The managerialism of today's university culture is no more than enshrining this duty in the procedures of faculty against the vested interests of academic staff. In response to this it can be said that there is obviously a duty to teach students well, to operate a fair admissions policy, as far as possible, to assess students' work fairly and accurately, and to allow students to have control over what they study even. Academic freedom is not a freedom to provide poor teaching or poor research. It is, in fact, a freedom to do good research and good teaching, whatever form this takes – and that is a judgement for the academic community. The problem with the managerialist approach is that its procedures have never been discursively redeemed in argument. Rather, performance indicators and working practices have been handed down by the state to the administrators of our universities based on business norms (Kedourie, 1989, pp. 27–34) which (generally) regard students and their families as consumers demanding higher education. Of course, this denies the legitimate authority of academic staff over their students, which is not to say that students have no claim to academic freedom, but, rather, that academic freedom could best be served through procedures settled on – though they remain fallible – by participants: the academic community (and not only its managers), the state and the wider public.

With regard to citizenship, however, universities not only help to create citizens through teaching students; they also, through the academic freedom of faculty staff, help to lead political debate in new, or old and forgotten, directions. The autonomy of the modern university is rooted, like the idea of the active citizen, in the protection of democracy against the threat of domination. The academic freedoms of scholars and universities guard against political repression for all citizens, not only scholars. This is so precisely because the rational pursuit of truth lies at the heart of the intellectual exercise.

But the freedom of faculty scholars does not have to be directly impinged upon to infringe the academic freedom of universities. Central to understanding this is the idea that an academic community of scholars creates its own scholarly standards. Democratic societies can 'foster the general freedom of conscious social reproduction within politics by fostering the particular freedom of defending unpopular ideas within universities' (Gutmann, 1999, p. 177). This marks the difference between populism and democracy. We can, and should, defend unpopular ideas if these ideas meet other standards of legitimacy. In this case, this means meeting standards of scholarly merit. To undermine academic freedom means to undermine an important distinction between democracy and populism. So, academic freedom (from accountability mechanisms and to cultivate civic engagement) is important to democratic citizenship because it serves as a block to a rather insidious form of tyranny. The scholarly university, that is, the true university, provides a space for action in which students and scholars share a public, civic-minded ethic and supports students and academics in their democratic forays into the public realm. The league-table obsessed, branded, performative empirical reality of universities in the twenty-first century may speak of widening participation, but the hierarchical system they represent only reinforces the inequality of citizens (Delbanco, 2012, p. 135). At the normative level, however, the university, insofar as it supports and encourages an active, worldly, republican conception of citizenship, in both teaching and research ought to be regarded as a public good, only guided by market norms at the margins, only steered by state bureaucracy peripherally. The resuscitation of the authority of the university depends upon such scholarly integrity.

Notes

1   Williams writes that 'Career is still used in the abstract spectacular sense of politicians and entertainers, but more generally it is applied, with some conscious and unconscious class distinction, to *work* or a *job* which contains some implicit promise of progress. It has been most widely used for jobs with explicit internal development – "a career in the Civil Service" – but it has since been extended to any favourable or desired or flattered occupation – "a career in coalmining". Career now usually implies continuity if not necessarily promotion or advancement, yet the distinction between a career and a *job* only partly depends on this and is often associated also with class distinctions between different kinds of work'.

References

Arendt, H. (1993) *Between Past and Future*. Harmondsworth: Penguin.

Barnett, R. (1997) *Higher Education: A Critical Business*. Buckingham: Society for Research in Higher Education and Open University Press.

Callan, E. (1997) *Creating Citizens: Political Education and Liberal Democracy*. Oxford: Clarendon Press.

Clarke, J. and Newman, J. (1997) *The Managerial State*. London: Sage Publications.

Delbanco, A. (2012) *College: What it Was, Is and Should Be*. Princeton, NJ: Princeton University Press.

Gottsegen, M. G. (1994) *The Political Thought of Hannah Arendt*. Albany, NY: State University of New York Press.

Gutmann, A. (1999) *Democratic Education*. Princeton, NJ: Princeton University Press.

Habermas, J. (1996) *Between Facts and Norms: Contributions to a Discourse Theory of Law and Democracy*. Cambridge: Polity Press.

Ignatieff, M. (1995) 'The Myth of Citizenship', in Beiner, R. (ed.), *Theorizing Citizenship*. Albany, NY: State University of New York Press, pp. 53–77.

Jessop, S. (2012) Education for Citizenship and 'Ethical Life': An Exploration of the Hegelian Concepts of *Bildung* and *Sittlichkeit*, *Journal of Philosophy of Education* 46(2): 287–302.

Kedourie, E. (1989) *Perestroika in the Universities*. London: The IEA Health and Welfare Unit.

Nussbaum, M. (1997) *Cultivating Humanity: A Classical Defense of Reform in Liberal Education*. London: Harvard University Press.

Ryan, A. (1999) *Liberal Anxieties and Liberal Education*. London: Profile Books.

Salter, B. and Tapper, T. (2000) The Politics of Governance in Higher Education: The Case of Quality Assurance, *Political Studies* 48(1): 66–87.

Sandel, M. (2012) *What Money Can't Buy: The Moral Limits of Markets*. London: Allen Lane.

Scott, P. (1995) *The Meanings of Mass Higher Education*. Buckingham: The Society for Research into Higher Education & Open University Press.

Shils, E. (1997) 'The Academic Ethic', in Shils, E. (ed.), *The Calling of Education: The Academic Ethic and Other Essays on Higher Education*. London: University of Chicago Press, pp. 3–128.

Smith, T. (1991) *The Role of Ethics in Social Theory*. New York: State University of New York Press.

Taylor, C. (1995) 'Liberal Politics and the Public Sphere', in Etzioni, A. (ed.), *New Communitarian Thinking: Persons, Virtues, Institutions, and Communities*. London: University Press of Virginia, pp. 183–217.

Touraine, A. (1997) *What is Democracy?*. Oxford: Westview Press.

Walzer, M. (1980) 'Political Decision-Making and Political Education', in Richter, M. (ed.), *Political Theory and Political Education*. Princeton, NJ: Princeton University Press, pp. 159–176.

Williams, R. (1988) *Keywords: A Vocabulary of Culture and Society*. London: Fontana Press.

7

The Interpretive Tradition and Its Legacy

Jon Nixon

And what is hermeneutical imagination? It is a sense of the questionableness of something and what this requires of us. (Hans-Georg Gadamer, 2004, pp. 41–42)

Universities are centrally concerned with the sustainability of research, scholarship and teaching. These practices – in varied combinations – constitute the field of higher education: research and scholarship inform teaching, which in turn helps disseminate research and enrich scholarly discourse.[1] The continuity of human understanding from generation to generation is preserved, therefore, through the practices of higher education within an institutional context of which universities are an important element. That continuity is often conceptualized as one of selective transmission: the accumulation of received wisdom culled from the past and carried forward into the future. Underlying this notion of continuity is a view of history as either inherently progressive (the so-called Whig view of history) or in terminal decline (a view associated more with a conservative cast of mind). In this chapter I present a different view of continuity.

I argue – with reference mainly to the work of Hans-Georg Gadamer – that, while the past may bequeath us some insights, its main legacy is the questions we ask of it and the 'questionableness' it requires of us. We do not simply receive history. We *make* it. We do so through a process of understanding that is inherently dialogical and that acknowledges the plurality of the human world. Although the chapter focuses primarily on higher education, the implications of the argument are by no means restricted to that sector. The aim is to explore – with reference to a particular framework of ideas – how education might be

In this chapter I develop and elaborate ideas previously discussed in Chapter 3 ('The Interpretive Tradition') of Nixon (2012a, pp. 32–45).

applied within a changing world. Implicit in that aim are two assumptions. First, philosophy is useful, practical: its beauty lies in its *usefulness*. Second, education is incomplete, provisional: its intrinsic value lies in it being *not-yet-finished*.[2] These two assumptions inform the argument throughout and ensure, I hope, that the chapter is not so much an exercise in the philosophy *of* education as an initial and highly partial attempt at developing a philosophy *for* education.

The primacy of the question

In mid-eighteenth-century Milan, an obscure professor of rhetoric named Giambattista Vico claimed to have uncovered 'the order of all progress from its first origins'. He elaborated this 'order of progress' in terms of what he termed 'the course of nations', central to which was 'the recurrence of human institutions': 'at first there were forests, then cultivated fields and huts, next small houses and villages, thence cities, and at last academies and philosophers' (Vico, 2001, p. 15). Implicit in his argument is that these human institutions are historically situated, but that they constitute a category that is sustainable across history. Writing both within and against the Enlightenment that had illuminated the scientific potential of the natural world, Vico was exercised by the idea that the divinely ordained natural world can only be understood in the light of the human world that had evolved and was still evolving in time.

That world, he sought to show, could only be understood chronologically. History was, as Vico saw it, the key to worldly understanding. He set out to establish an understanding of the evolution of human societies that was as revolutionary in its time as Darwin's application of the notion of 'evolution' to the life sciences over a hundred years later. He lay the foundations of what we now categorize as 'the humanities' and of what is now practised as 'anthropology', 'cultural studies', 'history', 'sociology', and so on – but never lost sight of the partiality of human understanding. 'There is always', as Edward Said (2004, p. 12) put it, 'something radically incomplete, insufficient, provisional, disputable, and arguable about humanistic knowledge that Vico never loses sight of'.

However, the impact of Vico's *New Science* extends beyond 'the humanities'. The third edition of this work published in the year of his death – and 'thoroughly corrected revised, and expanded by the author' – shows how all human knowledge is historically located and therefore open to interpretation. The 'rules' of science, as developed by contemporaries such as Newton, were not – he implied – absolute and for all time. They were necessarily relative to their age and, as such, open to question. They were *interpretable*. Vico routed the tradition of hermeneutic enquiry – that was as old as Socrates – into the modern age of scientific enquiry. He was virtually unrecognized in his day and his work had little influence, but his long-term impact is indisputable. The world is not entirely given but made through our own understanding of it; and, as Marx went on to argue, if the world is what we make of it, then we can struggle to make of it a better world. Vico's great, sprawling and (by our standards) unscholarly work is the hinge upon which the interpretive tradition turns towards historical consciousness.

Two insights in particular form the basis of that tradition. The first idea is that *in any attempt at interpretation we are interpreting that which has already been interpreted*. The object of our interpretation is a construct that we inherit from the historical layering of countless prior interpretations and re-interpretations. There is no blank page of history upon which we can inscribe our entirely original understandings. History is a palimpsest of layered inscriptions and layered commentaries. The second insight follows from the first. If all understanding is always already interpretation, then *the interpreter is always already part of what is being interpreted*. The subject that interprets is implicit in the object of interpretation. Notions of 'objectivity' and 'neutrality' as the privileged criteria of rationality become increasingly difficult to justify in the light of this second insight.

These two insights were implicit – rather than explicit – in *New Science*. Vico was feeling his way towards a new world view that was still embryonic. He was fascinated by pre-history and how, prior to a chronological and sequential notion of time, people nevertheless located themselves historically. He understood that the past was another country which had to be understood on its own terms rather than on our terms. His formulation of the 'epochs of world history' into 'the ages of gods, heroes, and men' may seem strange and esoteric to us, but in its time it was path-breaking in its insistence on past epochs as interpretive constructs expressed in terms of mythology, political constitutions and legal frameworks. History is what we make of it, and what we make of it is inextricable from how we understand it. These were ideas that would inspire and inform the work of Karl Marx and James Joyce. At the time, however, Vico was still finding a language and form within which to express and elaborate them.

A third insight follows from the first two and was developed in particular by Gadamer.[3] If all understanding is always already interpretation and the interpreter is always already part of what is being interpreted, then *all understanding necessarily involves an element of self-understanding*. Gadamer elaborated this insight with reference to the notion of 'application', which he understood as being implicit in all understanding from the moment of its inception. It is not that understanding is achieved and then applied but that the application is intrinsic to the process of understanding: 'in all understanding an application occurs, such that the person who is understanding is himself or herself *right there* in the understood meaning. He or she *belongs to* the subject-matter that he or she is understanding ... Everyone who understands something understands himself or herself in it' (original emphases). (Gadamer, 2001, pp. 47–48) The hermeneutical task, as Gadamer defines it, is to locate oneself within one's own field – or, as he would put it, 'tradition' – of understanding.

The idea of 'tradition' is central to hermeneutics as developed by Gadamer: 'we stand in traditions, whether we know these traditions or not; that is, whether we are conscious of these or are so arrogant as to think we can begin without presuppositions – none of this changes the way traditions are working on us and in our understanding' (Gadamer, 2001, p. 45). Traditions pose questions in response to which we define ourselves and our own sense of purpose. The coherence of any tradition, as understood by Gadamer, can only be defined with reference to its intrinsic plurality and potential for innovation. Traditions are constantly evolving as new generations interpret and re-interpret them and, by so doing, modify and elaborate them. Traditions may initially present themselves to us as assertions, but, as Gadamer (1977, pp. 11–13) insists, 'no assertion is possible that cannot be understood as an answer to a question, and assertions can only be understood in this way ... The real power of hermeneutical consciousness is our ability to see what is questionable'.

Central to the argument of Gadamer's (2004) *Truth and Method* is what he calls 'the hermeneutic priority of the question' (pp. 356–371). 'Understanding begins', as he puts it, 'when something addresses us. This is the first condition of hermeneutics' (p. 298). In becoming receptive to that which addresses us we are opening ourselves to the question it asks of us: 'the essence of the *question* is to open up possibilities and keep them open' (p. 298) (original emphasis). Interpretation is the process whereby we receive the object of interpretation as a question and thereby gain 'a sense of the questionableness of something and what this requires of us' (Gadamer, 2001, p. 42). Gadamer's major contribution to the interpretive – or hermeneutic – tradition is his insight into the dialogical nature of all interpretive acts. The inherent structure of that tradition, he argues, is that of question and answer.[4]

Understanding as dialogue

The interpretive tradition as understood and developed by Gadamer is not, therefore, a bounded and impermeable system but an open and dialogical process that relies heavily on *phronesis* ('deliberation' or 'practical reasoning'). Gadamer insists that *phronesis*, rightly understood, is not simply a process of applying general laws, rules or precepts to specific cases and thereby involving technical knowledge of the means. His central insight was that this process of application necessarily involves – in addition to, and in conjunction with, knowledge of the means – knowledge of the ends. *Phronesis*, in other words, is not just a form of technical reasoning but a mode of ethical reasoning requiring an understanding of the common good. 'It's clear', as Gadamer (2006, p. 35) put it towards the end of his life, 'that the knowledge of the means can't leave out of consideration the knowledge of the final end of every action'. Human understanding is, from this perspective, (1) a highly complex process of 'fusion' which (2) necessarily involves 'prejudices' or 'fore-meanings' and (3) cannot, given its inherent unpredictability, be reduced to 'method'.

The first of these elements relates to *the notion of 'the fusion of horizons'*. The idea of 'horizon' – as developed by Gadamer – relates directly to the importance he places in tradition as the legacy of the past to the future and the corresponding debt owed by the present to the past. In *Truth and Method*, Gadamer provides a general explanation of how and why he is using the concept: 'The concept of "horizon" suggests itself because it expresses the superior breadth of vision that the person who is trying to understand must have. To acquire a horizon means that one learns to look beyond what is close at hand – not in order to look away from it but to see it better, within a larger whole and in true proportion' (Gadamer, 2004, p. 304). The concept as applied by Gadamer invariably relates to our understanding of the past and of how we interpret the past with reference to the sources available to us. Gadamer's central point on this matter is that our horizons of understanding are never static: 'Every historian and philologist must reckon with the fundamental non-definitiveness of the horizon in which his understanding moves. Historical tradition can be understood only as something always in the process of being defined by the course of events' (Gadamer, 2004, p. 366).

The meaning to be derived from any act of interpretation is always *in between*: between the interpreted and the interpreter, between the object of interpretation and the interpreter as subject, between different historical positions and perspectives. This means that the object of interpretation does not simply surrender its meaning as a form of divine revelation or authorial intention. Notwithstanding its historical roots in biblical exegesis, hermeneutics is in this respect both secular and humanist in its assumption that neither divine authority nor authorial intention provides the final arbiter in any interpretive act. There can be no appeal to a divine purpose that lies outside the historical course of events or to a human will that is immune to the consequences of those events.

The *in between* nature of human understanding also means that interpretation is not simply imposed – as imported theory or pre-specified criteria – by the interpreter on the object of interpretation. Although the world is always already interpreted, every act of interpretation is a new beginning occasioning a necessary shift in the interpreter's self-understanding; or, as Joseph Dunne (1997, p. 121) puts it, 'the interpreter's horizon is already being stretched beyond itself, so that it is no longer the same horizon that it was independently of this encounter'. Because both interpreter and interpreted are located in the process of history – *in medias res* – the horizon of interpretation can never achieve permanent fixity. It changes constantly, just as our visual horizon varies with each step we take. Each interpretation is, therefore, both unique and open to reinterpretation – and 'the fusion of horizons', a process rather than an achieved state: 'horizons are not rigid but mobile; they are in motion because our prejudgements are constantly put to the test' (Gadamer, 2001, p. 48).

That brings us to the second element: namely, *the power of 'prejudices' or 'fore-meanings'* in the constitution of understanding.[5] What the interpreter brings to the process of interpretation is vitally important. We understand the world in relation to what we bring to it by way of prior assumptions, preconceptions and prejudices. We understand the world in and through our experience of the world. This perspective, as Gadamer (2004, p. 271) puts it, 'involves neither "neutrality" with respect to content nor the extinction of one's self, but the foregrounding and appropriation of one's own fore-meanings and prejudices'. If we are an integral part of the world that we are seeking to understand, then we can 'formulate the fundamental epistemological question for a truly historical hermeneutics as follows: what is the ground of the legitimacy of prejudices? What distinguishes legitimate prejudices from the countless others which it is the undeniable task of critical reason to overcome?' (p. 278) Prejudice – our historicity – is where interpretation begins: 'the concept of "prejudice" is where we can start' (p. 273). In any attempt at interpretation we consider prior values and assumptions that shape what and how we interpret

Gadamer insists that this importing of ourselves into the process of understanding is a necessary component of that understanding. However, he also insists that we must be aware of what we are importing. Some of our prejudices may assist understanding, while others may distort or deny understanding. A large part of the hermeneutical task involves self-examination through the sifting of prejudices. To have trust in an interpretation is to trust that the interpreter has undergone this process of self-examination in respect of the values and assumptions that have shaped that interpretation. Similarly, to trust in one's own interpretive capacity is not to have blind faith in one's own convictions but to trust in one's own commitment to questioning those convictions. Trust is a necessary condition of understanding and understanding is a necessary condition of our being in the world. If we trusted nothing in this world of ours, then it would be a world beyond our understanding – and a world beyond our understanding is no longer our world.

That is why Gadamer (1977, p. 8) argues that hermeneutics cannot be 'restricted to a technique for avoiding misinterpretation': misinterpretation through the application of inappropriate prejudices is to be avoided, but that avoidance does not in itself constitute understanding. I gain understanding not only by rejecting inappropriate prejudices but by using other of my prejudices to connect with what I seek to understand. In explicit opposition to the scientific ideal of objectivity devoid of all prejudice, Gadamer insists on the productive power of prejudice. He rejects as alienating the mistrust of the subject – and of 'subjectivity' – that he sees as implicit in that ideal. He argues, instead, for the necessity of trusting to the subject – and to 'subjectivity' – in all understanding.

Gadamer is not arguing on behalf of relativism: an ethics of 'anything goes'. Rather, he is arguing for an ethics of deliberation.[6] He is arguing on behalf of mutuality and reciprocity as the conditions necessary for whatever shared understanding is necessary for being together. Understanding implies – and requires as a necessary condition – recognition of both selfhood and difference and of the necessary relation between the two. To seek to understand is to adopt an ethical stance – not a moralistic or moralizing stance, but a stance which affirms the central importance of personhood (of the other and of the self). If our world is shaped by our understanding of it, and if that understanding is conditional upon our meeting of minds, then understanding is nothing if not ethical. The originality of *Truth and Method* lies in its injunction to overcome what Gadamer sees as the alienation implicit in the ideal of prejudiceless objectivity: acknowledge the presence of yourself in your own understanding; recognize the other person's understanding as central to your own understanding; develop your understanding as you would a dialogue. Above all, Gadamer insists, do not assume that human understanding can be reduced to method. That is not how human understanding works.

Beyond method

This third element – *the irreducibility of human understanding to 'method'* – is in part an attempt by Gadamer to distinguish 'the humanities' from 'the sciences'. However, it is also an attempt to resist what he saw as the methodological appropriation of the former by the latter. At the time when Gadamer was writing, 'method' was in the ascendancy. The idea of 'method' was particularly associated with scientific enquiry, but the idea of there being a pre-ordained methodology of enquiry across disciplines and fields of study held sway. For enquiry to be taken seriously – whether within the natural, human, or social sciences – it had to be conducted systematically and in accordance with pre-specified methodological procedures.

In its most extreme form, this scientific positivism – buttressed by the philosophical presuppositions of logical positivism or logical empiricism as it is sometimes termed – claimed that observational evidence is indispensable for knowledge of the world and that only when supported by such evidence could a belief that such and such is the case actually be the case (i.e. be 'true'). A methodical approach to the selection, gathering and analysis of empirical 'data' – and to the inferential process whereby 'findings' were derived from this approach – was and to a large extent still is the means by which scientific enquiry gained legitimacy and public recognition. 'Method' would enable one to gather and analyse 'data' which would then provide knowledge in the form of 'findings'. This became the dominant paradigm of scientific enquiry and exerted a strong influence on the social sciences generally and on social psychology in particular, where it was supported by the presuppositions of behaviourism.

Gadamer's starting point in *Truth and Method* is the 'problem of method' as he terms it (Gadamer, 2004, pp. 3–8). Understanding, he maintains, cannot be reduced to a method, although interpretive methods may contribute to our understanding. Gadamer does not deny that there are methods, but he denies that such methods are constitutive of human understanding:

> Of course there are methods and one must learn them and apply them ... As tools, methods are always good to have. But one must understand where these can be fruitfully used. Methodical sterility is a generally known phenomenon. ...

What does the truly productive researcher do?... Applying the method is what the person does who never finds out anything new, who never brings to light an interpretation that has revelatory power. No, it is not their mastery of methods but their hermeneutical imagination that distinguishes truly productive researchers. And what is hermeneutical imagination? It is a sense of the questionableness of something and what this requires of us. (Gadamer, 2004, pp. 41–42)

Implicit in Gadamer's critique of method is the idea that understanding involves self-formation and human flourishing that is open-ended in the extent and scope of its proliferation. The application of method, on the other hand, assumes a notion of rationality that seeks closure and predictability. Human understanding, argues Gadamer, must be true to the nature of humanity: a humanity that is necessarily fragile and vulnerable by virtue of its complex interconnectivities and its uncertain relation to the future. Gadamer saw this as a struggle between the human and natural sciences, with the latter imposing an inappropriate methodology on the former: when inappropriately applied to the human world, the scientific method insists upon an ideologically skewed version of humanity. Moreover, since the natural world is always already an interpreted world, the methodology derived from the natural sciences may be severely limited even when applied within its own traditional domain.

Worldly understanding

What Gadamer calls 'the hermeneutical imagination' begins and ends in dialogue. His attempt to elaborate the dialogical nature of human understanding remains hugely important in an increasingly globalized world of complex inter-connectivity. Almost all the problems we now face are collective problems – problems, that is, that cannot be resolved by individuals working in isolation. The global inter-connectivity of human life means that working together towards collective solutions is much more difficult and much more crucial than it was in the past. Our networks of inter-connectivity are no longer knowable and bounded communities, but they are boundless spaces – the full communicative potential of which is unknowable.

Our big problems are all 'bigger than self problems'.[7] Such problems – economic, environmental, religious and political – are, as Martha C. Nussbaum (2010, p. 79) argues, problems that require both collective and global understanding:

They have no hope of being solved unless people once distant come together and cooperate in ways they have not before. Think of global warming; decent trade regulations; the protection of the environment and animal species; the future of nuclear energy and the dangers of nuclear weapons; the movement of labor and the establishment of decent labor standards; the protection of children from trafficking, sexual abuse, and forced labor. All these can only truly be addressed by multinational discussions.

Such a list could, as Nussbaum points out, be extended almost indefinitely. The point is that our problems are increasingly not only collective problems but globally collective problems requiring globally collective solutions: problems which at every level of impact – the individual, inter-personal, institutional, national and international – are experienced globally. The collective solutions will emerge not from any totalizing consensus but from a willingness to reason together and in doing so to acknowledge and respect our differences. 'People love homogeneity and are startled by difference', Nussbaum (2008, p. 362) writes in her defence of religious equality; but it is the willingness to be 'startled by difference' that finally wins through in the long haul towards collective solutions: the collective, open-ended argument that constitutes deliberative democracy and locates within it mutual respect for our shared human dignity.

Globalization presents us not only with economic, political and social challenges but also with a huge hermeneutical challenge: How, in a world of difference, are we to engage in conversations that are both constitutive of and conditional upon shared understanding? Indeed, the economic, political and social terms within which debates on globalization are invariably couched may serve to obscure its impact on how we understand our world – and on how, in turn, that understanding impacts upon the economic, political and social construction of that world. How are we to learn to live together in a world of incommensurable difference? How are we to achieve understanding in – and for – the world?

Technical know-how (*techne*) and propositional knowledge derived from theory (*theoria*) are necessary resources for addressing such questions, but they are by no means sufficient. Indeed, as Gadamer seeks to show, they reveal a deficiency in the hermeneutical resources necessary for a worldly understanding of the world. Gadamer's notion of understanding as intrinsically dialogical – and of *phronesis* as a distinct dialogical and conversational form – reminds us that in the sheer ordinariness of human understanding we possess the resources necessary not only for addressing those questions but for responding to them creatively and collectively. As Raymond Geuss (2010, p. 152) points out, 'to speak of a "conversation" is to be very explicit about the inherently social nature of what makes us human and … directs attention away from trying to understand this activity as the activation of pre-given formal rules, or as aspiring to satisfy some antecedently given consensus of cogency, relevance, or accuracy'. That is, as Geuss acknowledges, an important part of the hermeneutical legacy bequeathed by Gadamer – and one which clearly has a bearing on the ends and purposes of higher education.

A critical legacy

But it is only part of that legacy. Given Gadamer's insistence on the significance of the question in the constitution of human understanding, a large part of his legacy also lies in the questions his work raises and the critiques it invites. This is crucial: Gadamer's framework of ideas provides us with an authoritative basis from which to critique that framework. Notwithstanding the power of any such critique, it is important to recall that 'answering back' is one of the defining features of Gadamer's hermeneutical emphasis on the primacy of the question. Gadamer invites – requires even – a critical response.

One such critique questions whether Gadamer's understanding of the dialogical – and of *phronesis* as a distinct dialogical and conversational form – fully acknowledges the powerful plurality that underpins it. Indeed, does Gadamer's avowedly liberal perspective lead to a denial of that plurality and the power implicit in that plurality? Is there an inherent exclusivity in Gadamer's conceptualization of *phronesis* that is unacknowledged – or repressed – within his conceptual framework? Is there a denial of radical difference? Such questions imply a critique of the critical capacity of Gadamer's hermeneutics; its capacity, that is, to expose to critical scrutiny not only its own presuppositions but also its own preconditions. Does Gadamer take sufficient account of the systematically distorted communication that constitutes ideology? Or is it the case that, as Jürgen Habermas argues, 'Gadamer's prejudice for the rights of prejudices certified by tradition denies the power of reflection' (Habermas, 1977, p. 358).[8]

These questions invariably lead to a consideration of the historical setting of Gadamer's life and work – and, in particular, Gadamer's relation to Nazism and the post-war reconstruction of Germany within Europe. Unlike Heidegger, Gadamer was not a member of the Nazi Party. Nevertheless, he did accommodate himself to Nazism sufficiently to remain in an academic post throughout the period that the Nazi regime controlled all the major institutions within Germany, including the universities. Reflecting back on that period in an audio-taped conversation with Dorte von Westernhagen in or shortly before 1990, he said: 'My cleverness [*Geschicktheit*] consisted in taking seriously as colleagues those who were Nazis but who were also at the same time genuine, rational scholars; avoiding, of course, political conversation' (Gadamer, 2001, p. 129). Interviewed in 1993 by Christiane Gehron and Jonathan Ree on behalf of *Radical Philosophy*, he re-asserted his earlier uneasy relation to Nazism: 'I think we could teach philosophising even under the Nazi system' (Gadamer, 1995, p. 31). It is difficult not to infer from such statements that, for Gadamer, philosophically collegial discourse could be based on both a shallow and a narrow consensus – one that clearly avoided 'political conversation'.[9]

Such an inference has a direct bearing on how we interpret Gadamer. If the sifting of prejudices and fore-meanings is central to his hermeneutics, then how does that sifting occur? Does, for example, the avoidance of 'political conversation' – albeit under exceptional circumstances – constitute an example of such sifting? Do we not sometimes – when, for example, refuting the claims of racist ideology – require the resources of 'scientific method' to help us in that task of sifting? If so, does Gadamer polarize humanistic and scientific modes of understanding in ways that may provide a rhetorical cutting edge to his argument but that are ultimately unhelpful in any attempt to gather the educative resources necessary for worldly understanding? The global citizens of the future will need to have not only a humanistic understanding of the world but also a technological and scientific understanding of the way the world works.[10] This requirement has important implications for how we conceive of education at every level and – in particular – how we conceive of an all-through, comprehensive further and higher education curriculum.

It also has pedagogical implications with regard to how radically different viewpoints, opinions and perspectives might be mediated and negotiated. How inclusive of difference is the dialogical component of understanding as assumed by Gadamer? We live within and across microcosms of difference: differences of race, class and gender; differences of value and identity affiliation; differences of sexual orientation and life style. We all have membership of different communities: to reduce individuals to a unitary identity is to violate the complexity of that identity.[11] We carry difference around with us in our heads and in the relationships that sustain and form us. Reasoning together requires a responsive understanding of these worlds of difference that constitute the self and the relationship of self with others. A consensus that denies these differentials – and the agonistic element that binds and divides them – denies also its own democratic authenticity.[12] The pedagogical task is to find ways of recognizing difference and valuing *dissensus*.[13] Given Gadamer's limited emphasis on plurality, his work may be of limited value in setting about this task.

That limitation is also evident in Gadamer's notion of tradition, which he defines almost entirely in terms of Western culture. This raises a number of questions: Is Western culture a single tradition? Is it one tradition among many? How are national differences accommodated within a tradition? Gadamer does not address these questions in any detail.[14] Yet, as Said (2003, p. 332) argues, such questions are highly germane to any discussion of how interpretation operates in the context of global interconnectivity and disconnectivity: 'debates today about "Frenchness" and "Englishness" in France and Britain respectively, or about Islam in countries such as Egypt and Pakistan, are part of that same interpretive process which involves the identities of different "others", whether they be outsiders and refugees, or apostates and infidels'.

Fazal Rizvi (2009, p. 265) explores the pedagogical implications of this perspective with reference to what he calls 'cosmopolitan learning'. Such learning, he argues, 'involves pedagogic tasks that help students explore the criss-crossing of transnational circuits of communication, the flows of global capital and the cross-cutting of local, translocal and transnational social practices'. In so doing it 'encourages students to consider the contested politics of place making, the social construction of power differentials and the dynamic processes relating to the formation of individual, group, national and transnational identities, and their corresponding fields of difference'.[15]

Similarly, Bob Lingard (2008, p. 210) writes about the need to 'deparochialize pedagogies': 'to construct and work towards pedagogies which make a difference in the distribution of knowledge and construction of identities and construction of global citizens who can work with and value difference'. Joelle Fanghanel (2012, pp. 108–112) also addresses these issues with reference to academic practice and the globalization of higher education.[16]

Conclusion

The interpretive tradition as presented in this chapter highlights the dialogical nature of human understanding and the significance of *phronesis* as a distinct dialogical and conversational form. It also, however, highlights the need to relate *phronetic* forms of understanding with technological (*techne*) and explanatory (*theoria*) forms of reasoning. That in turn has implications for how we conceive of method. As Paul Ricoeur (1977, p. 329) puts it, 'there are no rules for making good guesses. But there are methods for validating guesses'. Good students need to be able to make good guesses, but they also need to be good at validating their guesses. They need, that is, to operate across different modes of understanding: to be able to deliberate and reason together, to have the technical know-how appropriate to particular tasks and to find their way in and around different explanatory frameworks. In doing so, they also need to be able to recognize radical differences of received opinion, cultural values and beliefs, and intellectual background. Finally, they need to be able to relate to the complex inter-connectivities of a world in which the global saturates the local and the local permeates the global.[17]

What are required are *pedagogical processes* that provide opportunities for dialogical interaction between students and between students and teachers, *curricular frameworks* that give access to different modes of understanding and different ways of ensuring complementarity across the arts, humanities and sciences, and *institutional systems* that are inclusive, participatory and outward-looking. The risk is that at a time of shrinking resources – when universities are under threat and higher education is being increasingly deprived of public funding – such fundamental requirements will be seen as unrealistic accessories. The only acceptable utopias now, as Ronald Barnett (2012) reminds us, are 'feasible utopias'. All others are deemed to be either nostalgic yearnings or idealistic longings. What is central to higher education – and to academic practice – thereby becomes marginalized and isolated. If utopian thinking is limited to what is feasible, then we all too easily find ourselves inhabiting an alienated and alienating dystopia. 'We need', as Jan McArthur (2013, p. 160) insists, 'to resist our own acceptance of this isolation. We should cease to feel the need to apologize for academic work that shows its passionate motivations and committed values.' We need to reaffirm the central importance of both human understanding within an increasingly decimated higher education sector and also higher education within an increasingly stratified and fragmented university system.

The world view against which Gadamer was reacting was, as Richard Rorty (2000, p. 25) put it, 'dominated by the thought that there is something nonhuman that human beings should try to live up to – a thought which today finds its most plausible expression in the scientistic conception of culture'. Rorty went on to define Gadamer's legacy in the following terms: 'In a future Gadamerian culture, human beings would wish only to live up to one another... The relationship between predecessor and successor would be conceived...not as the power-laden relation of "overcoming" (*Uberwindung*) but as the gentler relation of turning to new "purposes" (*Verwindung*)'. In such a culture, Rorty concludes, 'Gadamer would be seen as one of the figures who helped give a new, more literal, sense to Holderlin's line, "Ever since we are a conversation" ("Seit wir ein Gesprach sind")'. He would also be seen, we might add, as one of the figures who helped envisage a more democratic, secular and cosmopolitan world.

Notes

1   See Carolyn Kreber's discussion of 'the inseparability of academic functions' in Kreber (2013, pp. 66–69).

2   Both ideas are central to the life and work of William Morris and to the Manifesto of the Socialist League which Morris drafted and which was adopted at the General Conference of the Socialist League on 5 July 1885. (see E.P. Thompson 1976, pp. 732–740).

3   Hans-Georg Gadamer was born on 11 February 1900 in Breslau (Germany) and died on 13 March 2002 in Heidelberg (see Jean Grondin 2003).

4   A similar argument had previously been advanced by R. G. Collingwood in Chapter 5 ('Question and Answer') of his autobiography which was first published in 1939 (see Collingwood, 1978, pp. 29–43). Fred Inglis's (2009) recent biography provides a readable and non-technical introduction to Collingwood's life and thought.

5   In his analysis of 'prejudice', Gadamer starts from the structure of the German word – *das Vorurteil* ('pre-judice'). Duska Dobrosavljev's (2002, p. 608) gloss on Gadamer's usage of the term is helpful: 'Prejudice is a soil where our judgement is grown'.

6   I discuss the topic of deliberative ethics more fully in Nixon (2012b, 2012c, 2008, 2004). See also Bruce Macfarlane (2004).

7   See WWF-UK (2010). Appendix two of this report provides a comprehensive review of the literature relating to this category of problem.

8   Habarmas's major and highly influential critique of Gadamer's *Truth and Method* was published in German in 1970 and subsequently translated into English in 1977 (see Habermas, 1977).

9   Dmitri N. Shalin (2010) provides a comprehensive overview of the ongoing debate on Gadamer's relation to Nazism. See, also, Yvonne Sherratt (2013).

10 It is worth bearing in mind that, as Albert Einstein and Leopold Infeld (1938) showed in their remarkable *The Evolution of Physics*, science is also deeply interpretive: 'Science is not just a collection of laws, a catalogue of unrelated facts.

It is a creation of the human mind, with its freely invented ideas and concepts'
(p. 310). See also Werner Heisenberg (2000).

11 See Amartya Sen (2007) for a fuller elaboration of this argument regarding the
violence imposed upon identity through the process of cultural homogenization.

12 See Chantal Mouffe (1993 and 2005) for a discussion of *agonistic* element in
democratic discourse. 'Democracy', she argues, 'is in peril not only when there is
insufficient consensus and allegiance to the values it embodies, but also when its
agonistic dynamic is hindered by an apparent excess of consensus, which usually
masks a disquieting apathy' (1993, p. 6).

13 See Jacques Ranciere (2010 and 2011) on the democratic significance of *dissensus*.

14 These questions were put to Gadamer in the 1993 interview conducted by
Christiane Gehron and Jonathan Ree on behalf of *Radical Philosophy*, but received
little in the way of detailed response (see Gadamer, 1995, p. 32).

15 Rizvi (2008) develops a similar argument.

16 See also my discussion of 'cosmopolitan imaginaries' in Nixon (2011, pp. 51–65).

17 Anatoly Oleksiyenko (2012) shows how what he terms a 'glonacal' (i.e. global–
national–local) institutional partnership in Central Asia involving the governments
of three diverse national regions – Kazakhstan, Kyrgyzstan and Tajikhstan – is
seeking to promote and support such learning.

References

Barnett, R. (2012) *Imagining the University*. Abingdon: Routledge

Collingwood, R. G. (1978) *An Autobiography*. Oxford: Oxford University Press.
(First published in 1939).

Dobrosavljev, D. (2002) 'Gadamer's hermeneutics as practical philosophy', *Facta
Universitatis: Philosophy, Sociology, Psychology and History* 2(9): 605–618

Dunne, J (1997) *Back to the Rough Ground: Practical Judgment and the Lure of
Technique*. Notre Dame, IN: University of Notre Dame Press.

Einstein, A. and Infeld, L. (1938) *The Evolution of Physics: The Growth of Ideas from the
Early Concepts to Relativity and Quanta*. Cambridge: Cambridge University Press.

Fanghanal, J. (2012) *Being an Academic*. London: Routledge.

Gadamer, H-G (1995)'Without poets there is no philosophy', (interview with C. Gehron
and J. Ree) *Radical Philosophy* 69, pp. 27–35.

——— (1977) *Philosophical Hermeneutics*. Ed. and Trans. Ling, D.E., Berkely, CA:
University of California Press.

——— (2001) *Gadamer in Conversation: Reflections and Commentary*. Ed. and Trans.
Palmer, R.E., New Haven, CT: Yale University Press.

——— (2004) *Truth and Method*. Trans. Weinsheimer, J. and Marshall, D.G.,
2nd Revised Edn. London: Continuum. (Originally published in German in 1960).

—— (2006) *A Century of Philosophy: Hans-Georg Gadamer in Conversation with Riccardo Dottori*. Trans. Coltman, R. and Koepke, S., London: Continuum.

Grondin, J. (2003) *Hans-Georg Gadamer: A Biography*. New Haven, CT: Yale University Press.

Geuss, R. (2010) *Politics and the Imagination*. Princeton, NJ: Princeton University Press.

Habermas, J. (1977) 'A review of Gadamer's *Truth and Method*', in Dallmayr, F.R. and McCarthy, T. (eds), *Understanding and Social Inquiry*. Notre Dame, IN: University of Notre Dame Press, pp. 335–363.

Heisenberg, W. (2000) *Physics and Philosophy: The Revolution in Modern Science*. London: Penguin Books.

Inglis, F. (2009) *History Man: The Life of R. G. Collingwood*. Princeton, NJ: Princeton University Press.

Kreber, C. (2013) *Authenticity in and through Teaching in Higher Education: The Transformative Potential of the Scholarship of Teaching*. Abingdon: Routledge.

Lingard, B. (2008) 'Pedagogies of indifference: Research, policy and practice', in Lingard, B., Nixon, J. and Ranson, S. (eds), *Transforming Learning in Schools and Communities: The Remaking of Education for a Cosmopolitan Society*. London: Continuum. pp. 209–235

Macfarlane, B. (2004) *Teaching with Integrity:Tthe Ethics of Higher Education Practice*. London: RoutledgeFalmer.

McArthur, J. (2013) *Rethinking Knowledge within Higher Education: Adorno and Social Justice*. London: Bloomsbury.

Mouffe, C. (1993) *The Return of the Political*. London: Verso.

—— (2005) *The Democratic Paradox*. London: Verso.

Nixon, J. (2004) 'Learning the language of deliberative democracy', in Walker, M. and Nixon, J. (eds), *Reclaiming Universities from a Runaway World*. Maidenhead: Open University Press/McGraw-Hill, pp. 114–127

—— (2008) *Towards the Virtuous University: The Moral Bases of Academic Practice*. Abingdon: Routledge.

—— (2011) *Higher Education and the Public Good: Imagining the University*. London: Bloomsbury.

—— (2012a) *Interpretive Pedagogies for Higher Education: Arendt, Berger, Said, Nussbaum and their Legacies*. London: Bloomsbury

—— (2012b) 'Universities as deliberative spaces: Learning to reason together', in Kossek, B. and Zwiauer, C. (eds), *Universitat in Zeiten von Bologna: Zur Theorie und Praxis von Lehr- und Lernkulturen*. Vienna: V&R unipress/Vienna University Press, pp. 153–164.

—— (2012c) 'The ethics of academic practice: Grasping what ethics is', in Su, F. and McGettrick, B. (eds), *Professional Ethics: Education for a Humane Society*. Newcastle upon Tyne: Cambridge Scholars Publishing, pp. 10–24.

Nussbaum, M. C. (2008) *Liberty of Conscience: In Defence of America's Tradition of Religious Equality*. New York, NY: Basic Books.

—— (2010) *Not for Profit: Why Democracy Needs the Humanities*. Princeton, NJ: Princeton University Press.

Oleksiyenko, A. (2012) 'Glonacal' partnership strategies in Central Asia', in Adamson, B., Nixon, J. and Su, F. (eds), *The Reorientation of Higher Education: Challenging the East-West Dichotomy*. CERC Studies in Comparative Education 31. Hong Kong: Springer/Comparative Education Research Centre, The University of Hong Kong, pp. 269–283.

Ranciere, J. (2010) *Dissensus: On Politics and Aesthetics*. London: Continuum

—— (2011) 'Democracies against democracy', in Agamben, G. and others, *Democracy in What State?* New York, NY: Columbia University Press, pp. 76–81.

Ricoeur, P. (1977) 'The model of the text: Meaningful action considered as a text', in Dallmayr, F.R. and McCarthy,T.A. (eds), *Understanding and Social Inquiry*. Notre Dame, IN: University of Notre Dame Press, pp. 316–334.

Rizvi, F. (2008) 'Education and its cosmopolitan possibilities', in Lingard, B., Nixon, J. and Ranson, S. (eds), *Transforming Learning in Schools and Communities: The Remaking of Educatioj for a Cosmopolitan Society*. London: Continuum, pp. 101–116.

—— (2009) 'Towards cosmopolitan learning', *Discourse: Studies in Cultural Politics in Education* 30(3): 253–268.

Rorty, R. (2000) 'Being that can be understood is language', *London Review of Books* 22(6): 23–25.

Said, E. W. (2003) *Orientalism*. London: Penguin Books (First published in 1978).

—— (2004) *Humanism and Democratic Criticism*. New York, NY: Columbia University Press.

Sen, A. (2007) *Identity and Violence: The Illusion of Violence*. London: Penguin Books.

Shalin, D.N. (2010) 'Hermeneutics and prejudice: Heidegger and Gadamer in their historical setting', *Russian Journal of Communication* 3(1&2): 7–24 (Winter/Spring).

Sherratt, Y. (2013) *Hitler's Philosophers*. New Haven, CT: Yale University Press.

Thompson, E. P. (1976) *William Morris: Romantic to Revolutionary*. London: Merlin Press. Revised edition. (First published in 1955)

Vico, G. (2001) *New Science: Principles of the New Science Concerning the Common Nature of Nations*. (3rd edition of 1744) Trans. Marsh, D., London: Penguin Books.

WWF-UK (2010) *Common Cause: The Case for Working with Our Cultural Values*. London: WWF-UK.

8

An Epistemic Monoculture and the University of Reasons

Richard Smith

To begin, here are some examples of the epistemic monoculture, the hegemony of instrumental reason, in which increasingly we live (I write throughout from a UK perspective, but I believe my points have wider interest). There is space here for only a few egregious instances. The President of the Royal British Legion (which 'provides help and welfare to the serving and ex-Service community and their families') resigned after he was discovered to have described the annual events to commemorate those killed in war, such as the ceremony at the Cenotaph in London's Whitehall, as a 'tremendous networking opportunity' in which he could help defence companies (i.e. arms manufacturers), lobby ministers and senior members in the armed services (*The Guardian*, 15 October 2013). I have elsewhere (Smith, 2012) quoted the mayor of London, Boris Johnson, welcoming the London Olympics as a 'gigantic schmooze-athon', the opportunity to show the world the 'wealth of ... amazing investment opportunities' in Britain. The website of the government's department of Business, Industry and skills (BIS) where this appeared without apparent embarrassment or shame quoted other politicians from the Coalition government, such as the Business Secretary, Vince Cable: 'Tomorrow we welcome the world to London as the 2012 Olympic Games get underway. This summer is more than just a great sporting spectacle – it is an unrivalled opportunity to promote the best of British industry and make the most of our openness to foreign trade and investment.' Thus sport, which one might have thought was above all something to be enjoyed for its own sake, or at least not for the sake of foreign trade and investment, becomes instrumentalized for the benefit of the economy. Another, recent, example, a headline from the *Guardian*, 27 December 2013, reads 'Tour de France to bring cash and cachet to Yorkshire'. A sub-heading reads 'organisers predict £100m lift for regional economy'. Nothing, it seems, is left untouched by this process. Hull's success in being named as UK's City of Culture for 2017 was reported in the local paper the *Hull Daily Mail* in almost exclusively instrumental terms as helping to deliver 'the £190m ten-year City Plan outlined by Hull City Council to create 7,500 jobs'. The newspaper's headline made the relative standing of culture clear by putting the money at the beginning of its headline: '£60m UK City of Culture boost for Hull is "start of the future"'. In similar terms, the *Ilkley Gazette* celebrated the 40th anniversary of its town's Literature Festival with the headline 'Literature festival estimated to boost economy by £2,50,000' (4 October 2013). Of course, these headlines do not come from nowhere: they probably recycle press releases from the organizations that have an interest in the various events they promote.[1] This is one more way in which the monoculture takes root.

What I mean, then, by saying that we are coming to live in an epistemic monoculture is that increasingly the only form of reason that is valued or even acknowledged is the instrumental, means–end kind. We are becoming insensible to the value of sport, the importance of remembrance, the complex delights and satisfactions of literature and other forms of the arts. With increasing speed we are coming to resemble those responsible for that other distinctive monoculture of our time, that of high-profit agriculture: where the profits made from the intensive farming of wheat or oil-seed rape (not to mention here the destruction of the rainforest) are made at the cost of grubbing out the hedgerows and over-using insecticides to the point where what used to be called the 'countryside' cannot sustain those other cultures such as wildlife and the people who once lived side by side with them.

I turn now to the way that what I shall simply call 'the university', for centuries widely held to be a place committed to the critical examination of thinking rather than to its ossification, and even to the generation of different forms of thinking, is now meekly collaborating in the triumph of instrumental thought. While my examples come from the United Kingdom (or at any rate England) in the second decade of the twenty-first century, since the political and economic forces affecting the United Kingdom are similar elsewhere in the Anglophone world, and beyond, my argument may have wider application. Here our condition, as I diagnose it, can be put briefly as follows. The ever-increasing reach of instrumentalism, stimulated by the growth of neoliberalism and the market, has brought us to the point where it has become difficult to imagine the purpose of university education in any other terms. Studying at university is now widely conceived as above all the acquisition of 'employability skills'. A degree is a passport to a career – or at any rate a job – that offers you the chance of enjoying at least a reasonable standard of living and, of course, being able to repay the fees that you have incurred. At the same time, university research and scholarship are more and more judged in terms of their 'impact', as if the ideal to which all research should aspire was the invention of a light-sabre or personal jet-pack. Under these circumstances, management and administration – often dignified as 'governance' by a curious twist of language that there is no room to explore here – naturally assume new significance, since it is precisely in the finding of means to achieve ends that managers are supposedly skilled (MacIntyre, 1981).

Critiques of the culture of managerialism, targets and performance indicators in the university are often suspected of nostalgia for an older and more relaxed vision of higher education associated with a time when numbers of students (and academics) were smaller and management was more collegial.[2] In order to pre-empt what is in my view a rather cheap dismissal of my line of argument, let me make it clear that I am not saying instrumental thinking has no place at all in the university. Clearly, it is good that academic researchers find cures for diseases and discover ways of ameliorating climate change. I reject too any suggestion that students who pursue university qualifications essentially as a means to an end are in some sense inferior to those who – whether now or in some imagined past – come or came in search of knowledge for its own sake. Perhaps I can best emphasize this by sketching two of my own recent students, with some composite features for the sake of anonymity.

Carol was a middle-manager in a Primary Care Trust (a local tier of the United Kingdom's National Health Service). Although she was very good at her job she had hit a ceiling beyond which she was unlikely to be promoted. Every year she saw colleagues who held university degrees being promoted above her. Eventually she took the risk – both financial and in terms of the potential damage to her self-belief if she did not succeed – of applying to university, at the age of 37, initially as a part-time student. After three years of this she changed to full-time study, partly to reach her goal more quickly and partly to do herself the justice she now saw she was capable of. She has her own family and bears significant responsibilities as one of the carers for her elderly mother. During her years of study she did not play university sport, go to student parties or involve herself with any of the numerous student societies – all the things which this particular university's vice-chancellor likes to recommend as ways of 'not letting your degree get in the way of your education'. She was seldom able to do more than the essential reading and certainly did not have time to explore 'the fascinating by-ways and nooks and crannies' of her subject that one lecturer insisted was the difference between real university education and a poor substitute for it. Towards the end of her final year Carol sat in a restaurant with a dozen fellow-students and shocked them with the revelation that this was the first time she had had any substantial social contact with other students over her six years of study. With her newly conferred degree she was quickly promoted. She talks now of her career, rather than her job, of her sense of status in her workplace and of her new self-respect.

Tom came to university as an eighteen-year-old from a rural background in the west of England. He liked to present himself as a country boy, more comfortable on a tractor than in the library. Nothing however could disguise his intelligence, ambition and capacity for hard work. He aimed to secure a place on the graduate scheme of one of the major consultancy and accounting firms. Despite being on route to the first-class degree that he eventually secured, he was unsuccessful in all his applications. He decided to take a master's degree in International Politics, reasoning that although he was not particularly interested in the subject, this would help him stand out from the hundreds of applicants who only held a bachelor's degree. Now his applications quickly led to offers. Throughout his time as an undergraduate he made his career plans known and defended them against those disposed to characterize them as 'selling out' or 'working for the man'. He doggedly used to explain that 'for someone like me' working in the city represented a crucial break from his roots, marking him out from the peers with whom he had grown up and taking him to a wholly new place (he never used the word 'class'). Tom enjoyed student life to the full, including sport; but his career goal was always paramount. For him university stood for more than many of his contemporaries could easily understand. If it was a means to an end, the meaning of that end was rich and complex.

As these two brief examples show, the pursuit of vocational ends by way of university study can be life-transforming. Instrumental thinking in higher education has its place. The problem is that instrumental thinking has now become dominant and pervasive, reaching into every aspect of the university and driving out other kinds of thinking or, as I shall put it, other modes of rationality. No clearer instance of this can be given than the way that media reporting and discussion of university education in England has for several years focused on the question of fees, the debts that graduates will incur and whether these will prove to have been a good investment in the light of the salaries they earn in the jobs or careers that they embark on. The question of the worthwhileness of university study thus becomes answerable in terms of calculating financial outlay against financial return. This is instrumental thinking of the crudest sort. Its inevitability is confirmed by TV news clips or newspaper photographs (the complicity of the media should again be noted) showing young people, wearing academic gowns and fresh from their graduation ceremonies, tossing their mortar-boards into the air. Text accompanying the pictures highlights the annual fees to be paid for tuition and the amount of debt incurred over the three (or more) years of study. The message is clear: any idea that the point of all this was pleasure in academic achievement or the acquisition of understanding for its own sake, the mastery of a subject or discipline or exhilaration in a sense of the boundlessness of knowledge, is shown up as naive against the ineluctable numbers, the reckoning of profit and loss.

Instrumental thinking here is closely bound up with the assumptions of neoliberalism: that university education is a market good whose purchase is entirely comparable to a house, car or any other commodity. The market knows only means–end, instrumental thinking. As Adam Smith memorably noted in *The Wealth of Nations*, the butcher, the baker and the brewer aim to please their customers not out of any benevolent motive but from the knowledge that this is the only way for their business to flourish. If they serve them badly, the customers will go elsewhere. So too the university is now reconceived as one more industry that must submit to 'the discipline of the market'. Students are now customers who must be served well if the institution is to survive and prosper. Any other kind of thinking, such as that the lecturer came into this line of work motivated by a desire to introduce the next generation to the fascination and frustration of her subject, is discounted. Whole batteries of information, known as 'Key Information Sets' (KIS), are now available online, allowing students to discover, for any course of study they are interested in, the percentage of graduates at work or further study after six months, the percentage of them in professional and managerial roles after six months, their satisfaction with the support and guidance they received, the costs of accommodation and so on. Accordingly, universities have made rapid progress in foregrounding the 'employability skills' their courses equip students with. Staff are encouraged to diversify modes of assessment, on the grounds that, say, having to make a presentation to other students in a seminar means that you can claim to have 'communication skills' on your CV. Any course or module making a plausible case to supply 'employability skills' now seems to enjoy a charmed passage through university validation committees. Again, the point is not that students should not acquire such skills (if we only knew what they were) or should not have data from KIS, but that other ways of thinking about what to study and where, and why, are rendered invisible.

Fully to grasp the extent to which instrumental thinking and neoliberal theory have colonized the English university is to be in a position to make sense of various other oddities of the educational landscape. Three examples will suffice. First, it is a phenomenon more remarkable than we tend to notice, having become familiar with it, that the universities of the United Kingdom are the responsibility not of the Department for Education, nor any other government department with 'education' in its title, but of the Department for Business, Innovation and Skills (colleagues from other parts of the world tend to find this beyond parody). This is commonly abbreviated to BIS, some image management consultant having decreed, or so I assume, that the abandonment of words and comma signify the urgent, businesslike and innovative discovery of means towards the skilling-up of the workforce (as the consultant would no doubt put it) in the interest of the economy. Secondly, the Coalition government put the key higher education funding proposals, including the massive increase in fees, to a vote in parliament in December 2010 and only then published a White Paper, *Higher Education: Students at the Heart of the System*, in June 2011. The usual practice is the other way round: White Papers set out principles and policies, from which follow consultation and discussion, and then the detailed draft legislation on which parliament eventually votes. Here instrumental considerations of how the university system was to be funded took priority over, or rather obviated, considerations of just what universities are for.

Thirdly, university research is now judged partly on its 'impact', that is on the extent to which it brings benefits to the world outside academe. As I noted above, in one sense this is unexceptionable, and there is a strong case in principle for saying that much of the research done by university departments and their staff should be in some way useful to the wider society, rather than merely being valued by other academics. Why else, it may be asked, should the tax-payer fund it? Yet the matter is far from straightforward. For a start, some subjects, such as philosophy, classics or English literature are bound to find it much more difficult to demonstrate such 'impact' than others such as physics or engineering. Any overt proposal to cease the teaching of the humanities (to 'disinvest' in them, no doubt) on the grounds that they are not socially useful would almost certainly cause public disquiet: it is obvious enough – or so we might think – that their value cannot be conceived in this kind of way. But the criterion of 'impact' seems likely to have a similarly disastrous effect, seeming to offer the humanities in particular the chance to succeed on a yardstick against which they can in fact hardly be measured while still being the kinds of subjects that they are.

Furthermore, it is well-known that even research that does have 'impact' seldom does so within the lifetime of a particular university research assessment period of roughly eight years. Peter Higgs' theorization of what has become known as the Higgs boson particle is often cited in this context: Higgs' seminal work was published in 1964 but the particle's discovery was not announced at CERN (the European Centre for Nuclear Research) until the summer of 2012, and it is still far from clear what the use of the discovery is even while it is widely agreed that it is of enormous scientific importance. (Higgs has observed that he would be unlikely to be kept on his university post these days, even supposing that he was appointed to one in the first place.[3]) To give your research maximum 'impact' you would need to publish or otherwise disseminate it at the beginning of a research cycle, but this only points up the arbitrary nature of whether research has 'impact', in the terms proposed, or not.

One of the most disquieting aspects of the introduction of 'impact' as a criterion is the way that it has colonized the academic imagination. For the forthcoming UK research assessment exercise, the 'Research Excellence Framework', 'impact' will actually acccount for no more than 20 per cent of a department's score (and thus for 20 per cent of its research income from central sources); 65 per cent is contributed by 'outputs', that is publications. The criteria for the quality of these is clear: they are originality, significance and rigour. Not only does 'impact' not figure here: research assessors are explicitly instructed not to let their judgements be affected by any thoughts they have about what the impact of publications is likely to be. Nevertheless, academics and their managers can be heard constantly talking as if research that has 'impact' is the only game in town. At my own university, for example, applicants for research leave are now required to indicate what they expect the impact of their proposed research – research not even started yet – to be. Similar demands are also made of lecturers attempting to pass their probation, or to secure promotion. A particular sort of academic, whose publications are indifferent but who likes to think of his or her research as on the jet-pack end of the spectrum, now has licence for self-importance.

It is not easy to see how this state of things can successfully be countered. It seems to be impervious to sound argument and criticism. I take this to be a clear sign that a particular kind of rationality and language have made themselves at home, and that its most fluent practitioners, the self-important especially, now seeing little around them except the monoculture which they themselves have helped to create, take this simply as the natural and given, and no doubt desirable, order of things. The philosopher Richard Rorty (1989) has written about the difficulty of mounting successful arguments against an entrenched language or viewpoint such as that constituted by instrumental reason. He thinks that radical social changes generally take place not because an individual thinker or even a group of thinkers puts forward a convincing argument: it is more that a language which has long seemed to be the only language to use starts to seem old-fashioned or inadequate. He gives the example (p. 12) of how 'the traditional Aristotelian vocabulary got in the way of the mathematical vocabulary that was being developed in the sixteenth century by students of mechanics'.

This line of thought seems plausible. What the monoculture of instrumental reason and its vocabulary 'gets in the way of', I would say, is a conception of rationality that allows us to do greater justice to human well-being and human needs, particularly the need to live a meaningful life. We do not have to invent such a conception *ex nihilo*. Other epochs have set out richer visions of rationality than we now enjoy, sometimes apparently in response to a similar narrowing of the prevailing horizons of thought. Perhaps the most obvious recent example is the Romantic movement of the late eighteenth and early nineteenth centuries, which countered the mathematical and geometric rationality of the Enlightenment with a celebration of spontaneity and irregularity (the poet Wordsworth was *wandering* when he happened to come upon the daffodils, as was William Blake through the 'charter'd' – that is, always for sale – streets of London) and recommended attunement to the natural world instead of mastery of it. I have written elsewhere (Smith, 1999) of Dickens' marvellous treatment of this in *Hard Times*, where he contrasts the rigid formalism of Mr Gradgrind's utilitarianism with the uncalculating élan of 'the horse-riding', the travelling circus. (*The Coketown Gazette* no doubt carried a headline: '100 guinea boost to Coketown economy when circus comes to town'.)

Elements of a strikingly similar 'romantic rationality' can be found in Plato. It is tempting to interpret this as a reaction against the *realpolitik* and knowingness that had ended in the disaster of the war against Sparta at the end of the fifth century BC. It is worth giving an example at length. In Plato's *Phaedrus*, the young man after whom the dialogue is named first appears in conversation with Socrates while walking in the countryside outside the city walls of Athens. His doctor has advised him of the health benefits of country walks. They are means to an end. Our suspicion that Phaedrus is the model of an instrumental thinker is confirmed when we learn that he has been listening to a presentation by the itinerant sophist Lysias. This was on the subject of love (*eros*, which has a stronger sexual connotation than our word 'love'): Lysias argued that an attractive and promising young man – rather like Phaedrus himself, perhaps – ought to offer himself not to an older man who is in love with him but to one who is not. Phaedrus has a copy of the speech and reads it to Socrates. A young man is best advised to trade what he has to offer in return for the support a more experienced and better placed (politically and financially, no doubt) man can give him in his pursuit of his ambitions.

> The fitting thing is rather to grant favours not to those who stand in great need of them but to those who are most able to pay a favour back; not to those who are merely in love with you but to those who deserve the thing you have to give; not to the sort who will take advantage of your youthful beauty but to the ones who will share their own advantages with you when you become older. (*Phaedrus*, 233e6–234a3)[4]

In Plato's dialogue Socrates offers Phaedrus a superior speech, but along the same general lines as Lysias'. Then he declares the conversation over and makes to leave. But some supernatural force prevents him. He explains that the speech he has just made was dreadful, as was Lysias'. Both speeches made the mistake of denigrating being in love as a kind of madness, and so praised relationships based on cool, prudential rationality. Socrates says: 'That would be rightly said if it were a simple truth that madness is a bad thing; but as it is, the greatest of goods come to us through madness, provided that it is bestowed by divine gift ... god-sent madness is a finer thing than man-made sanity' (*Phaedrus*, 244a6–244d3). And this is true about language itself, about speech and writing.

> The man who arrives at the doors of poetry without madness from the Muses, convinced that after all expertise will make him a good poet, both he and his poetry – the poetry of the sane – are eclipsed by that of the mad, remaining imperfect and unfulfilled. (*Phaedrus*, 245a6–245a10)

The dialogue asks us to open our minds to more than means–end calculation. The sensuality and magic of the setting, under a plane-tree by the river Ilissus, with the cicadas making their hypnotic music overhead, create an atmosphere in which both Socrates and Phaedrus become unusually receptive, both to the place and to each other. There is a heightened sense of awareness here in which their understanding of their ends re-shapes itself in ways that are only shadowed by the words that are written as having been spoken and are thus doubly removed from intention and calculation, the workings of dispassionate intellect. Can this vision of reason as an alternative to the relentlessly instrumental kind still speak to us today? The cynicism (some might call it 'realism') of the instrumental approach to human relationships that Lysias recommends can be appreciated if we place it in a modern setting (see Nussbaum, 1986, for an illuminating discussion along these lines). A young woman can look for the elusive 'real thing' in her personal life, or she can form a relationship with an older man in her workplace, her line manager, perhaps, or 'one of the partners', someone who can help her up the career ladder and take her out for better meals than her regular boyfriend can afford. Another modern parallel is supplied by the numerous Internet sites offering instructions on how to write a love letter. ('The purpose of a software program for love letters is to get your creative juices flowing by presenting you with a wealth of ideas, tips, and examples to help you compose a love letter that is deeply personal and effective – a letter someone will cherish for a long time.'[5])

The reaction against exclusively means–end thinking, and the attempt to articulate a different version of reason, can also be found in Aristotle's account of *phronesis*, variously translated as practical judgement, practical reasoning or practical wisdom, in the *Nicomachean Ethics*, written around 350 BC, some ten years after Plato's *Phaedrus*. Aristotle distinguishes *phronesis* from *techne*: the latter, often translated as 'skill', belongs in the realm of instrumental reason and has connotations of what in our own time we would call 'science'. *Techne* is displayed by the craftsman who plans and makes a chair. Once he has acquired the relevant skill or set of skills he can replicate the procedure more or less accurately and teach the procedure to others so that they can make a chair in just the way that he does (vases from the workshops of classical Greek potters are often hard to attribute to particular craftsmen for precisely this reason; so too paintings from, say, 'the school of Peter Paul Rubens'). He can give an explanation for making the chair one way rather than another, pointing out, say, that the legs characteristically splay slightly in order for the chair to have greater stability. Thus there is a rationale behind his craft which makes it possible to think of it as a distinctive kind of rationality.

The example of *phronesis* most-often cited, and used by Aristotle himself, is the activity of politics. Politics cannot consist simply in the pursuit of certain ends such as low inflation and territorial expansion while being indifferent to means. The good nation-state, in terms that Aristotle would recognize, is characterized by open and honest dealings among the citizenry, as opposed to corruption and what we would now call 'spin' and 'sleaze'. In the world of industry or commerce, similarly, the pursuit of such goals as competitive advantage does not justify using any means, including (e.g.) the hacking of one's rivals' communication systems, to ensure those goals are achieved. That is to say that particular values are internal to the practice of the good organization. Good teaching, management or professionalism in general by its very nature does its work with respectful adherence to values and ethical norms, which it is no less concerned to respect as it is to achieve 'external' ends such as profit, advantage over its competitors or a higher position in educational or other league tables. Internal goods include the professional integrity of those exercising judgement. If they are *phronimoi,* people who have good practical judgement, they cannot be treated simply as good technical operatives, possessors of skills in which the real value and usefulness is held to lie and which would in principle be no less and no more valuable if they were possessed by another operative (or 'hand', as the revealing word has it: someone whose value lies exhaustively in his dexterity). In practical judgement knowledge, wisdom and feeling hold together and inform each other. To draw on Lasch's (1984, p. 253) helpful way of putting it, 'the choice of means has to be governed by their conformity to standards of excellence designed to extend human capacities for self-understanding and self-mastery'. There are connections here, which I do not have space to explore, via the notion of *praxis* with Marxist ideas and with critical theory, which themselves can claim to be distinctive forms of rationality.

There are two features of *phronesis* that mark it out sharply from technical reason. First, it is marked by attentiveness to the particular case and by flexibility. This attentiveness is what Aristotle calls *aesthesis*: 'alertness' is sometimes used to translate the term. It comprises sensitivity and a kind of attunement to the subject, involving a degree of openness and passivity, where by contrast instrumental or technical reason is characterized by mastery and control. Whereas *techne* is marked by a high degree of pre-planning (the skilled maker of chairs may follow a blueprint), *phronesis* is more typically exercised in the course of what is sometimes called 'hot action'. It also involves being open to further experience. The *phronimos* does not rest content once she has achieved a satisfactory set of procedures but is aware of the danger of settling into unreflective routine. Here there are no algorithms to follow. In this too there is a connection with certain elements of critical theory, particularly its emphasis on personal development through reflection. Secondly, *phronesis* has an ethical side to it which technical rationality lacks. Questions of character, of what kind of person the individual exercising judgement is, are at issue here: it does not simply come down to what 'skills' he or she is exercising. A person who is open, alert, attuned and self-critical is a better person than one who is not. We only need to pause to consider whether we would prefer to have friends who were like this than ones who are obtuse, insensitive and lacking in the ability to reflect on their own judgements and decisions.

I have developed this second example at length in order to show that in the idea of *phronesis* there is a complex and highly coherent alternative to means–end reason, one that can properly be called a form of rationality since it offers a framework within which reasons can be given and justifications offered. It has attracted much interest in recent decades, partly through the work of Alasdair MacIntyre (1981, 1988), whose influence on this chapter is extensive, and the work of Joseph Dunne (1993). It has proved appealing to management theorists (see Dobson, 2009, for an overview and critique) and educational philosophers: a brief vignette from education may help to point up what is at issue here.

The history teacher cannot adopt a simple means–end approach to improving her pupils' understanding of the subject. It is not just that basic ethical and legal considerations rule out inflicting physical punishment on those failing to hand in their homework or to achieve adequate marks in tests: the good aimed for here is understanding history, which is to be achieved through the action – the action of learning to understand history – and not through some other means. This is why extrinsic rewards for good work are no less problematic than extrinsic punishments. They will not extend the children's capacity for 'self-understanding and self-mastery' (Lasch's words again), for example their capacity for coming to realize that they love history, or prefer science (as opposed to loving the rewards and hating the punishments), or for realizing that they need to read primary sources less carelessly and more critically (as opposed to simply perceiving that they need to score higher marks). The issue of capacity-building, as it is now often described in organizational contexts, applies, for all its industrial connotations, to the teacher too. The teacher whose teaching of history emanates from, and in turn nurtures, her own love of the subject is a different teacher from the one who is mainly concerned to increase the proportion of her pupils who secure good grades. Of course the pressures on schools now mean that there are more of the second kind of teacher than the first. The first kind of teacher is nourished by her work while the second risks being made exhausted (literally, 'drained') by it. This point, which cannot be emphasized too strongly, can be expressed by saying that practical judgement, learning and human flourishing are intrinsically and essentially linked.

If there were space here I would want to explore how the body of ideas that is usually described as 'postmodern' can helpfully be understood as the most recent way of trying to find an alternative rationality to the instrumentalism of our age, its characteristic features being playfulness and a refusal to construct systems, acknowledgement of the instability of language, interest in the marginal and ephemeral, *petits récits* rather than grand narratives, exploration of the sublime, of what cannot be said yet demands to be heard. There is a challenge in justifying this as any kind of cohesive theory or set of theories, not least because its proponents (e.g. Lyotard, Derrida) generally refuse to describe themselves as 'postmodernists', and in justifying it as a form of rationality. Its power to disrupt the neoliberal, instrumental assumptions of our age can however perhaps be detected in the denegration to which 'postmodernism' is routinely subjected, usually by those who have heard that it amounts to 'anything goes' and are anxious to position themselves on the side of those who are in the know about these things. 'Romantic' thinking can of course be dismissed with the same facility.

My final point concerns the position of the university with regard to the state of things I have described in this chapter. Having rushed, for instrumental reasons, to make common cause with the forces of neoliberalism and means–end thinking, it may seem an institution ill-fitted for challenging the new consensus. Yet the alternative notions of rationality that I have sketched here – ideas from Plato, Aristotle and romanticism, let alone postmodernism – are ones that are entirely familiar in the study of the humanities and social sciences, and ones that would hardly have been recovered or developed were it not for the university in the form we know it in western developed nations in our time. We thus have an ever-increasing tension between, on the one hand, what the university still, in its teaching and research, does, and the strategies, philosophies and rhetoric of its leaders and managers, on the other. Between the richness of ideas that may be uncomfortable, strange, even eccentric, and the self-destructive wasteland of a monoculture from which they offer us relief and, possibly, salvation.

Notes

1   I owe this telling point, as well as many other helpful suggestions, to Morgan White.
2   See, for example, Simon Jenkins' (2012) remarks on Stefan Collini's book, *What Are Universities For?*
3   http://www.theguardian.com/science/2013/dec/06/peter-higgs-boson-academic-system.
4   All translations are from Rowe (2005).
5   http://www.writeexpress.com/How-to-write-a-love-letter.html.

References

Department for Business, Innovation and Skills (2011) *Higher Education: Students at the Heart of the System*. London: HMSO.

Dobson, J. (2009) 'Alasdair MacIntyre's Aristotelian business ethics: A critique', *Journal of Business Ethics* 86:43–50.

Dunne, J. (1993) *Back to the Rough Ground: 'Phronesis' and 'Techne' in Modern Philosophy and in Aristotle*. Notre Dame, IN: University of Notre Dame Press.

Guardian (2012) http://www.theguardian.com/uk/2012/oct/15/royal-british-legion-president-quits [accessed 15 October].

——— (2013) *Royal British legion president quits in wake of lobbying claims'*, http://www.theguardian.com/uk/2012/oct/15/royal-british-legion-president-quits [accessed 15 October, 2013].

Hull Daily Mail (2013) *'The £190m Ten-Year City Plan outlined by Hull City Council to Create 7,500 jobs'*, http://www.hulldailymail.co.uk/60m-UK-City-Culture-boost-Hull-start-future/story-20111197-detail/story.html#ixzz2og9qLRyi. [accessed 21 November, 2013].

Ilkley Gazette (2013) *'Literature festival estimated to boost economy by £250,000'*, http://www.ilkleygazette.co.uk/news/news_local/10715765.Literature_festival_estimated_to_boost_economy_by___250_000/. [accessed 4 October, 2013].

Jenkins, S. (2012) 'Universities need the guts to break this Faustian pact with research', *The Guardian*, March 15 http://www.guardian.co.uk/commentisfree/2012/mar/15/universities-faustian-pact-research-academics.

Lasch, C. (1984) *The Minimal Self: Psychic Survival in troubled Times*. London: Picador/Pan.

MacIntyre, A. (1981) *After Virtue*. London: Duckworth.

——— (1988) *Whose Justice? Which Rationality?* Notre Dame, IN: University of Notre Dame Press.

Nussbaum, M. (1986) *The Fragility of Goodness Luck and Ethics in Greek Tragedy and Philosophy*. Cambridge: Cambridge University Press.

Plato trans. Rowe 2005 *Phaedrus*. London: Penguin.

Rorty, R. (1989) *Contingency, Irony, and Solidarity*. Cambridge: Cambridge University Press.

Smith, R. (1999) 'Paths of judgement: Tthe revival of practical wisdom', *Educational Philosophy and Theory* 31(3):327–340.

——— (2012) 'University futures', *Journal of Philosophy of Education* 46(4):649–662.

9

Towards an Anarchist Philosophy of Education

Judith Suissa

Two discernible trends can be found in recent work in philosophy of education, giving rise to significant internal tensions and debates. In what follows, I will identify the form and some of the key features of these trends and suggest how a critical, anarchist-inspired perspective on them can offer some fruitful ways of thinking about the important philosophical and practical educational questions that they address. I am not referring to 'rival conceptions' (Standish, 2007) of the discipline, or to the distinction between 'analytic' and 'continental' traditions. What I want to draw attention to is not primarily a question of philosophical tradition(s), style or method, but rather a question of how the relationship between education, schooling, the state and social change is conceptualized, and how this in turn structures the way we bring philosophical arguments to bear on educational questions. I do not claim to offer an exhaustive description of the current state of the discipline; there are certainly important themes developed by philosophers of education that do not fall neatly into this account. However, I do think that the themes I identify are significant in terms of their influence in setting the terms of the debate in which so much of our academic discussion takes place.

One strand is concerned chiefly with offering a clear, normative account of 'what education is for' that will, it is supposed, be of use to policymakers, teachers, educational theorists and, to a lesser extent, parents. Most of the work within this area is conducted in the form of tightly constructed philosophical argument, although it often draws on policy analysis, empirical sociology and history. In addition, the language in which it talks of education is predominantly that of the formal school system: curricula, teacher training and policies on access and provision. It is important to note that while this kind of work has obvious intellectual antecedents in what is usually referred to as the analytic tradition in philosophy of education, it has moved away from this tradition in significant ways. Although, as John White points out (White, 2010), it is doubtful whether even the classic work by key figures in this tradition such as Hirst, Peters, Dearden and Elliot was ever as narrowly confined to conceptual analysis, committed to social atomism, suspicious of articulating norms and values, or insulated from historical and political arguments as some of its detractors make out, the articulation of substantive political and moral positions has been far more explicit and prominent in recent work by theorists working within this tradition. Thus Harry Brighouse, Eamonn Callan, Graham Haydon, Meira Levinson, John White, Patricia White and Christopher Winch, to name but a few, have all developed accounts both of general educational aims and of subject-specific aims which, while written with the argumentative style and clarity so familiar to the analytic tradition, certainly do not aspire to offer a universal, 'neutral' or value-free account, and which are explicitly situated within a particular political and historical context.

The second strand is philosophically oriented to the Aristotelian or neo-Aristotelian tradition, or to post-structuralism, and is characterized by a suspicion of the project of offering either a conceptual analysis of the structure of aims or a defence of specific aims within a clearly articulated substantive moral or political position that is supposed to lead, logically and unproblematically, to prescriptions for educational policies, curricular design and classroom practice.

As Standish puts this, 'the suspicion that emerges is that stating the aims of education may lead to a kind of stifling' (Standish, 1999, p. 42). Many philosophers of education working in this second vein have developed accounts of 'the goods internal to education' – accounts that go hand in hand with a concern that conceptualizing educational success in terms connected to the productive, political and economic sphere runs the risk of subverting or displacing these intrinsic goods (see Dunne, 2005, Hogan, 2009, 2010, 2011).

I will argue that both these approaches, due to their unexamined and unarticulated assumptions about the state, lead to a constriction of our ability to think about education, the political, the social and the relationship between these. A consideration of the anarchist perspective can, I suggest, open up our thinking and, in doing so, suggest a more critical and dynamic role for philosophy of education.

Education without aims

As explained above, although contemporary philosophers of education working within the analytic tradition have long ago abandoned the aspiration to provide a purely conceptual, second-order account of educational concepts and are generally explicit about their commitment to a set of substantive (liberal) values, their work often, as Standish suggests (1999, p. 40), takes the same 'discursive form' as older analytic accounts within this tradition, which offered, for example, defences of autonomy as an educational aim.

What concerns critics like Standish is that this type of philosophizing about education seems to 'assume the possibility of an overview and the possibility of completeness' (Standish, 1995, p.133). In their critique of the idea of perfectibility and of the dominance of performativity in educational thought and practice (see Blake et al., 1998, 2000, Smith, 2002, Standish, 2007), these philosophers are not all invoking a defence of education as a practice; nor are they rejecting wholesale the traditional account of liberal education. Yet the suggestion that 'questions concerning the aims of education should then touch us with a faint sense of embarrassment' (Standish, 1995, p. 128) adds to the impression that any attempt to pin down and define education in a way that is 'too formulaic too explicit' (see Standish, 2012) risks losing something of its possibly ineffable qualities.

In this sense, Standish's work has affinities with that of philosophers like Dunne and Hogan who emphasize the intrinsic quality of educational practices and relationships. The political is often, in such accounts, implicitly regarded as something to be suspicious of. This is not to say that such accounts are devoid of political or historical analysis. Yet to the extent that politics appears at all in such work, it is either as something 'external' from which the practice of education must be protected in order to preserve its integrity or as a 'system' which pre-exists any form of educational practice and can be defended or criticized independently of anything we may wish to say about the practice of education.

Padraig Hogan defends this view particularly forcefully, arguing that educational practice needs to 'emerge from its historic subordination to paternalistic and bureaucratic masters, and to lay claim in an articulate and sure-footed way to its own identity as a human practice' (Hogan, 2011, p. 30). His recent work consists of an articulation of the 'inherent purposes' of this practice and 'a recognisable family of virtues' that arise from it (Hogan, 2011). While acknowledging that education is inescapably value-laden, Hogan wants to resist the idea that the values in question must be derived from 'particular individuals and groups'. 'Such a conclusion obscures the very possibility that education is a practice in its own right, with its own inherent purposes and ethical commitments. Instead, it defines education from the start as a subordinate practice' (Hogan, 2011).

From the perspective of this position, accounts like those of John White (1990, 2011), Reiss and White (2013), Levinson (1999), Brighouse (2006, 2010) and Callan (1997), which explicitly defend a view of the kind of education necessary in liberal state, both run the risk of 'subverting' education and distorting its internal goods and suggest a dangerous form of closure (Standish, 1995).

As I will suggest below, both these perspectives share a similarly narrow view of the relationship between politics and education. What accounts for this narrowness, however, is not a view of educational aims and practices as 'subservient' to 'extrinsic' political ones, nor anything 'formal or procedural' (Standish, 2007, p. 163), in particular philosophical approaches, but rather the assumption of the state and the institutional framework of state education as the conceptual territory on which all debates about education take place, and a connectedly narrow view about the meaning of and possibilities for social change. These assumptions, I suggest, involve a serious lack of philosophical imagination.

Politics and the state

The (capitalist) state is there implicitly in the work of theorists within the analytic tradition from the 1970s, and explicitly in the work of prominent contemporary theorists such as Harry Brighouse, Richard Pring, John White, Patricia White and Christopher Winch. Indeed, one could argue that while this tradition was once centrally concerned with a defence of 'liberal education', it is now more accurately described as focused on 'education in the liberal state'. The conflation of liberal education with the liberal state is sometimes explicitly defended, as in Alan Ryan's contention that liberal education is 'the kind of education that sustains a liberal society' (Ryan, 1998, p. 27). Yet the state itself is rarely argued for by philosophers of education who, like most political philosophers, seem to assume that, however imperfect, it is somehow inevitable.

It is certainly not true that in tacitly assuming the state as the normative framework for their discussion of education, theorists such as those mentioned above are ignoring wider, traditional 'liberal' aims to do with pursuing education for its own sake. Nor are such accounts devoid of critical political perspectives. Harry Brighouse (2003, 2010) and Christopher Winch (2000, 2005), for example, have defended accounts of liberal education that require far more interventionist policies of redistribution than those currently operating in most liberal state education systems. Winch's critical position, which combines a concern for those aspects of educational experience which cannot be reduced to instrumental or positional goods, with an engagement with the vocational aspects of education and the link between educational achievement and socio-economic outcomes, is most evident in his recent exchanges with James Tooley (see, e.g., Sarangapani and Winch, 2010).

Winch has criticized Tooley for ignoring the social and political implications of private educational provision, as well as for his failure to appreciate the public good nature of education alongside its positional value. Yet while I have a great deal of sympathy for Winch's view, I want to suggest that positions like this, which assume the (capitalist) state as an inevitable feature of our lives – the worst consequences of which can, perhaps, be ameliorated through educational provision – narrow the horizon of our political imagination.

Tooley's work is often described as 'radical', in that it imagines education without the state. Yet while Tooley (1996, 2000) has made an important contribution to philosophy of education in reminding us that 'education' is not equivalent to 'schooling' and in questioning the monopoly of state education, he begins, like his opponents, from the assumption that the state is the framework in which we are operating. In Tooley's market-driven alternative to schools controlled and funded by the state, the capitalist state is still very much there in the background – indeed, it constitutes the very structures and paradigms within which the market system can operate and within which the educational goods that it provides make sense.

Winch argues that re-constructing educational provision along the market-driven lines Tooley suggests will both encourage the kinds of attitudes and individual propensities that will undermine the humanistic elements of the form of liberal education that he wishes to defend and entrench socio-economic gaps, leading to vast inequalities. While I would not disagree with this argument, I do want to reject the implication that there are only two options to choose from: either education provided and controlled by the liberal state, hopefully configured in such a way as to meet at least a minimum requirement of social justice, or educational provision within a private system operating on the logic of free-market capitalism.

Similarly, Harry Brighouse, in arguing against Tooley and other proponents of market or quasi-market reforms or parental choice policies in educational provision, assumes that the basic structure of the capitalist state will remain the same; all we can do is ameliorate its worst injustices. The main quarrel between him and Tooley is that, *given this structure*, Tooley does not think that the socio-economic disparities produced by differential educational opportunities will be any worse under a market-driven system than they are in a state-controlled system.

While Brighouse is careful to acknowledge that trying to equalize educational opportunity alone will not resolve the deficit of social justice, he, like most philosophers of education, takes the normative and practical framework of the state as a given and suggests that the role for political philosophers is to propose and critically analyse policies with the aim of bringing it closer to the Rawlsian model of a truly liberal, just state. By focusing on the fact that '[i]t is unfair, then, if some get a worse education than others because, through no fault of their own, this puts them at a disadvantage in the competition for these unequally distributed goods' (Brighouse, 2010, p. 27), Brighouse diverts attention from the idea that the capitalist state is *characterized* by competition for unequally distributed rewards, with educational attainment causally linked to such rewards.

Likewise, John White, whose recent work focuses on the notion of well-being as an aim of education, assumes the state framework. His very focus on the question of 'what schools are for', rather than what education is for, is indicative of this assumption. His account is also perhaps the most clear-cut example of the kind of 'neatness' that Standish worries about; its discursive form is indeed one in which the philosophical task is to 'begin with overarching aims, then fill them out in greater specificity' (Reiss and White, 2013, p. 1). While White is only too aware of the socio-economic context of human flourishing and has emphasised throughout his work that 'basic needs have to be met' (Reiss and White, 2013, p. 6) before one can even talk of well-being, his account does not start from a serious enquiry into what kind of social and political arrangements are most likely to secure these goods but rather assumes the arrangements we have in place, albeit with a fairly critical view of their inadequacy. The state, here, is a given; our task is merely to delineate its 'proper role' (Reiss and White, 2013, p. 48) and limits in determining the aims of schools. Thus in arguing that schools 'have a contribution to make in encouraging young people to […] be sensible in managing money' (Reiss and White, 2013, p. 6), White fails to acknowledge the ways in which this very argument assumes the capitalist state structure as a given. Similar assumptions can be found in the work of Brighouse who, in arguing that we should 'use schooling to enable children to interact with the economy in ways that facilitate their flourishing in their leisure time' (Brighouse, 2006, p. 41), assumes 'the economy' as a background constraint on what schools are and what they can and should do, rather than seeing it itself as part of a malleable socio-political structure than can and should be reconceptualized and challenged. Brighouse, like White, has focused on the idea of education for human flourishing in his recent work, yet he does not seem to regard it even worth explaining how such an idea can slide unproblematically into the claim that 'this means four central ideals that should inform the curriculum and ethos of schooling' (Brighouse, 2006, p. 131), without justifying the framework of the state and state schooling.

So even theorists who acknowledge, with Reiss and White (2013, p. 48), that the question of what education is for 'is essentially a political issue' assume the state as the unquestioned backdrop against which all contemporary philosophical debates about education take place. In doing so, they essentially reduce 'the political' to a discussion of policy.

It is worth pointing out that this is no less true of accounts like Hogan's which explicitly reject the idea that education can have political aims. Thus when Hogan refers to 'the wide diversity of practices – from early childhood education to adult education to postgraduate research seminars – that education as a practice in its own right includes' (Hogan, 2011, p. 35), he is, in this very delineation, already assuming something like a state education system. I believe a similar assumption is operating in work by philosophers sympathetic to post-structuralist approaches. Thus one finds repeated references to 'the system' in the work of philosophers who have developed an eloquent critique of 'managerialist assumptions' (Blake et al., 1998, Hogan and Smith, 2003) and of what Richard Smith (2002) describes as 'the instrumentalism, the techno-rationalism that runs through education at all levels'. Yet the absence of any reference to the state in such work suggests a failure to seriously consider the ways in which it may be, in fact, features of the state itself that are bound up with the problems these theorists identify in their critique.

Both accounts that implicitly assume the state in arguing for educational practice to be freed from politics and accounts that explicitly defend the state out of a belief that it is the best guarantor of social justice show a serious lack of political and philosophical imagination. All of the theorists discussed above are, to be sure, critical, whether in their determination not to allow education to be harnessed to neoliberal agendas and to worsen socio-economic disparities; or out of a concern not to allow schools, teachers and pupils to be dominated by the language of instrumental rationality. Yet in assuming the (capitalist) state as the backdrop against which this critical view of education takes place, rather than as the very thing that needs to be constantly acted against, they undermine the force of their own critique.

How many philosophers have dared to go further than the warning that '[e]xcessive positional advantage conferred by education may lead to outcomes that are harmful both to individuals and society through the production of excessive relative inequalities of income' (Sarangapani and Winch, 2010, p. 501) and to imagine a social world in which the very structures which give rise to 'positional advantage' have ceased to be relevant? How many have dared to imagine not just a world where poor or working-class children's educational opportunities would not be restricted by their parental background, but in which there was no poverty and where society was not characterized by hierarchical divisions of class?

Brighouse states frankly that 'to achieve a fully just society [...] would require substantially more radical reform' (Brighouse, 2010, p. 65) than that which he is advocating, and admits that he sees 'no great prospects for such reform' (Brighouse, 2010). I want, in what follows, to explore what it would mean to take seriously, as anarchism does, the possibility of a truly equal and free society, organized non-hierarchically on the basis of cooperation, solidarity and mutual aid and to consider how the anarchist position also encourages a very different view of what radical social change actually means.

Yet in starting from such a radical idea, are we not already falling victim to the kind of trap that Standish warns us of: the temptation that if we can only work out what the perfect society would look like, we can then map out what kind of education we need to get us there, and work out how to 'deliver' it? An understanding of the anarchist view, as I will elaborate below, suggests that one can take seriously the point that education is bound up with political questions about the kind of social world we want, without falling into the trap described by Standish. The choice is not between defending the integrity of educational practice or allowing our educational thinking to become hostage to a kind of rational planning that runs the risk of subverting such practices by seeing them as subservient to political or economic ends. The anarchist position, I will argue, offers us an imaginative, critical and motivating vision of a good society, without proposing a programme of revolutionary social change that can be worked out in advance, or a total overthrow of the existing system. In so doing, it suggests a very different perspective on the relationship between education and social change.

Education as social self-liberation

Many readers will no doubt balk at the idea of beginning our work as philosophers of education from such a 'utopian' vision. It is important, then, to pause for a moment to consider the different meanings and uses of the term 'utopian'. Saul Newman has described how, in the contemporary political landscape, dominated by implicit or explicit references to the 'inevitability' of capitalism, free-markets and neoliberal assumptions, 'the word utopia has a precise ideological function: it operates as a way of stigmatising alternative political and economic visions as, at best, unrealistic and naive, and, at worst, dangerous' (Newman, 2009, p. 209). There is, in fact, an interesting history of derogatory use of the term 'utopian' towards anarchism, although the precise content of the charge has varied depending on who was making it. I have discussed elsewhere (Suissa, 2006) how both the charge that anarchists have a naively optimistic account of human nature, thus rendering their position 'impractical', and the conflation (famously found in Popper and Berlin) of the term 'utopian' with the idea of a static state of perfection or a form of totalitarianism can be rejected on the basis of a rigorous understanding of anarchist theory (see also Morland, 1997).

What I want to emphasise for the current discussion, though, are two points that are particularly pertinent to the educational questions under consideration. Firstly, the key point that the anarchist utopia does not consist of a blueprint for the future society; and secondly, the sense – so urgent and necessary in the current climate of 'no alternative' – in which utopian thinking, and the anarchist utopia in general – can fill the important positive function noted by so many theorists of utopia, namely that of 'generating constructive and dynamic critical thought' (Goodwin and Taylor, 1982, p. 27), and thereby 'relativising the present' (Bauman, 1976, p. 13). As Newman puts it, at a time when 'the very idea of utopia has been discredited', introducing a utopian dimension to political discussion and action can bring 'a kind of radical heterogeneity and disruptive opening into the economic, social, political and ideological constellation that goes by the name of global capitalism' (Newman, 2009, p. 208).

Taking on board these points, we can begin to see how anarchism suggests an understanding of the relationship between education and social change that sheds new light on the themes and tensions discussed above, and thus cannot be simply rejected as the kind of unrealistic 'more radical reform' that Brighouse refers to. For crucially, the kind of social transformation that anarchists envisage is one in which spheres of social action are gradually freed of relations of domination, a process which can go on within and alongside the existing structures of the state – as captured in the phrase 'building the new society in the shell of the old'. Thus anarchism, as Colin Ward explains, is 'not about strategies for revolution'; rather, 'far from being a speculative vision of a future society, it is a description of a mode of human organization, rooted in the experience of everyday life, which operates side by side with, and in spite of, the dominant authoritarian trends of our society' (Ward, 1973, p.18).

The modes of human organization that Ward documented and engaged with ranged from housing, allotments, use of urban space and education. All these arenas constituted spaces in which individuals working collectively could enact anarchism as 'an act of social self-determination' (Ward, in Wilbert and White, 2011, p. 261). So rather than see education – and schools – as either a process of preparing children for life in society as we know it, an inevitable reproduction of existing ideological structures, or a means to improving and strengthening liberal institutions through the nurturing of certain intellectual qualities or civic virtues, anarchism invites us to see educational activity as a site of social transformation. It is here that the key anarchist idea of prefigurative practice comes in, for it is central to the anarchist view that the means for creating the alternative, stateless society be commensurate with the ends; 'a transformative social movement must necessarily anticipate the ways and means of the hoped-for new society' (Tokar, in Gordon, 2009, p. 269).

On the anarchist view, as we do not and cannot know the form of the ideal society, it is essential to enable the free interplay of human imagination and experimentation as far as possible. This insistence, though, should not lead to the common misperception that anarchism means chaos or disorder. In fact, as Morris points out (2005, p. 8), '[anarchism] means the exact opposite of this. It means a society based on order. Anarchy means not chaos, or a lack of organisation, but a society based on the autonomy of the individual, on co-operation, one without rulers or coercive authority'. Likewise, it is misleading to see anarchism as focused simplistically on the abolition of the state. Yet while nuanced understandings of the operation of power, oppression and the symbiotic relationship between state power and capitalism can arguably be found in early anarchist thinkers like Kropotkin (see Morris, 2004), it is nevertheless true that the many new social movements that constitute the contemporary anarchist scene place particular emphasis on 'the generalization of the target of anarchist resistance from the state and capitalism to all forms of domination in society' (Gordon, 2009, p. 262). But, as Gordon argues, this resistance clearly does not lead to the positing of 'the idea of an end to "all" forms of domination' – indeed, such an idea would be nonsensical as 'we simply cannot think such a state of affairs since we do not possess the full list of features that should be absent from it' (Gordon, 2009, pp. 264–265).

In light of such conceptual arguments, one can appreciate how, as Gordon puts it, 'diversity itself has ascended to the status of a core value in contemporary anarchism' (Gordon, 2009, p. 266). Yet in many ways, this idea echoes the thought of earlier anarchist thinkers like Ward, especially concerning the demand for diversity in education. If we are truly to allow educational spaces to become spaces for prefigurative practice, it is essential that we give teachers, children, parents and educational theorists the freedom to engage creatively and experimentally with such spaces. As Ward says, 'experiment is the oxygen of education' (in Wilbert and White, 2011, p. 238).

On this view, educational activities become not just an important arena for prefigurative practice but, connectedly, a form of direct action. As Gordon notes, while direct action is often associated with actions undertaken in a 'preventative or destructive' approach, it also has a constructive sense central to the anarchist project whereby individuals, acting together, 'directly pursue not only the prevention of injustices, but also the creation of alternative social relations free of hierarchy and domination' (Gordon, 2009, p. 269).

Anarchism's utopianism, then, consists of an imaginative critique of the present, without imposing a static vision of the utopian future or a blueprint for how to achieve it. Crucially, the anarchist perspective on social change suggests a radically different view of the relationship between education and social change from that of philosophers of education concerned to emphasize the way in which our educational thinking must go beyond existing arrangements. Thus Bridges, for example, argues that '[w]e cannot really conceive of education without reference to some selection of the human qualities we want to cultivate and of the kind of social world we expect or perhaps want our pupils to occupy' – and that this requires 'an inescapable responsibility to invoke some normative conception of the human qualities and the social world we see as desirable' (Bridges, 2008, p. 466). But the anarchist view challenges this account both by positing a radically different view of 'the kind of social world we want our pupils to occupy' from that of the state and by insisting at the same time that the way to achieve this is not by working out in advance which human qualities are necessary to bring about and sustain it and nurturing them through education but by imagining and enacting this social world here and now in our social relationships – of which education is one.

What this suggests is, in fact, a reconceptualization of the social. The fixation on the state (see Miltrany, in Sylvan, 1993, p. 215) and its logic which, as I have argued above, characterizes both those philosophical positions on education which reject the political as a contaminating factor and those which emphasize the political aspects of education, gives rise to a narrow view of the political. It is the state, in fact, which is associated with what Martin Buber referred to as 'the political principle' and which he distinguished from the social principle. Whereas the political principle 'is seen in power, authority and dominion', the social principle is seen in 'families, groups, unions, cooperative bodies and communities' (Ward, in Wilbert and White, 2011, p. 268). While it seems naive to conceive of families and communities as devoid of issues of power and authority, nevertheless there is an important insight here, I think, in that it is the monopolizing of power by the state which weakens society conceived of as a network of spontaneous human self-organization. It is this same insight behind Gustav Landauer's famous remark that 'the state is not something which can be destroyed by a revolution, but it is a condition, a certain relationship between human beings, a mode of human behaviour; we destroy it by contracting other relationships, by behaving differently' (in Ward, 1991, p. 85).

The above discussion, in suggesting that we rethink the sense in which education is a social practice, may seem to be not that different from accounts by philosophers of education like Dunne and Hogan. Yet education, understood in the way I have discussed, cannot be a practice with its own 'internal goods' any more than 'society' is a practice with its own internal goods. We cannot, then, talk of education 'without aims'; nor can we articulate a set of aims derived from a fully worked-out model of 'the good society'. Any such model, without the built-in requirement of constant human experimentation, would be a dangerous abstraction that itself would undermine the possibilities for human freedom that it is intended to bring about. Yet concerns that thinking about the quality of educational practices in light of normative ethical ideas about the good society would somehow contaminate education, or that such normative ethical ideals go hand in hand with a dangerous form of closure are, in light of the above account, ill-conceived. A suspicion of closure and perfectibility should not lead us to abandoning the project of thinking about education as part of a normative, ethical project for transforming our life as individuals and as a society. For as Ward points out, 'The concept of a free society may be an abstraction, but that of a freer society is not' (in White, 2011, p. 97).

Interestingly, Blake et al., (1998), in developing the idea that educational institutions need 'to be released from the performativity...that has come to dominate them' (p. 189) make the point that there is no clear-cut prescriptive answer as to how to do this; the idea of a blueprint is, they say, 'at odds with' their very arguments, influenced as they are by post-structuralist thinkers, and they emphasize the need for more 'human scale' control (Blake et al., 1998). Their analysis could perhaps have been enriched by a serious consideration of anarchist thought, which, contrary to their claims about 'established traditions of progressive or radical theory' that they reject as not being 'dominant forces in the present educational scene' (Blake et al., 1998, p. 186), does not in fact hold an idealistic view of the social subject. For the anarchist position does not subscribe to an essentialist or metaphysical conception of human nature. Kropotkin, for example, was as scathing in his critique of Rousseau's notion of the benign, pre-social individual as he was in his rejection of the Hobbesian competitive, asocial individual. As Brian Morris points out, 'Marx, Bakunin and Kropotkin all critiqued – indeed ridiculed – these "abstract" conceptions of the human person long before Lacan and the poststructuralists' (Morris, 2009, p. 15)[1]

Joseph Dunne has discussed the way in which not just 'practical subjects but traditional academic subjects, can benefit from a conception of education more focused on the idea of a practice'. He defends the idea that it is, in the case of any subject, 'an ongoing practice that students need to be introduced to – a practice that embodies its own ways of conducting enquiry, asking fruitful questions, imagining or empathising with characters or situations, devising plausible hypotheses or interesting interpretations, sifting and weighing evidence, making creative connections or shifts of perspective […]' (Dunne, 2005, p. 156). Similarly, Hogan (2010, 2011) articulates and defends 'the virtues of teaching and learning'. But while I would not want to reject these rich accounts of teaching and learning, I would add that *the practice* of education always takes place in a social space which is itself reflective of and embodies particular modes of organization and forms of interpersonal relationships; there is no escaping the question of how these relationships are constituted and what qualities they embody; those of domination, hierarchy and competitiveness, or those of commensality, mutual aid and spontaneity?

Theorists like Wilfred Carr are concerned with the way education has come to be seen 'less as a "practice" and more as a "system"' that had to be organised, managed and controlled so as to make it responsive to the political and economic demands of the modern industrial state' (Carr, 2005, p. 41). Yet Carr's historical account notwithstanding, it would be a mistake, in the process of trying to reclaim this sense of education as a practice, to jettison the sense of the practice of education as being inextricably bound up with social and political ideas and values, whether those of the industrial nation state or those of a very different conception of social life.

Going back to Buber's distinction between the political and the social, an anarchist philosophy of education not only transcends the dichotomy between 'intrinsic and extrinsic aims of education' (a dichotomy that has become something of an orthodoxy within the discipline), but can contribute to a theoretical and practical reclamation of and reaffirmation of the social. The state fixation which characterizes so much work in political philosophy and philosophy of education has the effect not only, as I argued above, of seriously limiting our philosophical imagination, but also of squeezing out the social in the sense that Buber and Ward talk about it.

This point is developed by Bargu as follows:

> From the perspective offered by traditions of mutuality, the crisis of modernity lies less in the invasion of the political by the social than in the flattening out of the social by the hegemonic construction of the autonomy of the political and the progressive destruction of the social by the incursion of a capitalist market whose primary form of competitive and individualist action has been detrimental to communal practices and relations. (Bargu, 2013, p. 37)

For the social anarchist, the problem facing humans today is not, as Arendt would have it, 'the rise of the social and its invasion of the political' but rather the 'progressive constriction of the social by the juridical conception of the political based on rights and liberties, on the one hand, and by the commercial relations of private exchange in the market on the other' (Bargu, 2013, p. 50).

Imagining a self-governing anarchist society free from relations of domination means, then, imagining a radical reconfiguration of the present, but also committing ourselves to enacting this reconfiguration in countless diverse and possibly small ways, embodying the kind of prefigurative practice where 'subsistence and mutual aid, justice and fellowship are elements that we must seek in order to nourish, both literally and metaphorically, the new community' (Bargu, 2013).

Objections

It will be objected that, in the current political climate, to open up the possibility of siding with proponents of free educational experimentation outside the state system is a dangerous abandonment of the political terrain and a betrayal of the struggle for social justice, and will play into the hands of neoliberal reformers.

To this I would respond that to frame the debate as if one had to choose between a blanket defence of state education and an endorsement of neo-liberal, market-led forms of private educational provision is both to ignore the historical context of state education and to misrepresent the critical role of philosophy.

Educational philosophers on the political left are almost universally united against current proposals for 'free schools'. Yet as the history of working-class initiatives in cooperative education, free schools and experiments in cooperative living reminds us, the alternative to a state monopoly on education is not just free-market individualism or for-profit schools. Indeed, the tendency to polarize debates on issues like welfare and education can be seen as symptomatic of the ideological anti-utopian stance described above. We need to revisit and re-examine the history of these debates as part of an attempt to reclaim a more critical, emancipatory position. Carissa Honeywell (2011) has offered just such a contribution in her fascinating analysis of British social policy debates, drawing on the work of anarchist thinkers such as Ward, who describes how the political left in Britain 'invested all its fund of social inventiveness in the idea of the state, so that its own traditions of self-help and mutual aid were stifled for lack of ideological oxygen' (Ward, in Wilbert and White, 2011, p. 272). Revisiting these debates seems particularly urgent at a time when the traditional values of the socialist left are so much under attack. As Ward remarked bitterly in 2000, 'The socialist ideal was rewritten as a world in which everyone was entitled to everything, but where nobody except the providers had any actual say about anything. We have been learning for years, in the anti-welfare backlash, what a very vulnerable utopia that was' (Carissa Honeywell, 2011, p. 273).

Philosophers, sociologists and historians of education can contribute to the project of reclaiming notions like 'community', 'freedom' and 'fairness' from the right and challenging contemporary ideological positions by articulating and documenting alternative educational ideas and experiments. Some philosophers of education have in fact been doing just that; yet even these theorists often overlook the anarchist position. Fielding and Moss, for example, in their book *Radical Education and the Common School* (Fielding and Moss, 2011), explore and defend the pedagogical practice of radical educational experimenters such as Alex Bloom. Of course the book's title implies a tacit defence of the state (where, while the need for radical democratic education is rigorously defended, the need for *state* education is not). Yet even so, given that the notion of prefigurative practice features so centrally in their analysis, it is remarkable that the anarchist tradition, arguably the tradition most associated with this idea, and the most fruitful source of well-developed and rich accounts of its theoretical and practical implications, receives not even a passing mention.

Fielding and Moss, however, at least do an important job in reminding us that it is not state education as such that is a project worth defending, but only state education insofar as it instantiates human and social values such as justice, freedom and equality. This position is in fact implicit in accounts like those of Winch and Brighouse, who, in defending state education against attacks from right-wing libertarian and neoliberal positions, are simply arguing that, given the political system we have, the unfair positional advantage conferred by education is *more likely* to be produced by the private sector.

As discussed above, framing the discussion as if there are only two options – universal compulsory state schooling which, while far from perfect, is the best guarantor of a minimal standard of universal educational provision and the best protection against parents' ability to exploit their unequal economic resources to confer educational advantage on their children – or a private market in educational provision, shuts down the possibility of imagining and allowing schools and other educational experiments where the utopian idea of a radically different society could be enacted freely through the kind of transfigurative practice described above. The point I want to make here is that we do not have to choose between either daring to imagine and to prefigure a society radically different from the kind we have now, or trying to ensure that, given the kind of society we live in, educational provision is not shaped by policies that adversely affect certain groups and privilege others. We can do both. Indeed, as Chomsky reminds us,

> In today's world, I think, the goals of a committed anarchist should be to defend some state institutions from the attack against them, while trying at the same time to pry them open to more meaningful public participation – and ultimately, to dismantle them in a much more free society, if the appropriate circumstances can be achieved. (Chomsky, 1996, p. 75)

It is important to note, though, that in the same way as worries about the excesses of neo-liberalism and capitalism should not lead political theorists concerned with social justice into blindly defending state education, nor should anarchists assume that all 'free schools' are necessarily better than those provided by the state. The anarchist commitment to prefigurative practice goes hand in hand with the insight of contemporary anarchists that 'resistance to all forms of domination in society moves its notions of social transformation beyond their previous formulation as the abolition of institutions to the redefinition of social patterns in all spheres of life, institutional or otherwise' (Gordon, 2009, p. 263), thus making sense of the fact that many anarchist educators work within the state system (see Haworth, 2012). But equally importantly, one has to pay careful attention to the political context in which possibilities for 'freeing' education from the state are being proposed.

Buber's reference to 'the political surplus' of the state over society and the suggestion that we need to recover a richer notion of the social are reminiscent of Nikolas Rose's account of how, in neoliberal discourse, 'the unified space of the social is re-configured, and the abjected are relocated, in both imagination and strategy, in "marginalized spaces" [/...]' (Rose, 1996, p. 347). I have argued that an anarchist perspective demands that we reclaim and enact a multiplicity and plurality of spaces for 'the social', redefining – and possibly reclaiming – in doing so, the very notion of the social and associated notions like community. How, where and to what extent this can be done in the current political climate is an open question. Certainly the current UK Coalition government's policy on free schools and academies is very far removed from any truly social, grass-roots initiatives, and seems rather more like what Rose has described as another form of politically centralized and hegemonic control by the state of spaces once thought of as 'social'. The individuals within such spaces and their very configuration are also, of course, subject to what Rose calls 'government by audit' (Rose, 1996, p. 351) – in this case, educational forms of audit such as standardized testing and inspection regimes – which 'hold out the promise – however specious – of new distantiated forms of control between political centres of decision and the autonomized loci – schools, hospitals, firms, – who now have the responsibility for the government of health, wealth and happiness' (Rose, 1996).

Most 'free schools' in Britain today are indeed very different from the original free schools of the sixties and seventies, as Charkin (2011) reminds us. But nor should we be under the illusion that there was a golden age of 'free schools' in which such projects were immune to the kinds of entrenched privileges and social hierarchies which contemporary critics warn of. Jonathan Kozol, a leading member of the 1970s free school movement, talked scathingly, as early as 1972, of people who go out 'into the mountains of Vermont' to start 'an isolated upper-class rural free school for the children of the white and rich' while still profiting from the consequences of the deeply unequal and racialized power relations that characterize US society (Kozol, 1972, pp. 5–12). Free schools, he says, 'cannot with sanity, or with candor or with truth, endeavor to exist within a moral vacuum' (Kozol, 1972, p. 10). Yet this is not to say that there were not then, or now, and that one cannot imagine, genuinely free schools that engage with these issues of power, through a form of prefigurative practice, while at the same time perhaps exhibiting the 'virtues of teaching and learning' that philosophers such as Hogan have described. Indeed the history of radical educational experiments is full of examples of such schools (see Avrich, 2006, Gribble, 1998, Shotton, 1993, Smith, 1983). We should not, then, reject all free-schools outright simply because they do not fit in with a theoretical model of Rawlsian liberalism.

In defending Ward's particular brand of anarchism against Bookchin's claim about the 'unbridgeable chasm' between 'life-style anarchism' and 'social anarchism', Stuart White reminds us that a 'good deal of Ward's work is less concerned with mapping the possible future than with celebrating what people can and do experience here and now' (White, 2011, p. 98). Perhaps philosophers of education, as part of the project to reclaim and articulate a truly critical position, should do a bit less mapping and a bit more celebrating. It may be difficult and sometimes frustrating trying to negotiate the tensions described by Chomsky, but acknowledging them will make our discipline both more lively and more politically engaged than pretending that we have resolved them. 'There is a certain kind of revolutionary courage', Kozol insists (1972, p. 72) 'in fighting for a new world and still helping men [sic] to live without ordeal in the one that they are stuck with'. I am not so arrogant (or deluded) as to presume that being a salaried academic philosopher requires this kind of courage; but surely it is part of our role as philosophers to explore and articulate different conceptual and practical possibilities from the ones dominating our political and academic discourse. By such philosophical work, alongside a commitment to genuine educational experimentation, we can multiply 'the political and also the social and imaginary ties people are subjected to' (Bottici, 2013, p. 18) and thereby engage in a kind of utopianism of the present. For

> utopianism is above all about the present [...] The most utopian of utopianisms is also the most practical one. [...] It does not propose any 'metaphysics of presence' that posits an unmediated essential reality that somehow reveals to us its full being. Rather it is a radical empiricism of presence that allows what is present to present itself, to give itself as a miraculous gift. (Clark, 2009, p. 20)

My concern is that in our anxiety to shield education from the worst excesses of the language, logic and oppressive practices of managerialism, instrumental rationality, or free-market capitalism, we will forget that it is not just our education system, but our society that needs changing. And it is just possible that such change may come about not through a moment of revolutionary rupture, or through a scientifically worked-out programme of reform, but by allowing educational spaces to become sites for prefigurative practice. The task for philosophers of education, then, is to imagine what such spaces might look like; to articulate the values and ideas that they embody; to celebrate and engage with them, and to defend their possibility, while ever vigilant of their dangers.

Notes

1   In fact the anarchist position described here may have affinities with the kind of Emersonian perfectionism which Standish, drawing on Cavell, discusses in his work and contrasts with 'ideas of the realisable perfectibility of human kind' (Blake et al., 2000, p. 153).

References

Avrich, P. (2006) *The Modern School Movement; Anarchism and Education in the United States*. Oakland, CA: AK Press.

Bargu, B. (2013) 'The politics of commensality', in Blumenfeld, J., Bottici, C. and Critchley, S. (eds), *The Anarchist Turn*. London: Pluto Press.

Bauman, Z. (1976) *Socialism: The Active Utopia*. New York, NY: Holmes and Meier.

Blake, N., Smeyers, P., Smith, R. and Standish, P. (2000) (eds), *Education in an Age of Nihilism*. Abingdon: Routledge.

Blake, N., Smeyers, P., Smith, R. and Standish, P. (1998) (eds), *Thinking Again: Education After Postmodernism*. Westport, CT: Bergin & Garvey.

Bottici, C. (2013) 'Black and red: The freedom of equals', in Blumenfeld, J., Bottici, C. and Critchley, S. (eds), *The Anarchist Turn*. London: Pluto Press.

Bridges, D. (2008) 'Educationalization: On the appropriateness of asking educational institutions to solve social and economic problems', *Educational Theory* 58(4): 461–474.

Brighouse, H. (2006) *On Education*. Abingdon: Routledge.

——— (2010) 'Educational equality and school reform', in Haydon, G. (ed.), *Educational Equality*. London: Continuum, pp. 15–69.

——— (2003) *School Choice and Social Justice*. Oxford: Oxfrod University Press.

Callan, E. (1997) *Creating Citizens: Political Education and Liberal Democracy*. Oxford: Clarendon Press.

Carr, W. (2005) 'Philosophy and Education' in Carr, W. (ed.), *The RoutledgeFalmer Reader in Philosophy of Education*. Abingdon: Routledge, pp. 145–160.

Charkin, E. (2011) 'For a real free school look to postwar Pekham', *The Guardian*, Comment is Free,http://www.guardian.co.uk/commentisfree/2011/aug/30/free-school-peckham-education [accessed 30 August 2013].

Chomsky, N. (1996) *Powers and Prospects: Reflections on Human Nature and the Social Order*. Boston, MA: South End Press.

Clark, J.P. (2009) 'Anarchy and the dialectic of Utopia', in Davis, L. and Kinna, R. (eds), *Anarchism and Utopianism*. Manchester: Manchester University Press, pp. 9–29.

Davis, L. (2009) 'Introduction', in Davis, L. and Kinna, R. (eds), *Anarchism and Utopianism*. Manchester: Manchester University Press, pp. 1–5.

Dunne, J. (2005) 'What's the good of education?' in Carr, W. (ed.), *The RoutledgeFalmer Reader in Philosophy of Education*. Abingdon: Routledge, pp. 145–160.

Fielding, M. and Moss, P. (2011) *Radical Education and The Common School; A Democratic Alternative*. Abingdon: Routledge.

Goodwin, B. and Taylor, K. (1982) *The Politics of Utopia: A Study in Theory and Practice*. London: Hutchinson.

Gordon, U. (2009) 'Utopia in contemporary anarchism', in Davis, L. and Kinna, R. (eds), *The Politics of Utopia: A Study in Theory and Practice*. London: Hutchinson pp. 260–275.

Gribble, D. (1998) *Real Education; Varieties of Freedom*. Bristol: Libertarian Education.

Haworth, R.H. (2012) (ed.), *Anarchist Pedagogies: Collective Actions, Theories, and Critical Reflections on Education*. Oakland, CA: PM Press.

Hogan, P. (2009) *The New Significance of Learning: Imagination's Heartwork*. London: Routledge.

——— (2010) 'Preface to an ethics of education as a practice in its own right', *Ethics and Education* 5(2): 85–98.

——— (2011) 'The ethical orientations of education as a practice in its own right', *Ethics and Education* 6(1): 27–40.

Hogan, P. and Smith, R. (2003) 'The activity of philosophy and the practice of education', in Blake, N., Smeyers, P., Smith, R. and Standish, P. (eds), *The Blackwell Guide to the Philosophy of Education*. Oxford: Blackwell, pp. 165–180.

Honeywell, C. (2011) *A British Anarchist Tradition: Herbert Read, Alex Comfort and Colin Ward*. New York, NY: Continuum.

Johnson, R. (1987) ' "Really Useful Knowledge": Radical Education and Working Class Culture, 1790–1848', in Clarke, J., Critcher, C. and Johnson, Richard (eds), *Working Class Culture: Studies in History and Theory*. London: Century Hutchinson Ltd., pp. 75–102.

Kozol, J. (1972) *Free Schools*. Boston, MA: Houghton Mifflin Company.

Levinson, M. (1999) *The Demands of Liberal Education*. Oxford: Oxford University Press.

Morland, D. (1997) *Demanding the Impossible? Human Nature and Politics in Nineteenth Century Social Anarchism*. London: Cassell.

Morris, B. (2004) *Kropotkin: The Politics of Community*. Amherst, MA: Humanity Books.

——— (2005) *Anthropology and Anarchy: Their Elective Affinity*. London: Goldsmiths Anthropology Research Papers.

——— (2009) 'Kropotkin and the post-structuralist critique of anarchism', *Social Anarchism* 44: 5–21.

Newman, S. (2009) 'Anarchism, utopianism and the politics of emancipation' in Davis, L. and Kinna, R. (eds), *Anarchism and Utopianism*. London: Goldsmiths Anthropology Research Papers.

Reiss, M. and White, J. (2013) *An Aims-Based Curriculum; The Significance of Human Flourishing for Schools*. London: Institute of Education Press.

Rose, J. (2010) *The Intellectual Life of the British Working Classes*. New Haven, CT: Yale University Press.

—— (1996) 'The death of the social? Refiguring the territory of government', *Economy and Society* 25(3): 327–356.

Ryan, A. (1998) *Liberal Anxieties and Liberal Education*. New York, NY: Hill and Wang.

Sarangapani, P. M. and Winch, C. (2010) 'Tooley, Dixon and Gomathi on private education in Hyderabad: A reply', *Oxford Review of Education* 36(4): 499–515.

Shotton, J. (1993) *No Master High or Low; Libertarian Education and Schooling in Britain, 1890–1990*. Bristol: Libertarian Education.

Smith, M. (1983) *The Libertarians and Education*. London: George Allen and Unwin.

Smith, R. (2002) 'Sustainable learning', *The Trumpeter* 18(1).

Standish, P. (1995) 'Postmodernism and the education of the whole person', *Journal of Philosophy of Education* 29(1): 121–135.

—— (1999) 'Education without aims?' in R. Marples (ed.), *The Aims of Education*. London: Routledge, pp. 35–49.

—— (2007) 'Rival conceptions of the philosophy of education', *Ethics and Education* 2(2): 159–171.

—— (2012) *"Imputend practices"*, Paper presented at the Philosophy of Education Society of Great Britian annual conference, New college, Oxford.

Suissa, J. (2006) *Anarchism and Education*. London: Routledge.

Sylvan, R. (1993) 'Anarchism', in R.E. Goodin and P. Pettit (eds), *A Companion to Contemporary Political Philosophy*. Oxford: Blackwell.

Tooley, J. (1996) *Education Without the State*. London: Institute of Economic Affairs.

—— (2000) *Reclaiming Education*. London: Cassell.

Ward, C. (1973) *Anarchy in Action*. London: Allen & Unwin.

—— (1991) *Influences; Voices of Creative Dissent*. Bideford: Green Books.

White, J. (1990) *Education and the Good Life: Beyond the National Curriculum*. London: Kogan Page.

—— (2010) 'Elusive rivalry? Conceptions of the philosophy of education', *Ethics and Education* 5(2): 135–145.

—— (2011) *Exploring Well-Being in Schools*. Abgindon: Oxford.

—— (2011) 'Social anarchism, lifestyle anarchism, and the anarchism of Colin Ward', *Anarchist Studies* 19(2): 92–104.

Wilbert, C. and White, D. (eds), (2011) *Autonomy, Solidarity, Possibility; The Colin Ward Reader*, Oakland, CA: AK Press.

Winch, C. (2000) *Education, Work and Social Capital: Towards a New Conception of Vocational Education*. London: Routledge.

—— (2005) *Education, Autonomy and Critical Thinking*. London: Routledge.

Part Three

Religion

10

Buber, Religion and Inclusion

Alexandre Guilherme

Martin Buber (1878–1965), the well-known Jewish philosopher and theologian, is considered to be one of the greatest thinkers on education of the twentieth century. He was born in Vienna to an Orthodox Jewish family and spent most of his early life with his grandfather, who was a prominent scholar of *Midrash* (Rabbinic *dialogue* with the Torah, the Old Testament), in Lvov, the capital city of Galicia (today's Ukraine). He was awarded a doctorate by the University of Vienna in 1904, for a thesis on Christian mysticism during the Renaissance and Reformation, and worked at the University of Frankfurt until 1933 (he resigned from his position when the Nazis came to power and all Jews were excluded from the educational system). He was also part of the original committee that sought to set up the Hebrew University of Jerusalem and was involved very early on with the Zionist movement, continuously advocating dialogue with the Arabs in Palestine and proposing the foundation of a bi-national state, where both communities would share power once the British Mandate ended in Palestine.

Buber wrote his major work, *I and Thou (Ich und Du)*, between 1919 and 1922, and published it in 1923. It is a major philosophical-theological work that deals with the most profound issues of what it is to be human and of human relations. Buber's views as presented in this text have served as the basis for his views on education, something he developed further in texts such as *Education* (also known as *An Address to the Third International Educational Conference*, which was delivered at Heidelberg in 1925) and *The Education of Character* (also known as *An Address to the National Conference of Palestinian Teachers*, which was delivered at Tel Aviv on 1939); that said, it is also important to note that Buber's views in *I and Thou* have been applied by others to various fields, such as environmental ethics (cf. Friskics, 2001, Tallmadge, 1981).

This chapter is divided into two distinct parts. First, it provides the reader with a standard philosophical reading of Buber's concepts of *I-Thou* and *I-It* and revisits these concepts under the light of the Hasidic roots of Buber's thought while demonstrating the connections of these readings to the field of education. Second, this chapter will argue that the main implication of Buber's views for education is that 'education is inclusive per se' and that 'educational systems must be as inclusive as possible'.

Philosophical reading

When one peruses the secondary literature on Buber's views on *I and Thou*, a philosophical reading soon comes to the fore. This reading of Buber's views is founded on the premise that Buber was critical of Western philosophy and searched for that which he called a 'philosophical anthropology'. There is much supporting evidence for this reading as Buber himself referred to 'his own "philosophizing" as "essentially anthropological"' (Schillp (1967, p. 693) cited in Murphy (1988, p. 41)). Buber complained that Western philosophy (with the exceptions of the pre-Socratic Greek philosophers, Saint Augustine, Pascal and existentialist philosophers) failed to formulate and tackle fundamental questions, preferring to focus on particular philosophical problems and becoming increasingly detached from the human being and human experience. For Buber, any philosophical enquiry has to deal with issues such as 'what is the human being?' and 'how does the human being relate to the world?'. Thus, Buber was interested in understanding the human condition and its relation to reality – this is what is fundamental for philosophy, and something that places Buber within the existentialist philosophical school alongside the likes of Kierkegaard and Sartre (cf. Murphy, 1988, pp. 41–63).

According to this reading, in *I and Thou* Buber establishes a typology describing the kinds of human relations into which a human being can enter. For Buber, human beings

i. are relational beings;
ii. are always in a relation with either other human beings, or the world, or God;
iii. possess a two-fold attitude towards other human beings, the world or God, which is indicated by the *basic words* I-It (*Ich-Es*) and I-Thou (*Ich-Du*).[1]

Before considering the *basic words* in detail, it is important to note here that the idea that human beings are relational beings is not particular to Buber and was well established in the German philosophical tradition since Kant's publication of the three *Critiques*, where he argued strongly and convincingly about the importance of the relational aspect of the human being for the solution of epistemological, ethical and aesthetical problems (and this understanding was further developed by the post-Kantian idealists, namely Fichte, Schelling and Hegel); however, Kant's critical philosophy remained too compartmentalized and focused on particular problems to understand the importance of those fundamental questions that are key to a true 'philosophical anthropology'. In 'What is Man?' (1938), Buber (1938; 1961e, p. 135) says:

> Kant was the first to understand the anthropological question critically, in such a way that an answer was given to Pascal's real concern. This answer – though it was not directed metaphysically to the being of man but epistemologically to his attitude to the world – grasped the fundamental problems. What sort of a world is it, which man knows? How can man, as he is, in his altered reality, know at all? How does man stand in the world he knows in this way – what is it to him and what is he to it?

Buber, as a German-speaker, philosopher and theologian, was well versed in the German philosophical tradition and latched onto its relational theme and elaborated on it with great skill while conceiving the *basic words* I-Thou and I-It. The *basic words* are a 'linguistic construct created by Buber as a way of pointing the quality of the experience that this *combination of words* seeks to connote' (Avnon, 1998, p. 39; *my emphasis*), so that I-It and I-Thou are read as 'unities' indicating one's state of Being and attitude towards the *Other*, the *World* and *God*. This means that there is no *I* relating to a *Thou* or to an *It*; rather, what exists is a kind of relation encapsulated by the unification of these words. Avnon (1998, p. 40) comments insightfully that 'one may summarize this point by suggesting that the difference between the I-You and the I-It relation to being is embedded in the hyphen'. The hyphen of I-Thou indicates the kind of relation that is inclusive to the Other, while the hyphen of the I-It points to the sort of relation that is not inclusive to the Other, that in fact separates the Other. As such, these *basic words* are pivotal for a proper understanding of Buber's thought and consequently of his views on education. Let me now explain these *basic words* in further detail.

The I-Thou relation is an encounter of equals who recognize each other as such and it represents an *inclusive* reality between individuals. Buber argues that the I-Thou relation lacks structure and content because infinity and universality are at the basis of the relation. This is so, as when human beings encounter one another through this mode of being, an infinite number of meaningful and dynamic situations may take place in that which Buber calls the 'Between'. Thus, it is important to note that any sort of preconception, expectation or systematization about the Other prevents the I-Thou relation from arising (cf. Olsen, 2004, p. 17, Theunissen, 1984) because they work as a 'veil', a barrier to being *inclusive* towards the Other. Within I-Thou relations, the 'I' is not sensed as enclosed and singular but is present, open to and inclusive towards the Other (cf. Avnon, 1998, p. 39). Despite the fact that it is difficult to characterize this kind of relation, Buber argues that it is real and perceivable, and examples of I-Thou relations in our day-to-day life are those of two lovers, two friends, a teacher and a student.

Contrariwise, in the I-It relation a being confronts another being, objectifies it and in so doing *separates* itself from the *Other*. This is in direct contrast with I-Thou relations because the ' "I" of I-It relations indicates a separation of self from what it encounters' and '[b]y emphasising difference, the "I" of I-It experiences a sensation of apparent singularity – of being alive by virtue of being unique; of being unique by accentuating difference; of being different as a welcome separation from the other present in the situation; of having a psychological distance ("I") that gives rise to a sense of being special in opposition to what is' (Avnon, 1998, p. 39). Thus, when one engages in I-It relations one separates oneself from the Other and gains a sense of being different, special and arguably superior at the same time.

Buber understood that human existence consists of an oscillation between I-Thou and I-It relations and that the I-Thou experiences are rather few and far between. It is also important to emphasize that he rejects any sort of sharp dualism between the I-Thou and I-It relation. That is, for Buber there is always an *inter-play between the* I-Thou and the I-It rather than an *either–or* relation between these foundational concepts. I-Thou relations will always slip into I-It relations because I-Thou relations are too intense and we live in a worldly reality, requiring to use people to fulfil our basic needs; but I-It relations have always the potential of becoming an I-Thou relation, if we remain *on the watch*, open and inclusive of the Other. I draw the reader's attention to the fact that this oscillation is very significant for it is the source of transformation; that is, through every I-Thou encounter, the I is transformed and this affects the I's outlook of the I-It relation and of future I-Thou encounters. Putnam (2008, p. 67) notes that 'the idea is that if one achieves that mode of being in the world, however briefly … then ideally, that mode of being … will *transform* one's life even when one is back in the "It world" '.

Theological reading (or Hassidic reading)

The above reading of Buber's thought is so widespread in the secondary literature that arguably it has now become 'standard'. However, there is also a different reading of Buber's thought based on its Hasidic roots (cf. Avnon, 1998, Friedman, 2002, Weinstein, 1975, Yosef, 1985). The Hasidic influence on Buber's thought is something worth noting because, as Mendes-Flohr (1986, p. 118) notes:

> In Buber's gracefully written and elegantly produced books [Die Geschichten des Rabbi Nachman (1906) and Die Legende des Baal Schem (1908)], the Hasid, for so long an emblem of putatively backward, uncouth Ostjuden, was no longer an object of disdain and ridicule ... Buber disclosed a remarkable spiritual universe of mystical profundity. He rendered Hasidism respectable ... by integrating this distinctive expression of Jewish spirituality into the general discourse and idiom of the fin-de-siècle .... By virtue of Buber's inspired presentation, Hasidism – and the millennial Jewish mystical tradition from whence it emerged – was deemed relevant to the concerns of the educated individual [my brackets].

Hasidism is a popular religious movement within Judaism that emerged in the second half of the eighteenth century in Eastern Europe. During the nineteenth and twentieth centuries it spread to other regions, notably Palestine and the United States. It has a focus on communal life and charismatic leadership as well as on 'ecstasy', 'mass enthusiasm' and close-knit group cohesion (cf. Hasidism, 2007). The founder of this movement was Rabbi Israel ben Eliezer (1700–1760), more commonly known as the Baal Shem Tov (i.e. *Master of the Good Name of God* in Hebrew). Friedman (2002, p. 18) notes that originally he was 'a simple teacher, then later a magic healer', who 'finally gathered about him a group of disciples dedicated to a life of mystic fervour, joy, and love', and '[r]eacting against the tendency of traditional Rabbinism toward strict legalism and arid intellectualism', exalting 'simplicity and devotion above mere scholarship'. For Buber, the Baal Shem Tov was an exemplary figure, who created the conditions for a historical response for the demands of the hour, for the problems faced by the Jewish community at the time, without creating a new religion and a departure from Judaism; moreover, the Baal Shem Tov contrasted with Jesus, whom Buber also considered to be an exemplary individual and whose badly timed and 'premature emergence' caused his followers to break away from Judaism (cf. Avnon, 1998, pp. 102–118).

It is arguable that some of the most important texts on this aspect of Buber's thought are his *Tales of the Hasidim*, where he compiled various Hasidic stories disseminating moral and theological ideas, and his *Hasidism and the Modern Man* and *The Origin and Meaning of Hasidism*, where he characterized the movement and proposed that it led to the popularization of the Kabbalah (i.e. Jewish mysticism); hence, his involvement with Hassidism was quite substantial. It is also noteworthy here that he acknowledges the influence of this movement on his own thought in 'What is Man?', published in Between Man and Man (1947; 1961c). Buber (1938; 1961e, p. 224) says:

> Since 1900 I had first been under the influence of German mysticism from Meister Eckhart to Angelus Silesius, according to which primal ground of Being, the nameless, impersonal Godhead, comes to birth in the human soul; then I had been under the influence of the later Kabbala and of Hasidism, according to which man *has the power to unite the God who is over the world with his shekinah dwelling in the world* [*my emphasis*].

As Buber's own thought was influenced by Hasidism, it is also arguable that it was inspired by Kabbalistic influences, such as Rabbi Isaac Luria's teachings (i.e. Lurianic Kabbalah).[2] One very evident Hasidic and Kabbalistic aspect, which can be identified in the background of Buber's thought, is the incorporation of the idea that shards (i.e. 'sparks') of the divine remain contained in the material world and that *rightful deeds* (i.e. *Tikkun Olam* in Hebrew or 'repair of the world') by the pious will help in releasing this divine energy (cf. Silberstein, 1989, pp. 46–48) – and it is to this aspect that I now turn my attention.

To comprehend the notion from the previously quoted passage that the human being 'has the power to unite God who is over the world with his shekinah dwelling in the world', one must first attain an understanding of the Hasidic conception of creation, which is connected to the Kabbalistic notion of the divine 'shards' or 'sparks'. On commenting on this aspect of Buber's thought, Wodehouse (1945, p. 29) writes:

> The glory of God, said the Chassists, was poured out in the beginning over weak vessels that broke and could not hold it; but every fragment still retains a spark of that divinity, and the Presence of God goes into exile with these sparks, and man co-operates with it to bring them back into manifestation and into reunion with the one Light from which they came.

Hasidism understands that all genuine relations converge into the Eternal, and hence whenever human beings *genuinely* relate to one another, and to other entities, they relate to God – it is this aspect of Hasidism that greatly influenced

Buber. For Buber, allowing I-Thou relations to arise, that is, addressing the Other as a Thou, represents also an encounter with the eternal Thou (i.e. God), and that is why he says, 'In each Thou we address the eternal Thou' (Buber, 2004, p. 14).

This understanding turns I-Thou relations into the key to a religious life and religion, as establishing I-Thou relations in our daily lives brings sanctity to our daily tasks and routine (cf. Silberstein, 1989, p. 210). In *Le Hassidisme et l'homme d'Occident*, Buber (1957, np) acknowledges this point and the great contribution of the Baal Shem Tov, and of Hasidism, when he says:

> Le trait le plus important du Hassidisme est aujourdhui comme autrefois la tendance énergique, et se manifestant aussi bien dans l'existance personelle que dans cella de la communauté, de vaincre de plus en plus la séparation fondamentalle entre le sacré et le profane.[3]

For Buber, every time we allow I-Thou relations to arise in our daily lives, every time we address the Other as a Thou, we cease to be alone because we allow the 'spark' of the Eternal that resides in us to connect with the 'spark' of the Eternal that is in the Other. As such and according to the theological reading of the *basic words*, I-Thou relations do not consist merely in an encounter within an *inclusive* reality between individuals as the philosophical reading would have; rather, I-Thou relations are more than this, gaining a spiritual aspect through the 'uncovering and connecting of the divine sparks'. Hence engaging with the Other through I-It relations means to fail to uncover and connect with the 'divine spark' as well as to engage with the eternal-Thou, and the implications of this for the individual will become clear below.

This 'divine spark' is better characterized by referring to the Hasidic concept of shekhinah (i.e. divine presence). In *Hasidism and the Modern Man*, Buber (1958, p. 37) elaborates on this when he says that 'the sparks which fell down from the primal creation into the covering shells and were transformed into stones, plants, and animals, they all ascend to their source through the consecration of the pious [Hasid means *pious* in Hebrew] who works on them in holiness, uses them in holiness, consumes them in holiness' [my brackets]; and Buber (1958, p. 103) elaborates further by commenting that 'the sparks are to be found everywhere. They are suspended in things as in sealed-off springs; they stoop in the creatures as in walled-up caves, they inhale darkness and they exhale dread; they wait.' The Hasidic movement understands that we are responsible for finding, for drawing forth, for re-connecting with the sparks, and each and every entity must be approached with the intent of uncovering the spark and merging it with our own. However, sometimes the sparks become too hidden from us because of our own ignorance and/or choices and this creates a thick veil that enshrines them; as such our challenge is to escape from our own debilitating conditions and to seek to uncover these sparks (cf. Blenkinsop, 2004, p. 80). This means that as human beings this is part of our being, and consequently an individual who fails to do so, who continually engages with the Other through I-It relations, is an individual who is denying his own essence.

Furthermore, the failure to establish 'a dialogical between' leads one to experience an 'existential guilt', which prompts one to seek 'reconciliation with oneself and with the world'. This is described by Buber in 'A Conversion', a subsection of his *Dialogue*, when he says:

> What happened was no more than that one forenoon, after a morning of 'religious' enthusiasm, I had a visit from an unknown young man, without being there in spirit. I certainly did not fail to let the meeting be friendly, I did not treat him any more remissly than all his contemporaries who were in the habit of seeking me out about this time of the day as an oracle that is ready to listen to reason … Later, I learned that he had come to me not casually, but borne by destiny, not for a chat but for a decision. He had come to me, *he had come in this hour*. What do we expect when we are in despair and yet go to a man? Surely *a presence* by means of which we are told that nevertheless there is meaning. Buber (1929; 1961d, pp. 13–14; my emphasis)

The failure to establish *dialogue* led Buber to feel guilty, and this changed him because he felt the need to remind himself constantly of the importance of *I-Thou* relations, of establishing dialogue, entering into *inclusive* relations, connecting with the 'sparks'. What is important here is that the *I* is not just transformed by every *I-Thou* encounter; it is also transformed by the *I*'s realization that it failed to establish a dialogue with the *Other*, and that it has missed an opportunity to connect the divine shard within it to the spark in the *Other*.

These two readings, the philosophical and the theological, might be seen as complementary to, rather than competing with, each other. This is so because as Avnon (1998, p. 17) notes, 'Buber was a servant of two voices, of two masters. One voice sought to participate in the ordinary discourse – philosophical, literary, political and scholarly – prevailing in his time. That voice was grounded in the texts of the day and addressed contemporary philosophical and political concerns … Yet there was an additional, latent voice in the background.' The latent voice is the Hasidic voice, which was a source of much inspiration to

Buber and represents a sort of hidden dialogue, something concealed under the surface of his writings.

Implications for education: Inclusion

This leads me to the implications of Buber's thought for the field of education. What are these implications? Let me first deal with the philosophical reading of Buber's views for education before turning to the theological interpretation of the *basic words*, I-Thou and I-It.

Buber understands that both *I-Thou* and *I-It* relations play a role in education; however, he argues that *dialogue* should be at its centre. As a consequence of this, he was very critical of both teacher-centred and student-centred approaches to education, which were being practised in Germany in the early part of the twentieth century. In his 'Address on Education' (1925; 1961a), which builds on *I and Thou* (1923), Buber criticizes the teacher-centred approach for it gives too much weight to the role of the teacher, and he understands that this makes it difficult for *I-Thou* relations to arise. Within the teacher-centred approach, the teacher and students become trapped into *I-It* relations, in which the teacher provides students with facts and information; that is, the teacher *funnels* information *into* students and does not encourage their creativity. Buber also criticizes the student-centred approach for focusing too much on the role of the student, and he understands that this approach makes it difficult for *I-Thou* relations to arise as the student lacks proper guidance from the teacher and is left to *pump* his education *out* of his own subjective interests or needs within a given environment.

For Buber, *dialogical* education is one that places appropriate weight on the roles of both teacher and student, drawing in from both I-Thou and I-It relations. The role of the teacher is to set the curriculum, the framework, to provide the value platform for the student, which provides information and starting points for discussion – this is based on I-It relations; but this does not mean that the student's interests, creativity and needs are overlooked as the student develops these within the framework set by the teacher, and through discussions topics and elements of the course are constantly re-evaluated – this is based on I-Thou relations. Such an approach is now established in modern education which might indicate Buber's great influence on its theory and practice (Hilliard, 1973).

Another implication of Buber's defence of *dialogical* education and of his understanding of I-Thou relations and the attitude of *inclusion* implied by it is that the teacher must *accept* whoever presents themselves to him or her; that is, it is a fact that the teacher does not choose who is to be present and educated in his or her classroom. But this form of *inclusion* does not mean that the teacher must accept students as they *are*; rather, ' teacher must accept students as they *can be* and wrestle with them openly and compassionately to enable them to grow in an ethical sense' (Watras, 1986, p. 16). This means that the educator can only educate if able to build a relation based on *inclusion*, on true dialogue with students, which can only come to the fore if the student trusts the educator, if the student feels accepted. Cohen (1979, p. 87) notes that any attempt to impose an authoritative form of education, which restrains the child's expressive and creative faculties, will 'only bring the child to a state of resignation or drive him into rebellion'; this is the kind of education that remains within the realm of *I-It* relations and as such seeks to *separate* teacher from student by placing the teacher in a 'position' based on difference, superiority and uniqueness. Moreover, accepting students as they *can be* also implies that the student 'must take up the challenge of her/his becoming' and this 'not because we have made her/him do so'; that is, the student must take ownership of her/his education and turn towards the relationship and experience the educator has made available to her/him – and this raises challenges to our current practices (Blenkinsop, 2005, p. 293), which are, arguably, based on too much 'scaffolding' and 'spoon feeding'.

But it is not just the teacher–student relation that needs to be *inclusive*, which must fall within *I-Thou* relations, as the student–student relation must also fall within this category. Culturally we learn a great deal from other people who have different interests and experiences from our own. Arnstine (2000, pp. 236–237) notes that 'the inclusiveness criterion for the formation of groups supports multicultural education ... , for it includes ... equally important kinds of human diversity that are very important to the quality of the lives and learning of the young ... heterosexually disposed youth can learn from those who are homosexually inclined. Economically fortunate children can learn from the disadvantaged ... People who are able to learn from those who are disabled.' This demonstrates that it is by recognizing others as invaluable to one's own human development, one also recognizes them as individuals striving to live their humanity fully and truthfully, and this leads one to ascribe a greater meaning and depth to their lives. It is arguable that when students experience this, they become more inclusive of one another as they gain a better understanding of life in community and of humanity itself (cf. Laverty, 2007, p. 130). Thus, through bringing a wide range of students from the most varied backgrounds and walks of life together, as in most universities, and allowing them to learn from each other and to share experiences, it is possible to encourage *I-Thou* relations to arise, and *inclusive* attitudes to take hold, even if this takes time and commitment from all participants (Morgan and Guilherme, 2014, pp. 91–104). Noddings (1994, p. 116) comments on this point: 'Insistence on respect and loving regard leaves us open to influence; we are pledged to learning and exploring together … this is preparation for a moral life of openness, friendliness, trust and caring. It is preparation that takes time.'[4] It can be argued that the more *inclusive* education is, the more it will promote the positive aspects of the human being and of community (e.g. understanding of oneself and of the Other; pursuing a peaceful co-existence). Thus, I would suggest that education at all levels (i.e. formal, non-formal or informal), for both children and adults, should embrace *inclusion* as much as possible if these positive aspects are to take hold and flourish.

The danger of not pursuing *inclusion* in education becomes obvious when we consider that it is only through I-Thou relations (i.e. inclusion) that we are able to 'put a face' to the *Other* and recognize 'the validity of another person's views' (cf. Watras, 1986, p. 15), and in doing so the potential for objectifying the *Other* dissipates. It is arguable that this puts a stop to, or it at least hinders, the objectification of the *Other*, which makes it difficult for prejudices, preconceptions and racism to take a grip. In turn, this prevents the potential for conflict between individuals and communities to arise, and when conflict is already in place it provides individuals and communities with a chance to resolve it. This is an extremely important implication of Buber's philosophy given the potential positive implications for human society.

Through my discussion thus far, it becomes quite evident that *dialogical* education, based on inclusion as conceived by Buber, is always the education of *character*. In fact, in his 'Education of Character', Buber (1939; 1961b, p. 146) expresses education as

> a step beyond all the dividedness of individualism and collectivism … genuine education of character is genuine education for community … he who knows inner unity, the inner most life of which is mystery, learns to honour the mystery in all its forms.

Buber was aware of the implications of his thought for social and political development (as well as for spiritual well-being, which will be discussed later). The previously mentioned *inclusive* attitude between teacher–student and student–student is the keystone of what Buber calls a *dialogical community*. Guilherme and Morgan (2009, pp. 570–571) argue that such a *dialogical* community is for Buber *a third way* between absolute individualism (*I* without

Thous) and collectivism (*Thous* without an *I*). This is so because in such a community individuals hold an *inclusive* attitude towards the Other, while constantly engaging creatively and critically with the Other. Buber believed that this improves the quality of life for each of the members of the community, as well as encourages the continuation of the community as it increases social cohesion, sustains cultural creativity and dissipates the potential for conflict.

This shows that Buber was concerned about the need to differentiate between *dialogical* education and propaganda and indoctrination. The propagandist and the indoctrinator impose opinion and attitudes on *Others*; the educator, to the contrary, nourishes the *Other's* mind and recognizes it as unique and autonomous. I quote:

> [education is] a true, deep and persistent influence...teaching is not propaganda and must not be allowed to become such. What is needed is instruction, expression of feeling and thought, expression which is forthright and consequential, spontaneous and untendentious. What is needed is critical and responsible knowledge and articulation thereof, and nothing else. One who seeks to gain influence through an act which is *in lieu* of responsible articulation of critical knowledge, corrupts not only the act and his soul, but will fail to achieve what he sought, even though what he will achieve will bear resemblance to what he sought to achieve. I have said 'truth' and I say it again: by truth I mean human truth, truth given to human beings and this truth is based on emancipation from the matrix called tendentiousness.[5]

Friedman (2002, p. 213) and Blenkinsop (2004, p. 86) conclude that the propagandist is concerned not with the *Other's* development per se but only in exploiting the *Other* so as to fulfil and to expand the propagandist agenda; the educator, to the contrary, recognizes students as individuals with unique existential needs and tasks. The propagandist has no respect for pupils; the educator does. The propagandist always works within the *I-It* framework and as such holds an attitude of *separation* towards students, and encourages the *separation* of *Others* by them in turn, which invariably leads to conflict and to commit evil acts. The educator has always *I-Thou* relations in his mind and, in so doing, encourages an attitude of acceptance and of the *inclusion* of the *Other*, which advances ethical attitudes, defusing conflict between individuals and communities. Hence, *dialogical* education 'aims to develop certain propensities in the student: it aims particularly to promote a responsible exercise of freedom and the continuing authentication of all intentions and deeds in the moment of their occurrence' (Murphy, 1988, p. 146), and I would add that this has to be done in an ethical manner.

The above seems to be the direct consequence of the philosophical reading of Buber's views, and thus it is fair to ask here: What are the implications of the theological reading for education?

For Buber, the *zaddik* and *hasid*, rabbi and follower in a Hasidic community, are a pivotal example of teacher–student and student–student relationship. Boff (2009, p. 39) states that 'the Hasid is the person who lives intensely the duty to love God, who cultivates a great intimacy with him, who is sensitive to his intentions, which are expressed by the law as a living manifestation of his will. The pious person completely inserts himself or herself in the spiritual tradition of the people through a religious practice within the family, through taking part in the holy festivals, and through the weekly attendance of the synagogue'; the *hasid* (i.e. *pious* in Hebrew) becomes a *zaddic* (i.e. *just* in Hebrew) when he 'becomes a beacon of the community, educates the younger ones by example, conquers through acting righteously, and garners the trust of the rest of the community and thus becomes a reference for the collectivity'.[6]

Avnon (1998, p. 165) commented on this aspect of Buber's philosophy by noting:

> The dialogue between the *zaddik* and the Hasid, sealed by the common aspiration to realize higher levels of being, grants Buber's image of the *zaddik* an intrinsically *social* dimension. The dialogue among the members of the community is dialectically intertwined with the individual member's dialogue with Elohim. To unveil the deeper self, to come closer to one's being, one needs to enter into meaningful, purposeful, human relationships. To be capable of entering such human relationships, one needs an affinity to the greater reality represented by the idea of God. By serving as a living example of the way to conduct reciprocal relationships in the various circles of the community, Buber's *zaddik* exemplifies the paradigmatic conduct of one at the center of a community of persons committed to the fulfilment of this human need [i.e. *Hasids*].

This strong and profound connection between the *zaddik* and the *hasid* is established through *inclusive* relations, I-Thou relations (cf. Yosef, 1985, pp. 20–25), which is something discussed by Buber in the *Tales of the Hasidism*, where he says that 'one of the principles of Hasidism is that the Zaddik and the people are dependent on one another ... The *teacher* helps his disciples find themselves, and in hours of desolation the *disciples* help their teacher find himself again' (Buber, 1975, p. 8; my emphasis). The dynamic flow from teacher to student, from student to teacher, and between students is telling and demonstrates the level of *inclusiveness* incorporated by Hasidic communities, and why Buber saw them as prime examples for *dialogical* education and communities. It could be contended here that such levels of inclusion are not always easy to achieve; and this is perhaps true specially given the current framework of educational systems and the 'learnification' that has been implemented (cf. Biesta 2013), which focus on 'achievements' and considers 'relations' a desirable non-essential by-product. Despite this, teacher and students should strive for *inclusion* if 'education worthy of the name' (Buber 1947, p. 132) is to be achieved.

It is interesting to note here that in the Hebrew language the verb to teach *Lelamed* (ללמד) and to learn *Lilemod* (ללמוד) share the same root (*shoresh*), the letters *LMD* (למד), which are the basis for the conjugation of these verbs in all tenses, demonstrating a closeness in the understanding of 'what it is to teach' and 'what it is to learn'. Hence, the basic idea behind these verbs was closely inter-related in the mindset of ancient Hebrew speakers, and arguably in that of modern Hebrew speakers also. The aforementioned inter-dependent relation between the *zaddik* and the *hasid*, teacher and student, seems to mirror the idea of closeness portrayed by these two Hebrew verbs; this means that teaching-and-learning is not something unidirection happening only from teacher to student, but bidirectional happening also from student to teacher. The teacher also learns from the student; the act of teaching creates *feedback loops* from students that need to be considered and addressed by the teacher.

A direct consequence of the theological reading of Buber's views is that the teacher should not only provide students with information about reality and encourage in them critical thinking but should also encourage them to *perfect the world*; that is, the teacher provides students with the insight that their deeds exist in the world, but that the world also exists in their deeds (cf. Gordon, 1978, pp. 88–89). This is so because students must become aware of the idea that human beings must 'seek and connect with the divine shards or sparks', and failing to do so somehow diminishes us as humans (whether this is done overtly or not is a different question that cannot be answered here for matters of space). This gives education a spiritual tinge that is often overlooked by educators, and which, arguably, turns it into a more meaningful experience to both teachers and students. The idea of 'perfecting the world' is extremely important in Judaism and it is conveyed by the concept *tikkun olam* (literally, 'world repair'), which stands for the physical, social and spiritual improvement of the world. In Jewish circles it is now associated with actions such as charity (*tzedakah*) and kindness (*gemilut hasadim*) and other programmes connected with social issues; it can also be associated with the *Kabbalah* due to its connection with the 'shards' or 'sparks' of the divine, assuming a mystical meaning. Buber was certainly aware of it as it is a key concept in Judaism.

Final thoughts

The philosophical reading of Buber's thought when connected to education provides us with a strong argument in favour of different levels and kinds of *inclusion*. The theological reading further enriches this by providing a spiritual dimension to both *inclusion* and education. Moreover, Buber's understanding that the the *zaddik* and *hasid* relation 'could serve as an example of the dialogue principle in education' because 'the three components of this dialogue – contact, trust and envelopment [i.e. inclusion] are present in Hassidism' (my brackets) and because 'the Zaddik and his followers live together and he teaches them, through his entire being, as a living example' (Yosef, 1985, p. 24) was not defended just in theory but also in practice.

At first glance, and because of the strong focus of Buber's views on the importance of dialogical relationships for education, it might appears that he is asking educators to give up the idea that education is about certain pre-established suppositions about the human being, about how we learn, what makes us happy, which currently work as a compass for educational systems. However, I believe that this is not the case. Buber seems to demonstrate that if educators understand themselves to be more than mere agents of socialisation, then they must understand the crucial importance of relationships and of the encounter with the Other. [7] This does not mean that they are empty hands because Buber put this into practice both in Germany, when the Nazis came to power in 1933 when the Jewish community found itself excluded from the state educational system, and also in Israel, after the War of Independence (1948) in 1949 when the newly found state had to cope with the influx of immigrants who had survived the terrors of the Nazi Concentration and Extermination Camps along with those fleeing pogroms in Arab countries (cf. Morgan and Guilherme, 2014, pp. 71–90). In both occasions Buber set up important and innovative educational ventures, defending the role of education as a fundamental aspect for the formation and renewal of *community*. He encouraged teachers to live with their students and to pursue a pedagogical approach largely based on the study of texts through reading and critical discussions – it was expected that this would give rise to a *community* and ultimately encourage individuals to live in and form *communities*. Hence, these educational ventures and pedagogical approaches were fundamentally founded on the *inclusion* of the Other – the very cornerstone of *community formation* – as well as on connecting with the ultimate Other, the eternal Thou.

Notes

1   It is important to draw attention to the German word *Du*, which is present in the original German title as well as in the foundational concept *Ich-Du*. Walter Kauffman in his important and modern translation of the work points out that *Du* is the German personal pronoun one uses to address friends or family, people with whom one has a close relationship. *Du* is the informal personal pronoun and this is in contrast with *Sie* which is the personal pronoun used to address people one is not familiar with or that one does not have a close relationship or that is used as a sign of respect (e.g. to elders). This distinction is present in many languages (e.g. French: Tu and Vous); however, it has been lost in English. The English archaic personal *Thou*, which was the equivalent of *Du*, has lost its informal connotation in modern times, and as such it does not capture the idea of informality present in Buber's text. Perhaps, *Du* is better translated in English as *you*, which is something Kauffman actually does in his translation – he only kept the original *Thou* of the title (cf. Buber, 1972). That said, I have opted to keep *Thou* throughout the text so to follow the conventional terminology of the secondary literature.

2   Rabbi Isaac Luria (1534–1472), commonly known as Ha'Ari (the Lion), was born in Jerusalem and is considered a major figure of modern Kabbalah, and in the establishment of the Kabbalistic School of Safed (i.e. Safed is a town in Northern Israel).

3   This manuscript was found in the Buber Archives, Jewish National and University Library, Hebrew University of Jerusalem. Its archival number is ARC. MS. VAR. 350.04.23a and it was originally published as 'Le Hassidisme et l'homme d'Occident', in *Melanges de Philosophie et de Literature*, Paris: PUF, 1957.

4   Veck (2013) provides an interesting discussion focusing on Buber's thought and the issue of Special Educational Needs (SEN). He argues that Buber's conception of *inclusion* is a valuable corrective to the technical approach thus far taken by special education policy and theory, which turns relationships between educators and the young into a demarcated area characterized by pre-established and categorized needs. Veck (2013: 627) concluded that 'if such acts [i.e. acts of inclusion] were to inform our understanding of relationships in education, then our vision for an education and society that is inclusive might diverge from a distant terrain, accessible only through the exercising of specialist skill and technical mastery, and return us to "the Kingdom that is hidden in our midst, there between us" (Buber, 2004, p. 90)' [*my brackets*].

5   Letter from Martin Buber to Fischel Schneersohn, 31 March 1943, cited by Porat (1986, pp. 113–114).

6   In *Meetings*, Buber (1969, p. 39) wrote of the relation of the *zaddic* and the *hasid* while reflecting on his childhood experiences by saying: "I could compare on the one side with the head man of the province whose power rested on nothing but habitual compulsion; on the other with the rabbi, who was an honest and God-fearing man, but an employee of the 'directorship of the cult'. Here, however, was another, an incomparable; here was, debased yet uninjured, the living double kernel of humanity: genuine *community* and genuine *leadership*. The place of the *rebbe*, in its showy splendor, repelled me. The prayer house of the Hasidim with its enraptured worshippers seemed strange to me. But when I saw the *rebbe* striding through the rows of the waiting, I felt, 'leader', and when I saw the Hasidim dance with the Torah, I felt 'community'. At the time there rose in me a presentiment of the fact that common reverence and common joy of soul are the foundation of genuine human community."

7   Biesta (2008) makes this same point with respect to Levinas.

References

Arnstine, D. (2000) 'Ethics, learning and democratic community', *Studies in Philosophy of Education* 19: 229–240.

Avnon, D. (1998) *Martin Buber: The Hidden Dialogue*. Lanham, MD: Rowman and Littlefield Publishers.

Biesta, GJJ. (2008) "Pedagogy with Empty Hands: Levinas, Education, and the Question of Being Human", Levinas and Education: At the Intersection of Faith and Reason. Abington, Oxon: Routledge.

—— (2013) "Receiving the Gift of Teaching: From 'Learning From' to 'Being Taught By", *Studies in Philosophy and Education* 32, 449–461.

Blenkinsop, S. (2004) 'Martin Buber's 'Education': Imitating God, the Developmental Rationalist', *Philosophy of Education Yearbook* 79–87.

—— (2005) 'Martin Buber: Educating for Relationship', *Ethics, Place and Environment: A Journal of Philosophy and Geography* 8(3): 285–307.

Boff, L. (2009) *Saint Joseph: Father of Jesus in a Fatherless Society*. Eugene, OR: Wipf and Stock.

Buber, M. (1925, 1961a) 'The Address on Education', in *Between Man and Man*. London: Collins.

—— (1929, 1961d) 'Dialogue', in *Between Man and Man*. London: Collins.

—— (1938, 1961e) 'What is Man?', in *Between Man and Man*. London: Collins.

—— (1939, 1961b) 'The Education of Character', in *Between Man and Man*. London: Collins.

—— (1947, 1961c) 'Between Man and Man', in *Between Man and Man*. London: Collins.

—— (1957) 'Le Hassidisme et l'homme d'Occident', in *Melanges de Philosophie et de Literature*. Paris: PUF. The manuscript number is ARC. MS. VAR. 350.04.23a at the Buber Archives, Jewish National and University Library, Hebrew University of Jerusalem.

—— (1958) *Hasidism and modern men* (Trans Maurice Friedman,). New York: Harber and Row.

—— (1969) *Meetings*. Ed. and Trans. Mendes-Flohr, P., La Salle, IL: Open Court Publishing.

—— (1972) *I and Thou*. Trans. Kauffman, W., New York, NY: Charles Scribner's Sons.

—— (1975) *Tales of the Hasidim: The Early Masters*. New York, NY: Schocken.

—— (1960) *The Origin and Meaning of Hasidism*. New York, NY: Horizon Press.

—— (2004) *I and Thou*. London: Continuum.

Cohen, A. (1979) 'Martin Buber and Changes in Modern Education', *Oxford Review of Education* 5(1): 81–103.

Friedman, M. (2002) *Martin Buber: The Life of Dialogue*. London: Routledge.

Friskics, S. (2001) 'Dialogical Relations with Nature', *Environmental Ethics* 23(4): 391–410.

Gordon, H. (1978) 'An Approach to Martin Bubers Education Writings', *Journal of Jewish Studies* 29(1): 85–97.

Guilherme, A. and Morgan, W. J., (2009) 'Martin Buber's philosophy of education and its implications for non-formal adult education', *International Journal of Lifelong Education* 28(5): 565–581.

Hasidism (2007) in Berenbaum, M. and Skolnik, F. (Eds), *Encyclopaedia Judaica*. Detroit, MI: Macmillan Reference USA, pp. 393–434.

Hilliard, F. H. (1973) 'A Re-examination of Buber's Address on Education', *British Journal of Educational Studies* 21(1): 40–49.

Laverty, M. (2007) 'Dialogue as philosophical enquiry in the teaching of tolerance and sympathy', *Learning Enquiry* 1: 125–132.

Mendes-Flohr, P. (1986) 'Martin Buber's reception among Jews', *Modern Judaism* 6(2): 111–126.

Morgan, W. J. and Guilherme, A. (2014) *Buber and Education: Dialogue and Conflict Resolution*. London: Routledge.

Murphy, D. (1988) *Martin Buber's Philosophy of Education*. Blackrock, Co. Dublin: Irish Academic Press.

Noddings, N. (1993) 'Conversation as moral education', *Journal of Moral Education* 23(2): 107–117.

—— (1994) 'Conversation as moral education', *Journal of Moral Education* 23(2): 107–117.

Porat, D. (1986) 'Martin Buber and Eretz-Israel During the Holocaust Years, 1942-1944', in *Yad Vashem Studies*. XVII, Jerusalem, pp. 93–143.

Putnam, H. (2008) *Jewish Philosophy as a Guide to Life: Rosenzweig, Buber, Levinas, Wittgenstein*. Bloomington, IN: Indiana University Press.

Olsen, G. (2004) 'Dialogue, phenomenology and ethical communication theory', *Proceedings of the Durham-Bergen Postgraduate Philosophy Seminar* II: 13–26.

Schilpp, P. A. (1967) *The Philosophy of Martin Buber*. London: Cambridge University Press.

Silberstein, L. J. (1989) *Martin Buber's Social and Religious thought – Alienation and the Quest for Meaning*. New York and London: New York university Press.

Tallmadge, J. (1981) 'Saying *You* to the Land', *Environmental Ethics* 3(4): 351–363.

Theunissen, M. (1984) *The Other: Studies in the Social Ontology of Husserl, Heidegger, Sartre, and Buber*. Trans. Macann, C., Cambridge, MA: MIT Press.

Veck, W. (2013) 'Martin Buber's concept of inclusion as a critique of special education', *International Journal of Inclusive Education* 17(6): 614–628 (earlyview).

Watras, J. (1986) 'Will Teaching Applied Ethics Improve Schools of Education?', *Journal of Teacher Education* 37(13): 13–16.

Weinstein, J. (1975) *Buber and Humanistic Education*. New York, NY: Philosophical Library.

Wodehouse, H. (1945) Martin Buber's 'I and Thou', *Philosophy* 20(75): 17–30.

Yosef, I. A. B. (1985) *Martin Buber on Adult Education*. Tel-Aviv: Rotem Publishers.

11

A Philosophical Assessment of Spiritual Education

Ruth Wills

In schools within England and Wales, spirituality is required to be evident within all lesson planning and delivery. It should also be recognized within whole school community life (Ofsted, 2013, pp. 15–18). Mirroring the second aim of the National Curriculum which states that schools should 'aim to promote pupil's spiritual, moral, social and cultural development and prepare all pupils for the opportunities, responsibilities and experiences of life' (Qualifications and Curriculum Authority, 1999, p. 11), these four aspects of learning, often referred to together using the initials 'SMSC', have once again come to the fore in recommendations from government and the national standards agency, Ofsted (Office for Standards in Education, Children's Services and Skills). While there is no discrete curriculum area we might call 'spirituality' and existing separately from religious education, it is nevertheless a dimension pervading all aspects of school life that holds some meaning for children and is intrinsic to who they are.

As a nebulous concept, spirituality is not easy to define or measure; indeed, any definition might be perceived as antithetical to the essence of what spirituality might be (Priestley, 1996). Certainly, within literature pertaining to the spirituality of children and young people a range of views are presented (Watson, 2000, pp. 96–99). However, in 2004, guidelines were provided by Ofsted, which summarizes spiritual development as

> the development of the non-material element of a human being which animates and sustains us and, depending on our point of view, either ends or continues in some form when we die. It is about the development of a sense of identity, self-worth, personal insight, meaning and purpose. It is about the development of a pupil's 'spirit'. Some people may call it the development of a pupil's 'soul'; others as the development of 'personality' or 'character'. (Ofsted, 2004, p. 12)

In the absence of a theoretical underpinning, one questions the philosophical starting point for these guidelines. What is clear however is that spirituality is located outside of any exclusively religious domain and is identified as an aspect of being human. While the acceptance of what might be represented as 'religious' in education is under discussion (Watson, 2010, pp. 5–6), issues of knowledge and truth here pertain to children's own beliefs drawn from their personal lives. In the light of this, the Ofsted document promotes teaching methods which, for example, value pupils' questions to provide space for their own thoughts, ideas and concerns; enable pupils to make connections between aspects of their learning; encourage pupils to relate their learning to a wider frame of reference, for example, asking 'why', 'how' and 'where', as well as 'what' (Webster, 2004, p. 14).

This Osfted material is resonant of a debate spanning fifteen years or so, in which Clive Erricker, whose scepticism refuses to acknowledge absolute truth, has sought the liberation of spirituality from religion (2007, pp. 55–56; p. 58), arguing against scholars such as Andrew Wright who believe that without ultimate truth and divine revelation, spiritual education remains rootless (1998, p. 39). This dualistic positing sets the scene for the problematic which this chapter is to address.

Although having no official influence over Ofsted, the values of the global children's spirituality movement established in 2000 (www.childrenspirituality. org) by Erricker are resonant. This movement's belief in human spirituality (de Souza, 2013) and inductive teaching methods inspires an educational paradigm which recognizes the child at the centre of the learning experience (de Souza, 2010, p. 34) and engages in exploration and existential questioning (Webster, 2004, pp. 10–11) in a space designed to allow for enquiry and personal growth (Miller, 2000, pp. 3–4). I have termed this the 'experiential paradigm' based on Adams, Hyde and Woolley's assertion that spiritual education involves reflection on experiences and the meanings gained from them (2008, pp. 38–39). At a time when the frameworks for teaching and assessment are so tight and children are expected to acquire non-negotiable skills and knowledge, the inclusion of an open-ended aspect to learning is timely.

In this chapter I describe further the values of the experiential paradigm before locating these ideas within a Heideggerian framework for a philosophical underpinning. But I also raise points for critique. Although I am a member of this movement, I argue against dualism, highlighting the difficulties of placing of the personal over the universal and the possible over the certain in its epistemology. I propose that humanistic meaning placed in negation to meanings gained from religious traditions is illusory; based on a fear of error it may well be itself an error. Also I believe that as an educational paradigm, it is inadequate in itself.

Observing dualism as the result of negation and separation, I propose that it is a critical conversation with, and not a divorce from, religious traditions that is required for a challenging and life-giving process of education.

Discussion

Advocates of the 'experiential paradigm' consider children as spiritual entities in their own right. A commonly held view is that spirituality is both universal and innate: 'an ontological reality' (Adams et al., 2008, p. 14). It follows that spirituality is part of a child's being, embedded within lived human experience. For example, Hay and Nye argue that spirituality is an 'ever present aspect of being human' (2006, p. 134), and Hyde concurs, stating that 'there is reason to examine spirituality as an ontological reality for human beings' (2008, p. 29). It is also accepted that human beings have the capacity to experience a transcendent dimension within the everyday occurrences of life (Berger, 1969, p. 70; Hay and Nye, 2006, p. 60).

Influential authors in this field are David Hay (2006) and Tobin Hart (2003), who both provide empirical data to propose that as self and spirit are ontologically linked, epistemological authority subsequently lies with children. For Hart, spiritual learning begins with children's experiences from their 'secret spiritual worlds', rather than influenced by anything external (2003, p. 173); for this reason, the objectivity and influence of religious teaching for him is at odds with the development of an authentic self.

This position then is suspicious of any objective reality presented as truth. It is held that knowledge is partial; therefore nothing absolute can be totally known. It is temporary, as understanding gained by children is the truth of 'now'. It is contingent; therefore when perceiving what knowledge and truth mean, context will play a determining role. It is mediated; therefore absolute truth (such as a notion of 'God') cannot be known in a pure form. It is localized; therefore the form and certainty of religious metanarratives are traded for a truth founded on subjective knowledge already located in human consciousness.

While advocates such as Wright have confidence in the truth of their religious (Christian) beliefs and tradition, in this paradigm such assurance is treated with caution. Hay identifies religious knowledge as a culturally constructed illusion (2006, p. 25), while Hart suggests that to manipulate children's meaning-making into that acceptable as the 'truth' of any tradition is to do violence to the children's views themselves (2003, p. 178). This is perceived as an infringement on their rights. This view is most fervently advocated by Erricker and Erricker who place epistemological certainty under the microscope and throw into question the reliability of any reality represented by objective truth and form. They incite error on the part of those attempting to present such truth. Asserting that knowledge is always mediated, they claim it cannot be accepted as true truth (1996, p. 187) and write 'the only authentic criteria against which the truth claims embedded in language should be tested is that of reality itself' (2000, p. 46). They allege that spiritual education based on religious values has a 'deleterious ontological effect' on children (2000, p. 75).

The personalized meaning-making of their pedagogy negates the perceived epistemological hegemony of the dogmas, doctrines and rules of religion and places children at the centre of all enquiry. Free from the proclamation of truth claims or the requirement to accept agreed values and beliefs, it is the children's mode of discovery that motivates each to uncover subjective understandings and insights into their place in this world. They construct their own image of the other one might call 'God', creating meanings based on their own perceptions and located within their own cultural (Erricker and Erricker, 1996, p. 187) or private worlds (Adams, 2010, pp. 123–127).

These meanings in turn influence children's personal values (Hyde, 2010, p. 94). Such values inspire decision-making based on an ethical and moral code which is established from the 'reality' of each individual's life and not in response to contingent influencers. Furthermore, this has an impact on the child's decision-making. Adams et al. (2008, p. 48) suggest that a sense of being acknowledges the authentic self rather than the role played out through expected behaviours. Similarly, Jane Erricker argues that children should be 'given the opportunity to identify and continue to construct and change their own moral stances on existential issues. They should work out for themselves how they should behave and why they should behave in that way' (2000, p. 159).

In a Heideggerian sense these authors resist the child *falling* from his or her authentic self. Being suspicious of socially pre-determined modes of conduct and being, they aim to retain children's ontological validity when making meaning and value judgements to avoid situations where their innate spirituality is contaminated by the seen and unseen authority figures in their lives. The children individually are the beginning and end of their questions of identity and existence. The self is the director of the trajectory of the authentic self and of the values held therein.

A pedagogical path *away* from the epistemological problem veers *towards* methods such as existential questioning. Webster, an advocate of this approach, asserts that meaning-making will have more significance when the individual has made it on his or her own. He does not negate the idea of a transcendent other or deity, but he argues that meanings found in relationship with this phenomenon are a risk when presented objectively. Without any absolute certainty of truth, meaning-making must be true to the authentic self (2004, pp. 15–16).

Other scholars promote affective teaching and learning methods which again place children in the centre and draw on their inner life, senses and emotions. Noting that as the etymology of 'education' is 'to bring forth what is present' (Miller, 2000, p. vii), the teacher is at most a facilitator while the educational objective is to supersede epistemological mastery to assist children in constructing their own worldviews. Through strategies such as 'spiritual questing' (Hyde, 2008, p. 138), children 'gain ownership of their beliefs by self construction rather than imposed dogma' (Erricker and Erricker, 2000, p. 159). The arts, silence, iconography and physicality are all considered conduits for affective spiritual learning, and Miller outlines how visualization, storytelling and creative writing are examples of how a child's inner life might be developed (2000, p. 49; pp. 56–58). He suggests that by bringing 'soul' into the educational process, children can face the big questions of life and help 'bring vitality and a deeper sense of purpose and meaning to classrooms' (2000, pp. 9–10).

Having drawn on a statement regarding spirituality in an influential Ofsted document and acknowledged its resonance with the views of authors within an experiential paradigm, it has been identified that the child is considered both the beginning and end of all spiritual development and that education involves the primacy of an authentic self in learning, value formation and meaning-making. This view is posited against a spiritual education based on religious values or those who teach for certainty. I observe here a correlation with Heidegger's thinking and my reading of literature from the experiential paradigm, through a Heideggerian lens has brought to light similarities regarding the underlying assumptions of both the paradigm and the philosophy. In the next section then I will locate the material presented so far in a philosophical framework, drawing on Heidegger's *potentiality-for-Being* as its foundation.

Heidegger

As I have explored this paradigm, no detailed study has been brought to light which marries themes from Heidegger's philosophy with aspects of experiential spiritual education. Rather, fleeting references are interjected in a handful of articles and texts to reinforce the author's own intentions. For example, Champagne notes Dasein as the spiritual dimension of the child (2003, p. 45) and as an elemental quality disclosed *before* the 'discursive intellect' kicks in (Hay and Nye, 2006, p. 134); therefore, it is antithetical to systematic educational processes (Westermann and Newby, 1996, p. 48). Here I offer a slightly more nuanced philosophical perspective on the themes of spiritual education, mainly in the light of *Being and Time* (1962).

The primacy of the self in spiritual education is key and I suggest that Heidegger speaks to this through his philosophy of Being. Because for him, the Being of an entity is the primordial phenomenon, it *belongs to* that made manifest in appearance (1962, pp. 51–55). Being is essence, that is 'as it is', which is the a priori condition (1962, pp. 32–33) for the possibility of existence. This primordial state of Being, which is Being-in-the-world, is that which my colleagues note as ontological and consequently the platform for truth which is in-itself. But Dasein is more than this. Essence is already included *in* Dasein, which is described as the manner of Being which man possesses in its possibility, or *potentiality-for-Being*. It has a character all of its own and provides the condition for the possibility of all ontologies; thus it is pre-ontological and concerned with the constant advancement of Dasein. In this way, truth *from* Being will not be understood until the truth of the possibility *of* Being is acknowledged. The truth of Being is that in which Dasein has *potentiality-for-Being* thrown into its own possibility of existenz, ahead of itself in care (1962, p. 274).

Dasein is a manner of Being which has Being. It has a relationship with Being such that it understands itself in terms of Being-in-the-world as its basic state and the potentiality of what it might become. As Being, it is an issue for Being (1962, p. 274). Thus, it is both prior to and ahead of itself. Existenz (1962, p. 32) is not Being in its actuality but the designation of Being given to Dasein (1962, p. 67). It is the possibility of the truth of its Being in existence (1978, p. 227). Therefore 'I' as an entity must be recognized as exhibiting phenomenally the kind of Being which Dasein possesses in its possibility and interpreted existentially as the Being of Dasein and not as 'my' true self. It follows that the projected self which is encountered in the world of relation is not any actual representation of Dasein and should not be interpreted as reality. Appearance announces through something that is not itself (1962, p. 51).

Through disclosure however, Dasein is brought to the fore in a clearing of Being. In such a disclosure, clearing breaks down the disguises which prevent Dasein from being its own possibility and sweeps away any concealments (such as mediation or contingency) in order to draw on its pre-ontological way of interpreting Being (1962, p. 167). In this way a child's spiritual talk might be considered the more true representation of what he or she is feeling or has experienced, religiously or otherwise. Heidegger writes:

> [T]he existential analytic of Dasein. ... must seek for one of the most far reaching and most primordial possibilities of disclosure-one that lies in Dasein itself. The way of disclosure in which Dasein brings itself before itself must be such that in it Dasein becomes accessible as simplified in a certain manner. (1962, p. 226)

This dictates that phenomenology and other methods of enquiry are therefore more authentic as that which is seen issues from their own selves (1962, p. 58). The aim of enquiry is to lay bare the horizon for the interpretation of the meaning of Being (1962, p. 36):

> If the interpretation of Dasein's Being is to become primordial as a foundation for working out the basic question of ontology, then it must first have brought to light existentially the Being of Dasein in its possibilities of authenticity and totality.(1962, p. 276)

The self is viewed in its totality: 'in itself'. This is posited as separate from the contingent 'I' which is influenced by mediation within thought consciousness. The cleared Being is immersed in Being, which the child sustains in his or her relation with Dasein in care (1978, p. 225). Enquiry and its interpretation eradicate external influences; instead, Heidegger directs his thinking to the a priori state of Being which is present before thought and leaves it there. Responding to education today, there is no room for facts, information or non-negotiable skills: instead enquiry is about recognizing the potentiality of each child in their Dasein and drawing on this for primal meaning-making. Meaningmaking is that of possibility not actuality, and it is interpreted existentially from the clearing of a Being which is in its essence, as it is.

The existential analytic of Heidegger also asks as to the meaning of the Being of the inquirer (1962, p. 27). The Being of the inquirer in his or her search for meaning is already made *available within* his or her primordial Being. The child then is the beginning and end of all existential searching; that is, Being exists before one comes to an understanding or knowledge of the self as Being. This searching is considered an authentic expression of *potentiality-for-Being*.

This is posited in contrast to the inauthentic self which exists factically and therefore *fallen* from its primordial state of Being (1962, pp. 219–224). As identified earlier, spiritual educators fear inauthenticity and aim to prevent children from falling into such a state. For example, Chickering et al. assert that the gaining of authentic beliefs and values be 'rooted in our prior experiences and conceptions' (2006, p. 10) to evade falling into the error of the contingent biases and assumptions of the institutions or ideologies named by Heidegger as the 'they' (1962, pp. 164–165). Spiritual journeying (Hyde, 2008, p. 129), existential questioning (Webster, 2004, pp. 9–10) and other such methods instead allow children to inquire and search, free from the constraints of universal authority. As pure Dasein will always be in a state of Becoming, aspiring not to the truth of the present but to the truth of the 'not yet' (1962, p. 307), children will continue to be shaped and formed as time and experience direct, directed not by the 'they' or masterful teachers but from their own *potentiality-for-Being*.

Critique

Having focused on the expression of spiritual education which seems to be coming from our government's inspectorate and highlighting the problematic of dualistic positing, I now come to the point where I introduce speculative philosophy into the discussion. My task is to critique this problematic before exploring a solution. Although Heidegger's *Being and Time* announced the end of the tradition of systematic philosophy and whilst being the system Heidegger sought to overturn, Hegel's philosophy does speak to the current discussion. As Gillian Rose states that her essay *Hegel Contra Sociology* 'attempts to retrieve Hegelian speculative experience for social theory' (1981, p. 1), I will also undertake my critique of the experiential paradigm through a Hegelian lens drawing on Rose and Nigel Tubbs's commentaries as well as the primary sources.

The first aspect concerns liberation. In Hegel's illustration, natural consciousness (or the universal) is described as a master from whom his slave seeks to become free (1977, p. 123). Recognizing his dependence on the master for his identity and truth, and as its negativity, the slave views this truth as an illusion and eschews any relationship with it. In a life-and-death struggle for the recognition of his own self-consciousness, he supersedes his master so that he might understand himself in his totality (1977, p. 123). He strives to become an independent consciousness. The slave might be represented by Erricker et al. whose evasion of objective truth claims seeks to gain a personal spiritual identity and ascertain the validity of their own position.

However, by attempting liberation, the slave's positing actually prevents him from becoming known as self-consciousness in its totality. Freedom is also illusory. Tubbs writes, 'it is an illusion to be natural or in-itself' (2000, p. 57).

Hegel maintains that the master/slave relationship is actually intersubjective, which means that each only exists in his association *with* the other. The truth of the natural consciousness comes in his dependence on the slave. He needs the negativity of himself in order to establish his position. Equally, the slave without the master, although pursuing (in Heidgeggerian terms) possibility and authenticity, is free to become whoever he chooses in his own identity. But without the overarching framework of truth provided by the master, his liberation may well lead to his own demise. Rose writes, 'freedom cannot be conceived if opposed to necessity – this is the illusion of freedom to the relations or lack of identity which it reveals' (1981, p. 57).

Or it might follow that the slave in his freed state also becomes a master. The truth of the slave is that he is 'not' an independent consciousness but in becoming free *from* the oppression of the master *to* his own essentiality, he becomes a lord himself. His own dogmas are formed from the deconstruction of inherited dogmas. Hegel writes: 'It procures for itself the certainty of its own freedom and thereby raises it to truth' (1977, p. 124). This truth is equally illusory but the truth of its own illusion is not recognized.

Tubbs notes that as long as illusions are not recognized, they will only continue to repeat their domination (2000, p. 53). I doubt that Erricker and colleagues consider their liberationist position as lordship and their view of meaning-making drawn from children's own views as dogma. But if we are to suggest that liberation from mastery brings about spirituality 'in-itself', the creation of another form of mastery becomes evident and the illusion of this position as essential truth is perpetuated.

Hegel's dialectic thus inspires the need to gain a critical view of the illusion of both notions of truth and allows educators as Tubbs suggests, to recognize the illusion of the illusion (2000, p. 50). Both master and slave are contradictions of the same consciousness. Although dualistic, they exist side by side in a relationship of struggle. Consciousness sits uncomfortably with contradiction as Erricker might sit uncomfortably next to Wright. But the contradiction is within itself (1977, pp. 126–138), as two Janus-faced representations of the *same* consciousness (Tubbs, 2005, p. 113). Therefore, each should be acknowledged as a reflection of the other's truth (1977, p. 113).

Truth in its totality results not from freedom but from the recognition of the illusion of freedom. While contingency highlights the illusion of objective truth, the primacy of the self is similarly illusory when it does not recognize itself in the other. I suggest that when one negates perceived illusory truth without the recognition of his or her own illusory state, a precarious path is tread. In that case, both Erricker and Wright should become critically aware of the hegemony of both positions and look not to a compromise but to a position which recognizes the personal in the universal and vice versa.

The second point concerns error. Although illusion is not a Hegelian word, in the *Phenomenology* he does use the word 'error'. He suggests that this fear of error is actually the fear of truth itself (1977, p. 47). Reminiscent again of Erricker's position, Rose describes how a 'state of nature' which is absolute is considered by some to be an abstraction. She writes that advocates consider that 'social relations are contingent and transitory: a fiction of the basic truth of man's condition' (1981, p. 52). She continues that for those who hold this view, a 'state of nature' based on the relative life instead will 'abolish the evils of such a situation' (1981, p. 52). But Rose through Hegel attacks this separation and posits this latter view as a prejudice and an absolute itself 'for which empiricism knows no absolute' (1981, p. 53).

Sadly, we do see today extremist responses to some dogmas and we might quite rightly perceive these as error; but I also suggest that open-ended, self-proclamatory truths drawn from what is understood as possibility are also dangerous. The avoidance of perceived error might be as destructive as the error incited in the first place. When anything is possible, the possible can become anything.

While possibility is presented as allowing learning to evolve and grow from within, I wonder where the contingency which checks against unethical behaviour sits. For children who need boundaries, will possibility not lead to negative short-term effects such as behaviour on the playground or longer-term effects of mental and physical health? When morals are a choice and a personal narrative inspires meaning-making, is it too strong to suggest that this might inspire a kind of spiritual anarchy? Tubbs illustrates this by drawing on Heidegger's own contingent political position in war-time Germany (2005, p. 137), and while this is as an extreme instance of unchecked *potentiality-for-Being*, it presents a caution for those favouring an education based on possibility.

Having located the critique in a Hegelian framework, I now come to the place where his thinking becomes formative. As it has been identified that the truth of self and other is in their relation, the discussion now turns to an assessment of the middle space *between* the two partners. It is in this space that education can begin its search for spiritual truth. I propose that learning *through* the dualistic relationship is the truth of spiritual pedagogy and this is the place where meaningful learning begins.

The broken middle

Gillian Rose uses the term 'the broken middle' to describe the middle space in which dualisms are held in creative tension for learning. In the introduction to her work of the same name, she reinforces Hegel's distrust of duality, boldly suggesting that 'anti-utopia and anarchy turns into triumphant ecclesiology' (1992, p. viii). Instead, she claims that that which separates the two cannot actually be overcome: the broken middle explores the truth within and between each one (1992, p. xiv). I will explore this in more detail in the light of the three themes raised in the critique and suggest how speculative philosophy speaks to the issues of freedom, error and possibility for a paradigm of spiritual education which results from learning the truth of itself *as* learning (Tubbsm, 2008, p. 4).

As Hegel states in *Logic*, truth is not in the in-itself but in the middle term between the finite self in consciousness and objectivity (1975, p. 276). Truth lies in the unity in which the two are one (1975, p. 244). Rose describes this in terms of a philosophical situation in the neo-Kantian tradition. Arguing in *Hegel Contra Sociology* that dualistic thinking is an epistemological trap (1981, p. 42) and through an exploration of the dichotomies of the values of the positions of Durkheim and Weber respectively, she claims that the divergences actually 'rest on an identical framework'. (1981, p. 1). She also later argues that the church and the state although contradictory are the same (1981, p. 49).

This is difficult to fathom and just as difficult to put into practice. But Rose suggests that if dichotomies are seen as relations (as in that of the master and slave), both sides might exist in unity without being unified (1981, pp. 54–55). Tubbs explains that, as such, teachers need not choose one approach over another. They can find themselves in the broken middle of the relationship between them (2005, p. 12): in a space where the contradictions of the universal and personal find a place to meet. The middle is not a comfortable place to be and the dialectical relationship which involves contradiction is not an easy one; nevertheless, I propose that spiritual teachers neither negate the idea of authentic self nor separate the individual from the wider collective experience brought about by religion and tradition.

To put this into practice, children can be allowed to interpret the Bible and other sacred texts in the light of their own subjective experiences, making their own responses *through* the tradition. For example, using role play, creative responses to a guided meditation or creative writing, they can present their own understanding of the stories of Moses or Rama and Sita, tackling the issues presented by these characters empathetically. They can handle these personal meanings alongside those 'handed down' to them, like a hot potato, juggling between the two, creating a space for debate and the opportunity to think more creatively about what the story *can* mean for today. They can be given the opportunity to describe their own image of 'God' or transcendent other in their own terms or to challenge those presented to them. They can take part in learning experiences about the teachings of Jesus or other religious leaders, with permission to explore what these teachings mean for them and ensuring that their own perspective is brought to the learning process in relationship with the tradition.

When the teacher retains the tension which exists between two positions in the broken middle, each is recognized as illusory (or error) within the illusion of misrecognition. Rose suggests that for truth to become an issue for *subjective* consciousness, it must take an interest in its *object* and find itself in contradiction with itself. With this comes the recognition of the illusion of the illusion. Tubbs suggests that it is in the recognition of the illusion where spiritual learning begins; therefore truth is that which results from learning the error of itself in itself, and this recognition is learning (2008, p. 4). Having identified contingency and mediation as the concealments from which the authentic Being of Heidegger is cleared, and as elements which deny truth its universality, the speculative experience embraces rather than shuns them for learning. Located in the broken middle, contingency brings history into a relationship with the child's immediate experience and religious tradition into a creative tension with the culture in which he or she lives.

Again in practical terms, children 'in the middle' can learn creatively about ethics and morality. Through graffiti, rapping, poster-making and other means of expression, they can explore who the influencers on their lives are; they can assess what is good or bad and think about how they come to understand moral behaviour. Drawing on, for example, the Ten Commandments, they can explore 'why' such principles are good or bad and critically engage with the principles of sacred texts in the light of their own questions. Allowing for contingency provides the opportunity for children to be critical in order to establish new, creative and organic ideas about themselves and others in the light of their personal experiences.

The final point concerns possibility. In *Hegel Contra Sociology*, Rose brings us back to Heidegger who is referenced in terms of the neo-Kantian paradigm that Hegel sought to address. Here Dasein is noted as a pre-condition of life: 'the *a priori* of a new ontology' (1981, p. 23). She describes the condition of the possibility of experience as the condition of the meaning of experience. This is resonant with the suggestion made earlier that the child is both the beginning and end of all learning and enquiry, and Rose describes this as a Kantian hermeneutic circle. But she claims that the circle has no result (1981, p. 23). Its meaning lacks identity when the self only relates back to self. She argues that rather than projects (which might include the educational) justifying their own validity or rights, they should acknowledge instead epistemological circularity which embraces contingency for a 'different way' of examining knowledge (1981, p. 23). This cycle involves the negation (or loss) of the self to contingency and mediation, but in its return to self, finds negation negated for the truth of spiritual learning.

Rose cites the dialectic of Hegel and Kierkegaard's writings as an example of loss and return, worked out through *The Broken Middle*. In this text she treats the contradictory ideas as a relation and looks for the truth of each in the unity of the broken middle. This mirrors a theme in *Fear and Trembling*, in which the circularity of the dialectical relationship is illustrated in the loss and return to self of its protagonist. In this text, Kierkegaard explores the story of Abraham as a knight of faith who in anguish and despair suspends the ethical in order to lose himself in an absolute relation to the absolute (1985, p. 62). He does this in a leap of faith. The leap leads to infiniteness which neither loses nor overcomes the finite. The resonance here is clear. The self is lost through negation, but this does not lead to an abandoning to the absolute but to the relation with the absolute. After the leap comes a return. In his return to self, the knight of faith is brought back to the ethical for his own truth. This is the dialectical relationship, illustrated as a double movement of leap and return (1985, p. 57).

Rose writes that the existence of the middle implies that the ethical is not overcome but suspended (1992, p. 154). The action of the leap of faith is described as a danger: the leap and the return are a double danger which indicates the truth of the relationship between self and other. But Rose actually notes this as being the only undangerous position, being the only one that 'does not liberate from one dominion' (1992, p. 159). The middle is the only way to avoid spiritual introversion.

Finally, in practice, I suggest that teachers always keep learning in check. For Heidegger, learning is always a process of becoming that only finds its end in death (1962, p. 307). This to me is too vague. Learning, however exploratory and creative, must always make a return. In this case, when children engage personally with a scriptural text and allow their own meanings to take shape, their re-reading of the original text again is made in a different light. A meaning made without a return can mean anything. A meaning made with a return allows the text to remain the text 'as it is' but has more value for the child. When exploring morals and ethics, children have the space to question and explore for themselves the values by which they and others live. But morals explored that do not make a return can simply lapse into hedonism. A return to tradition, the state and religious values in the light of the children's own existential enquiry encourages children not to be suspicious of authority and to understand more fully the reasons for rules. It also allows them to critically engage with other influencers and consider what aspects of popular culture are moral, ethical and to be trusted.

Conclusion

In the light of this discussion, I draw on Nigel Tubbs for conclusions. He provides advice for teachers that is equally relevant to those responsible for spiritual development in schools. Asserting that the concept of the broken middle is a twenty-first-century expression of the suspension of the ethical (2000, p. 57), he suggests how teachers might embrace this idea in order to avoid the problematic of dualistic positing as described in this chapter. First, he suggests that teachers should be aware of the gap and the dilemma posed between any positions. Teachers should recognize but not evade the struggle or unrest caused by the broken middle. They should also guard against illusion and accept that truth learns its own truth as contradiction and mediation (2000, p. 56). He also argues that contingency forms the substance of speculative enquiry (2005, p. 12).

He writes: 'If (the teacher) recognizes her doubts to be the necessary negation of her identity, her power, authority, and teaches from within this experience, then she is master and servant, or a philosophical teacher' (2005, p. 146). Similarly, from my perspective, if the teacher of spiritual education retains the tension which exists between Being as possibility or as an entity, sees the truth of the subjective and objective as contractions of the same totality, and views meaning-making as a creative tension between both individual and traditional parties, each recognizing the illusion of the illusion of themselves in themselves, and teaching from within the middle, then he or she is also a philosophical teacher.

Finally, a quote from Hegel sums these conclusions up. He writes that education can 'learn from this impossibility of resolution is its own truth, a truth known in and as the form and content of the contradictory conjunction of abstraction and mediation. It is the truth within the relation of contingency to itself' (2005, p. 157). The middle is not a comfortable place to be and the dialectical relationship which involves contradiction is not an easy one. The task of recognizing each in the other might involve a painful and uncomfortable manoeuvre, but I do believe that the learning experience will be more meaningful and have greater impact for children and young people in the United Kingdom.

References

Adams, K. (2010) *Unseen Worlds*. London: Jessica Kingsley Publishers.

Adams, K., Hyde, B. and Woolley, R. (2008), *The Spiritual Dimension of Childhood*. London: Jessica Kingsley Publishers.

Berger, P. (1969) *A Rumor of Angels: Modern Society and the Rediscovery of the Supernatural*. New York, NY: Anchor Books.

Champagne, E., (2003), 'Being a Child, a spiritual child', *International Journal of Children's Spirituality* 8(1): 43–53.

Chickering, A., Dalton, J. and Stamm, L. (2006) *Encouraging Authenticity and Spirituality*. San Francisco, CA: Jossey-Bass.

de Souza, M. (2010) Meaning and connectedness: Australian perspectives on education and spirituality – an introduction, in de Souza, M. and Rimes, J. (eds.), *Meaning and Connectedness: Australian Perspectives on Education and Spirituality*. Mawson: Australian college of Educators, pp. 1–6.

——, (2013), *A Concept of Human Spirituality*. http://www.childrenspirituality.org [accessed 05 March 2013].

Erricker, C. and Erricker, J. (1996) 'Where angels fear to tread', in Best, R. (ed.), *Education, Spirituality and the Whole Child*. London: Cassell, pp. 184–195.

—— (2000) *Reconstructing Religious, Spiritual and Moral Education*. London: Routledge Falmer.

——. (2007) 'Children's Spirituality and Postmodern faith', *International Journal of Children's Spirituality* 12(1): 51–60.

Hart, T. (2003) *The Secret Spiritual World of Children*. Makawao, HI: Inner Ocean Publishing.

Hay, D., with Nye, R. (2006) *The Spirit of the Child*. (Revised Edition), London: Jessica Kingsley Publishers.

Heidegger, M. (1978) 'Letter on Humanism', in Heidegger, M. (ed.)*Basic Writings*, London: Routledge.

—— (1962) *Being and Time*. Oxford: Blackwell Publishers.

Hegel, G. (1975) *Logic*. Oxford: Clarendon Press.

—— (1977) *Phenomenology of Spirit*. Oxford: Oxford University Press.

Hyde, B. (2008) *Children and Spirituality: Searching for Meaning and Connectedness*. London: Jessica Kingsley Publishers.

—— (2010) 'Agency, play and spiritual development in the early years' curriculum', in de Souza, M. and Rimes, J. (eds.), *Meaning and Connectedness: Australian Perspectives on Education and Spirituality*. Mawson: Australian college of Educators, pp. 92–104.

Kierkegaard, S. (1985) *Fear and Trembling*. London: Penguin Books Ltd.

Miller, J. (2000) *Education and Soul*. Albany, NY: State University of New York Press.

Ofsted (2004) *Promoting and Evaluating Pupils' Spiritual, Moral, Social and Cultural Development*. Crown Copyright.

—— (2013) *Subsidiary Guidance: Supporting the Inspection of Maintained Schools and Academies from January 2012*. Manchester.

Priestley, J. (1996) *Spirituality in the Curriculum*. Essex: Hockerill Educational Foundation.

Qualifications and Curriculum Authority (1999) *The National Curriculum: Handbook for Primary Teachers in England*. London: QCA.

Rose, G. (1981) *Hegel Contra Sociology*. London: The Athlone Press Ltd.

—— (1992) *The Broken Middle*. Oxford: Blackwell Publishers.

Tubbs, N. (2000) *Mind the Gap: The Philosophy of Gillian Rose*. Thesis Eleven Pty, 60:42, Chicago: SAGE publications (downloaded 18 May 2008).

—— (2005) *The Philosophy of the Teacher*. Oxford: Blackwell Publishing.

—— (2008) *Education in Hegel*. London: Continuum International Publishing Group.

Watson, J., (2000), 'Whose model of spirituality should be used in the spiritual development of school children?', *International Journal of Children's Spirituality* 5(1): 91–100.

—— (2010) 'Including secular philosophies such as humanism in locally agreed syllabuses for religious education', *British Journal of Religious Education* 32(1): 5–18.

Webster, R.S. (2004) 'An existential framework of spirituality', *International Journal of Children's Spirituality* 9(1): 7–19.

Westermann, W. and Newby, M. (1996) *International Journal of Children's Spirituality*. 1(1): 44–51.

Wright, A. (1998) *Spiritual Pedagogy: A Survey, Critique and Reconstruction of Contemporary Spiritual Education in England and Wales*. Abingdon: Culham College Institute.

12

Theology as Partner for Educators

John Sullivan

For many people theology might seem irrelevant, perhaps a distraction, or even worse, a rival for educators. Notions such as revelation and holiness, practices such as prayer and worship, combined with a reverential attitude towards sacred texts and tradition, appear alien to the kinds of learning and education required today, instead of being envisaged as providing openings to alterity and as an engagement with a bigger picture of reality than that offered in contemporary education and through diverse media for communication. This chapter suggests ways in which theological perspectives can enrich understanding of central aspects of educational endeavour. *Who* we are as teachers and learners (the centrality of personhood and relationality); *what* we might teach and learn (content and types of rationality); *how* we might learn (methods and virtues); *why* we learn and teach (purpose and motivation) – our understanding of each of these could potentially be deepened and expanded through a dialogue with theological insights. Education is founded on an appreciation of anthropology, of relationships and of rationalities. Theology has something to contribute to each of these areas. As examples, I propose three areas for creative encounter, where theology can serve as a beneficial partner for educators, rather than as a hostile intruder: first, vulnerability; second, prayer as context for learning; and third, revelation.

My focus in this chapter is not on Christian education or on how Christians should use theology in their educational work. This is not an exercise in theology; nor am I advocating any one particular theological tradition from among the diversity manifested by Christian bodies. Instead, I make a tentative, very selective and incomplete proposal that educators, as part of equipping themselves to address their tasks, might benefit from considering theology as a source of possible insights. Such insights could be as valuable as those from other disciplines. Traditionally, educators have been encouraged to learn from philosophy and sociology, psychology and human development. They can also learn much from history, politics and literature. Those more interested in educational leadership and administration than in pedagogy, pastoral care or curriculum will find relevant insights from management studies and organizational analysis (see Heclo, 2008). Theology, however, is scarcely ever considered as a potential partner for educators. Although I will draw only on Christian theology here, there is every reason to expect that the theology stemming from other faith traditions will also have pertinent insights of value, from which educators can benefit, ones which both parallel and reinforce the points made in this chapter, as well as those offering contrasting insights. There are five sections in the chapter. In the first section I explain why it could appear counter-intuitive to think that theology might contribute anything worth taking into account by educators. Here I acknowledge negative expectations of theology together with past abuses by theologians and extremes to be avoided. Then, in the second section, I comment on the overlap of interests between education and theology, articulate my understanding of the nature and scope of theology and indicate some ways that it might have relevance for educators. Sections three to five illustrate the three themes named in the previous paragraph, around which a theological perspective might be claimed to have possible relevance for educators: vulnerability, prayer and revelation.

Expectations of theology

Theology is viewed with suspicion by some academics. Richard Dawkins refers to four kinds of discourse offered by theologians who make claims on behalf of religion. These are explanation, exhortation, inspiration and consolation.[1] In his view, and this would be shared by a significant number of scholars from different disciplines, all four are unwarranted in terms of evidence, lack rationality, are spurious, even dangerous because they lead people to base their lives on fantasy rather than reality. Furthermore, past abuses of theology can cause people to write off entirely its potential for offering a positive contribution to the growth of knowledge or, more specifically for this chapter, to thinking about education. Too often theologians have been come across as backward-looking, too confident in their assertions, insufficiently attentive to the methodologies of other forms of knowledge, confining rather than liberating in their effects on those who accept their findings, so focused on the path to heaven that they neglect earthly realities and too subservient to authorities (Bible, church, tradition) to display serious critical thinking and imagination. Even the virtues espoused by some theologians seem to offer little of value to education. As an illustration of this point, Aaron Ghiloni asks:

> [W]hat can obedience, silence, humility and yearning contribute to educational theory and practice? All four values could be interpreted negatively: obedience may be seen as a sign of indoctrination; silence may be seen as the exclusion of one's voice; humility may be seen as a sign of weakness and docility; imaginative yearning may be seen as impractical and fanciful. (Ghiloni, 2012, p. 145)

Despite these possible defects, however, Ghiloni proceeds to argue that theology can also be understood as inherently and centrally educational in nature. In a similar way to Ghiloni, I hope to show that theology *can* be a valuable partner for educators.

Those unfamiliar with theology might be tempted to think that theology is an esoteric form of thought that speaks of topics that seem completely outside the normal experiences of our shared life, of interest only to the specially pious, and making knowledge claims about another dimension and a Being that are both inaccessible to rational investigation and having little bearing on daily decisions and the realities of nature that people have to negotiate. In contrast, a common understanding of theologians, with regard to the nature and scope of theology, as articulated by Thomas Aquinas, is that it offers an account of all things in the light of God. Seen in this way, theology is not restricted to speaking of supernatural objects as removed from our natural world but attempts to appreciate how all things cohere and find their proper place within the whole, this whole being understood in the light of God. In this perspective, as John Webster observes, 'all sorts of cultural activities – making shelter and food, commerce, drama, arts of speech and speculation – are disclosive once they are "read" within the comprehensive context of creatureliness' (Webster, 2011, p. 51) and as a participation in and response to God's initiative.

There is always the danger that, because of this huge scope (all things in the light of God), theology might suffer from one or other of two extremes: *either* being so attentive to the divine source and goal of all things that the dimensions and workings of natural living are obscured, over-shadowed and insufficiently appreciated, *or* being so concerned to connect in a relevant way to our natural concerns and operations and to draw our knowledge from these that the divine is interpreted solely in light of the forms of experience and reasoning that derive from these natural activities and concerns. David Jasper labels these dangers respectively as 'hypertheism' and 'overhumanization'.

> Hypertheism denotes a conviction that locates all human life and experience within a vision of God to the endangerment of responsible support for and recognition of the rich diversity of human life while overhumanization denotes the exclusive triumph of human power in the shaping of our reality, which brings about, sooner or later, an inevitable foreshortening and over-definition of aims in materialist, economic or absolutist myopias. (Jasper, 2011, p. 65)

The problem with each of these extremes, in Jasper's view, is that they fail to develop 'a proper sense of the *integrity* of life, which is lived neither exclusively on the *horizontal* plane of the purely secular, not the *vertical* plane of the obsessively religious, but in a rich and complex mutual acknowledgement of both in the pursuit of all human flourishing'.

When applied to educational practice and to the study of education, one working out of an unbalanced emphasis on the divine or vertical dimension might be neglect of the human or horizontal aspects of development and learning. One working out of an unbalanced emphasis on the horizontal and human aspects might be a failure to attend properly to the divine, thereby closing down prematurely the possibility of being open to a more expansive understanding of the sources of knowledge and transformation available. My assumptions here are, first, that neither theology nor the other disciplines should be considered subordinate one to the other; second, that there should be dialogue between them (at university); and third, in educational practice at all levels openness to what a theological perspective might offer teachers and learners should be fostered, without this implying that the theological perspective must be adopted or embraced. As a recent collection of essays (about university education) suggests, though unfortunately without reference to education as field of study in its own right, dialogue between theology and other disciplines can facilitate the bringing together of consideration of 'the intelligibility of creation, purpose, grace, human flourishing, truth seeking, coherence and convergence of explanation, participation and representation, imagination and culture' (Crisp et al., 2012, p. 11).

Newman hints at the tensions between different kinds of knowledge when he distinguishes scientific from poetic knowledge.

> The aim of science is to get hold of things, to grasp them, to handle them, to comprehend them; that is, to *master* them, or to be superior to them.... Its mission is to destroy ignorance, doubt, surmise, suspense, illusions, fears, deceits.... The poetical ... demands, as its primary condition, that we should not put ourselves above the objects in which it resides, but at their feet; that we should feel them to be above and beyond us, that we should look up to them,

and that, instead of fancying that we can comprehend them, we should take for granted that we are comprehended by them ourselves.... Poetry does not address the reason, but the imagination and the affections; it leads to admiration, enthusiasm, devotion, love. (Newman, 2001, pp. 387–388)[2]

Poetic knowledge, whether or not it is envisaged as closely related to a theological perspective or a spiritual outlook, switches the focus away from conceiving learners as being prepared through education to be consumers and producers and goes beyond an emphasis on mastery via scientific and technological competence by nurturing an expansion of the capacity to receive and to appreciate. Alongside religious sensibilities, according to Adam English, it facilitates seeing every person as 'shot through with physicality and mystery, immanence and transcendence, finitude and immortality, sin and grace' (English, 2007, p. 49). Such an outlook is central to an approach to education considered by Coleridge as 'the harmonious development of those qualities and faculties that characterize our *humanity*' (Coleridge, 1972, pp. 33–34).

Theology's potential as partner for educators

Educators always hold in view simultaneously two notions of reality that rarely coincide. First, they seek to equip people for the world as it currently is. At different times this has meant education has been intended to serve the needs of hunters, farmers, fighters and religious disciples; it has also been intended to prepare people to be manufacturers and providers of various kinds of services and goods in society. Second, educators, at least implicitly, hold in view some picture of the world as they think it should be, in light of some over-arching vision or set of principles and ideals. Theology has something to say about both of these, each in light of the other. That is, a theological perspective comments in diagnostic fashion about the human condition as it currently appears to be, claiming that this diagnosis is illuminated by the prospect of a different expression of human personhood, one that can be achieved with divine assistance and on the pattern of a divine exemplar; at the same time, a theological perspective envisages the remedy it prescribes for human flourishing as one that directly addresses current shortcomings and that closely engages with current needs.

Theology offers a way of 'reading' reality, to enable those who dwell in a theological *habitus* to understand the world they encounter, to interpret it, to make sense of it and to appreciate it, in order to help them to participate in God's work in it more appropriately. If they are to do justice to the potentially huge scope of their work, theologians need to draw upon insights from other disciplines; they cannot comment usefully about the human condition by ignoring or by seeking to dictate to other disciplines how they should investigate the aspects of reality that each puts under scrutiny. If educators wish to promote human flourishing, then they can find valuable insights into the human condition in many disciplines, for example, in sociology, biology, psychology and economics. My claim is that they can also learn from theology. The case for suggesting that theology might be a useful partner for educators is weakened by the fact that often in the past theology has been abused by some of its exponents, being insufficiently respectful of the methods of other approaches to knowledge and inadequately attentive to the findings derived from these. Such *hubris* unsurprisingly leads to suspicion about theological claims. Often theology has seemed to comment merely extrinsically *on* the world, lacking intrinsic connection *to* it. I believe its task is less about bringing God in, as if from the outside, as finding God already at work within the world, and suggesting ways to participate in that divine work.

Theology is an intellectual endeavour carried out from the inside of a faith tradition, a reflection on the grounding, coherence and implications of the faith experience of religious communities. What is being suggested here is not that educators should do theology. This cannot be expected of people who are not insiders, who do not share the faith and who do not participate in its living tradition. What is being proposed is that educators could profitably consider theological insights, from the outside, as it were, for the light they might cast on aspects of education. Examining theological insights, from this external perspective, will very likely be an activity that is less comprehensive in coverage, less penetrating in depth and less efficacious in potential for personal transformation than it could be if done as an insider who accompanied such examination by living a religious life. However, even such a limited examination can still be suggestive of insights into the human condition, the personal context for learning and the nature of knowledge by expanding the range of considerations to be taken into account by educators. The use of theology I am thinking of here might be called a theology of the threshold, the vestibule, the forecourt, the entrance hall, the gatehouse or the atrium. It gets close to and learns from theology, without necessarily adopting the religious life and community experience on which theology reflects and which theology seeks to nurture.

Theology is about our relationship to the whole, to what we consider ultimate. If spirituality is revealed in what people give their energies and time to, theology reflects on and tries to make sense of the central goals of human intentionality, the God or gods they pursue. and it explores how this God or these gods relate to the whole and how individuals fit into the whole and relate to God or the gods. The Czech psychotherapist and theologian Tomáš Halík comments interestingly on this point. 'People did not worship gods; what they worshipped *became* their god or gods. Thus the word "god" did not originally denote any special "supernatural being", but it had a status similar to that of the word "treasure".... in its original use the word "god" or "gods" did not denote beings, things, or objects, but a *relationship*' (Halík, 2012, p. 113). Theology might play a role, alongside other disciplines, in identifying and unmasking the idols that are served or the gods that are pursued in contemporary educational policies and priorities.

I shall assume that transformative learning depends on learners being surprised and exposed, interrupted and shaken, and that these are necessary prerequisites if learning is to reorient their lives and give them a glimpse of a fuller way of being. This entails a degree of vulnerability and a sense of inadequacy in the face of experience as a preliminary to opening oneself to the possibility of a more abundant life. Thus I will devote the following section to a brief exploration of vulnerability and how theology might enhance our understanding of this feature of our experience. Theology finds its sources in and takes its shape from personal prayer and corporate worship. Central to all major Christian traditions is the importance of prayer for true perception and right living. In the practice of prayer, human dependency, desire, duty and direction all come together and cohere. In prayer there is an unending dance between receptivity and self-donation. Hence in the fourth section I consider prayer as a context for learning. Theology also relies heavily on an understanding of revelation as a guide to the knowledge which is of most significance for human flourishing. Therefore, in the final section I indicate some of the ways that an understanding of revelation might expand the appreciation of teachers and learners of the potential sources of knowledge available to them, with a view to help them to avoid closing down their options too early.

Vulnerability

As a counterbalance to emphases in education on agency, competencies, strengths, skills, autonomy and rationality, I suggest that teachers, students preparing to be teachers and those who facilitate reflection on education in initial teacher formation or in continuing professional development might benefit from taking into account other aspects of human experience, for example, limitation, weakness, vulnerability, dependency, receptivity and relationships. I focus on vulnerability here as a way of opening up for attention these dimensions of our condition. Vulnerability is integral to the process of learning (just as it is for discipleship). When we open ourselves up to learn there is always the risk that we will experience deep discomfort, that we will feel anxious and confused, disoriented and incompetent. I treat the sense of vulnerability as an intelligent as well as emotional response to the limitations we experience. Each of us is limited by inheritance and endowment, so that the repertoire of gifts that is available to us to develop is restricted, rather being entirely open-ended. We are also limited by the environment in which we grow up and the influences we are subject to. Thus, the opportunities available to us vary considerably, from person to person, in ways beyond our control. We are limited too by our choices, by how we exercise our freedom. As some doors open, because of the steps we take and the direction in which we move, so other paths remain untaken and we find that they now seem no longer as accessible to us as once they might have been. In fact, if we reflect on our choices, we can experience internal divisions and incoherence, a constant and seemingly unbridgeable chasm between our ideals and our actions, a feature of humanity described poignantly by St Paul in his Letter to the Romans 7: 15–24, where he speaks of not doing what he wants but the opposite and of encountering conflict between intention and practice.

Vulnerability accompanies any reliance we might place on goods that do not last, that cannot be made secure. From a theological, as well as more generally from an ethical perspective, our reliance on goods can be misdirected. Those who trust in or aim for wealth, popularity, comfort, independence, power, reputation and career advancement are likely to disappointed in the long run. Theologians, along with secular moral thinkers, direct our attention instead to the importance, for human well-being, of integrity, fidelity, forgiveness, love, patience, compassion, service and gratitude. Where theologians may differ from secular moral thinkers in their advocacy of these qualities is that they are likely to stress the central role played by worship as a context for developing an appropriate interpretation of virtues as responses to and a participation in the activity of God; they are also likely to privilege, as an exemplar for humankind to emulate and identify with, the person of Jesus Christ.

Curriculum is often directed at developing mastery in a range of competencies. Students are encouraged to break through all barriers that hold them back and to learn how to get on in the world, to be a winner, to achieve success. While necessary, this is incomplete, for a major dimension of human life is the experience of limitation or finiteness and the associated sense of vulnerability (and perhaps frustration). Education should also assist learners to recognize, interpret and cope with such limitation and vulnerability. Losing as well as winning is part of life, for ourselves and our fellow human beings, and reflection on this should form part of educational experience. Education should, in addition to equipping people for success, develop the capacity to cope with losing and, in so doing, nurture the capacity to respond sensitively to others who suffer set-backs or who are vulnerable. Educators should be conscious that their priorities and emphases, the allocation of their energies and their deployment of reward systems in schools and universities, might be misinterpreted by some learners as valuing so highly independence and control, achievement and success, as to neglect also developing a capacity for recognizing and responding sensitively to people who are apparently failing, unpopular, dependent or impoverished. Teachers and students should be encouraged to be hospitable to vulnerability, in themselves and in others.

The philosopher John F. Crosby, in a book that probes the dimensions of human personhood, devotes a chapter to finitude (Crosby, 1996). He points out (pp. 248–252) that only part of the plenitude of personhood is realized in each person. To put this differently, we find ourselves suspended between potentiality and actuality (pp. 257–260); there is always something within us that remains unfulfilled or not fully realized. We also experience our finiteness in relation to time (pp. 253–256), for the past cannot be held onto and the future cannot be controlled. In his analysis, furthermore, we discover a discrepancy between being and consciousness (pp. 257–260), since full self-knowledge escapes us. In facilitating the growth of self-knowledge among students and in encouraging them to have hope for the future, teachers should also help them to take into account the limitations and vulnerability that are inescapably part of human life.

Crosby's analysis on finitude is a rare foray into aspects of limitation and vulnerability in philosophical analyses of the human condition. An exception here is MacIntyre's examination of vulnerability and dependency as central to human experience (MacIntyre, 1999). MacIntyre's focus on vulnerability and dependence, however, is with a view to showing why human beings need the virtues. His concern is less to do with exploring the parameters of vulnerability and appreciating their existential 'weight' than it is to indicate the implications of taking vulnerability and dependency, as basic features of human life, into account when developing an adequate rationale for and approach to the virtues.

Theologians too have tended to neglect many aspects of vulnerability (with the major exception of the attention they have given to the workings of sin). In their analyses of what constitutes the image of God in human beings – the theological topic that explores most deeply the nature of human personhood – they have tended to emphasize most often such features as rationality, free will and conscience.

In contrast to such emphases, the therapist Molly Haslam, who has substantial experience of working with individuals with a variety of disabilities, including those with profound intellectual disabilities, draws on her experience to argue that traditional theological approaches to identifying what is integral to the notion of *imago Dei* in human beings end up by lacking inclusivity and thereby rule out as less than human a significant minority of people. Her central thesis is that although those with profound intellectual disabilities cannot display what are normally considered important features of personhood, for example, rationality, the exercise of choice or the ability to communicate in language or symbols, they do, however, display an ability 'to participate in mutually responsive relationships – to respond to the world around them and to evoke a response from others' (Haslam, 2012, p. 57). 'What defines human being is not located internal, or external, to the self but rather is located in the human-to-human relationship and in the relationship of human beings to God' (p. 14). It is in relationships of mutual responsiveness, she argues, that we find our humanity; the temptation to limit what we recognize *as* a response to the use of language or symbols should be resisted. She shows that individuals with profound intellectual disabilities 'still express themselves in a variety of ways through body motion, sound, changes in body temperature and behavioural state' (p. 42).

Her analysis of human personhood in relational terms builds not only on her lengthy experience as a physical therapist but also on her reading of the work of Martin Buber, especially his book *I and Thou* (Buber, 1958). For Buber, our humanity is called forth when we meet another in a relationship that is mutually responsive, immediate and where the other person is encountered as a whole – not in the sense that we have comprehensive knowledge of him or her, but in the sense that we meet them as they are without this being because of any particular feature or isolatable characteristic or capacity which they display. Something is called forth on both sides of such an encounter, even if their respective contributions are asymmetric.

Although it is unlikely that most teachers will find themselves working with those with profound intellectual disabilities, nevertheless, Haslam's theological reflection on vulnerability and relationships that are mutually responsive provides a salutary reminder that we should approach those we seek to educate with an attentive, respectful and inclusive openness, avoid judging them by inappropriate yardsticks and seek to engage them as whole persons rather than merely at the cognitive level. Although the development of this kind of sensitivity does not *depend* on theology being brought to bear, since such sensitivity can evidently be fully developed without reference to theology, I believe that a theological perspective on vulnerability, limitation and finitude can offer valuable additional conceptual and motivational resources that both assist in the interpretation of what is stake in a situation and reinforce the capacity to act according to this interpretation.

Prayer and learning

What claims might theologians make for prayer as a context for enriching learning? Prayer can assist people in their relentless struggle against distraction from what matters most. It can sharpen their focus and facilitate their willingness to free themselves from encumbrances that prevent them from developing further or even from starting afresh. It can break through the distorting lens of the compromises and projections and the ways we conspire to live by surface appearances rather than in accordance with realities in their depths. It can expose attempts at self-delusion. It can bring into view our connectedness to the whole. In prayer one is not in control of the agenda but opens oneself to the agenda of Another. Daily life is the site for the working out and the practical expression of our devotion and desire, but prayer provides a context for seeing more truly our disfigured relationships, our self-defeating strategies, our blindness to the needs of others, our capitulation to unworthy pressures, our readiness to accept hollowness rather than wholeness at the centre of life. Prayer nurtures gratitude and reverence, perseverance and compassion, honesty and hope, patience and humility. It can encourage us to slow down, to step away from the constant effort to 'manage' situations and people, to give space to others, especially to our students; it invites us to acknowledge mystery in ourselves, in our students, in the world. It can nurture a willingness to avoid always relying on control, technique and power. If in the context of prayer we can grow in self-knowledge and humility, and thereby recognize how easy it is to interpret the words and actions of others through the distorting lens of our own fears and needs, and if conscious that we stand before One who knows us intimately and from whom we cannot pretend, we come to admit that we have sometimes acted towards others in ways that protect or promote our own interests rather than theirs, we may become empowered to approach others in a way that is more liberating and life-enhancing for them. Again, I am not claiming that such honesty, willingness to change and reversal of selfish orientations *depend* on one having a theological perspective, merely that a theological perspective, built upon the practice of prayer, can be a valuable prompt to such features in our character and behaviour.

It may already be apparent how such qualities can enhance both the breadth and the depth of the diverse kinds of learning that education can foster. Prayer has the potential to add to, to deepen and to help us to see in a different light the kinds of knowledge already being developed in other ways in education. Such knowledge might be about oneself, other people, the human condition or the world around us. In prayer, Christians believe, one can learn who we are and who we are related to, because we are related to God. In the processes of prayer our perceptions and passions can be healed and purified, recontextualized and reframed, reoriented and reformed, reinvigorated and redirected. In its stillness and silence, our 'hearing' of self, other people and situations can be sharpened and made more acute and discerning, allowing us to sift the more from the less important. Making room for the sacred helps us to become de-centred from putting self first and simultaneously opens up space for others within our attention and emotional repertoire. This cannot be irrelevant for any educational endeavour that seeks to promote human flourishing. Many of the key verbs used in worship and prayer seem to have a bearing on education. In his study of worship, Christopher Irvine picks out some of its central verbs as change, conform, form, fashion, partake, reflect, renew, restore, reveal, strengthen, transform (Irvine, 2005, p. 72). To this list one might add other verbs that are often integral to the activity of worship: read, receive, relinquish and respond – all of which are relevant to the tasks of learning.

Prayer and engagement with the world feed into each other. There is a mutual, reciprocally interactive relationship between them.

> We will understand or realize authentic prayer only as we commit ourselves to an attentive, affectionate, and responsible engagement with the world.... We need the instruction that follows from our practical commitments and care, that builds upon our availability to the world's dynamism and grace. Without this deep commitment, we will remain adrift, insulated from the very action of divine life that would inspire and correct our intentions and desires. (Wirzba, 2005, pp. 95–96)

According to this view, prayer needs the contact with and friction aroused by work in the world around us. In turn, our work in, with and on the world – for which education seeks to equip us – needs to be informed by a proper appreciation of the respective role played by each part within it and a respect and reverence for particularity and the whole; and here prayer can contribute to this appreciation, respect and reverence since it places each person, creature or situation in its broadest context, in a shared dependence on and relationship with the One who creates, sustains, renews and brings all to fruition, if they are open to receive. This work must be understood expansively, as the production of anything; as examples of the breadth of work to be included here, Wirzba suggests the following: 'breakfast, friendships, gardens, tables, solidarity, community institutions' because such work 'serves as our most direct (though by no means linear) entry into the ways of grace and so call forth our capacity to express gratitude and demonstrate care' (Wirzba, p. 97).

Prayer can foster a range of religious affections or capacities that might assist us in reading and responding to the world. Hotz and Mathews (2006, p. 8) refer to the following as examples: awe, humility, gratitude, a sense of direction, a sense of rightness, a sense of well-being, contrition, a sense of mutuality and interdependence, a sense of obligation, delight, self-sacrificial love and hope.

> When we refer to a religious affection, we mean a deep abiding feature of the human personality that grounds and orients us in all that we know, do, and feel. The religious affections form our fundamental disposition and attunement to the world around us. … [They] constitute in us a kind of readiness to experience the world in certain kinds of ways. (Hotz et al., 2006, p. 9)

These authors see these religious affections as all being interrelated, with each one flowing into and out of the others. For them worship plays a central role in the development, nurture, integration and orientation of such affections or capacities.

> Worship *evokes* particular religious affections. … it also *shapes* them individually and *orders* them by establishing relationships between the affections that assure that they comprise a coherent constellation rather than merely an aggregation. Worship gives us the opportunity to *express* these well-ordered affections. Worship *sustains* our religious affections. Finally, worship *directs* our religious affections toward God in such a way that we are brought into fitting relationships with other creatures. (p. 73)

Although they have in mind particularly the corporate worship of faith communities, their points also apply to personal prayer. While many educators and many students may not belong to a faith community, nor have any wish to do so, I suggest that the kinds of qualities and perceptions that can be fostered by prayer deserve some consideration by them, not least in terms of offering ways to 'read' and respond to the world that would augment those currently being developed in schools, colleges and universities.

Revelation

Revelation is a contested idea, with regard to its source, nature, scope and effects; also contested is its relation to the rest of our knowledge and how it might be recognized and verified. Different models of revelation have been used among Christian theologians. Principally these have been the following: revelation as propositional statements, as historical acts, as inner experience, as transcendent and transforming presence and as new awareness. Revelation is considered by believers to be something that comes to us unbidden, unexpected, as gift, not as the outcome of our searching or the exercise of our reasoning (though not by-passing, contradicting or denying reason). Revelation is viewed as God's initiative, offering humankind intimacy with God and calling forth a response in faith. Avery Dulles, in a thorough analysis of the diverse models of revelation in play among Christians, has summarized competing definitions as follows:

– Revelation is divinely authoritative doctrine inerrantly proposed as God's word by the Bible or by official church teaching.
– Revelation is the manifestation of God's saving power by his great deeds in history.
– Revelation is the self-manifestation of God by his intimate presence in the depths of the human spirit.
– Revelation is God's address to those whom he encounters with his word in Scripture and Christian proclamation.
– Revelation is a breakthrough to a higher level of consciousness as humanity is drawn to a fuller participation in the divine creativity. (Dulles, 1983, p. 115)

My concern here is not to comment on the respective merits and defects of these models; instead it is to indicate the potential bearing of the notion of revelation on our understanding of education and learning. After claiming that a proper understanding of revelation, far from demanding the complete passivity of learners and an overriding of personal freedom, instead requires of them the full engagement of all their critical faculties and releases them into a much deeper kind of freedom than is usually allowed for, I pick out three potentially valuable prompts for educators, drawn from the notion of revelation: first, the connection between identity and being known; second, an awareness of inhabiting an ultimate environment; and third, a stress on the necessary role of unlearning or letting go of familiar categories of interpretation of experience.

In a study of the connection between divine revelation and human learning, David Heywood treats revelation as 'a process of learning in which the learner is open to God' (Heywood, 2004, p. 9). He goes to great pains to argue that revelation should not be treated as closing down questions, requiring passivity or denying the active role of recipients. As he suggests, there is a danger that the faith process involved in appropriating revelation can become the 'receiving of a cultural hand-me-down and not the wrestling with Jacob's angel that leads to authentic commitment' (p. 172). And he stresses that 'God's gift of new identity', part of what is received within the acceptance of revelation, 'is not an "identikit"' (p. 177). That is, it does not crush or override our unique individuality; it does not prescribe for us a life-script that prevents significant creativity on our part in the way we seek to build a path for ourselves or to contribute to the world; in conforming us more closely to the image of God, revelation does not render us clones; it releases us into real freedom.

Heywood approaches the topic of revelation by a focus not on the content on revelation – *what* is communicated, nor on *who* gives it – but on the *receiver*. His claim is that 'to recognize how revelation might be *received* supplies the key to recognizing the way in which it might be *given*' (Heywood, p. 118). He sees close connections between revelation and self-knowledge, openness to the transcendent and a sense of our ultimate environment, within which we can 'place' our experiences and all that we encounter. As for self-knowledge, it is this that 'prepares us to know God, yet without knowing God a clear knowledge of ourselves is impossible' (p. 115). Heywood's argument (over-abbreviated here) proceeds thus:

> We could only come to a true knowledge of the people we really are in relation with a person who actually knew. … (L)earning about the world and the growth of identity go hand in hand … (L)earning about God in revelation must involve a consequent change in identity. … (T)he search for identity is the key which opens people to revelation. … We shall discover that revelation flows from a relationship with the person who knows the answer [to the question "who am I?"]. (p. 96)

Whether or not this line of argument is regarded as cogent, educators might at least ponder on whether or not their efforts succeed in assisting learners to develop self-knowledge and they might consider Heywood's point that such self-knowledge is not gained purely by introspection but in the process of encounter with others (and, if Heywood is right, with God), others who see aspects of ourselves which we are unwilling to acknowledge or to which we can remain blind. We come to know ourselves in the light of how we find ourselves to be known. Revelation invites us to envisage ourselves being known more deeply and comprehensively by God than in any other relationship.

As for the notion of inhabiting an ultimate environment, the psychologist and religious thinker James Fowler claims that '[o]ur images of the ultimate environment determine the way we arrange the scenery and grasp the plot in our life's plays' (Fowler, 1981, p. 29). Not only do individuals live within the context of an ultimate environment; so too do communities and cultures. Our sense, whether implicit or explicit, of being within an ultimate environment 'locates' us within our universe and helps us to find significance in our relationships, endeavours and commitments and provides a foundation for our sense of identity. One of the functions of revelation is to give us the capacity to recognize our ultimate environment. This environment might be quite different from and much richer than the one that is conveyed to us through pressures to secure levels of educational achievement prescribed by government or to pursue the material goods marketed by merchants.

Heywood argues that revelation is conveyed through the normal processes of human learning, assimilation and accommodation. Thus 'previous experience … or cultural inheritance' will affect the reception and assimilation of revelation, but, in turn, 'these categories are themselves transformed by the implications of revelation' (Heywood, p. 166). Human interpretation and ingenuity are not bypassed or superfluous when touched by divine revelation.

Theologian and educator Aaron Ghiloni echoes this view that there are close parallels between the ways that revelation 'works' and the operations of human learning when he comments:

> Doctrines of revelation that place the initiative completely on God's side leaving humans wholly passive are more like "divine rote" than divine pedagogy, more like indoctrination than experimental inquiry. … To argue for human learning is *not* to argue for the elimination of divine teaching; to promote activity is not to demote passivity. [But] divine teaching without human learning is not revelation. (Ghiloni, 2012, pp. 168–169)

Ghiloni identifies three aspects of Rowan Williams' writing on revelation as being fertile for educators: revelation as active learning, as generative disruption and as reconstruction (Ghiloni, p. 193). Williams, however, not only stresses the importance of human agency in receiving revelation; he also emphasizes the divine initiative, for, with revelation, something is happening *to* humans: 'a strange gift, an odd interruption, a foolish surprise, an uncontrolled passion, an unavoidable call' (Ghiloni, p. 197). Ghiloni quotes Williams on revelation as breaking 'existing frames of reference'. ... 'The "generative" event is one which breaks open and extends possible ways of being human' (Ghiloni, p. 198). Puzzlement plays an important role here. Humans cannot adequately grasp revelation or explain it satisfactorily; it eludes all our attempts to describe or interpret it with any finality; there always remains more to be said, more to be understood, more to be internalized. Such puzzlement acts as stimulus and it forces individuals and faith communities to engage in life-long exploration of revelation (Ghiloni, p. 199). Ghiloni also usefully retrieves another insight on revelation from Williams: it requires a constant process of *un*learning before learning, *stripping away*, a putting off the old self in order that a new self may be born (Ghiloni, p. 199). In addition to revelation requiring on our side active learning, and as well as experiencing it as disruptive of who we are in a way that is fertile, Ghiloni finds parallels between philosopher of education John Dewey and Rowan Williams in the way that both stress the need for a reconstruction of experience. For each of these prolific thinkers, such reconstruction of experience sought not to repeat the past (unfortunately too often a temptation of those who consider themselves defenders of revelation) but to use it as equipment for interpreting and addressing present experience. For both, 'Reconstruction is creative, forming something new and useful' (Ghiloni, p. 201).

The understanding of revelation in both Heywood and Ghiloni opens the way to worthwhile dialogue between educators and theologians and shows that at least some understandings of revelation are compatible with learning as understood by secular thinkers. First, openness to the possibility of revelation as a source of knowledge might prompt reflection on the connections between personal identity and being known by someone who sees us in our totality, rather than partially. Second, some familiarity with the notion of revelation can turn our attention to and facilitate a sense of inhabiting an ultimate environment that includes but transcends the immediate world of our everyday encounters and transactions. Third, openness to the possibility of revelation might encourage learners to allow for disruption to their existing frames of reference and bring home to them the need to be willing to let go (conceptually) whatever might tempt them too smoothly to assimilate knowledge according to already settled patterns and categories of interpretation rather than allow for these to be radically reconstructed by new insights and experience.

Conclusion

In this chapter I have invited educators to consider theology as a potential partner, along with, not instead of, other disciplines, in order to cast light on aspects of teaching and learning. Both in the initial period of pre-service training of teachers, as they seek to establish an overall picture of, or framework for, the kind of human endeavour they are preparing to engage in, and again in periods of reflection during ongoing professional development or as part of higher studies, when they can take account of growing experience as an educator, there can be some benefit in considering theological perspectives. The themes considered in this chapter – vulnerability, prayer and revelation – could deepen the appreciation and enhance the sensitivity of educators with regard to, respectively, the human condition, the qualities or capacities worth nurturing in learners and the sources of knowledge.

Notes

1   Dawkins, from a talk he gave in 2007, as quoted by Richard Holloway, Honest Doubt series, BBC Radio 4, 18 June 2012.

2   For two historical studies of holistic approaches to education that display sympathy for a religious perspective, see parallels between this and poetic knowledge and which recommend an integration of poetic, spiritual and scientific knowledge in aid of the promotion of wisdom, see Olson (1995) and Taylor (1998).

References

Brittain, C. C. and Murphy, F. A. (eds) (2011), *Theology, University, Humanities*. Eugene, OR: Cascade Books.

Buber, M. (1958) *I and Thou*. Trans. Smith, R. G., Edinburgh: T & T Clark.

Coleridge, S. T. (1972) in Barrell, J. (ed.), *On the Constitution of the Church and State*. London: J.M. Dent & Sons.

Crisp, O. D., D'Costa, G., Davies, M. and Hampson (eds) (2012), *Christianity and the Disciplines*. London: T & T Clark.

Crosby, J. F. (1996) *The Selfhood of the Human Person*. Washington, DC: Catholic University of America Press.

Dulles, A. (1983) *Models of Revelation*. Dublin: Gill & Macmillan).

English, A. (2007) *The Possibility of Christian Philosophy*. London: Routledge.

Fowler, J. (1981) *Stages of Faith* San Francisco, CA: Harper & Row.

Ghiloni, A. J. (2012) *John Dewey Among the Theologians*. New York, NY: Peter Lang.

Halík, T. (2012) *Night of the Confessor*. New York, NY: Image Books.

Haslam, M. C. (2012) *A Constructive Theology of Intellectual Disability*. New York, NY: Fordham University Press.

Heclo, H. (2008) *On Thinking Institutionally*. Boulder, CO: Paradigm Publishers.

Heywood, D. (2004) *Divine Revelation and Human Learning*. Aldershot: Ashgate.

Hotz, K. G. and Mathews, M. T. (2006) *Shaping the Christian Life Worship and the Religious Affections*. Louisville, KY: Westminster John Knox Press.

Irvine, C. (2005) *The Art of God*. London: SPCK.

Jasper, D. (2011). 'The New Theological Humanism and the Political Future', in Brittain and Murphy (eds), *Theology, University, Humanities*. Eugene, OR: Cascade Books, pp. 64–74.

MacIntyre, A. (1999) *Dependent Rational Animals*. London: Duckworth.

Newman, J. H. (2001) in Tillman, M. K. (eds), *Rise and Progress of Universities and Benedictine Essays*. Leominster: Gracewing.

Olson, P. A. (1995) *The Journey to Wisdom*. Lincoln: University of Nebraska Press.

Taylor, J. S. (1998) *Poetic Knowledge*. New York: State University of New York Press.

Webster, J. (2011). '*Regina Artium*: Theology and the Humanities', in Brittain and Murphy (eds), *Theology, University, Humanities*. Eugene, OR: Cascade Books, pp. 39–63.

Wirzba, N. (2005). 'Attention and Responsibility. The Work of Prayer', In Bruce Ellis Benson and Norman Wirzba (eds), *The Phenomenology of Prayer*. New York, NY: Fordham University Press, pp. 88–100.

13

Essential Features of a Catholic Philosophy of Education

David Torevell

In 1996, while serving their Muslim neighbours, seven Cistercian monks[1] of the monastery of Tibhirine were kidnapped and brutally murdered by terrorists. Xavier Beauvois' film *Des Hommes et des Dieux* (Of Gods and Men, 2010) not only captures their exemplary martyrdom but also invites those who see it to reflect on the choice which confronted the monks at that time – whether to leave the monastery altogether and abandon their vocation or to remain and endure the unknown consequences. To flee or to stay. The bitter ordeal and the final decision they take as a community in Christ directly parallels the words of scripture they have imbibed, the liturgy they have embodied and the vow of stability they have undertaken as professed contemplatives (Kiser, 2002).

This chapter highlights why the film is important for understanding constituent aspects of a philosophy of Catholic education and why I consider it to be a resource of immeasurable richness and beauty. Teachers working in Catholic schools, and beyond, have here a moving story based on the tortuous but redemptive drama of the Christian life itself. As such, it is rooted in the paschal mystery of Christ and its intrinsic association with the sacraments of baptism and the Eucharist. It is a film, therefore, which positions itself at the very heart of Catholic theology, identity and education. It should not be overlooked.

The Cistercian community at Tibhirine in Algeria faced a difficult dilemma in the mid-nineties when an extreme Islamist terrorist group began to murder foreigners in the vicinity of their monastery. What was going to be their response, both individually and collectively, to this situation? They had been assisting their Muslim brothers and sisters by acts of charity for many years and had come to recognize that their community's vocation was to live among the poor who needed their physical and spiritual sustenance.[2] But the extraordinary circumstances they were now faced with compelled them to investigate anew the meaning of the life they have pledged themselves to by following the Rule of St. Benedict. They were well aware that, at baptism, their own bodies had been incorporated into the death and resurrection of Christ and that monastic life was a continuous call to *conversio* until death, when the white garment which had been wrapped around their bodies at birth would be used again to wrap their bodies in death. Such ongoing conversion demanded ascetical practices, periods of suffering and time (Huerre, 1994). But they were now confronted to live out that paschal mystery in very different circumstances to the one to which they were accustomed. It seemed that their newly clothed identity as baptized Christians and as solemnly professed monks beckoned them to something else: to put into practice what they had learned about powerless vulnerability to the terrors of a fallen world, just as their Saviour had. And to partly redeem the world by this submission.

'New creature': A philosophy of baptismal incorporation

The monastic life would have rehearsed them – to some degree – to face this ordeal, but this does not mean that accepting the full significance of their baptismal incorporation was an easy one – far from it. The Trappist monk Thomas Merton writes that the monastic life directly encourages an awakening to a kind of death to the exterior life and that it is a difficult learning process encompassing huge risks of faith: ' we will dread his coming in proportion as we have identified with this exterior self and attached to it. But when we understand the dialectic of life and death we will learn to take the risks implied by faith, to make the choices that deliver us from our routine self and open to us the door of a new being, a new reality' (Ford, 2009). The alternative to taking such risks is to live the life of a prisoner to conventional ideas and to one's own desires. Freedom only comes through accepting 'an unfamiliar truth' and a 'supernatural desire'. The baptized must let go of the familiar and consent to what is new and unknown: 'I must learn to "leave myself" in order to find myself by yielding to the love of God', he writes. Their lives as monks were already a public and radical consent to this 'newness', to the embrace of an alternative understanding, to dying in order to live. But the threat of Islamic terrorism was to become their greatest testing of this consent.

Monks are aware that all Christ is by nature, they can become by grace. But they also realize that this growth in deification, which they so earnestly desire, is at jeopardy if they fail to live up to the promises they made at baptism. As

Collins writes, ' the intimate relationship with God into which baptism grants admittance entails recognizing a staggering truth clearly taught in the New Testament and reiterated by Christians throughout the centuries...: all that Christ is by nature we invited to become by grace' (2010, p. 226). Crucially, a dynamic of radical internalization is necessary if the pattern of Christ's life is to embed itself into the heart and to be instantiated in their everyday actions: 'Monastic spirituality with its various disciplines aims to help believers do just that: to keep alive the constant memory of God (*memoria Dei*) by focusing one's whole existence on his presence in the heart' (Collins, 2010, p. 226). A Catholic philosophy of education is rooted in this kind of pragmatic anthropology – charitable and loving actions come about as the fruit of *conversio*.

Clearly then, the sacrament of baptism has enormous repercussions for ontology, self-understandings and daily living (Radcliffe, 2012). Since the baptized are made and encouraged to stand outside the self, the Christian life is always an adventure into living an ecstatic life (*ekstacis* in Greek), of being taken outside and forgetting oneself, since the person to whom the baptized devote their lives is not themselves but Christ and his body, the Church. When one leaves the old body behind and endorses a 'new' one, the self becomes gradually deified. This is primarily enhanced through prayer, grace, the sacraments and acts of love (Pope Benedict XVI, 2005). The 'new' body also learns to re-situate itself to a larger body, the Church, of which Christ is the head: 'Baptism is never, therefore, a private act, but is always a public proclamation of the beginnings of a Christian life rooted in the Word...and made real in the body through the sacramental life of the Church, a series of events which are enacted from birth to death' (Torevell, 2011, p. 30).

This beginning and ongoing formation of a 'new creature' is of paramount significance for it claims that such newness is nothing other than the experience of being an adopted son or daughter of God (2. Cor. 5:7; Pt. 1.4.), whereby their bodies become a temple of the Holy Spirit (Catechism, 1994, p. 1265). This signifies that the baptized have been marked by Christ to live according to His teachings, and since they are incorporated into His body, they no longer belong to themselves and their own concerns but to Christ who died and rose (1 Cor. 6:19; 2 Cor. 5:15). Thus, the Christian life after baptism becomes an ongoing performance of witness to Christ. The baptized are consumed by the first performance of the biblical rite which releases a new but demanding life which gradually conforms itself to Christ. Just as Christ abandoned Himself to the waters of baptism on the banks of the river Jordan (although he had no need of this) so, too, Christians commit themselves to the waters of new life. But this first baptismal abandonment signifies other abandonments which will follow, maybe even to the cross: As Collins puts it, Christ's 'obedient descent into the waters in solidarity with sinners is a mystery in the strictest sense, a symbolic act charged with the grace of spiritual energy, by means of which Christ manifests his passage from death to an endless life' (2010, p. 221). It signifies and involves a descent into the waters of death, having undergone capture into the hands of the violent.

All those involved through baptism in Catholic education will have to face similar if not such dauntingly intensive experiences of estrangement that the community at Tabhirine endured. All Christians' intimate, adoptive relationships with Christ are a source of consolation at such times, but they are also the fulcrum around which those experiences rest. More hopefully, they entail the mystical identification with all the baptized which removes any sense that the self is isolated or abandoned, since their bodies are handed over to the one Body. No Catholic pupil is ever alone. S/he is trained to recognize and delight in this one body, where all barriers of race, cultures, class and gender are dissolved. This extends to those outside the Christian body, since nothing that is truly human fails to find an echo in the hearts of Christians who 'cherish a feeling of deep solidarity with the human race and its history' (Flannery, 1992, pp. 903–904). Once the gift has been received and recognized, then gratitude is its most natural response; the Christian life is always one of thankfulness and praise, never abandonment. But we shall see later that sometimes agonizing feelings of abandonment are paradoxically the path to a recognition of this truth.

The opening paragraph of *The Religious Dimension of Education in a Catholic School* (Congregation for Catholic Education, 1988) reiterates this crucial aspect of baptismal newness: 'Catholic education tries to guide the adolescents in such a way that personality development goes hand in hand with the development of the "new creature" that each one has become through baptism' (para 1). This is one of the hallmarks of the distinctiveness of Catholic schools and governs its philosophy of education in relation to the personal development of each student (Morris, 2012). It is why Catholic schools and colleges insist that one of their criteria for admission is baptism. There is already a different ontology for the one who enters the school's gates after baptism. The challenge is to foster that ontology over time. This difference continues to be formed and shaped by the liturgical and especially sacramental life of the Church: 'The performance of baptismal liturgy was the drama of the beginnings of a new life, a performance which would be repeated through the receiving of the sacraments throughout life, especially the Eucharist' (Torevell, 2011, p. 29). As early as 1943, Maritain was arguing that Catholic education was about shaping the person's disposition and that it must resist attempts to place young people in a one-dimensional universe where the only yardstick is practical utility and the only value is economic and technological progress (Maritain, 1943). All this is true, but such shaping within a new transcendental horizon means recognizing that the paschal mystery transcends all times 'while being made present in them all' (Catechism, 1994, p. 1085).

During the Middle Ages, and to a large extent still today, three sources were used by monks for the protection and enhancement of this 'new creation': scripture, the patristic tradition and classical literature (Leclercq, 1982, p. 71).[3] Reading (unlike modern practices) involved a bodily and performative exercise which was part of a wider enactment of liturgy. Its *meditatio* element consisted in applying oneself attentively to this practice with total memorization and the repeated mastication of the scriptural words were invariably couched in a lexicon of spiritual nutrition, including eating, chewing and digesting. It was a corporeal act, affecting the en-souled body. Such mastication of the text was able to release its fullest flavour. Accumulating knowledge discursively was never a largely cognitive practice but an embodied experience of prayerfully *savouring* the Word, the source of all life. Not about mastering, but of inwardly absorbing the words, monks became attuned to beauty and symbolism and transformed by listening with 'the ear of the heart' (Caldecott, 2009, pp. 39–49; Cook, 2013, pp. 7–12). It consisted in a passive openness to the fruits which the text might yield with patient attention. Foster admits that this entails learning to tune into a different level of the text's meaning than is normally associated with critical reading which resulted in a feeling of transformative rest (Foster, 2007, p. 4).

All this is associated with a contemplative and intimate approach to reading and flows naturally from a philosophy of Catholic education which acknowledges all life and knowledge as gift, what Ward terms an 'ontological scandal' since it 'concerns God's uncreated power to call something into being from nothing, bring flesh from bread. The scandal is the gift of being itself – that something should be rather than not be – which the transformative Word of God announces' (2000, p. 89). *Pace* Ward, Griffiths' insights into the foundations of Christian learning encourage us to recognize that such creation *ex nihilo* entails believing that everything created is good. Knowledge of that goodness through learning is therefore a blessed thing to do and is recommended by the Church (Griffiths, 2011, p. 106). To know something, therefore, is to know something of what God has made. It is 'to become intimate with it; and since to become intimate with a good is itself a good, the conclusion is unavoidable and delightful in itself, that all knowledge and all thinking are goods' (Griffiths, 2011, pp. 106–107). This is an exercise of gratitude for the gift of goodness given in the created order. The heart expands as a result (Torevell, 2009, p. 26). Prayer, then, is the wise thing to do before studying, since it reminds the one who studies that their understanding does not come from themselves but from God, the source of all wisdom. Beauvois cleverly positions a shot of the monks in silent reading in their library directly after a scene of them praying and chanting in the chapel; reading is another form of prayer. It demands a humble act of leaving oneself, of moving away from the trappings of self-consciousness and narcissism, enabling a process of *ekstasis* to take place. It is why the intellectual life can be so beautiful and transformative. Students in Catholic schools, colleges and universities should be encouraged to learn in this manner, for it is associated with a distinctive Christian philosophy of gift.[4]

A philosophy of living powerlessly

In accepting and drawing from the liturgical and sacramental life of the Church, the baptized are able to withstand and bear any 'defeat' by those who would profess otherwise. It equips them to understand the weaknesses of others, even those who instigate violence: 'Recognizing our own weaknesses, I accept those of others. I can bear them, make them mine, in imitation of Christ', speaks Brother Christian. It might not be too adventurous to suggest here that in this recognition of their own and others' weaknesses, they learn to forgive those who will eventually wrong them, just as Christ forgave those who crucified Him before he died. The Christian paradox, of course, at the heart of the gospel and the film is that such apparent weakness is not weakness at all but rather its opposite – courage: 'The apostle's weakness is like Christ's. It is neither resignation nor passivity. It requires *beaucoup de courage* and incites one to defend truth and justice.' The latest statement by the Congregation for Catholic Education, *Educating Together in Catholic Schools: A Shared Mission Between Consecrated Persons and the Lay Faithful* (2008), makes exactly this point about powerlessness in relation to the notion of communion: Catholic education is 'not given for the purpose of gaining power but as an aid towards fuller understanding of and communion with people, with events and with things' (2008: para 39). The word 'communion' is important here, implying a deep bonding of humanity resulting from one's communion with Christ. What the monks seek and attempt to live out is this communion with others, where all barriers are broken down. That is why they care for their enemies and why Brother Christian prays over the dead body of Ali Fayattia, one of the terrorist leaders, much to the disgust of the government authorities. Jamison sums it up nicely: ' communion in the Catholic school leads to a deeper communion with God and with the world' (2013, p. 12).

This inculcation into liturgical agency is framed within cyclical time, not metronomic time, which is subject to the law of measure and finitude. The body learns to adjust itself to a new way of living outside temporal time-space coordinates. Death is experienced not as the end of linear time and as annihilation but as part of a personal and cosmic drama, where death gives way to a different form of life. The eschatological learning and desire for the heavenly Jerusalem is never far from the monks' finite existence, since it is the framework that the liturgy they encounter each day and hour endorses (Leclercq, 1982, pp. 53–70). This prayerful submission to this repetitive cycle echoes the body's gradual and intimate engagement with the quotidian challenges of dying to the self and repeating that dying until the end of time. The Christ-child, the minute he is born, is the child who is destined, from all eternity, to die a tortuous death and to take on Himself the sins of the world and then to rise in glory. A Catholic philosophy of education takes seriously this eschatological framework and students are entitled to be introduced to this 'new' way of being in the world, for it will most certainly determine the manner in which they live their lives (Griffiths, 2013). The preparation for death has always been a hallmark of Catholic education and is not a dark fascination for the end of things. As Haldane suggests, 'It is not morbid to think often of mortality when the point of doing so is to reflect back on one's present condition .... It is within this context that a catholic philosophy of education should be developed' (1999, p. 192). The cadences and rhythms of the liturgy, including the undulations of poetic form within sacred scripture, penetrate the folds of the body with their 'virtually endless modulations' (Fodor, 2004, Burton-Christie, 1993) assisting participants to attune to the resonances of Christ's passion, death and resurrection. It is a formation released by entering systolic time which is a characteristic of heavenly time (Griffiths, 2013).

For the duration of the film, Beauvois cuts back to the chapel scenes on a regular basis, as the film's frequent shots of the monks' worship – in particular their chanting in front of the paschal candle, the altar of sacrifice and the crucifix – highlight the liturgical cycle to which they conform their own bodies as one body in Christ. To be born anew each day is to allow oneself – through prayer – to enter into this mutual exchange, by receiving the life of Christ. This entails a

Christian anthropology which is theandric – that is, it involves a divine–human exchange most clearly expressed by St. Augustine's homily to neophytes on Easter day, when he encourages them to wake up and celebrate the exchanges of life offered by Christ in exchange for his own death: 'I receive death from you: receive from me life. Wake up: see what I give, what I receive' (quoted in Leachman, 2009, p. 175). Christ has given his body for the world, but it requires an antiphonal giving from those baptized, patterned on His own life and giving. The monks' response to their oppressors is a desire to imitate Christ whom they encounter in the liturgy and absorb into their own flesh at the Eucharist. Their actions gradually become the actions of the One whom they adore and eat, whom they imitate, whom they love and praise around the altar of sacrifice. In gathering there as one body, the monks prepare themselves for those times when they too will be called to replicate in their own lives the love of Him, whom they worship. The film traces this bitter trail which they take. The constant echoing of the road to Golgotha endures throughout the film. There is no easy imitation of submission. Theirs, like Christ's, is an agonizing one, of excruciating self-doubt and resistance, demanding nothing less than the relinquishing of their own wills to the Father's.

This obedient submission is what the feast of Christmas calls attention to, encompassing what liturgical agency involves. The agonizing question of Carlo Caretto, 'Why is faith so bitter?' is partly answered by the Biblical birth narrative which proclaims that relationships in Christ are never built on power or prestige but on a fragile powerlessness where innocence is often desiccated. What the film so genuinely represents is the struggle the monks endure in relation to this incarnational theology. Eventually, painfully, *Je reste* (I stay) becomes translated into the plural – we stay – and the monks speak and act as one voice and one body. They are certain that they will have to confront the 'unknown' and that although their lives would be at risk each day from the violence of the terrorists, it is a risk worth taking, since it is the risk of faith. Although they do not seek martyrdom and did not choose the monastery, as Brother Christophe comments, 'to commit collective suicide', their collective decision is at the heart of their faith. They know that the Good Shepherd does not abandon his flock to the wolves, since they have listened to this teaching time and again, year on year. The audience become convinced of this, too, as the camera captures in wide-angle shots the hills and countryside where sheep roam and graze. The monks walk among them, are one with them, shepherd them. By not abandoning their Muslim brothers and sisters, they acknowledge they will not be abandoned by God. Any leaving would simply constitute an unfruitful, non-paschal dying.

Consenting to this type of 'communion' with their fellow monks and Muslim neighbours is rehearsed in the Eucharistic food they share and eat. The camera takes time to focus the audience's attention on the paten and the host (the body of Christ) and the chalice (the blood of Christ). The blood of the victims of the terrorists who have their throats cut and the killing of the monks themselves become associated with the blood of Christ in the Eucharistic liturgy they share each day (Cavanaugh, 1998). The spilling of their blood is therefore never without meaning, since their innocent victimhood becomes at one with the victimhood of Christ. If Girard is right, then this is a cultural and perpetual cycle of violence and is only ever assuaged by the killing of the scapegoat (Girard, 1977, 1986, 1987). They chant their communal identification with the bloodied One they adore: 'Because he is with us in this time of violence/ … Who beckons us from the cross'. His passion is their passion too. They know why they open their lips and why their mouths proclaim His praise, for he is the One of whom they sing, 'He sacrificed Himself, loving to the end'. The title of the film is taken from psalm 81: 'You are gods, sons of the Most High' reminds the audience that although in their baptismal adoption they are 'as gods', they 'shall die like men and fall like princes'.

A philosophy of redemptive abandonment

In light of this claim, it is not surprising that Catholic education will, at times, be about tears. Let me explain why with reference to one of the final scenes before the monks are bullied and frog-marched to their deaths in the forest. After all agreeing that they will stay and after their final talk by Brother Christian, they share their final meal together. Obviously, this is an echo of the Last Supper of Christ with his disciples and in silence the monks drink of the cup of wine which they have all agreed to drink. The audience hear Tchaikovsky's evocative *Swan Lake* overture as this takes place. As the camera records close-up shots of the monks' faces, one by one, it captures their intense oscillation between joy and sadness, their brotherly love of each other, their Oneness in Christ and their resignation to their destiny, the will of the Father. Tears flow down the cheeks of Brother Christian and Brother Amédée. This shedding of tears is a familiar monastic practice which was termed *penthos* (compunction) or the 'gift of tears' by some of the earliest monastic communities (Leclercq, 1982). It is associated with the whole of a monk's life which, as I have hinted at earlier, is one devoted to *conversio*. The experience of *penthos* came as a result of the direct piercing of the heart by the Biblical text. As one student suggested in a class discussion about the decision of the monks to stay, '[t]here is an unspoken recognition that they must stay and this is confirmed by the readings they have listened to'. The film has revealed already how dependent upon scripture the monks are, so it is not surprising that weeping is shown on screen; it is 'an expression of one's utter dependence upon God and in the firm hope that God's mercy will soon be made manifest' (Burton-Christie, 1993, p. 187). Such a life entailed both the judgement and mercy of God and a radical dying to the old self, with a commitment to the new. Resisting the temptation (or demon) to flee from the demands of the scriptures was an ever-present struggle for monks, but they also believed that such scriptures possessed an additional power to deliver them from the evil which they encountered in the world and, at times, in their own hearts.

The film prepares the audience for the inevitable death of the monks. They offer the full abdication of their own wills to the Father as a sacrifice of themselves to God. After the example of Christ, who came to do the Father's will, they are led to serve all their brothers and sisters to the end. If the suffering of Christ is the paradigmatic salvific event to which the monastic community gives allegiance, then there is no option but to centre their own lives around this witness. To avoid this is to move themselves away from the passion of Christ, even as they gather themselves around the altar of sacrifice each day. Here sacred geography comes into play, for the liturgical space they inhabit trains them to instantiate that space in the outside fallen world, the world of mistrust, reprisals and violence. It demands that they witness another ground which is alien to the one upon which power and violence makes its claims. Not to do so is to betray the sacred ground upon which they stand. None of this, of course, is easy. Staying, rather than fleeing the monastery, is the decision they take after agonizing turmoil. Brother Christian's final talk to his brothers is contextualized within the theology of innocence. This is how they will make sense of their fate. He reminds them that day by day they have learned to embody the Christ-child who was born so absolutely helpless and so threatened from the time of his birth. They must bring the child that they embody to the world and teach it that whoever saves his life will lose it and whoever loses his life will inherit eternal life. This claim is at the heart of any Catholic philosophy of education.

This wrestling is represented in a number of scenes within the film. Brother Christophe tells Brother Christian that he is deeply confused about whether to go or to stay. God has become silent – when he prays, he hears nothing. In his cell, alone, his anguished prayer, 'Don't abandon me. Help me', is heard by his fellow monks; his bitter experience is theirs too (Kennedy, 2013).[5] This is not only an echo of the Gethsemane experience of Christ the night before he died, when he 'was deeply grieved and agitated' (Luke 26: 37), just before the raw acceptance of the will of the Father, but an echo of the cry of desolation uttered by Christ on the cross, 'Why God, my God, why hast thou forsaken me?' (Mk, 15:34; Mt, 27: 46). This can only be fully appreciated as the other side of the experience of intimacy with Christ begun at baptism and developed throughout monastic life (Collins, 2010, p. 22). The scene then cuts to Brother Christophe kneeling silently before the chapel altar, head down in agonizing prayer. 'Why *is* faith so bitter?' might be the audience's question. But the camera also catches rays of light emerging from the window to the left of the frame. The scene is one of intense struggle, but hopeful endurance which comes from considering the path he knows he must follow and which has been laid before him at his baptism and throughout his monastic life. There is no other path – what is at stake is his determination and courage to follow it. Other scenes reflect a similar agitation within the abbot himself; even though he encourages the community to stay from the very start, his solitary walk over the hills and beside the lake during the rainstorm is no less bitter than Brother Christophe's struggle.

Nevertheless, in the midst of this inevitably lonely trail where each monk has to make up his own mind, Beauvois includes memorable shots of brotherly embrace and resolve. When Brother Christophe tells his superior he cannot pray, they finally embrace one another in mutual support; as the deafening noise of the government forces' helicopter drowns their prayers, they gather together, arm in arm as one body corporately defying the invasion of their chants, when Brother Luc embraces and then kisses the bosom of the crucified Christ in the painting, when Brother Amédée embraces the last surviving monk, after the remainder of the community have been captured and marched to their deaths. These physical and communal acts of brotherly love become the visible expression of their Christian identity. As they walk to their martyrdom in the snowy, bitter landscape, the audience gradually lose sight of their bodies as they fade silently into the mist. The audience grieve for their loss but applaud with admiration on how their baptismal promises have been kept to the very end.

Conclusion

In summary then, Catholic educators have in the film *Of Gods and Men* a vitally important resource for their students. Its beauty lies first in representing a courageous living out of the paschal mystery in difficult circumstances. In so doing, it draws attention to the ontological change that takes place at baptism and how those who have been plunged into its waters begin a 'new' life devoted to joyful self-sacrifice. Having been handed over to the One who assists them to see and live life as a gift, the monks witness to what a holy and happy life signifies. In the story of the Cistercian monks at Tibhirine therefore, students are given encouragement to imitate such fortitude in their own daily lives, if not to the same agonizing degree. Ultimately, the philosophy rests on the Biblical claim that those who lose their lives for the sake of justice and truth shall find it, and those who gain their life shall lose it. A philosophy of Catholic education starts from this paradoxical teaching and is rooted in the nature of the baptized self and all that demands. There is nothing morbid or pessimistic about such a view, for it offers a redemptive and hopeful understanding of what love means and entails, as well as how death might be conquered.

Second, the film highlights that it is not possible to understand any Catholic philosophy of education without referring to the Church's liturgy. The acceptance of the redemptive powerlessness which underpins the community's final decision to remain in the monastery is made sense of through their adoration of the Saviour's birth, whom they already know never resorted to retaliation or violence and who learned, as they must, to submit to the will of the Father. This is not a philosophy of weakness, but of courage, made possible through grace. Third, a Catholic philosophy of education teaches that there are some things in this life which are worth dying for and that martyrdom still has a role to play in the Christian life. This understanding pierces so deeply the hearts of the monks, because they have become attentively receptive to the Word and strengthened by the Eucharist. Because metronomic time gives way to systolic time so abundantly within the monastery, such a view appears right and proper. My hope is that this demanding but beautiful philosophy of life – so sensitively portrayed on screen by Beauvois – might also appear right and proper to students and the only one ultimately worth following.

Notes

1   The Cistercian Order was formed in 1089 after a group of twenty-one monks and their abbot left their Benedictine monastery in Burgundy to set up a new community in Cîteaux (Latin, *Cistercium*) unreservedly devoted to simplicity and austerity. Their Order is characterized by a uniformity of strict custom, discipline and architecture. Probably the most famous Cistercian is St. Bernard of Clairvaux (1090–1153), who in letters, sermons and treatises set down the

ideals of the Cistercian founders. In 1892 a further reform was established – the Order of Cistercians of the Strict Observance, popularly known as the Trappists. Thomas Merton belonged to this Order, which became known for its dedication to a highly disciplined form of asceticism and to almost perpetual silence. Today, many Cistercian monasteries still exist and their monks continue to lead a hidden life of contemplation and prayer dedicated to the Rule of St. Benedict. They live a life of solitude and silence. Prayer, reading and work make up their daily routine and undivided attention is given to the liturgy around which their entire existence revolves. Each community is also dedicated in a special manner to the Blessed Virgin Mary who is never far from Cistercian monks' hearts.

2   The film is remarkable in its representation of the dialogue and friendship which have been established between the Christian and Muslim communities around Tabirhine. Not only is the chanting of Qur'anic verses harmoniously set side by side with the chanting of Gregorian chant, but the leader of the terrorist group shows deep respect for the festival of Christmas and for the birth of Jesus on his first raid on the monastery, made all the more significant in light of his terrorist activities. Further work needs to be done on the implications of the film for the future of Christian–Muslin encounter.

3   During the Middle Ages two features dominated a monastery's literature. The first was centred around compunction whose aim was to foster a desire for God. This was invariably expressed in the language of the spiritual senses, especially taste. Monastic life was one of pre-libation, resulting in a kind of intoxication brought about by the anticipation and fore*taste* of the heavenly abode in fellowship with the angels. The monastery became a place of waiting and desire for the heavenly city (Leclercq, 1982, p. 56). The other was *otium* – leisure, which had a very different meaning from the one which is given to it today. For the Greeks, 'not-leisure' was the time of everyday work. Christian monasticism developed this idea and thus leisure became associated with a life dedicated to contemplation and the 'work' of the liturgy in which one found rest and peace (Pieper, 1998, Cook, 2013, pp. 46–47).

4   If this Catholic philosophy of education is to be taken seriously, then a corresponding pedagogy is demanded. It needs to be rooted in a contemplative approach where silence and stillness become essential features of the learning environment. See Grace, F. (2011) and my chapter 'Like a Jar of Wine in Left in a Place for a While … Clear, Settled and Perfumed' in Schmack, J. Thompson, M, Torevell, D., and Cole, C., 2010. pp. 171–184.

5   Kennedy's moving account weaves together her own work as a human rights lawyer with the theme of abandonment and situates them within the Lenten liturgy: 'To reinforce our belief in human rights, we only have to consider the life and death of Christ – the corrupted intelligence which came from Judas, Christ's arrest, persecution and torture, the travesty of a trial, the washing of hands by those

in power, the denial of him by his friend, Peter, the fear generated amongst his disciples by the horrifying events and then the slow, excruciating execution. "*Eli, Eli, lama sabachthani*", "Father, Father, why hast thou forsaken me?" Christ too felt abandoned' (2013, p. 17).

References

Burton-Christie, D. (1993) *The Word in the Desert: Scripture and the Quest for Holiness in Early Christian Monasticism*. Oxford: Oxford University Press.

Caldecott, S. (2009) *Beauty for Truth's Sake. On the Re-enchantment of Education*. Ada, MI: Brazos Press.

Cavanaugh, W. T. (1998) *Torture and the Eucharist: Theology, Politics and the Body*. Oxford: Blackwell.

Congregation for Catholic Education (2008) *Educating Together in Catholic Schools: A Shared Mission Between Consecrated Persons and the Lay Faithful*. www.vatican.va [Accessed date 25 May 2014].

Collins, G. (2010) *Meeting Christ in his Mysteries. A Benedictine Vision of the Spiritual Life*. Dublin: The Columba Press.

Cook, B. (2013) *Pursuing Eudaimonia. Re-appropriating the Greek Philosophical Foundations of the Christian Apophatic Tradtion*. Cambridge: CSP.

Flannery, A. (1992) *Vatican Council II. The Conciliar and Post Conciliar Documents*. (New Revised Edition), Dublin: Dominican Publications.

Fodor, J. (2004) 'Reading Scriptures: Rehearsing identity, Practising Character', in Hauweras, S. and Wells, S. (eds), *The Blackwell Companion to Christian Ethics*. Oxford: Blackwell, pp. 141–155.

Ford, M. (2009) *Spiritual Masters for all Seasons*. Dublin: Columba Press.

Foster, D. (2007) *Deep Calls to Deep. Going Further in Prayer*. London: Continuum.

Girard, R. (1977) *Violence and the Sacred*. Baltimore, MD: John Hopkins Press.

—— (1986) *The Scapegoat*. Baltimore, MD: John Hopkins Press.

—— (1987) *Things Hidden from the Foundation of the World*. London: The Athlone Press.

Grace, F. (2011) 'Learning as a Path, Not a Goal: Contemplative Pedagogy – Its Principles and Practices', *Teaching Theology and Religion* 14(2): 99–124.

Griffiths, P. (2011), 'From Curiosity to Studiousness: Catechizing the Appetite for Learning', in Smith, D. and Smith, J. (eds), *Teaching and Christian Practices. Reshaping Faith and Learning*. Grand Rapids, MI: Wm.B. Eerdmans, pp. 102–122.

—— (2012–2013) 'The End. An Eschatological Asaay', Stanton Lectures, University of Cambridge. [online] Available at: http://www.divinity.cam.ac.uk/news-and-events/the-stanton-lectures [accessed 13 March 2013].

Haldane, J. (1999) 'The Need of Spirituality in Catholic Education', in Conway, J. (ed.), *Inside-Out/Outside-In*. Dublin: Lindisfarne Books, pp. 188–206

Hancock, C. L. (2005) *Recovering a Catholic Philosophy of Elementary Education*. Pine Beach, NJ: Newman House Press.

Huerre, D. (1994) *Letters to My Brothers and Sisters. Living by the Rule of St. Benedict*. Collegville, MN: The Liturgical Press.

Jamison, C. (2013) 'God has created me to do him some definite service' (Cardinal Newman): Vocation at the heart of the Catholic curriculum', *International Studies in Catholic Education* 5(1): 10–22.

Kennedy, H. (2013) 'Right at our heart', *The Tablet* 16, 2 March 2013.

Kiser, J. (2002) *The Monks of Tibhirine: Faith, Love and Terror in Algeria*.

Leachman, J. G. (2009) *The Liturgical Subject. Subject, Subjectivity, and the Human Person in Contemporary Liturgical Discussion and Critique*. Notre Dame, IN: University of Notre Dame Press.

Leclercq, J. (1982) *The Love of Learning and the Desire for God*. New York, NY: Fordham University Press.

Maritain, J. (1943) *Education at the Crossroads*. New Haven, CT: Yale University Press.

(2011) in Matthews, J. and Torevell, D. (eds), *Performing Life, Living Performance*. Cambridge: Cambridge Scholars Publishing.

(1989) in McDonnell, T. P. (ed.), *A Thomas Merton Reader*. New York, NY: Doubleday.

(2012) in Morris, A. (ed.), *Catholic Education. Universal Principles, Locally Applied*. Cambridge: Cambridge Scholars Publishing.

Of Gods and Men (2010) [Film] Directed by Xavier Beauvois. France: Armada Films.

Pope Benedict XVI (2005) *Encyclical Letter: Caritas in Veritate*. [online] Available at: http://www.vatica.va.com [accessed 13 March 2013].

Pieper, J. (1998) *Leisure: The Basis of Culture*. South Bend, ID: St. Augustine's Press.

Radcliffe, T. (2012) *Take the Plunge. Living Baptism and Confirmation*. London: Bloomsbury.

Stock, M. (2012) *Christ at the Centre*. London: Catholic Truth Society.

The Religious Dimension in a Catholic School. (1988), in Franchi, L. (ed.) 2007. An Anthology of Catholic Teaching on Education. London and New York: Scepter, pp. 247–296.

Torevell, D. (2000) *Losing the Sacred. Ritual, Modernity and Liturgical Reform*. Edinburgh: T&T Clark.

—— (2007), *Liturgy and the Beauty of the Unknown. Another Place*. Aldershot: Ashgate

—— (2009), 'Keeping a Balance: The Sacred Space of the Heart and the Modern University', in Brie, S., Daggers, J. and Torevell, D. (eds), *Sacred Space. Interdisciplinary Perspectives within Contemporary Contexts*. Cambridge: Cambridge Scholars Publishing, pp. 23–38.

—— (2010), ' "Like a Jar of Wine Left in its Place for a While … Clear, Settled, and Perfumed": Evagrius of Pontus and the Purifying Engagement of Stillness', in Schmack, J., Thompson, M., Torevell, D. and Cole, C. (eds), *Engaging Religious Education*. Cambridge: Cambridge Scholars Publishing, pp. 171–184.

Ward, G. (2000), *Cities of God*. London: Routledge.

Index